D0640696

TEXTBOOK OF MEAT INSPECTION

Including the Inspection of Rabbits and Poultry

BY

HORACE THORNTON

B.V.Sc., M.R.C.V.S., D.V.H., F.R.S.H.

Senior Meat Inspection Adviser, Department of Veterinary Services, Ministry of Agriculture, Rhodesia. Formerly Chief Veterinary Officer, City and County of Newcastle upon Tyne, Lecturer in the Inspection of Meat and Other Foods, Rutherford College, Newcastle upon Tyne; and in the Science of Meat, College of Commerce, Newcastle upon Tyne.

FIFTH EDITION

LONDON

BAILLIÈRE, TINDALL AND CASSELL

FIRST EDITION .	. 1949
SECOND EDITION	. 1952
THIRD EDITION .	. 1957
FOURTH EDITION	. 1962
Reprinted .	. 1965
FIFTH EDITION .	. 1968

7020–0238–0

7 and 8 Henrietta Street, London, W.C. 2

Published in the United States by The Williams & Wilkins Company, Baltimore

PRINTED IN GREAT BRITAIN AT
THE UNIVERSITY PRESS
ABERDEEN

CONTENTS

LIST OF COLOURED PLATES

PREFACE TO FIFTH EDITION

The need for a textbook covering the whole field of meat hygiene in a simple yet comprehensive manner induced the author to write this book, the first edition of which was published in 1949; since then three further editions have appeared.

Meat hygiene in any country never stands still; it either progresses or regresses, and it is a matter for sober satisfaction that the need for greater efforts in this field is now appreciated in many countries of the world. There are various reasons for the undoubted progress that has been made, and one factor which has focused attention on the necessity for greater attention to hygienic practices in regard to meat and meat products has been the increase in the number of cases of human gastro-enteritis which have been shown to be due to secondary bacterial contamination of originally sound food. Another factor was the public interest and concern which arose following on the outbreak of typhoid fever in the north of Scotland in 1964, and this outbreak, attributed to a can of corned beef of South American origin, had the salutary effect of bringing into being more stringent procedures in the many countries which exported, and wished to continue to export, their meat and meat products to the United Kingdom.

The deleterious effects of untoward stress factors on animals destined for slaughter are gradually being appreciated by those engaged in the meat trade and this subject is dealt with at some length in the present edition. Tuberculosis in cattle and pigs still constitutes a problem in some countries, but in others the eradication of the disease has relegated it to one of but minor importance in meat inspection. The section of the book dealing with tuberculosis has therefore been reduced but reference has been made to the more severe code of judgment now prescribed in the meat inspection regulations of Western Germany. Amongst the various parasitic diseases affecting animals destined for human food, bovine cysticercosis continues to be a major problem throughout the world and the section of the book dealing with this affection has been almost entirely rewritten.

In the last decade scientific literature has indicated the world-wide distribution of organisms of the salmonella group and the important role they play in diseases of both animals and man. Salmonellosis is now perhaps the greatest bacterial hazard which confronts the public health worker concerned with foods of animal origin. Considerable additions have therefore been made in this edition to the problems of abattoir and meat factory hygiene, and the author's visit to numerous establishments in the United States, Canada, New Zealand and Australia in 1965 afforded him the opportunity of observing the latest techniques and developments in this field. New material in this edition includes the ways in which bacterial contamination occurs in abattoirs and meat works, the routine bacteriological procedures by which such contamination can be assessed, and the methods by which a reduction in surface bacterial contamination can be attained.

Though the book was written primarily for those concerned with meat inspection in the United Kingdom, its acceptance in many other countries of the world has made it essential to refer to certain affections of animals which are peculiar to these countries; a number of affections, in addition to foot and mouth disease, have become of increasing importance as the trade in meat and meat products between one country and another has tended to increase from year to year. Sections of the book now deal with rinderpest and African swine fever; certain parasitic infections such as anaplasmosis and schistosomiasis have also been included. The long-existing parochial attitude to meat hygiene cannot now be justified and the deliberations of the member states of the European Common Market indicate that universal acceptance of uniform codes of practice and judgment may yet be achieved.

The author has produced the various editions of this book unaided over a period of eighteen years, but accepts the fact that the services of a co-author must now be enlisted if the continuity of the book is to be ensured. He has been fortunate in obtaining the acceptance of Dr. J. F. Gracey, Ph.D., B.Agr., M.R.C.V.S., D.V.S.M., F.R.S.H., City Veterinarian, Belfast, Northern Ireland, to become a co-author in the next edition, and Dr. Gracey has perused the manuscript of this, the fifth edition, and has made a number of valuable contributions to it. These include a section on chemical residues in meat, a subject which has assumed greater importance for the meat hygienist in recent years because of the many compounds being used to promote increased productivity in agriculture. Another addition has been to the section on abattoir hygiene, with which those concerned with abattoir operation have to be conversant; it is one matter to discuss the importance of hygiene but quite another to know how to achieve it in an efficient, practical and economical manner. Because of the great contribution which the abattoir can make in furthering research into and the control of animal disease, a section on the important sphere of abattoir statistics has also been included.

I feel sure that, with Dr. Gracey as my co-author, the book will continue to be of value to those concerned with the animals destined for human food.

Salisbury, Rhodesia H. THORNTON

CHAPTER I

THE FOOD ANIMALS

In civilized countries the animals which furnish food for human consumption are drawn almost entirely from those which consume plant food, as hay, straw, roots or grain. The flesh of carnivorous animals, including the cat and dog, is repugnant to many, though at one time it constituted a proportion of the protein diet of the labouring classes of certain large German towns, particularly in Saxony and Bavaria. Except in times of famine when rats too have been consumed, notably in the siege of Paris, the consumption of cat and dog flesh has now practically ceased in all civilized countries.

In Europe horse flesh forms an important article of human diet and the prejudice that once existed against it was largely based on its prohibition by proclamation of the Christian Church, as horses were then slaughtered for sacrificial purposes. The Danes reintroduced the consumption of horse flesh into Europe as a result of economic stress during the siege of Copenhagen in 1807, and slaughter of horses and sale of the flesh for human consumption is now well established in Denmark, Belgium, Holland and Germany. During wartime horse flesh has been consumed in Great Britain to augment rationed meat, but the demand has disappeared with the resumption of normal supplies of the accepted meat foods, and horse flesh is now largely used for feeding of cats and dogs.

The rabbit forms a subsidiary but important source of meat food, the demand in Great Britain being largely met by the importation of fresh rabbits from Ireland and by those imported from Australia in a frozen condition. Poultry and fish are also subsidiary but valuable articles in augmenting the meat diet.

The great majority of animals slaughtered in all countries for human consumption consist of cattle, calves, sheep and pigs, the modern demand being for meat from a young fattened animal with highly developed musculature. In 1965, in the United Kingdom, the total of meat consumed per head of the population was beef 44·2 lb., mutton and lamb 23·2 lb., pork 25·8 lb. and bacon and ham 25·9 lb.

CATTLE

Cattle in Britain are fattened for slaughter in two main classes, by summer grass feeding, the finished product being marketed between June and December, and by winter feeding, these cattle being slaughtered between January and May. The two sections of the industry are of almost equal size.

A factor which has in some measure affected the popularity of English beef is that about 75 per cent. of the beef produced in England and Wales originates from dairy herds and consists either of beef produced from bull calves, surplus heifers from dairy herds, or from cows. Of the 3·3 million cattle slaughtered annually in the United Kingdom, approximately 2·5 million are either beef cattle, dual-purpose cattle or the progeny of dairy cows reared for beef, 500,000 are discarded dairy cows, and rather more than 250,000 are fat cattle imported alive from Eire and Northern Ireland.

In 1963 the approximate cattle population of some of the principal countries of the world were, in millions, India 255 (cattle and buffaloes); United States 107; U.S.S.R. 87; Brazil 80; Argentina 40; France 20; Australia 16; Canada 12; United Kingdom 12; and New Zealand 6.

Carcase Yield

This is also known as the killing-out percentage or dressing-out percentage, and in cattle denotes the weight of the two sides of beef, including the kidneys, but minus the head, skin, blood, fat and viscera. For beef purposes the butcher requires an animal which will yield a good percentage of carcase, i.e. an animal in which the proportion of offal parts, as the head, feet and intestines, is small. It should also have a good thickness of muscle compared with length of bone, with a smooth covering of fat over the whole carcase. The carcase yield, which is arrived at by comparing the dead weight with the live weight, is expressed as a percentage of the live weight of the animal and varies with the breed, feeding and age of the animal but a high dressing percentage is desirable only if it is brought about by an increased growth of saleable meat without a depression of value due to overfatness.

Breed. British breeds of cattle which fatten readily are the Aberdeen Angus, Beef Shorthorn, Devon and Hereford. Of these the Aberdeen Angus is the outstanding butcher's beast, with its fineness of bone, ability to fatten early and excellent yield of lean meat. The percentage of roasting beef obtainable from the Aberdeen Angus is high and the flesh is of such texture that it commands the highest market quotation. The Beef Shorthorn, also an excellent feeder, will show a daily gain in weight

Fig. 1.—Aberdeen Angus heifer, aged 2 years 1 month and weighing 14 cwt. 14 lb. Note straight top and underline, short leg and smooth level back. The Angus bull is excellent for crossing purposes, and crossed with horned cows produces 100 per cent. black polled calves.

of 1·93 lb. and weighs 12½ cwt. when 2 years old. The Devon, though a slow feeder, shows an excellent carcase yield, but the Hereford, though it fattens early, is not so impressive in this respect.

Argentina is the premier country in the world for the fattening of beef cattle, for the temperature is equable and the great amount of sunlight is an important factor in encouraging growth of young stock. The Shorthorn is the animal in greatest favour, and there are more of this breed than any other, though the Hereford and Aberdeen Angus breeds are also fattened extensively. Britain is Argentina's best customer, most of the prime cattle slaughtered being exported in a chilled condition, while poorer grade animals are exported frozen.

In all fat cattle fineness of bone is an important feature, for no less than one-fifth of the weight of the dressed bovine carcase consists of bone.

FEEDING. Well fattened cattle have a higher carcase yield than animals in poor condition. The state of repletion of the digestive tract also has an obvious bearing on the proportion of dead to live weight, for the average weight of the stomachs and intestines constitutes 16 per cent. of the live weight of the animal. In indigestion, where the stomachs are engorged, the weight of stomachs and intestines may reach 42 per cent. of the animal's live weight.

AGE. The best age for the slaughter of cattle is between 2 and 2½ years, for cattle under 18 months are not mature enough, while over 3 years of age the flesh may be coarser, dark and fibrous. In the United States, where greater importance is placed on tenderness than on flavour, prime cattle are slaughtered at 12 to 14 months old. Though the carcase yield, expressed as a percentage of the live weight, varies little between younger and older animals, it is agreed that cattle between 2 and 2½ years have better form, thickness and quality. A trade which, however, has shown considerable development in Britain, particularly in the northern counties and in Scotland, is the feeding for baby beef. For this trade calves born in April are usually suckled, sold as stores in the autumn, and then fattened indoors throughout the winter, being in prime fat condition by the months of April to July. Baby beef cattle will weigh 7½ to 8½ cwt. alive at the age of 1 to 1½ years and such animals will produce 5 stones of carcase to every 8 stones live weight, a carcase yield of 62 per cent. Exceptional conditions of breeding, feeding and husbandry may even improve on this figure, for prime Scotch cattle which are never permitted to lose their calf fat and are regularly handled and groomed develop an equable temperament which encourages fattening, and may show a carcase yield of as high as 70 per cent. Well nourished young bulls may also show a carcase yield of 70 per cent., though the average in Britain is 54 per cent., while the world's record is that of a spayed Aberdeen Angus heifer with a carcase yield of 76·75 per cent.

The production of baby beef and prime Scotch cattle is only possible by intensive methods of feeding and husbandry, and is outside the scope of the average farmer; generally speaking, good average bullocks and heifers in Britain will show a carcase yield of 53 to 54 per cent. at 2½ years of age, prime bullocks and heifers 60 per cent., and cows 48 to 55 per cent., with an average of 51 per cent. Prime cattle fattened in Argentina for the export trade in chilled beef to Britain have a carcase yield of between 58 and 62 per cent. A useful rule-of-thumb method in assessing the carcase yield in cattle is to estimate it as four-sevenths of the animal's live weight.

The desirable features in a beef animal are a straight top and underline with massive, symmetrical body on short legs set wide apart, back level, smooth and broad throughout its whole length, brisket well forward, and well sprung ribs with thigh full and wide to the hocks. The palatability of beef is enhanced up to a point at which rather more than one-third of the roasted joint is fat and the greatest palatability is obtained in animals with a carcase yield of 58 per cent. In European countries, e.g. Yugoslavia, where beef containing a high proportion of fat is not

FIG. 2.—Hereford heifer. The animals of this breed are good grazers and excellent for ranching purposes where water and fodder may be difficult to obtain and long distances have to be covered.

favoured by consumers, it is common practice to leave male cattle uncastrated so that they will grow rapidly and yield beef with the minimal amount of adipose tissue.

Hormone Treatment of Beef Animals

Castration of male animals was introduced to make them more manageable and to avoid the dark flesh associated with testosterone secretion in later life. Similar results can also be achieved by the administration of hormones to castrated animals, and in effect one is reintroducing into these castrates some of the sex hormones which have been removed, but without the disadvantages of an intact testis and the excessive excitement and danger associated therewith. The purpose, then, of hormones is to enable the feeder to grow his animals fast and market them at an earlier age. Treated animals will gain appreciably in weight compared with untreated animals without alteration in the final dressing percentage, but over-dosage tends to make the meat dark. Similarly in lambs there is an appreciable weight gain but over-dosage tends to produce a carcase with dark meat and heavy shoulders.

Definitions

Bull.	An uncastrated male bovine.
Heifer.	A female up to its first calf.
Cow.	A female which has had one or more calves.
Steer or Bullock.	A castrated male (usually castrated at 6 to 12 weeks old).
Stag.	A male bovine castrated late in life, and therefore presenting a more masculine conformation than the bullock. Some authorities state that cattle castrated by means of the bloodless castrator frequently have a " staggy " appearance.

CALVES

Though beef, pork, mutton and lamb form the main portion of the meat diet in Britain, veal is in great demand on the Continent, particularly in France and Germany. Veal, to be of first quality, must be from calves fed on milk and milk alone, and the calves should be well grown and relatively fat when they are born ; the excellence of veal on the Continent is well known, the calves being specially fed for the purpose.

In Britain the supplies of veal are met almost entirely from home-fed and home-killed animals. These are largely bull calves of dairy breed which, if they were to be kept alive and reared to a more mature age, would consume a gallon of milk daily. They are therefore uneconomical to rear and are slaughtered when 1 to 7 days old, being known as " bobby " calves, and, possessing little muscular development, their flesh is fit only for use in manufactured food products. The proportion of bone in the carcase of a " bobby " calf is high, and represents 50 per cent. of the dressed carcase weight.

The veal calf is slaughtered at 2 to 4 months old, the carcase then weighing about 150 lb. and the proportion of bone in these animals is about 25 per cent. of the dressed carcase weight. The weight of the calf's stomach and intestines in relation to the animal's live weight is less than in adult cattle because of the fluid nature of the digestive contents, and may be put at 11 per cent. of the live weight, as compared with 16 per cent. in adult cattle. The carcase yield is therefore correspondingly greater in calves, and may be estimated as 63 per cent. of the live weight. Male calves intended for sale as veal are not castrated because of the check this operation gives to development.

SHEEP

Sheep feeding may be broadly divided into two similar divisions as in the fattening of cattle, i.e. grass feeding and root feeding. In Britain about 11 million lambs are born yearly, and of these 6 million are

FIG. 3.—Cheviot wether sheep, a hill breed which can live and thrive well on the poorest land and fattens readily when brought down to lower ground.

slaughtered as lamb, 2½ million are slaughtered as mutton, while the remaining 2½ million go into the breeding flock and eventually reach the market as ewe mutton when 5 to 7 years old. Ewes are retained in the breeding flock until sterility, loss of incisor teeth which hinders grazing, or mastitis which diminishes the milk yield, renders them of no further value. Such animals are described as cast ewes.

Various breeds of sheep are crossed to produce a type of lamb which matures early for summer slaughter and one which will also grow and fatten so as to make winter feeding a paying proposition. Generally speaking, long-woolled sheep tend to produce carcases which are too fat for modern requirements, and it is the mountain sheep which furnish mutton of the choicest quality and flavour.

The Half-bred sheep, which is the product of the Border Leicester ram and Cheviot ewe, is one of the foremost utility sheep in Britain for though the flesh of the Border Leicester carries an excessive amount of fat and is lacking in lean meat, while the Cheviot flesh is close and lean, the product of their cross produces a tender, succulent flesh.

The Half-bred ewe is crossed with a Suffolk, Oxford or Hampshire ram, the cross lambs being in great demand for summer slaughter or winter keep. The Ryeland and Southdown ram is also occasionally mated with the Half-bred ewe, while the Scottish Blackface, or Hill ewe,

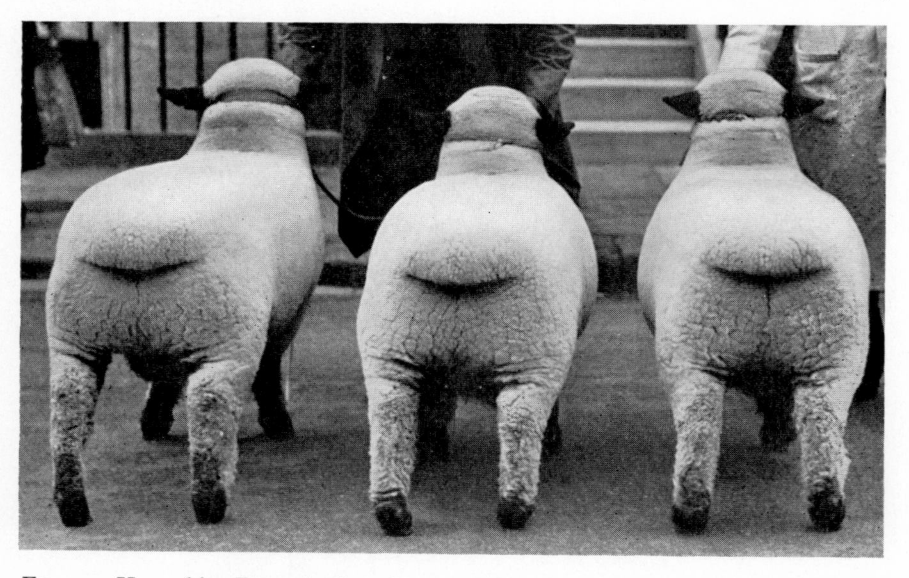

FIG. 4.—Hampshire Down lambs. Note short, very thick legs, with great breadth across thigh and broad flat back. The two legs account for at least 25 per cent. of the weight of the dressed carcase.

crossed with the Border Leicester ram produces the mule lamb which is in great demand for summer slaughter, the flesh being very tender and the joints of meat small and ideal for modern requirements.

The Southdown is an outstanding butcher's sheep, and the success of the imported New Zealand lamb trade is largely due to the export of the Southdown breed from Britain to that country, and has enabled the New Zealand farmer to produce a lamb suitable in weight and grade to meet the public demand in Britain. The Romney Marsh crossed with the Southdown is used extensively in the South Island of New Zealand. The Southdown is deservedly popular for, with the exception of the Welsh Mountain breed, it produces the smallest of all joints, and a Southdown sheep of 8 stone weight will provide as much prime meat as a 10 stone sheep of other breeds, the bones being small and the flesh finely grained. It is also an excellent sheep for crossing, for cross Southdown lambs mature very early, and lambs born in January are frequently sold fat to the butcher in April. The Merino is essentially a wool breed and in Australia accounts for 75 per cent. of the sheep population ; about 28 per cent. of the sheep population consists of Merino wethers kept for wool production.

The desirable features required by the butcher in both lamb and mutton carcases of any breed are short, stocky plump legs, thick full loin, broad full back, thick fleshy ribs with a wide breast and shoulder, a good depth of chest cavity and a short plump neck. Lamb is now more in demand than mutton, for it is more tender and contains less fat.

In 1963 the approximate sheep populations in some of the principal countries in the world were, in millions : Australia 159 ; U.S.S.R. 134 ; China 59 ; New Zealand 50 ; United States 30 ; United Kingdom 29, and France 9.

Carcase Yield

All fat sheep in wool should show a carcase yield of 50 per cent. or over. The Suffolk and Half-bred sheep will show a carcase yield as high as 54 per cent., while old thin ewes in full fleece have a carcase yield as low as 35 per cent. A useful practical method for the estimation of the weight of a sheep carcase is to take 50 per cent. of the animal's live weight and deduct or add 2 to 4 lb. according to quality.

Definitions

Lamb.	A sheep from birth to weaning time (generally at 3½ to 4½ months old). Butchers apply a more generous interpretation to the term lamb, and use it to denote a sheep from birth until shearing time the following year ; by this interpretation a sheep 13 months old is still classed as lamb.
Tup or Ram.	The uncastrated male.
Hogg or Wether.	The castrated male sheep (usually castrated at 3 weeks to 3 months old).
Gimmer.	A female which has not yet borne a lamb.
Ewe.	A female which has borne lambs.
Cast Ewe.	One which has been removed from the breeding flock.

PIGS

The chief characteristic of the pig is that it matures within a shorter period than any other domestic animal, i.e. in about 9 months. It also has greater powers of reproduction, and will produce about ten pigs in each litter and frequently two litters in a year. Pigs intended for human food may be classified into porkers, bacon pigs, sows and boars.

Pork pigs yield carcases of 80 to 120 lb. dead weight, the main demand being for carcases of 100 to 120 lb. A prime porker should be the carcase of a hog pig or virgin female pig, the latter being preferred by the pork butcher as it grows more slowly and does not carry as much fat as the hog.

Desirable features in a good pork pig are a moderately long carcase, line of back not dished, good depth of loin, with even distribution of back

FIG. 5.—Crossbred pork pigs (Large White × Middle White), aged 4 months. Note good thick chine, full sides, and long flat back.

fat of not more than ½ inch and not less than ¼ inch depth at any point behind the shoulder.

Bacon pigs weigh between 140 to 250 lb. dead weight, the ideal commercial weight for manufacture into bacon being about 160 lb. In Denmark a markedly uniform carcase is produced for export to Britain as mild-cured bacon, this carcase being the product of a cross between the native Landrace and the British Large White pig, animals of both these breeds being large and long and putting on less fat at the required slaughter weights. It weighs about 180 lb. live weight, and yields a carcase of about 145 lb. (i.e. 70 per cent.). Desirable features in a good bacon pig are a long body more or less slab-sided, level back without too much fat, light shoulders, and hams full to the hock. A pig of this type will produce a side of bacon with the correct proportions of fat and lean.

Sows weigh from 250 lb. to 280 lb. or more dead weight, but these, together with boars and stags, are not cured for bacon but are utilized by the pork butcher for the manufacture of pork sausage.

In 1963 the approximate pig populations in some of the principal countries of the world were, in millions : U.S.S.R. 69 ; United States 59 ; Brazil 56 ; Western Germany 15 ; Poland 12 ; France 9 ; United Kingdom 7. The figures for China are unavailable but are probably astronomical, for in 1959 the pig population was estimated at 180 million.

FIG. 6.—Bacon pig of the White Landrace breed. Note light shoulder, good length, flat deep side and good ham. The fore-end is reduced as far as is consistent with need for lung and heart room, wasteful fat is eliminated, while the increased length gives a maximum of the highest-priced cuts of bacon.

Carcase Yield

The dead weight in pigs is the weight of the carcase, including the head and kidneys, but minus the viscera. A useful practical method for assessing the weight of a pig carcase is to remove the head and weigh it, when the weight of the head in pounds approximates closely to the weight of the carcase in stones. The carcase yield is estimated, as in cattle and sheep, by comparing the dead and live weight, and is expressed as a percentage of the live weight; it is influenced by breed, age, sex and weight, and generally speaking may be put at 75 per cent. In Denmark it is stated that good pork pigs will show a dressing-out percentage of 80, and bacon pigs 70 per cent.

Definitions

Boar. The uncastrated male.

Hog. The castrated male (usually castrated at 6 to 8 weeks).

Stag. A male pig castrated late in life to facilitate fattening and obviate the strong " boar " odour of the carcase.

Rig. A male pig with one undescended testicle. The retained testicle, somewhat smaller than normal, can usually be found lying close to one of the kidneys.

Gilt. A female which has not had a litter. Known also as a " clean " pig.

Sow. A female which has had a litter.

TRANSPORT

The importance of the careful handling of the food animals before slaughter cannot be exaggerated, for unsuitable conditions of road or rail transport frequently lead to injury, lameness, suffocation or transit fever. The danger is greater for fat animals than for lean, and is accentuated the more closely animals are loaded, the higher the temperature, and the longer the journey. In Britain there is a specific legal enactment which prohibits the transportation of an animal in any vehicle if owing to illness or injury it cannot be carried without unnecessary suffering.

Regulations concerning transport of live stock are laid down in Great Britain by the Transit of Animals Order, 1927. This order prescribes that all bulls shall be securely tied, and horned stock travelling in the same wagon as a bull shall be securely tied or be separated from it by a partition. Calves, sheep, goats and swine, if carried with any head of cattle, shall be separated therefrom by a partition. Shorn sheep shall only be transported between the 1st November and the 30th April if the sides of the railway truck are covered by a tarpaulin. Water assists all animals to withstand heat, and provision must be made for the supply of water to sheep during a journey of 36 hours or over and, in the case of cattle and swine, for a period of 27 hours or over. No specific requirements with regard to floor space are laid down, but railway stock wagons are of two common sizes, the large being $17\frac{1}{2}$ feet × $7\frac{1}{2}$ feet, and the medium 15 feet × $7\frac{1}{2}$ feet. The table on p. 13 shows the generally accepted maximum numbers of stock carried.

American regulations prescribe the minimum floor space required for animals during transport as $4\frac{1}{3}$ square feet for pigs, $2\frac{3}{4}$ square feet for sheep, and $3\frac{1}{2}$ square feet for calves. Cattle placed crosswise in the wagon require 22 to 26 inches of the car length.

Amongst the food animals, fat pigs are the most likely to become

	Large Wagon	Medium Wagon
Cattle (fat) . .	10-11	9-10
Cattle (store) .	14-15	11-13
Pigs (bacon) . .	31-34	28-30
Boars and Sows .	14-16	10-12
Sheep (small) .	50	42
Sheep (medium) .	40	35
Sheep (large) . .	35-40	30-35

deleteriously affected during transport as their heat-eliminating powers are very limited and they soon succumb to over-exertion. Suffocation due to badly ventilated lorries is not uncommon and is assisted by the habit of breeders giving pigs a heavy meal before the journey with the object of preventing loss during transport. The ventilation of the lorry is also important because pigs become more aggressive under conditions of high temperature and relative humidity, and also when exposed to the direct rays of the sun.

Bruising and bite marks on the surface of the skin of pigs cause depreciation in market value and it has been shown that most bruises occur during transport, a minor proportion during loading and unloading. Pigs from different farms loaded on to the same lorry behave comparatively quietly once the lorry is in motion but commence to fight as soon as the lorry stops, and it has been shown that by reducing the stopping periods by one half the incidence of bite marks is reduced by 25 per cent.

Sheep are frequently found dead as a result of suffocation during transport. Sheep in full wool rarely bruise in transit, though lifting by the fleece of the back causes damage and in New Zealand this is known as "wool burn". In cattle, bruising occurs commonly, and authorities in Kenya have shown that bruising as a result of transport occurs more frequently in horned cattle than in polled animals, exotic breeds are more susceptible than indigenous breeds, provision of bedding in the wagon reduces the incidence of bruising by about half, and a similar reduction in bruising incidence is secured if the sexes are kept separate. In South Africa it was stated that about 12 per cent. of beef carcases were rejected for the export trade because of bruising and that improvements in methods of handling and transport could reduce bruising losses to 1 to 2 per cent.

Loss of Weight during Transport

Animals consigned to a market or abattoir for slaughter will lose weight during the journey. The loss in live weight, which is primarily due to sweating, exhalation, and the excretion of urine and faeces, is controlled by the bodily condition of the animal, state of repletion before transport, season of the year and duration of the journey. This loss, being essentially due to the excretion of waste matter from the body, is of little or no significance and occurs most readily in pigs, less readily in sheep, and still less readily in cattle. Pigs will lose 5 to 12 lb. of their live weight during 24 hours transport, sheep 2 to 4 lb. if kept in a lairage for 24 hours and up to 8 lb. during transport, while a calf of 330 lb. live weight loses 9 lb. during its first day of travel and 4 lb. on the second day. A bullock weighing 12 cwt. will lose 66 to 88 lb. during the first day of travel but only 11 to 15 lb. on subsequent days.

Of much greater importance, though difficult to assess, is the actual loss of flesh during transport. With bacon pigs the loss in actual carcase weight is about 2 lb. for every day of their journey, and it is probable that both muscular and fatty tissues are affected and that there is an abnormal loss of water from the muscular tissues. The effect of over-exertion, excitement and strange surroundings on pigs during transit may also cause a loss of 6 to 7 per cent. in the weight of the liver. Short or long journeys appear to have little effect on carcase wastage in sheep. In the United States cattle transported by rail are stated to lose 1·48 per cent. of carcase weight for journeys of up to 100 miles and 2·10 per cent. for journeys of 250 to 300 miles. Tissue shrinkage begins during the early part of a journey, continues at a relatively uniform rate for 90 hours, then tends to diminish. Some shrinkage occurs even though animals receive food and water during transport, but tissue shrinkage is less if these are provided during long journeys. In some South American countries the native Criollo cattle are involved in road journeys of a week or more on their way to the slaughterhouse, and these animals, which weigh about 450 lb. when alive, are stated to lose 20 to 40 lb. in actual carcase weight during the journey. Cattle from the northern parts of Australia lose so much weight and quality in their long overland trek to the slaughterhouse that they must be placed on pastures for up to a year to regain the weight and quality needed to meet export demands. The practice of trekking cattle several hundred miles is, however, gradually giving way to motor haulage and by 1962 more than half of the cattle in that area were transported by motor vehicle.

Affections Induced by Transport

Transit fever is a catarrhal and often fatal disease which chiefly affects store cattle in poor condition that have become fatigued due to a long journey by rail or sea without a sufficiency of food. The affection is noticed particularly during the colder months and post-mortem lesions take the form of a lobar pneumonia, the interlobular septa being sometimes thickened due to serous infiltration. Acute enteritis is usually present, though the spleen appears normal and, as the affection does not respond well to treatment, early slaughter is advisable before the onset of septic lung changes.

Transit tetany occurs under similar circumstances but almost invariably in cows, particularly those in advanced pregnancy and in the warmer months of the year. It is a disease which bears a resemblance to milk fever and affected animals usually respond to calcium therapy. There are no specific post-mortem lesions. The transportation of young calves from one part of the country to another and their subjection to exhaustion, dietary changes and chilling on the journey may increase their susceptibility to infection and cause a latent salmonella infection to assume an acute and septicaemic form.

The Effect of Stress During Transport

During the journey of an animal from farm to abattoir, and again in the abattoir pens while awaiting slaughter, an animal is subjected to a number of disturbing and unfavourable stimuli. This produces in the animal a state of tension or stress, a term which may conveniently be defined as any deviation from that enjoyed by the healthy well-fed and properly rested animal. Stress becomes apparent when the environmental changes are unusually severe and the responses of the body exceed those which are considered physiological. Environmental changes take the form of strange surroundings, strange noises, strange attendants, rough handling, extremes of temperature and starvation, and the response of the animal to these unfavourable factors results in stimulation of the central nervous system by way of the hypothalamus and pituitary body, and thence to various organs causing the increased production of adrenalin and its release into the bloodstream. One effect of the release of adrenalin into the blood stream is to cause depletion of the glycogen reserves in muscular tissue and a resultant rise in the level of blood sugar. A second effect is to bring about an increased blood flow to the muscles and this is compensated by a decreased blood flow to the digestive organs. Further effects of adrenalin are a contraction of the spleen thus emptying its reserve of blood corpuscles into the blood, strong enhancement of the clotting power of the blood, and a dilation of the bronchioles of the lung thus permitting greater intake of oxygen. Of the various effects of stress the depletion of muscle glycogen and the increased flow of blood into muscular tissue are particularly undesirable in an animal about to be slaughtered.

The effects of stress in animals destined for beef and bacon have been studied closely and more recently similar work has been done on lambs. It is a known fact that stress factors increase the susceptibility of animals to infectious diseases and it is also recognized that influences such as hunger, fatigue and fear trigger off a chain of events which affects dressing percentage, microbial content of the tissues, onset of rigor mortis and the keeping quality of meats both fresh and preserved. Workers in Australia and elsewhere have shown further that undesirable stimuli operating shortly before slaughter may affect not only the keeping quality of beef but also its tenderness and flavour and the investigations have shown that individual cattle show considerable variation in their reaction to stress. The meat of those animals which exhibit fear or pronounced excitability prior to slaughter may undergo undesirable changes and amongst such changes are the production of so-called black beef, bone taint, which is a form of internal anaerobic spoilage, and the condition in pig muscle known as watery pork. Not only do unfavourable stimuli affect muscular tissue but they may also produce irreversible changes in colour and consistency of the liver, and to this the term " stress liver " has been applied. Inasmuch as stress may bring about serious deterioration in the marketability and value of a carcase it has been recommended that stress factors could be minimized in an animal by the administration of tranquillizers.

TRANQUILLIZERS. Though it has been shown that the administration intra-muscularly of tranquillizers to cattle 24 hours prior to a long journey may bring about a significant lowering in weight loss, the method has certain disadvantages. Some of the tranquillizers used have caused severe tissue reaction in the form of gelatinous infiltration, haemorrhage, and muscle changes of a necrotic nature at the site of injection, and this entails considerable trimming, often as much as 5 lb., of the affected carcase. It is probable that the condition encountered most frequently in animals which have undergone transport is traumatism, which likewise entails considerable trimming of tissue from the carcase, but tranquillizers do not appear to be efficacious in lowering the incidence or degree of bruising.

THE TREATMENT OF ANIMALS PRIOR TO SLAUGHTER

Resting

It is desirable to rest an animal before slaughter, as an animal slaughtered without an adequate period of rest may show a reduction in the keeping quality of the flesh due to incomplete development of acidity of the muscles and also due to early invasion of the system by putrefactive bacteria from the intestinal tract. These bacteria are the essential cause of bone taint in cattle and of ham taint in pigs. Though the meat of animals slaughtered while exhausted appears dark and fiery and gives the impression that bleeding of the animal has been incomplete, this dark coloration must be attributed in some degree to changes of a chemical nature which take place in the muscle of the fatigued animal, for in such animals there is a decreased oxygenation of the blood haemoglobin and muscle myoglobin with a consequent darkening of the muscle pigment. A minimum period of 12 to 24 hours detention and rest in a lairage is therefore essential before slaughter, and though cattle subjected to stress for a short period may recover rapidly, those subjected to stress for a long period may take several days to regain physiological normality.

Watering

Animals should receive ample drinking water during their detention in the lairage as this serves to lower the bacterial load in the intestine and facilitates removal of the hide or pelt during dressing of the carcase. Stunning of animals by electrical means is rendered more efficacious if they have received unlimited water, but no food, during their detention prior to slaughter.

Feeding

Among butchers throughout the world the practice of withholding of food from animals prior to slaughter has long been observed, it being contended in support of this practice that fasted animals bleed better, that the carcase is easier to dress and that it has a brighter appearance. Scientific evidence for such assertions is lacking and the hungry animal does not settle as well as an animal which has been fed. It is also a known physiological fact that although cattle and sheep are better able to withstand cold than are the other farm animals, resistance to the shock of a severe fall in atmospheric temperature is greater in the fed animal than in one which has been starved.

In the case of pigs the resting of these for 24 hours after a journey does not restore them to normality unless they are fed. Indeed, the fatigue and restlessness engendered by hunger in pigs, in which a definite excitement pyrexia appears to occur in those animals not used to handling, may render the flesh unsuitable for those preserved meat products which are not consumed until some considerable time later. One authority records a loss of 7 per cent. in carcase weight and 30 per cent. in liver weight of pigs rested for 72 hours without feeding, but when pigs were fed milk and sugar the loss in carcase weight was reduced to 3 per cent. and the loss in liver weight to 8 per cent. In cattle detained for two days in a lairage a 25 per cent. loss in liver weight may occur, and in one works in Chicago the effects of stress in cattle are reduced by incorporating molasses in the drinking water. In sheep detained for two, three or four days there is a significant loss in carcase weight and up to 29 per cent. of loss in weight of the liver, and even four days resting and feeding of sheep in a lairage is insufficient to reverse the effect of carcase and liver wastage. There is, however, justification for withholding food from cattle for a period of 12 hours prior to slaughter and in this way minimizing the emigration of bacteria from the intestinal tract, which occurs during digestion.

It will be seen that there are convincing reasons for avoiding thirst, hunger and fatigue in animals awaiting slaughter but there are also cogent reasons against detaining animals too long in the lairage pens. Cross-infection with salmonella organisms may occur, particularly when mixed collections of animals are grouped together. This frequently occurs in calves, and in one experiment in calves awaiting slaughter it was shown that after a few hours' detention only 0·6 per cent. of the animals harboured salmonellae, whereas after a detention period of two to five days 55·6 per cent. contained salmonellae in their intestine. Other authorities have recorded the finding of salmonellae in 7 per cent. of farm pigs, in 25 per cent. of pigs in the lairage pen, in 50 per cent. of pigs on the slaughter floor, while 75 per cent. of lairage drinking water was found infected. Very young calves cannot be induced to take food in lairage pens and because of the danger of cross-infection they should be slaughtered forthwith on arrival at an abattoir. Small pens with solid bases to the partitions will considerably lower the risk of cross-infection with salmonella organisms.

ANTE-MORTEM INSPECTION

This most desirable practice is of great value, for it aids in the detection of animals suffering from scheduled or infectious diseases, particularly anthrax, rabies and glanders, which are communicable to man. It is not uncommon for swine fever to be first detected at an abattoir, and a visit to the farm or piggery from which the pigs were consigned is indicated. Similarly, where foot and mouth disease or sheep scab is detected in an abattoir, a " tracing back " is likely to be of value, and in the majority of cases disease may be found on the premises as a result of such a visit. Further, many diseases of a toxic or infectious nature are difficult to detect in the carcase and organs after slaughter, and ante-mortem inspection is of particular value in the recognition of diseases such as septic metritis and mastitis, sturdy in sheep or tuberculous meningitis in young cattle. In specific diseases such as tetanus or rabies the recognition of the typical symptoms is of the greatest value, for in these diseases the post-mortem findings are but slight and of little diagnostic value; indication of disease detected in the live animal calls for its segregation, and a detailed examination after slaughter. Ante-mortem inspection is also of value in the prevention of food-poisoning outbreaks, for many of these outbreaks can be traced to the consumption of meat from animals slaughtered while obviously ill but whose carcases and organs may show little noticeable change on post-mortem examination. In Australia the isolation of slaughter cattle which show symptoms of shivering and diarrhoea has proved a valuable procedure in limiting salmonella infections.

Routine ante-mortem inspection calls for an entirely different procedure in countries such as North and South America, Canada or Australia where the animals are range cattle, compared with Great Britain and Europe, where the animals can usually be approached and handled. In

FIG. 7.—Ante-mortem examination in a U.S.A. abattoir. The ear is being tagged to indicate the animal is not healthy and that a detailed inspection will be required after slaughter.

every case an inspection should be carried out daily and the final examination should take place within 24 hours of slaughter. Where any of the food animals are recumbent and unable to stand, the temperature should be taken ; a rise in temperature may be the first indication of communicable disease, although in moribund animals the temperature may frequently be subnormal. In sheep, temperature may be a somewhat misleading guide as, of all the food animals, its temperature is subject to the greatest daily fluctuation ; variations between 102° F. and 104° F. are common, and in heavy-woolled sheep in summer the temperature may reach 105° F. In pigs the body temperature can vary between 100·9° F. and 104·5° F. in healthy animals, but pigs which show a temperature of 106° F. or over, and cattle and sheep which show a temperature of 105° F. or higher, should be isolated until the temperature falls or diagnosis of the disease is estab-blished for, if slaughtered while suffering from this degree of fever, the carcase will be congested and will invariably require condemnation.

In the United States all animals slaughtered in Federally inspected establishments and showing symptoms of rabies, tetanus, milk fever or transit fever are condemned on ante-mortem inspection, except that cattle affected with milk fever or transit fever may be detained for treatment under official supervision; of other animals marked as suspect during

FIG. 8.—Ante-mortem inspection on horseback at a South American frigorifico. The cattle are dehorned Hereford bullocks, castrated within 2 months of birth, and are never housed from birth to slaughter. Dehorning greatly lowers the losses due to bruised meat. (Dr. M. T. Morgan.)

ante-mortem inspection, 25 per cent. are subsequently condemned as a result of post-mortem examination.

Diseases and Abnormalities Encountered in Ante-mortem Inspection

Cattle. These are tuberculosis, actinomycosis and actinobacillosis, emaciation, blackleg, tumours, ringworm, mange, mastitis and transit fever. Lameness may be the result of "foul of the foot" or foot and mouth disease, while a common injury encountered in cattle is when an animal slips, "does the splits" and injures its pelvis. Animals which are dead or dying, or which show symptoms of tetanus, rabies, anthrax, or blackleg should not be dressed for human food, but should be destroyed. In 1965 in the United States the principal conditions for which cattle were condemned on ante-mortem inspection were, in the following order, moribund, epithelioma, pyrexia and emaciation.

Calves. In the ante-mortem inspection of these animals the following conditions must be looked for: immaturity, calf diphtheria, ringworm, cowpox or white scour.

Sheep. Search must be made for emaciation, sheep scab, tetanus, foot and mouth disease, caseous lymphadenitis and pneumonia. Pneumonia is common in old ewes and often follows a railway journey, especially in winter and spring, while smothered sheep are not uncommonly encountered in lairage inspection.

Swine. Ante-mortem inspection is of value in the detection of atrophic rhinitis, gut oedema, foot and mouth disease, rabies, actinomycosis of the udder, herniae, tumours, injured animals, particularly those with fractures of the limbs, and abscess formation. Ante-mortem inspection is also of value in detection of cases of swine fever and swine erysipelas, and pigs which have recovered from an acute attack of swine erysipelas and are affected with the chronic disease have a dry scaly skin, exhibit pain on movement and have a typical unthrifty appearance.

1. *Tetanus*. The pig acquired the infection a week previously during castration. When startled the animal fell to the ground and exhibited arching of the back with rigid extension of the limbs and pricking up of ears and tail. Death occurred some twelve hours later.

2. *Contagious Pustular Dermatitis or Orf*. An acute virus affection occurring in lambs in early summer and characterized by an eruption around the mouth and formation of warty masses on mouth and nostrils, sometimes at the extremities of the limbs. Infection may be conveyed to the udder and teats of the ewe and give rise to an acute staphylococcal mastitis.

3. *Gut Oedema (Bowel Oedema) in Swine*. There is incoordination of movement, which is progressive until the animal walks with a pronounced staggering gait, and when an affected pig tries to rest the front legs may be extended forwards. Swelling of the eyelids, seen also in this illustration, is a frequent symptom.

4. *Atrophic Rhinitis in Swine*. Sneezing and nasal haemorrhage may occur and discharge from the eyes with collection of dust causing dark patches on each cheek. The face becomes distorted upwards or, as in this case, sideways and this is usually accompanied by marked wrinkling of the skin of the nose and face.

5. *Johne's Disease*. Friesian bullock showing characteristic early wasting of the buttock muscles and the typical pipe-stem diarrhoea. This is usually profuse, painless but persistent, very foul smelling and often mixed with gas bubbles and flakes of mucus. (W. D. Rankin.)

6. *Parasitic Gastro-enteritis in a Goat*. There is loss of weight and progressive weakness with anaemia and oedema of the dependent parts of the body and submaxillary space (" bottle neck ") . Diarrhoea, which is dark due to the presence of blood, may be observed in infection by certain species of stomach worms but in others there is obstinate constipation.

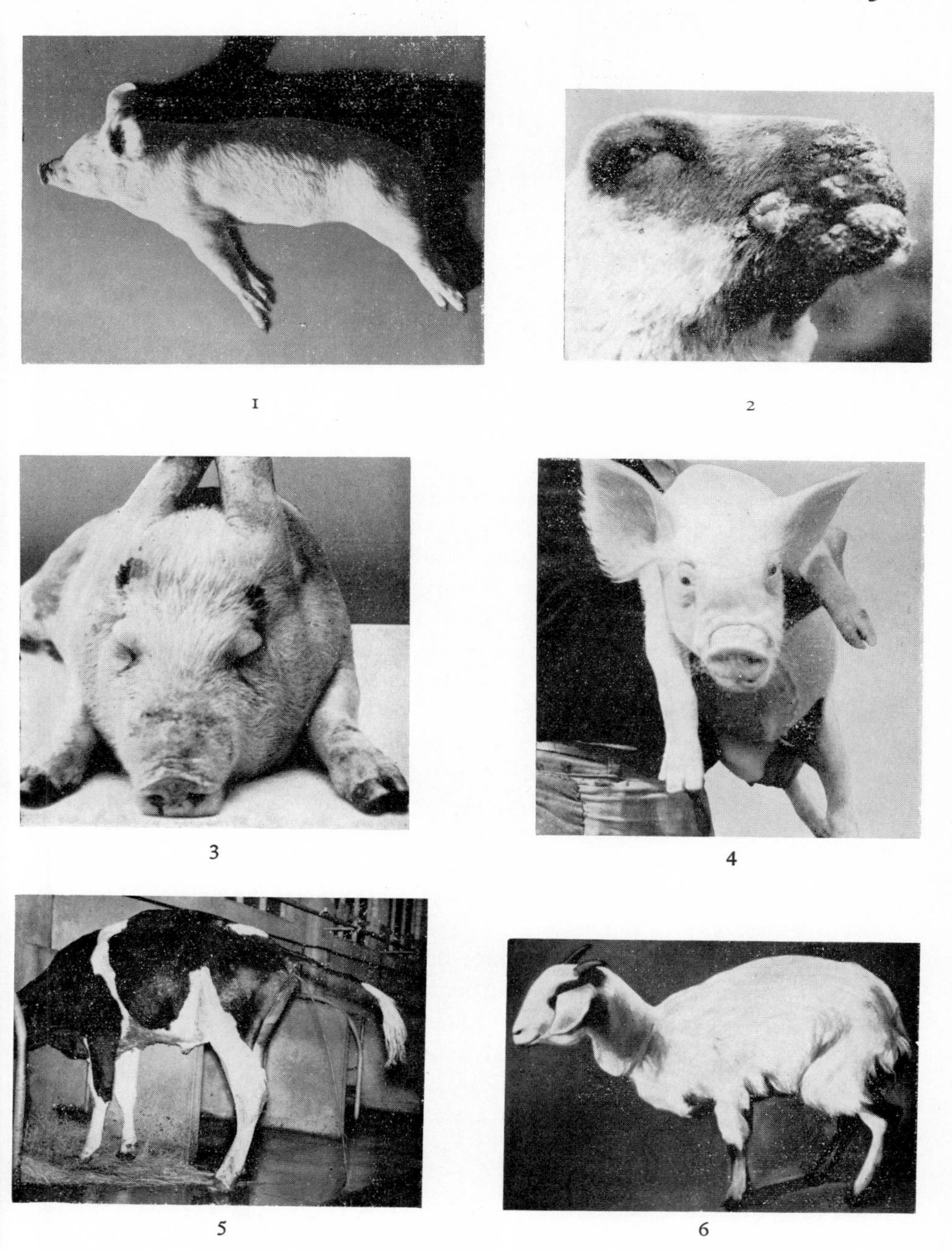

FIG. 9.—Some important affections of animals and the typical symptoms which may be observed during ante-mortem inspection.

CHAPTER II

ABATTOIRS

GENERAL CONSTRUCTION AND LAYOUT
METHODS OF SLAUGHTER

GENERAL CONSTRUCTION AND LAYOUT

In European practice abattoirs are usually provided by a local authority although these cannot be classed as municipal enterprises comparable to a municipal electric supply or transport undertaking. In the case of abattoirs the municipality owns the buildings and is also responsible for certain essential services, such as cleansing, feeding of animals in the lairage and the renting of cold storage accommodation. Public abattoirs are open to all who wish to slaughter animals for human food, the revenue of the abattoir being derived from lairage fees, slaughter charges, cold-storage charges and the operation of a by-products plant.

The first step in planning an abattoir is to ascertain the ultimate maximum daily kill of each class of animal and the proposed disposal and treatment of the edible and inedible by-products. The actual system of operation must also be determined and this may comprise (*a*) a complete factory abattoir on one, two or three floors, (*b*) an abattoir adapted to allow for slaughter and dressing by individual butchers, or (*c*) a building of the factory abattoir type but with dressing accommodation rented by individual butchers. The above three groups are capable of many variations and combinations to suit local conditions. The factory abattoir principle denotes employment of regular whole-time slaughtermen to deal with all the livestock and it is a method that ensures economic handling of the by-products, which include the hides, offals, glands, blood and condemned meat. The factory abattoir also reduces the overhead charges on buildings, equipment and labour.

Site

It is usual for an abattoir to be erected near to a cattle market so that animals need not be driven long distances through the streets. With the advent of motor transport for livestock this argument, other than on the grounds of expense to the wholesale butcher, is not now of such importance. The contiguity of railway sidings is also a desirable feature, but the main essentials of an abattoir site are that there should be available an ample supply of water, adequate facilities for sewage disposal, an electricity supply and if possible a gas supply and good road facilities. Whether grazing land should be provided contiguous to an abattoir for accommodation of cattle and sheep is a matter of opinion, though it is contended that animals settle better on grazing land than in an enclosed lairage.

FIG. 10.—South American frigorifico showing ramp up which stock is driven to the fifth floor where slaughter takes place. Fractious cattle are readily induced to ascend the ramp by use of the electric goad, but beating with sticks results in bruising and is forbidden. (Dr. M. T. Morgan.)

In England and Wales the hygienic requirements in respect of construction, layout and equipment of slaughterhouses, and the practices to be observed are laid down in the Slaughterhouse (Hygiene) Regulations, 1958. The provisions directed towards the avoidance of unnecessary suffering in animals awaiting slaughter are laid down in The Slaughter of Animals (Prevention of Cruelty) Regulations, 1958.

In a modern abattoir the following buildings must be provided:

1. Lairage.
2. Isolation Block.
3. Slaughter Hall.
4. Cooling Hall.
5. Hide and Skin Store.
6. Guttery and Tripery.
7. Offices and Condemned Meat Room.

1. Lairage

The importance of suitable lairage accommodation for animals awaiting slaughter cannot be overestimated, for a period of rest of 24 hours before slaughter has a markedly beneficial effect on the appearance and subsequent marketability of the carcase. Cattle detained in cold, damp lairages may suffer depletion of their glycogen reserves, and the incidence of "black beef" may be greatly reduced if cattle, particularly stall-fed animals, are housed in lairages which are not too cold and free from draughts and are provided with adequate food and water from leaving the farm until the time of slaughter.

Lairage space sufficient for 3 days' supply of cattle and 2 days' supply of sheep or pigs is regarded as ample. It is desirable that pig and sheep pens should be interchangeable and some of the sheep pens should also be adapted for the temporary lairage of cattle.

CATTLE LAIRAGE. Accommodation may be of the tie-up type, similar to a cow-byre, the neck chain being attached to a sliding ring on a vertical bar, thus permitting the animal to stand or lie down in comfort. The vertical bar should permit of easy withdrawal, so that an animal in danger of being strangled can be quickly released. The tie-up form of lairage is necessary for cows, bulls and pugnacious cattle, and under the Slaughter of Animals (Prevention of Cruelty) Regulations horned stock and those likely to injure other animals must be separated from other stock, and if two such animals are kept together, they must be restrained so as to prevent injury to each other.

Under the above Regulations drinking water must be available to animals at all times and each pen should be provided with a gravitational water supply, one cistern being sufficient to feed three troughs, but automatic water bowls, though satisfactory for cows, are less suitable for young cattle as they tend to cause fright. In a lairage of the tie-up type, long water troughs in front of the cattle are quite satisfactory and are more easily cleansed than individual troughs or bowls. Hayracks must be provided, and it is a legal obligation that animals must be fed twice daily except on the morning of the day of intended slaughter or the afternoon preceding the morning of intended slaughter. In the case of horses, however, they must be fed on the afternoon preceding the day of intended slaughter.

Hydrant points should be placed conveniently, so that all parts of the lairage can be reached by a sufficient supply of water for cleansing, and the water supply of an abattoir should be estimated on the basis of 150 gallons per beast slaughtered. An important factor which facilitates cleansing is that the lairage should be provided with a passage wide enough to admit entry of a vehicle suitable for the removal of manure, and this also aids in rapid removal of a dead animal.

SHEEP LAIRAGE. The height of the sheep pens should be 3 feet, with passages 3 feet wide between the pens, while to prevent animals putting their heads through the lower rails of the pens these rails should not be more than 6 inches apart. Double-hinged gates should be used in all sheep and pig pens, as they greatly facilitate entry and exit of stock, and two adjoining pens can be utilized to accommodate an overflow of animals if a sliding gate is provided between the pens. Sheep pens must also be provided with water troughs, for sheep drink quite freely, and these troughs should be placed some 10 inches from the floor as, if placed too low, they easily become fouled. Hay racks should also be provided above the level of the sheep's head.

Calf pens may be provided as an integral part of the sheep lairage, as it is customary for calves to be slaughtered in the same abattoir section and by the same slaughtermen engaged on the slaughter of sheep. It is, however, a prescription of the Slaughter of Animals (Prevention of Cruelty) Regulations that young animals unable to take swill or solid food must be slaughtered as soon as practicable. There is no objection to cattle and sheep lairage being provided in the same building, while pigs and sheep may be housed together without detrimental effect. Cattle, however, do not appear to rest well in the company of pigs.

PIG LAIRAGE. Pig pens are preferably constructed of stouter pattern rails and gates than in the sheep lairage, and the lower horizontal rails of the pen should not be more than 6 inches apart to prevent pigs putting their heads between the rails and becoming fixed. The feeding troughs should be so designed that the pigs cannot gain access to them while the troughs are being cleansed and filled.

In the pig lairage several smaller pens should be provided for the accommodation of one sow or two or three pork pigs. It is a mistake to have the pig lairage building too lofty, as pigs readily become victims of pneumonia, especially when moved from an overheated sty to a cold lairage.

MANURE. Considerable quantities of lairage waste in the form of bedding and dung require periodical removal, and this should be conveyed to an elevated covered site near to the lairage, from which it can be conveniently reloaded for removal, usually by contractors. The manure obtained from the stomachs and intestines of slaughtered animals requires separate treatment.

2. Isolation Block

This important building is actually a miniature abattoir, and is provided with lairage for up to four cattle, together with a slaughter hall and hanging room. It should be situated near to the suspected meat detention room, and should also be in direct communication with the by-products department. Under the Slaughterhouse (Hygiene) Regulations animals which are diseased or suspect must be lairaged apart from other animals and such animals must be taken to that part of the lairage provided for the segregation of such animals.

3. Slaughter Hall

The transference of animals from lairage to slaughter hall is a matter

FIG. 11.—Water bath and holding pen in a meat works in Western Australia. As cattle enter the abattoir they are sprayed from above while in the water bath (beyond the gate). The bath is 30 feet long and 6 feet in width and filled with water to a depth of 3 feet for large cattle, but this level can be adjusted for calves. The animals then enter the holding pen (in foreground), the floor of which consists of raised octagonal sections of concrete which are 12 inches in width and 1 inch high, and this prevents slipping without impeding drainage. A similar design and material is used in the lairage pens, but in the water bath and the race from lairage to stunning box the raised sections are of cast iron to withstand severe wear.

of no difficulty if the abattoir is well designed, and if a top or killing floor is used and the site is on a slope it will be possible to walk the animals directly on the level on to the killing floor. Alternatively, a ramp of easy gradient can be provided up which the animals walk, and cattle and sheep can readily be driven up a ramp as steep as 1 in 6 though the ramp should be provided with a man-way. In certain abattoirs trained sheep or goats are used to lead flocks of sheep up the ramp to the killing floor. In some cases animals are stunned on the ground level then hoisted after bleeding for subsequent dressing on the top floor. Many abattoirs spray the cattle from above as they move along the race connecting the mustering pen and stunning pen, a procedure of doubtful value except in reducing the

FIG. 12.—Single-throw cattle stunning pen, showing guillotine and rectangular orifice through which the pistol is inserted and the animal shot. (North British Lifting Co.)

number of hairs that may be transferred from the hide to the surface of the dressed carcase. On the other hand, cleansing of the bellies, legs and feet by horizontally directed water sprays fitted on both sides of the race, or alternatively, by directing the animals through a water bath (Fig. 11), can be strongly recommended.

The size and type of slaughter hall for cattle depends on which of the slaughtering systems is adopted, but in all cases it should be an open hall which is well ventilated and lighted. The Slaughterhouse (Hygiene) Regulations prescribe that efficient natural and artificial light of an intensity of 20 ft. candle power be provided, except where inspection takes place when it shall be not less than 50 ft. candles. All floors in lairs, slaughter-halls, work rooms, hanging rooms and room for condemned meat must be

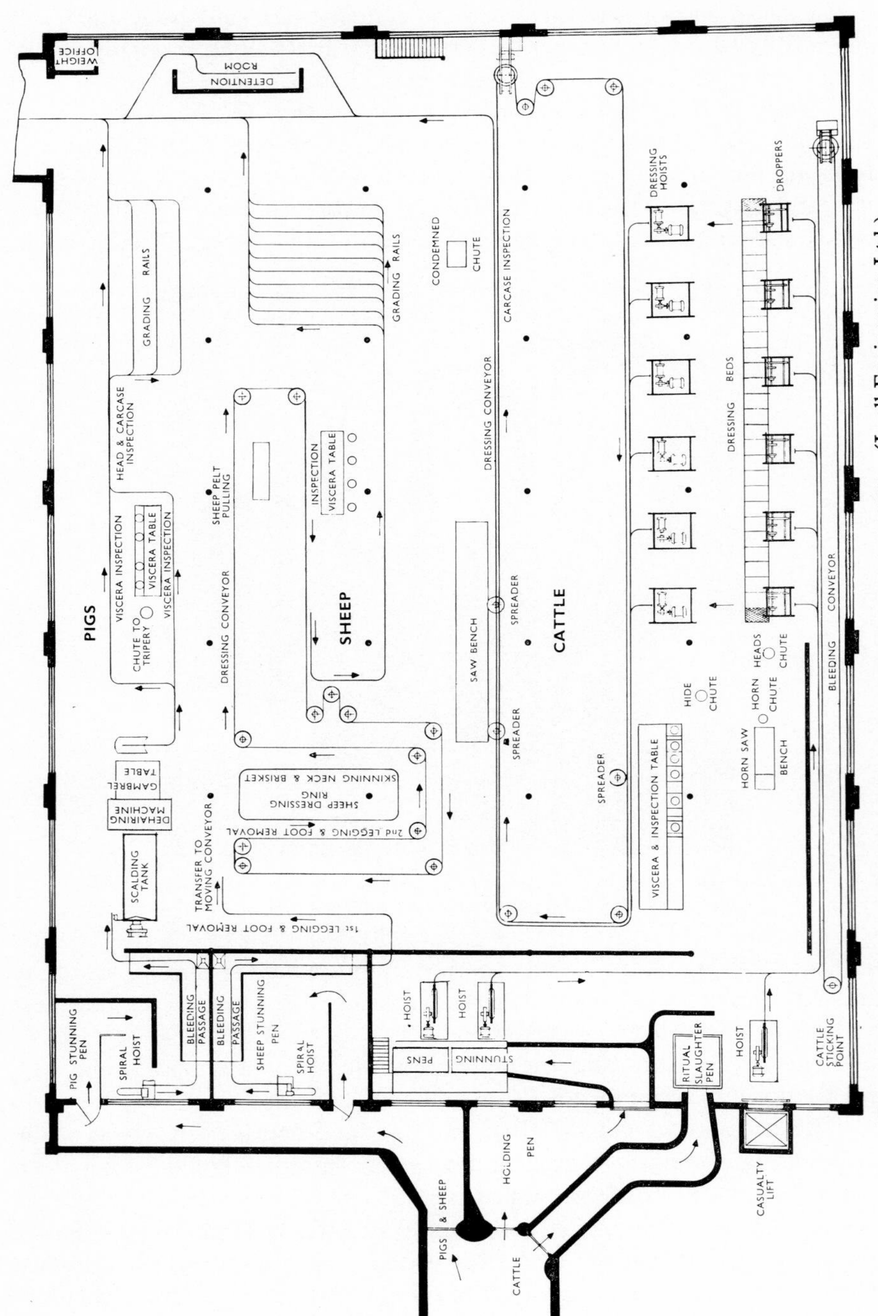

FIG. 13.—LAYOUT OF SLAUGHTER FLOOR FOR CATTLE, SHEEP AND PIGS. (Iwell Engineering Ltd.)

FIG. 13

There is a single entrance from the lairage for all classes of stock and these are all dealt with on a single open slaughter floor. The size of the floor is approximately 100 ft. by 150 ft. and the layout is designed to deal with an hourly throughput of 60 to 80 cattle, up to 150 sheep and up to 150 pigs.

The procedure in slaughtering and dressing of each class of animal is as follows :—

(1) *Cattle.* From the lairage the animals enter a holding pen and are then driven along a passage to the stunning pens of which there are two arranged in series. After stunning, the animals are hoisted by one or both hind legs to an overhead rail leading to the cattle sticking point. Provision is also made for the ritual slaughter of adult cattle which enter the slaughter pen by a separate passage and after the throat is cut and bleeding completed the animal is hoisted to the overhead rail leading to the mechanized bleeding conveyor. Provision is also made for dealing with casualty animals, i.e. injured animals, which can be raised by lift from ground level to the level of the slaughter floor and a common hoist serves both ritually slaughtered and casualty animals. Animals which are ill are dealt with in a separate isolation block.

At the cattle sticking point the throat is cut, which on the line system is usually carried out by severance of all the neck vessels with one transverse cut. Bleeding continues for not less than six minutes and when completed the head is removed from the body, horns sawn off on the saw bench and both head and horns then fed into chutes to the lower floor. By means of a dropper the carcase is then lowered on to one of the six dressing beds, where the feet are removed, removal of the hide commenced, and the carcase then raised by a dressing hoist to the mechanized dressing conveyor. (By this method no beef trees are used between the tendons to keep the hind legs apart so each hind leg is attached to a roller on the dressing conveyor and the carcase moves sideways along this rail.) The hide is now removed and passes down the chute provided, the carcase being then moved to the first spreader where the hind legs are separated to a distance of 3 ft. to facilitate evisceration on the raised viscera table. After inspection the various organs are dropped by chutes to the lower floor.

At the second spreader the distance between the two hind legs is extended to 4 ft. to facilitate the first part of the sawing operation, this being carried out on a raised saw bench, while the third spreader widens the legs to 5 ft. for the lower part of the sawing operation. This is followed by inspection of the two sides of beef, which are dispatched to the cooling room if passed, to a detention room if further inspection is required, or placed in the chute provided if they are condemned.

(2) *Sheep.* Sheep are stunned in a stunning pen, elevated by a spiral hoist to a round bar rail, and bled in the bleeding passage for not less than five minutes. The first legging operation and foot removal takes place on the bleeding rail before transference of the carcase to the overhead moving conveyor, on which the second legging and foot removal takes place. On the dressing ring the skinning of the neck and brisket is performed and the pelt removal commenced, the pelt being finally pulled off before the carcase is eviscerated at the viscera and inspection table. The dressed carcase is then propelled manually to the grading rails or direct to the cooling room. Where necessary, calves are also slaughtered and dressed on the sheep line.

(3) *Pigs.* Pigs are stunned, hoisted by spiral hoist to the bleeding rail where they are bled for six minutes. Normal bacon factory procedure then follows, the animals proceeding from scalding tank to dehairing machine, then to the gambrel table for a final scraping, and then hoisted to an overhead round bar rail for evisceration. Two lines are provided at which viscera removal and inspection take place, and this is followed by a final inspection of the head and carcase.

of non-slip material, and slaughterhall and workroom floor must be laid so as to have a fall of not less than two inches in every ten feet.

Blood must not be allowed to gain access to the gullies, as it congeals and quickly blocks the drains. It must either be collected in shallow trays, 20 inches diameter and 4 inches deep, which is the usual method when the blood is required for manufacture into black puddings, and the Slaughterhouse (Hygiene) Regulations prescribe that blood intended for human food must be properly stored and identifiable with the carcase. Alternatively, the animal may be bled so that the blood is diverted into a special glazed blood drain which empties into a container for removal.

Under the above Regulations the interior wall surfaces of slaughterhalls, workrooms, hanging rooms and room for condemned meat must be faced with smooth, hard, impervious material up to a height of not less than 6 feet from the floor. The hot water tap should be of the decompressor type for wastage of hot water is a serious factor in an abattoir. Under the above Regulations facilities must be provided for the sterilization of cloths, knives and other equipment.

Mechanical stunning of all animals is now obligatory in Britain, and under the Slaughter of Animals (Prevention of Cruelty) Regulations, subject to certain provisions, stunning pens must be provided for adult cattle and no animal must be slaughtered in the sight of another. The passage from lairage to stunning pen should be a narrow one to facilitate the driving of a fractious animal.

The fewer the number of stunning pens commensurate with a smooth slaughtering throughput the better, and the provision of a bleeding rail renders a minimum number of pens necessary and is an essential feature where cattle are slaughtered on the line system. The bleeding rail system entails the shackling of one or both hind limbs and the raising of the beast after shooting, to a rail, where the animal is bled and then conveyed to a slaughtering bay. By this system animals are bled at a central point and the subsequent dressing of the carcase in the slaughtering bay is carried out under vastly more hygienic conditions.

LINE DRESSING. The development of this method of dressing carcases has emanated from the practice in the American Continent and consists essentially in propelling the carcase along an overhead rail where the process of dressing is divided up into various single stages, each undertaken by an operator who performs his allotted task as the carcase reaches him ; without the line method of dressing it would be impossible to reach the output maintained in factory abattoirs, which in some of the Argentine frigorificos amounts to 5,000 cattle, 10,000 sheep and 1,000 pigs every 10 hours. The advantages of such a system over the " booth " method of dressing are that semi-skilled labour can be used to the best advantage, the output per man is considerably increased, the floor space required is relatively small, and as mechanical equipment is not duplicated unnecessarily it is utilized to its maximum advantage. In British practice it has been shown that one stunning pen with bleeding rail and carcase droppers can deliver some 15 cattle per hour to the dressing areas, while after dressing is completed a single mechanical saw can split some 25 carcases per hour if the line plan is adhered to. It is, however, important not to economize unreasonably in the matter of space of the actual slaughter floor, for the difficulties of the inspector are greatly magnified unless adequate space and facilities for inspection are provided.

SHEEP SLAUGHTER HALL. Though larger installations are best served by retaining the cattle slaughter hall for cattle only, in smaller establishments where cattle and sheep killing are not likely to take place at the same time a portion of the cattle hall can be adapted for slaughter and dressing of sheep. Sheep are driven to a passage-way adjoining the slaughter hall, being then carried by hand into the slaughter hall and placed on crates preparatory to stunning and dressing. Metal crates, which permit of easy cleansing, are greatly preferable to wooden ones, and the Slaughterhouse (Hygiene) Regulations prescribe that equipment and fittings in the slaughter-hall shall be of easily cleansed, non-corrosive materials and shall not be of wood except in the case of brooms, chopping and cutting blocks and handles. An admirable arrangement is the provision of a low, metal-covered bleeding bench sufficient to accommodate ten sheep, with a gutter along one side to catch the blood, and this method is considered preferable to a bleeding rail for sheep, for the rate at which sheep are dressed makes it difficult with a bleeding rail to ensure that individual owners receive their animal from the rail for dressing at the moment their operators require it. Line slaughter is frequently carried out on sheep, and by this method a gang of 10 to 12 men can slaughter and dress 60 to 70 sheep per hour.

PIG SLAUGHTER HALL. Pig slaughter is invariably carried out in a separate hall from that used for cattle and sheep, as the moist atmosphere which is inseparable from the scalding of pigs is not conducive to the good setting and drying of carcases of beef and mutton.

Pigs are conducted from the lairage through a narrow passage to a metal-walled compartment where they are stunned. After bleeding, pigs are scalded and then scraped to remove the hair; in the smaller abattoirs scraping is done by hand, but in large abattoirs and bacon factories the process is carried out by a mechanical dehairing machine. It is estimated that if there is a regular throughput of some 200 pigs on two to three days per week the installation of a dehairing plant should be seriously considered. An extraction system which removes steam from the canopies over the scalding tanks and keeps the temperature of the steam raised by heated air serves to prevent condensation and fogginess in the pig slaughter hall.

Provision must be made so that the offals from each animal can be easily identified with the carcase. Some authorities prefer the offals to be placed on galvanized tables prior to inspection, and then removed by offal carriers. In many large abattoirs, and in frigorifico practice, the viscera are consigned to the offal rooms by means of sloping chutes, where the stomachs are opened, the intestines cleaned, and the ingesta collected and its moisture content reduced. This material is then driven along pipes by a pneumatic automatic ejector system for compression and removal. Separate chutes are also provided for the removal of hides and skins from the slaughterhouse floor.

4. Cooling and Chilling Room

The treatment of the carcase immediately after dressing is of importance, a desirable condition being rapid cooling in a dry atmosphere, and continental practice has shown that the capacity of an abattoir to deal with increases in throughput which develop as a township grows are related directly to the lairage accommodation and to the facilities provided for the chilling of the carcases. With adequate accommodation for holding the kill this can be spread if necessary to 5 to 5½ days per week instead of being concentrated in 2 or 3.

In large slaughtering centres a space is necessary for pre-cooling with good ventilation, this space acting as a convenient point to facilitate quick loading of the chill room. Chilling space should be ample to accommodate at least two days' kill and it is preferable to provide several small chill rooms than one large one. The problem of chilling is to hold the meat in good condition without destroying the " bloom " and for this purpose temperatures between 30° F. to 40° F. have proved most satisfactory. Continual opening and closing of the chilling room doors causes undesirable fluctuations in temperature, and a method of obviating this is the use of an air curtain consisting of ambient air passed through ducts fitted over the coldroom doorway. Alternatively, a method effective for chill rooms is a system of flexible doors which extend only to a height over which men can see with ease; the amount of warm air entering through the open upper portion has been found to be extremely small.

An important requirement is the provision of facilities for cleansing of overhead runners and meat hooks, particularly those on which cattle livers are suspended. This may be done by passing the equipment through a water bath, or alternatively they may be sterilized by scrubbing with hot water containing 5 per cent. washing soda (sodium carbonate), and it is a desirable hygienic procedure which is frequently overlooked.

MEAT MARKET. A cooling hall of large and commodious capacity may also serve the purpose of a meat market, or a separate market hall may be provided. The overhead running rails should be so arranged that sections may be leased to individual wholesale meat traders, while each section should be provided with an office and telephone.

FIG. 14.—Washing of meat hooks, Copenhagen Abattoir. The hooks are cleansed by passing through a water bath for 40 seconds at 170° F.

The loading of quarters of beef and carcases of the other animals on to transport wagons can be done either at ground level or from a platform, but the latter is generally considered unnecessary.

5. Hide and Skin Store

This need not be extensive, as it should be cleared daily during slaughtering periods. Sheep skins in summer weather should be laid flat so that the animal heat can be dissipated; they should be well salted and can then be arranged in piles, for if stacked immediately after slaughter they rapidly decompose. Hides may be conveniently marked for subsequent identification by clipping of the hair with a pair of scissors.

6. Guttery and Tripery

A boiler house and engine room, gut-scraping rooms, tripe rooms, stores and by-products plant should be placed at convenient sites for handling the material dealt with, but they should form a separate unit or units from the main building. Stomachs may be cleansed and converted into tripe, and feet cleansed and cooked by employees of the local authority, or alternatively, the renting of the tripery and guttery may be put up for auction and let to the successful firm on a yearly contract.

7. Offices

In addition to office accommodation provided in the meat market, the administrative offices should occupy a central position and have a good viewpoint therefrom. This block may conveniently be contiguous to the carcase detention room and laboratory.

Up-to-date lavatory and dressing accommodation, with lockers for clean and working clothes for workmen, who under the Slaughterhouse (Hygiene) Regulations are obliged to wear protective clothing, must be provided.

METHODS OF SLAUGHTER

It is generally agreed that the two essentials in the slaughter of food animals are that they shall be dispatched without unnecessary suffering and that the bleeding of the animal shall be as complete as possible. Good bleeding is ensured if the animal is healthy, but is retarded in all affections which deleteriously affect the action of heart, lungs and muscles, and animals suffering from febrile conditions, from severe indigestion, or from severe heart and lung affections, bleed badly and the flesh is therefore of poor durability. Of the total amount of blood in the animal body, only one-half is extracted during bleeding.

It is generally regarded as undesirable that an animal awaiting slaughter should view the slaughtering process, but though the higher animals undoubtedly share some sensations with human beings it is questionable whether any trepidation is felt specifically by an animal at the sight and smell of blood or as a result of witnessing the dressing operation; nevertheless fear is undoubtedly engendered by strange noises, movements, surroundings and smells, and this fear is accentuated by the separation of the animal from its fellows and the consequent disappearance of the feeling of protection that a gregarious animal enjoys in the presence of its comrades.

In countries such as America, Canada and Australia where many of the cattle are range cattle and difficult to approach and handle, the factory methods employed require a rapid throughput of animals, and on these grounds the stunning of cattle is chiefly carried out by the use of the felling hammer or a rifle which discharges what is known as a frangible bullet that obviates the danger of ricochets. A number of efficacious devices are in use to distract attention and arrest movement of the animal when it enters the stunning box, amongst these being the provision of a mirror at the far end of the box, a knotted rope suspended in the box, or two strong electric lamps at the level of the animal's head and which operate automatically as the animal enters the box and cause temporary blindness. In Britain, where cattle can usually be handled with safety, the use of a mechanically operated instrument for stunning of all animals is now required by law, and similar legislation is in force in most other European countries. The instruments generally employed are of the captive-bolt type, though the use of a gun discharging a free bullet may at times be necessary for the stunning of bulls, boars and large sows. The captive-bolt pistols usually employed are the Cash, the Temple-Cox and the Schermer and produce immediate unconsciousness by physical brain destruction, changes in intracranial pressure, and the sudden jerk producing what is known as acceleration concussion.

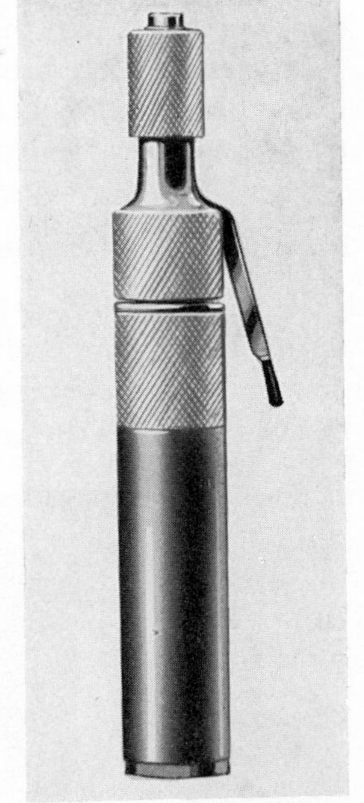

FIG. 15.—Douglas-Schermer mechanical killer. (Lockerbie and Wilkinson.)

PITHING. After cattle are stunned they are sometimes pithed before bleeding, this being done by inserting a long thin rod into the aperture made in the skull by the bolt of the pistol. The insertion of this rod destroys the medulla oblongata, so that reflex muscular action will not take place when the act of sticking takes place or when dressing of the carcase is commenced. The purpose of pithing is to enable the slaughterman to proceed more rapidly and with safety with the dressing of the carcase; it is a method purely directed towards the saving of time. There is little practical evidence that destruction of the medulla interferes to any appreciable degree with the satisfactory bleeding of the carcase, but the pithing rod or cane should not be of greater length

FIG. 16.—Cash captive-bolt pistol.

than 24 inches, for if too long a cane is used the spinal cord roots of the great splanchnic nerve, which is the main vasoconstrictor of the abdominal cavity, are destroyed. The resultant dilatation of the splanchnic blood vessels causes congestion of the liver, kidneys and intestines, and, in addition congestion and enlargement of the spleen, the so-called slaughter spleen. The operation of pithing in cattle appears to be confined to the European countries and is not usually carried out in factory abattoir practice abroad.

Methods of Slaughter in Different Countries

Legislation in Britain require that all animals slaughtered in an abattoir, except those slaughtered by the Jewish and Mohammedan ritual, shall first be rendered unconscious by mechanical means and similar requirements are laid down in most of the countries in Europe. In Spain, parts of Italy and some South American countries, however, it is the practice to slaughter cattle by the neck-stab or evernazione method, a short double-edged knife known as a puntilla being plunged into the occipito-atlantal space at the nape of the neck, thus severing the medulla oblongata. In the Arctic Circle reindeer are killed by a curved, single-edged knife, which, after being inserted into the occipito-atlantal space, is directed forwards to destroy the brain.

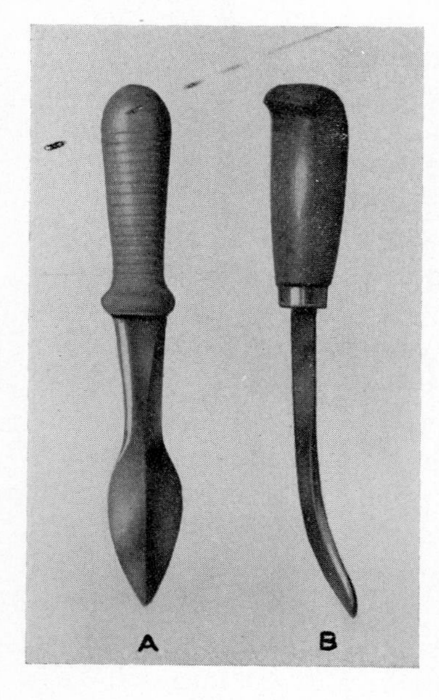

FIG. 17.—A. Puntilla, a type of knife used in some countries for slaughter of cattle. The knife is inserted into the occipito-atlantal space to sever the medulla oblongata. B. Knife used in Lapland for slaughter of reindeer.

In India and in the Far East practically all animals are slaughtered without first being rendered unconscious. In India the majority of sheep and goats are killed by the Halal or Mohammedan method in which the throat is cut transversely as in the Jewish method of slaughter. The Sikh or Jatka method is also practised, the sheep or goat being decapitated by one stroke of a sword ; in parts of Northern India skilled operators can decapitate buffaloes by a single stroke of a special sword. It may be remarked that the Mohammedan ritual does not forbid stunning of the animal prior to bleeding provided the stunning instruments have never been used on pigs.

verse cut and immediately bleeding is completed the head is removed from the body. The advantage of a bleeding rail is that it permits of a centralized collection of blood and also accelerates the throughput of animals, allowing them to be stunned and removed in quick succession through the same stunning pen.

Whichever method of bleeding is employed it should continue for 6 minutes, the average amount of blood obtained in cattle slaughter being 30 lb. Cows yield more blood than bulls or bullocks of the same weight, in some cases up to 50 lb. in old cows.

Sheep. In the slaughter of sheep, bleeding is carried out by an incision in the jugular furrow and close to the head, severing both carotid arteries. At the same time the head is jerked back sharply to rupture the spinal cord where it enters the skull, the purpose of this, as in the pithing in cattle, being to obviate reflex muscular action when the dressing of the carcase is commenced. Bleeding of the sheep carcase should last for 5 minutes, the amount of blood obtained from a slaughtered sheep being 4 to 5 lb.

Calves. In calves the incision was at one time made at the side of the neck and the jugular vein severed. The purpose of this was to produce slow bleeding after the carcase was hung up prior to dressing, for slow bleeding ensures the desirable white colour of veal. Calves are now bled rapidly, and yield 6 lb. of blood.

Pigs. In pigs the knife is inserted in the middle line of the neck at the depression in front of the sternum, and is then pushed forward to sever the anterior vena cava at the entrance of the chest; sometimes the carotid artery is also pierced. Care should be taken not to insert the knife too far as it may penetrate into the shoulder, allowing blood to run back into the shoulder " pocket " beneath the scapula. This may cause subsequent tainting of the meat from early decomposition of the blood, especially in hot weather, and may render the carcase unfit for bacon curing. Where pigs are bled without being previously stunned the heart continues to beat for 2 to 9 minutes, and the carcase should therefore not be placed immediately in the scalding tank; too large a sticking wound and contaminated scalding water facilitate the entry of micro-organisms into the carcase tissues by way of the jugular vein, and may lead to taint in bacon or ham. In some abattoirs pigs are stunned, then hoisted and bled while suspended, but urination occurs while the pig is bleeding and renders the blood unmarketable by contaminating the blood tray. In some continental slaughterhouses this objection is overcome by introducing a rubber funnel into the sticking wound, the funnel leading to a rubber tube which discharges the blood into a blood vat. Pigs should be allowed to bleed for 6 minutes, as during this period the muscles relax and the hair is more readily removed during scalding. The slaughter of pork pigs yields 5 lb. of blood, bacon pigs 7 lb., while boars and sows yield 8 lb.

In certain abattoirs in the United States, and primarily in the Hormel plant in Minnesota, the prone-sticking of pigs has been adopted. After being rendered unconscious the animal is discharged on to a conveyor belt and is stuck while lying prone, the blood draining into a trough running parallel to the conveyor. Immediately after sticking the animals come under a holding-down belt which continues the full length of the conveyor and restrains the involuntary struggling that may occur. The advantages of prone-sticking are the more efficient recovery of blood, which amounts to $\frac{3}{10}$ lb. per animal on a dried basis, and it completely eliminates ruptured joints and joint capsules which are a troublesome condition in pigs bled while suspended and are the cause of the so-called internal ham bruising (Fig. 213).

The efficiency of bleeding has a most important bearing on the subsequent keeping quality of the carcase, and experiments have been conducted on pigs which show the amount of blood yielded by the various methods of slaughter. If the amount of blood remaining in the carcase after shooting and delayed bleeding be 100 parts, then the amount remaining after shooting and immediate bleeding is 86 parts, after direct bleeding without previous stunning 70 parts, while after stunning by the electrical method and subsequent bleeding, only 60 parts of blood remain. Experiments on 110 bacon pigs showed that in pigs stunned by the hammer the blood yielded was 2·67 per cent. of the body weight, while pigs stunned by the electrical method yielded 3·14 per cent.

Jewish Slaughter

Regulations for the slaughter of animals for Jewish consumption have existed since A.D. 500 and, according to the Mischna of the Talmud, a blow on the head of an animal whose flesh is intended for Jewish consumption is forbidden, as perforation of the membranes of the brain constitutes one of the eight mutilations which render meat " terepha ", or unfit for food. The only animals which may be slaughtered according to the Jewish faith are cattle, calves, sheep, goats, deer, and all kinds of poultry; slaughter of these animals is therefore carried out without previous stunning. The effects of the round worm *Trichinella spiralis* and the tapeworm *Taenia solium* were probably responsible for the ancient Jewish prohibition against the consumption of pork. Slaughtered animals which are found on examination to be fit for Jewish consumption are described as " kosher ", and about 50 per cent. of the meat consumed in New York City is from animals slaughtered by the Jewish ritual method.

In Britain the use of a casting pen of the Weinberg, Dyne, or North British rotary type for the slaughter of adult cattle by the Jewish or Mohammedan methods is obligatory under the Slaughter of Animals (Prevention of Cruelty) Regulations, 1958, the purpose being to place the animal in a position convenient for the severing of the neck vessels. An incision across the neck is then made by one rapid thrust of a sharp knife which severs the skin, muscles, oesophagus, trachea, carotid arteries and jugular veins. This method of slaughter is known as " Schechita ", and is carried out only by the cutter or " Shochet ", assisted by a sealer or " Shomer " who stamps the kosher seal on each part of the carcase which is passed for Jewish food.

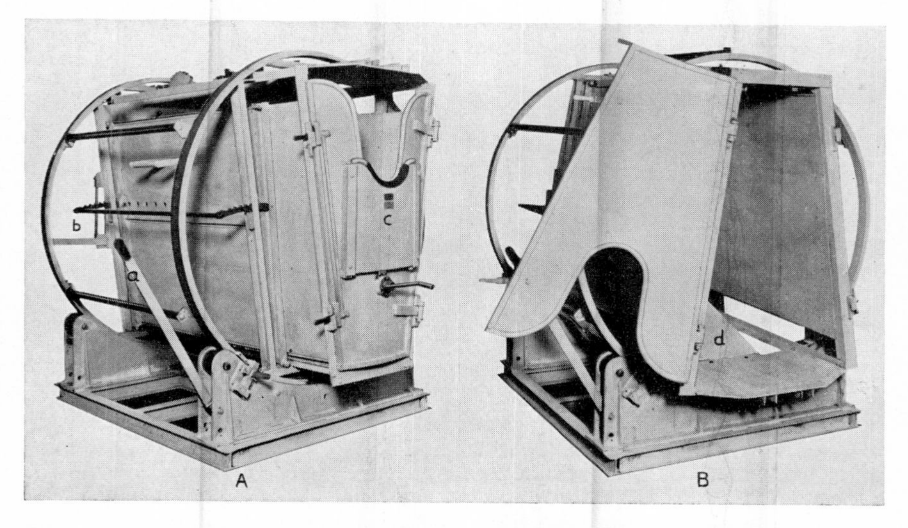

FIG. 20.—Jewish slaughter pen. A. Front view showing brake lever (a), locking device (*b*), and adjustable auxiliary door (*c*) to suit height of animal's neck. B. Pen rotated into slaughtering position showing roof (*d*) canted to facilitate removal of animal. (Dyne Engineers Co.)

The five principles of Schechita, in their traditional order, are that the neck incision shall be completed without pause, pressure, stabbing, slanting or tearing, while if the knife receives any nick, however small, during the operation of cutting the throat, the slaughter is not correctly performed and the use of the animal is not permitted for Jewish food. Likewise, animals which lie quiet and cannot be made to get up by striking with a stick must not be slaughtered according to Jewish ritual, and it is further forbidden to eat the meat of animals which exhibit no movement during or after the process of slaughter. This early recognition of the inadmissibility of the ill or moribund animal for human food is worthy of note.

The dressing of the carcase proceeds until the diaphragm is exposed, when the Shochet pierces this and subjects the thoracic organs to a manual examination, the operation being known as searching. Any adhesions of the lungs found are examined visually and, if deemed detrimental to the animal when alive, the carcase is pronounced terepha or unfit for Jewish food.

Carcases found fit for Jewish consumption must have the meat "porged" by removing the blood vessels prior to retail sale of the meat. It is for this reason that forequarters of kosher beef, which include twelve ribs and are easily porged, are consumed by the Jews, while the hindquarters, stated to contain over 50 blood vessels, can only be porged by highly skilled kosher butchers, and hindquarter beef is therefore rarely eaten. Kosher meat must be sold within 3 days of slaughter and, failing this, must undergo a further religious ritual.

FIG. 21.—Knives used for Jewish slaughter. Above, cattle knife; centre, sheep knife; and below, knife used for poultry. (One-fifth natural size.)

It is claimed that the Jewish method of slaughter does not involve any act of cruelty for the reasons that the knife is particularly sharp, the cut is made dexterously by a trained person, and the severance of the carotid vessels is followed by a very rapid fall in blood pressure within the cerebral arteries. It is therefore contended that the occurrence of anoxia resulting from the diminished blood supply to the brain tissue brings about almost immediate unconsciousness.

The persistence of the eye reflex, and also the convulsions which occur in the animal some time after the neck cut has been made, have been advanced by the opponents of Jewish slaughter as evidence that consciousness persists in the animal for quite considerable periods; these reflexes are not associated with consciousness and their significance may therefore be discounted. Opponents of the Jewish method of slaughter have also contended that inasmuch as there is an additional supply of blood to the brain, namely by way of the vertebral artery and therefore independent of the carotid supply, an appreciable volume of blood may still reach the brain and prolong the period of consciousness. There is evidence, however, that if the blood flow from the cut carotid arteries is uninterrupted the supply of blood to the brain by way of the vertebral artery is insufficient to maintain the animal in a state of consciousness.

A factor of considerable importance, and to which not enough attention has been paid in considering the problem of Jewish slaughter, is that after the carotid arteries of cattle are severed transversely they tend, by virtue of their elasticity, to retract rapidly within their own external connective tissue coat, and as a result sealing of the cut ends of the vessels may occur. As the blood pressure in the anterior aorta will then be maintained by the persistence of the function of the heart, the blood pressure in the vertebral artery may likewise be maintained at a substantial level and unconsciousness therefore delayed. Such sealing can and does occur, in some cases very rapidly, and provides an explanation as to why some cattle, the throats of which have been cut by the Jewish method, have been known to regain their feet and have walked a considerable distance before they have eventually succumbed some minutes later. In the past when such occurrences have been witnessed they have been attributed, perhaps for want of a better explanation, to the fact that all the neck vessels may not have

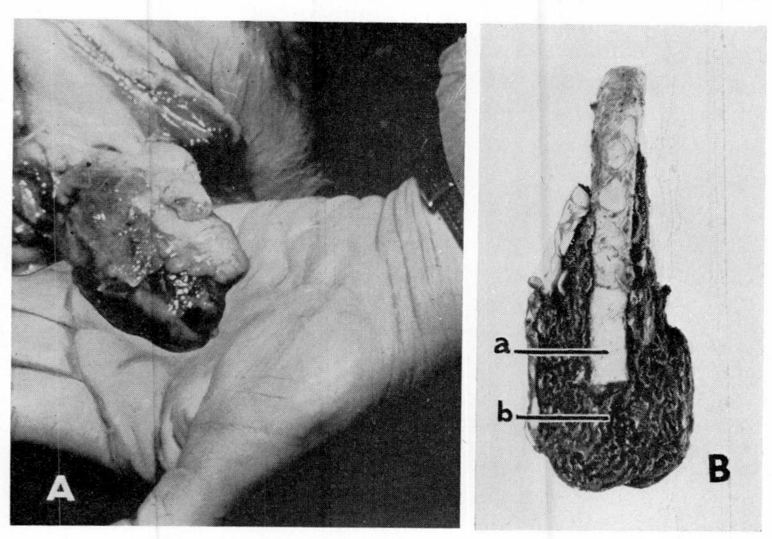

FIG. 22.—A. Severed end of carotid artery of ox slaughtered by the Jewish method. Sealing of the cut end of the artery has occurred rapidly due to retraction of the vessel within its connective tissue coat. B. Dissection of end of carotid artery shown in A. (*a*) End of severed vessel, (*b*) connective tissue coat which has become suffused with blood and has arrested further haemorrhage.

been severed completely, but observations on the Jewish method of slaughter lead one to the conclusion that the cut is invariably made dexterously and the efficiency of the technique is rarely in question. There is therefore considerable doubt as to whether unconsciousness always follows rapidly in cattle after the severance of the neck vessels, for by the very nature of the neck cut made in Jewish slaughter it is impossible to ensure that self-sealing of the cut ends of the carotid arteries will not occur.

The assertion by supporters of Jewish slaughter that bleeding of the animal is more complete than in other methods of slaughter has been challenged by some authorities who contend that the paler colour of the flesh of Jewish slaughtered animals is due to the violent respiratory efforts which accompany ritual slaughter, these having the effect of increasing the proportion of oxyhaemoglobin in the blood, thus rendering the residual blood in the carcase paler than normal and giving the flesh a well-bled appearance.

Certain continental countries have introduced legislation requiring that animals slaughtered for Jewish consumption shall be rendered unconscious by mechanical means before the throat cut may be made. Legislation to this effect is in operation in Upper Austria, Norway, Switzerland and Sweden, and in Stockholm a type of electrical stunning apparatus known as the Elther is used to anaesthetize cattle prior to ritual slaughter.

FACTORS INFLUENCING BLEEDING

The stunning of an animal by any means produces a rise in the blood pressure of the arterial, capillary and venous systems, and in sheep the normal arterial blood pressure of 120–145 mm. of mercury may rise to 260 mm. or over when the animal is shot prior to bleeding. This is accompanied by a transitory increase in the heart rate, and as an increase in blood pressure and heart rate assists bleeding, advantage can be taken of these facts to carry out bleeding immediately after stunning. The importance of immediate bleeding is obvious when it is realized that the rate of flow from a cut vessel is five to ten times more rapid than in the intact vessel, and not until an appreciable amount of the blood in the body has been lost does the blood pressure begin to fall. If an undue interval is allowed to elapse between stunning and bleeding, the carcase may be imperfectly bled, and this may be accompanied by " blood splashing ".

Muscular Haemorrhages or Splashing

The condition known variously as blood splash, blood extravasation or shot meat is characterized by the presence of blood spots or streaks in various parts of the carcase musculature. It appears typically as dark-coloured streaks somewhat resembling brush marks, or as a collection of dark spots not unlike those seen on a used blotting pad and varying in size from those scarcely visible up to $\frac{1}{4}$ or $\frac{1}{2}$ inch in length.

The muscular portion of the diaphragm is the area most frequently affected, though splashing may also be seen on the inner aspect of the thoracic or abdominal wall, and in cattle is particularly common in the muscles of the neck and longissimus dorsi. In the pig it may be found in any muscle but most frequently in the hip and thigh and muscles of the loin, diaphragm and shoulder; at times the lymph nodes draining tissues affected with splashing are suffused with blood. The frequency of the

SPLASHING OF MUSCLE

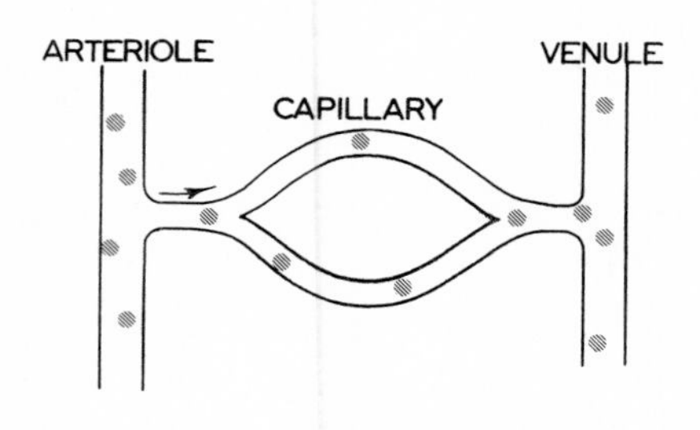

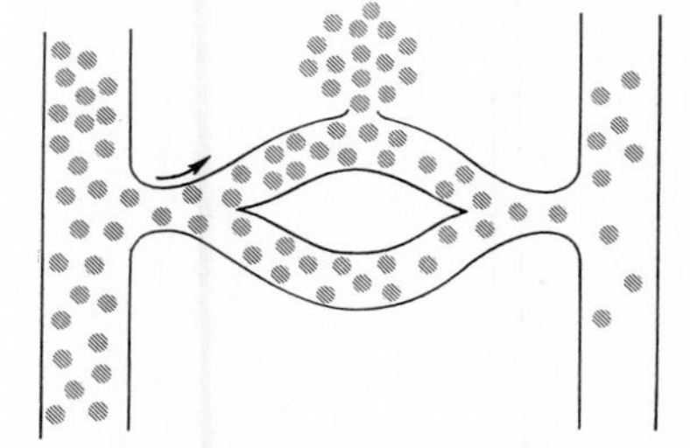

FIG. 23.—The mechanics of blood splashing. Rupture of the capillary wall occurs when vaso-constriction of the arteriole is succeeded by vaso-dilatation and the capillary blood pressure is suddenly raised.

occurrence of blood splash in pigs is related to the fact that these animals are kept closely confined in sties and have little opportunity for exercise, with the result that the muscles are heavily infiltrated with fat and are particularly liable to rupture.

Much research has been carried out as to the factors causing splashing and the method of its prevention. One factor which has been stressed as of importance is delay between stunning and bleeding, while other observers have stressed the importance of the violent inco-ordinated muscular contractions and rise in arterial and venous blood pressure which occur when animals are stunned. Blood pressure is likely to be already raised above normal in animals fatigued after a long journey, or in animals which have been chased into a slaughter pen, and it is noteworthy that the incidence of splashing in these animals is higher than in those which have been rested. In the United States it has been observed that the condition most commonly affects well finished animals in hot weather, and fat stall-fed cattle are likely to show splashing if they are excited prior to slaughter and the bleeding operation is delayed. There is no justification for condemnation of meat affected with splashing as it is not less durable and may safely be used in finely minced made-up foods.

When an animal is stunned, either by the captive bolt pistol or by electrical means, there is a rise in arterial blood pressure, though this is a predisposing and not a causative factor in the splashing of muscular tissue. The mechanics of blood splashing are illustrated diagrammatically in Fig. 23. The rise in arterial blood pressure following stunning is brought about by vaso-constriction of these vessels, but this vaso-constriction does not occur in the capillaries, which are virtually passive tubes, and their diameter is therefore controlled by the state of tone of the blood vessels supplying them. When the vessels of the arterial system are in a state of constriction the capillaries contain relatively little blood, but when the stimulus which causes vaso-constriction ceases, as when the tongs are removed from the head of an electrically-stunned pig, the arterioles undergo immediate vaso-dilatation and the effect of this is to cause a rush of blood into the capillaries. (An apt analogy is what occurs when the flood gates of a dam are opened and water crashes on to the bed of the empty stream below.) The effect of this sudden suffusion of the capillaries, which are already weakened by anoxia or oxygen lack, is to cause rupture of the capillary wall and haemorrhage into the surrounding tissue.

The higher the arterial blood pressure the more severe will be the impingement of blood on the capillary wall when vaso-dilatation occurs. Any factor, such as excitement, that tends to elevate unduly the blood pressure of an animal immediately prior to slaughter will therefore predispose the muscles of that animal to splashing. Conversely, any procedure which will rapidly reduce the systemic blood pressure following on the act of stunning, as, for example, immediate bleeding, will tend to reduce the incidence of splashing. Another way in which the blood pressure can be rapidly reduced is destruction of the medulla oblongata after stunning, and in one establishment in Australia where splashing of beef carcases presented a serious problem, the condition was virtually eradicated following the introduction of pithing.

Electrical Stunning

This method consists in passing a low voltage alternating current through the brain of the animal, the instrument most commonly employed being one which resembles a pair of tongs. It is a method permitted under the Slaughter of Animals Act, 1958, and widely used in bacon factories and abattoirs for the stunning of pigs, and also in some abattoirs for the slaughtering of sheep and calves.

When electrical stunning was first introduced little was known as to its efficacy in producing complete unconsciousness. It must be agreed that if certain requisites are not complied with the method may be inhumane, for the electrical current may produce a condition known as "missed shock" in which the animal, though paralysed, is fully conscious. Provided certain conditions are observed, however, the electrical method of stunning may be regarded as efficacious and humane inasmuch as it gives rise to a cerebral stimulation which causes inco-ordination of the cerebral nerve cells and what may be aptly defined as a confusional state of the brain. The desiderata necessary for the production of genuine anaesthesia are as follows :

1. The strength of the electric shock, measured in ampères, should be of sufficient magnitude ; this is dependent on two factors, (*a*) the strength of the current, which should not be less than 250 milliampères and (*b*) the voltage, which should not be less than 75 volts.

2. Provided the current in milliampères exceeds the requisite minimum, a genuine electroplectic shock will be induced if the current is applied for a sufficient time, and it is recommended that this period should be one of 10 seconds. It should, however, be noted that the voltage of mains current may fluctuate considerably and at times fall to a dangerously low level in the stunning apparatus ; it is therefore most desirable that every electrical stunning apparatus should be fitted with indicators which provide a warning when the current falls short of the requisite milliampères and if the time of application falls short of 10 seconds.

3. The electrodes should be correctly positioned so that the current will pass through the thalamus and cortex, the chief sensory centres in the fore-brain. The electrical resistance of the hair and skin may be lowered by ensuring that the skin under the electrodes is clean and moist, and for the same reason the caloric intake of the animal should be reduced and its state of hydration increased ; this is achieved by allowing the animal unlimited drinking water but no food.

4. The animal should be bled immediately after unconsciousness has been produced, otherwise it may regain consciousness though still remain paralysed.

There is little doubt that failure on the part of operators of electrical stunning instruments to observe these criteria has been the cause of criticism of electrical stunning methods, firstly on the grounds that the method was not always a humane one, and secondly on the grounds that haemorrhages were often observed in the muscular tissue of animals stunned by electrical means. The production of a genuine electroplectic shock may be assumed if after application of the current the hind legs are stretched out violently, for this extensor-tonus of the hind legs always occurs when the stimulation is sufficient to cause unconsciousness. In addition, the fore legs should be stiff, the head bent back, and there should be cessation of respiration ; in the absence of these manifestations it may be assumed that the animal has not been effectually stunned. Undue

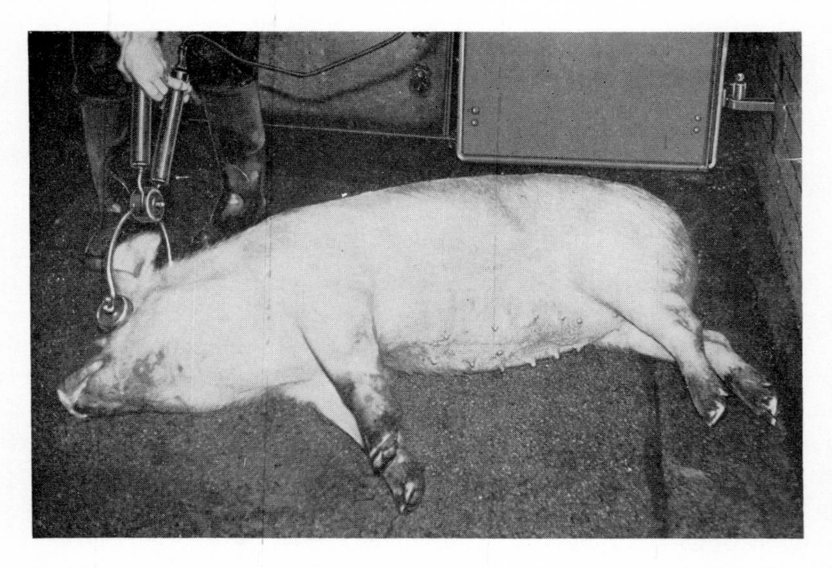

FIG. 24.—Genuine electroplectic shock produced in pig stunned by the electrical method. The limbs are rigidly extended, head bent back and there is cessation of respiration.

importance has perhaps been laid on the production of haemorrhages in the muscular tissue and lungs of animals stunned by electrical means. Muscle haemorrhages can be obviated or reduced to negligible proportions provided the animal is rested, stunned correctly, and the act of stunning is followed by immediate bleeding. In Denmark great importance is attached to the latter factor, and in pigs the electrical apparatus is kept in position on the head and vaso-constriction maintained until the moment the throat cut is made.

The excellence of bleeding which occurs after electrical stunning would appear to be related to (*a*) the continuance of function of the heart and also the maintenance of the arterial blood pressure at a higher level than that obtaining when animals are stunned by instruments of the captive-bolt type, and (*b*) the nature of the muscular contractions which expel the maximum amount of blood from the skeletal muscles in a manner similar to the squeezing of a sponge. The violent and inco-ordinated muscular contractions which are common in other methods of stunning are noticeably absent after electrical stunning and during the act of sticking.

The electrical method of stunning has found its widest application in the case of pigs but it is also used satisfactorily for the slaughter of sheep and calves. In sheep proper unconsciousness may be assumed if there is immediate flexion of all four limbs, closing of the eyes followed in a few seconds by extension of the hind limbs. After some ten seconds this is

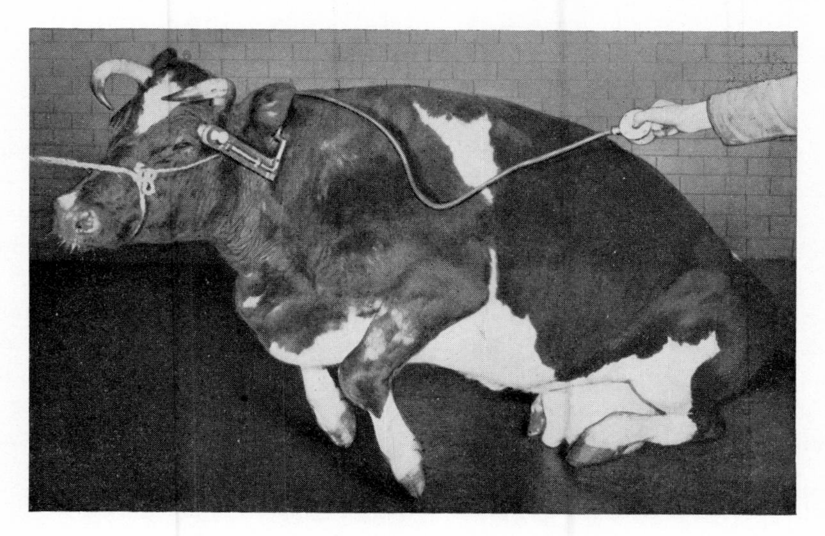

FIG. 25.—Stunning of cow by the Elther electrical method. The apparatus resembles a pair of earphones and a current of 285 watt-seconds is being applied for a period of one second.

followed by gradual muscle relaxation and then vague walking movements of the hind limbs, the eyelids being usually open at this stage and the eyes rotated upwards so that the pupil cannot be seen. Until recently electrical stunning had not proved entirely satisfactory for the anaesthetization of cattle, possibly because of the insulating effect of the fine hairs on the animals' head, but certain continental authorities have now shown that cattle may be anaesthetized satisfactorily by electrical means. These workers have demonstrated that the efficacy or otherwise of electrical anaesthesia is not dependent on the individual factors of voltage, ampèrage or time, but on the total quantity of electrical energy supplied. This quantity is expressed in watt-seconds (watt-seconds = voltage × ampèrage × time) and an apparatus known as the Elther has been devised by which a large quantity of electrical energy can be administered over a very short period. An application of 285 watt-seconds for a period of 1 second is ample to anaesthetize cattle, while an application of 198 watt-seconds for 1 second is effective for the stunning of pigs, sheep and calves. This method of stunning renders the animal instantaneously and completely unconscious and it is significant that cattle stunned by this method exhibit the same syndrome as do animals stunned by the ordinary electrolethaler. It is claimed that the bleeding of animals stunned by the Elther apparatus is very rapid and complete, muscular haemorrhages do not occur, and that the method is superior to the electrolethaler inasmuch as devices are incorporated in the apparatus by which the current supplied to the stunning electrodes and the period of application are carefully controlled.

Washing of Carcases

This has long been an accepted practice in bacon factories after dehairing and scraping, and done by means of a shower, and the washing of beef carcases has become a routine procedure in the majority of modern establishments. In some abattoirs this is done by cold water, but in others a water spray at about 300 lb. per square inch pressure heated to 95° F. is applied and it is claimed that water heated to this temperature secures a greater reduction in surface bacterial contamination and a better carcase appearance. Subsequent to washing, the sides are in some cases shrouded in sterile linen sheets soaked in a 10 per cent. salt solution, this helping to minimize cooler shrink and improve the external appearance of the carcase.

Inflation of Carcases

This is an old practice which developed in relation to slaughter of calves because it was said to facilitate the removal of the calf skin and thus avoided deleterious cutting. An incision is made on the fore shanks and on the belly of the calf just posterior to the sternum, air being pumped into these incisions, while at the same time the carcase is beaten with the hand or a stick to permit infiltration of air throughout the subcutaneous tissue. Formerly air was introduced by the mouth, but legislation in Britain now forbids this though it permits of inflation by means of a pump. Certain countries have adopted legislation forbidding inflation, or " blowing " as it is called, by any method, maintaining that the practice is a fraudulent one in that it misrepresents the bodily condition of the carcase and also makes the inspection of bobby calves difficult, particularly where signs of immaturity and lack of muscular development have to be judged. Again, where calves are inflated and the skin left on, the detection of arthritic changes is rendered more difficult. The practice of inflation is also carried out on sheep carcases, air being introduced through an incision made near the hock.

Carcases of veal, mutton and lamb can be dressed satisfactorily without inflation, and there is little doubt that the practice conceals the lack of muscular development of the carcase, for no matter how it is conducted

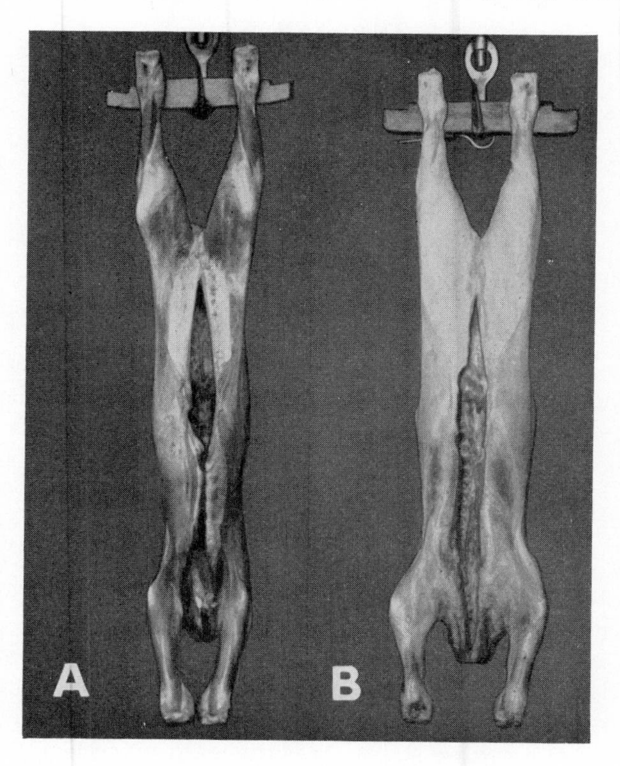

FIG. 26.—Inflation of carcase of veal, carcase A being uninflated and carcase B inflated. The animals were of a similar age, weight and size.

some air will infiltrate into the intermuscular connective tissue ; it is therefore fraudulent and should not be permitted. Inflation of carcases is now forbidden in the United States, and also in Germany where carcases found inflated are regarded as contaminated and the inflated portions condemned. In Switzerland carcases inflated by the mouth may only be sold on the Freibank.

CHAPTER III

POST-MORTEM INSPECTION

A routine post-mortem examination should be carried out as soon as possible after dressing of the carcase is completed, for carcases of beef and pork set rapidly, and if this inspection be delayed, particularly in cold weather, the examination of the carcase lymph nodes is rendered more difficult.

Inspection of carcases by artificial light is unsatisfactory, especially in the judging of those which are badly bled, fevered, or in cases of icterus, and such carcases should always be detained for a further inspection in daylight. In some Danish abattoirs the examination of the submaxillary lymph nodes in pigs is facilitated by the employment of a metal cradle which is placed behind the carcase and tilts it to a level at which the head and throat region can readily be examined.

Inspection of a carcase and its organs should proceed in the following order which should always be adhered to, though in countries where bovine tuberculosis has been eradicated suitable modifications in the routine technique may justifiably be made.

CATTLE

Head. In addition to the sex, a record of the age of the animal should be made, as this serves as a method of identification of the carcase and also enables accurate records to be kept of the incidence of disease at different ages and in the various sexes. This preliminary examination is followed by an inspection of the gums, lips and tongue for foot and mouth disease, necrotic and other forms of stomatitis, actinomycosis and actino-bacillosis, the tongue being palpated from dorsum to tip for the latter disease. Incisions of the internal and external masticatory muscles for *Cysticercus bovis* should be made parallel with the lower jaw and in most European countries the tongue is also incised.

Routine incisions of the retropharyngeal, submaxillary and parotid lymph nodes should be made for tuberculous lesions, and in old cows the latter node should always be included. Symptoms of roaring in cattle are associated with enlargement of the retropharyngeal lymph nodes and may be due to tuberculosis, actinobacillosis or encapsulated abscesses. Snoring is a milder form of the same condition and may be due to similar causes, but it has also been observed as a physiological condition in fat, short-necked dairy cows. The tonsils of cattle and pigs frequently harbour tubercle bacilli, and regulations which apply in the United States to

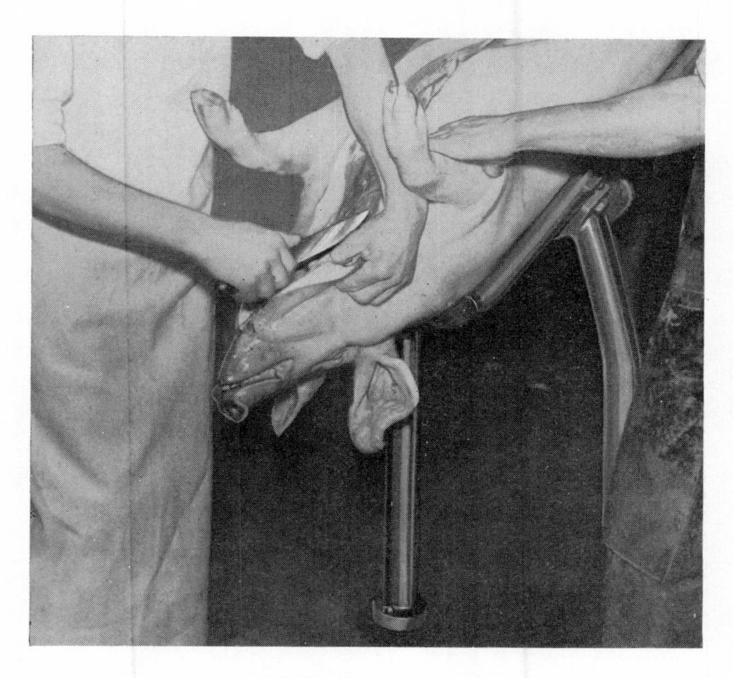

FIG. 27.—Carcase of pork manipulated on to an inclined metal cradle to facilitate examination of the submaxillary lymph nodes.

Federally inspected establishments, and also abattoirs in Western Germany, prescribe that the tonsils shall be removed and shall not be used as ingredients of meat food products.

Lungs. Visual examination, which should be followed by palpation, should be carried out for evidence of pleurisy, pneumonia, tuberculosis, fascioliasis, and hydatid cysts. The bronchial and mediastinal lymph nodes should be incised for tuberculosis, and the lung substance should be exposed by a long, deep incision from the base to apex of each lung.

Heart. The pericardium should be examined for traumatic or tuberculous pericarditis. The heart ventricles may then be incised, particular attention being paid to the presence of petechial haemorrhages on the epicardium or endocardium, or for cysticerci or hydatid cysts in the myocardium. A flabby condition of the myocardium is often associated with septic conditions in the cow.

FIG. 28.—South American frigorifico practice, showing examination of superficial inguinal and precrural lymph nodes. The inspectors do not handle the carcase, but use the knife in one hand and a hook in the other. (Dr. M. T. Morgan.)

Liver. A visual examination should be made for fatty change, actinobacillosis, abscesses, telangiectasis, and such parasitic infections as hydatid cysts, *Cysticercus bovis*, fascioliasis or linguatulae; the larval stage of *Oesophagostomum radiatum*, which is not uncommon in Britain, may also be found in the ox liver. In examination for fascioliasis a routine incision may be made in the thin left lobe of the liver, and this also facilitates drainage of the organ when it is subsequently hung up by the portal notch. The portal lymph nodes should also be incised.

Stomach and Intestines. The serous surface of these organs may show evidence of tuberculosis or actinobacillosis, while the anterior aspect of the reticulum may show evidence of penetration by a foreign body. Routine incision of the mesenteric lymph nodes should be made for tuberculosis or linguatula nodules. It is of interest to record that, as a result of the virtual eradication of bovine tuberculosis from the United States, it is not now considered necessary in that country to incise the mesenteric lymph nodes in routine examination; except in the case of reactors to the tuberculin test, the mesentery is now examined by simple palpation.

Spleen. The surface and substance should be examined for tuberculosis, anthrax, haematomata, or the presence of infarcts.

Uterus. This may be opened and examined for septic conditions, but evidence of pregnancy or of recent parturition in the well-bled and well-set carcase are of no significance.

Udders. In some districts these are the slaughterman's perquisite and are sold by him to pork butchers as an article of human food; they should therefore be carefully examined by multiple deep incisions about two inches apart. Abscesses or septic mastitis may be present, and the supramammary lymph nodes, even in the dry cow, should be incised for evidence of tuberculosis.

Carcase. An external inspection should be carried out for bruising or injuries, especially of the angle of the haunch. The assessment of the age of bruises can be determined with reasonable accuracy by the following indications. Bruises inflicted within a few hours of slaughter are red and haemorrhagic; when about 24 hours old they are dark coloured; from 24 to 38 hours they commence to show a watery condition, while bruises three days old or more have a rusty orange colour and are soapy to the touch, indicative of a normal healing process. When bruises are very severe they may take up to six weeks before they heal completely. Inspection of the thoracic and abdominal cavities should be made for inflammation, abscesses or tuberculosis, and the diaphragm should be lifted, for tuberculous lesions may be hidden between the diaphragm and thoracic wall. The cut surface of the carcase bones should be examined, the kidneys loosened and visually inspected, and the renal lymph nodes incised. If the above routine examination reveals no evidence of abnormality the carcase may then be passed for food.

In 1965 in the United States the number of bovine carcases condemned as a result of post-mortem inspection was 0·3 per cent. of the total slaughtered, the affections, in order of frequency, being neoplasms (mostly epithelioma and malignant lymphoma), pleurisy and pneumonia, emaciation, pericarditis and septicaemia.

Calves

It is unnecessary to carry out routine examination of the lymph nodes of the head, but a visual examination of the mouth and tongue should be made for foot and mouth disease and calf diphtheria. In calves attention should also be paid to the abomasum for evidence of peptic ulcers, the small intestine for white scour or dysentery, and the liver, portal lymph nodes and posterior mediastinal lymph nodes for evidence of congenital tuberculosis. The lungs, kidneys and spinal cord should be examined for evidence of melanotic deposits and the umbilicus and joints for septic omphalophlebitis; the consistency of the synovial fluid of the hock joint can be readily determined by puncturing the protusion on the inner aspect of the joint with the point of a knife.

Sheep

These require a less detailed inspection than cattle, calves and pigs, but the carcase should be examined for satisfactory bleeding and setting, the lungs for parasitic infections, especially hydatid cysts or nematodes, and the liver for fascioliasis. In Australia and New Zealand it is a routine procedure to palpate the carcase for evidence of arthritis, caseous lymphadenitis, inoculation abscesses and lesions due to grass seed awns.

Pigs

Skin lesions in the pig are an important diagnostic feature in the recognition of swine erysipelas, swine fever and urticaria. The skin should also be examined for " shotty eruption " and the udder for mastitis or actinomycosis. The viscera of pigs require inspection in the manner detailed for cattle, with particular attention to pneumonia and the secondary complications that develop in virus pneumonia, mainly pleurisy, pericarditis and, to a lesser extent, peritonitis. In every carcase examination of the submaxillary lymph nodes, together with the bronchial and mesenteric lymph nodes, should be made for tuberculosis. Abscesses in the submaxillary lymph node in pigs may be caused by the passage of sharp foreign bodies through the wall of the pharynx, and in some countries a beta-haemolytic streptococcus has been shown to be the cause of abscessation of this node. The substance of the pig liver need not be incised except when it appears cirrhotic, but abscesses may be found in the liver and often contain portion of a stiff bristle from a broom. The portal lymph nodes, if not removed with the mesentery, should be incised as a routine procedure and the kidney surface should also be examined.

It will be seen that post-mortem examination in both the ox and pig should include incision of the following lymph nodes as a routine procedure : (1) The retropharyngeal and submaxillary in cattle, and the submaxillary in pigs, (2) bronchial and mediastinal, (3) portal and (4) mesenteric. In Holland the incision of the mesenteric lymph nodes of pigs has been discontinued because of the frequency with which knives became contaminated with salmonella organisms present in the nodes.

Sterilization of the Meat Inspector's Knife

Under The Slaughterhouse (Hygiene) Regulations, slaughtering tools, etc. must be sterilized after contact with diseased meat and at the end of the day's work.

A method for the rapid sterilization of a knife is to immerse it in a metal case containing alcohol, withdraw the knife and apply a flame to the blade, holding the knife point downwards. Alternatively, a contaminated knife may be sterilized by boiling in water for 30 minutes, or in a special apparatus which contains hot dry air maintained at 330° F., and similar results may be achieved by prolonged immersion of the knife in formalin vapour generated in a metal cabinet. Other satisfactory methods are by heating the knife for 10 to 15 minutes in oil, liquid petroleum jelly or glycerine maintained at a temperature of 248° F. to 266° F.

The sterilization of anthrax-contaminated equipment requires particular care, and is dealt with in consideration of that disease.

Meat Marking

The purpose of meat marking is threefold. It indicates that the carcase has been inspected and is therefore a guarantee to the consumer ; it will prevent the substitution of sound organs for diseased ones, and it forms a ready means of identification of meat about which questions may subsequently arise.

The marking of meat may be done in three ways, by the use of a stamp, by branding, or by the use of tags or labels, but the latter method is useless unless the label can be fastened to the carcase by means of wire, the ends of which must then be sealed. The best and most convenient method is by the use of a metal stamp which is more durable and therefore preferable to a rubber stamp. The stamping ink must be harmless, adherent, quick drying and readily visible, and a 1 to 2 per cent. solution of fuchsin fulfils all these requirements. The fuchsin is dissolved in just enough acetic acid to bring about its solution, glycerine then being added to make up the required quantity of ink ; where a quick-drying ink is required, methylated spirit may be substituted for glycerine. Before applying the stamp the surface of the meat should be slightly damped, but water must not be added to ink which has a glycerine basis, as the penetrating power of such ink depends on the hygroscopic properties of the glycerine. Though stamping is the method generally employed for the marking of carcases, lungs, etc., it is a method unsuitable for the marking of livers owing to their dark colour, and this organ is best marked by branding with a hot iron. In many countries carcases are graded according to quality, and in New Zealand are marked with distinctive coloured stripes which enable the purchaser to recognize the type and quality of the meat purchased.

THE DETERMINATION OF AGE AND SEX OF THE FOOD ANIMALS

This is of importance in the keeping of records of disease found on routine examination, and also in the recognition of the carcase of the cow, ewe and sow, animals in which dangerous affections of a septic nature are the most likely to occur. It is also of value where a system of mutual insurance of animals intended for slaughter exists and an inspector may be called upon to pass expert judgment as to the age and sex of any animal in dispute. It is chiefly in the decision as to whether a bovine is a maiden heifer, or whether she has had one calf, that his judgment will be required. Where meat is supplied to public institutions there is possibility of the substitution of cow meat for that from bullocks or heifers, of or the substitution of ewe mutton for that of lambs or young sheep. Here again the judgment of the inspector will be of value.

Determination of Age

In the food animals this may be estimated with reasonable accuracy by the teeth, the horns in cattle, or by the carcase bones.

Teeth

Ox. The age is estimated by the period at which the permanent incisor teeth erupt and come into wear; these periods are subject to variation, depending on sex, breed and method of feeding.

At birth or soon after, the ox shows eight temporary incisors or milk teeth in the lower jaw, these being considerably smaller than the permanent teeth. The average time of appearance of the permanent incisors is indicated on p. 63, but all four pairs of teeth may appear 3 months earlier or 3 months later than the average period. Again, if the milk or temporary teeth are drawn artificially the permanent or broad teeth will erupt earlier than normal.

The first change in incisor dentition begins at 2 years, the central pair of milk teeth being replaced by the permanent teeth. The next pair, the lateral central incisors, appear at 2 years 6 months, the lateral pair at 3 years, and the corner pair at 3 years 6 months; the animal is then said to have a "full mouth". The corner pair of permanent incisors are subject to the greatest variation in the time of eruption, and well-bred cattle or animals which are well fed and well housed tend to erupt their teeth earlier than scrub animals or those which are poorly fed and poorly housed. In pedigree cattle the corner incisors may appear soon after completion of the third year, and in bulls they are not uncommonly present at 2 years 10 months.

The formula for the temporary teeth may be shown as follows, the teeth being viewed from in front, and the upper and lower figures corresponding to the teeth of the upper and lower jaw:

Molars	*Incisors*	*Molars*
$\frac{3}{3}$	$\frac{0}{8}$	$\frac{3}{3} = \frac{6}{14} = 20$

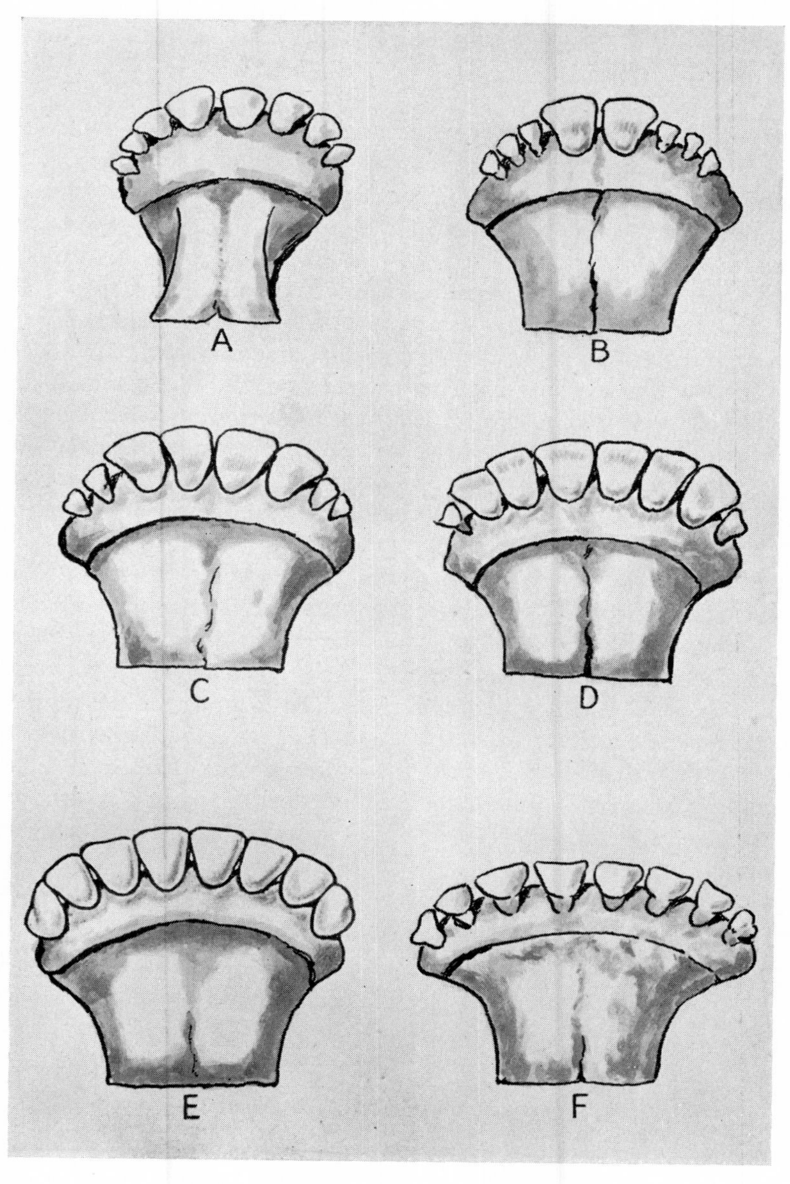

Fig. 29.—Incisor dentition of ox at various ages. (A) Calf teeth; (B) 2 years old; (C) 2 years 6 months; (D) 3 years; (E) 3 years 6 months; (F) 7 to 8 years old; the cutting edges have become thick and "square-cut" or hollow, while the roots of the teeth have become exposed and show a well-marked neck.

The formula for the permanent teeth is :

Molars	*Incisors*	*Molars*
$\frac{6}{6}$	$\frac{0}{8}$	$\frac{6}{6}=\frac{12}{20}=32$

After the permanent incisor teeth have erupted, the degree of wear on their cutting surface, and the amount of neck visible above the gums, are a guide to the animal's age. The neck of the central pair of incisors is perceptible at the sixth year, that of the lateral centrals at 7 years, of the laterals at 8 years, and of the corner incisors at 9 years. Subsequent to this the incisor teeth are small and much worn and it is then possible to confuse an animal $1\frac{1}{2}$ years of age, and therefore possessing all its milk incisors, with an animal of about 10 years, but this can be avoided by recognition of the exposed roots of the teeth in the older animal due to shrinkage of the gums and projection of the roots from the alveolar sockets.

Sheep. The milk incisors in sheep are all present at birth or shortly after, and remain until the animal is 1 year old. Where sheep are folded on turnips, however, a number of the temporary incisors may be broken off before the animal is 1 year old.

The first pair of permanent incisors appear between 12 and 18 months, the next pair between 18 months and 2 years, the laterals between 2 years 3 months and 2 years 9 months, while the corner incisors erupt between 2 years 9 months and 3 years 3 months. A notch develops between the central pair of incisors at 6 years of age. The formula for the temporary and permanent dentition in sheep is identical with that in cattle.

Goat. It is generally accepted that up to 4 years the goat is as many years old as it has pairs of permanent incisor teeth. Thus a goat in which the last pair of permanent incisors have erupted may be estimated as 4 years old.

Pig. The period of eruption of temporary and permanent teeth in pigs is subject to considerable variation, and dentition is not a really satisfactory or accurate guide to the animal's age. Estimation of the age in pigs is only likely to be necessary in the case of show animals in connection with their eligibility for particular age classes.

The formula for the temporary dentition of the pig is :

Molars	*Canines*	*Incisors*	*Canines*	*Molars*
$\frac{3}{3}$	$\frac{1}{1}$	$\frac{6}{6}$	$\frac{1}{1}$	$\frac{3}{3}\ \frac{14}{14}=28$

The formula for the permanent teeth is :

Molars	*Premolars*	*Canines*	*Incisors*	*Canines*	*Premolars*	*Molars*
$\frac{6}{6}$	$\frac{1}{1}$	$\frac{1}{1}$	$\frac{6}{6}$	$\frac{1}{1}$	$\frac{1}{1}$	$\frac{6}{6}=\frac{22}{22}=44$

There is slight variation in the figures quoted by various authorities as to the ages at which the permanent incisors appear in the various animals. Sisson gives the following :

	1st Pair.	*2nd Pair.*	*3rd Pair.*	*4th Pair.*
Ox .	1½-2 yrs.	2-2½ yrs.	3 yrs.	3½-4 yrs.
Sheep .	1-1½ yrs.	1½-2 yrs.	2½-3 yrs.	3½-4 yrs.
Pig .	1 yr.	16-20 mos.	8-10 mos.	Canines 9-10 mos.
Horse	2½ yrs.	3½ yrs.	4½ yrs.	Canines 4-5 yrs.

Horns

Estimation of the age of cattle by means of the horns entails counting the number of rings upon the animal's horns, but these rings must not be confused with the small wrinkles situated at the root of the horn which are an indication that the animal has been ill-fed during its growth. The first ring appears at about 2 years and thereafter one ring is added annually so that the age in years in cattle equals the number of rings plus one. In cows it is not unusual for the rings to be removed by scraping, and greater accuracy as to age may be obtained by examination of the incisor teeth or carcase bones.

Bones

Where the teeth of a bovine animal are unavailable for examination the age can be estimated with reasonable accuracy by examination of the carcase bones, this estimation being based on the degree of ossification of certain parts of the skeletal system; the most valuable of these are the cartilaginous extensions of the spines of the first five dorsal vertebrae. Ossification in these spines develops as follows :

At 1 year old the extension is entirely cartilaginous, being soft, pearly-white and sharply delimited from the bone, which is soft and red.

At 2 years small red islets of bone appear in the cartilage, and at 3 years the cartilage is greyish, and red areas are more numerous.

Between 4 and 5 years the area of ossification within the cartilage extends until the proportion of bone is greater than that of cartilage.

At 6 years the cartilage has ossified into compact bony tissue, though the line of junction between cartilage and bone can still be defined.

In cows these changes take place more rapidly and the cartilage has ossified after 3 years.

A further useful guide as to age can also be obtained from the ischio-pubic symphysis. In cattle up to 3 years of age this can be cut with a knife, but after this age a saw is necessary. Similarly, the red bone marrow of the vertebrae is gradually replaced by yellow bone marrow, and distinction can also be drawn between the soft vascular bones of the young animal with cartilage discernible at the joints, and the hard white bleached appearance of the bones in old cows. In young bovines cartilage is discernible between the individual segments of the sternum but after 5 years of age begins to be replaced by bone; at 8 years two or three cartilaginous divisions are still apparent but at 10 years the cut surface of the sternum presents a uniform bony structure.

In sheep the break at the carpus, or knee joint, is a valuable guide as to age. In lambs the joint breaks in four well marked ridges resembling the teeth of a saw, the ridges being smooth, moist and somewhat pink or congested. In older sheep, as wethers or ewes, the surface of the joint is rough, porous, dry and lacks redness. The determination by X-ray of the amount of cartilage present at the epiphysis of a long bone in a joint of meat provides unassailable evidence in cases where there is dispute as to the age of the animal from which the meat was derived. The degree of ossification, determined by X-ray, in the ischial portion of the pubic symphysis enables a leg of lamb to be differentiated with certainty from that of an old sheep.

Determination of Sex

CATTLE

Differentiation must be established between the carcase of the bull, stag, bullock, heifer and cow.

Bull. The outstanding characteristic in the bull carcase is the massive development of the muscles of the neck and shoulder, the forequarter, except in well-bred animals, being better fleshed than the hindquarter. This development of the crest is diagnostic in bulls, and in some American packing houses the funicular portion of the ligamentum nuchae is cut at its insertion to the dorsal vertebrae, the effect being to make the carcase approximate more in appearance to that of the bullock.

In the dressing of the bull carcase the testicles and spermatic cord are removed, leaving an open external inguinal ring partly covered by scanty scrotal fat. The pelvic cavity is narrow and can be spanned with the hand, while the pelvic floor (ischio-pubic symphysis) is angular and the pubic tubercle strongly developed. The bulbo-cavernosus muscle, often referred to as the erector and retractor penis muscle, is well developed, and the cut adductor, or gracilis muscle, is triangular in shape ; in young bulls, however, the posterior portion of this muscle is not covered with fat, and the gracilis muscle therefore appears bean-shaped. The muscle of young bulls is light or brick red in colour and similar to that of the bullock, but in older bulls it is dark red, dry and poor in fat.

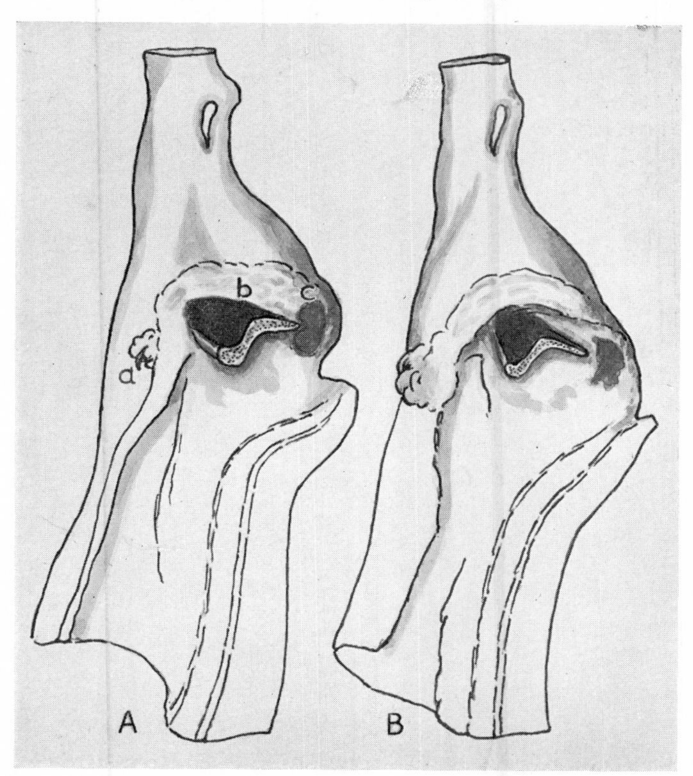

FIG. 30.—(A) Hindquarter of bull showing (*a*) scanty scrotal fat with open external inguinal ring, (*b*) triangular gracilis muscle, and (*c*) strong bulbo-cavernosus muscle. (B) Hindquarter of bullock with abundant scrotal fat and smaller bulbo-cavernosus muscle.

In the northern countries of South America cattle are rarely castrated and it is the custom in dressing the carcase to leave the testicles attached to the hindquarters. These organs are much in demand by the population, who regard them as an aphrodisiac.

Stag. If the male bovine is castrated later in life, at perhaps a year old, it will have developed certain masculine characteristics, chief of which are the strong development of the muscles of the neck and shoulder. Such animals are known as stags and, except for the muscular development of the forequarter, differ little in appearance and quality from the normal bullock.

Bullock. The muscles of the neck and crest are not so strongly developed as in the bull, but fat is more evenly distributed over the carcase and is particularly abundant in the pelvic cavity ; the scrotal fat, too, is abundant, and completely occludes the external inguinal ring. The pelvic cavity is narrow and can be spanned with the hand, but though the pelvic floor is angular and the pubic tubercle prominent, these characteristics are not so marked as in the bull carcase.

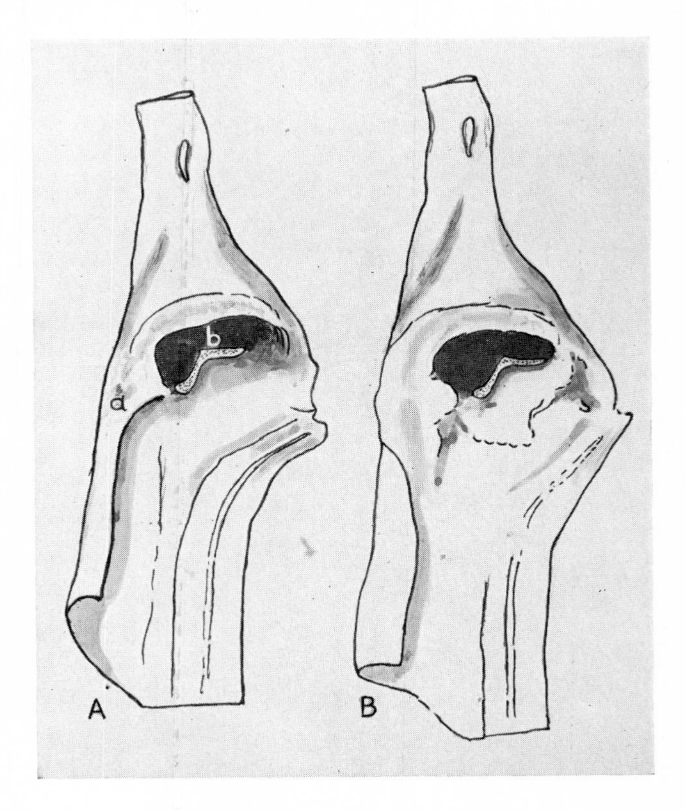

FIG. 31.—(A) Hindquarter of cow showing (*a*) area from which udder has been removed, and (*b*) bean-shaped gracilis muscle. (B) Hindquarter of heifer with smooth, convex udder composed almost entirely of fat.

The posterior or ischial portion of the gracilis muscle, which presents a triangular appearance, is covered with fascia and fat, while there is a well marked bulbo-cavernosus muscle, though this is less strongly developed than in the bull. Bullock flesh is lighter than bull flesh and has a brick red colour with a shiny, marbled appearance due to the presence of intermuscular fat.

Heifer. In the dressing of the heifer carcase the udder remains on each side of beef, and is characterized by its smooth, regular convexity and, on section, by the predominance of fat and lack of evidence of glandular tissue. The absence of a bulbo-cavernosus muscle may be noted, and a useful feature in distinguishing the forequarter of the heifer or cow from that of the bullock is the enlargement at the end of the foreshank (radius). In the cow and heifer the bone is slim and rather straight, but in the bullock it is markedly enlarged. In the heifer and cow remains of the broad ligament of the uterus are apparent on the inner abdominal wall, about a handsbreadth below the angle of the haunch. The differential features of the uterus itself are described on page 89.

Cow. The cow carcase is more slender and less symmetrical than that of the bull or bullock, and shows a long tapering neck, a wide chest cavity, curved back and prominent hips. The pelvic cavity is wide and can scarcely be spanned with the hand, while the pelvic floor is thin, only slightly arched, and the pubic tubercle but slightly developed. The exposed gracilis muscle is crescentic or bean-shaped, but no bulbo-cavernosus muscle is present. The udder, except occasionally in animals which have only had one calf, is removed, leaving a triangular ragged space on the outer aspect of the abdominal wall. In the cow both external and internal fat is irregularly distributed and yellowish in colour.

Calf. In the dressed bobby calf the bull may be recognized by the presence of testicles and the open external inguinal ring, and a transverse cut with a knife just above the pubic tubercle will expose the root of the penis. In the heifer calf the rudimentary udder remains on the carcase.

SHEEP

These include rams, wethers, gimmers and ewes.

Ram. The carcase has strong muscular development of the forequarter, the inguinal rings are open, and the scrotal or cod fat is sparse or absent.

Wether. The carcase is usually well proportioned, with evenly distributed fat and abundant, lobulated cod fat. The root of the penis can be exposed by a transverse section with the knife above the pubic tubercle and in the wether is no thicker than an ordinary pencil.

Gimmer. The carcase is characterized by its symmetrical shape and the presence of the smooth convex udder.

Ewe. The carcase is angular in shape, with long thin neck and poor legs. The udder is brown, spongy, and never sets; it is removed in dressing, leaving a roughened area on the outer abdominal wall, though portions of the supramammary lymph nodes frequently remain on the carcase.

PIGS

Differentiation must be established between the carcase of the boar, hog, gilt, and sow.

Boar. The boar possesses an oval, strongly developed area of cartilage over the shoulder region which may become calcified in old boars, and is known as the shield. The scrotum is removed in the dressing of the

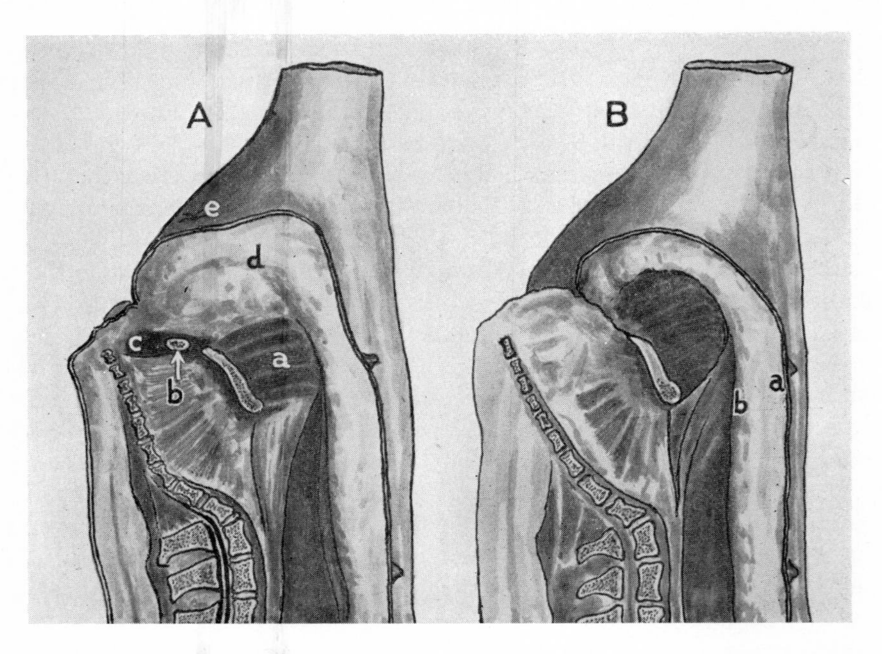

FIG. 32.—(A) Hindquarter of hog. The gracilis muscle (*a*) is partially covered with fat, particularly at the middle of the muscle, and in well fattened animals appears triangular or irregularly rhomboid in shape. Portions of corpus cavernosum of the penis (*b*) may be seen, and in recently castrated animals the bulbo-cavernosus (erector penis) muscle (*c*) may be apparent. A groove (*d*) in the fat indicates the position of the penis, while at (*e*) is the scar left after castration. (B) Hindquarter of gilt. The gracilis muscle is bean-shaped and clearly defined from the adjacent fatty tissue. The surface skin (*a*) and inner bacon line (*b*) are parallel in the region of the gracilis muscle.

carcase, the area of removal being apparent on the inside of the thigh. The cut gracilis muscle is triangular, while the root of the penis will be present on one of the sides when the carcase is split, and a strongly developed bulbo-cavernosus muscle will then be apparent. Strong, curved canine teeth (the tusks) are present in the boar.

Castration of the adult boar produces an animal known as a stag, which is both heavier and fatter and commands a higher price than the boar carcase. Stag pigs show some reduction in the density of the shield as a result of castration, but as both boars and stags are fit only for manufacturing purposes, being skinned and boned out, this reduction of the shield is not of great importance and the chief advantage is in the diminution of the boar odour.

Hog. The differentiation of the hog and gilt carcase frequently presents difficulty, as teats are present in both male and female pigs, though in the male they are small and undeveloped. Evidence of castration in the hog is seen as two puckered, depressed scars, and in both the hog and boar there is evidence of the removal of the preputial sac. The belly fat on one side of the abdominal incision is grooved, and on the floor of this groove can be seen the retractor penis muscle, which is long, thin and pale red in colour. When the carcase is split, remains of the bulbo-cavernosus muscle can be seen, while the gracilis muscle is covered with connective and fatty tissue.

Gilt. In the gilt, the space left below the tail after removal of the anus and vulva is greater than in the hog, the abdominal incision is straight and uninterrupted and the cut surface of the gracilis muscle is bean-shaped. In sows there is greater development of the udders and teats, and though canine teeth are present in the female pig, they do not develop.

Substitutions and Differentiation of the Various Carcases

Apart from fish, in which substitutions are common and difficult to detect, the chief substitutions of inferior flesh for that which is more highly valued are those of horse flesh for beef, goat flesh for mutton and, occasionally, cat for rabbit. Of these the chief substitution, particularly in wartime, is that of horse flesh for beef, though an inspector is unlikely to encounter horse flesh in carcase form as the flesh is invariably cut up or minced if intended for retail sale. In Eire, donkey has been recorded as being substituted for venison.

Differentiation of Carcase of Horse and Ox

(1) In the horse the unusual length of the sides is noticeable, together with the great muscular development of the hindquarters.

(2) The thoracic cavity is longer in the horse ; this animal possesses 18 pairs of ribs and, because it gallops, needs large lungs.

(3) The ribs in the horse are narrower but more markedly curved.

(4) The superior spinous processes of the first six dorsal vertebrae are more markedly developed in the horse and are less inclined posteriorly.

(5) In the forequarter the ulna of the horse only extends half the length of the radius ; in the ox it is extended and articulates with the carpus.

(6) In the hindquarter the femur of the ox possesses no third trochanter ; the fibula is only a small pointed projection, but in the horse it extends two-thirds the length of the tibia.

(7) In the horse the last three lumbar transverse processes articulate with each other, the sixth articulating in a similar manner with the sacrum. They do not articulate in the ox.

(8) The horse carcase shows considerable development of soft yellow fat beneath the peritoneum, particularly in the gelding and mare, but in the stallion the fat is generally of a lighter colour and almost white. In the ox the kidney fat is always firmer, whiter and more abundant than in the horse.

Differentiation of Carcase of Sheep and Goat

(1) In the goat carcase the sharpness of the back and withers is noticeable compared with the round back and well-fleshed withers of the sheep.

(2) The thoracic cavity of the goat is flattened ; in the sheep it is barrel shaped.

(3) The goat tail is thinner than that of the sheep. In India it is a common practice to provide the purchaser with a means of differentiating the carcase of the goat and sheep by leaving a portion of wool on the tip of the sheep tail.

(4) In the goat the shank bone, or radius, is twice the length of the shin bone, or large metacarpus. In the sheep it is $1\frac{1}{4}$ times as long.

(5) The scapula in the sheep is short and broad, and the middle of its superior spine is bent back and thickened. In the goat the scapula has a distinct neck, while the superior spine is straight and narrow.

(6) In the goat the lateral borders of the sacrum are thin and sharp ; in the sheep they are thickened in the form of rolls.

(7) The darker, coarser flesh of the goat may have a characteristic goaty odour, while the subcutaneous tissue is sticky and goat hairs may be found adhering to the surface of the carcase.

CHAPTER IV

COMPARATIVE ANATOMY OF THE TISSUES AND ORGANS AND THEIR FOOD USES

The most convenient method of studying the anatomical features of the organs and tissues of the food animals is to group them into various systems.

1. THE SKELETAL SYSTEM AND SKIN

The Bones

It has been seen that the carcase bones form a useful method of distinguishing the food animals, especially where substitution is suspected. Though a proportion of carcase bone is sold with the retail joints, the head bones, thigh bones, etc., are retained by the butcher after the meat is boned out and are collected by bone works for processing. The proportion of bone in the dressed carcase of beef, i.e. the two sides, varies between 12 to 28 per cent., according to breed and bodily condition, being about 15 per cent. in a good beef carcase and increasing with the age and weight of the animal. It is lowest in cattle of the Aberdeen Angus breed, but is as high as 28 per cent. in second quality cows. The following is the average percentage of bone in the various carcases: mutton 25 per cent., bobby calves 50 per cent., veal calves 25 per cent., and pork 12 to 20 per cent.

Bone is composed of the following constituents :

Animal matter	30·5 per cent.
Calcium phosphate	57·5 ,,
Calcium carbonate	7·0 ,,
Calcium fluoride	3·0 ,,
Magnesium phosphate	2·0 ,,
	100 ,,

The animal matter is the only edible constituent of bone and forms gelatine. This is extracted from the bones by hot water, and as it is utilized for culinary or confectionery processes or for ice cream manufacture, it is desirable that only butcher's bones from a known hygienic source should be utilized for its preparation.

Two types of bone marrow may be distinguished, the red marrow, and the white which is fatty and gelatinous. In the foetus and newborn animal the bone marrow has a heavy haemogenetic responsibility and is red in colour. Later, when the adult equilibrium is established, the marrow in the medullary cavity of long bones is converted into white bone marrow which is rich in fat, yellowish in colour and may weigh 15 per cent. of the weight of the bone; the marrow in the epiphyses of long bones usually remains red. Another important position of red bone marrow in the adult is in those bones which possess no medullary cavity, such as the bodies of the vertebrae, the scapula and pedal bones. The presence of red, semi-fluid bone marrow in the medullary cavity of bones in the adult animal is suggestive of osteomalacia, osteomyelitis or leukaemia.

USES

Bones, in addition to yielding gelatine, contain much fat in the medullary cavity, and this is used as stock for the preparation of soup.

The Skin

The skin of the ox and sheep is not used for human food, but in the pig the skin is left on the carcase, being scored and constituting the crackling. In Britain the shield of the boar is regarded as inedible and is removed, but in Germany it is transformed by boiling into a swollen, digestible mass, which, being glutinous in nature, forms a common constituent of sausage, particularly blood sausage.

Portions of muscle which remain on the inside of hides, particularly the ear muscles, are sometimes trimmed off and used for human food. Inasmuch as contamination of hides and skins on the slaughterhouse floor is extensive, this practice should be forbidden.

2. THE DIGESTIVE SYSTEM

The Tongue

Ox. In the ox tongue the filiform papillae are horny and directed backwards, and impart to the tongue a rasp-like roughness which aids in the prehension of food. The posterior part of the dorsum, i.e. the upper surface, is prominent, and defined anteriorly by a transverse depression which is frequently the seat of erosions due to actinobacillosis. On either side of the mid-line on the prominent dorsum are 10 to 14 circumvallate papillae, and the epiglottis, if left on the tongue, is oval in shape. Black pigmentation of the skin of the tongue is frequently observed, but is quite normal and of no pathological significance.

Sheep and Goat. In these animals the tongue is similar to that of cattle, but the centre of the tip is slightly grooved and the papillae are not horny. The sheep tongue may be differentiated from that of the calf by the fact that it is narrower, the dorsal eminence is more marked, the surface is smoother and the tip more rounded. Black pigmentation of the surface of the tongue is common in black-skinned sheep.

Pig. The tongue is long and narrow and there is no dorsal ridge. One, or possibly two, circumvallate papillae are present on each side of the mid-line near the base of the tongue, and the surface is studded with fungiform papillae.

Horse. The tongue is long and flat with spatulate end, there is no dorsal ridge and only one circumvallate papilla is present on each side. The epiglottis is pointed. Pigmentation is never seen on the surface of the horse tongue.

Uses

The tongue of the ox, sheep, pig and horse are used for food either fresh or salted.

The Stomach

Ox. The oesophagus is comparatively short and wide, being about $3\frac{1}{2}$ feet long and 2 inches wide. The voluntary muscle, by which the reverse peristaltic action in rumination is performed, weighs about $\frac{3}{4}$ lb. and is used for sausage meat; after removal of this muscle the serous covering of the oesophagus is utilized as a sausage casing.

The stomach consists of four compartments, the rumen, reticulum, omasum and abomasum, the latter being the true digestive stomach and secreting gastric juice. The rumen occupies three-quarters of the abdominal cavity, its left side being in contact with the abdominal wall, its anterior extremity bounded by the reticulum and part of the omasum, while on the right side it is in contact with the remainder of the omasum, the abomasum and intestine. The reticulum is placed transversely between the anterior extremity of the rumen and the posterior surface of the diaphragm, to which structure it is adherent. The omasum and abomasum are attached to the posterior surface of the liver by means of the omentum or caul fat, the root of this membrane being apparent on the posterior aspect of the liver to the left of the portal lymph nodes when the liver is removed

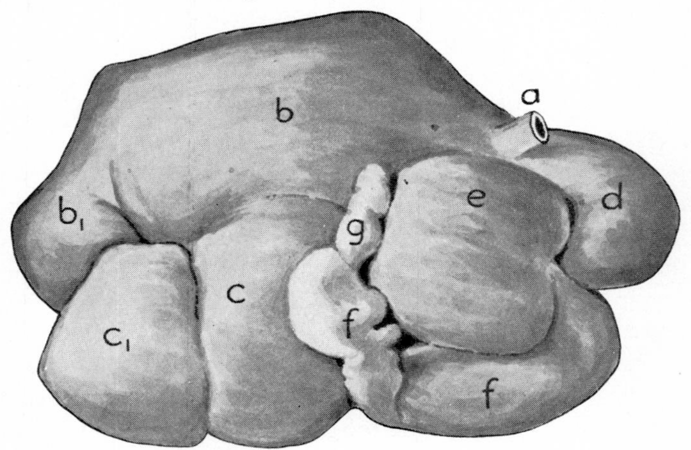

FIG. 33.—Stomach of ox viewed from right side: (*a*) oesophagus; (*b*) left sac of rumen; (b_1) its posterior blind sac; (*c*) right sac of rumen; (c_1) its posterior blind sac; (*d*) reticulum; (*e*) omasum; (*f, f*) abomasum; (*g*) duodenum. (After Sisson.)

from the carcase (Fig. 34). The omentum, after connecting the liver and omasum, is continued to the lesser curvature of the abomasum and thence to the duodenum. The anatomical relations of the bovine stomach play an important part in the aetiology of traumatic pericarditis.

A feature of the calf stomach is the relatively large size of the abomasum as compared with the small size of the rumen, which remains small until the animal is weaned. As the calf commences to take solid foods the size of the rumen increases until in the adult animal it is responsible for 80 per cent. of the total stomach capacity, the abomasum for 7 to 8 per cent.

USES

Both ox and sheep stomachs are similar in structure and constitute the raw material from which tripe is prepared.

TRIPE. In the preparation of ox tripe the rumen and reticulum are processed together, the omasum and abomasum separately. The stomachs are first emptied and washed and the fat, weighing about 3 lb., is trimmed off. The stomachs are then scalded in water containing washing soda, scraped and placed in cold water to cleanse them, and finally cooked for 3 to 3½ hours at a temperature of 120°-140° F. The weight of tripe obtained from an average ox stomach is 15 lb., this being made up of rumen and reticulum 9 lb., omasum 4 lb. and abomasum 2 lb., about 40 to 45 per cent. of the green weight of tripes being available as finished product. Though in some countries the omasum is made into tripe, in others it is considered uneconomical because of the difficulty of removing the mucous membrane, and this stomach is therefore discarded. Rennet is manufactured from the abomasum of the suckling calf.

Sheep. The sheep stomach is similar in structure to that of the ox, and has an average capacity of four gallons. The first and second stomachs together yield 2 lb. of tripe, the fourth stomach being also used, but the third stomach is often discarded. The sheep rumen is also used in Scotland as a container for haggis. This article of diet, the national dish of a people once so poor that they could not afford to discard any edible part of the sheep carcase, is manufactured from the chopped liver, heart and lungs of sheep, mixed with oatmeal, fat and spices. The mixture is packed into the rumen, which is then sewn up and cooked for 5 hours. Sometimes the ox bung is used as a container. Mechanical methods for the cleaning of both ox and sheep stomachs are now operating satisfactorily in modern triperies.

Pig. The pig stomach (Fig. 49) is a simple one, semilunar in shape, with a small pocket or diverticulum at the cardiac, i.e. oesophageal, end. The mucous membrane of the cardiac end of the stomach is pale grey in colour, while the central fundic region is reddish-brown, becoming paler and corrugated towards the pyloric end.

The pig stomach and large intestines are cooked and sold for food as chitterlings, and pepsin is extracted from the mucous membrane of the stomach and is used for pharmaceutical purposes.

Horse. The horse stomach is a simple one, the mucous membrane of the whitish oesophageal portion being clearly distinguishable from the fundic and pyloric portions which are reddish, soft and vascular (Fig. 191).

The Intestines

The average length of the intestines is as follows :

	Small Intestines	*Large Intestines*
Cattle	120 feet	30 feet
Horse	80 ,,	20 ,,
Sheep	84 ,,	20 ,,
Pig	56 ,,	16 ,,

Thus for practical purposes the ratio of the length of the small intestines to large intestines is 4 to 1.

Uses

In all the food animals the cleansed and scraped intestines are used as containers for sausage meat.

Gut Cleaning and Scraping

Ox. The external fatty tissue is removed before decomposition commences, the intestine is then turned, slimed by drawing it between the thumb and a piece of hard wood to remove the mucous membrane, and finally salted. The treated small intestines of the ox are termed runners, the caecum is termed the bung, and the colon is termed the middle. Ox runners are used as a container for black pudding, white pudding, polony and salami, or as a container for lard instead of the more usual pig's bladder. The middles are used as large food containers, as in liver sausage, while the bungs are used for luncheon sausage. With the exception of sheep and pig intestines, all casings of animal origin are turned, so that the outer surface of the gut is in contact with the contained food product. The serous covering of the ox caecum is used for goldbeaters' skin. Mechanical methods are now widely employed for the cleaning of the intestines of all the food animals.

Sheep. The sheep intestines are sometimes allowed to stand in a tub of water, it being claimed that this aids in the detachment of the mucous membrane. They are then placed on a cleansing board and slimed without being turned, for the small diameter of sheep and pig intestines renders this impracticable. They are finally salted and put up in 100 yards bundles, the small intestines being known as runners, the caecum and colon being termed the large gut. Sheep runners are mainly used for the ordinary beef or pork sausage ; they are also made into surgical catgut, and the runners of small sheep and lambs, filled with prime pork and seasoned, constitute the popular chipolata sausage.

Pig. The treated pig intestines, being thicker than those of sheep, are preferred by some butchers for casings and are used for pork sausage and saveloys. Animal casings should be stored after salting for at least one month in order to ensure the destruction of any pathogenic organisms that may be present.

With the exception of ox runners, the supply of sausage casings in Britain from home killed animals cannot meet the demand, and as a result considerable quantities of sheep runners are imported into Britain from

New Zealand, Australia and Russia. Pig runners are imported from Holland, Denmark, United States and Canada.

Horse. The intestines of this animal are not used in Britain as food containers, but considerable quantities of horse runners are salted and barrelled in Britain and exported under veterinary certificate to the Continent.

The Liver

With the exception of the horse, the livers of all the food animals are reddish-brown in colour.

Ox. The liver is poorly divided into three lobes, a thin left lobe, a thicker right lobe and a caudate lobe or thumb piece. The left and right lobes are divided by a slight notch known as the umbilical fissure which indicates the point of entry of the umbilical vein while the calf is *in utero*. In the cow the left lobe of the liver is thin, elongated, and often markedly cirrhotic. Running transversely across the upper border of the liver is the posterior vena cava, and on its posterior aspect the liver shows the root of the omentum, the gall bladder, portal vein and portal lymph nodes, the vein and lymph nodes being partly concealed by the pancreas. The weight of the ox liver is about 12 lb. The calf liver, which is relatively larger than in the adult, weighs 2 to 2½ lb.; its tenderness and usual freedom from parasitic and other pathological conditions, together with the fact that it has a therapeutic value in the treatment of anaemia, ensures the highest price for the calf liver.

Sheep. The liver is similar in shape to that of the ox, but the caudate lobe is more pointed and its edges are well defined; this is a useful distinguishing feature between the liver of the sheep and calf, the caudate lobe in the latter being more rounded and having a blunter extremity which frequently extends beyond the lower edge of the liver. When the calf liver is laid on the table, anterior surface uppermost, the caudate lobe fits into the liver in the form of a neat carpenter's joint. The weight of the sheep liver is 1 to 1½ lb.

Pig. This possesses five lobes, two small inner, two small outer and a caudate lobe. The oesophageal notch is prominent but a diagnostic feature of the pig liver is the large amount of visible interlobular tissue; the lobules are thus mapped out sharply, are polyhedral, and the organ, because of the amount of interlobular tissue, is less friable than in the other food animals; its weight varies from 2 lb. in pork pigs to 7 lb. in sows.

Horse. The liver possesses three distinct lobes and a thumb piece which terminates in a point, while a notable feature is the absence of a gall bladder. The horse liver is purplish in colour and weighs about 10 lb.

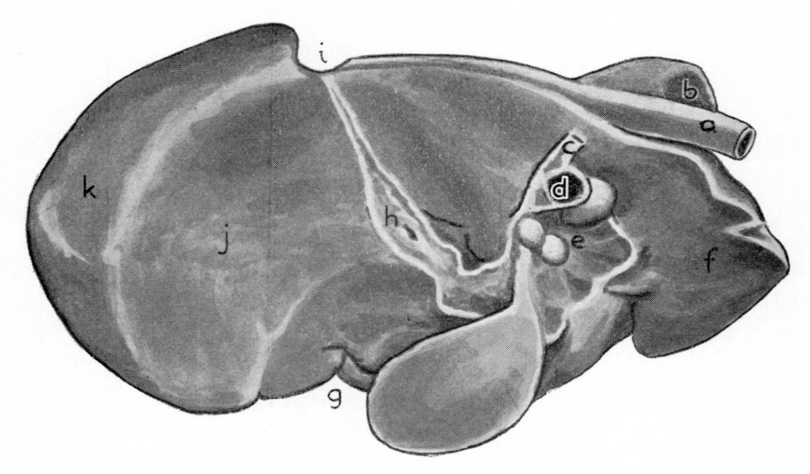

FIG. 34.—Ox liver showing: (*a*) posterior vena cava; (*b*) renal impression; (*c*) hepatic artery; (*d*) portal vein; (*e*) portal lymph nodes (to the right of the portal vein is the node which drains the pancreas); (*f*) caudate lobe; (*g*) umbilical fissure; (*h*) root of omentum; (*i*) oesophageal notch; (*j*) omasal impression; (*k*) reticular impression. (After Sisson.)

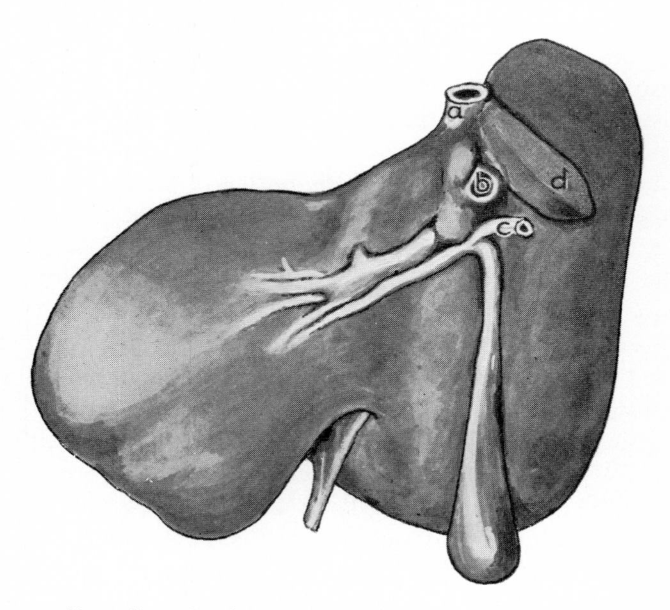

FIG. 35.—Sheep liver showing: (*a*) posterior vena cava; (*b*) portal vein; (*c*) bile duct; (*d*) caudate lobe. Note that the caudate lobe is somewhat pointed, and does not project beyond the edge of the liver. The remains of the umbilical vein, which becomes occluded and cord-like after birth, can be seen entering the umbilical fissure but has usually disappeared completely by the time the animal is slaughtered.

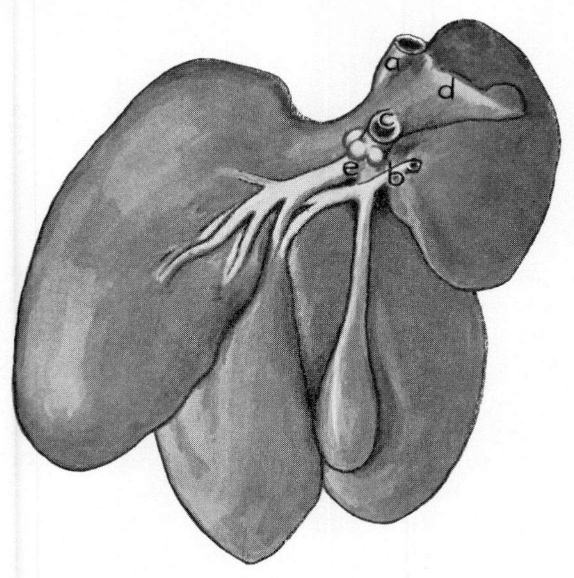

FIG. 36.—Pig liver showing: (*a*) posterior vena cava; (*b*) bile duct; (*c*) portal vein; (*d*) caudate lobe; (*e*) portal lymph nodes; these frequently become detached during evisceration, and may then be found in the fat attached to the lesser curvature of the stomach (see Fig. 49).

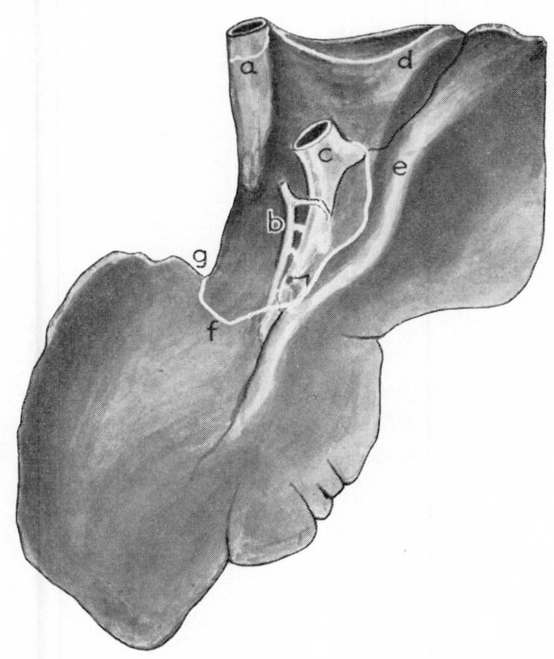

FIG. 37.—Horse liver showing: (*a*) posterior vena cava; (*b*) bile duct; (*c*) portal vein; (*d*) caudate lobe; (*e*) duodenal impression; (*f*) root of omentum; (*g*) oesophageal notch. Note the absence of a gall bladder. (After Sisson.)

Uses

The liver is usually sold fresh; a medicinal extract is also obtained from it for the treatment of pernicious anaemia. Bile is used as a cleanser and by the leather industry for polishing purposes.

The Pancreas

The ox pancreas is yellowish-brown in colour, loosely lobulated, and roughly the shape of an oak leaf. It is attached to the back of the liver and is deeply notched to accommodate the portal vein, around the entry of which vessel into the liver are situated the portal lymph nodes.

Uses

The pancreas, known to butchers as the gut-sweetbread, is frequently sold for food as the true sweetbread, but this practice is a dishonest one as the true sweetbread is the thymus gland. The medicinal product insulin, which is used in the treatment of diabetes, is obtained from the pancreas. The weight of the ox pancreas is 8 to 12 oz.

The Spleen

Ox. The spleen of the ox is related to the left dorsal side of the rumen and also to the diaphragm. In the young bovine it is elongated, slightly convex with rounded edges, reddish-brown in colour and lymph follicles are apparent on the cut surface. In the cow the organ is flat, the edges are sharp, the extremities rounded and it is bluish in colour; its weight is 2 to 3 lb.

Sheep. This is usually found attached to the pluck, being removed with it in the dressing of the carcase. It is oyster-shaped, soft or elastic to the touch and weighs 2 to 3 oz. In both ox and sheep the spleen is adherent to the rumen.

Pig. The pig spleen is connected to the greater curvature of the stomach by the serous membrane known as the gastro-splenic omentum (Fig. 49). The organ is elongated, tongue-shaped and triangular in cross section, while its under surface shows a well marked longitudinal ridge to which the omentum is attached; its weight is 4 to 15 oz. The relatively loose attachment of the pig spleen to the stomach often leads to splenic rotation, resulting in torsion and acute swelling of the organ (Fig. 67).

Horse. The spleen is flat and sickle-shaped, bluish in colour, and weighs 1 to 2 lb. (Fig. 120).

Uses

The spleen is usually referred to by butchers as the melt, and is used as food for cats or dogs.

3. THE RESPIRATORY SYSTEM

The pleura lines the chest cavity and in the healthy animal is a smooth glistening membrane divided into a right and left sac. Each sac covers the chest wall (the parietal pleura), and also the lung (the visceral pleura),

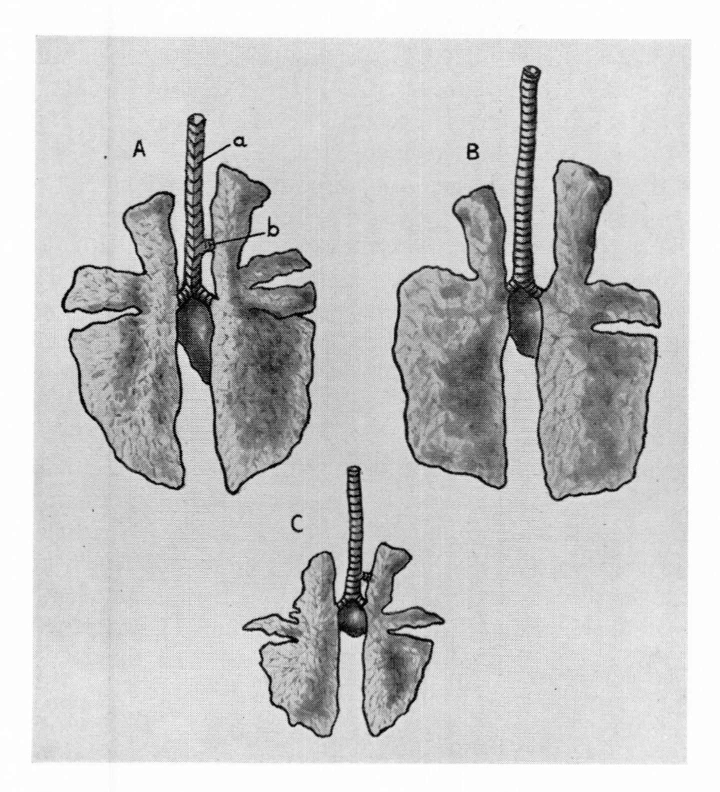

FIG. 38.—A. Ruminant lungs (ox and sheep) showing posterior tracheal ridge (*a*) and accessory bronchus (*b*). B. Lungs of horse showing absence of posterior tracheal ridge and accessory bronchus. C. Lungs of pig; there is no posterior tracheal ridge but an accessory bronchus is present.

the two sacs joining in the central mediastinal space in which are situated the mediastinal lymph nodes and which is traversed by the aorta, oesophagus and trachea. The lungs only remain expanded by virtue of the negative pressure which exists in the pleural cavities, and when the thoracic cavity is opened the elasticity of the lungs causes them to lose their form and collapse to one-third of their original size.

Lungs

Ox. The cartilaginous rings of the ox trachea meet at an angle and form a distinct ridge along the dorsal aspect of the trachea. The left lung has three lobes named, from before backwards, the apical, cardiac and diaphragmatic. The right lung has four or five lobes, its apical lobe receiving an accessory bronchus from the trachea. The lung lobulation is well marked due to the large amount of interlobular tissue, and is particularly evident in old cows. The pair of ox lungs weigh 5 to 7 lb.

Sheep. The sheep lungs resemble those of the ox in the division of the lobes, but their consistency is more dense and leathery, they are duller in colour, and the lobulation is less distinct. They weigh $\frac{3}{4}$ to 2 lb.

Pig. The number of lobes varies, there being two to three on the left and three to four on the right, this variation being due to possible further subdivision of the apical and cardiac lobes. The tissue is very spongy and compressible, and the surface lobulation is particularly well marked. Of all the food animals, pig lungs show the greatest variations in colour, varying from red to a light pink, but these variations are due to slight differences in the amount of blood left in the lungs after bleeding and are of no pathological significance. The pig lungs weigh $\frac{3}{4}$ to 1 lb.

Horse. The lobar divisions are very indistinct in the horse, and only two left lobes and three right lobes can be clearly distinguished. The horse lungs are long, and may be further differentiated from those of the ox by the absence of surface lobulation and the absence of an accessory bronchus, while the ends of the cartilaginous rings of the trachea, if they meet, overlap in the manner of a piston ring. The horse lungs weigh 5 to 7 lb.

The Pluck

In the pig, sheep and calf the internal organs comprising the larynx, trachea, lungs, heart and liver (and the spleen also in sheep) constitute the pluck. In the pig pluck the oesophagus remains attached and is related to the trachea, which is short and consists of 32 cartilaginous rings. In the sheep the oesophagus is removed with the stomachs in the dressing of the carcase, and the trachea is long and composed of about 50 rings.

Uses

The lungs of the food animals are used as an ingredient of white puddings and for cat and dog meat.

4. THE CIRCULATORY SYSTEM

The Heart

This is reddish-brown in colour in all the food animals, the myocardium being firm in consistency, and the epicardium and endocardium smooth and glistening. The right and left ventricles may readily be distinguished by palpation, the wall of the left ventricle being three times as thick as that of the right, while the mitral valve and its chordae tendineae are stronger than the tricuspid valve of the right side. A certain amount of blood clot is found normally in each of the ventricles after death.

Ox. The ox heart shows three ventricular furrows on its surface, and two ossa cordis, which are cartilaginous until four weeks after birth, develop at the base of the heart in the aortic wall. The ox heart weighs 4 to 5 lb., and in pregnant cows and in those suffering from a septic infection is frequently pale, flabby and friable.

Sheep. There are three ventricular furrows, while in later years a small os cordis may develop on the right side. The weight of the heart is 3 to 4 oz.

Pig. Only two ventricular furrows are normally present in the pig's heart, although a rudimentary posterior furrow may be present ; the apex is more rounded than in sheep, and the heart cartilage ossifies in older animals. The weight is 6 to 7 oz.

Horse. The heart possesses two ventricular furrows, the aortic cartilage becoming partly ossified in older animals. The average weight is 6 lb. though much greater in racehorses ; in the thoroughbred horse Eclipse the heart weighed 14 lb.

Uses

The hearts of all the food animals are sold fresh.

In considering the circulatory system reference must be made to the portal circulation and to the foetal circulation. The former is of importance in the study of ascites, or abdominal dropsy, and is also of importance in certain parasitic infections, e.g. hydatid disease, and in the spread of tuberculosis throughout the animal body. The foetal circulation plays an important rôle in the occurrence of congenital tuberculosis in the calf and in the distribution of lesions.

The Portal Circulation (Fig. 39)

The portal vein is formed by two main branches, the gastro-splenic and mesenteric veins which drain the stomach and intestines, while the portal vein also drains blood from the pancreas. Venous blood from these organs is conveyed by the portal vein to the liver, this organ being drained by the hepatic veins which enter the posterior vena cava, wherein the blood is conveyed to the heart.

Bacteria or parasites which gain entry to the portal vein may be arrested within the capillaries of the liver, but this organ is an imperfect filter and organisms may thus pass through its substance and be conveyed to the heart and thence to the lungs. Evidence of the imperfect filtering properties of the liver is shown by the presence of hydatid cysts in the lungs, and by the occasional presence of liver flukes in the bovine lung tissue.

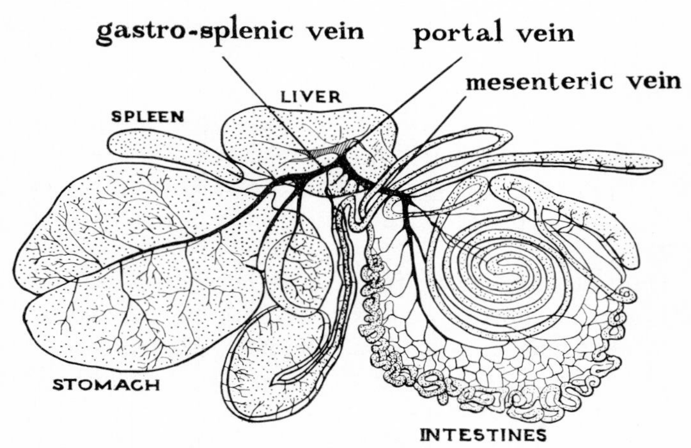

FIG. 39.—The Portal Circulation of the Ox.

The Foetal Circulation (Fig. 40)

Though the foetus *in utero* receives oxygen and nutrient material from the mother there is no actual passage of blood from mother to foetus. Transference of essential materials is rendered possible by the intimate contact of the mucous membrane of the maternal uterus with the foetal membrane, this contact being attained by means of the cotyledons. Corresponding to each maternal cotyledon (Fig. 42) is a foetal cotyledon containing fine branches of the umbilical vein, these branches being received into the sponge-like structure of the maternal cotyledon, and the close contiguity of the two blood supplies is thus assured. Foetal blood, which has received oxygen and nutriment from the mother, is conveyed from the placenta by the umbilical veins, two in number in the ox and sheep, to the umbilicus where they join to form a single vein. This main umbilical vein passes forward from the foetal umbilicus along the floor of the abdominal wall to the liver, which it enters at the umbilical fissure. In the blood circulation of the foetus the umbilical vein is the only vessel which carries unmixed arterial blood.

In the foetal calf a portion of the blood borne by the umbilical vein, having entered the liver, passes into the ductus venosus and thus discharges directly into the posterior vena cava. The amount of blood side-tracked in this way is insignificant compared with the amount which passes through the liver substance, but whichever route the blood takes through the liver its essential destination is the right auricle of the heart and thence to the lungs.

The lungs do not function in the foetus, as oxygen is supplied to the foetus through the placenta, and the blood requirements of the foetal lungs are accordingly small. Blood which reaches the right auricle is therefore largely directed from right to left auricle by way of the foramen ovale, an orifice situated in the inter-auricular wall. A certain amount of blood, mostly draining from the head, does pass from the right auricle to the right ventricle and into the pulmonary artery, but a large portion of this blood passes from the pulmonary artery into the ductus arteriosus, a connecting vessel to the posterior aorta, and consequently does not reach the lungs. The blood supply to the foetal lungs, then, is the minimum amount necessary for the growth of these organs.

Blood which supplies the foetal structures through the aorta and its branches is eventually collected by two umbilical arteries which arise from the two iliac arteries in the pelvic cavity. These pass back to the umbilicus and thence to the placenta, where the blood receives fresh oxygen and nutriment. After birth the umbilical arteries retract and, like the umbilical vein, ductus venosus and ductus arteriosus, become cord-like and cease to function, while the foramen ovale becomes occluded. Though the elastic umbilical arteries retract within the abdomen of the calf immediately after birth, the umbilical vein remains open for a day or so. This is filled with liquid blood and forms an ideal avenue for infection, and it is by this channel that the causal organisms of navel ill in calves gain entry to the body.

Though the placenta acts as an excellent filter, normally preventing the passage of bacteria into the umbilical veins and thence into the body of the foetus, certain foreign invaders do, at times, enter the umbilical vein from the placenta. It will be obvious that where bacteria or parasites gain entry to this vein the place where these organisms are most likely to be arrested is the foetal liver.

THE UMBILICAL CORD. In the cow this cord from membranes to umbilicus is 9 to 18 inches long, the foetal calf being born free of its membranes. In both cow and ewe the umbilical cord is embraced in a jelly-like tissue which contains the following vessels: two umbilical

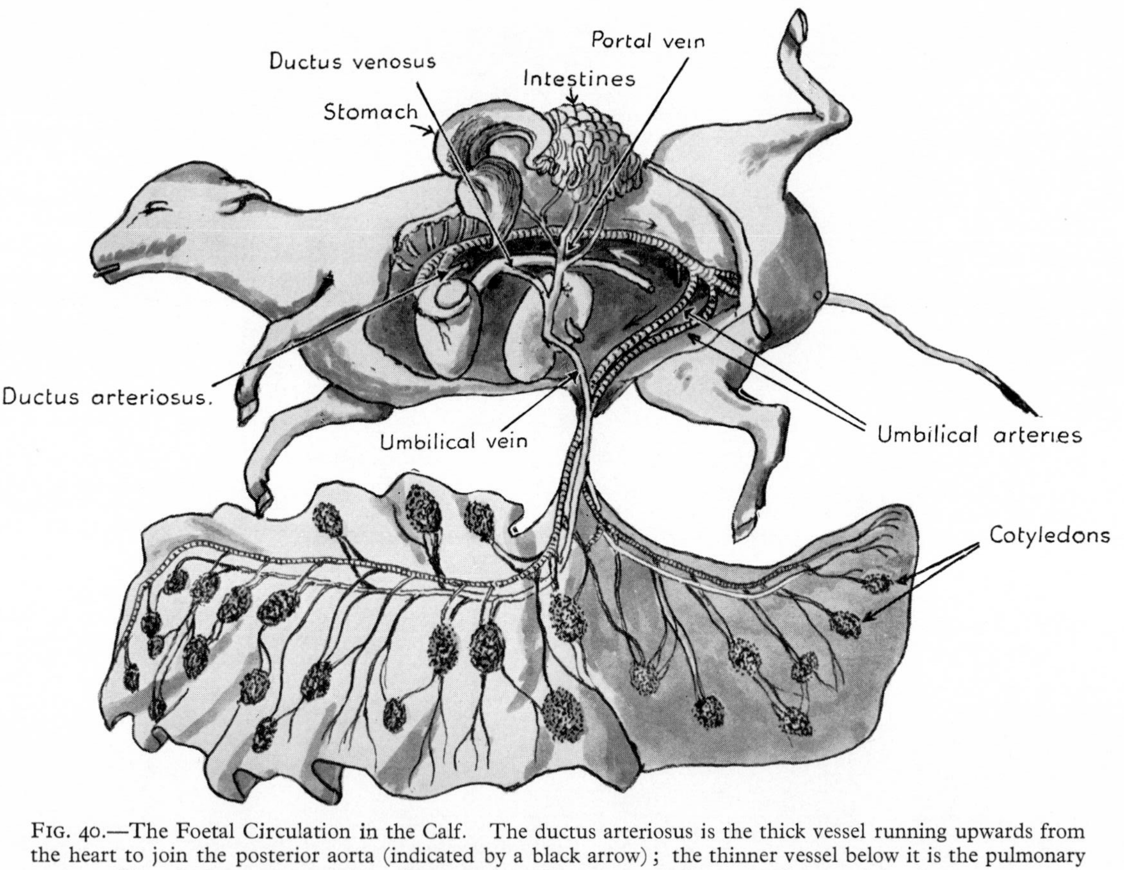

FIG. 40.—The Foetal Circulation in the Calf. The ductus arteriosus is the thick vessel running upwards from the heart to join the posterior aorta (indicated by a black arrow); the thinner vessel below it is the pulmonary artery. The ductus venosus is the thin vessel running upwards from the liver to join the posterior vena cava (white arrow).

veins, two umbilical arteries and the urachus, the latter being the tube which drains the foetal bladder.

The Blood

Blood obtained from the food animals at slaughter contains 77 to 82 per cent. of water and 18 to 23 per cent. of solids, of which nine-tenths are protein in nature. It therefore forms an article of food, an essential preliminary process being the whipping or defibrinating of it to prevent clotting. Defibrination should be carried out with a sterile metal fork, while if any suppurative lesion, however slight, or other gross lesion of infection be found the blood should be discarded for food purposes. Further, the blood of animals slaughtered by the Jewish method is contaminated by stomach contents and should be rejected. There is much to be said for the use of anticoagulants such as sodium citrate or sodium phosphate to prevent coagulation of blood intended to be used for human consumption. In Holland the addition of such substances is permissible but not in a proportion in excess of 1 per cent., i.e. 1 lb. to 10 gallons of blood.

FIG. 41.—Mechanical blood defibrination. This apparatus is water-jacketed to cool the blood and defibrination is carried out by the central rotating agitator arms.

USES

The fibrin removed when blood is defibrinated is digestible and nutritious but has never been in demand in Britain as an article of diet, though in Continental countries it forms an ingredient of blood sausage. In Russia blood bread bakeries were instituted some years ago, the product consisting of seven parts of rye flour and three parts of defibrinated ox blood, while defibrinated blood is also used in America and Germany as a constituent of blood sausage or blood paste, and in Britain as the main ingredient of black puddings. Blood which has been defibrinated is composed of nine-tenths haemoglobin and one-tenth globulin, but as haemoglobin is converted in the stomach into indigestible haematin, food products of which the main constituent is defibrinated blood have comparatively little nutritive value.

Black Puddings. Ox blood is preferred for the manufacture of these as it is said to be the thickest, though sheep and pig blood is also used, and a common formula is 18 gallons of defibrinated blood, 14 lb. of flour, 20 lb. of boiled barley, and cubes of pork fat. The casings used are ox runners or middles, the mixture being poured in with a funnel and the casings tied with string every 9 inches. These are then cooked for half an hour at 190° F., an extra 15 minutes being required for old blood. The temperature of the water must be kept below boiling point, as otherwise the casings will burst, and a black pudding is sufficiently cooked when no blood emerges after insertion of a skewer. Washing soda is frequently added to the water before cooking, as by this the brown colour of the cooked product is turned to a more attractive black colour. The casings may be finally rubbed with olive oil to produce a sheen.

Edible blood plasma, collected hygienically from animals which are certified on post-mortem examination to be free from disease, can be used as a human food. During collection an anticoagulant is added, the corpuscles removed from the liquid by centrifuging, and the plasma is then dried by a process similar to the spray method for the manufacture of dried milk. The dried powder is used, though not in Britain, in bakeries as a substitute for white of egg, one pound of dried plasma being equal to the whites of 500 eggs. It can also be used as a binder for sausage, but in Germany its use is not permitted for edible purposes, though it is exported for this purpose to other countries.

5. THE EXCRETORY SYSTEM

The Kidneys

Ox. These are reddish-brown in colour and composed of 15 to 25 lobes which are fused at their deeper portions; each of these lobes terminates in a blunt process or papilla, visible when the kidney is split. When the rumen is empty the left kidney lies to the left of the vertebral column, but as the rumen becomes filled it propels the kidney towards the right side of the body, and injury due to pressure on the kidney tissue is thus prevented. This orientation of the left kidney is rendered possible by its loose attachment in the lumbar region and, by virtue of this attachment, the butcher terms the left side of beef the "open" side. The left kidney, by reason of its movability, is roughly three-sided and of a somewhat twisted appearance, but the right kidney has a more regular, elliptical outline. The weight of each kidney is 10 to 12 oz.

Sheep and Goat. The kidneys are dark brown in colour, bean-shaped and unlobulated, and possess a single renal papilla. As in the ox, the left kidney of the sheep and goat is freely movable. The weight of each kidney is 2 to 3 oz.

Pig. The kidneys are smooth and bean-shaped, reddish-brown in colour, but thinner and flatter than in the other food animals; ten to twelve renal papillae are present internally. The weight of each kidney is 3 to 6 oz. In the pig the bladder is large with a long neck and the ureters enter the bladder posteriorly in the region of its neck. This predisposes the animal to hydronephrosis, for when the bladder is filled it hangs down into the abdominal cavity, the long neck presses against the pubis, thus closing the ureter openings and interfering with urination.

Horse. The right kidney is triangular or heart shaped, the left is bean shaped and longer than broad. The weight of each kidney is 1½ lb.

USES

The kidneys of all the food animals are sold fresh.

6. THE REPRODUCTIVE SYSTEM

The Uterus

Cow. This consists of a small body, less than 1 inch in length, and two cornua or horns about 15 inches long. A characteristic of the uterus of the cow and ewe is the presence of cotyledons on the mucous membrane of the body and uterine horns; these are oval prominences about 100 in all, and in the non-gravid bovine uterus are about ½ inch by ¼ inch in size. During pregnancy, and as the foetus develops, the cotyledons hypertrophy, becoming pitted or sponge-like, and then measure up to 4 or 5 inches in length and 1½ inches in width. Evidence as to whether a slaughtered female animal is a heifer or a cow is sometimes requested and may be established by opening each horn of the uterus and cutting transversely through the wall, including the diameter of a cotyledon (Fig. 43). Generally, in the uterus of a heifer the cotyledons are seen to be surrounded by a shallow moat, (A,A) whereas in the cow this moat usually disappears. The blood vessels in the exposed wall of the uterus in the cow are contorted and bulge from the surface (C,C). In the heifer the blood vessels can be seen clearly but do not bulge and show little contortion. The blood vessels in the cotyledon (B, B) are the most valuable guide; in the heifer they are very fine and straight, whereas in the cow the blood vessels are distinct and contorted and bulge slightly from the cut surface of the cotyledon. This method assumes that the cotyledons enlarge if the animal is in-calf and regress in the non-pregnant uterus, i.e. that the animal must have been at least three and half months or longer in calf.

Ewe. The uterine horns are relatively long, the cotyledons being circular, pigmented and much smaller than in the cow, while in advanced pregnancy the centre of each is cupped or umbilicated.

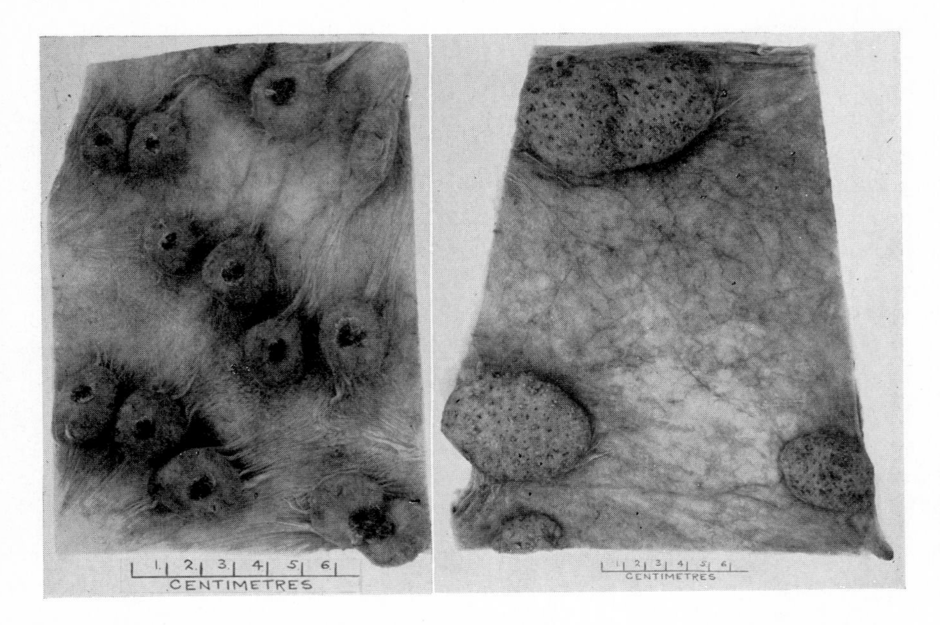

FIG. 42.—Cotyledons on the mucous membrane of the gravid uterus of a ewe (*left*). Cotyledons in the gravid uterus of a cow (*right*).

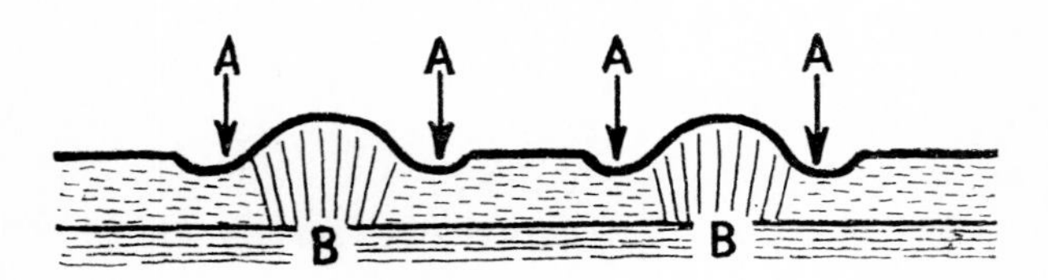

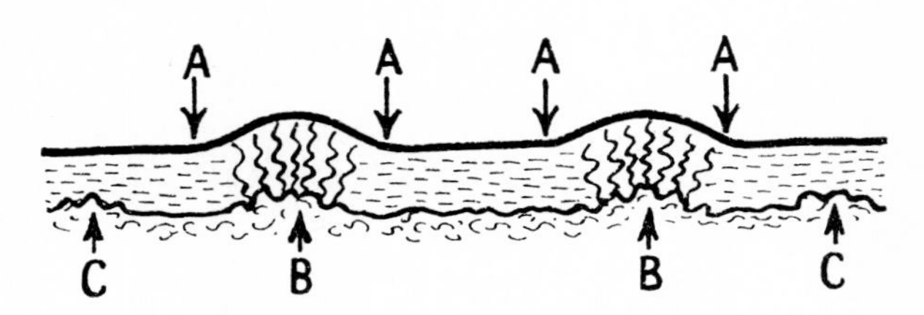

FIG. 43.—Differential features of heifer (above) and cow (below) shown by a transverse section through the uterine wall.

Gilt and Sow. The uterine horns are long and arranged in coils. The mucous membrane possesses no cotyledons but is arranged in numerous thin longitudinal folds. The ovaries are rounded with an irregularly lobulated surface. Differentiation between the sow and gilt carcase may not only be established by the condition of development of the udder and teats but by examination of the uterine arteries. An animal may be judged to be a sow if the udders are enlarged and if examination of the middle uterine arteries, visible in the broad ligaments of the uterine horns, shows the peripheral branches of these arteries to be tortuous. This stretching of the arterial vessels only results during pregnancy, and in the gilt the arterial network is less evident and the vessels are almost straight and not tortuous. Characteristic changes also take place in the walls of the uterine arteries during and after pregnancy, for the elastic fibres in the wall of the artery increase markedly in number and are readily demonstrable on microscopical examination of a suitably stained specimen.

The Udder

Cow. The right and left sides of the udder are separated anatomically by a tendinous septum, and although a strong septum does not exist between the fore and hind quarters of the same side, all four quarters are anatomically distinct, and injection of different coloured fluids into the four teats shows that they each drain separate and distinct areas.

The smooth udder of the heifer, which is composed almost entirely of fat, must be distinguished from the pendulous, fleshy udder of the cow in which glandular tissue predominates and which is grey to yellowish-white in colour.

Ewe. The udder is composed of two halves, each with one small teat. In the goat the udder is similar, but the halves are more pendulous while the teats are more strongly developed and directed forwards.

Sow. The mammary glands are ten to twelve in number, and arranged in two parallel rows ; each gland possesses a flat triangular teat and the glandular substance appears whitish-red on section.

USES

The udder of both cow and ewe is boiled and used for food.

Estimation of Age of the Bovine Foetus

By the end of the first month of pregnancy the foetus is about $\frac{2}{5}$ inch long. At the end of the second month the foetus is 2 to $2\frac{1}{2}$ inches long and digits and depressions for mouth and nose appear.

After 3 months the foetus is $5\frac{3}{5}$ inches long, stomach divisions are present and hoofs and horns appear.

In the fourth month there is little change except growth, but towards the end of the fifth month hair appears and the testes descend into the scrotum. At the end of 5 months the foetus is 12 inches long.

During the next 3 months the foetus attains a length of 24 inches, and by the end of the eighth month the eyes are open, the limbs covered with hair, and the hoofs hardened. At the end of the 9th month the foetus is full size, about 3 feet long and 80 lb. in weight, this being an average weight for a new-born calf, though variations occur according to the breeds; the Friesian cow may produce a calf which weighs up to 100 lb. at birth.

7. THE LYMPHATIC SYSTEM

Lymph is the medium by which oxygen and nutritive matter are transferred from the blood to the body tissues, and the medium by which waste products from these tissues are removed. Although the blood capillaries approximate to the individual cells of which the body is composed, actual contact with these cells is through the lymph. The presence of lymph around the tissue cells is maintained by a slow exudation of this fluid through the capillary walls and into the surrounding tissue; this fluid is similar to the plasma of the blood but is thinner, more watery, and poorer in protein as this latter substance cannot pass readily through the capillary walls. As the exudation of lymph from the capillaries is continuous, it is obvious that there must be a channel by which lymph is reabsorbed into the system.

After lymph has fulfilled its function of feeding the tissue cells it is forced by the animal's muscular movements into fine-walled vessels, the lymph vessels. These are similar to veins, but possess thinner walls and are provided with more numerous valves; when distended with lymph they have a characteristic beaded appearance. Practically all lymph vessels discharge their contents into lymph nodes and, with rare exceptions, all of the lymph throughout the system passes through at least one lymph node before it returns into the blood circulatory system. In every case the direction of flow of lymph in an organ is from the centre of the organ towards its surface.

Lymphatic vessels conveying lymph to a lymph node are known as afferent lymphatics, and the area drained by the particular lymph node is known as its drainage area. An appreciation of the drainage areas of lymph nodes is of particular value in the judgment of septic infections and of the tuberculous carcase.

After passing through one or more lymph nodes, and thereby ridding itself of some impurities, lymph is conveyed by efferent lymphatics to discharge eventually into larger lymph collecting vessels, the direction of the lymph flow in every case being towards the heart. The largest of these lymph collecting vessels is the thoracic duct, which commences as a thin-walled dilatation about $\frac{3}{4}$ inch in width and known as the receptaculum chyli. This dilatation is situated in the abdomen, lying above the aorta at the level of the last dorsal vertebra, and receives lymph from the lumbar and intestinal trunks ; it is the main receptacle for lymph from the posterior part of the body. The thoracic duct is about $\frac{1}{4}$ inch in width, passes forwards through the diaphragm, traverses the thorax, and opens into the anterior vena cava or other great vessel in the anterior thorax. Lymph from the anterior part of the body is carried towards the heart by two tracheal lymph ducts, which commence at the lateral retropharyngeal lymph nodes, pass down the neck on each side of the trachea and oesophagus, each duct discharging into the jugular vein of its own side.

The response of a lymph node to an irritant is normally rapid, with enlargement and congestion of its substance and possibly a breaking down of its tissue ; thus the size, colour and consistency of lymph nodes form a valuable guide in the estimation of disease processes in the animal body.

The size of lymph nodes varies from that of a pin-head up to that of a walnut, though the posterior mediastinal lymph node of the ox may reach a length of 8 inches. Lymph nodes are generally round or oval, and somewhat compressed ; in the ruminant they are of large size and few in number, but in the horse they occur in large numbers and in clusters. The size of lymph nodes is relatively greater in the young growing animal than in the adult.

The colour of lymph nodes shows considerable variation, and may be white, greyish-blue or almost black. The mesenteric lymph nodes of the ox are invariably black in colour, but in the pig the lymph nodes are lobulated and almost white, with the exception of those of the head and neck which are reddish in colour.

The consistency of lymph nodes varies in different parts of the body, the nodes of the abdomen being generally softer than those of the thorax. A physiological oedema of the supramammary and iliac lymph nodes will invariably be encountered in the lactating animal.

Lymph Nodes of the Ox

P. Position. D. Drainage area. E. Destination of efferent lymph vessels of node.

Nodes of the Head and Neck

SUBMAXILLARY. P. One on each side, just inside the angle of the jaw and embedded in fat. D. Head, nose and mouth. E. Lateral retropharyngeal nodes.

PAROTID. P. One on each side, on the edge of the masseter muscle and covered by the parotid salivary gland which must be incised to expose it. It is a flat node 3 inches long by 1 inch wide, and should always be examined in old cows. D. Muscles of head, eye and ear, tongue and cranial cavity. E. Lateral retropharyngeal nodes.

RETROPHARYNGEAL. These are divided into two groups (*a*) the INTERNAL RETROPHARYNGEAL nodes, two to four in number and situated between the hyoid bones. D. Pharynx, tongue and larynx. E. Lateral retropharyngeal nodes. (*b*) The LATERAL RETROPHARYNGEAL nodes (Fig. 76) situated beneath each wing of the atlas and therefore usually located at the neck end of the dressed carcase. D. Tongue, and receive efferents from submaxillary, parotid and internal retropharyngeal nodes. E. Tracheal lymph duct.

MIDDLE CERVICAL. P. Situated in the middle of the neck on each side of the trachea and often absent in cattle. They vary in number from one to seven and also in position and size. D. Lateral retropharyngeal nodes. E. Prepectoral nodes.

Nodes of the Chest and Forequarter

PREPECTORALS. These are known also as the lower cervicals, and may be considered anatomically as a continuation of the upper and middle cervical chain. The middle cervical group may, in fact, extend to the upper group, or may reach back almost to the prepectorals.

P. The prepectorals are two to four in number on each side, and are embedded in fat along the anterior border of the first rib. The main node of this group is superficially situated about the middle of the first rib and just anterior to it; haemo-lymph nodes are usually present in the fat around this group. The second node of this group is on the same level and just anterior to the main node, but is deep-seated and is exposed by making an incision 4 inches long and 2 inches deep through the triangular-shaped scalenus muscle. D. Efferents from upper and middle cervical nodes, together with efferents from the prescapular; thus all lymph from the head and neck passes through the prepectoral lymph nodes. E. Thoracic duct.

COSTO-CERVICAL. P. This may be found on the inner side or just anterior to the first rib and close to its junction with the first dorsal vertebra. It lies adjacent to the oesophagus and trachea and is frequently removed with these in the dressing of the carcase, being then found anterior to the heart and lungs. D. Neck, shoulder, parietal pleura and first few intercostal nodes. E. Thoracic duct.

PRESCAPULAR. P. This node is elongated, commonly 3 to 4 inches long and 1 inch or more in width. It lies about 4 inches in front of the point of the shoulder and a deep incision 6 inches long and 2 inches deep must be made to expose it. The node is embedded in fat and its exposure is greatly facilitated if the carcase is examined before the onset of rigor mortis. D. Head, neck, shoulder and forelimb. E. Thoracic duct.

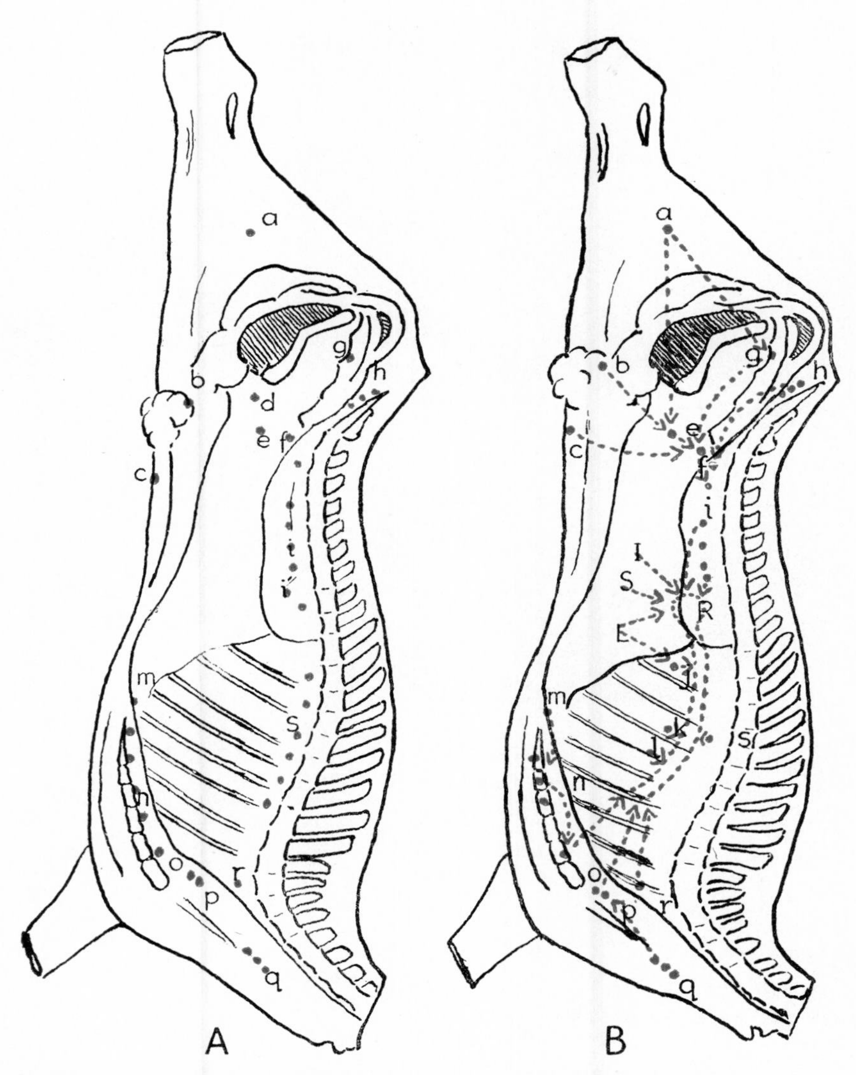

FIG. 44.—(A) Carcase of bullock showing position of lymph nodes: (*a*) popliteal; (*b*) superficial inguinal; (*c*) precrural; (*d*) deep inguinal; (*e*) external iliac; (*f*) internal iliac; (*g*) ischiatic; (*h*) sacral; (*i*) lumbar; (*i''*) renal; (*m*) xyphoid; (*n*) suprasternal; (*o*) presternal; (*p*) prepectoral; (*q*) middle cervical; (*r*) costo-cervical; (*s*) intercostal.

(B) Direction of the lymph flow. (I) lymph from intestine; (S) lymph from stomach; (L) lymph from liver; (R) receptaculum chyli; (*j*) lymph from posterior mediastinal lymph node discharging into thoracic duct; (*k*) lymph from bronchial lymph nodes; (*l*) lymph from anterior mediastinal lymph nodes.

The importance of the prescapular lymph node in relation to bovine tuberculosis lies in the fact that not only does it drain the head, neck, shoulder and forelimb, but also muscle and bone. When lesions of tuberculosis, therefore, are found in the prescapular node without lesions being

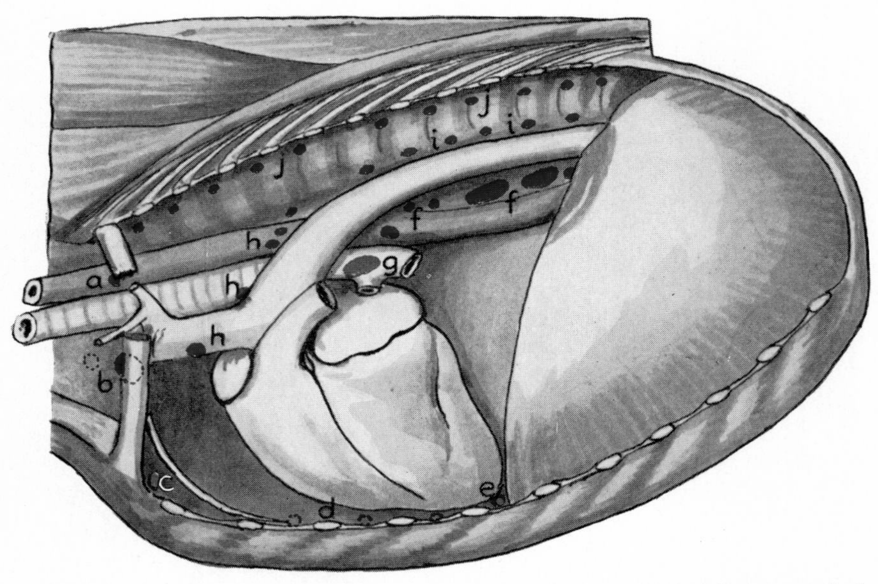

FIG. 45.—Lymph nodes of the bovine thorax viewed from left side: (*a*) costo-cervical; (*b*) prepectoral, lying on inner aspect of first rib. The deep prepectoral lies anterior to the main node, and is indicated by a dotted circle; (*c*) presternal; (*d*) suprasternal, indicated by dotted circles; (*e*) xyphoid; (*f*) posterior mediastinal, lying below the posterior aorta and above the oesophagus, both of which are seen passing through the muscular portion of the diaphragm; (*g*) left bronchial; (*h*) anterior mediastinal; (*i*) subdorsal; (*j*) intercostal.

present in the head or its lymph nodes, it is strongly suggestive that the infection of the node is either the result of local inoculation or of haematogenous dissemination.

INTERCOSTAL. P. Known also as the dorso-costal, these are situated in the intercostal spaces at the junction of the ribs with their vertebrae, and are deep-seated, being covered by the intercostal muscle. Most of these nodes are small, and not all of the spaces may contain nodes. D. Muscles of dorsal region, intercostal muscles, ribs, and parietal pleura. E. Mediastinal lymph nodes.

SUBDORSAL. P. This superficial group lies in the fat between the aorta and the dorsal vertebrae. The nodes are irregular in arrangement, varying in length from ½ to 1 inch, and are frequently removed with the lungs in the dressing of the carcase; they may then be found by incising the upper surface of the mediastinal fat between the lungs. The style of dressing of the carcase, however, has a bearing on whether these lymph nodes will remain on the carcase, for in some areas the thoracic portion of the posterior aorta is left attached, and the subdorsal lymph nodes, which run down each side of the vessel wall, will then be found on the carcase. The more posterior nodes of the group, no matter how the carcase is dressed, usually remain on the forequarter, and can be found by incising the fat below the dorsal vertebrae just anterior to the diaphragm. D. The same structures as the intercostals, and also the mediastinum, pericardium, diaphragm and efferents from the intercostal lymph nodes. E. Thoracic duct.

SUPRASTERNAL. P. Known also as the sternocostals, these nodes lie between the costal cartilages and are covered by muscle. They may be exposed by an incision 3 inches from, and parallel to the cut surface of the sternum, and are found at the junction of the internal thoracic vein with a line continuing the posterior border of each rib. The node in the fourth intercostal space is large and readily exposed but nodes are not present in every intercostal space. The largest of this group, known as the PRESTERNAL or anterior sternal node, is superficially placed and embedded in fat on the first segment of the sternum. D. Diaphragm, abdominal muscles, intercostal muscles, parietal and visceral pleura and peritoneum. E. Thoracic duct and prepectoral nodes.

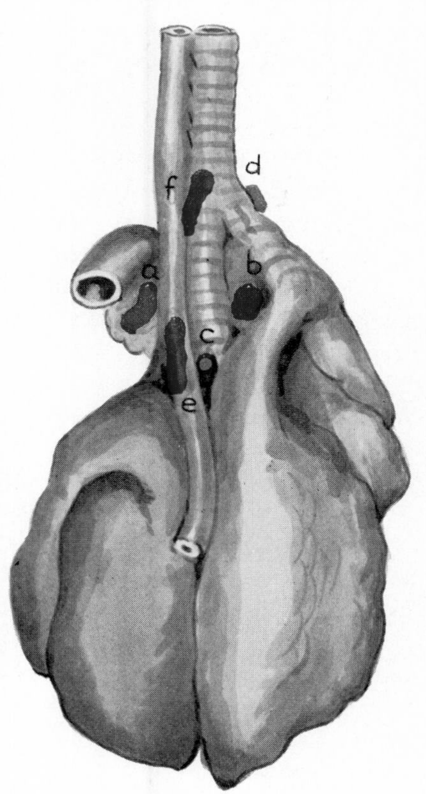

FIG. 46.—Lymph nodes of the bovine lungs: (*a*) left bronchial, partly covered by the aorta; (*b*) right bronchial; (*c*) middle bronchial; (*d*) apical; (*e*) posterior mediastinal; (*f*) anterior mediastinal, related inferiorly to the oesophagus and trachea. (After Baum.)

BRONCHIAL. P. There are two main bronchial nodes, the right and left, together with two smaller nodes. The left bronchial is $1\frac{1}{2}$ inches by 1 inch in size, often irregular in shape, and found close to the left bronchus, being embedded deeply in fat and partly covered by the aorta. The right bronchial is related to the right bronchus, is usually smaller than the left and partly hidden by the right lung; it is absent in 25 per cent. of cases, while in some cases two nodes may be found here. The middle bronchial node is situated in the middle line above the bifurcation of the trachea, but is absent in 50 per cent. of cases; a further node, the APICAL, is placed on the accessory bronchus where it enters the apical lobe of the right lung. D. Lungs. E. The left bronchial node discharges into the thoracic duct, the right bronchial node into the posterior mediastinal node or thoracic duct, the middle bronchial and apical into the anterior mediastinal nodes. When the right bronchial node is absent the lymphatics of the diaphragmatic lobe of the right lung discharge into the posterior mediastinal and left bronchial node.

A node known as the INSPECTOR'S NODE is present in 75 per cent. of cases and is situated at the junction of the two cardiac lobes of the right lung.

ANTERIOR MEDIASTINAL. P. These are numerous, lying in the mediastinal space anterior to the heart, and are related anatomically to the oesophagus, trachea and anterior aorta. D. Heart, pericardium, mediastinum and thoracic wall, and receive efferents from apical and middle bronchial lymph nodes. E. Thoracic duct.

POSTERIOR MEDIASTINAL. These nodes are eight to twelve in number and situated in the fat along the dorsal wall of the oesophagus. The largest and most posterior of these nodes lies posterior to the heart, being up to 8 inches in length and extending almost to the diaphragm; in some cases this large node is replaced by two smaller ones. D. Lungs, diaphragm, and, *via* the diaphragm, the peritoneum, surface of the liver and spleen. They receive efferents from the right bronchial node. E. Thoracic duct.

AXILLARY. P. Known also as the brachial, this node is about 1 inch in length, is covered by the scapula, and is situated in the muscle external to and about midway along the second rib. D. Muscles of shoulder and forelimb. E. Prepectoral node.

XYPHOID (Ventral Mediastinal). P. Found in the loose fat at the junction of the sternum and diaphragm at the level of the sixth rib, and related anatomically to the apex of the heart. This node is absent in 50 per cent. of cases. D. Pleura, diaphragm and ribs. E. Suprasternal lymph nodes.

Nodes of the Abdomen and Hindquarter

The position of these nodes is described as if the hindquarter were suspended by the hock in the normal manner.

LUMBAR. P. These are situated in the fat covering the lumbar muscles and are related anatomically to the aorta and posterior vena cava. Some of these nodes are superficial, others being embedded in the loin suet, and haemo-lymph nodes are common in this region. D. Lumbar region and peritoneum. They receive efferent vessels from the external and internal iliacs, sacral and popliteal nodes. E. Receptaculum chyli.

PORTAL. P. Known also as the hepatic, these form a group around the portal vein, hepatic artery and bile duct, and are covered by the pancreas. Another group, which includes the lymph node draining the pancreas, lies between the edge of the pancreas and the caudate lobe of the liver. The portal nodes vary from ten to fifteen in number. D. Liver, pancreas and duodenum. E. Receptaculum chyli.

RENAL. P. This node belongs in reality to the lumbar group, and is found in the suet at the entrance to the kidney. In this position a split blood vessel is found and the node can be exposed by making an incision lengthwise through this vessel and continuing the incision 1 inch deep into the lumbar suet. D. Kidneys and adrenal body. E. Receptaculum chyli. The renal lymph nodes vary in size and number.

MESENTERIC. P. These comprise a large number of elongated nodes which lie between the peritoneal folds of the mesentery and receive lymph from the intestines. These nodes may be divided into a small duodenal group which drains the duodenum, the efferent lymphatics passing to the portal nodes of the liver, and a jejuno-ileal group ranging in number from 10 to 50, and $\frac{1}{4}$ inch to 4 feet in length. The long nodes form the main chain parallel to and some 2 inches from the intestine, while the small nodes are scattered throughout the mesentery between the small intestines and the colon. D. The small intestine (jejunum and ileum). E. Receptaculum chyli.

SPLENIC. Splenic lymph nodes are absent in the ox, and lymph drained from the spleen passes to the gastric chain of lymph nodes.

GASTRIC. P. These are numerous and difficult to group satisfactorily; a number form a chain along the right and left longitudinal grooves of the rumen (Fig. 97). D. Walls of stomach and spleen. E. Receptaculum chyli. The gastric group are rarely incised in meat inspection.

ILIACS. These are situated near the terminal branches of the aorta and are embedded in fat.

INTERNAL ILIAC. P. This may be exposed by an incision level with the junction of the sacrum and last lumbar vertebra. Several nodes are present, lying some 7 inches from the vertebrae and $\frac{1}{2}$ to 2 inches in length. D. This node drains muscle and pelvic viscera, including muscles of the sublumbar region, pelvis and thigh, the femur, tibia, patella, tarsus and metatarsus, the male and female genital organs and kidneys. It receives efferent vessels from the external iliac, precrural, ischiatic and superficial inguinal nodes. E. Lumbar lymph nodes and receptaculum chyli.

External Iliac. P. A single or double node ½ to 1 inch in length and situated laterally to the internal iliac. It lies beneath the external angle of the ilium at the bifurcation of the circumflex iliac artery, but is sometimes absent on one or both sides. D. Abdominal muscles, sublumbar area, posterior part of the peritoneum, and some efferents from the popliteal node. E. Internal iliac and lumbar lymph nodes.

Superficial Inguinal (Male). P. These lie in the mass of fat about the neck of the scrotum and behind the spermatic cord. D. External genitals and adjoining skin area. E. Deep inguinal when present, or, failing this, the internal iliac.

Supramammary (Female). P. These lie above and behind the udder ; there are usually two present on each side, one large and one small, the larger pair, about 3 inches in size, approximating to each other, the smaller pair being found above or in front of the larger pair and ¼ to ½ inch in size. In the heifer these nodes may be found on a straight line level with the cut pubic tubercle, and they therefore appear to be placed in the udder substance rather than in the posterior position which they occupy in the cow. D. Udder and external genitals. E. Deep inguinal when present, or internal iliac.

Deep Inguinal. P. In the inguinal canal and frequently absent; when absent the internal iliac functions in its place. D. Hind limb and abdominal wall. E. Internal iliac. According to some authors the deep inguinals are part of the external iliacs.

Ischiatic. P. This lies on the outer aspect of the sacro-sciatic ligament, and is exposed by a deep incision on a vertical line midway between the posterior part of the ischium and the sacrum. D. Posterior pelvic organs and also receives efferents from popliteal node. E. Internal iliac.

Sacral. P. These are not constantly present and are unimportant.

Precrural. P. This node is known also as the prefemoral and is embedded in fat ; it may be exposed by an incision at the edge of the tensor fascia lata, the incision being made about 7 inches down from the apex of this muscle. D. Skin, prepuce and superficial muscles. E. Internal iliac nodes.

Popliteal. P. This is deeply seated in the round of beef and is exposed by a deep incision along the superficial seam or division which connects the ischium and os calcis, the node lying midway between these and 6 inches deep. D. Lower part of leg and foot. E. Lumbar and iliac nodes and also ischiatic node.

The Location of the Carcase Lymph Nodes of the Ox in relation to butchers' joints

The method of the cutting up of carcases into convenient marketable joints differs considerably in various countries and, indeed, in different areas of the same country. This difference is largely dictated by the greater or lesser demands for certain joints and this, in turn, is controlled by custom and the economic status of the purchasers.

The recognition of the carcase joints is of importance, as on it depends the ability of the inspector to expose the lymph nodes associated with them. This is of particular value where a carcase, suspected to be diseased, has been jointed and is deposited or exposed for sale on a butcher's premises; in such cases examination of the deep-seated carcase lymph nodes is likely to form a valuable guide as to the presence of tuberculosis.

The following table outlines the butcher's joints and alternative terms, together with the carcase bones and lymph nodes associated with them:

(1) HEAD. Contains the submaxillary, parotid and retropharyngeal lymph nodes.

(2) CLOD (Neck). Contains the cervical vertebrae and the middle cervical group of lymph nodes.

(3) STICKING (Sloat). Contains the prescapular node.

(4) BACK RIBS (Thick Chine). Contains the first five dorsal vertebrae, upper part of the first five ribs and the scapula, together with the costo-cervical and intercostal lymph nodes.

(5) FORE RIBS (Thin Chine). Contains the sixth to ninth dorsal vertebrae with corresponding ribs, and intercostal lymph nodes.

(6) TOP RIB (Thick Rib). Contains part of the first five ribs with the prepectoral and axillary lymph nodes. The main prepectoral node, however, is likely to be removed by the butcher in the trimming of this joint.

(7) FLAT RIBS (Thin Ribs). Contains part of the sixth to ninth ribs.

(8) BRISKET. Contains the greater part of the sternum with its costal cartilages, and the presternal and suprasternal lymph nodes.

(9) PLATE. Contains the posterior portion of sternum and its xyphoid cartilage, the costal cartilages, together with the xyphoid lymph node.

(10) SIRLOIN. Contains the last three or four dorsal vertebrae with their ribs, all five lumbar vertebrae, and the lumbar and renal lymph nodes.

(11) RUMP STEAK (Steak Piece). Contains the sacrum and shaft of the ilium with the deep inguinal, external iliac, internal iliac and sacral lymph nodes. The incision made by the butcher in dividing the sirloin and rump steak may also expose the external iliac lymph node.

(12) RUMP AND SHELL BONE (Izal and Rump). Contains the ischium and pubis and ischiatic lymph node.

(13) ROUND. This joint is divided into an inner topside and an outer silverside. The topside contains the superficial inguinal lymph nodes in the male and the supramammary lymph nodes in the female. The silverside contains the femur and popliteal node.

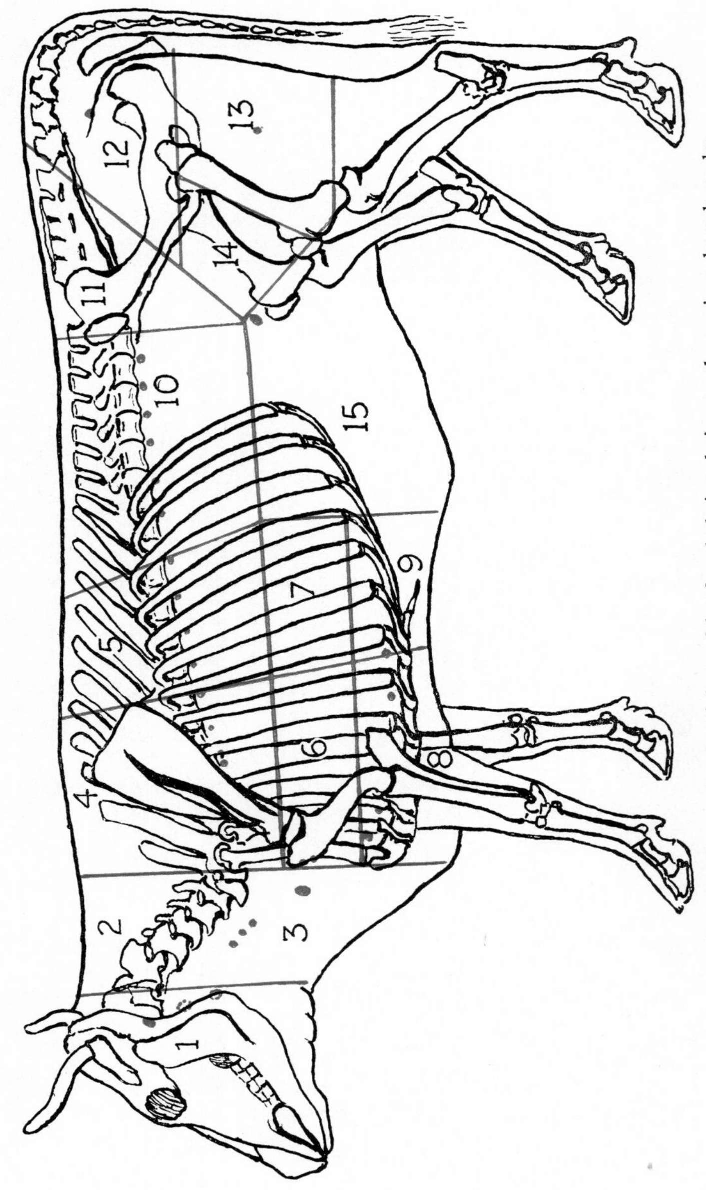

FIG. 47.—Carcase of ox, showing joints of beef and their relation to the various lymph nodes. The numbered joints correspond to those described on page 101.

(14) THICK FLANK. Contains the patella and part of the precrural lymph node.

(15) THIN FLANK. Contains portions of the last three or four ribs and part of the precrural lymph node.

Lymph Nodes of the Pig

The nodes of the head and neck are numerous and somewhat difficult to group satisfactorily. They include:

SUBMAXILLARY. These lie anterior to the submaxillary salivary gland near to the angle of the jaw, and are covered by the lower part of the parotid salivary gland. There are commonly two nodes on each side, one large and one small.

ANTERIOR OR UPPER CERVICAL. Known also as the accessory submaxillary, these lie a short distance behind and above the preceding nodes, being separated from them by the submaxillary salivary gland.

PAROTID. There are several nodes on each side which are red in colour, one of the largest being situated just posterior to the masseter muscle of the lower jaw and partly covered by the parotid salivary gland. One or two nodes may be left on the inner side of the jaw after the head is removed.

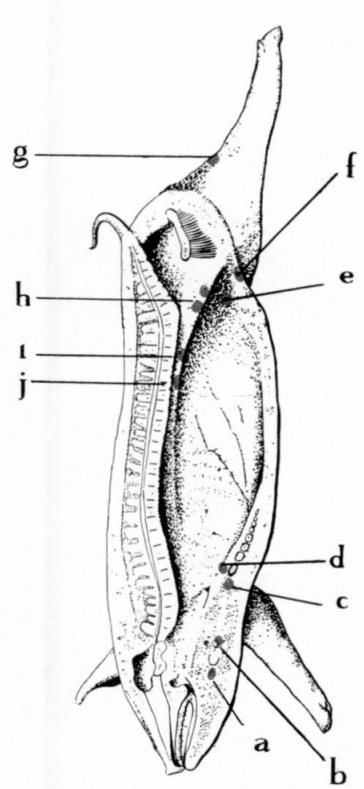

FIG. 48.—Side of pork showing position of lymph nodes. (*a*) submaxillary; (*b*) anterior or upper cervical; (*c*) prepectoral; (*d*) presternal; (*e*) precrural; (*f*) superficial inguinal; (*g*) hock node; (*h*) iliac; (*i*) lumbar; (*j*) renal.

PRESCAPULAR. On account of the short neck of the pig these nodes lie close to the parotid salivary gland, being partly covered by its posterior border. They form an oblique chain which is directed downwards and backwards to the shoulder joint. This chain really includes all the superficial cervical nodes and is best exposed by a long incision, made on the inside of the carcase, from the nape of the neck to the lower border of the neck and just anterior to the shoulder joint. The prescapular lymph nodes in the pig receive lymph from the submaxillary, parotid and upper cervical nodes and thus may become tuberculous as a result of a primary infection of the lymph nodes of the head. Enlargement of the prepectoral node in pigs may occur as a result of arthritic changes in the forelimbs.

Other lymph nodes of the pig which require mention are:

PRECRURAL. In adult pigs this is up to 2 inches in length by 1 inch wide, and is most easily exposed by an incision through the peritoneal aspect of the carcase deep into the fat and 1 inch in front of the stifle joint, the incision being made at right angles to the vertebral column.

POPLITEAL. When present these are superficial, but are absent in 50 per cent of cases. A small subcutaneous node, known as the hock node or Hartenstein's gland, can constantly be found, and is superficially placed on the posterior aspect of the limb about a hand's breadth above the tuber calcis.

GASTRIC. These and the pancreatic nodes are situated on the lesser curvature of the stomach.

BRONCHIAL. In addition to the right and left bronchial, this group includes one on the bifurcation of the trachea and another at the apical bronchus of the right lung. The posterior mediastinal nodes are rudimentary or absent.

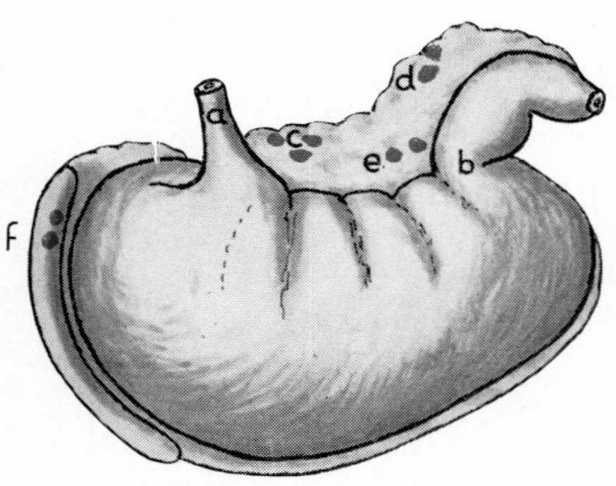

FIG. 49.—Stomach of pig and its related lymph nodes. Three groups of nodes are situated in the fatty tissue connecting the oesophageal opening (*a*) and the pyloric ring (*b*). They comprise the chain of gastric lymph nodes (*c*), the portal lymph nodes, bluish-red in colour (*d*), and in the immediate vicinity of the pyloric ring the pancreatic nodes (*e*). The small splenic nodes (*f*) lie in the gastro-splenic omentum at the upper extremity of the spleen.

PORTAL. Several nodes are present about the portal vein, the largest being about 1 inch long. The portal lymph nodes may be removed during evisceration of the carcase, and can be then found on the mesentery beneath the pancreas or in the fat attached to the lesser curvature of the stomach.

Haemo-Lymph Nodes

These are deep red or almost black in colour, oval in shape and up to a pea in size, but differ from lymph nodes in their anatomical structure and in the absence of afferent and efferent lymphatics. Haemo-lymph nodes are supplied by arteries which break up in the gland substance and discharge their blood into tissue spaces; in this respect these nodes bear a resemblance to the spleen, and may, in fact, be described as accessory spleens. Like the spleen, they contain numerous white blood corpuscles together with red blood corpuscles in various stages of disintegration, this process being responsible for the red coloration of the nodes.

Haemo-lymph nodes are numerous in the ox and sheep but are not found in the horse and pig. In cattle they occur especially along the course of the aorta and in the subcutaneous fat, while in sheep and lambs they are commonest beneath the peritoneum in the sublumbar region, being larger and more numerous in animals suffering from anaemic and cachectic conditions. The red lymph nodes of the head and neck of the pig are frequently mistaken for haemo-lymph nodes.

The Ductless Glands

The recognition and situation of these is of importance as they are used for the preparation of valuable medicinal products, while the thymus is used as an article of food. The ductless glands discharge their secretions direct into the blood stream, the secretions being known as hormones.

Thyroid

In the ox this consists of two lateral lobes lying on either side of the trachea immediately posterior to the larynx. These lobes are flat, dark red in colour, about 3 inches in length, and are connected inferiorly by a narrow isthmus which is band-like and about ½ inch in width. The thyroid gland is about ½ oz. in weight, 1 lb. of raw glands being recovered from about 25 cattle.

In the sheep these are dark red in colour, resembling muscle, and are about 2 inches long and ½ inch in height. Each lateral lobe is long and elliptical and covers the first five rings of the trachea, but the isthmus is indistinct.

In the pig the lobes are large, dark red, about 2 inches long and irregularly triangular in shape; they are situated some little distance from the larynx and are connected with each other inferiorly. The dark red colour of the thyroid gland is due to its rich blood supply.

Action. The active principle of the thyroid gland is thyroxine, which has the effect of accelerating most of the body activities. In the young animal thyroid secretion stimulates growth, whereas deficiency retards development and, in children, leads to cretinism.

Over-activity produces exophthalmic goitre in humans, while atrophy of the gland in later life produces a condition known as myxodema, characterized by a general physical and mental degeneration. Thyroid extract is used in human medicine in the treatment of obesity.

Parathyroids

The position of the parathyroids relative to the thyroid glands is subject to variation but they may sometimes be found near the posterior extremity or on the deep surface of the lateral lobes of the thyroids and are little larger than a grain of wheat. Their small size and similar colour to the thyroid makes them difficult to identify. They control the calcium and phosphate content of the blood, and have a steadying effect on muscles and nerves.

Thymus

This gland, which is pinkish-white in colour, is distinctly lobulated and constitutes the true sweetbread. It consists of two portions, a thoracic portion, or " heart bread ", which is rich in fat and roughly the shape of the palm of the hand ; this portion lies in the thoracic cavity and extends back as far as the third rib where it is in contact with the base of the heart. The second portion, or " neck bread ", is poor in fat, and consists of two lobes joined at their base and extending up the neck on either side of the trachea ; these lobes diverge and diminish in size as they pass up the neck and reach almost to the thyroid gland.

In the calf the thymus is at its greatest development at 5 to 6 weeks, and then weighs 1 lb. to 1½ lb., but gradual atrophy then takes place, and by the onset of sexual maturity little of the cervical portion remains. It is very small in 3-year-old cattle, but a vestige of the thoracic portion may be seen in cows even after 8 or 9 years. In the pig the thymus is large, greyish-yellow in colour, and reaches to the throat.

Action. The thymus, which is richly vascular, hastens the onset of sexual maturity, reproductive development being delayed if the gland is removed from the young animal. It is also concerned with the production of lymph cells and undergoes progressive atrophy with age.

Adrenal Bodies

In the ox these are related to the two kidneys, and lie anterior to them. The left adrenal body is in contact with the dorsal sac of the rumen, though it does not rotate in company with the left kidney when the rumen is distended. After dressing of the carcase, portions of the right adrenal body may sometimes be found attached to the posterior aspect of the liver, or sometimes to the central muscular portion of the diaphragm.

In the sheep both the adrenals are bean-shaped, but the left is not in contact with its kidney. In the pig the adrenals are long and narrow, each lying on the inner aspect of the kidney.

Action. The adrenals are reddish-brown in colour, and section of them reveals a well-marked cortex and medulla. The active principle produced by the medulla is adrenalin, which exerts profound physiological effects on almost every system in the body, an important one being the acceleration of the conversion of glycogen to lactic acid in muscle. Untoward factors such as excitement, stress or pain, by increasing the secretion of adrenalin, lead to depletion of the glycogen stored in the muscular tissues. Cortisone is a hormone derived from the cortical portion of the adrenal body and is used in the treatment of certain systemic diseases and allergic conditions.

Pituitary Gland

This is situated on the lower aspect of the cerebrum, being connected to it by a short stalk, and rests in a pit of bone formed by the base of the skull. It produces a number of hormones influencing growth of bone, stimulation of the mammary gland, ovary and testicle, and also stimulation of the muscular wall of the uterus; in this way it hastens parturition, and pituitary extract is therefore a glandular product which is of value to the veterinary practitioner.

Testicles

In the bull these have an elongated oval outline, each being about 5 inches in length and 10 to 12 oz. in weight. The epididymis is narrow, but is closely attached to the testicle along its posterior border. In the sheep the testicles are large, pear-shaped, and more rounded than in the ox, being 4 inches long and 9 to 10 oz. in weight. In the boar the testicles are very large and irregularly elliptical, while the epididymis is well developed and forms a blunt conical projection at both ends of the testicle.

Action. The testicles are responsible for development of male secondary sexual characters, and if removed early in life these characters fail to appear.

Ovaries

Action. The ovarian hormones are responsible for the development of female secondary sexual characters. They also control cyclical changes in the reproductive system which ensures development of breeding seasons when weather conditions, temperature, food, etc., are suitable for reproduction.

Though valuable pharmaceutical products are prepared from the ductless glands, it is only when there is a very large weekly kill that their collection becomes an economic proposition. It takes 180 cattle, for example, to produce enough pituitary glands to make 1 lb. of the green product and this is further concentrated to one-fifth of its original volume, so that 900 cattle are required to make 1 lb. of dry pituitary extract and the cost of such a process is necessarily high.

The following table shows the number of animals required to produce a given quantity of glandular product:

	No. per lb. fresh	*No. per lb. finished product*
Pituitary (entire gland)	180	900
Pituitary (posterior lobe)	2,000	12,000
Ovary (cow)	80	480
Ovary (pig)	144	864
Ovary (sheep)	600	3,600
Parathyroid	450	4,500
Suprarenal (cattle)	40	25,200

Successful utilization of glands entails careful handling from the moment the animal is killed. The glands should be removed immediately, freed from surrounding fat or tissue, and either frozen to a temperature of 14° F. or placed in acetone according to the variety of gland. In the case of the pancreas care must be taken to leave the gland whole and not to remove adjoining portions of the duodenum whereby trypsin might be liberated and the insulin destroyed.

8. THE MUSCULAR SYSTEM

This comprises voluntary or striped muscle which, together with fat and connective tissue, forms flesh or butcher meat.

Butcher meat is a valuable part of the human diet because: (*a*) it is the most concentrated and easily assimilable of nitrogenous foods, and is a good source of first class protein, i.e. it contains those amino-acids which are essential for human life; (*b*) it is stimulating to metabolism due to its high protein content, i.e. it assists the body in the production of heat and energy; (*c*) it is satisfying, for the presence of fat in the diet delays emptying of the stomach. Meat contains fat, and therefore remains in the stomach for some hours and allays hunger; (*d*) after suitable treatment, which includes the processes of ripening and of cooking, meat acquires a palatable flavour, acts as a stimulant to gastric secretion and is readily digested.

A vegetable diet, compared with a meat diet, is usually incomplete in essential amino-acids; the vegetable proteins are less easily digested and remain in the stomach for a shorter period than meat protein, with the result that a feeling of hunger recurs more rapidly.

The Chemical Composition of Muscle

Generally speaking, muscle contains 72 to 80 per cent. of water and 20 to 28 per cent. of solids, though the flesh of fat bulls, bullocks and heifers may contain only 48 per cent. of water and the flesh of fat pigs as little as 43 per cent. The meat from young animals contains more water than that from older animals, but the weight of lean muscular tissue, as distinct from fat, in beef animals is always approximately one-third of the animal's live-weight, whether the animals are fat or lean. Protein is the most important muscle constituent and consists of myosinogen and albumen, while there are also present in meat small amounts of glycogen and inorganic salts, together with extractives which are nitrogenous substances extracted from the meat by water.

Glycogen, for which the liver and muscle are the main storehouses in the animal body, is present in small but varying amounts in animal muscle, being particularly abundant in horse meat and in foetal flesh. It plays an important part in the production of rigor mortis after slaughter or death. The glycogen content in muscle diminishes to a trace within a few days.

The inorganic salts of meat are those of potassium and sodium, chiefly the chlorides and phosphates, and amount to 1 to 1·5 per cent. The largest quantity of potassium salts is found in fowl flesh (4·65 per cent.), while pig flesh is poor in potassium salts but rich in sodium.

Though the main sources of nitrogen in muscle are the proteins myosinogen and albumen, certain other nitrogenous substances, being water soluble, can be extracted from meat by water. These are known as extractives and are the substances which lend to meats, including game, their characteristic flavour. The extractives include creatine, phosphocreatine, carnosine and inosinic acid and are present in greater amounts in the flesh of full-grown animals than in young immature animals, being particularly abundant in the muscles which are much exercised and less tender. The flesh of animals which are properly rested prior to slaughter yields more extractives than that of unrested animals, has a better flavour and readily releases its flavour on cooking. These extractives are the principal constituents of the commercial extracts of beef and are obtained by concentrating waters in which beef muscle and offal parts have been soaked and cooked, or by concentrating the liquor in which beef has been cooked prior to canning; it requires about 30 lb. of lean meat to yield 1 lb. of extract. The food value of extractives is small, but as they stimulate the flow of gastric juice and aid in the digestion of the protein and carbohydrate of vegetable foods they play an important, though indirect, part in nutrition.

The only vitamins present in appreciable amounts in flesh are those of the B group, although the liver is a storehouse for A, B, D, and even a little C. Vitamin A is present in small amounts in beef, though not in mutton or pork, but is present in large amounts in the liver. The vitamin B complex is composed of several substances, some being unstable to heat and all being dissolved by water; butcher meat is a useful source of vitamin B. Vitamin C is present in small amounts in muscle, this being proved by the fact that the exclusive meat diet of the Eskimos is sufficient to prevent attacks of scurvy, an affection associated with an insufficiency of vitamin C in the diet.

Reducing bodies, which possess an enzyme action with marked oxidizing properties, are also present in meat; their action is manifested typically in carcases affected with icterus, for the yellow coloration of the tissues caused by the presence of the bile pigment, bilirubin, may often disappear if the icteric carcase be detained for 24 hours.

Connective Tissue

This is present in two forms in the animal body, the white and yellow, a typical example of white connective tissue being the fascia connecting

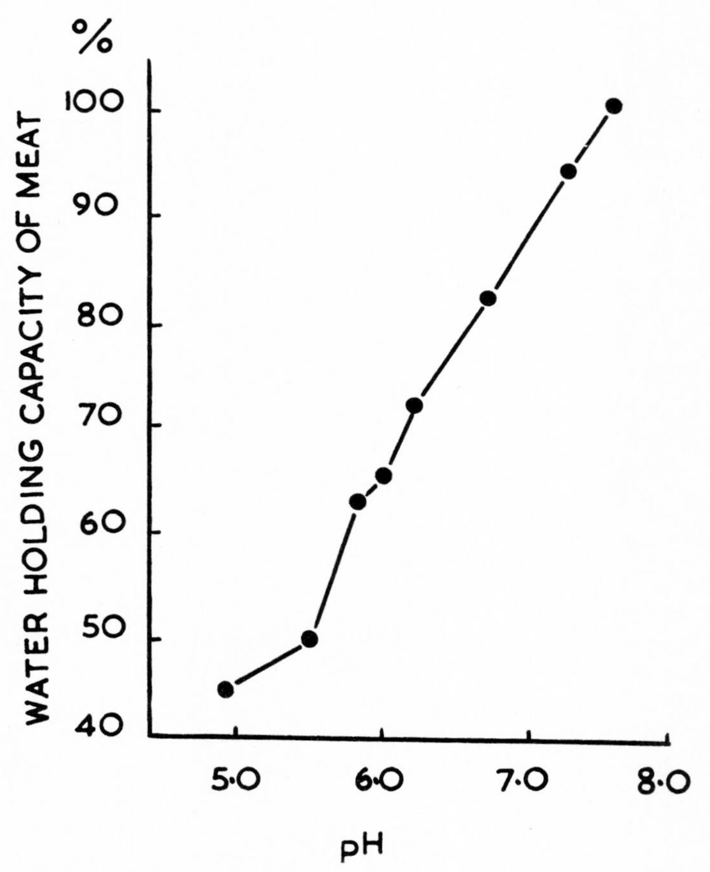

Fig. 50.—Water-holding capacity of fresh meat at various levels of pH. When the pH is at its highest the water-holding capacity is at its highest, and on this was based the old empirical practice of overdriving old cows just prior to slaughter in order to raise the pH of the flesh and increase its water-holding capacity for sausage manufacture.

the muscular bundles. The main constituent of white connective tissue is collagen, which is converted into gelatine by boiling. Yellow connective tissue, as seen in the yellow fascia covering the abdominal muscles or in the ligamentum nuchae, consists of elastin which is resistant and cannot be softened by boiling.

Physical and Chemical Properties of Voluntary Muscle

The colour of the muscle in the various animals is directly related to its myoglobin content, this substance being chemically identical with haemoglobin but distinguishable from it by spectroscopic methods. Pale muscle, as is seen in calves, lambs and young pigs, has a low myoglobin content but becomes darker with age and exercise, and the desirable cherry-red colour of prime beef cannot be obtained unless the animal has had sufficient exercise during its life.

Considerable changes occur in the nature of meat within one to two days after the animal is slaughtered. Shortly after death the meat appears dark, is sticky and adherent when minced, water can only be squeezed from it with difficulty, it is resistant to the penetration of salt and sugar and its electrical resistance is high. A day or so later the meat is lighter in colour, is wet but not sticky when minced, over 30 per cent. of fluid can be squeezed from it and the electrical resistance drops to one-fifth of its initial value. The rate at which meat undergoes such a change depends on the atmospheric temperature, but the change cannot take place unless adequate amounts of glycogen are present and the pH falls to a satisfactory level ; for this reason the meat of exhausted animals, in which the glycogen content is depleted, remains dark and fiery, though there is little concrete evidence that this state is due to incomplete bleeding.

Dark Cutting Beef

Dark cutting beef, also termed black beef, is a troublesome condition in which the colour of the musculature of freshly killed animals is appreciably darker than normal. The condition is most likely to be seen when cattle are exposed to inclement weather, injury, excitement or muscular fatigue either during marketing or in detention in a cold, damp lairage, particularly in autumn when the days are warm and nights cold and temperature shock is likely to occur. In the United States it is significant that dark cutting beef occurs only in the colder latitudes.

When cattle are subjected to untoward conditions there is a strong stimulation of the sympathetic-adrenal mechanism and a consequent increase in the amount of adrenalin discharged into the blood stream. The effect of this is to deplete the muscle glycogen, and laboratory investigations made on dark cutting beef have shown that there is both a depletion of the glycogen content and an abnormally high pH of the muscular tissue. The presence of an attractive bright-red hue on the exposed surfaces of meat is due to oxygenated myoglobin and is related to the considerable amount of oxygen the muscle myoglobin is able to absorb. The effect of a high pH in meat is to increase the activity of those muscle enzymes which utilize oxygen and to hinder the penetration of oxygen into

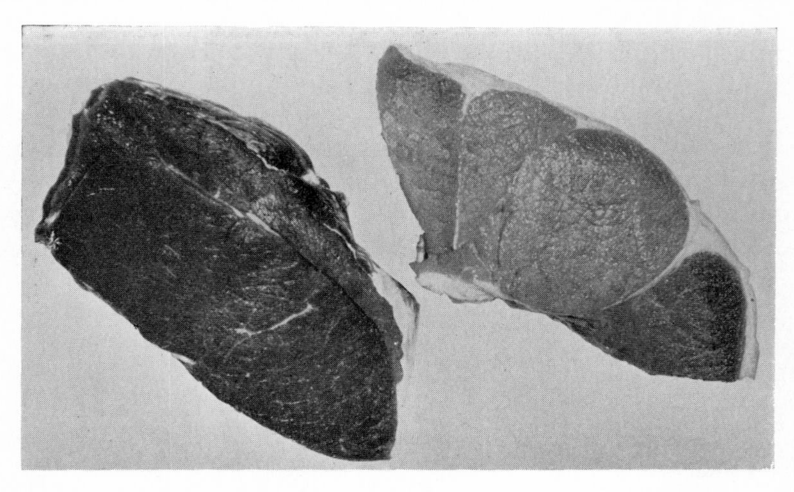

FIG. 51.—Dark cutting beef from a freshly slaughtered animal. On right is a portion of muscle from a normal animal.

the meat substance; the unpleasant purplish-red colour of dark cutting beef is therefore due to the fact that the myoglobin of the meat is only partly converted to oxymyoglobin.

In animals which have been travelled for long periods there is evidence that the stress of excitement rather than the continued fasting and exercise is the most significant factor, and although all cattle do not react alike to a given stress they must be subjected to such conditions for one day or longer, as it is only when stress is prolonged that muscle glycogen is depleted and dark cutting beef occurs. When stress has been severe, cattle may require rest and feeding in a lairage for several days before they recover physiological normality, and the incidence of the condition may be greatly reduced by the avoidance of chill and the provision of comfortable lairaging for the appropriate period with an adequate supply of food and water.

Rigor Mortis

The first and most considerable post-mortem change which occurs in muscle is the production of rigor mortis. The phenomenon is characterized by a hardening and contraction of all the voluntary muscles, by a loss in transparency of the surface of the muscle, which becomes dull, by stiffening of the joints, and it is accompanied by a slight rise in temperature of the carcase to 3° F. or more above normal in the case of beef carcases, the temperature then gradually dropping to that of the surrounding atmosphere. Rigor mortis affects first the muscles that have been most active and best nourished prior to death and commences at the head and neck, extending backwards to involve the body and limbs. In a physiologically normal animal it does not appear until 9 to 12 hours have elapsed after slaughter, and maximum rigidity is attained after 20 to 24 hours and then gradually declines.

The development of rigor mortis is influenced by (*a*) the atmospheric temperature, a high temperature accelerating its onset whereas a low temperature retards it, and (*b*) the health of the animal; where an animal is slaughtered while affected with a febrile condition rigor mortis may be absent or scarcely apparent. Certain drugs are said to encourage the early onset of rigor mortis, including sodium salicylate, alcohol and ether, but one of the most important factors controlling the production of rigor mortis is (*c*) the degree of muscular activity prior to slaughter.

Rigor mortis occurs when, after death, the muscles are no longer supplied with oxygenated blood, and it was at one time thought that the phenomenon was due to coagulation of the myosin of muscle by lactic acid derived from the muscle glycogen. Though all the chemical processes involved in rigor mortis are not known it is now considered to be related to breakdown of the muscle enzyme adenosine triphosphate (ATP), the breakdown of this substance providing energy for the muscular contraction which occurs during rigor mortis. The gradual disappearance of rigor is probably attributable to softening of the coagulated myosin by autolytic ferments. Under certain conditions the onset of rigor mortis after slaughter may be very rapid and may pass off as rapidly, as, for example in hunted animals, for any factor which reduces the glycogen of muscle during life will reduce the time course of rigor mortis. In other words, the longer rigor mortis takes to appear the longer is its duration. Rigor mortis may occur without any change in the pH of the muscle tissue.

In the meat trade the occurrence of an adequate degree of rigor mortis and a low ultimate pH of the flesh are desirable characteristics, for the low pH is inhibitory to bacterial growth while the lactic acid present brings about the conversion of the collagen of the connective tissue into gelatine and the meat when cooked is more tender.

Rigor mortis is inseparably connected with muscular acidity, and during maximum rigidity the concentration of lactic acid in muscle is ten times that of living muscle, i.e. from about 0·05 in living muscle to 0·5 to 1 per cent. in muscle 24 hours after slaughter. Immediately after slaughter of an animal the flesh has a neutral or slightly alkaline reaction, but in cattle, pigs and horses it becomes acid in $1\frac{1}{2}$ hours if the weather is warm, though it may be delayed for 3 hours if the weather is cold. In sheep this acid change is not so constant and may not appear for 7 hours. In freshly slaughtered cattle the pH of the flesh is about 7·0, eventually dropping to 5·6 or 5·8, and then gradually rising due to the formation of alkaline substances associated with protein breakdown (Fig. 205). In fatigued animals the muscle may remain alkaline for 2 to 3 days before becoming acid, while in animals slaughtered when suffering from fever the meat may remain permanently alkaline until decomposition commences.

It will thus be apparent that absence of rigor mortis in the carcase may result from unfavourable ante-mortem treatment such as fatigue or the fear and excitement engendered during transport, or it may result from an illness of an animal before slaughter, and though carcases of animals coming within the former class cannot usually be regarded as unfit for food they are difficult to cut up, the joints lose their shape, there is more waste and the durability of the meat is lowered. These undesirable changes also occur where absence of rigor mortis is due to illness of the animal before slaughter, but here must also be taken into account the possibility that the meat, in addition to being less durable, may contain organisms harmful to man or may be suffused with deleterious toxins. Conversely, the too rapid development of rigor mortis, as sometimes occurs in cattle and pigs, is indicative that the meat is likely to undergo early putrefactive change.

Fat

Fat develops in connection with connective tissue, and has an important influence on both the odour and flavour of the different meats. It varies in consistency according to its composition, this, again, being controlled by the species of the animal, the method of feeding, and the site of the fat in the carcase. Fat with a high stearin content, as in the ox and sheep, is firm, while in the horse it is richer in olein and is soft and greasy.

The deposition of fat between the muscle fibres, seen particularly in young well nourished cattle, is a desirable feature and is known as "marbling". It does not occur in older animals, and fat in them tends to be deposited subcutaneously, as is seen on the hips and pin bones of fat cows. Marbling of fat does not occur in the horse, while in the pig it is the presence of fat cells between the individual muscle fibres which prevents the gastric juice from reaching the fibres and thus renders pork so indigestible.

The Uses of Edible Fat

The edible fat from the ox carcase, other than that intermixed with the muscle, is obtained from certain well defined positions. These are the omentum, mesentery, stomach, mediastinum and kidney, and from these sources an average yield of 42 lb. of edible fat is obtained, varying between 25 lb. in the lean cow to 65 lb. in the well finished bullock; of the various by-products, the edible fat ranks only second to the hide in value. Abnormal amounts of kidney fat, in some cases up to 200 lb. in weight, are sometimes encountered; these are known as "balloon kidneys", the fat of which is both marketable and edible. The butcher may render down his edible beef and mutton fat to produce dripping, but in wartime all edible beef fat is converted into dripping. On a commercial scale edible fat is converted into oleo oil and oleo stearin, both being used in margarine manufacture, the former for best and the latter for inferior grades; oleo stearin is also used for soap and candle manufacture and is mixed with cooking fats to harden them.

Characteristics of Muscle and Fat of Food Animals

Beef

In young bulls the flesh is light red and attractive, but the muscle becomes darker, due to testosterone secretion, in later life. It also becomes coarse and shows little intramuscular fat, and in old bulls the dried surface of the meat appears very dark. Bull beef possesses good binding qualities, i.e. the power to take up and hold water; forequarters of bull beef are therefore in demand by manufacturers of pork sausage, a proportion of bull flesh being added to the pork. In the United States bull carcases are boned out immediately after slaughter, and the flesh, while still warm and before the pH falls, is chopped up with ground ice; by this method lean bull flesh will absorb its own weight of water. (See Fig. 50.) Bullock flesh is light red to dark red in colour with well marked "marbling" and in these and in young cows the fat is white or whitish-yellow and firm. In older cows the fat tends to be yellower and looser in consistency.

Veal

In calves a few days old the flesh is often pale and watery and the fat of a jelly-like consistency, but in the milk-fed calf the fat soon becomes white and firmer. The white colour of the flesh and the clear white baby fat of veal are desirable features and are maintained by keeping the calf indoors and allowing it to suckle its mother twice daily; it must not be pail fed or allowed to run with the cows or consume grass and in France when calves are allowed out on pastures they are muzzled. In calves of the Jersey or Guernsey breed the fat is white, becoming yellow as age increases and grass forms part of the diet, but this yellow coloration is confined to the fatty tissues and therefore should not be confused with icterus. After the veal carcase has hung for a day or so in its skin, a trade procedure adopted to prevent dryness but now forbidden in Western Germany, it becomes distinctly sour due to the formation of lactic acid.

Mutton

Mutton flesh is light to dark red in colour with fine, firm fibres. The muscles are not intermixed with fat, but in the well-nourished animal there are fat deposits which lie between the various muscles. Mutton fat is firm, white and odourless.

Goat

Goat's flesh resembles mutton, but the kidney fat is always abundant even where the subcutaneous fat is sparse, and there is practically no fat between the muscles. The typical goat odour is invariably transferred from the skin to the carcase during the process of dressing.

Pork

The colour of pork varies according to age, condition of nutrition, and the part of the body, both pale and dark muscle being observed in the same carcase. Of all food animals pork is the least firm, the colour varying from whitish-grey to red in young pigs, but of a strong red colour in boars and sows, particularly in the muscles of the back. A characteristic of pig flesh is the marked deposition of subcutaneous fat, this being white, soft and of a greasy consistency, and a further characteristic of pig flesh is that it becomes nearly white in colour when cooked, while in other animals the meat grows darker on cooking.

Horse

Horse flesh is dark red or even bluish after cutting, that of blood horses being almost black in colour ; the odour is sweet and repulsive, and the connective tissue fascia is more strongly developed than in other food animals as a result of muscular exercise. The fat may be yellow, soft and greasy, but it frequently resembles the fat of good class cow beef and may be firm in consistency, especially in young horses fed on oats and hay. It is characteristic of horse flesh that it does not exhibit the marbling with fat which is one of the most desirable characteristics of prime beef. After some hours horse flesh develops a rusty colour.

Influence of Feeding on Animal Tissue

The effect of feeding on the colour and texture of animal tissue is much more evident in fat than in muscle. The fat in grass-fed cattle is a rich, yellow colour, particularly noticeable in animals which have come off grass in early summer, though in animals coming off grass later in the year, and also in stall-fed cattle, the fat is almost white.

The yellow colour of fat due to grass feeding is linked up with the presence of carotene, a pigment converted in the animal body into vitamin A and abundantly present in fresh young grass, some varieties of maize, certain root crops such as carrots, and linseed and cotton cake. Mammalian fat consists of three substances, olein, stearin and palmitin, which are present in varying proportions, and of these the palmitin acts as a solvent of carotene so that animals such as cattle, horses and, to a lesser extent, pigs, which have a large proportion of palmitin in their fat will accumulate carotene if fed on carotene-containing foods and produce fat of a yellow colour. Where, however, such animals are fed on foods such as grain, hay or straw, which contain little or no carotene, the fat remains white in colour.

In the case of sheep, goats and buffaloes very little palmitin is present in their fat so that they can assimilate only small quantities of carotene and the fat remains white in colour irrespective of the nature of the feed. If the body fat should be lost, however, as in undernourishment or in the case of cows where the fat is lost due to the production of calves and milk, such carotene as is present in the body fat is either used up more slowly or completely left behind, becomes more concentrated, and the fat becomes yellow in colour.

In Jersey and Guernsey breeds of cattle a typical yellow fat is, however, a normal breed characteristic, and it is highly probable that in these animals this natural coloration is due to a genetic factor influencing the deposition of carotene or other pigments from grass, etc., to which fat owes its yellow colour. In young calves of the above breeds of cattle the fat is white, but becomes yellow when the animals are taken from their mothers and fed on grass and other foods. The deep yellow coloration of the fat occasionally seen in sheep carcases is a condition well known in Iceland and Ireland and is attributed to the fact that sheep so affected are unable to oxidize the yellow pigments, the xanthophylls, in their foodstuffs due to a recessive hereditary factor. The abnormal coloration may be so marked as to render the carcase unmarketable.

Pigs fed too long on swill develop a fat which is soft and unattractive and possesses an insipid taste, this softness being due to the fact that the fatty tissues contain insufficient fat, though the fat usually hardens as more and more of it is laid down. The undesirability of the soft fat of swill-fed pigs is that it renders the carcase difficult to cut up, causes heavy loss in frying, and contains a high proportion of unsaturated fatty acids leading to early rancidity. The feeding of pigs on fish meal produces fat of a brownish-yellow colour, a condition known as brown fat disease (Plate I) and attributable to an acid-fast pigment caused by the presence of excessive unsaturated fatty acids in the meal.

The Food Value of Meat from Lean and Prime Carcases

The chemical composition of meat from animals of the same species shows considerable variation, depending on the breed of animal and the degree to which it has been fattened, and variations also occur in different locations of the same carcase. The average percentage composition of meat from lean and fat animals of the same species is as follows :

	Water	*Nitrogenous matter*	*Fat*
BEEF			
Lean	65	16	18
Medium	56	15	28
Very fat	48	13	38
MUTTON			
Lean	75·0	18	5·7
Medium fat	65·2	14·5	19·5
Very fat	46	10·2	43·2
PORK			
Lean	58	14·6	24·6
Fat	43	11·4	43·9
VEAL			
Bobby calf	74	18	6
Fat calf	65	17	17

From consideration of the above table it will be seen that approximately three-quarters of the total weight of meat is composed of water, and that the ratio of water to protein is within the region of four parts of water to one of protein. A comparison of lean and fat meat shows that the main difference in chemical composition is in the proportion of water and fat ; the more fat there is present the less the proportion of water, fat replacing water as the animal gains weight. Conversely, meat from lean or young immature animals contains more water than meat from prime animals. Though fat replaces water it does not replace protein, so that the gain in the nutritive value of meat as the animal becomes fatter is an absolute one, and it is not obtained at the expense of a loss in protein value.

Though a few people prefer lean meat, the majority choose meat with an adequate amount of fat, as is obtained from well-nourished animals. This preference for fat meat is almost entirely an aesthetic one ; it is based on the greater palatability of fat meat, for it has been found that beef attains its greatest palatability when rather more than one-third of the roasted joint is fat, and this proportion is reached when a bovine animal has a dressing-out percentage of around 58.

In addition to its greater aesthetic value, fat meat has also a higher satiety value than lean meat. This denotes the period after consumption of the meat before hunger reappears, and depends on the amount of fat present; in fat meat it is about 5 hours, but in lean meat the satiety value is 3 hours. A further factor to be considered in assessing the food value of meat is its calorific value, which increases with the proportion of fat. The calorific value of lean beef is about 910 calories per pound of meat, and in prime beef 1840 calories per pound. Similarly, the flesh of bobby calves has a calorific value of about 567 calories per pound, and that of veal calves 995 calories per pound.

It will therefore be apparent that, weight for weight, fat meat is more valuable than lean meat because of its greater palatability and calorific value. Where there are recognized standards of quality, as when meat is graded and stamped as coming within a particular grade, the purchaser would be entitled to redress if it were proved that he or she had expressly stipulated meat of a specific standard, e.g. prime, but had been supplied with lean meat, which is definitely of a lower calorific value; in other words, the leaner the meat sold to the consumer, the more water he is purchasing at meat prices. It will also be apparent that when the bodily condition of an animal has deteriorated beyond the stage of leanness and has reached the stage of emaciation, i.e. the water content of the meat has still further increased at the expense of fat, the flesh in such cases is so lacking in fat, and its palatability, satiety value and calorific value so diminished, that it ceases to be meat in the recognized sense of the word. On these grounds the carcases of emaciated animals may be seized and condemned; similarly, the flesh of young bobby calves may contain such a high proportion of water and low proportion of fat that the carcase may be condemned on the grounds of immaturity.

As the amount of water in lean meat is greater than that in fat meat it is, on first thoughts, surprising that the sausage-maker prefers lean meat, maintaining that it absorbs more water than fat meat. It is undoubtedly true that lean meat which is chopped while still warm and mixed with ice can absorb its own weight of water, though this absorptive property diminishes progressively as the pH of the meat falls. The desirability of lean meat for sausage may therefore be based on several factors: (*a*) it can absorb a certain amount of water, this property being greater when the meat has a high proportion of gelatine, as in meat from bull forequarters (it is recognized in the meat trade that the colour and palatability of the type of sausage known as coarse-cut is considerably improved when a proportion of bull beef is added); (*b*) the absence of fat in lean meat permits the cereal and water added in sausage-making to form a more perfect emulsion than if fat were present, and in this way greater quantities of water can be absorbed; (*c*) lean meat is cheaper than fat meat, and this enables the sausage-maker to produce an article which commands a ready sale.

Chemical and Biological Means for the Differentiation of Meats

The differentiation of the muscle and fat of animals is of importance in connection with the possible substitution of inferior, and at times repugnant, meat for that of good quality. The substitutions that may be practised are that of horse flesh for beef, goat's meat for mutton, mutton for venison, and occasionally the flesh of the cat for that of the rabbit or hare.

There is little difficulty in differentiating the flesh and fat of these animals in the carcase form or in joints, but the recognition of horse flesh or other meats in mince or in sausage depends on tests of a chemical or biological nature and therefore comes properly within the province of the analytical chemist or the bacteriologist.

Chemical Tests

The statement that horse flesh is richer than the flesh of other food animals in glycogen is correct, and on this fact a number of differential chemical tests are based. Glycogen, however, commences to disappear from meat from the time the animal is slaughtered and, unless the examination is made soon after the carcase is cut up, very little may be found. Further, the liver of all animals, particularly the pig, contains appreciable quantities of glycogen, and if this organ is used as an ingredient of sausage a positive result to a glycogen test might occur from the presence of liver. Any deductions made from the presence of glycogen, particularly in sausage, should therefore be advanced with extreme caution.

A recently developed method of identifying horse fat when admixed with lard or beef and mutton fat is by demonstrating the presence of 1 to 2 per cent. of linoleic acid. In other animal fats this is not present in proportions higher than 0·1 per cent.

A valuable test for horse fat depends on estimation of the iodine value. This test is based on the amount of iodine absorbed by the unsaturated fatty acids present in the fat, and varies in the different animals. In the horse the iodine value of fat is 71 to 86, in the ox 38 to 46, in the sheep 35 to 46, and in the pig 50 to 70, good lard having an iodine value of 66.

A further valuable test for fats which can be liquefied by heat and thus converted into oil is by the estimation of the refractive index. All liquids, including oils, possess a specific refractive index, and by the aid of a refractometer it may be shown that the refractive index of horse fat is 53·5, ox fat not above 40, and pig fat not above 51·9.

BIOLOGICAL TESTS

Three methods are employed for the differentiation of the flesh of various animals by biological means. They are the precipitation test, the complement fixation test and the anaphylactic test; the tests are particularly applicable to mince or sausage meat, the precipitation test being the most valuable and depending on the fact that certain antibodies develop in the blood of an animal which receives repeated injections of blood serum from another animal. If, for example, it is desired to test for horse flesh, a rabbit is injected periodically with blood serum from the horse; the rabbit, as a result, develops antibodies for horse serum, and these antibodies are specific and possess the property of precipitating proteins of the horse but of no other animal. When blood serum from the injected rabbit is therefore mixed in a test tube with a filtered extract from the suspected meat, a turbidity of the solution first occurs if horse meat be present and this is then followed by a definite precipitation. The precipitation test is a protein reaction and is of value for the detection of flesh, organs, fat or intestines; it is of greatest value with raw meat, for if meat is very well boiled or fried it will be impossible to extract protein from it. Provided meat has not been cooked at a temperature higher than 176° F. for 10 minutes it is, however, possible to extract enough soluble protein to arrive at a definite conclusion, while drying, smoking and salting do not affect the test, though the salt should be extracted from salted meat by immersing in water before the test is applied. The test is a specific one except for closely related species of animals, as the horse and donkey, or sheep and goat, whose proteins have almost the same antigenic structure. However, it is now possible to render the prepared anti-serum more specific by absorbing the non-specific proteins common to mammalian sera and, by the subsequent use of the haemagglutination test, even the most closely associated species of animal can be differentiated.

The Effect of Cooking on Meat

Cooked meat is more completely assimilated than raw meat, for though the muscle proteins are coagulated in cooking, this coagulation renders them more easily acted on by the digestive enzymes. The advantages of cooking meat are (*a*) it is rendered easier to assimilate; (*b*) it becomes more tender because of the chemical change which takes place in the collagen of connective tissue during cooking, and (*c*) bacteria and parasites, some of which may be harmful, are generally destroyed.

Meat loses considerable weight during cooking due to loss of water, and the vitamins present in the meat may be destroyed, though this depends on the method of cooking. There is also a loss in extractives, in some cases as high as 60 per cent., but the loss of meat extractives is unimportant as they are present in the stew or gravy after meat is cooked and are therefore consumed.

Meat is not a good conductor of heat, and in ordinary cooking of joints weighing 6 lb. or over, the centre of such joints is very unlikely to attain a temperature of 212° F., a temperature which is regarded as a minimum to ensure efficient sterilization. The temperature of the interior of joints of this size may only reach 183° F. or less after cooking for 3½ hours, while boiling a large ham for 2 hours may only raise the temperature at the centre to 95° F., 6 hours boiling to 149° F. and 10 hours continuous boiling to 185° F. In another experiment a 12 lb. ham was placed in cold water and brought to the boil. When the water boiled the temperature in the interior of the ham was only 80° F. and only reached 95°-104° F. after half an hour. In the cooking of black puddings care must be taken that the temperature of the water does not reach boiling point, and the temperature of the contents may only reach 140° F.; in the quick frying of sausage the temperature at the centre may not exceed 84° F.

Boiling and cooking, however, are sufficient to destroy any smeared tuberculous material or salmonella organisms on the surface of a joint of meat, a factor of considerable importance, for surface contamination of meat with pathogenic organisms is much commoner than infection of the muscle itself. The most trustworthy method of cooking is by boiling, the next best method is by roasting in an oven, while the least trustworthy is by roasting in front of a fire.

CHAPTER V

PATHOLOGY OF THE FOOD ANIMALS

Inflammation

The basis of pathology, whether human or veterinary, is inflammation, and may be described as the series of changes that take place in living tissue as the result of an injury which has not been sufficient to cause the death of the tissue.

Injury or trauma to living tissue is caused by bacteria or their toxins, by parasites, chemical poisons, physical agents such as heat or cold, and by mechanical damage. Physical and chemical injuries are likely to be localized and are usually of less importance than bacterial injuries, though changes in temperature, as sunburn or frostbite, may act by reducing the vitality and resistance of a tissue and permitting the invasion by pathogenic bacteria.

Though inflammation may assume various forms according to the type of tissue attacked, the series of changes in the tissue follows a definite order. These changes have been recognized from time immemorial, and are revealed by the so-called cardinal signs of heat, pain, redness and swelling of the affected part, together with disturbance of its function; they are sometimes referred to by the Latin names *calor*, *dolor*, *rubor*, *tumor* and *functio laesa*.

When a tissue becomes injured an early dilatation of the arterioles and capillaries is observable, followed by a slowing of the blood stream due to swelling of the cells which form the capillary walls. Leucocytes, which previously occupied the centre of the blood stream, now cling to the vessel walls and, by lining these walls, retard still further the passage of blood along the blood vessels. The swollen and damaged cells of the capillary wall permit the passage of an abnormal amount of lymph through the walls, so that lymph suffuses and distends the surrounding tissues, while the leucocytes of the body, which possess power of amoeboid movement, now migrate through the capillary wall and are attracted to the area of inflammation. The accumulation of leucocytes, which if excessive

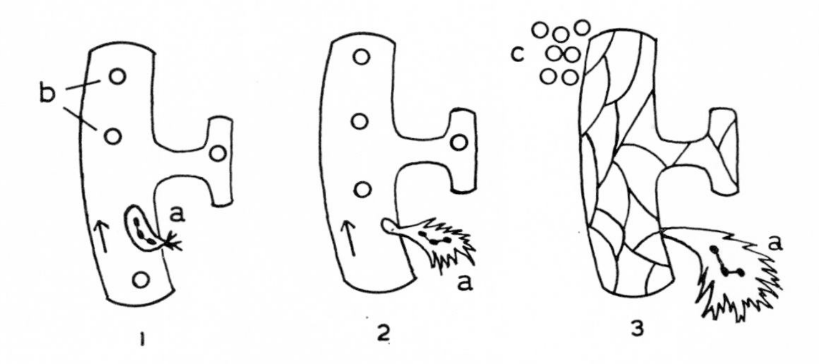

FIG. 52.—Stages (1, 2, 3) in the diapedesis of a polymorphonuclear leucocyte (*a*) through the wall of a capillary in an inflamed area, the arrow indicating the direction of the blood flow. (In healthy tissue the diameter of a capillary is only slightly greater than that of a red blood corpuscle.) In diagram 3 is shown the outline of the cells which make up the capillary walls. When a septic condition is present, bacterial toxins cause weakening of the capillary walls, and red blood corpuscles (*b*) pass through the binding material between the cells to produce a petechial haemorrhage (*c*).

produces pus, is part of the defensive mechanism of the body, and is not necessarily an unfavourable indication but is rather an indication that the agent producing the inflammation is being combated.

If the body defences are adequate, inflammatory changes in a tissue may terminate in recovery, and an inflammation in which the changes in tissue reaction are rapid, and in which recovery or death is also rapid, is described as acute. Typical examples of acute inflammation occur in anthrax, blackleg, braxy, or in acute miliary tuberculosis. Where an injury to a tissue is in a mild form but is prolonged, the changes in the blood supply of the part are not so well marked, and exudation of lymph and emigration of leucocytes is but slight. Such an inflammation is described as a chronic one, and the tendency in inflammation of this type is for tissue cells known as fibroblasts to proliferate in the inflamed part, and for the amount of fibrous tissue to be increased. Typical examples of chronic inflammation are seen in such diseases as cirrhosis of the ox liver, chronic tuberculosis of the serous membranes or in actino-bacillosis. An acute inflammation may become a chronic one, as is seen in the case of acute tuberculous pleurisy which invariably assumes the chronic form ; similarly, an acute attack of swine erysipelas which does not end fatally may resolve into the chronic form of the disease.

The following are the chief types of inflammation :

Catarrhal Inflammation is the term used to denote an affection of the mucous membranes characterized by the increased production of mucus with desquamation of the lining epithelium. Nasal catarrh, as may be seen in glanders, atrophic rhinitis (Figs. 4, 68) or calf pneumonia, is a typical example of this form of inflammation.

Serous Inflammation is characterized by the presence of a fluid transu-date, seen particularly in the thoracic and abdominal cavities. The peritoneal effusion encountered in sheep which have died of braxy is an example.

Fibrinous Inflammation is common on serous and mucous membranes, and is manifested by coagulation of the exudate and the deposit of fibrin. When it occurs on opposed surfaces, as in the pericardium in traumatic pericarditis or swine erysipelas, the surfaces present an appearance as if two pieces of buttered bread had been pulled apart (Fig. 73).

Diphtheritic Inflammation occurs when the superficial layers of a mucous membrane become necrotic and, together with a fibrinous exudate, form a membrane. Typical examples are seen in calf diphtheria, in swine fever, fowl pox, and in septic enteritis (Fig. 136).

Haemorrhagic Inflammation is characterized by the presence of excessive numbers of red blood corpuscles in the exudate which lend to it a reddish or chocolate colour. It may be associated with serous inflammation, as in braxy, or in the blood-stained anal discharge in bovine anthrax or calf dysentery and also in severe parasitic gastro-enteritis (Fig. 9).

Suppurative Inflammation is manifested by the usual series of changes associated with inflammation, together with the formation of pus, and is chiefly caused by the ordinary pyogenic organisms, including streptococci, staphylococci and members of the *E. coli* group. It may also be caused by specific micro-organisms as in glanders and actinomycosis, but it is not now considered that the tubercle bacillus is a pyogenic organism, for tuberculous caseous material resists liquefaction, and tuberculous lesions contain few leucocytes ; if suppuration is present the infection is probably mixed. The suppurative form of inflammation must be regarded as the most serious in meat inspection, for not only is an organ containing a suppurative lesion unfit for food, but there is also possibility that the lesion has extended to produce a septicaemia or pyaemia.

A collection of pus circumscribed by fibrous tissue is known as an abscess. Should the reaction of the body tissue be sufficient to overcome the activity of the micro-organisms contained in the pus, the abscess may remain localized and be eventually absorbed, inspissated or calcified.

Abscess formation in pigs is responsible for condemnation of 1·7 per cent. of carcase parts in the United States, the highest incidence being found in hams and attributed to hypodermic needles, followed by bellies, backs and shoulders respectively. Abscess formation also occurs in the submaxillary or retropharyngeal lymph nodes of pigs, and it has been shown that the condition is caused by a beta-haemolytic streptococcus and in some abattoirs may be responsible for 7 per cent. of condemnations of pig heads. Abscess formation may occur in the udder of sows due to actinomycosis, and in the udder of cows, the so-called summer mastitis, as a result of infection with *Corynebacterium pyogenes*.

High Body Temperature

A rise in temperature above normal is encountered in animals closely packed in over-heated railway trucks, though it will be realized that this is a passive heat accumulation and must be distinguished from true fever. A high body temperature is associated with excessive perspiration and has a retarding effect on the fattening of animals, and it is for this reason that thick coated Scottish Highland cattle are never fattened by stall feeding in the winter, though the Aberdeen Angus, possessing the thinnest and lightest hide of all beef cattle, fattens readily by stall feeding. In pigs not used to handling there may be elevation of the temperature due to excitement. Heatstroke is also accompanied by a rise in body temperature and, where an animal is slaughtered before it is allowed to cool, the carcase may show varying degrees of imperfect bleeding which may be so marked as to render the carcase unfit for food.

Pyrexia or Fever

Bacteria and their toxic products, and also protozoal organisms as in redwater in cattle, are the chief causes of pyrexia. It is manifested usually, though not invariably, by an elevation of body temperature, by an increase in respiration and pulse rate, and a diminution in the secretion of saliva, urine and bile. The carcase of an animal slaughtered whilst suffering from pyrexia is uniformly congested, giving the carcase surface a pinkish hue, while on closer examination the subcutaneous blood vessels are apparent, though not normally visible in the healthy carcase. The liver, kidneys and heart show evidence of cloudy swelling and, where the pyrexia has been of prolonged duration, cloudy swelling may have been succeeded by pathological fatty change, together with marked wasting of the muscular and fatty tissues. In some cases the typical appearance of a fevered carcase may not become evident until 24 hours after slaughter, and in winter this period may extend to 48 hours. Detention for at least 24 hours should therefore be a routine procedure in the case of suspected febrile carcases, and is compulsory under French meat inspection law.

The congestion of the blood vessels in pyrexia is an active hyperaemia associated with disease, and is accompanied by an increase in the alkalinity of the muscular tissue with a consequent decrease in the durability of the carcase. Carcases affected with pyrexia should therefore be condemned.

Imperfect Bleeding

It is of prime importance to distinguish between the congestion of a carcase resulting from active hyperaemia and that of a carcase which is imperfectly bled due to mechanical causes. The former is a condition associated with pyrexia and is therefore likely to be accompanied by systemic changes in the parenchymatous organs. Imperfect bleeding due to mechanical causes is, on the other hand, unaccompanied by systemic changes and is seen in animals slaughtered at the point of death on account of injury, suffocation, heart failure and lightning stroke, or in cases of severe indigestion or extensive afebrile affections of the heart and lungs.

In imperfectly bled animals the left ventricle usually contains blood, the subcutaneous blood vessels appear injected, and the flesh is dark and the organs congested, flabby and watery. The high blood content of the visceral organs is most apparent in the lungs, while the lymph nodes, particularly the prescapular, are suffused with blood though they are not enlarged. A useful feature in the detection of imperfect bleeding in a carcase is that the intercostal veins are easily discernible, and the incision of the masseter muscles made in cattle for the detection of *C. bovis* may be examined, for blood exudes from the cut surface in the imperfectly bled animal.

The malachite green test has recently been recommended for the determination of the efficiency of bleeding of a carcase, the reagents used being acid malachite green and 3 per cent. hydrogen peroxide. A meat extract is prepared by scraping 6 grams of meat, adding this to 14 ml. of water in an Erlenmeyer flask, allow to stand for 15 minutes then remove the sediment. The test is conducted by adding 0·7 ml. of the extract to an agglutination tube, adding one drop of malachite green, mix and add one drop of hydrogen peroxide. For measuring the malachite green reagent a pipette delivering 40 drops per ml. should be used. The mixture is shaken until it foams slightly then left to stand for 20 minutes. If bleeding is satisfactory the fluid is clear and of a blue colour ; if a moderate degree of imperfect bleeding is present the fluid is cloudy and of a green colour, while if there is a marked degree of imperfect bleeding the fluid is cloudy and olive-green in colour.

The flesh of a carcase which is imperfectly bled due to any of the above causes would be harmless if consumed immediately and would actually be more nutritious than that from a well bled carcase, for blood itself has a certain nutritive value, but consideration must always be given to the fact that a variable period of time must inevitably elapse between the slaughter of an animal and the consumption of its flesh in the form of butchers' joints. Unbled or badly bled carcases undergo rapid decomposition and must therefore be condemned, though in some cases where bleeding has been attempted prior to death and has been partially successful it may be possible to extend a favourable judgment. In emergency slaughtered animals, especially those consigned to an abattoir after slaughter on a farm and where the ante-mortem history is unobtainable, there is always a possibility that if imperfect bleeding is present it may be the result of a febrile condition and carcases so affected therefore call for a severe judgment. The judgment of young calves, particularly, should always err on the side of safety.

Dead Animals

In these animals there is absence of a regular slaughter, with marked fullness of the subcutaneous blood vessels and a high blood content of the lungs, kidneys and liver. The muscular tissue is dark, there is an objectionable odour when the abdominal cavity is opened, and a greenish hue is apparent on the abdominal walls, particularly on the kidney fat. The liver surface also possesses a yellow or greenish hue and this is due to imbibition of bile from the gall bladder. In cases where death is due to suffocation from drowning or from overcrowding while in transit, the lungs are congested with dark non-aerated blood, and as a result the right side of the heart will be full of blood but the left side empty. The carcases of dead animals are unwholesome, liable to rapid decomposition, and are unfit for food.

Malformations

These are not infrequently encountered in meat inspection, and examples are a double spleen in pigs, herniation of portion of the liver through the diaphragm, extra lobes of the liver, or malformation of the skeletal bones as seen in pigs as the result of an earlier attack of rickets. Where there is no alteration in the texture of an organ, malformations are of no significance and do not affect its marketability.

Infiltrations

This term denotes the collection of abnormal fluids or substances in body tissues or cavities, and includes oedema and fatty change.

Oedema

Oedema, or dropsy, denotes the presence of abnormal amounts of body fluid in the tissues or the body cavities, and is often associated with chronic affections of the liver, heart, lungs and kidneys. The important forms of oedema encountered in meat inspection are (*a*) hydrothorax, or oedema of the pleural cavities ; (*b*) ascites, or oedema of the abdominal cavity ; and (*c*) anasarca, in which the subcutaneous and connective tissues are infiltrated with lymph. Anasarca is the most important form of oedema encountered in meat inspection, and as the fluid is free in the tissues and easily influenced by gravity it is frequently seen in dependent and less compact tissues, such as the dewlap of cattle affected with traumatic pericarditis, or the intermaxillary space of sheep with severe parasitic infections. (Figs. 9, 176.)

Fig. 53.—Oedema (anasarca) of hind limbs of Friesian bull, the result of tuberculous pericarditis. More commonly the symptoms of this affection are stiffness of movement and a fullness and tenseness of the jugular vein. (Dr. H. Magnusson.)

Physiological oedema occurs in the udder of the newly calved cow, and is characterized by a tenseness of the udder and the presence of large flat plaques discernible by palpation on the udder surface. The condition is known as " seeding ", and must not be confused with the induration associated with mastitis.

Cardiac or circulatory oedema due to circulatory disturbances is common in meat inspection, and may be brought about in various ways. An increased blood pressure in the veins may result in the passage of an abnormal amount of lymph through the capillary walls ; thus ascites is encountered in cirrhosis of the liver in sheep, or in extensive hydatid infection of that organ, and may be associated with interference to the passage of venous blood through the liver resulting in increased pressure in the radicles of the portal vein.

Oedema may also be produced by an increase in permeability of the capillary walls as a result of damage due to toxins or to an increased filtrability of the blood. It is seen particularly in sheep as a result of severe roundworm infestation of the stomach and small intestines, the chronic anaemia giving rise to a deficiency in blood protein with a consequent reduction in the colloid osmotic pressure of the blood and the development of oedematous areas in various parts of the body. Anasarca is frequently associated with emaciation and it is probable that the latter affection, which occurs as a result of disease, is responsible for an increased permeability of the capillary walls and infiltration of the body fluids into the subcutaneous and connective tissues. A peculiar form of oedema, known as bull oedema, occurs in young male animals in Northern Australia and parts of Africa and is characterized by the fact that the carcase is well fleshed and the musculature of normal appearance but the fat, particularly of the kidneys and pelvic cavity, is yellow and gelatinous. The affection has been attributed to the severe working of young bulls in a hot climate on a falling plane of nutrition, and it has also been seen in young bulls which have undergone an arduous journey on foot. The procedure recommended is to detain the carcase overnight in a chiller and bone out the carcase the following morning. The overnight chilling may bring about considerable improvement and enable unaffected musculature to be released for food.

Judgment. Ascites and hydrothorax are of less serious import in meat inspection than anascara. In the two former conditions the detention of the carcase for 12 hours is advisable and, if the serous cavities have dried out and the carcase has set moderately well, it may safely be passed for food. In anasarca involving the subcutaneous and connective tissues, or in any form of oedema accompanied by emaciation, the carcase should be condemned. In healthy cattle the bone marrow contains not more than 25 per cent. of water, while if anasarca is present it contains more than 50 per cent. and a valuable test for estimating the water content of marrow is illustrated in Fig. 54. Pieces of marrow the size of a pea are obtained from a long bone and placed in beakers containing alcohol at strengths of 32°, 47° and 52°. Where the specimen floats in all of the three vessels this is an indication that the water content of bone marrow is not greater than 25 per cent. and the carcase may be released, whereas if the water content of the marrow is shown to be 50 per cent. or over the carcase may be regarded as unfit for food. The judgment of carcases in which the water content of the bone marrow is shown to lie between 25 and 50 per cent. depends on the facilities of the particular country. Where meat inspection regulations include a provision for "conditional release" of carcases the inspector may decide that the carcase can be dealt with under this category and be passed for cooking or sold in the Freibank at a reduced price. Where no

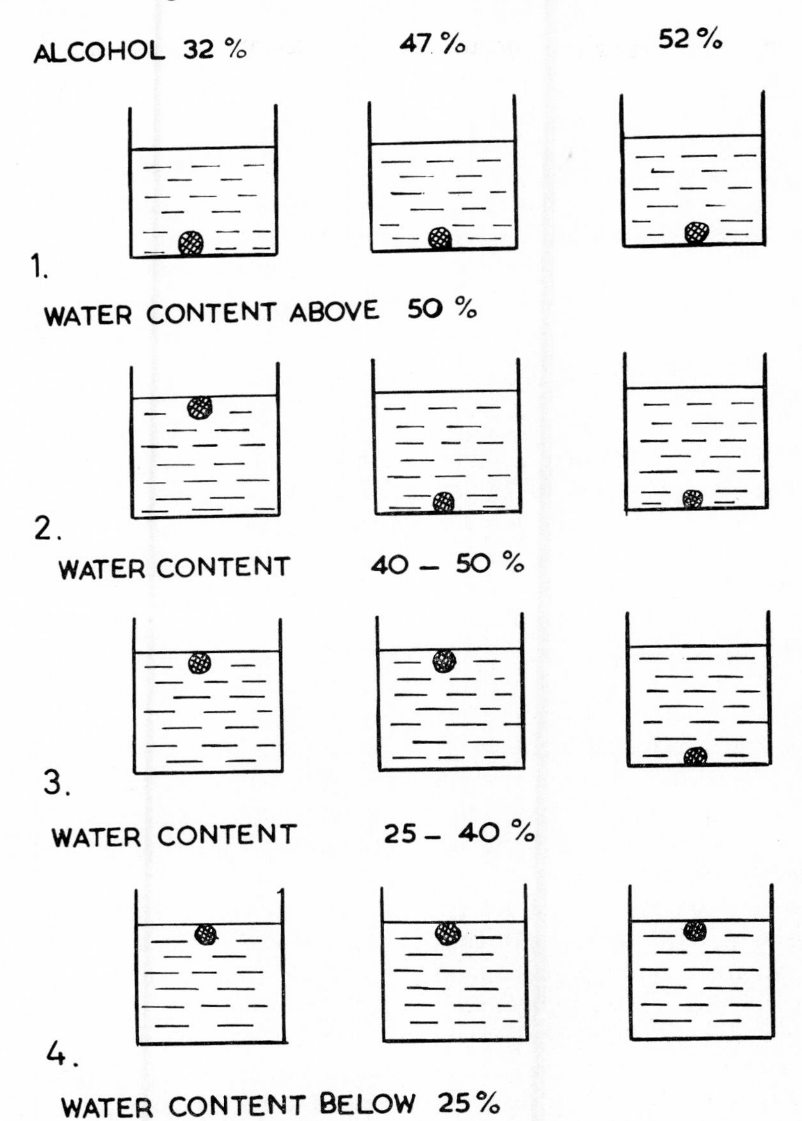

FIG. 54.—The bone marrow test for oedema.

such provision exists in the regulations the inspector's decision will be guided by correlating the result of the test with a visual assessment of the degree of oedema in the carcase. A fraudulent practice in some countries in the Far East is the " watering " of pork. This is carried out by opening the thorax as soon as the pig is bled, introducing a hollow bamboo cane into the heart and pumping water into the tissues by way of the arterial blood stream. The water content of duck carcases is likewise increased by the injection of water into the subcutaneous tissue beneath the wings.

Fatty Change

For many years fatty degeneration was said to be distinguished from fatty infiltration, and the terms caused considerable confusion. It is now known that all degenerations are infiltrations in the sense that they are an accumulation in the cells of fat coming from outside. Depending upon the amount of visible fat one might pass, almost insensibly, from a small amount, truly physiological, to a more severe condition which still might be included within the range of normality, e.g. fatty liver of pregnancy, and thence to a final stage where there is gross replacement of normal tissue by fat. The first two conditions might then stand as examples of " infiltration " and the last as " degeneration ".

Physiological Fatty Infiltration. The presence of a moderate amount of visible fat in the liver is a physiological process which is reversible, the degree depending on the nature and amount of the feeding; it is formed partly by the storage of fat direct from the food, or by the liver cells themselves. Physiological fatty infiltration chiefly involves the liver, though the condition is also encountered in the heart and kidneys, and is manifested by an excess of fat in these organs, this excess being induced by a diet which is too rich in fats and carbohydrates.

A liver affected with physiological fatty infiltration is larger and heavier than normal, its edges are rounded, while it is yellow or yellowish-brown in colour, soft in consistency and dimples on pressure with the fingers. On section with a knife the tissue projects beyond the cut edge and possesses a fatty lustre, and on microscopical examination the cells of an affected organ are seen to contain single fat globules which may be so large as to displace the cell nucleus to the edge of the cell; the normal cell structure, however, remains intact. The clear, glistening capsule of the liver affected with physiological fatty infiltration is a characteristic feature, for in cloudy swelling and pathological fatty change the capsule has a dull, turgid appearance. All animals in prime condition tend to show a physiological fatty infiltration of the liver and it may commonly be seen in well-nourished lambs and aged very fat cows. The condition very frequently accompanies advanced pregnancy in both cows and ewes and is also seen in many healthy animals slaughtered shortly after parturition. Adverse factors such as fractures, contusions and rough transport, which may occasion considerable physical pain thus resulting in an increase in the amount of adrenalin discharged into the blood stream, may cause changes in the colour in the liver of slaughtered animals to a brownish-yellow or yellow. This change, the so-called " stress liver ", may also be seen in animals slaughtered after travelling long distances without food, or in animals detained in a lairage for undue periods without feeding. In South Africa yellow coloured livers have been encountered in heavily-fleeced sheep transported over long distances in hot weather. In the cases where the untoward stress factor is starvation, it is the internal secretion of the pancreas that is of importance, for owing to the absence of food in the digestive tract the bowel wall fails to produce secretin and there is no production of insulin by the pancreatic gland ; the fat in the body cannot therefore be converted into glycogen and accumulates in the liver. It will be apparent that the increased production of adrenalin or the production of insulin as causal factors in the production of stress liver bears a direct relation to the nature of the stress and the period of its duration.

Physiological fatty infiltration is seen in sheep slaughtered as a result of pregnancy toxaemia (pregnancy disease), an affection which occurs during the last 2 to 4 weeks of pregnancy, usually in well-nourished ewes carrying twins of triplets and often following very severe weather. The condition is attributed to an inadequate supply of carbohydrate in the diet with the result that the liver glycogen is depleted and is replaced by fat, the hepatic fat being thus increased from the normal 3 to 4 per cent. to as much as 35 per cent. Should the animal recover, the liver histology returns completely to normal. Pregnancy toxaemia is a condition unassociated with fever, and slaughtered animals which have bled well may safely be passed for food. A liver affected with physiological fatty infiltration is quite fit for food, though its change in consistency and colour may induce a butcher to suggest that it is unmarketable.

PATHOLOGICAL FATTY INFILTRATION. This condition frequently succeeds cloudy swelling, and is seen as a result of acute febrile and toxaemic conditions, while it also occurs in cases of chemical poisoning by phosphorus, arsenic, chloroform or carbon tetrachloride. In addition, intestinal diseases in cattle such as indigestion are often associated with a pathological fatty infiltration of the liver. Bacterial necrosis of the liver, particularly the acute form, may be accompanied by pathological fatty infiltration, and Danish authorities record that in transit tetany in cattle the liver usually shows a similar fatty change. The organs chiefly affected are the liver, kidneys and heart, which are pale in colour, and in severe cases the liver and kidneys are of a clay-like or reddish colour and are both friable and greasy to the touch. Though the organs may show a uniform change in colour, the fatty change may be irregularly distributed, so that the organ presents a patchy or, more frequently, a spotted appearance. The liver is not usually enlarged, but shrinkage eventually takes place with a wrinkling of the liver capsule, and in extreme pathological fatty change of the heart the organ bears a resemblance to boiled meat; in human medicine this condition is often referred to as " thrush breast ". In pathological fatty change the cell substance, when examined microscopically, is seen to be broken down into numerous fat droplets and the cell nucleus disappears, whereas in physiological fatty change the fat globules are large and displace the intact nucleus to the edge of the cell. Organs affected with pathological fatty infiltration must be regarded as unfit for food.

Pigmentation

Melanosis

The healthy epithelial cells of any pigmented skin, together with the ingrowths of skin such as the mouth and anus, contain a substance in the

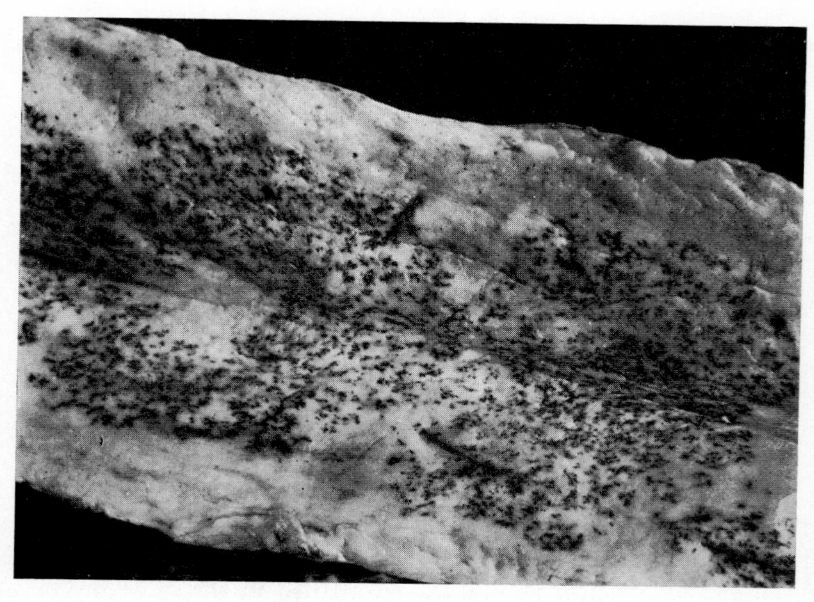

Fig. 55.—Melanosis (seedy cut) of sow's belly.

form of microscopic yellow or black granules which gives the skin its colour. This colouring substance, melanin, is protein in nature and is found not only in the skin but on the surface of the palate, tongue and cheeks of cattle and sheep and in the mouth of dogs. It is also found in the hair, horns and eyes, the deposits being jet-black in colour, of irregular size and shape, and frequently resembling ink splashes.

Abnormal deposits of melanin are encountered chiefly in the calf or ox, but they also occur in the sheep and pig, and there is little doubt that melanosis is congenital and that the pigment is deposited in early foetal life. Melanotic tumours may be seen in any animal, but a particularly malignant form, the melanoma, occurs in the horse. In the ox melanosis is commonly found in the lungs, liver, and on the brain membranes or spinal cord where it usually involves the pia mater, more rarely the dura mater, and is termed by the butcher " black pith ". Black coloration of the kidneys of adult cattle, commonest in animals of the Red Danish breed, is said to be due to deposits of melanin but a similar condition in the kidneys of cattle in Australia has been shown to be due to lipofuscin, an endogenous pigment closely allied to melanin. In calves, the liver and cortex of the kidney are frequently affected, but blackish coloured kidneys also occur in very young calves, the coloration in this case being attributed to biliverdin. In the sheep melanosis is commonest in the liver but the pigmentation in almost all sheep, as well as other animals, grazing in certain districts in Australia is due to lipofuscin, and at Brisbane abattoir about 3 per cent. of livers are condemned annually because of this discoloration. In the pig the common seat of melanotic deposits is in the belly fat or in the udder of females, these deposits being less dense than in the ox or calf and frequently seen as radiating lines or patches distributed along the ducts of the mammary gland. The condition is said to be due to the crossing of a black boar with the white sow, being mainly seen in females, and then only in coloured breeds, but it is becoming rare due to the disappearance of the black pig for bacon purposes.

In addition to the above common sites, melanosis may be found on the pleura or peritoneum, in cartilages and bone, or in the fascia between muscles.

Judgment. The only objection to the sale of flesh or organs affected with deposits of melanin or lipofuscin is from the aesthetic point of view, as the abnormal coloration renders them unmarketable. Affected organs should be condemned ; the pleura, if affected, may be stripped, while the spinal cord or affected vertebrae may be removed. In the pig the belly tissue affected with " seedy cut " may be trimmed off. Where there is involvement of the fascia between muscles the carcase should be jointed and the normal muscular tissue passed for food, but pigmentation which is generalized throughout the muscular tissue requires total condemnation of the carcase.

Three other forms of pigmentation have been occasionally observed in food animals :

Xanthosis

Lipochromes are fat-like substances which contain yellow pigments, including carotene and xanthophylls present in plants eaten by animals. When organs or other tissues undergo atrophy the discoloration becomes very prominent and is yellow, brownish-yellow or almost black. The muscles chiefly affected are the tongue, masseters and heart, though sometimes the diaphragm or muscles of the neck or leg may be affected.

Ochronosis

This affects cattle, calves and horses, and is caused by a yellowish brown or chocolate-coloured pigment which is allied to that causing melanotic deposits. It involves the cartilages, tendon sheaths and joints, and is sometimes generalized.

Osteohaematochromatosis (Plate III)

This is a congenital condition and occurs in calves, young cattle and pigs, affecting all the bones of the skeleton, and is attributed to an iron-containing pigment, porphyrin. A characteristic change in the carcase is the dark brown, chocolate colour of the cut sternum and ribs, though the pleura and peritoneum are normal. Further examination shows all the bones of the skeleton to be affected, including the vertebrae and the bones of the head, while the enamel and roots of the teeth may even be involved, together with the lungs, kidneys, liver and lymph nodes.

In cattle and sheep affected with schistosomiasis a grey pigmentation may be seen of liver, lungs and mucosa of the intestine due to the blood pigment haematin.

Judgment. The above conditions may be judged in exactly a similar manner to melanosis. Where bony structures are alone involved consideration should be given to " boning out " the carcase and releasing the unaffected muscular tissue for food. In local affection of muscles the affected parts need only be removed and condemned, though this procedure may scarcely be justified where melanotic deposits are found in the carcase of a young bobby calf. Generalized involvement of muscular tissues requires total condemnation of the carcase.

Degeneration

This term denotes the breaking down of the complex structure of a tissue or organ into simpler substances. Of the various forms of degeneration that of cloudy swelling is of most importance in meat inspection for it may be associated with fever and severe bacterial intoxication of the live animal.

Cloudy Swelling

This is the simplest of the degenerations and affects the liver, kidney, heart and muscular tissue. Affected organs are slightly enlarged, paler and softer than normal, lustreless and, in pronounced cases, have the appearance of having been boiled. On section with a knife the dull lustreless appearance is more obvious and the swollen tissue bulges on the cut surface.

The changes in cloudy swelling are essentially the breaking down of the cells of tissues or organs into fine granules which are protein in nature, this change being manifested microscopically by a turbidity of the affected cells. The animal may recover from the condition but, where the toxic influences are severe, cloudy swelling may be succeeded by pathological fatty change. An organ affected with cloudy swelling is unmarketable.

Judgment of Degeneration. Cloudy swelling and pathological fatty change are indicative that the animal may have suffered from severe systemic disturbance. Affected organs and muscles are unmarketable and unfit for food, and their detection is an indication for a more detailed examination of the carcase.

Necrosis

Necrosis, or death of tissue which is still part of the living body, occurs chiefly as a result of bacterial or toxic action, or by the arrest of the blood supply to a part. Necrotic tissue is pale and firm, and may be surrounded by an area of hyperaemia, perhaps best illustrated in the infarcts of the kidney or spleen. Necrotic areas which occur superficially, as in the skin, may be sloughed off with the formation of an ulcer, while necrosis of deep-seated tissues or organs may be followed by encapsulation and eventual absorption of the necrotic tissue, with the formation of a scar. On the other hand, the centre of necrotic areas may soften and degenerate, seen typically in the lesions of bacterial necrosis of the ox liver.

Necrosis of fat may be seen in the back fat of pigs, and in the mesentery, brisket fat and kidney fat of cattle ; it is sometimes observed in the kidney fat of the ox where there are liver abscesses in close proximity. It is also encountered in the subpleural, subperitoneal and subcutaneous fat, and is attributed to the enzymes trypsin and steapsin of the pancreatic cells entering the lymph stream. As there are lymphatic connections between the abdominal and thoracic cavities, lesions may also occur in the latter cavity. Necrosis of brisket fat, which occurs in cattle and occasionally in sheep, is termed putty brisket, the necrotic tissue being firm in consistency, dull white or yellowish in colour, and tending to undergo eventual calcification. Dry necrosis of the subcutaneous fat sometimes occurs on the sides

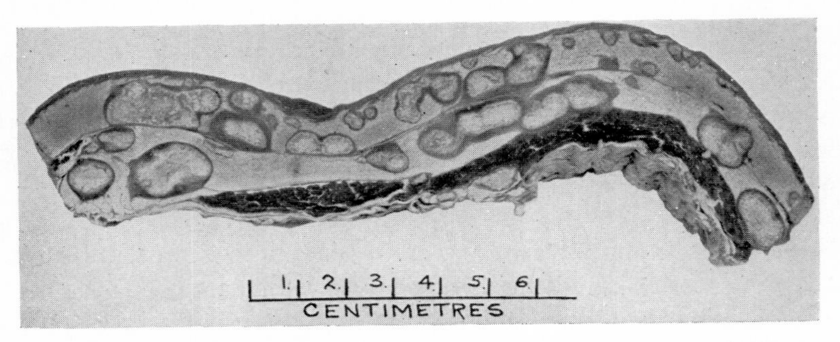

FIG. 56.—Necrosis of back fat of pig. The necrotic areas are lustreless, putty-like, and sharply delimited from the healthy fatty tissue. Eventual absorption of the necrotic tissue may cause a dimpling of the skin surface.

of cattle and is attributed to ante-mortem traumatism, and in New Zealand fat necrosis is often seen in crutched sheep around the tail. The removal and condemnation of necrotic areas is all that is required.

CASEATION

This degenerative change is manifested by the conversion of firm, dry necrotic tissue into a cheesy, pasty mass composed of fine fat droplets and protein granules, and is diagnostic of tuberculosis. Where the defensive mechanism of the body is adequate the caseated material tends to become encapsulated and eventually calcified, but where the defences are inadequate the normal semi-dry consistency of caseation gives place to a creamy yellow fluid which, in tuberculosis particularly, must be regarded as an unfavourable indication.

CALCIFICATION

This denotes the deposit of lime salts in the tissues, and may be regarded as a reaction on the part of the defensive mechanism of the body to enclose and immobilize some foreign agent. It usually occurs in necrotic tissue and is most commonly encountered in connection with chronic tuberculous lesions, or in parasitic infections of the food animals such as trichinosis or *Cysticercus tenuicollis*. Parasitic infections in the sheep, and tuberculous lesions when they occur in that animal, show a marked tendency to undergo calcification.

GANGRENE

This denotes the invasion of necrotic tissue by putrefactive bacteria. Gangrene may occur after an injury to a limb, but in meat inspection is most frequently observed in the udder of the cow as a sequela to septic mastitis, while it also occurs in the lungs of cattle as a result of septic pneumonia following faulty administration of drugs or due to penetration by a foreign body from the reticulum (Fig. 70). It may also be seen in the skin, ears and tail of pigs following an attack of swine erysipelas. Gangrenous tissue is soft, swollen, foul smelling and dark or greenish in colour, and in gangrene of the cow's udder the greenish or violet coloration of the affected tissue is separated from the normal tissue by a well marked haemorrhagic line of demarcation.

Gangrene is a serious indication in meat inspection, and all gangrenous areas should unhesitatingly be condemned. A carcase containing a gangrenous area requires close inspection, and evidence of septicaemic or toxaemic infection requires condemnation of the entire carcase.

Metaplasia

This term is used to denote a change of one kind of tissue into another, and is occasionally observed in meat inspection. Examples of such change are the conversion of the mesenteric fat or pelvic fat into bone, or the conversion of the scar wounds of castrated or spayed pigs into bone. The spaying of gilt pigs to facilitate fattening is regarded with disfavour by bacon curers, for the thin plate of bone which may develop in the flank at the site of the abdominal incision both deteriorates the value of the side of bacon, may damage the bacon-slicing machine, and is unacceptable to the consumer.

Circulatory Disturbance

Hypostasis

Immediately after death the blood may gravitate into the veins of the lowermost parts of the body and cause hypostatic congestion of the skin, which is usually only discernible in pigs. The lungs may also show evidence of hypostatic congestion, most frequently in the ventral and anterior portions of the diaphragmatic lobe of the side on which the animal has been lying, and the condition may be distinguished from lobar pneumonia by the fact that in hypostasis the lung substance is easily penetrated by the fingers.

The above conditions are not necessarily serious, for recumbency may have been due to injury, but the possibility of it being due to an acute or chronic disease must not be lost sight of, and the presence of hypostasis calls for a detailed post-mortem examination.

Thrombosis

This denotes the formation of blood clots within the blood vessels during life. These may be found in any part of the vascular system but must not be confused with post-mortem clots, the result of blood coagulation after death. Post-mortem clots are dark, soft and jelly-like, and easily removed from the blood vessels, though they may become entangled in the chordae tendineae of the heart valves. Thrombi, on the other hand, are adherent to the wall of the blood vessel, are laminated, and tend to become paler; they are frequently found in the heart, particularly on the mitral or tricuspid valves in chronic swine erysipelas.

A thrombus may become absorbed by the development of young connective tissue; on the other hand, it may break down to form emboli.

Embolism

Abnormal substances attached to some part of the vascular system, such as heart vegetations, thrombi or parasites, may become detached and carried with the blood stream to lodge in various organs, particularly the kidneys, lungs, liver or spleen. If these emboli are non-septic in nature they bring about the formation of infarcts, but if septic they produce a pyaemia. In new-born animals detachment of emboli from a septic thrombus in the umbilical vein leads to formation of multiple abscesses in the liver and other organs (Figs. 139, 140).

Infarcts

The spleen, kidneys, brain, heart, lungs, and possibly the liver, possess a peculiarity in that their arteries finally divide into branches having little or no lateral connections with neighbouring arteries. Occlusion of such an artery, either by an embolus or a thrombus, cuts off completely the blood supply to the part, with the result that necrosis develops, the necrotic area being typically wedge-shaped, with the point of the wedge towards the centre of the organ and with its base situated on the organ surface. All infarcts are originally haemorrhagic (Plate 1), but after 48-72 hours red infarcts become pale with a red margin and eventually completely pale or anaemic, and they may be absorbed by connective tissue with the formation of a scar. In the pig kidney, scar formation due to infarcts may result in considerable distortion of the organ, while anaemic infarcts are frequently seen in the kidneys of cows and are often mistaken for tuberculosis. Splenic infarcts of a non-septic nature are often seen in cases of acute swine fever (Fig. 112).

Haemorrhage

This denotes the escape of blood from blood vessels, the commonest cause being wounds or injuries. Where fractures are present, the carcase shows an area around the fracture in which the tissue is suffused with clotted blood, while the surrounding tissues show a jelly-like infiltration; areas of this nature are usually localized, for slaughter is

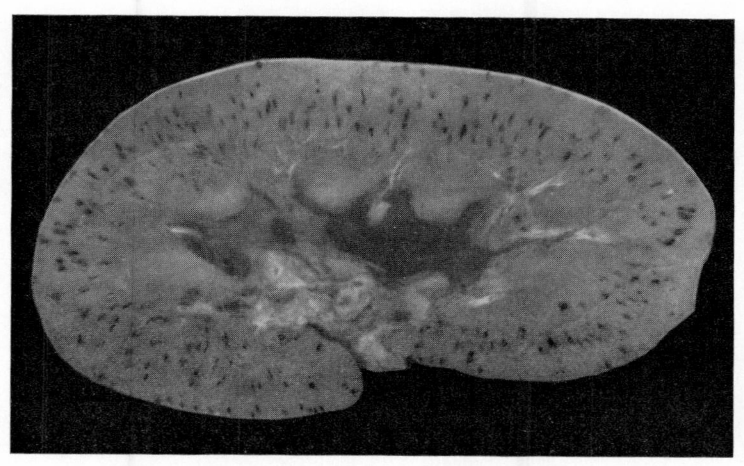

FIG. 57.—Section of pig kidney showing petechial haemorrhages in the superficial and deep cortex. From a case of acute swine fever. (T. M. Doyle.)

generally carried out expeditiously as soon as the injury is observed. It is therefore sufficient to remove the affected tissue, but haemorrhagic and bruised tissue should be removed when the carcase is still warm, otherwise

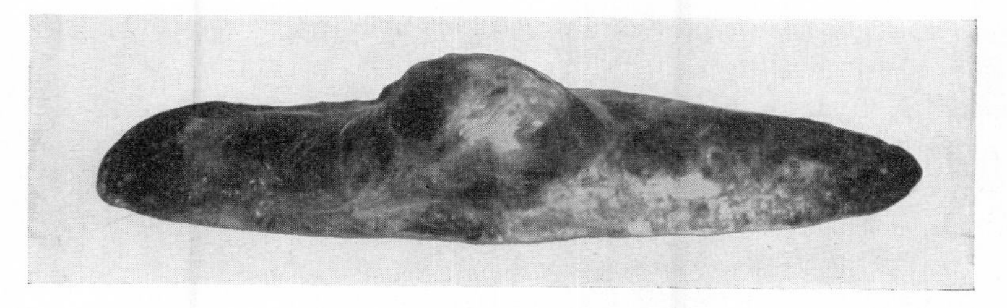

FIG. 58.—Haematoma of ox spleen.

serum will infiltrate downwards between the muscles of the suspended carcase. In many cases it is advisable, where a carcase is badly bruised, to cut it into joints, for the jelly-like infiltration may be found to have extended considerable distances, and removal of affected tissue should be done generously.

Haemorrhage into an organ or tissue results in the formation of a large clot known as a haematoma. This is usually traumatic in nature, and is not uncommonly observed in the spleen of cattle and of pigs. It is a local affection, only requiring condemnation of the affected organ.

A more serious form of haemorrhage in meat inspection are the petechial haemorrhages encountered in septicaemia and in acute infective diseases. These haemorrhages are small, pin-point in size, and are produced by nutritive disturbance of the wall of the capillaries ; they are small because the injury is to the capillary wall and only a small amount of blood escapes (Fig. 52). They may be found on serous or mucous membranes, skin, in the subcutis, fascia, muscles, lymph nodes, and particularly the kidneys, and are unaffected by the bleeding of the animal at slaughter.

Atrophy and Hypertrophy

Atrophy or waste of tissue occurs in muscles and in the internal organs. Though atrophy may be a physiological process, as in the gradual disappearance of the cervical portion of the thymus gland of the calf as age increases, it is usually pathological and associated chiefly with old age or starvation. Pressure atrophy due to interference with the nutrition of a part is also common in meat inspection and is seen typically in hydronephrosis of the kidney as a result of back pressure of urine. Marked atrophy of an organ requires its condemnation.

Hypertrophy is the opposite condition to atrophy, and is manifested by an increase in the size and number of cells of which an organ is composed. It may occur physiologically, as in the mammary glands during pregnancy, but is seen in pathological form in the increase in size of one organ in order that it may do the work of another ; compensatory hypertrophy of the healthy kidney may occur when one kidney has undergone congenital atrophy or is affected with hydronephrosis. An organ which is hypertrophied is perfectly marketable.

Tumours

As the incidence of tumours increases with the age of the animal, the fact that most of the food animals are slaughtered early in life renders tumour formation uncommon.

Distinction must be drawn between the simple or benign tumours such as the papillomata of the ox skin or mucous membranes, and malignant tumours such as sarcomas and carcinomas, which spread by the blood or lymph stream and form metastases in distant organs and parts. When malignant growths are found, usually in visceral organs and most often in the liver, search should be made for metastases in the lymph nodes draining the organ or in other visceral organs ; it may be necessary to divide the carcase into joints and examine these for evidence of secondary growths. Lymphosarcomas are of most importance in domestic stock and may be found in all the species of food animals, particularly in cattle and pigs. In the United States the neoplasms most commonly encountered in cattle are epithelioma and lymphosarcomas.

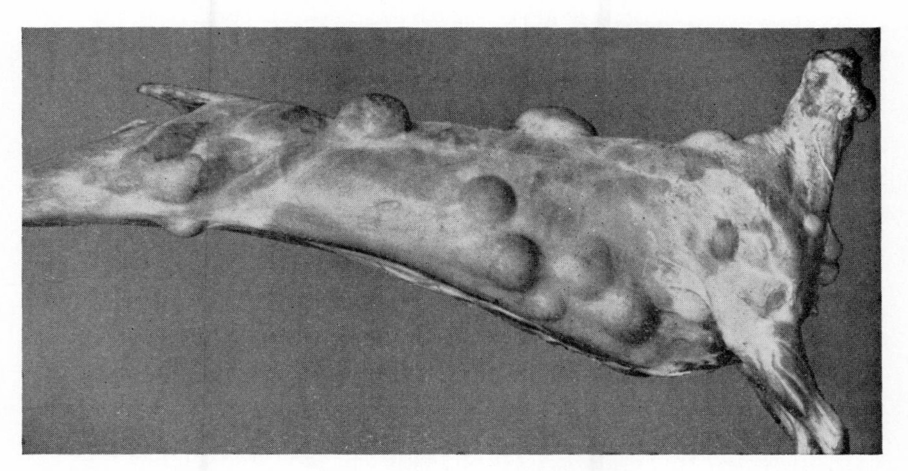

FIG. 59.—Multiple sarcomata in carcase of a ewe. The histological report indicated that the neoplasm was a highly malignant one and had extensively infiltrated the muscles.

Judgment. The presence of a benign tumour requires condemnation of the affected organ. Malignant growths may be treated similarly, though it is advisable that the carcase be jointed and, as stated, examination made of muscle, bone and lymph nodes. The objection to the consumption of meat which contains neoplasms is largely an aesthetic one, and judgment should not be unnecessarily severe. In the United States, Federal regulations prescribe that any individual organ or part of a carcase affected with a malignant neoplasm should be condemned ; if the malignant neoplasm involves any internal organ to a marked extent or affects the muscles, skeleton or carcase lymph nodes, even primarily, the carcase shall be condemned. If metastasis has occurred to any other organ or part of a carcase, or if metastasis has not occurred but there are present secondary changes in the muscles (serous infiltration, flabbiness or the like) the carcase shall be condemned.

Flesh of Foetuses and Stillborn Animals

At one time it was a not uncommon practice for unscrupulous butchers to market the flesh of unborn or stillborn calves, though such carcases were rarely sold as retail joints of meat, but were minced or used as an ingredient of sausage. The glycogen content of foetal veal is high, about

1·6 per cent. in a nearly full-time calf, but the submission that a sausage which contained flesh with a high glycogen content was indicative of the addition of foetal veal might be contested on the ground that liver, which also contains a high percentage of glycogen, had been added during the sausage manufacture. Horse flesh, too, contains appreciable amounts of glycogen, and deductions made from a high glycogen content in mince or sausage may be severely tested in a court of law and should only be advanced with caution.

It is doubtful whether consumption of the flesh of unborn or stillborn calves would be prejudicial to health, but the sale of such flesh is unjustifiable for the following reasons :

(*a*) Consumption of the flesh of unborn animals is repugnant to most of the civilized races.

(*b*) The commonest cause of dairy cows giving birth to stillborn calves is infection with *Brucella abortus*, the infective micro-organism being present in large numbers throughout the system of such aborted calves, and the entry of *Br. abortus* into the human system may give rise to undulant fever. Again, a proportion of cows suffering from tuberculous metritis may give birth to stillborn calves which are likely to be affected with congenital tuberculosis, and on these grounds the flesh of foetal or stillborn animals may justifiably be condemned.

The undressed foetal or stillborn calf may be recognized by the following signs :

(*a*) The skin presents a sodden appearance, the claws are soft and yellowish and the pads of the sole convex, a condition usually referred to as the " golden slipper ".

(*b*) The remains of the umbilical cord can be seen attached to the open umbilical ring, while the umbilical arteries and veins are patent and contain liquid blood.

(*c*) The stomach and intestines are free of coagulated milk, and the lungs are collapsed (atelectasis) and sink in water. Though the throat may have been cut to simulate bleeding, the edges of the throat wound in unborn calves are not infiltrated with blood.

When the carcase has been dressed the hoofs, intestinal tract and umbilical cord will have been removed, but the points of origin of the umbilical arteries from the internal iliac arteries will be apparent, the ductus arteriosus and urachus are wide open, the entire carcase has a sodden appearance, and the muscles are loose and flabby.

Occasionally a new-born calf may live for a brief period after birth, and in the lungs of these animals a few lobules may be seen inflated with air, while other lobules and portions of lung tissue are collapsed due to blocking of certain branches of the bronchi with amniotic fluid and phlegm aspirated at birth ; small collapsed areas of lung tissue are indicative, then, that the calf lungs have not fully functioned after birth. It was at one time a practice to attempt to deceive inspectors by artificial inflation of the lungs of foetal or stillborn calves, but lungs so inflated may be recognized by the fact that the individual lung lobules are distended in varying degrees, several lobules showing evidence of alveolar emphysema, while small ruptures of lung tissue give rise to an interstitial or subpleural emphysema.

The skin of foetal calves has a value in the fur trade and the skinning of such animals is therefore permissible.

Immaturity

The only food animal which is likely to be slaughtered and exposed for sale whilst in an immature condition is the calf, though immature carcases of pigs, kids and lambs may occasionally be encountered.

The seizure of immature carcases is justified for the following reasons: (*a*) The consumption of the flesh of newly born or very young animals, though admittedly not prejudicial to health, is repugnant to the vast majority of purchasers, and flesh is usually regarded as unwholesome until the muscle and fat has reached a stage of development which brings it within the definition of meat in the generally accepted sense of the word ; (*b*) Grounds for seizure may also be based on the fact that immature veal contains little or no fat, has a high proportion of water (usually over 76 per cent.) and a high proportion of bone. Its value as a food in terms of calorific value, satiety value and palatability is therefore so low that a purchaser of immature veal is largely buying bone and water at meat prices, and the sale of such meat may therefore be described as fraudulent and on these grounds should be forbidden.

The necessity for slaughter of young calves is in most countries controlled by economic factors, for it is considered unremunerative by farmers to retain bull calves of dairy breeds until they are 3 to 4 months old. They are therefore sold and slaughtered within a few days of birth, and it is the carcases of such animals that may come within the classification of immaturity.

Legislation is in force in some countries, and formerly in Germany, by which the marketing of veal from animals less than 3 weeks old is prohibited, while in other countries, including Britain and Denmark, it is now the rule to judge such carcases not on their age but on the condition and degree of development of the meat and fat. On the Continent, where veal is an esteemed article of diet, calves are regularly slaughtered when 6 to 8 days old, and in the United States each State has its own regulation concerning the age at which calves may be slaughtered, ranging from the statement that veal must be wholesome (Pennsylvania), to 3, 4, 6 or 8 weeks of age. In the Australian State of Victoria no person may sell for human consumption a veal carcase of less weight than 40 lb., including the skin but excluding the entrails, head and feet, or if such calf is less than 14 days old. The following code of judgment is prescribed in the United States Federal regulations:

"Carcases of young calves, pigs, kids and lambs are unwholesome and shall be condemned if:

(*a*) the meat has the appearance of being water-soaked, is loose, flabby, tears easily, and can be perforated with the fingers; or

(*b*) Its colour is greyish-red; or

(*c*) Good muscular development as a whole is lacking, especially noticeable on the upper shank of the leg, where small amounts of serous infiltrates or small oedematous patches are sometimes present between the muscles; or

(*d*) The tissue which later develops as the fat capsule of the kidneys is oedematous, dirty yellow or greyish-red, tough and intermixed with islands of fat."

In the Meat Inspection Regulations 1963, which are applicable to England and Wales, it is prescribed that the inspector shall regard as unfit for human consumption any stillborn or unborn carcase and any immature carcase which is oedematous or in poor physical condition, together with any offal or blood collected therefrom.

The estimation of the age of a calf may be of value in support of the seizure of a carcase of veal for immaturity, and may be arrived at by examination of the hoofs, teeth, and umbilicus. In the newly born calf the hoofs are soft and have conical processes on their solar surface. At birth calves are usually born with eight incisor teeth, but if only six are present at birth the last pair will erupt in 2 to 6 days. The gum is at first highly reddened and almost covers the incisors, but in 7 to 10 days it retracts and assumes a more rounded form; a calf in which the gum tissue still shows traces of blue coloration is not more than 5 days old, while if retraction of the gums is complete it is at least 10 days old. After a fortnight the central and lateral central incisors have assumed their free, shovel formation, and in 20 days this free, shovel shape is apparent on the corner incisors. By 1 month all the incisor teeth have emerged from the gums, which now possess their permanent pale pink coloration.

The umbilical cord becomes dry and black in 4 to 5 days, and falls off from the umbilicus between the 8th and 16th day to leave a sensitive surface which is soon covered by a scab. In 2 to 3 weeks the umbilicus forms a cicatrix or scar, the scab disappearing after 4 weeks. Infection of the umbilicus by pyogenic organisms, which frequently occurs at birth, will delay the process of healing, but in all cases the umbilical vein is open and filled with liquid blood during the first week of life. It may also be noted that during the first 2 weeks of life the kidneys are of a deep violet-red or greenish colour.

Poorness

Poorness or leanness is a physiological condition caused by an intake of nutriment inadequate for the animal's normal requirements, and is seen in young growing animals, in cows which are milking heavily, or in those on an insufficient diet ; all young growing animals at some stage of their life and all store animals, as in many Irish imported cattle, come within the definition of poorness.

The condition is characterized by the sparse development of fatty tissue, but a certain amount remains in particular locations, such as the orbits of the eyes, even although it may have disappeared almost entirely from the intermuscular and subserous tissue. Such fat that is present on the carcase is of normal appearance and composition, and the muscular tissue is firm though darker than normal.

Physiological leanness is of no significance in meat inspection, for though the meat is tough due to an increased development of connective tissue in the muscles, the carcases of such animals are marketable and have a definite value for manufactured food products.

Emaciation

Emaciation is a pathological condition which develops during the course of an illness, and is due to a lowering of the intake of food during illness or to an increase in the normal metabolic rate of the animal. It may develop rapidly as a result of acute disease, but frequently it is a chronic condition associated with such bovine diseases as tuberculosis or Johne's disease, and it is a characteristic of the latter affection that atrophy of the muscular tissues occurs before there is a loss of carcase fat. In sheep, emaciation is most often caused by parasitic infections, including fascioliasis and round-worm infestation of the stomach and intestines, while emaciation in the pig presents the most striking post-mortem appearance, as this animal is normally well endowed with fat both on the carcase surface and in the body cavities. In the pig emaciation is usually the result of swine fever, swine erysipelas or pig paratyphoid.

Emaciation is characterized by an abnormal retrogression in the bodily condition of the animal, together with a diminution in the size of the organs, particularly the liver and spleen, and muscular tissue, but the outstanding characteristic is a diminution in the amount of body fat and an alteration in its consistency. The locations which normally carry fat, including the subcutaneous tissue and the perirenal, subserous and intermuscular connective tissue, are shrunken, and such fat that remains in these positions is of abnormal appearance, being infiltrated and having a jelly-like consistency and a sickly yellow colour. The loss of intermuscular

FIG. 60.—Cow affected with tuberculous emaciation. Note the tightness of skin over the ribs, the dull eye, and that the head is held low and "poked out".

fat gives rise to a loose, flabby appearance of the muscular tissue, which may be pale should emaciation be accompanied by anaemia; there is also an increase in the connective tissue of muscles resulting from atrophy of the actual muscular cells. On chemical analysis of the flesh of emaciated animals there is an increase in water compared with that in the normal carcase, but there is a decrease in the proportions of protein, fat and inorganic salts. In extremely emaciated animals the percentage of water present in muscle is about 80 and the percentage of protein about 19, giving a ratio of water to protein of over four to one; in lean but healthy animals the percentage of water is not above 76·5 and the percentage of protein about 22, and the water-protein ratio is therefore less than four to one. It is suggested that the ratio between water and protein may be of value in distinguishing between carcases which are very thin and those which are emaciated. The lymph nodes, especially in young emaciated animals, are enlarged and oedematous, and the marrow of the long bones is red, watery, poor in fat or may be replaced by a damp slimy material. An emaciated carcase does not set in the normal manner and has a moist appearance both on its surface and in the body cavities, the changes in the consistency of the fat being well seen around the base of the heart, the mediastinum, the kidney region or between the spinous processes of the vertebrae.

Judgment of the emaciated carcase is based on the degree of wasting and on the nature of the disease. Tuberculosis with emaciation justifies total condemnation of the carcase, and many bovine animals in Britain, particularly cows, show evidence of emaciation as a result of Johne's disease. In "border-line" cases of emaciation, where there is little obvious sign of disease sufficient to cause the condition, it is sometimes advisable to detain the carcase for 12 hours; at the end of this period there may be considerable drying of the body cavities and, in the absence of serous infiltrations of the muscles, the carcase may receive a favourable judgment. Emaciation and oedema frequently coexist in the same carcase and the testing of the bone marrow for water content will assist the judgment in such cases. Emaciated carcases which show marked change in the consistency of the carcase fat, together with serous infiltration of the connective tissue between the muscles, should be condemned. Federal regulations in the United States prescribe that carcase of animals too emaciated or anaemic to produce wholesome meat, and carcases which show a slimy degeneration of the fat or a serous infiltration of the muscles, shall be condemned.

Abnormal Odours

Abnormal odours are commonly encountered in carcases or in meat, and may be acquired from outside sources, as from the consumption of certain foodstuffs, from drugs administered as medicine, or by the absorption of the odour of strong smelling substances whilst the meat is stored. Abnormal odours may also be intrinsic, as in the odour of acetone in the carcase of cows, or in the sexual odour of certain male animals.

The causes of abnormal odours in meat may be classified as follows:

1. FEEDING. The most common example of abnormal odour acquired as a result of feeding is the fishy odour of pig flesh due to excessive feeding on fish meal, and results in pork or bacon with a fishy odour and taste, while the fat of the carcase is soft in consistency and greyish-yellow in colour. Fishiness in pork or bacon is attributed to the high percentage of fat present in fish meal, and it can therefore be avoided if the fat content

of the meal is lowered to between 3 and 7 per cent., but although it is claimed that the fishy odour in pork can be obviated if the feeding of fish meal is discontinued 6 weeks prior to slaughter, it is questionable whether this period is sufficient and a minimum of 4 months should be regarded as a safer period. The feeding of cod-liver oil, particularly the cheaper brands, to pigs also produces pork or bacon with a fishy odour and brownish coloration of the fat, and it is the practice in Denmark that where pigs are to be slaughtered for bacon at 7 months old the feeding of cod-liver oil is discontinued after the animal has reached 110 lb. live weight; where pigs are fed on restaurant swill the flesh may possess a similar odour and taste to that of pigs fed on fish meal. In cattle an abnormal odour of the flesh is observed when animals are slaughtered after being moved from grass in the autumn and feeding on turnips has commenced; this turnipy odour in the flesh of cattle is only present during the first week of turnip feeding, and the continuance of root feeding after that period produces no odour. A turnipy odour of the flesh may also be present in carcases of bovines slaughtered due to obstruction or rupture of the oesophagus by a portion of root, and the odour may be so marked as to render the carcase unmarketable. In sheep the feeding of turnips rarely produces an abnormal odour of the flesh, but a rancid odour and soapy taste may occur in the flesh of sheep fed on fermenting beet; this would appear to be due to the beatine present in beet, for the feeding of sugar-beet tops in excessive quantities to cows is known to produce an abnormal flavour of the milk. The eating of young garlic leaves by rabbits and sometimes cattle gives the carcases a strong odour resembling phosphorus.

2. Absorption of Odours. Abnormal odours and taste of flesh due to the administration of drugs are commonly encountered in cattle, particularly in dairy cows, and attention should be paid in emergency slaughtered animals to the stomach contents, detection of an odour of drugs calling for an examination as to whether the odour is also present in the flesh. Drugs which may affect the meat adversely in this way are linseed oil, turpentine, carbolic acid, ether, chloroform, asafoetida, nitrous spirits of ether, aromatic spirits of ammonia, and aniseed. In addition, it is inadvisable to administer aloes, magnesium sulphate, treacle, chloral hydrate and bromides to animals which are likely to require emergency slaughter; the odour of drugs persists longest in the thickest parts of the carcase. Apart from abnormal odours caused by the administration of drugs shortly before slaughter, abnormal odours may occasionally occur due to the inspiration of air containing the vapour of chlorine or carbolic acid used in the cleansing of transport vehicles. The drinking of water impregnated with tar may likewise render the flesh unmarketable.

Certain of the chlorinated hydrocarbons, including D.D.T., used externally on animals as insecticides and ascarides, may accumulate in the fat as a result of spraying or by the animal consuming contaminated feeds, and in the United States the fat of meat in interstate commerce may not contain more than 7 p.p.m. of D.D.T. Organo-phosphorus compounds are also used externally for a similar purpose but do not create a hazard to the consumer when properly used on animals destined for slaughter.

In the imported meat trade the absorption of abnormal odours by refrigerated meat during transport or storage is a common cause of depreciation of value and even of condemnation. Meat tainted by the odour of oranges or citrus fruit may occur during a sea voyage if the fruit becomes over-ripe or unsound and the excessive generation of gas filters through to an accompanying meat cargo. Such odours are readily absorbed by meat, particularly by the fat, and odours of oil or tar in meat may occur in a similar way.

3. Products of Abnormal Metabolism. The existence of a peculiar odour, described as sweet but repugnant, is frequently observable in the flesh of cattle which have been affected with fever, or which were close to parturition prior to slaughter; it is often apparent also in cows suffering from milk fever which have been slaughtered owing to failure to respond to treatment by calcium injections. This odour is caused by appreciable amounts of acetone present in the flesh and is most readily detected in the large connective tissue sheets, in the kidney fat or in the muscular tissue. The odour, which does not disappear from the meat even when grilled, may be sufficient to render it unfit for sale, and for this reason a boiling test should always be applied on the flesh of animals slaughtered while suffering from fever, or those in an advanced stage of gestation, especially where the liver shows evidence of fatty change.

4. Sexual Odour. In male animals the meat may possess an abnormal odour and taste, which may be so marked as to lower its marketability and depreciate its value. This sexual odour, which is specific for each animal and may be described as resembling stale urine, is markedly apparent in the boar and male goat, though of little or no significance in bulls and rams. In boars it can be prevented by treatment of the animal with oestrogens. In castrated boars, i.e. stags, the degree of odour depends on the the length of time between castration and slaughter, as well as on the age of the pig and the length of time it has been used for breeding; it is most marked in older, coarser, animals. Boar odour persists in flesh for a considerable time after the animal is castrated and, according to Danish authorities, can only be completely obviated if the boar pig is castrated before it is 4 months old; about 11 days after castration the meat is odourless, but the boar odour persists in the fat for 10 weeks before it finally disappears. In Denmark boar carcases are marked with a special

boar stamp, for it is appreciated that the odour is not sufficient to warrant complete condemnation of the carcase, and the purpose of the boar stamp is to draw attention to the fact that the meat is not suitable for ordinary cooking or frying, but may be used for manufacture of sausage. A pronounced sexual odour may also be present in the flesh of cryptorchid pigs, and the carcases of hermaphrodite pigs often possess an abnormal odour, which, however, is distinguishable from the odour of boars.

Male sexual odour is most apparent in the meat immediately after slaughter, particularly in the fatty tissues and while the carcase is still warm. The odour largely disappears as the carcase cools but may reappear when the meat is boiled or fried, and for this reason animals exhibiting a marked sexual odour immediately after slaughter are detained for 24 hours in German and Danish abattoirs and a boiling test then applied to a portion of flesh.

In Denmark regard is also paid to the sexual odour which may be present in the gilt or sow, and though this odour disappears from the flesh in 3 weeks after slaughter, it may persist in the subcutaneous fat for 2½ months. The sow odour is most marked in the parotid salivary gland, and it is the practice to apply a boiling test to this gland and, if the female sexual odour be present, to subject portions of meat and fat to a further boiling test.

Judgment of Abnormal Odours. In Britain the meat of boars, of castrated boars and cryptorchid pigs (rigs) is of lower value than the flesh of sows because of the boar odour. The flesh of these animals and of sows is, however, used regularly as an ingredient of sausage, and the existence of a sexual odour cannot be regarded as justification for seizure of the meat as unfit for human food. In addition, the low price paid for such meat is sufficient to ensure that the practice of slaughtering boars is not encouraged, while the boar odour is minimized if the carcase be expeditiously cooled after slaughter, and largely disappears during the mincing and preparation for sausage. It is, however, inadvisable to add more than one part of boar meat to 20 parts of other meat ingredient. In England and Wales the Meat Inspection Regulations 1963 prescribe that the presence in a carcase of abnormal odour associated with disease or other conditions prejudicial to health shall be regarded as rendering the carcase, offal and blood unfit for human consumption. Regulations in the United States which apply to Federally inspected plants prescribe that carcases which give off the odour of urine or a sexual odour shall be condemned, but when the final inspection of carcases is deferred until they have been chilled the disposal shall be determined by the heating test.

Flesh with a pronounced odour of drugs or disinfectants must be regarded as unfit if the abnormal taste and smell are still apparent by a boiling test after the carcase has been detained for 24 hours. A marked and persistent fishy odour in pork may be regarded as sufficient to render the flesh unmarketable, and it should be condemned. In imported meat the odour caused by absorption of gases from cargoes of fruit during storage, and also superficial taint in meat due to oil or tar, can be removed almost entirely by subjecting the meat to long periods of ozonization.

BOILING TEST FOR ABNORMAL ODOUR AND TASTE

Abnormal odours, and particularly the male sexual odour, are most apparent immediately after slaughter and before the meat and fat have cooled ; these odours may disappear after cooling but reappear when the meat is cooked, and for this reason a boiling test for abnormal odour should not be carried out on meat until a period of 24 hours after slaughter has elapsed. A further factor in favour of adopting a 24 hours' waiting period is that the meat of freshly killed animals subjected to the boiling test has a specific odour which may be confused with sex odour or other abnormal odours.

The boiling test is carried out as follows : A pan should be filled with cold water and in it should be placed a piece of meat the size of the palm of the hand and preferably rich in fat. The pan lid is replaced, the water brought to the boil and, when boiling commences, the lid should be lifted and the vapour smelled ; the odour is often more readily detected as the water begins to cool. When the meat is boiled completely its taste, and that of the liquid also, should be noted, for an abnormal odour in meat is frequently accompanied by an abnormal taste. It is claimed by some that abnormal odours may be better detected by frying a portion of the meat than by boiling, especially in estimating the marketability of the fatty tissues. The application of the frying test to meat containing no fat may be carried out if a small amount of clean normal fat be previously added to the frying pan.

Advanced Pregnancy

The objection to the slaughtering of an animal carrying a nearly full-time foetus is that the purchaser who buys the animal alive obtains, in the case of the cow, some 80 lb. of useless material, whilst slaughter also prevents the birth of what may have proved to be a valuable animal. Though the flesh of the hindquarters of an animal slaughtered in advanced pregnancy may be somewhat moister than normal and the liver, particularly if the animal has travelled long distances shortly before slaughter, may show a degree of physiological fatty change, there is no scientific foundation for the condemnation of such a carcase provided no odour of acetone can be detected, but where the foetus or foetuses have died *in utero* and putrefactive changes are present in the maternal uterus, the carcase should be condemned.

Extra-uterine Pregnancy

This is a rare condition, occurring when the fertilized ovum develops outside the uterus and in the abdominal cavity. Development of the ovum may take place in the Fallopian tube, which becomes distended and eventually ruptured as the foetus grows, the mummified foetus being found embedded in fat in the abdominal wall. The condition is usually observed in the ewe and may be treated as a local one by removal of the foetus and surrounding tissues from the abdominal wall.

Recent Parturition

Regulations in the United States which apply to Federally inspected abattoirs provide that carcases of animals in advanced stages of pregnancy (showing signs of parturition), also carcases of animals which have within 10 days given birth to young and in which there is no evidence of septic infection, may be passed for sterilization, otherwise they shall be condemned. There is little doubt that this judgment is too severe, and there is usually no justification for condemnation of an animal which has recently delivered its young provided that the parturition is unaccompanied by septic or toxic infection.

Oestrum and its Effect on the Carcase

It is contended, particularly amongst those who slaughter and cure their own pigs for bacon, that the slaughter of a sow or gilt during its period of " heat " will produce bacon of poor keeping quality and liable to taint. This empirical belief may have a certain scientific foundation (see p. 450), though thousands of gilts and sows are slaughtered during oestrum in bacon factories, and without any subsequent deleterious effect on the meat. It is a further belief, still widely held in country districts, that no woman during menstruation should be permitted to participate in the slaughter or curing of pigs for pork, as it is maintained that her presence will cause subsequent taint of the bacon; this contention is entirely erroneous.

CHAPTER VI

AFFECTIONS OF SPECIFIC PARTS

1. Skin.
2. Digestive System, including Pancreas, Spleen and Peritoneum.
3. Respiratory System.
4. Circulatory System and Blood, including Icterus, Uraemia and Milk Fever.
5. Excretory System.
6. Reproductive System, including Uterus and Udder.
7. Lymphatic System.
8. Skeletal System, including Joints.
9. Muscular System.
10. Nervous System.

1. AFFECTIONS OF THE SKIN

The hair in cattle, and the wool in sheep, render the recognition of skin discoloration difficult, and it is only in the pig that skin changes can readily be detected. Acute skin congestion in the pig may be widespread, or it may be confined to local areas ; it is seen in swine fever, swine erysipelas (Fig. 115), urticaria, pig paratyphoid, transit erythema, swine pox and heatstroke, the skin changes being greatly accentuated after the carcase has been scalded. Urticaria, or nettle rash, is attributed to dietetic errors and is characterized by small circular areas or weals on the skin all over the body ; the rash can be distinguished from that formed in swine erysipelas, as urticaria is usually seen in the form of circular weals which are seldom more than ½ inch in diameter, and when the weals burst they leave small circumscribed red areas all over the body. It is a local condition having no effect on the marketability of the carcase, though removal of the skin may be necessary before the carcase is released.

Transit erythema usually affects pigs travelling on long journeys by rail, and takes the form of red patches on the skin where the animal's warm body has come in contact with the floor ; the affection is usually localized along the belly and hams, and is attributed to the irritant effect of disinfectant and urine on the floor of the railway truck, it may also occur in pigs transported in winter after being moved from a heated sty. Affected portions may usually be skinned off, but where the irritation is severe, with extravasations of blood into the subcutaneous fat, it becomes necessary to remove all discoloured adipose tissue, and in very severe cases the lymph nodes may be congested and the carcase so " fevered " in appearance as to require condemnation. In the slaughterhouse a diffuse reddening of the skin occurs in pigs which gain entry to the scalding tub when alive or which are stunned and placed in the tub before bleeding and reflex movements have ceased. The absence of lymph node congestion facilitates diagnosis in such carcases, which may usually be skinned and released for food.

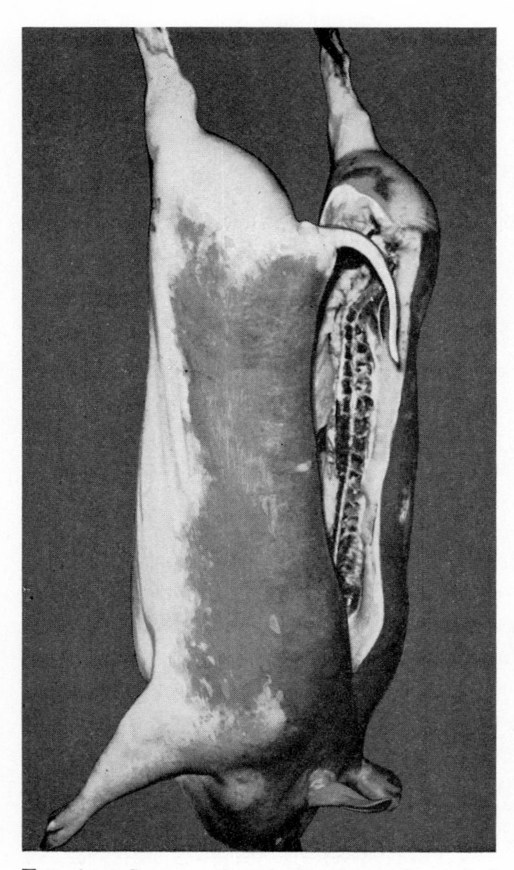

FIG. 61.—Carcase of pork showing well marked transit erythema caused by exposure of the live animal to the cold air during transport by motor vehicle to the slaughterhouse. The reddening in this acute skin congestion is due to the abundance of red blood corpuscles in the dilated skin capillaries.

Acute skin congestion must be distinguished from post-mortem skin discoloration which occurs in the dependent parts of the body, is purple in colour, and disappears on pressure with the fingers as the blood is intracapillary and does not clot. Hypostatic engorgement of the subcutaneous blood vessels may be observed if an animal has been recumbent for some time and this, together with a purplish post-mortem discoloration of dependent parts, as in the jowl and abdomen of the pig, forms a ready means for the detection of the dead animal.

Of the specific diseases, glanders may be manifested on the horse skin by a knotted, cord-like condition of the lymphatic vessels or by ulceration, and similar superficial lesions may be observed in epizootic lymphangitis of the same animal. Cloven-footed animals affected with foot and mouth disease may show vesicles or ulcers on the lips and muzzle or on the skin around the hoofs (Figs. 103, 104). Tuberculous ulceration of the skin in either the ox or pig is extremely rare, but in the ox local nodules or abscesses occur beneath the skin and constitute the so-called tuberculous " skin lesions " (Fig. 131). Necrosis of the tail and tips of the ears may occur in pigs as a sequela to an attack of acute swine erysipelas.

Sheep and swine pox are extremely rare in Britain, but varying stages of the affection may be seen, ranging from the formation of a papule to that of a vesicle, pustule and crust. Similar lesions, chiefly involving the lips and feet, occur in contagious pustular dermatitis, or orf, in sheep (Fig 9); the disease is mainly seen in lambs in the border districts of Scotland, but in meat inspection may be regarded as a local condition necessitating condemnation of the affected parts, though care should be taken in handling the latter for it is a virus infection transmissible to man. Subcutaneous emphysema may be encountered in connection with specific disease, as in cattle affected with black-quarter or in malignant oedema in horses, but it may also be traumatic in origin and associated with injury to the trachea or thoracic cavity. In the latter affection the subcutaneous tissue of the forequarter, particularly along the back and sides, is distended and puffy, but the condition, being of local significance, only requires condemnation of the affected musculature.

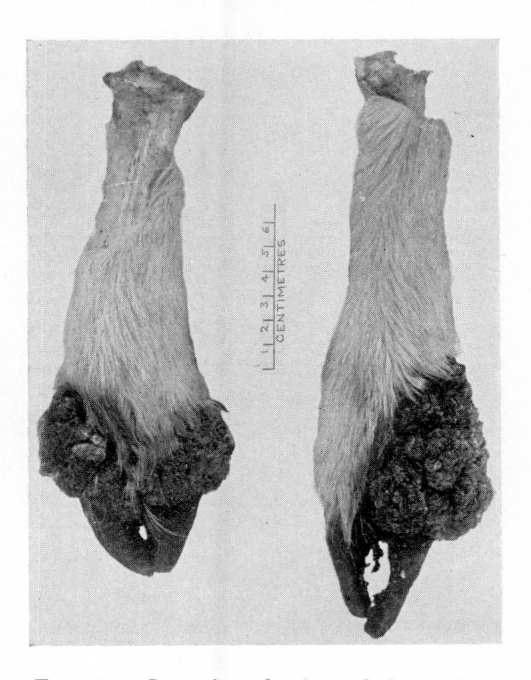

FIG. 62.—Contagious foot rot of sheep, showing marked development of granulation tissue around the coronet. Affected animals have difficulty in feeding and may become rapidly emaciated. The same causal organism (*Fusiformis necrophorus*) is responsible for calf diphtheria.

Common skin affections in young oxen are ringworm and papillomata, the so-called angleberries, but these are of no significance in meat inspection, for the skin of cattle is removed at slaughter. Contagious foot rot may be seen around the coronet of sheep and may be the cause of emaciation, while foot rot of a non-contagious form, which primarily involves the horny tissue, may also be seen. In pigs hypotrichosis cystica, or " shotty eruption " of the skin, is frequently observed and consists of numerous hard circular papules in which curled-up bristles may be found. The condition is not an infective process but a disturbance of growth in which the hair follicle does not develop properly, the hair being retained in the hair sac, with dilatation of the sac by a dark liquid which consists of the secretion from the sebaceous glands together with desquamated epithelial cells. As the skin of the pig is consumed as part of the joints of pork, constituting the " crackling ", all local skin lesions, including shotty eruption, mange, eczema, or marked skin discoloration, should be dealt with by removal of the affected parts. Awns of stipa grass may occasionally be present in the subcutaneous tissue of carcases of mutton in Africa, South America and Australia.

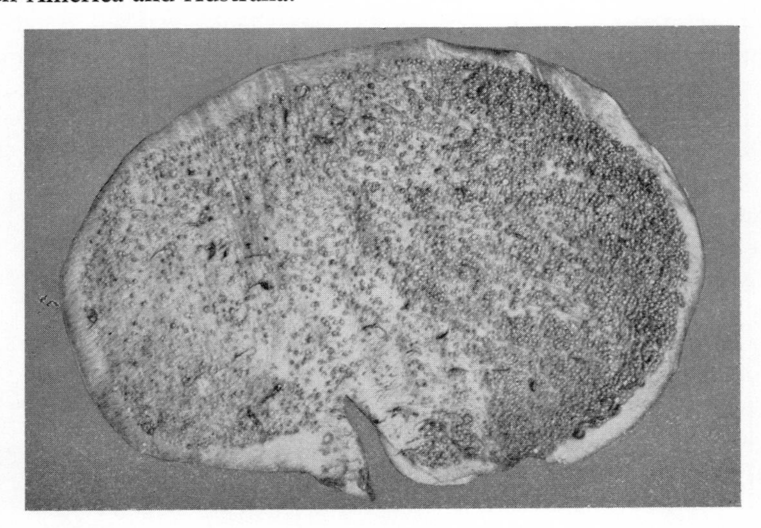

FIG. 63.—Shotty eruption of skin of pig. Scalding and scraping of the carcase have not removed the papules and curled up bristles which characterize the affection.

2. AFFECTIONS OF THE DIGESTIVE SYSTEM

Head and Tongue

Most of the affections of head and tongue are of a specific nature, and include actinomycosis (Fig. 90), actinobacillosis (Fig. 93), foot and mouth disease (Fig. 103), catarrhal stomatitis, cattle plague, atrophic rhinitis and fowl pox (Fig. 228). In rinderpest occurring in calves there is a diphtheritic inflammation, with cheese-like deposits in mouth and pharynx, and necrotic areas on the tongue or gums are seen in calf diphtheria (Fig. 99), and may simulate foot and mouth disease. Swelling of the tongue is a symptom in haemorrhagic septicaemia. In rabbit myxomatosis (Fig. 224) the eyes are shrunken into the swollen eyelids, which may be encrusted with dry matter.

The commonest lesions of tuberculosis in the ox head are found in the retropharyngeal lymph nodes, and in the pig in the submaxillary nodes, both of which may be primary infections ; post-pharyngeal abscesses in pigs are generally traumatic in origin and due to swallowing of some sharp foreign body with the food.

Of the parasitic conditions, *Cysticercus bovis* may be found in the internal and external muscles of mastication of the ox (Fig. 172), or in the musculature of the oesophagus, heart, tongue or diaphragm. Larvae of *Hypoderma lineatum* may be encountered in the oesophagus of the ox (Fig. 190), though the larvae of *Hypoderma bovis* are not found in this position, while sarcosporidia are frequently seen in the oesophagus of adult sheep (Fig. 182) and bear a resemblance to pieces of fat or small abscesses. Nematodes of the genus *Gongylonema* are commonly found in the mucosa of the oesophagus of sheep and cattle slaughtered in the United States, South America and Europe, these being small, filiform worms lying parallel to the long axis of the oesophagus and assuming a typical spiral formation; their economic significance is that they render the oesophagus undesirable for use in meat food products. In pigs *Gongylonema pulchrum*, ½ to 1½ inches in length, is found in the mucosa of the tongue, pharynx and oesophagus, the affection being particularly common in the Southern States of America, and it is the practice to treat infested tongues by scalding in water at a temperature of 145° F. or higher, drenching in cold water, and stripping off the mucous membrane.

Stomach and Intestines

Peptic ulcers are frequently found in the abomasum of 8 to 10 weeks old calves, the ulcers being round or oval, sharply defined and usually found at the pyloric end of the abomasum; they are occasionally seen in the abomasum of adult cattle, or in the stomach of pigs or horses.

Actinobacillosis may occur in the wall of the bovine rumen or reticulum (Fig. 94), and is manifested by lesions of a nodular or ulcerative character, with marked development of fibrous tissue in the stomach wall. Ulceration of a specific type also occurs in the stomach in acute and chronic swine fever, though congestion and diphtheresis of the gastric mucous membrane is more commonly seen in this disease; diphtheritic inflammation of the pig stomach is also seen in infection by the nematode *Hyostrongylus rubidus*. Tuberculosis of the bovine stomach is rare, but tuberculous ulceration of the small intestine may occur and is usually associated with breakdowns of lung lesions and the swallowing of massive doses of tubercle bacilli.

Both the rumen and reticulum in the ox may show inflammation due to traumatic influences, frequently resulting in peritonitis and adhesion of these organs to the posterior aspect of the diaphragm. Foreign bodies from the reticulum not infrequently penetrate the diaphragm to give rise to traumatic pericarditis, but a common lesion associated with traumatic penetration of the ox stomach is the presence of a large abscess situated between the stomach, liver and diaphragm. Multiple haemorrhages in the stomach and intestine of cattle and pigs are usually caused during slaughter and often coexist with "splashing" of the muscular tissue; haemorrhages in the stomach and intestine of pigs may also occur in cases of acute swine fever.

Gut oedema is an acute non-contagious though highly fatal condition of young pigs and an early diagnostic symptom is oedema of the eyelids (Fig. 9) and with this may be seen oedema of the ears and face. Gut oedema appears to be a specific enterotoxaemia in which certain types of haemolytic *E. coli* are involved, and the most consistent post-mortem lesion is oedema of the stomach wall, mainly along the greater curvature between the muscular coat and the mucous membrane and up to 1½ inches thick. The folds of mesentery supporting the spiral colon are also frequently affected and the intestinal coils appear as if they are situated in a jelly-like mass. In pigs recovering from an attack of gut oedema the peritoneal fat may only show a patchy brownish coloration or a slightly haemorrhagic discoloration, but when acute cases of gut oedema in young pigs are encountered they are best dealt with by total condemnation because of the nature of the incriminating organism.

Enteritis may be of an acute or chronic type. Acute enteritis, which is associated with symptoms of fever and intoxication in the live animal, may be caused by organisms of the salmonella group of bacteria, and the affection, particularly if of a haemorrhagic or diphtheric form (Fig. 136), calls for total condemnation of the carcase. Catarrhal enteritis, which is unaccompanied by fever or systemic disturbance, may occur in cattle as a result of heavy feeding on roots, but does not affect the marketability of the carcase. Enteritis of a specific type is seen in pig paratyphoid (Fig. 114), as well as in swine fever, but in bovines the commonest form of chronic enteritis occurs as a result of Johne's disease (Fig. 109).

Terminal ileitis is a condition sometimes seen in slaughtered pigs in which the ileum is so thickened as to resemble a thick-walled rubber hose and the mucous membrane may be thrown into folds similar to that seen in Johne's disease. Though the aetiology of this affection is unknown, in the cases encountered in slaughterhouses the carcase is usually otherwise normal and it may be treated as a local condition.

The parasitic infections of stomach and intestine are numerous, and include invasion by tapeworms and adult or larval nematodes. *Ascaris lumbricoides* (var. *suis*.) may migrate up the bile ducts from the pig intestine (Fig. 78), and, if the infestation is severe, may set up biliary stasis and icterus. Larval nematodes of the genus *Oesophagostomum* may be found in the intestines of the ox and sheep (Fig. 146) and give rise to nodules in the submucous tissue, these varying from a pin-head to a pea in size and greenish or yellowish-brown in colour. The larger nodules are visible through the muscular and serous coats of the intestine, and the significance of the affection in meat inspection is that it renders the intestines valueless for sausage casings. Parasitic infections of the intestinal wall may be differentiated from tuberculosis by the greenish coloration of the parasitic lesions, the absence of caseation in the mesenteric lymph nodes and by the microscopical demonstration of the parasitic larvae if the nodules are cleared with glycerin or dilute caustic potash.

Hairballs, composed of hair, vegetable fibre and other substances are common in the abomasum of calves, but are of no significance in meat inspection.

Liver

The liver is the first organ of the body to undergo macroscopic changes when an animal suffers from an acute infectious disease and is the last organ to assume normality should the animal survive. It is therefore a valuable guide as to the presence of toxic changes, and these may be manifested by cloudy swelling of the organ or, at a later stage, by pathological fatty change. The liver is also the organ most commonly affected with neoplasms.

TELANGIECTASIS. This condition, which is extremely common in old cows, was formerly designated cavernous haemangioma and is known to

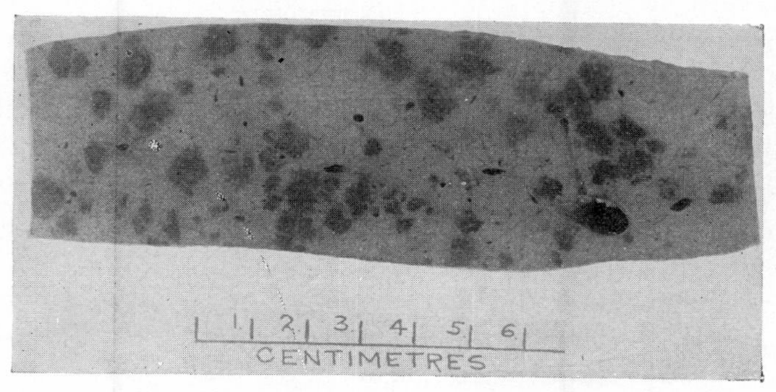

FIG. 64.—Section of liver of cow showing lesions of telangiectasis (cavernous haemangioma). The condition may be distinguished from melanosis by the fact that in the latter condition the lesions are irregularly distributed, are frequently large and do not cause depressions beneath the liver serosa.

slaughtermen as "plum pudding liver". An affected liver presents numerous bluish-black areas which are found beneath the serous capsule and throughout the liver parenchyma. These lesions are irregularly shaped and have a spongy appearance, while microscopically they are seen to consist of dilated capillaries filled with blood and lined with endothelium. Livers containing a few lesions may be seen in heifers and bullocks, though not in the extensive form encountered in cows, and the condition is not uncommon in the horse and has also been observed in the sheep and fowl. Though the aetiology of telangiectasis is still obscure there is some evidence that a feeding factor may be concerned, for in California it has been shown that the incidence of the affection is significantly higher in cattle fattened by intensive winter feeding than in animals on grass feeding alone. The only justification for the condemnation of a liver affected with telangiectasis is that it may be unmarketable, and though severely affected livers must be condemned, those which are slightly affected may be passed for food.

Enlargement of the liver with accentuation of the interlobular tissue may be observed in leukaemia (Fig. 77), and strangulation of the left lateral lobe of the liver in sows occasionally occurs due to torsion, resulting either in fatal haemorrhage or atrophy or necrosis of the affected lobe.

Bacterial Infections of the Liver

Bacterial Necrosis. This is seen most commonly in the liver of the ox, but is also encountered in the sheep and is caused by infection with *Fusiformis necrophorus* (*B. necrosis*), an organism which is a frequent inhabitant of the intestinal tract of herbivora. The bacteria penetrate the intestinal wall and enter the portal vein to reach the liver, in which organ the affection may assume an acute or chronic form, though the latter is much the commoner encountered in meat inspection. In acute cases of bacterial necrosis the animal exhibits symptoms of fever, intoxication, and not infrequently icterus, probably due to rupture of the intercellular bile canaliculi and to bile thrombi, and on post-mortem examination the liver is very much enlarged and exhibits cloudy degeneration or pathological fatty change with numerous necrotic foci throughout the substance. More commonly bacterial necrosis is seen as a chronic condition in which the liver is much enlarged and shows yellowish areas of coagulation necrosis, these being raised slightly above the liver surface, more or less spherical in shape and the size of a shilling or larger. In the early stage of this affection these lesions may be surrounded by a hyperaemic zone, and the causal organism may be demonstrated at the junction of the healthy and necrotic tissue, but at a later stage the necrotic areas become encapsulated by fibrous tissue, which may be up to $\frac{1}{8}$th inch in thickness and enclosing a pale yellow necrotic material. The liver capsule may be thickened where it covers the superficial prominences, and should degeneration eventually take place the centres of the necrotic foci contain a greenish purulent fluid.

Liver abscesses are common in cattle, particularly in animals kept under intensive methods of feeding, such as the barley beef of the United Kingdom in which the animals reach slaughter at under one year of age, or the feedlot system in the United States in which 1 to 2 year-old range-reared cattle are finished for about 4 months on high-energy cereal diets. In the North of Scotland in 1964 the incidence of liver abscesses in barley beef cattle was 22·2 per cent., while throughout the United States the incidence is in the region of 5 per cent., rises to 10 per cent. in the Rocky Mountain area, and is as high as 100 per cent. in cattle from certain feedlots. In approximately 85 per cent. of cases *Fusiformis necrophorus* in pure culture has been found and it is considered that the early lesion is a coagulative necrosis with eventual degeneration of the necrotic material. Necrosis of

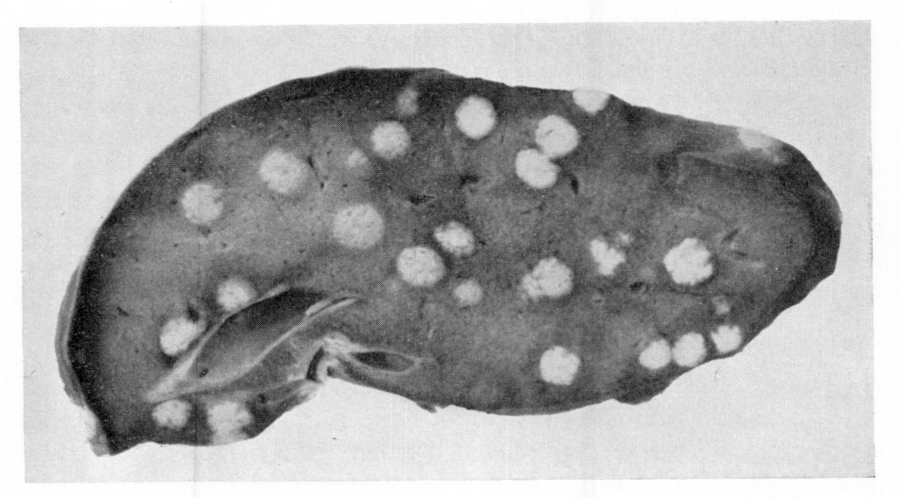

FIG. 65.—Bacterial necrosis of sheep liver. Note that the necrotic areas are raised slightly above the cut surface, and are sharply delimited from the surrounding liver tissue. The unaffected liver tissue is pale and indicative of pathological fatty change.

the kidneys, manifested by an abnormal paleness of the organ, and also of the myocardium, may accompany liver abscesses in animals under intensive methods of feeding. There is evidence that liver abscesses may be associates with inflammatory changes or ulceration of the rumen resulting from a highly concentrated grain diet and fall in pH of the rumen contents, and this permits passage of the causal organism into the portal blood stream. Such diets are often responsible for the blackening and clumping of the villi of the ruminal mucosa, and this abnormality, along with a possible low vitamin A content in the diet, may also be partly responsible for the high incidence of liver abscesses. It is claimed that the incidence of liver abscesses is reduced when antibiotics are incorporated in the animals' food and also when more roughage is introduced into the feed.

Liver abscesses in young animals may arise as the result of an umbilical infection, and in all animals they may occur in cases of pyaemia (Fig. 139).

Abscesses in the liver may also occur in cattle due to penetration of the hepatic tissues by foreign bodies from the reticulum, and in pigs due to penetration of a foreign body from the digestive tract. In the absence of systemic changes liver abscesses or bacterial necrosis may be regarded as a local condition.

CIRRHOSIS OF THE LIVER. Cirrhosis denotes the proliferation of fibrous connective tissue in the liver substance, with resultant induration and distortion of the organ, and in Britain is the commonest condition which renders the liver unfit for food. In the ox and sheep cirrhosis usually occurs as a result of infestation with *Fasciola hepatica*. In the pig there is little evidence that liver cirrhosis is caused by the feeding of fermented swill but in some cases it may be attributed to an allergic reaction in a pig previously sensitized by larvae of *Ascaris lumbricoides* (var. *suis*). It is also thought that some cases of liver cirrhosis in pigs may be due to the toxic action of certain moulds, both *Penicillium rubrum* and *Aspergillus flavum* being capable of causing hepatitis in cattle and pigs. In the horse, cirrhosis of the liver is associated with pernicious anaemia, and in cattle and horses the ingestion of ragwort (*Senecio jacobea*) in the fodder may cause marked enlargement and a diffuse cirrhosis of the organ.

PARASITIC AFFECTIONS OF THE LIVER

In acute fascioliasis of the ox liver the organ is enlarged but of a normal colour, while the chronic stage of the affection is characterized by dilatation and "pipiness" of the bile ducts, together with cirrhosis of the liver parenchyma. In sheep the affection is manifested by extensive proliferation of fibrous connective tissue resulting in marked distortion of the organ, but it is a characteristic of the ovine affection that the bile ducts, though dilated, do not become calcareous. Immature forms of *Fasciola hepatica* in the sheep liver may also give rise to irregularly distributed nodules and serpentine-like tracks which are often markedly calcareous; in pigs, white spherical nodules, usually situated superficially in the liver, are attributable to the same parasite. Hydatid cysts are not uncommon in the liver of ox, sheep (Fig. 163), pig (Plate IV) and horse, and *Cysticercus tenuicollis* is commonly seen beneath the serous covering of the liver of the sheep and pig, though it is rarely seen in the ox. In countries where schistosomiasis occurs in cattle and sheep, small white pin-head sized lesions, which contain schistosome ova, may be seen on both surfaces of the liver. Linguatula larvae are sometimes found in the liver of the food animals, appearing as small greenish nodules beneath the liver capsule, and their recognition may be facilitated by teasing out the nodule on a microscope slide and identifying the typical hooklets (Fig. 194).

Cysticercus bovis in the ox and *Cysticercus cellulosae* in the pig are only rarely encountered in the liver, and parasitic cysts which are found in the substance of the liver of the ox, sheep and pig are almost certainly hydatid cysts, while the vast majority of parasitic cysts situated superficially beneath the serous capsule of the liver of the sheep and pig are *Cysticercus tenuicollis*. The surface of the horse liver frequently presents numerous whitish foci which are caused by the larvae of intestinal nematodes, the lesions being serpentine in shape, raised above the liver surface and usually markedly calcareous.

An affection known as "milk spot" is common in the pig liver (Fig. 143), and is caused most commonly by migrating larvae of *Ascaris lumbricoides* (var. *suis*.), but occasionally by *Cysticercus tenuicollis*, while in South American countries lesions of a similar type are caused in pigs by the larvae of *Stephanurus dentatus*. There is also evidence that an ascarid foreign to pigs can be responsible for milk spot lesions and that *Toxacara canis* and *Toxacara cati*, common ascarids of the dog and cat respectively, can produce such lesions, as also can larvae of the pig lungworms. Milk spot lesions are essentially areas of interstitial inflammation and are situated superficially on both surfaces of the liver, possessing a white, opaque centre from which radiate thickened interlobular septa which merge more or less imperceptibly into the surrounding healthy tissue. Milk spot is found in the livers of about 10 per cent. of all pigs in Great Britain, the incidence being as high as 50 per cent. in porkers and store pigs, but less common in bacon pigs and sows; in Germany the incidence of the affection is stated to be between 20 and 25 per cent. A liver affected with milk spot need only be condemned if the lesions are so extensive as to render the organ unmarketable but an irregular surface mottling is commonly seen in pig livers when evisceration takes place, and this disappears if the liver is hung up for a period. It is recommended that judgment of pig livers be delayed for 1 hour, and by adoption of this practice one authority reports a fall of 10 per cent. in the number of livers condemned for this affection.

The rabbit liver is very commonly affected with the protozoan parasite *Eimeria stiedae*, the organ being studded with white, irregularly shaped lesions which consist of dilated bile ducts filled with a white purulent fluid; the lesions are scattered more or less uniformly throughout the liver substance, and render the organ unfit for food. Sharply circumscribed caseous or caseo-calcareous nodules in the livers of food animals are usually indicative of a parasitic origin, and may be differentiated from tuberculosis by the absence of lesions in the portal lymph nodes.

Pancreas

Fat necrosis may be seen in the fat around the pancreas of pigs and other animals. The lesions have a dry, putty-like consistency and are usually seen in the mesentery or omentum, though they occasionally occur in the subperitoneal or subpleural fat or the subcutaneous tissue (Fig. 56). Calcareous concretions encountered in the pancreas of the ox or pig represent the final stage of areas which have undergone fat necrosis. The multiple adenomas reported in the bovine pancreas may actually be lesions of hyperplasia.

Spleen

Acute enlargement of the spleen may be seen in certain specific diseases and occurs in redwater, anaplasmosis and theileriosis in cattle and in acute swine erysipelas, anthrax and other septicaemias. Chronic enlargement of the spleen may be seen in liver stasis resulting from swine erysipelas, and it

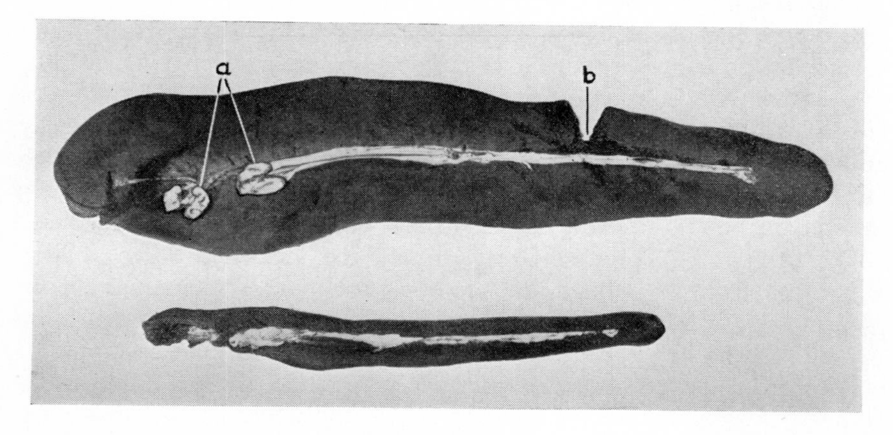

FIG. 66.—Spleen of pig affected with lymphatic leukaemia (a normal spleen of an animal of similar size is shown below). The splenic lymph nodes (*a*) are also greatly enlarged and are leathery-like and haemorrhagic. The animal died shortly after being delivered at an abattoir and post-mortem examination showed that death was caused by internal haemorrhage due to rupture (*b*) of the splenic capsule.

occurs in cattle as a result of traumatic pericarditis. Chronic splenic enlargement is also seen in leukaemia (the so-called " burst spleen ") and in chronic salmonella infections in cattle (the so-called " board spleen "). Infarcts of the spleen, caused by the occlusion of end-arteries, are not uncommon and may be associated with an ulcerative endocarditis ; splenic infarcts are initially haemorrhagic, being wedge-shaped on section and raised above the spleen surface, but eventually they become organized and cause considerable shrinkage and distortion of the organ. Haemorrhages or haemorrhagic infarcts in the pig spleen are regarded as a valuable diagnostic lesion in swine fever (Fig. 112). Tuberculosis of the spleen substance is evidence of a haematogenous infection and is common in the pig, though less common in adult cattle. Parasites occasionally found in the spleen are echinococci, encysted liver flukes, or linguatula larvae.

Abnormalities of the spleen due to mechanical causes are not uncommon. Haematomata may be seen in all food animals and are traumatic in origin, usually occurring as a result of injury during transport. In cattle necrosis of portions of the spleen may occur due to penetration of foreign bodies from the reticulum, a feature of the lesion being that it disintegrates on handling. Torsion of the spleen in pigs may occur by virtue of the loose attachment of this organ to the stomach, the whole spleen or its lower portion rotating on its long axis to cause passive congestion and acute swelling of the organ. Similarly, interference with

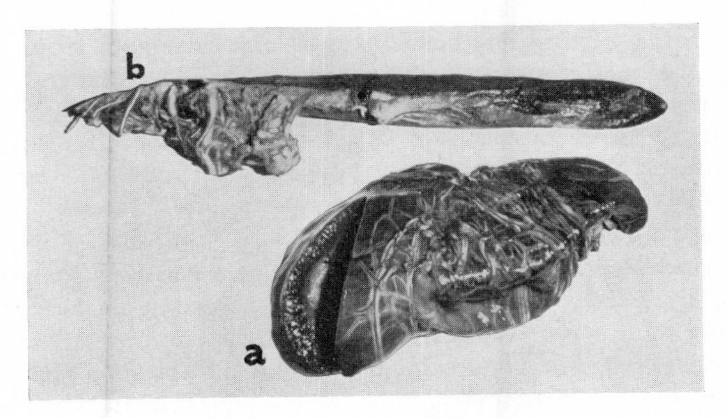

FIG. 67.—(*a*) Strangulation of spleen of pig by portion of the omentum causing passive congestion and great enlargement of the organ. (*b*) Normal spleen of an animal of similar age and size.

the arterial blood supply to the spleen may result in complete necrosis of the organ, but the condition is not uncommon in healthy pigs and pathological changes of the pig spleen due to mechanical causes have little or no effect on the health of the animal or its bodily condition. Splenic congestion and enlargement may occur in cattle due to use of an inordinately long pithing cane and constitutes the so-called " slaughter-spleen ". The condition has been observed in Germany in pigs slaughtered by certain types of captive-bolt instruments and is sometimes seen in pigs stunned by electrical means, while in Central America it has been observed in pigs placed in the scalding tub before they are unconscious.

Peritoneum

Acute peritonitis may occur in calves due to perforation of peptic ulcers, and in adult animals may arise from the rupture of the bladder or stomach, from liver or kidney abscesses, or in females from inflammatory processes in the uterus or oviduct. Well-marked congestion of the peritoneal membrane is an indication for total condemnation of the carcase, and although congestion may be absent in rupture of the bladder, the carcase should be condemned if a marked urinous odour is present. Chronic localized peritonitis is frequently seen in sheep in the form of adhesion of the liver to the posterior surface of the diaphragm, and usually occurs as a result of extensive infestation of the liver with the common liver fluke, whilst in the ox adhesions may be seen between the reticulum and diaphragm as a result of traumatic influences. Widespread lesions of actinobacillosis are occasionally seen on the bovine peritoneum but chronic localized peritonitis only requires condemnation of the affected tissue or organs.

Areas of fat necrosis may be found in the omentum, kidney fat, between the layers of mesentery, or in the pelvic region. A condition known as bovine lipomatosis is sometimes observed, particularly in cattle of the Jersey breed, in which masses of fatty tissue are found in the abdominal cavity and usually involving the rectum and large intestines. Immature fasciolae $\frac{1}{80}$th inch to $\frac{1}{8}$th inch in size may occasionally be found beneath the parietal portion of the bovine peritoneum.

Mesenteric emphysema (Plate II) is seen occasionally in the pig, very occasionally in sheep and poultry, and is characterized by single or multiple clusters of thin, colourless cysts which contain gas and bear a resemblance to a bunch of grapes. The condition is attributed to infection by a coliform organism which penetrates the wall of the intestine and sets up gas formation by virtue of its fermentative properties ; mesenteric emphysema is usually seen in the region of the ileum or jejunum, occasionally the large intestine, and may involve the wall of the intestine or, in severe cases, the lymph nodes and mesentery. It may be regarded as a local condition.

3. AFFECTIONS OF THE RESPIRATORY SYSTEM

Nasal Cavities

Febrile conditions in the food animals are often accompanied by nasal catarrh, and a purulent nasal discharge may be seen in calf pneumonia caused by *Corynebacterium pyogenes*, while in malignant catarrhal fever of the ox and sheep the nasal mucous membrane may show a catarrhal or diphtheritic inflammation. In glanders the nasal mucosa of the horse presents a nodular or ulcerative condition (Fig. 107), and a purulent nasal discharge is seen in equine strangles and in infestation of the nasal passages of sheep with the larvae of *Oestrus ovis*. Partial obstruction of the nasal passages in cattle may occur through tumours or, more commonly, through actinobacillotic nodules, and tuberculosis of the bovine nasal mucous membrane may be seen in the form of nodules or chronic ulceration. In atrophic rhinitis in pigs (Fig. 68) the nasal bones tend to turn upwards from the lower jaw, the snout becomes " dished " and there is a wrinkling of the

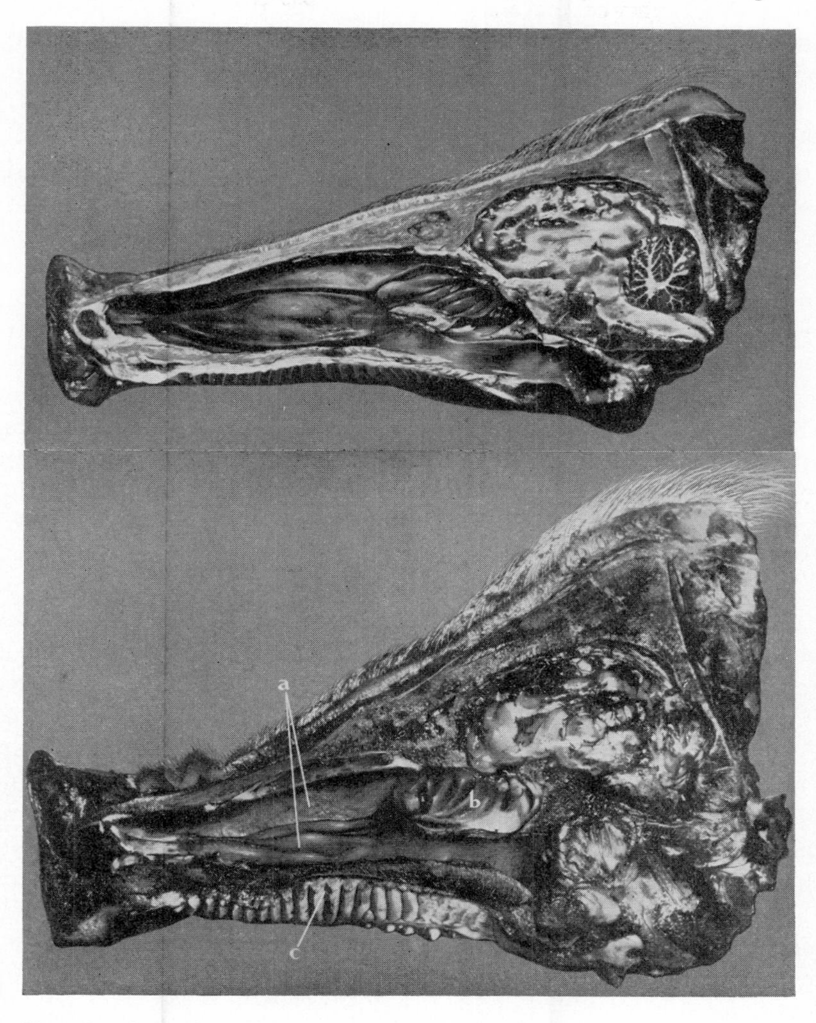

FIG. 68.—Atrophic rhinitis of head of pig. Above is seen a sagittal section of head of a normal pig. Below is head of a pig with a severe atrophic rhinitis infection ; the turbinate bones (*a*) are shrunken and distorted, the ethmoid (*b*) is also damaged, while the corrugation of the skin over the snout and the undulation of the hard palate (*c*) reflects the foreshortening of the upper jaw.

skin over the distorted area. On splitting the head the turbinate bones show atrophy, marked congestion and may exhibit areas of necrosis. In the absence of systemic changes the affection may be regarded as a local one.

Larynx

Lesions of actinobacillosis, which are flat or pedunculated, may be seen in the larynx of the ox. In swine fever the epiglottis may show evidence of petechiation or ulceration, and in calf diphtheria deposits of a diphtheritic nature may sometimes be found in the larynx.

Trachea

Exposure of the tracheal mucous membrane by a longitudinal incision through the tracheal cartilages is adopted as a general practice in some countries as it has a value in the detection of aspirated stomach contents or of parasitic infections involving the respiratory tract. In France it is a routine procedure to incise the horse trachea for evidence of glanders ulcers. A chronic tracheitis, which is manifested by the presence of mucus, blood and worm larvae in the lumen of the trachea, occurs in hoose in sheep and calves. Cases of suffocation in sheep are associated with intense congestion and thickening of the tracheal mucous membrane, whilst food may be aspirated into the trachea of cattle or sheep during slaughter, especially in animals slaughtered according to Jewish ritual.

Bronchi

Inflammation of the bronchial tubes chiefly occurs in the food animals as a result of infection with parasitic nematodes, which give rise to a chronic bronchitis, usually referred to as husk or hoose; the parasites commonly implicated in this affection are *Dictyocaulus viviparus* in calves, *Dictyocaulus filaria* in lambs (Fig. 147), and *Metastrongylus elongatus* (*M. apri*) in pigs. Bronchitis of parasitic origin may give rise to areas of alveolar emphysema, this change being particularly well manifested in the lung of the pig, in which marginal areas of pulmonary tissue are white, swollen and glistening and sharply defined from the adjacent healthy lung tissue. A streptococcal bronchitis occurs in cattle independently of hoose.

The upper respiratory passages are not generally the seat of affections which are of great importance in meat inspection, and attention must be chiefly directed towards the lungs and pleura.

Lungs and Pleura

Interstitial emphysema is chiefly seen in the lungs of old cows and also in the lungs of cattle slaughtered by the Jewish method and in cattle severely affected with hoose. It is characterized by a marked dilatation of the pulmonary interstitial tissue and arises as a result of rupture of a lung alveolus with resultant penetration of air into the interlobular connective tissue and accentuation of the lobulated appearance of the lung surface.

Though the affection is usually a local one, emphysema may extend to the mediastinum and finally to the subcutaneous tissue over the thorax and abdomen, thus rendering the affected muscular tissue unmarketable. Bovine lungs affected with interstitial emphysema are commonly encountered in meat inspection, particularly in old cows, but there is little or no justification for the condemnation of affected lungs.

Pneumonia

This affection is usually bacterial or viral in origin, although it may be caused by traumatic influences as in the penetration of the lung by a

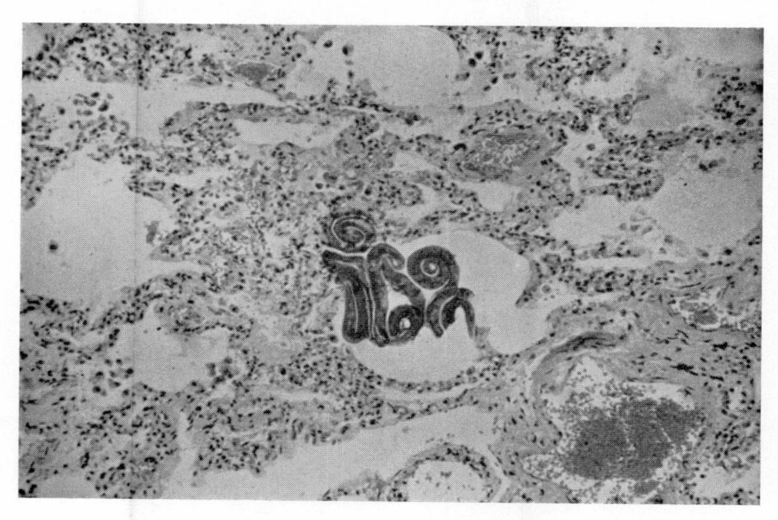

Fig. 69.—Larvae of *Ascaris lumbricoides* (var. *suis*) free in alveoli of lung of pig.

foreign body from the bovine reticulum or by accidental inhalation of liquids during the administration of drugs. Pneumonia may also be caused by adverse weather conditions, but is frequently seen in meat inspection in connection with specific diseases such as swine fever, or in extensive parasitic infections of the respiratory tract, including the passage of ascaris larvae from the lung capillaries into the alveoli in pigs. Virus pneumonia in pigs is a common affection encountered in bacon factories and as many as 30 per cent. of slaughtered animals are found so affected. Invasion of the lungs by moulds may also give rise to pneumonia, but this affection is rare in the food animals and is most likely to be encountered in poultry.

Bronchopneumonia. This form of pneumonia is characterized by the formation of small pneumonic foci around the bronchioles, pneumonic areas being thus intermixed with areas of normal lung tissue. In parasitic bronchopneumonia there is primarily a bronchitis, followed by obstruction of the bronchial tubes which prevents the return of inspired air and gives rise to an alveolar emphysema; the mature parasitic worms

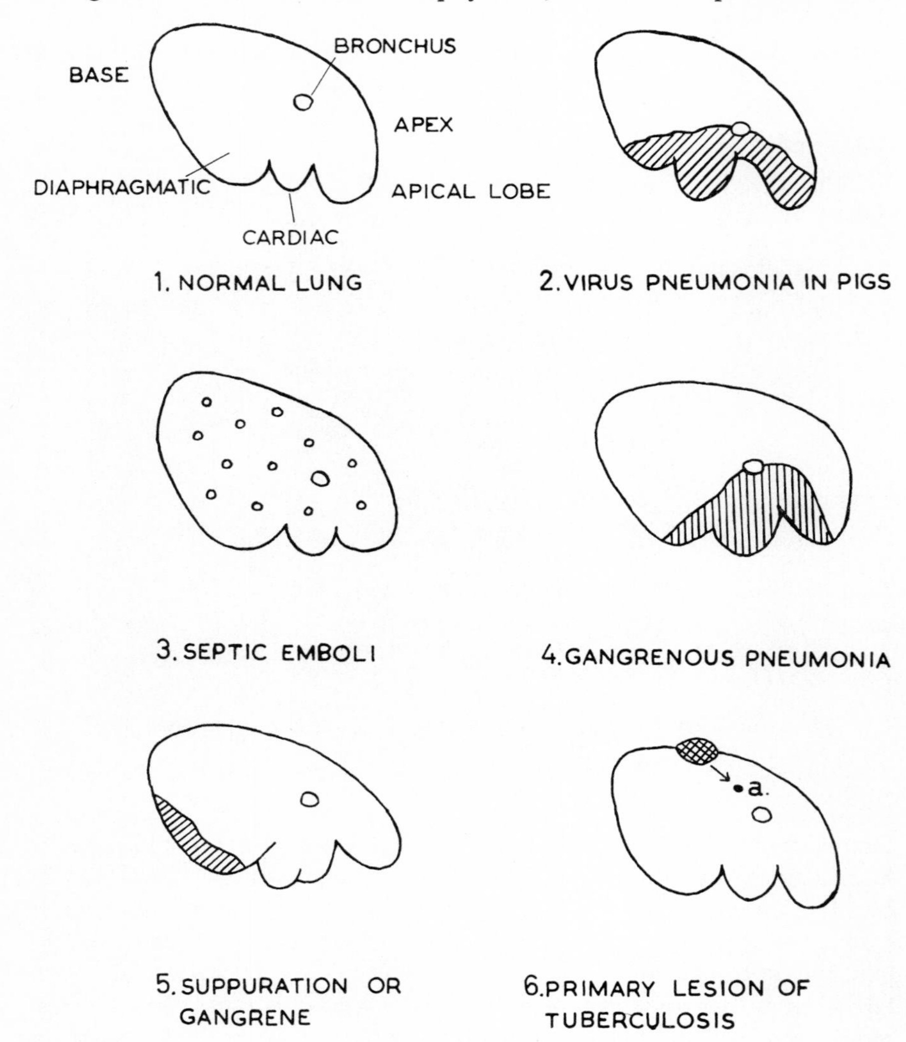

FIG. 70.—Lung lesions which may be encountered in meat inspection.

produce ova which develop into larvae, and these penetrate to the finest bronchioles and produce local areas of bronchopneumonia. Bronchopneumonia may also occur from inhalation of drugs administered in the liquid form; this affection is likely to give rise rapidly to a septic and, eventually, a gangrenous pneumonia, and in cattle is a frequent cause of emergency slaughter.

Lobar Pneumonia. This is frequently caused by bacteria which are normal inhabitants of the respiratory tract, and is characterized by the involvement of the whole or greater part of the lobe of a lung, the hepatized or consolidated tissue being more or less uniform in appearance and separated from normal lung tissue by a sharp line of demarcation.

Both lobar and bronchial pneumonia may be associated with necrosis of the lung tissue, the necrotic areas appearing as sharply defined foci which vary in size from a pinhead to a fist and rapidly become purulent with the production of a septic pneumonia. Septic pneumonia due to *Bacterium purifaciens* is frequently encountered in sheep, the lung containing several abscesses filled with a thick yellowish-green pus, while lobar pneumonia, which is common in Irish cattle affected with transit fever, occurs within a day or two of their landing in Britain, rapidly becomes septic, and early slaughter and salvage of affected animals is therefore advisable. Gangrene of the lung may develop if necrotic tissue is invaded by putrefactive organisms and is a common sequel to an attack of septic pneumonia or to penetration of the bovine lung by a foreign body from the reticulum.

Simple lobar or bronchial pneumonia is rarely an indication for total condemnation of the carcase, for it usually has little effect on its bleeding, setting or marketability. Carcases affected with septic or gangrenous pneumonia must be judged on the presence or absence of systemic

---

FIG. 70.

1. Left lung, normal, seen from inner aspect.
2. *Virus pneumonia in pigs.* Infective material passes into the bronchi and settles in the ventral portions of the lung below the tracheal bifurcation to produce a chronic pneumonia. This involves the postero-ventral portion of the apical lobe, the entire cardiac lobe and the antero-ventral portion of the diaphragmatic lobe. The areas of chronic pneumonia are clearly demarcated from the normal lung tissue by a narrow zone of active inflammation. Patchy areas of pneumonia may be seen if considerable bronchitis is present.
3. *Septic emboli.* These are of haematogenous origin and manifested by numerous abscesses distributed throughout both lungs, and usually in kidney, liver and other organs. In cows the primary focus of infection is frequently the uterus following on retention of the foetal membranes.
4. *Gangrenous pneumonia.* This occurs in the ox as a result of entry of drugs into the trachea due to faulty administration. Material enters the lower part of the lung below the entrance of the bronchi into the lungs and produces dirty grey foci of putrefaction.
5. *Suppuration or gangrene.* This occurs in the ox when a foreign body from the reticulum passes through the diaphragm and penetrates the diaphragmatic lobe of the lung. A fistulous tract, often with hard bluish-grey walls, usually shows the path of the foreign body from the reticulum.
6. *Tuberculosis*, primary lesion. In the ox, and also in man, the primary lesion is in the lung in about 90 per cent. of cases, usually in the well-aerated upper border of one of the main lung lobes. The associated bronchial lymph node (*a*) invariably shows caseous lesions. (After Runnells.)

disturbance, but in sheep it is common to find one lung extensively affected and resembling a bag of pus, the septic focus being markedly encapsulated by the thickened pleura, and if such carcases show no evidence of systemic change they may receive a favourable judgment.

In both cattle and sheep, foodstuffs are readily regurgitated from the rumen during slaughter, the foreign matter entering the respiratory tract during inspiration ; contamination of the lungs with ingesta is particularly common in cattle and sheep slaughtered according to the Jewish ritual, and pressure on the flank of cattle to facilitate bleeding also brings about regurgitation. Where there is suspicion of contamination, the main bronchi of the lungs should be incised, and if stomach contents are found to be present the lungs should be condemned. Incision of the bronchi of cattle, calves and sheep lungs is a routine requirement in abattoirs under United States Federal control.

The trachea may be severed at the same time as the neck vessels are being cut, especially in Jewish slaughter, with the result that blood is inspired into the bronchi and lungs. The condition is also seen in pigs, and may be detected when the lungs are incised by the red coloration of certain lung lobules, these lobules being intermixed with areas of normal lung tissue. The presence of inspired blood in the lungs may be differentiated from bronchopneumonia by the fact that in blood aspiration the bronchi will be seen to contain blood whilst the surrounding pulmonary tissue is normal. Lungs containing considerable amounts of aspirated blood are unfit for food and should be condemned, and also lungs of pigs which contain water aspirated during the scalding process ; for this reason the regulations in the United States which apply to Federally inspected establishments prescribe that pig lungs may not be used for edible purposes. In certain Continental countries this contamination is avoided in pigs by insertion of a wooden chock into the mouth and larynx, or by incising the neck region and applying a metal clamp to the trachea before the animal is immersed in the scalding tank.

PNEUMONOMYCOSIS. This is a fungoid condition of the lungs, the result of invasion by moulds of the genus *Aspergillus* or *Mucor*, and occurs most commonly in fowls, ducks and geese. The infection is usually encountered in young birds, being termed brooder pneumonia, but is not likely to be met with in table birds and is only occasionally seen in lambs, pigs and cattle. The condition is characterized by diffuse hepatization of the lungs, with numerous small grey or greenish spots scattered throughout the lung substance, together with a thin deposit of mould in the bronchi ; the fungus can be demonstrated on microscopical examination of the bronchioles and alveoli, and in adult well-nourished birds the affection may be regarded as a local one.

PARASITIC INFECTIONS OF THE LUNGS. The commonest parasite affecting the lung is undoubtedly *Muellerius capillaris* of sheep, and though the pathogenic effects of this parasite are but slight, it is responsible for the greenish nodules and raised pithy patches which are encountered so commonly in the lungs of adult sheep and usually attributed to *Protostrongylus rufescens*. In addition to the parasitic nematodes causing broncho-pneumonia in cattle and sheep, the lungs of these animals frequently contain hydatid cysts and, less commonly, these cysts may be seen in the lungs of pigs. Immature forms of *Fasciola hepatica* are also

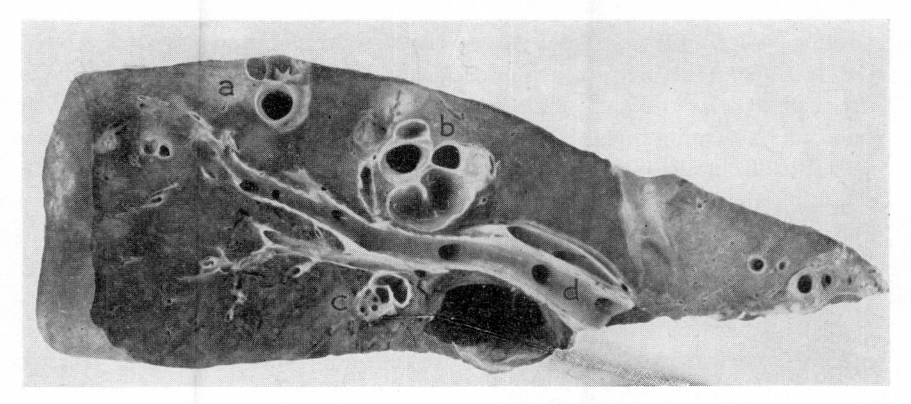

FIG. 71.—Section of sheep lung showing fertile multilocular hydatid cysts at *a*, *b*, and *c* A main bronchus, *d*, has been incised and shows the openings of six bronchioles.

seen in the lungs of cattle, though they are not found in the lungs of sheep, and grey fibrous nodules caused by nematode larvae may be seen in the lungs of horses.

All the above parasitic infections are of local significance, and only require condemnation of the affected organ.

PLEURISY

Pleurisy in the food animals is usually associated with pneumonia, and in the acute stage is characterized by the presence of a fibrinous exudate which, in cattle, has a red and velvety appearance. Acute pleurisy in cattle may at times be confused with " back bleeding " which occurs if the pleural membrane at the entrance to the chest be punctured during the act of sticking, with the result that blood is aspirated into the thoracic cavity and eventually dries on the parietal pleura, particularly along the posterior edges of the ribs.

Acute pleurisy tends to assume a chronic form with the production of fibrinous adhesions between the parietal pleura and the lung surface. In Denmark chronic pleural adhesions are very common in bacon pigs, and are of economic significance as only carcases of pigs with a clean pleura may be exported to Britain. Small haemorrhages beneath the parietal pleura, or beneath the visceral pleura covering the lungs, may occur during the act of slaughter, but being of mechanical origin and without other changes in the carcase are therefore of no significance; subpleural petechial haemorrhages may, however, be seen in many septicaemias, including swine fever and swine erysipelas. Tumour formations on the pleura are rare, though neuromata of the intercostal nerves are occasionally encountered and are seen as thickenings of the nerve sheaths, in some cases reaching the size of a pea, and visible beneath the parietal pleura; when multiple they are spaced regularly and parallel to the ribs but are of no significance and do not affect the marketability of the forequarter. In the pig small encapsulated abscesses containing a pale green pus are sometimes seen on the pleura in the region of lung abscesses caused by *Corynebacterium pyogenes*.

4. AFFECTIONS OF THE CIRCULATORY SYSTEM AND BLOOD

Heart

PERICARDIUM. The commonest affection of the bovine pericardium is traumatic pericarditis, and is seen most commonly in cows over 4 years of

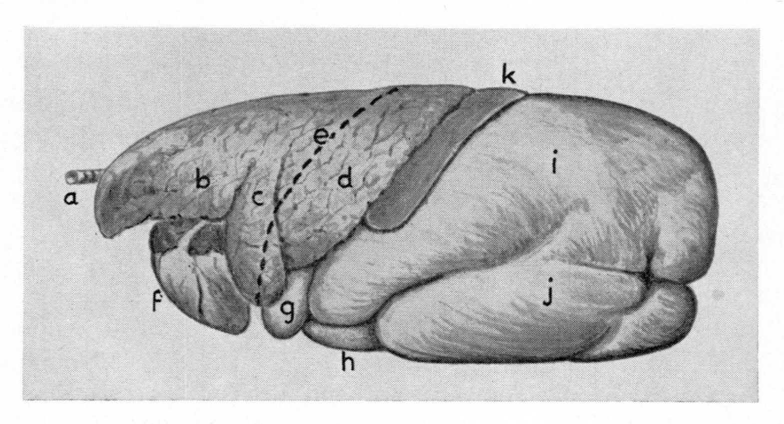

FIG. 72.—Anatomical relationship of bovine heart and reticulum. (*a*) trachea; (*b*, *c*, *d*) apical, cardiac and diaphragmatic lobes of left lung; (*e*) position of diaphragm; (*f*) heart; (*g*) reticulum; (*h*) abomasum; (*i*, *j*) left and right sacs of rumen; (*k*) spleen.

age, often shortly after parturition. The frequency of this affection is related to (*a*) the habit of these animals of licking various objects and often swallowing them, for the backward direction of the filiform and conical papillae of the mucous membrane of the tongue tends to prevent such bodies from falling out of the mouth, (*b*) the structure of the mucous membrane of the reticulum, the honeycomb-like conformation of which is likely to arrest foreign bodies, particularly nails, needles and pieces of wire, and (*c*) the anatomical relationship of the reticulum and apex of the heart which are not more than two inches apart during the act of expiration and one inch apart during inspiration. The regular movement of the diaphragm during respiration facilitates the penetration of sharp foreign bodies through the antero-ventral aspect of the reticulum and diaphragm to reach the pericardial sac opposite the apex of the heart; at times these

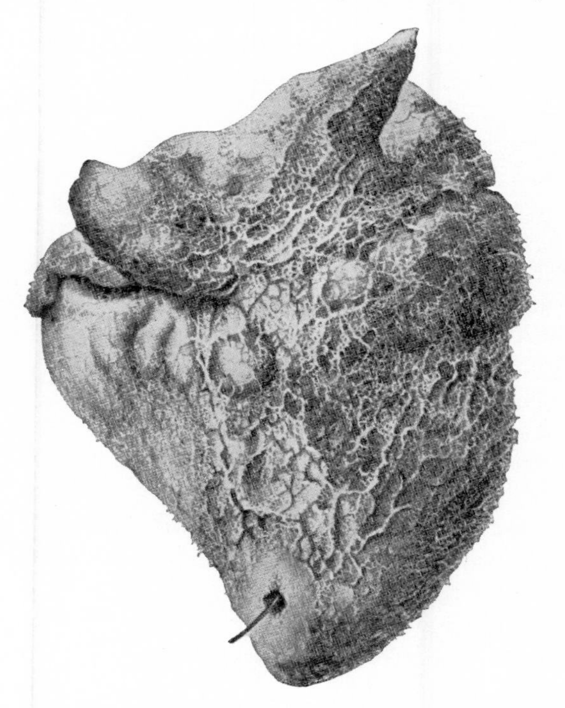

FIG. 73.—Fibrinous pericarditis of ox heart, the result of penetration of a piece of wire into the wall of the left ventricle. Penetration of the foreign body into the chamber of the left ventricle rarely occurs because of the thickness of the myocardial wall.

bodies may penetrate the myocardium or lung (Fig. 70) and occasionally the pleura, liver or spleen. The passage of the foreign body gives rise to the formation of a fistulous tract, often with hard bluish-grey walls, between the reticulum and pericardium, and a mixed bacterial flora, of which *Corynebacterium pyogenes* is the commonest and which may include anaerobic gas-forming bacteria, enters the pericardial sac to produce a suppurative exudate which may contain bubbles of gas; less commonly a fibrinous pericarditis may occur. A local chronic peritonitis is frequently present in association with the fistulous tract and may give rise to adhesions between the diaphragm, pericardial sac, and anterior aspect of the reticulum; abscess formation, usually single and of a large size, may sometimes be seen between the diaphragm and liver, or between the reticulum and omasum.

In the live animal traumatic pericarditis is manifested in the early stages by fever due to toxic disintegration of proteins, while pressure on the vena cava due to the effusion of fluid into the pericardial sac results in circulatory disturbance and stasis of the larger vessels of the venous system. This gives rise to oedema of the intermaxillary space, the oedematous fluid soon gravitating down the neck to cause distension of the brisket, and continued disturbance of the circulatory system may lead to serous infiltration of the muscular tissues and eventual emaciation. Though bacteria may pass from the infected pericardial sac into the blood stream to produce a septicaemia, this is not common as the infective material in the pericardial sac is likely to remain encapsulated, but absorption of toxic products from the suppurative sac may lead to a chronic toxaemia resulting in cachexia and general wasting of the musculature. Purulent or ichorous changes in the pericardial sac are less likely to produce a septicaemic infection than is generally supposed, and such changes as do occur in the carcase of an animal affected with traumatic pericarditis may usually be attributed partly to a chronic toxaemia and partly to circulatory disturbance resulting from gross interference with the action of the heart.

Judgment of traumatic pericarditis must therefore be based on the presence or absence of fever, the general bodily condition of the animal, and whether the circulatory disturbance has had the effect of producing serous infiltration of the muscular tissue. In the absence of fever, or of extensive serous infiltrations or emaciation, a favourable judgment may be given to the carcase, and a local oedema confined to the brisket region may be dealt with by removal of the brisket and plate. Emaciation, or the presence of extensive serous infiltration of the musculature manifested by lack of setting, dictates total condemnation of the carcase.

Tuberculosis of the bovine pericardium (Fig. 124) usually occurs as an extension from tuberculosis of the lungs. In pigs a fibrinous pericarditis, often accompanied by adhesions to the parietal or visceral pleura, may be seen as a result of an attack of swine erysipelas, and pericarditis of an effusive or fibrinous form due to *Pasteurella suiseptica* infection also occurs in cases of swine fever.

EPICARDIUM. This serous layer, also known as the visceral pericardium, is a common seat for petechial haemorrhages which occur in affections of a septicaemic or toxaemic nature. Haemorrhages of the pericardium may also occur during the death agony of slaughter and are caused by the lack of oxygen and spasmodic contraction of the tissues.

MYOCARDIUM. The chief affections of the myocardium are cloudy swelling or fatty change, and are associated with toxic affection of the carcase. All infectious febrile conditions may give rise to degenerative changes or to myocarditis, and in foot and mouth disease the myocardium may show patchy areas of pathological fatty change which appear on the heart surface as light grey or yellow streaks and spots, and to which the term "tiger heart" is applied; muscular degeneration or myocarditis is also seen in such affections as tetanus, septic metritis and septic mastitis, or in colic in horses. Brown atrophy of the bovine heart may occur in connection with wasting diseases, especially tuberculosis, the heart being reduced in size, flabby, wrinkled, and brown in colour due to accumulation of numerous pigment granules in the muscular substance, while the coronary arteries are prominent and tortuous. Abscesses may be seen in the myocardium of cattle due to penetration of foreign bodies from the reticulum, and metastatic abscesses may be found in the myocardium in cases of pyaemia, not infrequently as a result of septic metritis.

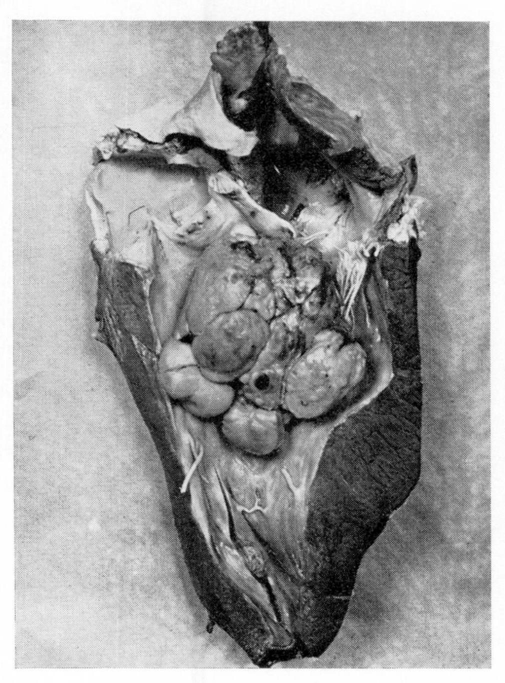

FIG. 74.—Heart of cow, showing lesions of chronic ulcerative endocarditis. Several thrombi have developed on the ulcerated surface of the heart valves, and have become organized. Endocardial vegetations are usually present on the side of the valve which faces the blood stream, and arise at points where one valve cusp is in contact with another.

In cattle one of the predilection seats of *Cysticercus bovis* is the myocardium (Fig. 173), and the heart muscle is also a predilection seat of *Cysticercus cellulosae* in the pig. Hydatid cysts are occasionally seen in the heart, and *Cysticercus ovis*, usually completely calcified, may be found in the myocardium of sheep. Larvae of linguatula have been found beneath the bovine epicardium and appear as a hard, elastic nodule with a necrotic centre which is greenish-yellow in colour.

ENDOCARDIUM. The commonest affection of the endocardium in the food animals occurs in the pig; it takes the form of a verrucose endocarditis (Fig. 116), and is a valuable diagnostic lesion in chronic swine erysipelas. The heart valve most commonly affected is the mitral, from which emboli of a nonpyogenic nature may become detached and give rise to infarcts of the liver, kidneys or spleen. Ulcerative valvular endocarditis, due to streptococci or *Corynebacterium pyogenes*, is occasionally seen in the ox and may give rise to the production of septic emboli and metastatic abscesses which are particularly likely to be found in the kidney. Ulcerative endocarditis may be seen in horses due to infection with *Streptococcus*

FIG. 75.—Periarteritis nodosa lesions in heart muscle of an ox. A small blood vessel is sometimes discernible in the white spherical nodules of fibrous tissue.

equi, and in pigs due to streptococcal infection. Differentiation between a streptococcal infection in pigs and that due to *Erysipelothrix rhusiopathiae* may usually be established by microscopical examination of a stained smear, for in a streptococcal infection only an occasional coccus will be evident whereas in erysipelas infection the smear will reveal the small slender bacilli in great numbers. Subendocardial haemorrhages, particularly in the left ventricle, are common in septicaemia and in sheep dead of entero-toxaemia (Fig. 98). They also occur in animals bled to death, as in the case of those slaughtered according to Jewish ritual, and are caused by the violent terminal beating of the heart.

BLOOD VESSELS. The affections of these are of little importance in meat inspection, though parasitic aneurisms in the abdominal aorta of the horse may rupture and cause death from internal haemorrhage. Death from internal haemorrhage may also take place in heifers, particularly in very fat animals, due to rupture of the internal pudic artery caused by injury at calving. More commonly internal haemorrhage occurs as a result of rough handling of pigs or sheep during transport, and in all the food animals, if death from internal haemorrhage is followed by prompt evisceration and provided the possibility of anthrax has been discounted, it is usually possible to release the carcase for food. In old cows the aorta may show thickening of its wall due to calcareous deposits, while miliary tuberculosis of the bovine lungs is frequently associated with a tuberculous endarteritis of the aorta, the intima at the level of the aortic arch presenting roughened, ulcerated areas which have a ridged appearance. Lesions which bear resemblance to degenerated *Cysticercus bovis* and from a pin head to a barley grain in size, are sometimes seen in the ox heart. The condition is knows as periarteritis nodosa and is caused by development of fibrous tissue in and around the smaller blood vessels ; lesions may also be found in muscles such as the masseters and tongue, and in organs such as the kidney and spleen.

Affections of the Blood

Anaemia

This may be defined as a deficiency in blood or a diminution in the number of red blood corpuscles. It is usually an indication of severe systemic disturbance and in cattle is most frequently associated with emaciation due to tuberculosis, Johne's disease or redwater ; in sheep it may be caused by severe parasitic infection of the stomach, intestine or lungs. Anaemia is difficult to detect in the live animal other than by a slight paleness of the mucous membranes, especially of the conjunctiva in sheep, whilst in the dressed carcase the flesh may show little change in colour and all that may be observed are emaciation and impaired coagulation of the blood. A moderate degree of anaemia in the lean but otherwise normal carcase is not sufficient grounds for condemnation, but carcases which show anaemia and marked emaciation should be condemned.

Hydraemia

This denotes a condition in which the blood is more watery than normal, being poorer in red blood corpuscles, while its water content is increased. Hydraemia is characterized by the transudation of watery fluid from the blood vessels into the subcutaneous tissues of body cavities, causing them to be water-soaked and oedematous. The condition, therefore, bears a close resemblance to oedema or dropsy, in which the subcutaneous tissues, intermuscular connective tissue, or body cavities may show an abnormal fluid content, and hydraemia is regarded by some as a form of oedema in which the predisposing cause is the abnormal, watery condition of the blood. Hydraemia and anaemia frequently co-exist in chronic wasting diseases, particularly in fascioliasis (Fig. 176) or parasitic gastro-enteritis of sheep ; hydraemia, though less common in pigs and adult cattle, may also be seen in chronic kidney affections such as hydronephrosis.

Carcases showing a moderate degree of hydraemia should be allowed to hang for 24 hours in dry, airy surroundings, as considerable improvement in the appearance of the carcase will often result due to evaporation, dripping, and reabsorption of the fluid by the muscular substance. Carcases of beef, however, should not be released at the end of this period until they have been quartered and the cut surfaces examined, and it is advisable to leave two ribs on the hind-quarter as this ensures that quartering is not done too low down, where setting is more difficult to judge. The neck and axillary region should also be examined and incised for the accumulation of fluid, and " drip " may be seen on the sawdust beneath the suspended carcase. Where the carcase is still oedematous after 24 hours, or where hydraemia is associated with emaciation, total condemnation is necessary.

Leukaemia

This is a chronic disease characterized by an increase in the number of white blood corpuscles in the general circulation, and caused by a proliferation of the leucocyte-forming tissues of the body. If the proliferative changes involve the bone marrow the condition is termed myeloid leukaemia, while if the lymph nodes and spleen are affected it is known as lymphatic leukaemia. The disease in animals is almost always of the lymphatic form and is commonest in older animals, particularly cows. Pigs and sheep are less often affected, though leukaemic conditions (leucosis) are relatively common in fowls.

The typical post-mortem lesions of leukaemia may be evident wherever lymphoid tissue is present ; thus the lymph nodes, spleen, liver, kidneys stomach and intestines may be affected, though the changes in the various organs vary considerably in extent. In affected cattle the lymph nodes are greatly enlarged, greyish-red in colour and resembling bacon fat, while they are often interspersed with blood spots or larger haemorrhagic areas. A characteristic lesion in the lymph nodes of bovines is the presence of orange-yellow, sharply delimited areas of necrosis, particularly in the marginal areas of the node. The spleen in all animals is often enormously enlarged (Fig. 66) and there may be subcapsular haemorrhage, which, if the capsule ruptures, may cause death due to internal haemorrhage. In the kidneys lesions of leukaemia may take the form of

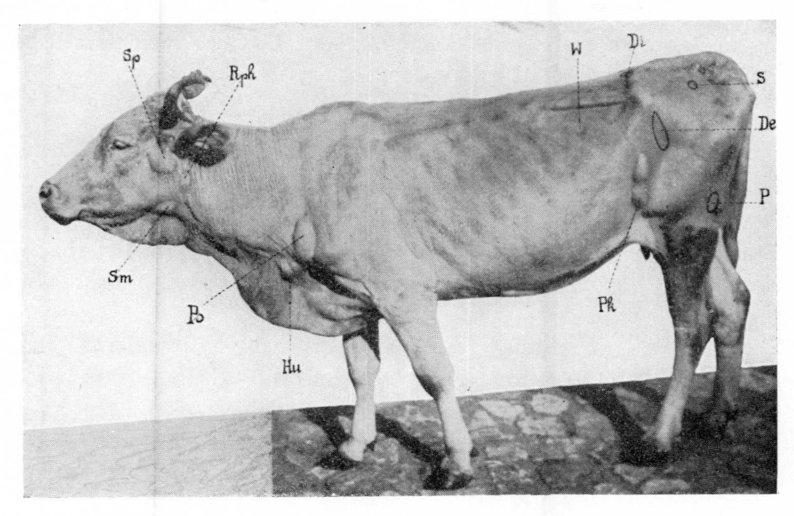

FIG. 76.—Cow affected with lymphatic leukaemia showing great enlargement of superficial lymph nodes. Sp, parotid lymph node; Sm, submaxillary; Rph, lateral retropharyngeal; Ps, prescapular; Hu, prepectoral; W, flank; Di, internal iliac; De, external iliac; Pk, precrural; S, ischiatic; P, popliteal node. (In countries where bovine theileriosis exists a valuable diagnostic lesion in the live animal is enlargement of the parotid, prescapular and precrural lymph nodes.)

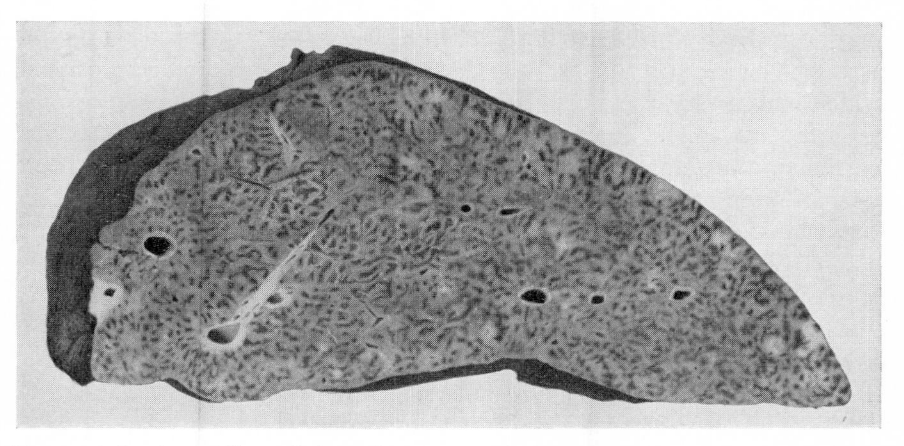

FIG. 77.—Section of liver of sheep from a case of lymphatic leukaemia. The liver was soft, greyish-red in colour, and shows white patches and marked accentuation of the interlobular tissue. The organ weighed 8 lb., and the spleen was also greatly enlarged and weighed $1\frac{1}{2}$ lb.

greyish-white nodules which vary in size and project above the surface of the organ. Leukaemia is regarded as a form of tumour formation and affected carcases are unfit for food. The regulations in the United States which apply to Federally inspected abattoirs prescribe that carcases showing lesions of leukaemia, pseudo-leukaemia and the like, which affects the system of the animal, shall be condemned.

Haemoglobinaemia

This condition is manifested in the live animal by a haemoglobinuria with a dark red or black coloration of the urine. In cattle haemoglobinuria is most commonly seen in redwater fever, and is symptomatic of the destruction of red blood corpuscles by the protozoan parasite *Babesia bovis*.

The carcases of animals affected with haemoglobinaemia may be passed for food if the animal has bled well and if there are no marked changes in the muscular or fatty tissues. Where slaughter has been delayed the carcase may show evidence of decubitus, imperfect bleeding and icterus, and certain of the muscles may be pale and fish-like in appearance ; such carcases should be condemned.

Icterus

Icterus, or jaundice, is a symptom of the presence of bilirubin and biliverdin in the circulating blood, these pigments being constituents of bile and normally excreted by the liver into the duodenum. The affection is caused by reabsorption of bile pigment into the circulatory system, and may occur from mechanical obstruction to the flow of bile by such agencies as calculi or parasites in the bile ducts ; in pigs the commonest parasite which may invade the bile ducts from the small intestine is *Ascaris lumbricoides* (var. *suis.*). Icterus may result from severe cirrhosis of the liver, particularly in the pig, but it is a rare sequel to cirrhosis in cattle or sheep. The affection may occur in the form of a haemolytic icterus in which there is increased destruction of blood elements by infective organisms ; this form of icterus may be seen in redwater and anaplasmosis in cattle, while in pigs it may be caused by leptospira transmitted by the faeces and urine of infected rats. Icterus is caused most frequently by toxic changes in the liver due to bacterial action and less commonly results from obstruction of the bile ducts due to mechanical causes. In haemolytic icterus the yellow colour is less well marked than in the obstructive or toxic form.

Suspicion that a carcase may be icteric is aroused by the yellow coloration of the superficial fatty tissues, of the fat depôts within the visceral cavities, and of the serous membranes, and closer inspection of the carcase

PLATE I

1. Haemorrhagic infarcts in kidney of pig affected with chronic swine erysipelas. The infarcts are caused by non-septic emboli from the cardiac vegetations.

2. (*Right*) Side of pork affected with brown fat disease caused by excessive amounts of unsaturated fatty acids in the feed. (*Left*) Normal side of pork.

3. Diphtheritic metritis of uterus of sow caused by retention and death of a foetus.

4. Small intestine of pig (opened) showing enteritis and necrotic foci caused by strangulation of an umbilical hernia. Note also congestion of mesentery and mesenteric lymph nodes.

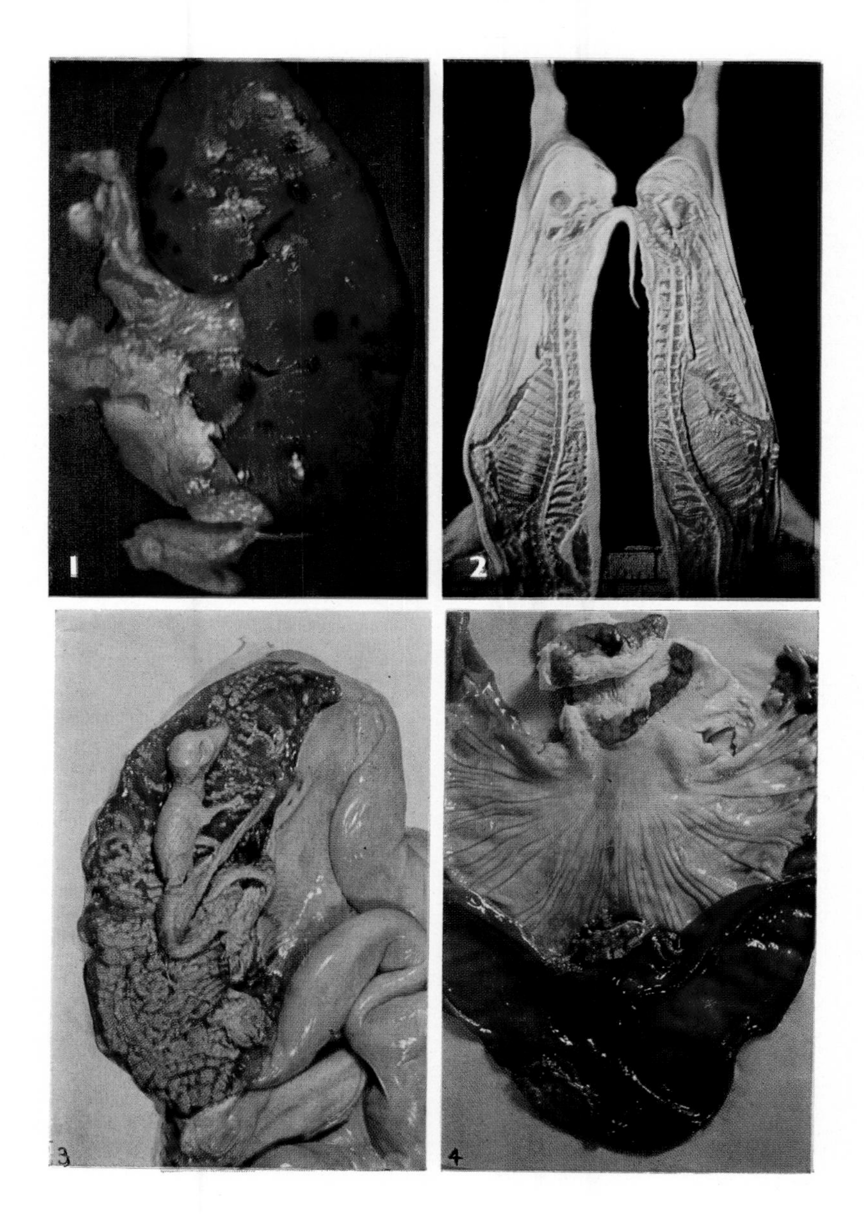
1
2
3
4

connective tissue may then show an abnormal coloration which varies from a lemon colour to an orange-yellow or greenish-yellow. An incision should be made through the kidney fat, where the icteric colour, being of haematogenous origin, is well marked at the more vascular periphery but becomes less obvious towards the centre, and if the kidneys are sectioned the yellow coloration may be seen in the cortex of the organ and also in the calyces and renal pelvis. Yellow pigmentation may also be sought for in the large nerve trunks and in the endothelial lining of the medium-sized

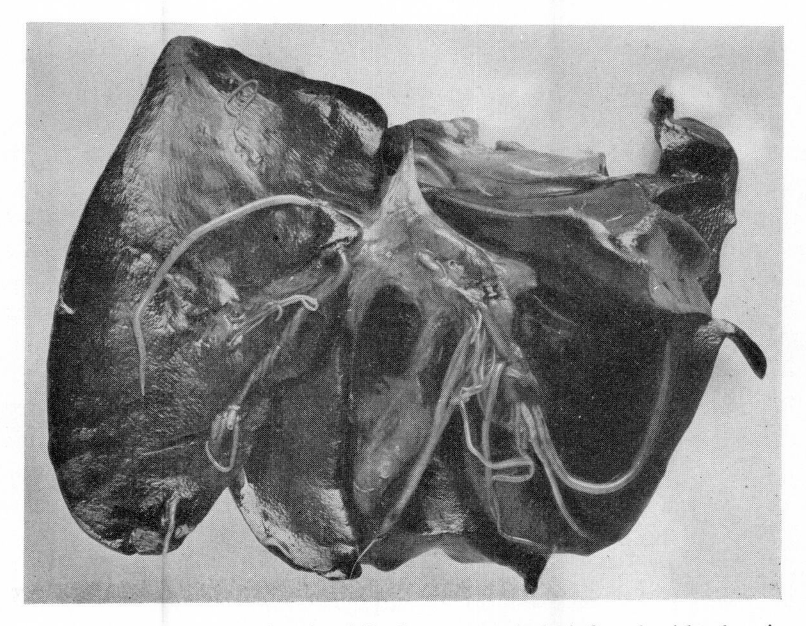

FIG. 78.—Liver of pig showing bile ducts extensively infested with *Ascaris lumbricoides* (var. *suis*).

arteries such as the internal and external iliacs, brachial and femoral, and even in slightly icteric carcases the lining of these blood vessels, when examined in natural light, exhibits a pale yellow coloration, or a yellow colour slightly tinged with orange. Other locations in which the icteric coloration may be sought for are in the lungs, sclerotic membrane of the eye, serous membranes, liver, tendons and cartilaginous extremities of the long bones.

The objections to the sale of a carcase affected with icterus are that the yellow coloration due to the presence of bile pigments may render the carcase repugnant and unmarketable, and in some cases, particularly those associated with cirrhosis of the pig liver, the flesh may possess an abnormal odour and taste due to the presence of bile salts. Where icterus is detected in the well-nourished carcase it should be detained for 24 hours and then re-examined, for the enzyme action of the reducing bodies normally present in muscular tissue may bring about the disappearance of the yellow colour ; if the yellow colour is but slightly evident after 24 hours' detention the carcase may be released for food. Icterus in the pig which is associated with cirrhosis of the liver may also be accompanied by an abnormal odour and taste, and in these animals the yellow coloration may deepen after cooling and hanging overnight, the skin then appearing as if coloured with deep yellow freckles. Icteric pig carcases should therefore be detained for a similar period and then subjected to a boiling test for the presence of abnormal odour and taste, but in the absence of these changes the slightly icteric carcase may be released for food. In all animals, a marked degree of icterus present after the carcase has been detained 24 hours dictates total condemnation. The importance of examining an icteric carcase in daylight must be stressed, for abattoir practice has repeatedly shown that grey, yellow and green tints of muscle, connective tissue or fat can only be recognized with difficulty under artificial light. The regulations which apply in the United States to Federally inspected establishments prescribe that no carcase retained for icterus may be passed for food unless the final inspection thereof is completed under natural light. Those carcases which then show any degree of icterus with a parenchymatous degeneration of organs, the result of infection or intoxication, and those which show an intense yellow or greenish-yellow discoloration without evidence of infection or intoxication, shall be condemned.

Icterus must be distinguished from the yellow coloration of fat which is common in old cows and in certain dairy breeds, and is occasionally seen in pigs, sheep and lambs. Yellow coloration confined to the fatty tissues is due to the presence of the pigment carotene and is either a normal breed characteristic, as in Jersey and in Guernsey cattle, or is the result of assimilation of carotene-containing foods. A marked yellow coloration of the fatty tissues is sometimes seen in sheep and is attributed to a hereditary factor rendering the animal unable to oxidize the yellow pigments, the xanthophylls, in its food. Differentiation between icterus and the normal yellow coloration of fat may be established by the generalized systemic coloration in icterus, and further confirmation may be obtained by the following test. Place 2 grammes of fat in a test tube and add 5 ml. of a 5 per cent. solution of caustic soda. Boil for 1 minute, shaking frequently, then cool under a tap until comfortably warm to the hand. Add one-half or up to an equal volume of ether, and if bilirubin is present it forms a water-soluble sodium salt and remains in the lower layer which is thereby coloured a greenish-yellow. In physiological yellow coloration of the fat the upper ether layer is coloured yellow, while if both pigments are present the upper layer is yellow and the lower layer greenish-yellow.

URAEMIA

The normal secretion of urine by the kidneys and its excretion by way of the bladder and urethra may be obstructed in various ways, with the result that the carcase may emit a strong urinous odour which renders it unfit for food. Gross structural changes of one kidney, as may occur in pyelonephritis or in extensive cyst formation, are followed by a compensatory hypertrophy of the healthy kidney without the production of uraemia ; even where bilateral pyelonephritis or hydronephrosis is present uraemia rarely supervenes, and by far the commonest cause of this condition is obstruction of the urethra, particularly in the ram and boar. The sigmoid flexure of the penis renders the urethra of these male animals particularly prone to obstruction by urinary calculi, the locations at which this is most likely to occur being the ischial arch, behind the sigmoid bend of the penis and, in the case of rams, at the vermiform appendix of the urethra. Urinary calculi occur only rarely in cattle though they are reported to be more frequent in feedlot cattle in the United States, and calculi are very rare in females because of the shortness and dilatability of the urethra. Obstruction to the normal excretion of urine may cause rupture of the bladder, or the presence of a urethral calculus may give rise to necrosis of the urethra, and urethral necrosis may also occur through faulty use of the Burdizzo castrator; in such cases this leads to infiltration of urine into the tissues and the production of a uraemic odour of the carcase. Rupture of the bladder is associated with a strong urinous odour when the abdominal cavity is opened, and this persists after the latter is irrigated, but the odour is only apparent for a few hours and the peritoneal membrane may be only slightly reddened. Necrosis of the urethra is manifested by infiltration of urine into the subcutaneous tissues along the belly, but the urinous odour also disappears rapidly after slaughter and becomes less marked as the carcase cools. Urine rapidly decomposes into urea, ammonia and carbon dioxide, so that a uraemic carcase may possess little more than a slight ammoniacal odour.

Uraemic carcases are unfit for food, but " border-line " cases possessing a slight odour of uraemia should be detained for 24 hours and a portion of the meat then subjected to a boiling test. The detection of a urinous or ammoniacal odour on boiling dictates condemnation of the carcase, but in the absence of odour the carcase may be passed for food.

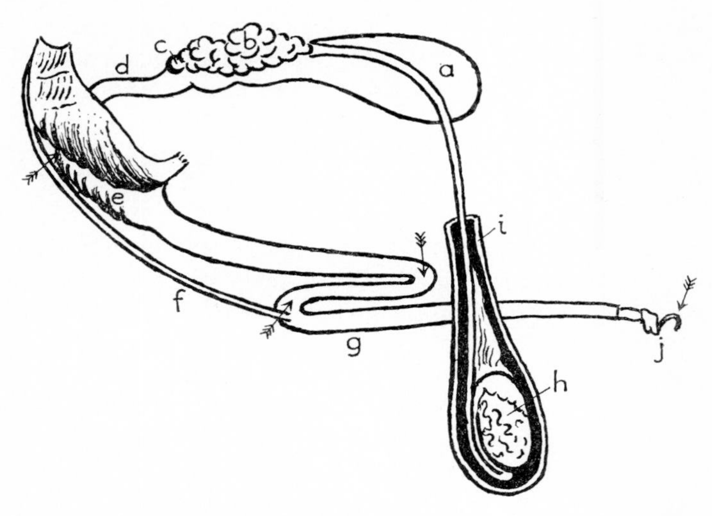

Fig. 79.—Genital organs of ram: (*a*) bladder; (*b*) vesicula seminalis; (*c*) body of prostate; (*d*) urethra; (*e*) bulbo-cavernosus muscle; (*f*) retractor muscle of penis; (*g*) sigmoid flexure of penis; (*h*) testicle; (*i*) tunica vaginalis (opened); (*j*) vermiform appendix of urethra. The arrows indicate where urinary calculi are likely to be arrested.

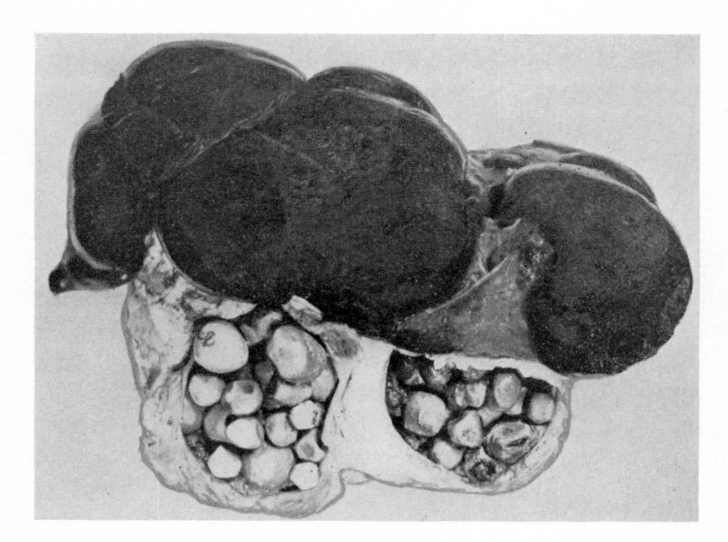

Fig. 80.—Urinary calculi in pelvis of ox kidney. Calculi situated in the kidney pelvis usually only produce slight superficial lesions of the mucous membrane, even when present in large numbers, but become of more serious import when they, or vesical calculi, become lodged in the urethra.

MILK FEVER

This condition is encountered in dairy cows, and may be regarded as a blood affection as it is related to a lowering of the normal calcium content of the blood. Milk fever, which occurs usually within a few days after calving, particularly in good milking cows, is manifested in the live animal by depression, coma and paralysis, but the term milk fever is a misnomer, for the body temperature is only slightly elevated in the early stages of the affection and rapidly becomes normal or subnormal. Though the majority of affected cows recover rapidly after treatment by inflation of the udder or by the subcutaneous injection of calcium gluconate, a number of animals do not respond to treatment and are usually consigned to a slaughterhouse in an attempt to salvage the carcase. The post-mortem findings in milk fever may be slight or absent and are out of all proportion to the cachectic state of the animal before slaughter, though if the animal has been recumbent there may be evidence of bruising on the sternum and hips, while the side of the carcase on which the animal has lain may be oedematous. The uterus is usually strongly contracted and without abnormal contents, but if slaughter has been unduly delayed the carcase and organs may show evidence of imperfect bleeding and an area of bruised tissue may be apparent in the neck or dewlap, indicating the site of a subcutaneous injection. Acetonaemia is often present in cases of milk fever which do not respond to calcium injections, and as a result the carcase may possess the sweet, repugnant odour associated with the presence of acetone.

In the absence of septic infection of the uterus, and if there is no evidence of imperfect bleeding or abnormal odour due to drugs or acetone, the carcase may usually be passed for food, and bruised tissues may be removed by trimming. Carcases which are oedematous, imperfectly bled, or which possess an abnormal odour should be condemned.

5. AFFECTIONS OF THE EXCRETORY SYSTEM

Multiple cysts, which are of congenital origin and usually bilateral, are common in the kidneys, particularly of the sheep and pig, and though at times nearly all the kidney tissue may be affected, there is usually sufficient normal tissue to maintain the animal in health. These cysts develop while the foetus is still *in utero*, being irregularly distributed throughout the kidney, usually no larger than a lentil in size, and caused by failure of a ureter to develop. The presence of extensive congenital cyst formation warrants condemnation of the kidneys, but there is no justification for condemnation of these organs if only one or two small cysts are present. Hydronephrosis, caused by mechanical obstruction to the flow of urine along the ureters, is seen in all animals, but is particularly common in pigs. The ureter and pelvis of the kidney are dilated (in this way the condition can be distinguished from cysts of congenital origin) and urinary pressure may lead to eventual obliteration of the kidney tissue with the formation of a large thin-walled cyst containing urine. Unilateral hydronephrosis is most commonly caused by a twist and occlusion of a ureter, and the most extensive kidney lesions are seen in unilateral affections, whereas bilateral hydronephrosis may be due to a chronic cystitis or to an obstruction in the lumen of the urethra as a result of calculi.

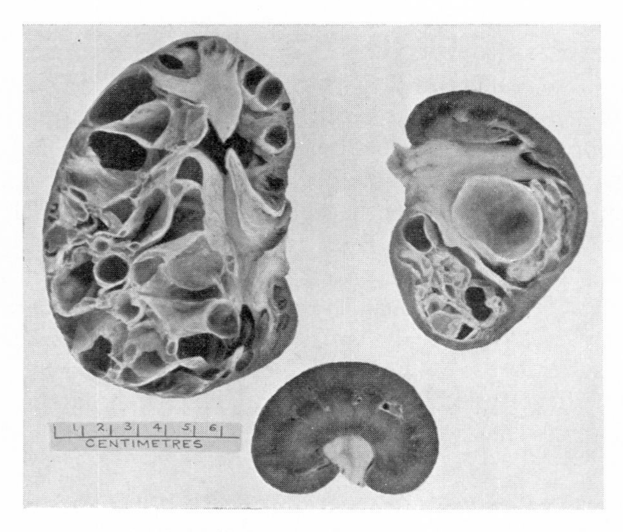

FIG. 81.—Section of left and right kidney of sheep affected with congenital cysts. Small areas of normal kidney tissue are present at the periphery of the organs, and provided one-quarter of the uriniferous tubules in the two kidneys remain they are sufficient to maintain the animal in health. A normal sheep kidney is seen below.

Unilateral hydronephrosis has no deleterious effect on the carcase, the affected kidney alone requiring condemnation, but bilateral hydronephrosis requires more careful consideration, for the flesh of the surrounding parts may be oedematous or, more rarely, the carcase may present a urinous odour. Where bilateral hydronephrosis is present, or where a cystic kidney has ruptured into the abdominal cavity, it is advisable to subject the meat to a boiling test, and the presence of a urinous odour in the flesh or of oedematous areas in various parts of the body dictates total condemnation of the carcase. In bacon factory inspection about 6 per cent. of pig kidneys are condemned, mainly on account of retention cysts and a small number on account of nephritis and hydronephrosis.

The kidneys of the food animals frequently show degenerative changes as a result of toxic affections, and these take the form of cloudy swelling or pathological fatty change. Kidney infarcts (Plate I) caused by detachment of non-pyogenic emboli from a verrucose endocarditis may be seen in chronic swine erysipelas, and may lead to considerable distortion of the organ and unevenness of its surface. Kidney infarcts may also result from a pyogenic ulcerative endocarditis or from a pyaemia, with lodgment of septic emboli in the kidney and the formation of numerous abscesses in

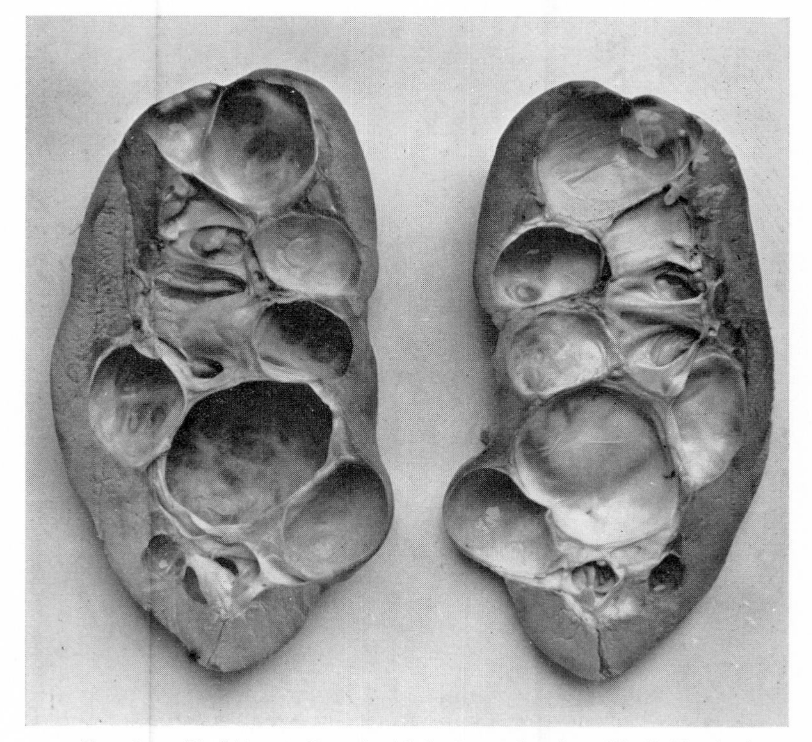

FIG. 82.—Pig kidney affected with hydronephrosis. (G. O. Davies.)

the kidney cortex ; it is a characteristic of pyaemic abscesses in the kidney that their number is inversely proportional to their size (Fig. 140).

Pyelonephritis is occasionally seen in sows, rarely in calves, but is more common in cows and generally occurs as a sequel to parturition, especially where there has been retention of the foetal membranes. The condition is essentially an infection of the renal pelvis with a mixed flora of bacteria, including streptococci, which are the most pathogenic in this affection, while coliform bacteria and nearly always *Corynebacterium renale* may be present. Pyelonephritis may be unilateral or bilateral, and is manifested by catarrh and dilatation of the renal pelvis which is filled with a slimy, glairy fluid, while at times the fluid may contain fibrinous clots or pus and possess a strong ammoniacal odour. The ureters are generally thickened and contain a similar material, and should infection extend fan-wise from the pelvis of the kidney along the uriniferous tubules it may give rise to abscesses in the kidney cortex and the formation of irregular yellowish-grey areas on the kidney surface. Occasionally the infective material may cause complete obliteration of the kidney substance, so that the kidney appears as a purulent sac. The judgment of pyelonephritis depends on whether the affection involves one or both kidneys, and on the bodily condition of the animal. In unilateral pyelonephritis the carcase is usually otherwise

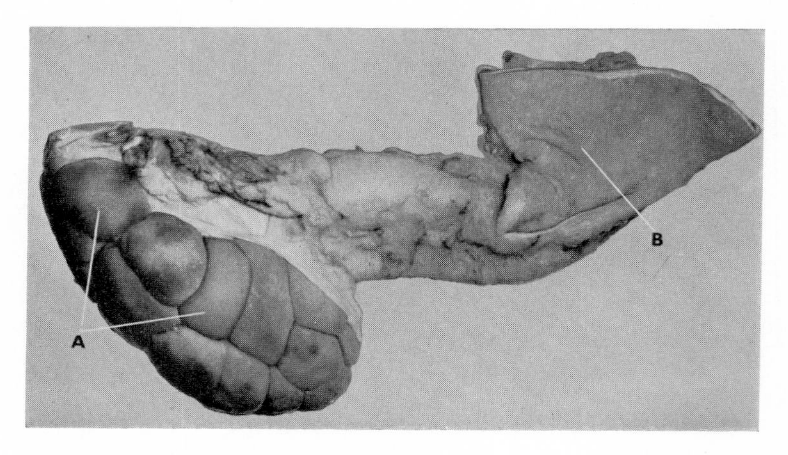

FIG. 83.—Pyelonephritis in a cow. The surface of the kidney (A) shows irregular yellowish-grey areas and the mucous membrane of the ureter (B) is inflamed, covered with a slimy exudate similar to that found in the renal pelvis, while the ureter itself is greatly thickened and dilated.

normal and judgment may be favourable, but a bilateral affection is a more serious condition, and, if associated with oedema and emaciation or with evidence of uraemia, toxaemia or pyaemia, dictates total condemnation of the carcase.

Other forms of nephritis are of but minor importance in meat inspection, for they appear to have little or no effect on the health or bodily condition of the food animals. Carcases of sheep which have died or been slaughtered as a result of entero-toxaemia show a haemorrhagic and pulpy state of the kidneys, this change being particularly apparent if the animal has been dead for some hours.

Green or black coloration, the latter bearing a resemblance to melanosis, is sometimes seen in the kidney cortex of very young calves and is attributed to the bile pigment biliverdin. White spotted kidney, or nephritis fibroplastica, is occasionally seen in young calves, and is attributed to arrested embryonic kidney development, or to infection with *Brucella abortus*. The surface of the kidney presents numerous white spots which are wedge-shaped or circular on cross-section, and it is stated that about 1 per cent. of calves slaughtered show the affection, though the white spots disappear during the first year of life, usually before the animal is 6 months old ; the condition may be regarded as a local one, kidneys alone requiring condemnation. Tuberculosis of the kidneys, which is seen in the ox and pig and indicative of a haematogenous infection, may take the form of small isolated caseous nodules scattered throughout the kidney substance, but more commonly the caseation in the ox involves part or the whole of a kidney lobe.

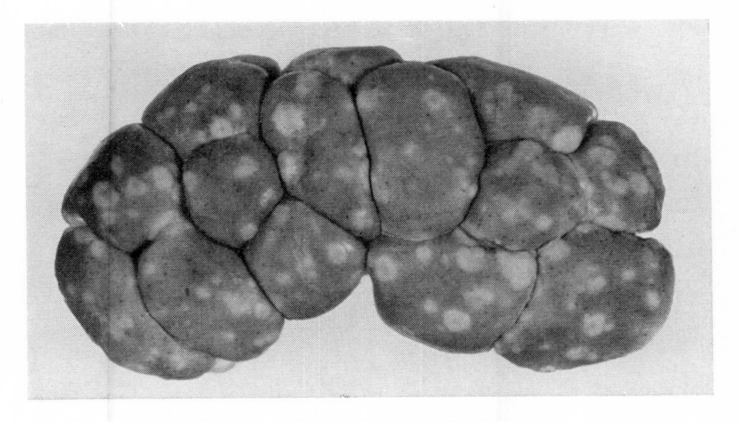

FIG. 84.—Kidney of three months old calf with fibroplastic nephritis.

Parasites are not common in the kidneys of food animals, though the giant kidney worm, *Macracanthorhynchus hirudinaceus*, which normally inhabits the small intestine of the pig, may occasionally be found in the pelvis of the kidney, and cysticerci and hydatid cysts are sometimes found in the kidney substance if the infestation is severe. Kidney worm disease, caused by *Stephanurus dentatus*, is a serious disease of pigs in the southern States of North America and in the exporting districts of Australia. In countries where schistosomiasis exists the ova or cercariae of *Schistosoma mattheei* may give rise to small haemorrhages in the kidneys of cattle or sheep.

Tumour formations in the kidneys are rare, but in leukaemia the kidneys are enlarged and of a mottled grey colour due to lymphocytic infiltration, while in avian leucosis infiltration of the kidneys may be seen in the form of nodules. Embryonal nephroma is a tumour which is not infrequently seen in cattle and is situated at the anterior end of the kidney in contact with the adrenal body; it is usually a local tumour, well encapsulated, the size of an orange or larger, and apparently the result of a congenital displacement of tissues in the kidney. On section the tumour shows areas of necrosis and connective tissue, these areas being interspersed with patches of haemorrhage and yellow tissue resembling that of the adrenal cortex. In the United States embryonal nephroma is regarded as the most common tumour of swine. Affections of the bladder and urethra in the food animals are rare, and occur chiefly in male animals in which the sigmoid flexure of the urethra readily becomes occluded by calculi.

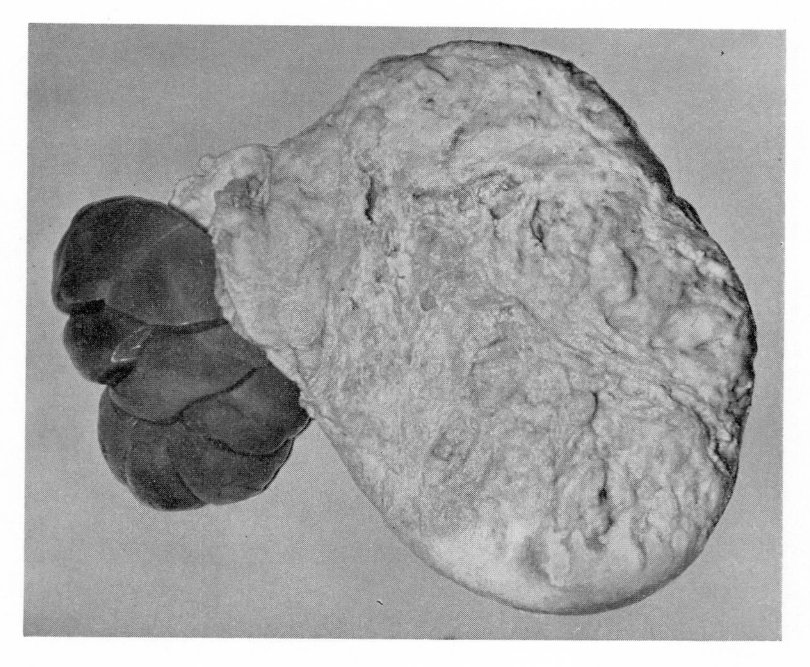

FIG. 85.—Embryonal nephroma or hypernephroma in an ox. The tumour is usually found at the side of the kidney, as in this case, and in contact with the adrenal body. In most cases it is a simple tumour, though it may be malignant, and in this case was unusually large and weighed 30 lb.

6. AFFECTIONS OF THE REPRODUCTIVE SYSTEM

Septic infections of the udder and uterus are common, particularly in the cow, and are of great importance in meat inspection. These septic infections are associated with a condition of fever, and the carcase may therefore be congested, badly bled and the flesh of poor durability, but their greatest importance lies in the fact that septic metritis or mastitis may so lower the resistance of the body as to permit of systemic invasion by organisms which are pathogenic to man, and outbreaks of food poisoning may thus occur if the flesh or organs of such animals are consumed.

Testicles. Tuberculosis of the epididymis or testicle may occur in both ox and pig and is of haematogenous origin, though affection of the tunica vaginalis, which is a pouch-like extension of the peritoneal serous membrane, may occur as an extension of a tuberculous peritonitis and without involvement of the testicular substance. Primary tuberculosis of the glans penis (Fig. 129) and prepuce of the bull may result from the service of a cow suffering from tuberculous metritis. Orchitis is seen in the bull as a result of *Brucella abortus* infection, and may result in complete necrosis of the testicular substance (Fig. 100). An affection known as scirrhous cord is not uncommon in castrated pigs and often confused with scrotal hernia. In scirrhous cord the tumour-like scrotum contains necrotic foci, often with fistulous tracts and the presence of a foul-smelling fluid, and affected pigs are usually stunted, oedematous and unfit for food.

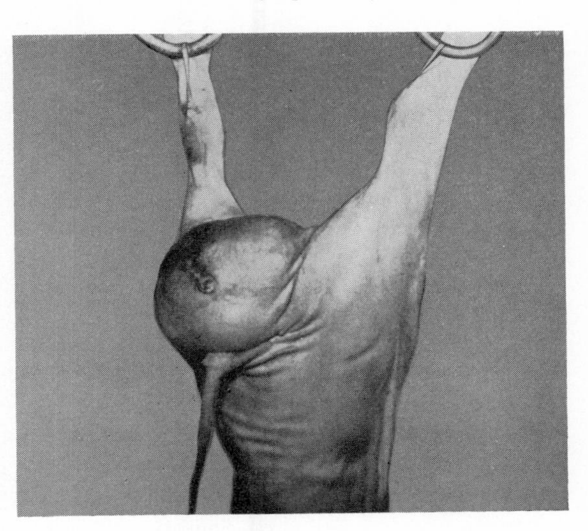

FIG. 86.—Scirrhous cord in a castrated pig.

Uterus. Metritis, or inflammation of the uterus, is bacterial in origin and usually occurs as a result of a retained placenta after parturition, or after injury or rupture of the uterine mucous membrane during parturition; less commonly it may arise as a result of decomposition of the foetus *in utero* (Plate I). Septic metritis is of serious import, being manifested by fever and great constitutional disturbance, and the carcases of such animals call for a severe judgment. Chronic endometritis, on the other hand, is a common affection in cows, being characterized in the live animal by a mucopurulent vaginal discharge, but without fever or constitutional disturbance, and may be regarded as a local condition. Pyometra, or the accumulation of pus in the uterus, likewise often occurs without systemic change, though it may eventually lead to emaciation, and judgment of this affection must be based on the nutritive condition of the animal. Pyometra is occasionally seen in maiden heifers suffering from " white heifer disease ", which usually occurs in white coloured animals of the Shorthorn breed and is caused by the presence of an imperforate hymen with the consequent retention of the uterine secretions. Mummification of the foetus may also take place *in utero*, the process being an aseptic one in which the foetus becomes dehydrated and appears dry and odourless ; though the dam is rendered sterile by the presence of the foetus, and for this reason is usually consigned to a slaughterhouse, there is an entire lack of constitutional disturbance and the condition exerts no deleterious effect on the maternal carcase. Similarly, the foetus may become macerated *in utero*, the foetal tissues becoming transformed into a grey, soft, odourless mass containing loose bones which may be discharged from the uterus during the animal's life. This condition, as in mummification, is of no significance in the judgment of the maternal carcase. Hermaphroditism is not uncommonly encountered in the pig, the animal resembling a gilt pig but usually possessing an enlarged clitoris which projects backwards through the vulval lips ; anatomical defects or abnormalities of the sex organs are responsible for about 50 per cent of the cases of sterility in pigs but are only of local significance in meat inspection.

Vagina. Traumatism of the vagina, which may occur during copulation, is of less serious import than injury to the uterus, for the vaginal wall is not lined externally by the abdominal serous membrane, and peritonitis with severe systemic disturbance, is therefore not so likely to occur. Difficult parturition in both cow and ewe is a common cause of emergency slaughter on the farm, and though the pelvic cavity may show evidence of bruising and congestion, particularly at the anterior borders of the pelvis, such carcases may safely be passed for food provided bleeding and evisceration have been carried out expeditiously and there is no evidence of septic uterine changes.

Vulva. Necrosis of the vulva due to infection with *Fusiformis necrophorus* is common in calves, the lesions being removed in the normal dressing of the carcase. If the condition has caused no systemic effects the carcase may be passed, but in some cases the ischiatic lymph nodes are enlarged and congested, and if this occurs in adult well-nourished calves, the hindquarters should be removed and the remainder of the carcase passed ; if the ischiatic nodes are enlarged in young bobby calves the carcase should be totally condemned. Necrotic lesions may also be seen on the genitalia and on the lips and muzzle of wild rabbits and constitute the so-called rabbit syphilis, while in myxomatosis in this animal fleshy tumours may develop round the anus and genital organs.

Udder. Mastitis, or inflammation of the udder, is commonly encountered in the cow, but less commonly in the sow, while chronic mastitis in the ewe is one of the main causes for the casting of the animal from a breeding flock and consigning it, after fattening, to a slaughterhouse. In the cow the commonest form of mastitis is caused by *Streptococcus agalactiae*, the affection being essentially a catarrh of the milk ducts which tends to assume a chronic form, with proliferation of fibrous connective tissue and induration of the affected quarter or quarters. A thick ropy secretion is produced when the milk is drawn, and this secretion is also observable in the milk ducts when the udder is incised during post-mortem examination. Simple catarrhal mastitis is unaccompanied by systemic disturbance, and only requires condemnation of the udder. Incision of the cow's udder will frequently reveal the presence of abscesses caused by *Corynebacterium pyogenes* which are characterized by pale greenish-yellow purulent centres surrounded by an inner slate-grey or yellowish membrane of soft granulation tissue and an outer capsule of dense connective tissue. They may also be seen in virgin heifers and constitute the so-called summer mastitis which is usually a local affection but may at times give rise to a severe or fatal toxaemia.

Septic mastitis, on the other hand, is a highly acute affection characterized by its rapid progress and severe systemic disturbance; it is essentially an involvement of the whole glandular tissue of the udder as well as the milk ducts, and is usually associated with infection by staphylococci. Septic mastitis may be succeeded by gangrene, in which the udder

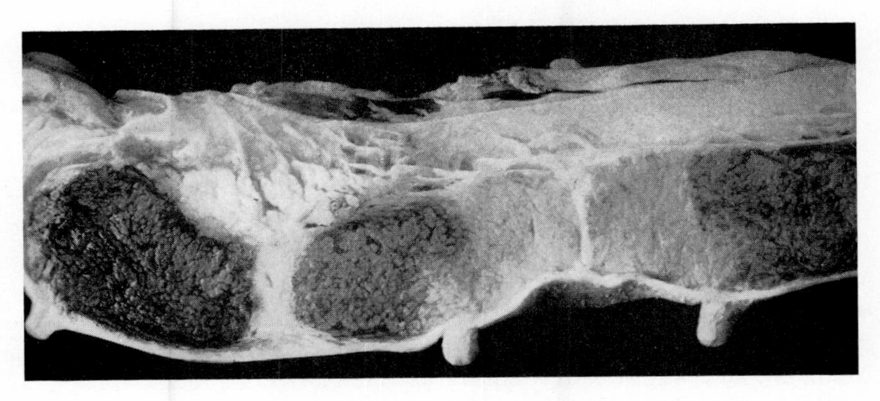

FIG. 87.—Udder of sow affected with acute streptococcal mastitis. The mammary glands at the centre and right of the illustration contain areas of white unaffected glandular tissue.

tissue is of a grey, brownish or bluish colour and contains a dark, thick malodorous liquid often mixed with blood. Carcases affected with acute septic or gangrenous mastitis should be condemned. In countries where brucellosis exists it is questionable whether the udders of cows should be regarded as admissible for human food.

Tuberculosis of the cow's udder (Fig. 130) is most frequently of haematogenous origin, being usually chronic in nature and involving one or more of the quarters of the udder, particularly the hindquarters; the majority of cases of tuberculous bovine mastitis are associated with generalized disease throughout the carcase. The so-called actinomycosis of the udder of the cow is a misnomer, for the condition is essentially a chronic mastitis due to infection with *Staphylococcus pyogenes aureus*, the udder showing nodular lesions the size of a bean or hazel-nut and containing purulent material in which may be found small yellow granules resembling those in lesions of actinomycosis. Primary actinomycosis of the udder is, however,

FIG. 88.—Actinomycosis of sow's udder caused by *Actinomyces bovis*. Only rarely does the affection reach this pendulous, tumour-like form.

the commonest form of chronic mastitis encountered in the sow, and takes the form of thick-walled abscesses embedded in indurated udder tissue (Plate II), while occasionally the teats may be gangrenous; approximately 75 per cent. of cases of chronic mastitis in sows are due to *Actinomyces bovis*, the remaining 25 per cent. being caused by *Staphylococcus pyogenes aureus*. Chronic mastitis of the sow may be regarded as a local condition, and only requires removal of the affected glandular tissue. In ewes the udder is often affected with mastitis, including the acute catarrhal, indurative, suppurative, and particularly the gangrenous form. Though the udder of the ewe is removed in the dressing of the carcase, portions of the supramammary lymph nodes usually remain *in situ*, and evidence of mastitis of an acute and serious form may sometimes be recognized by congestion of these lymph nodes together with oedematous infiltration of the external abdominal wall and a resultant enlargement of the precrural nodes.

7. AFFECTIONS OF THE LYMPHATIC SYSTEM

The examination of the lymph nodes of the carcase and organs is perhaps the most valuable guide as to the nature and extent of toxaemic or septicaemic processes in the animal body, and it is also of the greatest value in the judgment of the tuberculous carcase. In pigs, sheep and calves the iliac nodes provide a useful indication as to the presence of fractures or arthritic changes in the hind limbs.

Pigmentary changes in the lymph nodes, particularly of the bronchial group, are seen as a result of inhalation of particles of coal dust, and this condition, known as anthracosis, is particularly common in animals fed in urban districts or near to collieries. Lymphadenitis, or inflammation of the lymph nodes, may be acute or chronic, the acute condition being manifested by swelling and oedema of the node, which is therefore softer than normal and may be congested ; this latter change is seen particularly well in the " strawberry " lymph nodes associated with acute swine fever, or in the deeply congested lymph nodes in anthrax. Changes in the size, colour and consistency of the lymph nodes are also valuable indications in acute septicaemic or pyaemic conditions, though these changes may be absent if the animal has been slaughtered in the early stages of the affection.

Chronic lymphadenitis is manifested by the development of fibrous connective tissue in the affected node which therefore becomes enlarged and indurated ; such changes are constantly observed in caseous lymphadenitis of the sheep, actinobacillosis of the ox, glanders of the horse, or tuberculosis in any of the food animals, while caseation of the lymph nodes is a diagnostic feature in caseous lymphadenitis and tuberculosis. In tuberculosis of a lymph node the erosion of a caseous lesion into a blood vessel may result in the entry of bacilli into the blood stream and in the production of an acute lymphadenitis, so that a chronic and acute tuberculous lymphadenitis may coexist in the same lymphatic node (Fig. 118).

Parasitic affections of lymph nodes are not uncommon, and linguatula larvae (Plate IV) or immature specimens of *Fasciola hepatica* may be found in the mesenteric nodes of the ox. Both of these parasitic conditions tend to undergo caseation and calcification and may therefore be confused with tuberculosis, but the typical greenish colour of the caseated parasitic foci, together with the ease with which they can be shelled out from the affected lymph node, are reliable methods of differentiation. Lymphadenomatous growths, characterized by progressive enlargement of the lymph nodes and lymphoid tissue of the carcase, are seen in lymphatic leukaemia.

8. AFFECTIONS OF THE SKELETAL SYSTEM

Bone. Pigmentation of bone, which assumes a brown colour, is seen in osteohaematochromatosis of the calf, young bovine (Plate III), and pig.

Rickets is unlikely to be encountered in meat inspection as it is an affection which generally occurs in the months after weaning, and affected animals, except in the case of the calf, are therefore too young for slaughter. It is, however, sometimes encountered in pig carcases where the animal,

FIG. 89.—Friesian bull calf showing severe rachitic infection of the fore limbs. The knee joints are enlarged due to continued production of cartilage at the epiphyses of the long bones.

fed on a diet deficient in vitamin D, i.e. on grain, but with little milk or green foodstuffs, has been unable to absorb the lime salts necessary to produce adequate rigidity of bone. Rickets is characterized by softening, swelling and curvature of the skeletal bones, with which is associated a swelling of the joints, and in advanced cases these changes are manifested in the live animal by lameness and curvature of the spine and bones of the limbs. It is a characteristic of rickets, and also of osteomalacia, that the ends of diseased bones are easily penetrated with a scalpel, and where a rib is bent at right angles to the vertebral column it will bend and break like a piece of cardboard, whereas a normal rib will crack and splinter. Rachitic young pigs may exhibit little more than swelling of the joints and button-like swelling on the ribs, but the affection is usually associated with emaciation, and affected carcases, unless they possess a moderate amount of normal flesh, should be condemned.

Osteomalacia, which may be described as rickets of the adult animal, is caused by an actual decalcification of bone and not, as in rickets, by a failure of the animal to absorb the necessary lime salts. Decalcification may be so pronounced that only a thin shell of bone is left, and the abnormal softness and fragility of the bones may result in fractures, particularly of the ribs and pelvis. A characteristic of osteomalacia is that the periosteum peels off easily from the bone, while the bone marrow is of a dark red, jelly-like consistency which can be most readily detected on examining the sawn surface of the sternum (Plate III). In myeloid leukaemia there may be a similar softening of bony tissue. In the early

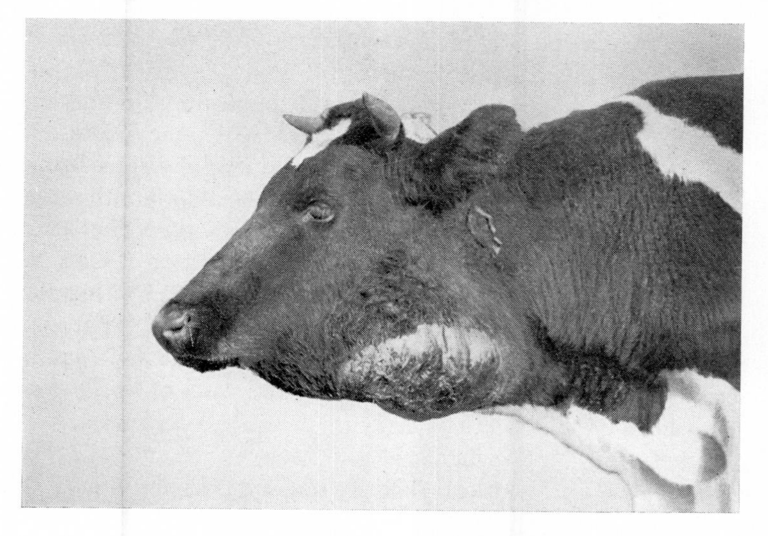

FIG. 90.—Actinomycosis of bovine lower jaw caused by *Actinomyces bovis*. The condition has initiated as a primary affection of the bone of the lower jaw, but has eroded through the skin to produce a hard tumour covered with red, wart-like granulations.

stages of osteomalacia the animal may be well nourished, and it is then only necessary to " bone out " the carcase, the flesh being released for manufacturing purposes. As osteomalacia progresses the muscular tissue undergoes atrophy and serous infiltrations develop in the intermuscular connective tissue, and when these changes are present the flabby and watery condition of the carcase dictates its total condemnation.

Fractures of the ribs, pelvis and bones of the limbs are a frequent cause of emergency slaughter, particularly in the sheep and pig. Recent fractures are associated with the presence of considerable amounts of blood clot and gelatinous infiltration around the seat of fracture, whilst the adjacent lymph nodes are infiltrated with blood ; such cases may be dealt with by removal of the affected tissues. Old fractures which have healed by the production of a callus are common in the ribs of sheep, cattle and pigs.

Presternal calcification, commonly termed "putty brisket", is sometimes seen in the cushion of the brisket in cattle, less frequently in sheep; it is traumatic in origin, and is probably caused by repeated bruising of the presternal tissues during the act of lying down. The condition is primarily one of fat necrosis and is manifested by irregular putty-like masses in the presternal fat, the necrotic tissue eventually becoming calcareous due to infiltration with lime salts and bearing a resemblance to tuberculosis.

The commonest specific affection of bone occurs in actinomycosis in cattle, and usually involves the lower jaw (Fig. 92), with the formation of hard tumour-like lesions which may break through the skin and appear as red, fungoid proliferations. Parasitic infections of bone are rare, though hydatid cysts are occasionally seen and may be distinguished from tuberculosis by the absence of involvement of the associated lymph nodes.

Joints. Arthritis may be of an acute or chronic type, the latter being much more frequently encountered in meat inspection. Chronic non-suppurating arthritis is seen commonly in the stifle and fetlock joints of sheep, and in the knee, hock and stifle of pigs; in the latter animal it is usually the result of a previous attack of swine erysipelas, and many of the so-called cases of rheumatism in the pig are in reality old cases of swine erysipelas. The same causal organism causes arthritis in lambs a few months old, and chronic non-suppurating arthritis is also seen in rickets. The synovial fluid of a joint affected with arthritis of a non-suppurating form is opaque, sometimes blood-coloured, and there is a proliferation of the synovial villi which gives the synovial membrane the appearance of being covered with a red pile (Plate III). The joint contents are usually sterile, but *Erysipelothrix rhusiopathiae* may be found in the arthritic joints of sheep and pigs, and if the affection is in the hind limb the iliac lymph node of the affected limb is usually greatly enlarged and reddish-brown in colour. Carcases showing chronic arthritis of a non-suppurating form only require removal of the affected joint and contiguous tissue, but a "flare up" of a chronic erysipelas arthritis is probably the commonest cause of petechial haemorrhages in the kidney of pigs.

Septic infection of a single joint is only likely to arise as a result of a penetrating joint wound, but multiple septic arthritis, especially of the hock or stifle joints, is seen in calves in septicaemic conditions or in infections of umbilical origin, joint symptoms generally appearing 3 to 4 weeks after birth. It is also seen in the acute form of pyaemia which sometimes occurs in cows as a result of septic metritis subsequent to parturition. Joints affected with septic arthritis are swollen, the synovial membrane is oedematous and thickened, and the synovial fluid is increased in amount, turbid, and often contains flocculi; at times it may be purulent in character, the contents of the joint having the appearance of a hen's egg which has been mixed, while the adjacent tendon sheaths may be serously infiltrated. Multiple septic arthritis is caused by various organisms, including coliform bacteria and occasionally members of the salmonella group, and as the condition is indicative of a septicaemic process affected carcases must be totally condemned. Regulations in the United States applicable to Federally inspected abattoirs prescribe that carcases affected with arthritis or polyarthritis when localized and not associated with systemic change may be passed for food after removal and condemnation of all affected parts provided the carcases are otherwise in good condition. Carcases affected with arthritis or polyarthritis characterized by the presence of periarticular abscesses which may or may not be connected with similar suppurative foci within the epiphyses of the bones shall be condemned in cases manifesting suppurative lesions in more than one joint. Otherwise the condemnations shall be restricted to the affected parts if such carcases are otherwise in good condition.

9. AFFECTIONS OF THE MUSCULAR SYSTEM

A chocolate-coloured pigmentation of the muscular fibres occurs in xanthosis, while muscular haemorrhages, known as "splashing" (Fig. 23), are not uncommon and are due to mechanical causes associated with the act of slaughter.

Muscular tissue may undergo degeneration, cloudy swelling being seen in severe toxic disturbance, while hyaline degeneration occurs in haemoglobinaemia in horses and in milk fever in cattle. Hyaline degeneration may be regarded as a sign of severe systemic disturbance, affected muscles appearing cloudy, very pale in colour, and somewhat resembling the flesh of fish; the condition may also be seen in the diaphragm, abdominal and intercostal muscles in pigs, and in these animals the affected muscular tissue is so watery that it can be easily penetrated by the fingers.

Interstitial myositis, known also as muscular fibrosis, is usually encountered in imported hindquarters of beef, but also occurs in home-killed stock. The normal muscular tissue is replaced by bands of white fibrous connective tissue, the affection being usually localized in the round of beef but occasionally seen in the lumbar and shoulder muscles. The condition has been attributed to hyaline degeneration, and in some cases sarcosporidia have been found, but it is probable that the affection is traumatic in origin, and affected muscular tissue must be regarded as unmarketable and should be condemned.

Advanced fatty change of muscle occurs in the ox and pig, being characterized by the replacement of normal muscle by fatty tissue, and is regarded as being due to retarded development of the blood vessels supplying the muscle, resulting in the development of mucoid tissue between the muscles, this material eventually undergoing advanced fatty change. The condition is less likely to be localized than in muscular fibrosis and may extend for varying distances, particularly in the loin; in the pig the

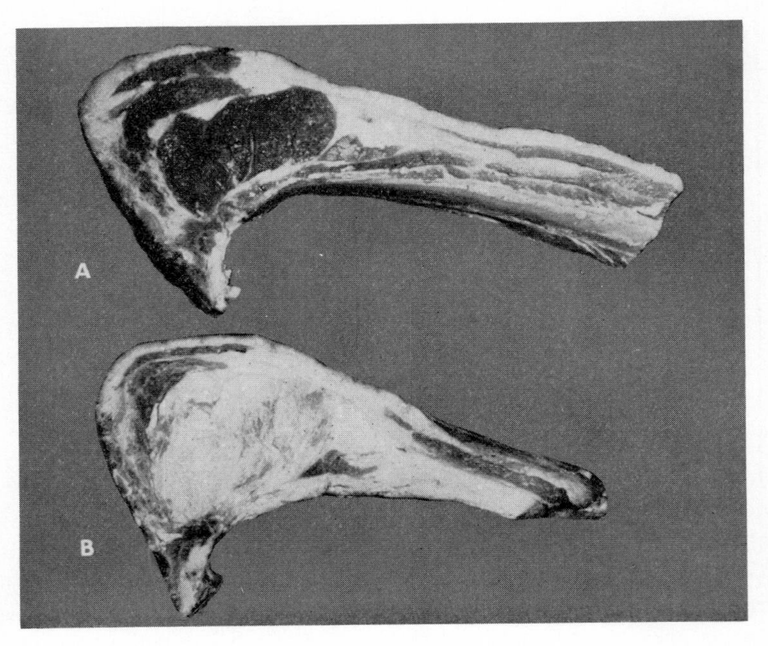

FIG. 91.—Muscular fibrosis in beef (B) compared with a portion of normal muscle (A).

latissimus dorsi muscle of the back may be involved, and fatty tissue may replace normal muscle to such an extent that only a few muscle fibres remain. A condition in calves termed muscular dystrophy or white muscle disease has been recorded in Scotland, and particularly in northern Germany and Scandinavia, and has been attributed to a deficiency in vitamin E. The affected areas of muscular tissue are conspicuous by their bilateral symmetry and creamy white colour, and a symmetrical muscular degeneration is sometimes seen in lambs in southern Australia.

Actinobacillosis is a common affection of the masseter muscle and tongue muscles of the ox and takes the form of an interstitial myositis, with enlargement and induration of the muscle which has a white glistening appearance when it is sectioned with a knife.

Nodular Necrosis. This condition is known also as Roeckl's granuloma, and is found occasionally in cattle, affecting animals of all ages and both sexes, but most frequently older cows. It may occur in animals in excellent condition, but is commoner in animals in moderate or poor condition, and is characterized by the presence in the muscular tissue of nodules from a walnut to a golf ball in size. These are localized chiefly in the muscles of the neck, shoulder, back, croup, and almost constantly the tail, being superficially placed and not usually deeper in the musculature than one inch. Palpation in the live animal will show that the nodules are intramuscular and not attached to the skin, but even when very numerous they do not become confluent. The nodules are rounded or elongated in the direction of the muscle fibres, are greyish-yellow in colour, not easily enucleated, being slightly elastic and rather dry or waxy on section. The larger nodules sometimes contain yellow pin-point foci, and microscopically are seen to consist of a central zone of necrosis, sometimes with calcification, and surrounded by a connective tissue wall. These granuloma have been attributed to the result of chronic inflammation, while other authorities classify them as blastomycomata, the blastomyces being one of the pathogenic fungi. From the meat inspection point of view they may be regarded as local tumour formations and, as they occur only in the superficial musculature and do not involve the viscera, the presence of a few nodules on the muscular surface may be dealt with by removal of the affected areas of superficial muscle. In extensive affection in a poorly nourished animal the carcase should be condemned.

Parasitic infections of muscle include *Cysticercus bovis* in the ox (Fig. 172), *Cysticercus cellulosae* in the pig (Fig. 168), *Cysticercus ovis* in sheep, sarcosporidia in the ox, sheep and pig, and *Trichinella spiralis* in the pig. In severe infestation hydatid cysts may be found in the muscular tissue, and the cysts of *Multiceps multiceps*, the cause of sturdy in sheep, have occasionally been recorded in the skeletal musculature. Parasitic infections of muscle show a marked tendency to degenerate and become calcified, and greenish foci or calcareous nodules encountered in the muscular tissue of food animals are almost certainly of parasitic origin.

10. AFFECTIONS OF THE NERVOUS SYSTEM

Conditions which may affect the central nervous system of food animals are tuberculous meningitis in cattle and sturdy in sheep.

Tuberculous meningitis in the bovine is evidence of a haematogenous infection of congenital origin, and is usually encountered in young cattle up to 1½ years old, affected animals being often unthrifty and showing inco-ordination of movement. On post-mortem examination, the meninges may show lesions which are irregularly distributed over the pia mater and up to a lentil in size. Tuberculous abscesses may occur in the vertebrae of the lumbar region of pigs, and in the live animal produce a peculiar inco-ordinated gait due to pressure of the lesion on the spinal cord ; in sows they are sometimes responsible for prolonged recumbency which necessitates emergency slaughter.

Hydatid cysts may occasionally be found in the brain of the food animals, while *Multiceps multiceps* is not uncommon in the brain of sheep (Fig. 160), and *Cysticercus cellulosae* may be found in the brain of over 40 per cent. of pigs affected with this parasite. Melanotic deposits are seen in the spinal cord and meninges of calves, but in the absence of generalized deposits throughout the carcase are only of local significance.

Certain affections in the live animal are associated with symptoms of nervous derangement and often necessitate emergency slaughter. Lactation tetany, due to a magnesium deficiency, occurs in milch cows, usually in about a fortnight after the animals are turned out to grass in springtime ; eclampsia may occur in sows, generally within 24 hours of farrowing, and pregnancy toxaemia is seen in pregnant ewes. There are few typical post-mortem lesions in these affections, though a physiological fatty infiltration of the liver is invariably present in pregnancy toxaemia, and judgment of such carcases must be based on the degree of bleeding and the presence or absence of rigor mortis.

CHAPTER VII

BACTERIAL AND VIRAL DISEASES OF THE FOOD ANIMALS

ACTINOMYCOSIS

This is an infective disease pursuing a chronic course and occurring commonly in cattle and pigs, less commonly in sheep, horses and man. The disease is caused by several different forms of micro-organisms which are classified as follows :

(1) *Actinomyces bovis* is responsible for actinomycosis of bone in cattle and is the main cause of udder actinomycosis in the pig.

(2) *Actinobacillus lignièresi* is the principal cause of actinomycosis (actinobacillosis) of the tongue, skin and parenchymatous organs.

(3) *Staphylococcus pyogenes aureus* is the cause of udder actinomycosis in the cow and a minor proportion of cases of udder actinomycosis in the pig.

In investigation of 20 cases in cattle where bone was involved, it was found that the causal organism in every case was *Actinomyces bovis ;* in 90 cases of tongue involvement *Actinobacillus lignièresi* was found exclusively, and in 115 out of 117 cases of udder actinomycosis of the cow the causal organism was found to be *Staphylococcus pyogenes aureus.* The affection of bone may be regarded as the true form of actinomycosis, while affection of the softer tissues of the body, such as tongue, lips, palate, lungs, stomach and intestines are caused by the actinobacillus. Lesions which show affection of the adjacent lymph nodes may with certainty be attributed to the latter organism.

The term actinomycosis has been conveniently used to include all the above affections, and in each form of the disease the typical granules in the older lesions are characteristic. These granules can be felt when purulent lesions are incised, and under the low powers of the microscope appear rosette-shaped, with the centre of the granule composed of numerous

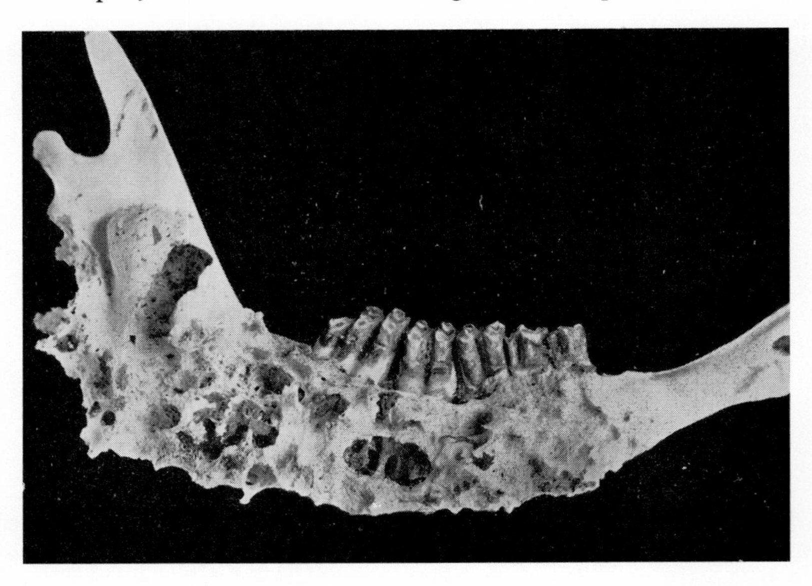

FIG. 92.—Actinomycosis of lower jaw of ox. The external layer of bone has become thickened due to periosteal inflammation, and the interior is replaced by a soft, sarcoma-like tissue interspersed with a wide-meshed network of bony tissue.

branching filaments and the periphery of radially arranged clubs. It is these colonies which give the pus its granular feel and appearance.

Pathogenesis. It is probable that the causal organism is naturally parasitic in the animal body, gaining entry to the tissues during the change of teeth or after infective diseases which involve the mouth and gums. There are records on the Continent of severe outbreaks of actinobacillosis in cattle which had been affected with ulceration of the tongue, mouth and gums as a result of foot and mouth disease. The bovine tongue is particularly liable to injury and infection, as the depression on the dorsum of this organ acts as a stop to torn off or prehended straw, and for this reason cases of actinobacillosis are more common in straw-fed cattle than in those during summer grazing.

On entering the tissues the organism proliferates and a small nodule develops. These nodules extend by growth and coalescence to form large tumours in which there is considerable development of fibrous tissue, the centres of these tumours being grey or yellowish in colour and containing a yellowish purulent substance in which fine sulphur-yellow granules are just visible to the naked eye. Extension from the primary lesion may occur by contiguity, or by way of the lymphatic stream, to involve the neighbouring lymph nodes, and secondary infection of the internal organs may occur by way of the blood stream. It is a peculiarity of the disease that actinobacillosis of the internal organs seldom coexists with lesions of the tongue.

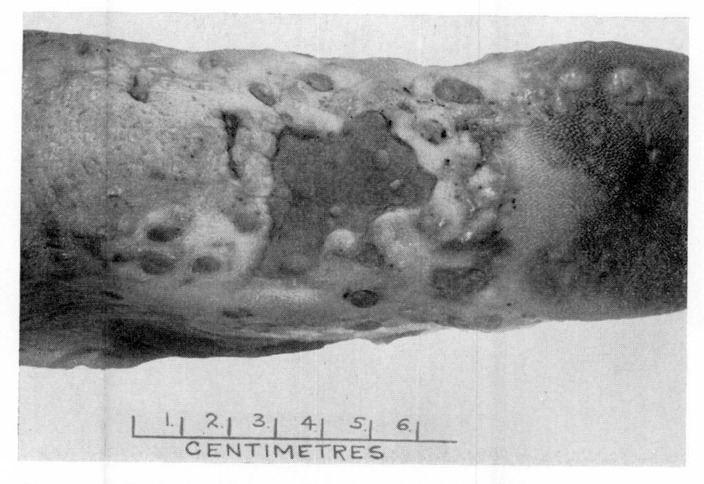

FIG. 93.—Actinobacillosis of bovine tongue, showing ulceration in the dorsal depression, together with a number of actinobacillotic nodules at the base of the ulcer and on the tongue surface.

Lesions. In cattle the lesions of actinomycosis are usually confined to the head, and may involve the jaw bones to produce the so-called lumpy jaw. The lower jaw is more often affected than the upper, the bone being thickened but rarefied and presenting a honeycombed appearance on section. The disease process may extend from the bone to involve the buccal cavity, with the formation of ulcers on the cheeks or gums, or it may extend outwards to erode through the skin and produce red, wart-like granulations (Fig. 90). More frequently head lesions are due to actinobacillosis and take the form of great thickening and induration of the outer muscles of mastication, and these on section show a marked development of white fibrous tissue; this form of the disease is the one more commonly encountered in the slaughterhouse. Actinobacillosis may spread from the head along the neck muscles even as far as the shoulder, so that the forequarter should always be examined when the head is severely affected.

Actinobacillosis involving the tongue may be seen as a well-defined ulcer which possesses indurated edges and is usually situated in the depression on the dorsum of the tongue. In other cases, and sometimes coexistent with the ulceration, are flattened nodules, up to a hazel nut in size, which are distributed about the lateral aspect of the tongue and cause elevations of the mucous membrane; these nodules may also erode through the epithelium of the tongue to produce small ulcers. Ulceration or nodule formation in the tongue is associated, as in the jaw lesions, with a marked development of fibrous tissue which gives rise to the term wooden tongue.

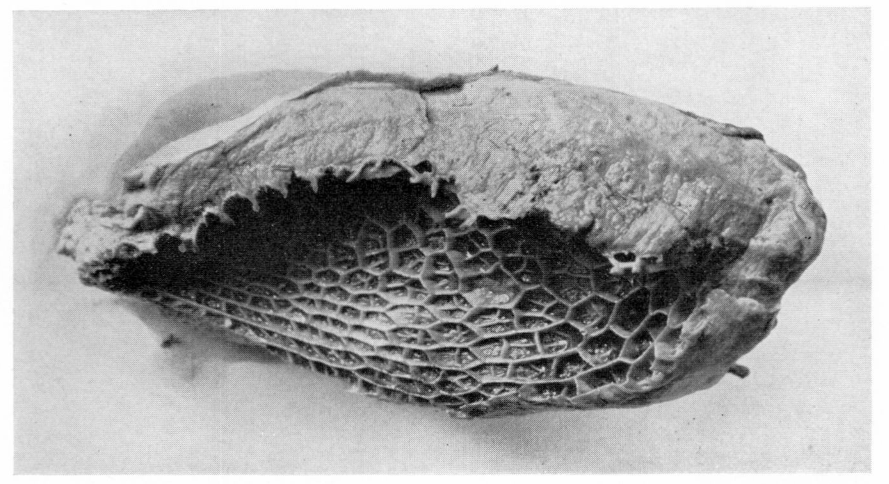

FIG. 94.—Actinobacillosis of bovine reticulum, showing marked fibrous thickening of reticular wall. (H. L. Torrance.)

Actinobacillotic lesions of the tongue or masticatory muscles are frequently associated with lesions in the associated lymph nodes, i.e. submaxillary, retropharyngeal, parotid, and occasionally the mediastinal nodes. In the early stages the lymph nodes are enlarged and of a firmer consistency than normal, while on section the cut surface of the node appears somewhat convex and shows small, yellowish glistening nodules, not unlike pellets of shot embedded in fibrous connective tissue. These nodules are arranged characteristically in the peripheral portion of the cortex, frequently in irregular clusters towards one end of the node, but in older lymph node lesions the centres tend to degenerate and contain several foci of yellow purulent matter which can be expressed when the lymph node is squeezed.

Lesions of actinobacillosis in the ox stomachs may be seen in the rumen or reticulum, and arise as a result of mechanical injuries or by ingestion of infective material from a lesion in the buccal cavity. The stomach lesions take the form of raised plaques on the mucous membrane; these may undergo ulceration and are associated with marked fibrous thickening of the stomach wall which on section shows numerous yellow nodules embedded in the indurated tissue. The affection may also involve the lower portion of the oesophagus, the walls of which are often 1 to 2 inches thick due to infiltration with a yellow gelatinous fluid which exudes when the oesophagus is incised.

The liver, diaphragm and lungs are frequently involved in cases where actinobacillotic infection has occurred by penetration of the reticulum and has spread by simple contiguity. Actinobacillotic lesions which occur on the peritoneum usually involve the left flank and appear as cauliflower-like projections attached to the serous membrane by a delicate pedicle, or they may assume the form of low convex growths, and incision and close inspection of their cut surface will reveal a number of minute yellowish spots. Peritoneal lesions are often associated with lesions in the liver, the substance of which shows circular nodules up to 2 inches in size and consisting of fibrous tissue in which are embedded numerous small yellow foci. In the lungs the smaller lesions are fibrous, somewhat irregularly shaped, and when incised show a distinct convexity of the cut surface but no pus. Older lung lesions may reach a great size, and consist of white fibrous tissue intermixed with areas containing a greenish-yellow pus which can be readily expressed when the lesion is squeezed. The larger lung lesions have a typical marbled appearance when incised, and a striking feature is the deposition of a greenish-black pigment which radiates from the centre of the lesion in rough irregular lines. Very occasionally actinobacillosis may appear in a miliary form in the lungs of cattle. Actinobacillosis may also be found on the skin surface and takes the form of sessile, fibrous tumours. In sheep actinobacillotic lesions occur on the lips and face and may also be found in the lymph nodes of the neck and lungs.

In the sow actinomycosis is usually confined to the udder tissue (Plate II), infection being probably introduced into the udder by the bites of suckling pigs in which the organism is parasitic in the mouth cavity and whose teeth are particularly sharp. Lesions may appear on the udder in the form of indurated ulcers, but more commonly the organ is partially or totally converted into a hard tumour containing abundant fibrous tissue embedded in which are rounded, thick-walled abscesses up to a walnut in size. About 75 per cent. of cases of chronic mastitis in the sow may be attributed to actinomycosis, the remainder to a staphylococcal infection, and in Malmo abattoir, Sweden, it is recorded that 25 per cent. of older sows have actinomycosis of the mammary glands.

ACTINOMYCOSIS IN MAN. Farmers and those tending cattle are most commonly affected, with the formation of fibrous tumours of the jaw muscles. The affection is probably acquired by sucking or chewing straw or grains, but there is no evidence that man has ever acquired the infection from animals, either through milk or meat or by accidental inoculation. It is considered that the strains affecting man and animals are specifically distinct and that the strains from man should be regarded as *Actinomyces israeli* and the strains from animals as *Actinomyces bovis*. In regard to actinobacillosis there has only been one authenticated record of human infection with this organism.

Judgment. Affected organs, such as head, tongue, stomach or lungs, should be condemned. In some countries it is recommended that where there is an isolated tongue lesion this may be excised and the remainder of the tongue passed for food. Where actinobacillosis of the serous membranes, usually the peritoneum, occurs in well-nourished animals, the carcase may be released after removal of the affected membrane. Regulations in the United States which apply to Federally inspected abattoirs prescribe that heads affected with actinomycosis or actinobacillosis, including the tongue, shall be condemned, except that when the disease of the jaw is slight, strictly localized, and without suppuration, fistulous tracts, or lymph node involvement, the tongue, if free from disease, may be passed, or, when the disease is slight and confined to the lymph nodes, the head, including the tongue, may be passed after the affected nodes have been removed and condemned. In cases where the disease is slight and confined to the tongue, with or without involvement of the corresponding lymph nodes, the head may be passed after removal and condemnation of the tongue and corresponding lymph nodes.

BOTRIOMYCOSIS

This is a chronic infective disease occurring particularly in the horse, more rarely in the ox, sheep and pig, and characterized by the formation of large fibrous tumours. The condition is now very rare and should more properly be termed staphylococcal granuloma.

The causal micro-organism, *Staphylococcus pyogenes aureus*, can be demonstrated microscopically in grape-like clusters which are enclosed in a strong connective tissue wall. Macroscopically the tumours resemble fibromata, with yellowish-brown centres projecting above the cut surface and containing yellowish " sand grain " granules. In the horse the predilection seats are the spermatic cord after castration, or the skin surface as a result of harness erosions, and these primary superficial lesions may extend by metastases to the lungs, other internal organs, udder, ribs or muscle.

Judgment. Although cases of staphylococcal granuloma in man occasionally occur, there is no evidence that the disease is transmissible from animal to man. All affected portions of a carcase, however, should be condemned as unfit for human food.

ANTHRAX

Anthrax is primarily a disease of animals, and man is infected secondarily, the affection being an acute, infective septicaemia caused by *Bacillus anthracis* and in Great Britain occurs chiefly in cattle, though all the food animals are susceptible. The pig is somewhat more resistant than the sheep and horse, while among wild animals there are records of numerous cases in zoological gardens where lions, tigers and leopards have died as a result of consuming the flesh of an animal which has died of anthrax. Infection may also occur naturally in the cat, dog, mink and elephant, and in Sweden outbreaks occur frequently in silver foxes fed on raw cow meat. Domestic poultry and other birds possess a high degree of immunity which can be artificially overcome as, for example, experimentally, if the body temperature is lowered several degrees by immersion of the bird in cold water.

Bacteriology. Bacillus anthracis is 5 μ long by 1·5 μ broad, being one of the largest micro-organisms amongst the pathogenic bacteria, whilst in the spore form it is one of the most resistant to destructive influences such as heat and disinfectants. The bacilli are square-ended rods which occur in the body fluids either singly or as short chains of three to eight links. On culture media longer chains are formed, appearing microscopically as wavy, hair-like growths.

Bacilli obtained from the body fluids, including the blood, are surrounded by a very typical capsule formation, and this capsule is of great diagnostic value in differentiating *B. anthracis* in the blood of a dead animal from the putrefactive bacteria which invade the blood soon after an animal's death.

Examination of Blood for B. anthracis. As the invasion of the blood by putrefactive bacteria arises from the intestines and extends in an out ward direction, it is advisable, in examining a dead bovine for anthrax, to obtain a blood smear from a part of the body furthest removed from the intestines, for in this way confusion between anthrax and putrefactive bacilli may be largely avoided. A blood smear is usually obtained from one of the small veins on the inner aspect of the ear, or from an incision on the under aspect of the tail and close to its attachment to the sacrum ;

a smear may also be obtained by an incision through the skin of a limb just above the coronet. The two latter methods have the advantage that the incision can be readily bandaged and thus further escape of blood prevented, but it is generally agreed that the tail is the most satisfactory position from which a blood smear may be obtained.

After a drop of blood is placed on a slide, it is spread with the edge of another slide held at an angle of 45°, and the smear is then dried in air or with a flame, care being taken that the slide is not overheated. A 1 per cent. aqueous solution of methylene blue is added, poured off after 1 minute, and the smear dried between two folds of blotting paper. Anthrax bacilli may then be searched for by microscopical examination, particularly at the edge of the smear, and if present they appear blue and are surrounded by definite capsules which are purple in colour; this typical staining characteristic is known as McFadyean's reaction. Capsulated anthrax bacilli have been demonstrated microscopically in the circulating blood 16 to 18 hours before a bovine animal's death, but are extremely unlikely to be present in the milk of affected cows. Some of the bacillary capsules disintegrate, producing a purple groundwork between the bacilli, and this is so characteristic that the purple coloration of a positive blood smear can be even detected by the naked eye. This purple coloration of the capsular material and detritus is very persistent, and empty capsules, known as "shadow forms", may still be demonstrated in blood smears after the anthrax bacilli themselves have been eliminated by putrefactive anaerobic bacteria from the intestines.

In sheep the disease is also septicaemic in character, and a blood smear may be taken in a similar manner to that in cattle, but in the horse and pig the bacilli tend to remain localized in the region of the throat, and in such animals it is frequently difficult to demonstrate the micro-organisms in the circulating blood. A smear is therefore usually taken from a submaxillary lymph node or from the oedematous swelling of the throat.

Under favourable conditions, chief of which is the presence of sufficient oxygen, the bacilli form spores. These spores, which are centrally placed, are not found in the living animal or in the intact carcase, and are only formed between a temperature range of 53° F. to 110° F. and when the oxygen supply is adequate. These optimum conditions for spore formation can only take place when bacilli, having exhausted the oxygen of the blood, gain access to the outer air by way of the nasal or anal discharges, or if the blood is spilt during the dressing of an affected carcase. The sporulating form of *B. anthracis* is markedly more resistant to destructive influences than the bacillary form, and for this reason, when dealing with anthrax or suspected anthrax, it is necessary to prevent the effusion of blood from all natural openings as well as other parts of the carcase.

Resistance of Anthrax Bacilli and Spores. Anthrax bacilli are easily destroyed by the common disinfectants, by the gastric juices in 20 minutes, and by moist heat at a temperature of 136° F. in 15 minutes. In the intact and unopened carcase they will not survive longer than 4 days.

The spores, on the other hand, are resistant to the action of the digestive juices and when ingested may produce intestinal or generalized disease. The dried spores may survive for as long as 32 years but they are destroyed in 10 minutes by moist heat at a temperature of 212° F. to 222° F. In the soil, anthrax spores may survive for 3 years or longer, this fact accounting for the so-called anthrax fields where there has previously been a death from anthrax, and where infective blood has been shed; in many cases it may be unsafe to graze stock of any kind on these fields even after an interval of several years. Though the ridding of such fields of infection is impossible, adequate disinfection of cowsheds, slaughterhouses, etc., after a case of anthrax, can be ensured by the use of 1 in 1000 corrosive sublimate for 10 minutes, 1 to 2 per cent. formaldehyde, 5 per cent. potassium permanganate, or 5 per cent. fresh chloride of lime.

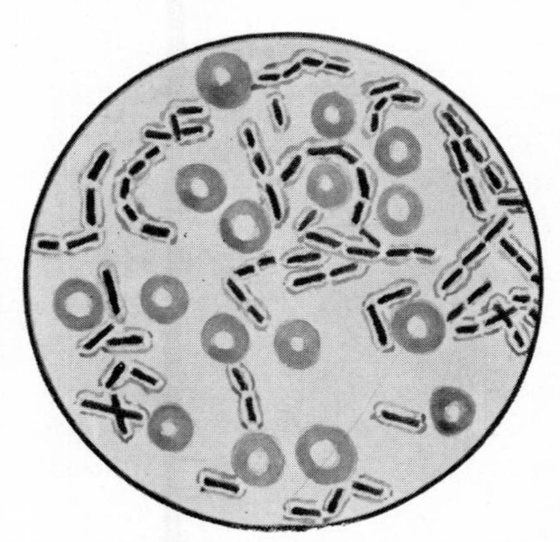

FIG. 95.—Anthrax bacilli in blood smear stained with methylene blue to show short chains of bacilli surrounded by the typical capsule formation.

Pathogenesis. Infection in the ox, sheep and horse usually occurs from the ingestion of anthrax spores contained in the food, the period of incubation varying from 1 to 3 days, though it may be as long as a fortnight. Infection may take place from grazing on infected pastures after a previous death of an animal from anthrax; by grazing on a field which has been dressed with unsterilized bone manure, or by the feeding of imported cattle cake which has become contaminated in the holds of ships which had previously carried hides. Again, shoddy waste from glove making, or the effluent from knackeries or tanyards, may discharge into streams and infect cattle grazing on the banks. During the war of 1914-1918, a marked fall in the number of cases of anthrax was recorded in Britain, this being due to the restriction on imported feeding stuffs, but it then rose, so that between 1919-1928, 68 per cent. of anthrax outbreaks in Britain were attributed to this method of infection. A similar sharp fall occurred in the 1949-1945 war, but rose again in the post-war period.

In the pig and dog the chief mode of infection is by the consumption of blood and flesh from affected animals, but infection through a skin wound, which is the common method in man, is rarely observed in animals.

Symptoms. In the ox the chief characteristic of anthrax is its acute nature and the rapidity with which death follows. The disease is sudden in its onset and is manifested by high fever, a bloody diarrhoea, with a discharge of dark red, tarry, uncoagulated blood from the nose, mouth and vulva, while in the lactating animal there is a complete cessation of the milk yield. In the dead, uneviscerated bovine a characteristic is the rapid abdominal distension. In the sheep the disease is very acute, and post-mortem abdominal distension is even more rapid than in the ox for the fleece prevents the quick dissipation of heat after death.

In the horse and pig the disease tends to become localized in the region of the throat, and is characterized by the presence of pharyngeal oedema, with stiffness of the head and neck and difficulty in swallowing.

Lesions. A post-mortem examination should never be undertaken if anthrax is suspected or diagnosed in the intact dead animal, and although anthrax carcases are unlikely to be opened in an abattoir, it is of interest to record the post-mortem changes in this disease. In cattle there is a marked effusion of a blood-stained serous fluid into the connective tissues of the body, together with engorgement of the superficial veins of skin and muscle, the carcase thus presenting a bright pink or a fiery red colour; these manifestations of hyperaemia may, however, be slight and easily overlooked in animals slaughtered at the point of death and subsequently well bled. The heart, liver and kidneys are red, swollen and friable as a result of cloudy swelling, while the intestinal canal, especially the small intestine, shows a haemorrhagic inflammation of the mucous membrane. When examined externally the intestines therefore present a reddish-blue coloration, and the associated lymph nodes, especially where gelatinous infiltrations are present, are enlarged, haemorrhagic and oedematous. Rigor mortis in the carcase is absent, and the blood is dark red, tarry, and does not coagulate; if a string of clot can be drawn from a blood-vessel the existence of anthrax can be discounted. The most marked and characteristic change is seen in the spleen, which is acutely swollen, up to five times its normal size, its substance being usually dark red, soft, and even fluid; the spleen may show little change, however, if the animal is slaughtered in the incubative stage of the disease. In the dressed carcase of beef a blood smear for diagnostic purposes may be made from the kidney, flesh or a lymph node, but in French abattoirs it is an accepted procedure to cut through the fore shank (radius) and obtain material for microscopical examination or culture from the bone marrow.

In sheep the lesions are similar to those in cattle, though splenic enlargement may be absent, but splenic changes are rarely seen in the pig and horse, and in these animals search must be made for a gelatinous blood-stained infiltration of the pharyngeal region, with enlargement and a haemorrhagic condition of the submaxillary lymph nodes. The swelling of these parts is due to the fact that here the organism multiplies rapidly in the lymph, and probably also in the lymph nodes and adjoining tissue, and distension of the bacillary capsules due to their gradual absorption of fluid causes blockage of the capillaries and lymph vessels with resultant pharyngeal oedema. Under certain conditions *B. anthracis* also produces a lethal toxin which has both an oedema-producing and a tissue-damaging action and this explains why death may occur in animals such as the horse and pig in which the bacilli are often few in number in the blood stream. A local intestinal form of anthrax occurs occasionally in the pig, and in these cases bacilli may be demonstrated microscopically in smears from the congested mesenteric lymph nodes or the peritoneal effusion. In the pig, affected lymph nodes of the head or mesentery may undergo necrosis, the degenerated material becoming surrounded by a thick fibrous capsule with eventual recovery of the animal, for though bacilli may remain alive in the necrotic material they gradually die, and healing takes place by scar formation. In the chronic localized form of anthrax the lymph nodes may be enlarged and fibrous and the cut surface presents a mottled appearance, parts being brick-red in colour, parts having a dark grey parboiled appearance together with necrotic foci which may be of a dry and caseous nature. In Germany this local form of anthrax is fairly common in the pig, and though in that country the carcase is released if a bacteriological examination proves negative, in Denmark total condemnation is the rule.

Differential Diagnosis. The diseases with which anthrax may be confused are blackquarter, malignant oedema, septicaemia, and cases of splenic enlargement which may be seen in redwater, anaplasmosis, infarction, leukaemia, swine erysipelas, torsion of the spleen in pigs and the so-called " slaughter spleen ". It is inadvisable to attempt to differentiate these affections from anthrax by naked-eye examination alone, and in all cases of splenic enlargement a smear should be made from the organ or from a kidney or lymph node, particularly one which is associated with an area of gelatinous infiltration. There is evidence, however, that the antibiotic treatment of animals suffering from anthrax renders it extremely difficult to demonstrate *B. anthracis* in smears made from the peripheral blood either before or after death, and when death occurs there may be an absence of typical post-mortem lesions and it may not be possible to demonstrate the organism in the internal organs by smear or by the usual bacteriological methods. In pigs, as in cattle, antibiotic therapy prior to the death of the animal may render diagnosis more difficult.

Judgment. The meat from anthrax-infected animals is definitely dangerous to man, as although anthrax bacilli are readily destroyed by gastric juice the spores are resistant and, if the meat is consumed, may gain access to the system through abrasions of the mouth or mucous membranes. The carcase, including blood, hide, fat and all internal organs, must be destroyed.

PROCEDURE WHEN ANTHRAX IS DETECTED. In Great Britain the Anthrax Order of 1938 forbids the skinning or bleeding of any animal which has died of anthrax or suspected anthrax, and if the disease is suspected this fact must be reported forthwith to the police. Investigation is carried out by a veterinary inspector who, if the carcase is not diseased, issues a certificate to that effect, and the carcase can then be disposed of by the owner, while restrictions are withdrawn by the local authority. If the veterinary inspector suspects anthrax to exist, the case is certified as one of suspected disease and the local authority proceeds to dispose of the carcase by burning or burial, and disinfection. In Britain confirmation or otherwise of the existence of anthrax may only be made by the Ministry of Agriculture, Fisheries and Food.

Where an animal has died in a lairage, steps should immediately be taken to prevent the flow of blood from the body openings and thus prevent the production of bacillary spores. This may be done by packing the nose, vulva and anus with tow or cotton wool and by fitting a sack round the animal's head, while pools of blood already evacuated may be absorbed with earth or sawdust; peat, because of its humic acid content, is particularly recommended for this purpose, and such materials, together with any faeces, must be destroyed by burning.

ANTHRAX IN A SLAUGHTERHOUSE. The detection of anthrax in the dressed carcase is of much more serious import than in the uneviscerated dead animal, for the skinning and opening of the carcase favours the formation of spores, with increased danger of human infection, especially to the slaughtermen through cuts and abrasions.

As soon as disease is suspected any further dressing of the carcase should be forbidden. If dressing of the suspected carcase has been completed and the same slaughtermen have commenced work on a further carcase, the danger of contamination of the second carcase is so great that it, too, must be condemned. Carcases which have been dressed prior to the suspected animal, but are contiguous to it, may possibly have been contaminated by blood splashes, and such carcases may be released to a manufacturer, e.g. for pie making, provided the meat is cooked under supervision for 3 hours; if this is impracticable, the carcase should be condemned. All knives, shooting instruments, saws and choppers should be boiled in water for half an hour or, alternatively, they may be thoroughly cleansed in a hot 5 per cent. solution of sodium hydroxide, the solution being prepared immediately before use by dissolving 2½ lb. of sodium hydroxide in 5½ gallons of hot water. The solution should be applied as near scalding as possible and protective clothing in the form of rubber gloves, boots and goggles should be worn. Alternatively a 0·5 per cent. solution of sodium hypochlorite (5,000 parts per million) may be used. The value of hot sodium hydroxide lies in its ability to remove fat and grease, and it can be also recommended for the efficient cleansing of the floor and walls after anthrax has been detected in a slaughterhouse; this application may be made by a mop, or preferably by means of a pressure spray, and the liquid should be allowed to act for one hour. The sterilization of blood splashes and awkward crevices may be ensured by aid of a painter's blow lamp, and clothing and aprons of the slaughtermen may be disinfected by steam pressure in an autoclave, using 15 lb. pressure for 30 minutes. Leather equipment, however, cannot be sterilized satisfactorily without serious deterioration of the material, and contaminated boots, knife sheaths, leather aprons and belts should therefore be destroyed by burning. Expenditure in the form of reimbursement for the destruction of such articles may properly be incurred by a local authority, in the absence of any wilful act or neglect by the owner of the animal or his employees, in fulfilment of its public health obligations.

The collection and destruction of all the products concerned with slaughter is of the greatest importance, and these include not only the carcase but hoofs, horns, blood, viscera, fat and hide. In some cases blood from the infected animal may have been collected in a blood can, and, as many of these are rusty and unhygienic and difficult to cleanse satisfactorily, it should be destroyed with its contents. The hide may have been removed to a tanyard, and on tracing this it may be found that the infected hide has been salted and laid in a heap with other hides. Though the hide from the infected animal must be destroyed, it is permissible to carry out disinfection of those hides which lie in immediate contact with the infected one. This may be done by the Seymour-Jones method, which consists in immersing the hide in a 1 in 5000 solution of bichloride of mercury to which 1 per cent. of formic acid has been added; after 24 hours' immersion, the hide should be detained for a period of 2 weeks before being released. An alternative form of treatment can be carried out by the Shattenfroh method and consists of soaking the hide for 48 hours in a solution which contains 2 per cent. hydrochloric acid and 10 per cent. sodium chloride.

ANTHRAX IN MAN. Human infection is usually contracted by inoculation through a skin wound. Less frequently, cases may occur by inspiration of anthrax spores during wool sorting, or, still less frequently, by the ingestion of anthrax-infected flesh; perhaps the greatest danger is to the housewife who may cut her hands when chopping up infected meat, and since 1960 human anthrax in Britain has been made a notifiable disease.

Infection by inoculation is likely to occur in those working with hides, skins and wool, and also in slaughtermen and those engaged in the tending of live stock. In Great Britain in 1963 anthrax was reported in 15 persons, infection arising from wool in six cases, from bones and bone products in two cases while two cases occurred in dock workers and five in persons connected with farming and butchery. Though the death rate in persons suffering from anthrax was previously around 25 per cent., this has been very considerably reduced in recent years by appropriate antibiotic treatment, while the danger of human infection from imported wool and hair has been obviated in Britain by the setting up of a government disinfecting station at Liverpool, where the material is washed in hot alkaline suds, followed by treatment in hot 2 per cent. formaldehyde and subsequent storage for several days in a holding room. The number of human cases occurring annually throughout the world has been estimated at about 9,000, though a true incidence figure may be between two and ten times this reported figure.

BLACKQUARTER

This is also known as blackleg, and is an acute infective disease of the ox and sheep caused by *Clostridium chauvaei*. It is a disease resulting from infection from the soil and it is therefore more commonly encountered in grass-fed than in stall-fed animals. The period of incubation is 2 to 5 days.

Pathogenesis. The bacterium is 3 to 5 μ long and 0·5 μ broad, being rod-shaped and slightly curved but, unlike anthrax, never tends to form chains; it is found in the intermuscular and connective tissues, but never in the circulating blood. If spore formation takes place the spore is placed centrally or towards one end of the bacterium and is of greater diameter than the bacterium itself; the latter therefore presents an outline resembling a snowshoe. Blackquarter spores are very resistant to destructive influences and may retain their virulence in dried muscle for 10 to 12 years, while they may live indefinitely in the soil. The disease is confined to certain districts and even to particular fields on a farm, and being less common on cultivated land is more likely to be observed in cattle on high permanent pastures.

Methods of Infection. Susceptible animals may be infected by inoculation or, more commonly, by the ingestion of spores in soil, dust, food or drinking water. By far the greatest proportion of cases in cattle occur in animals between 6 months and 2 years of age, animals in good bodily condition being most often attacked. The disease is therefore commonly observed in bullocks, often after bruising or injury, for clostridia are frequently present in tissues of animals showing no evidence of infection, and traumatism causes necrosis of muscular tissue and here the organisms multiply and spread rapidly. When the disease occurs in the cow it is found that this is associated with a recent movement from an uninfected to a blackquarter district.

Sheep may be attacked at any age, and outbreaks of the disease are associated with wound infection which arises after shearing, docking or castration. It is probable that gangrenous metritis in ewes, which sometimes occurs after difficult lambing, is also a manifestation of blackquarter. In both ox and sheep the death rate is high, probably in the region of 98 per cent., but the disease does not affect man.

Symptoms and Lesions. In the ox, infection is followed by crepitant swellings which develop in the subcutaneous connective tissue and spread rapidly. These swellings are usually observed on the shoulder, neck, breast, loins or thigh, the reason that blackquarter occurs in these locations being that they are muscular areas most subject to traumatism.

Carcases of animals which have died of blackquarter emit a peculiar rancid odour, though they do not tend to decompose as rapidly as animals which have died of anthrax. On examination of the crepitant swellings the connective tissue of the part is seen to be infiltrated with a yellow gelatinous substance which may be haemorrhagic and permeated with gas bubbles. The muscular tissue of the swelling is blackish-red in colour and oedematous at the periphery of the swelling, but has a dry spongy texture in the interior due to separation of the muscle fibres by numerous gas bubbles. The lesion has a strong odour resembling rancid butter, and section with a knife has a feel and sound as though a piece of lung were being incised. The neighbouring lymph nodes are acutely enlarged and may be haemorrhagic, and the pleural and peritoneal cavities contain a quantity of blackish-red fluid, but the spleen is unchanged or only slightly enlarged, and the blood, though dark red in colour, coagulates readily.

Of the visceral organs the liver and kidneys show the most marked changes, being enlarged and congested and developing brown, porous areas a few hours after death; after 24 hours these areas have enlarged up to the size of a walnut and the spongy appearance is more marked, due to further gas formation. These post-mortem changes of the liver and kidneys are responsible for the so-called "foaming organs" of blackquarter.

In sheep the lesions are similar to those in the ox, but as the disease occurs by inoculation the swellings may appear in the jaw, head or tongue after wounds of the head, or in the pubic region after castration or docking.

Though the crepitant swellings are similar to those appearing in the ox, the characteristic changes in the liver and kidneys do not occur.

Differential Diagnosis. Blackquarter is often mistaken for extensive bruising, and occasionally a calf, usually of the larger veal type, is con-

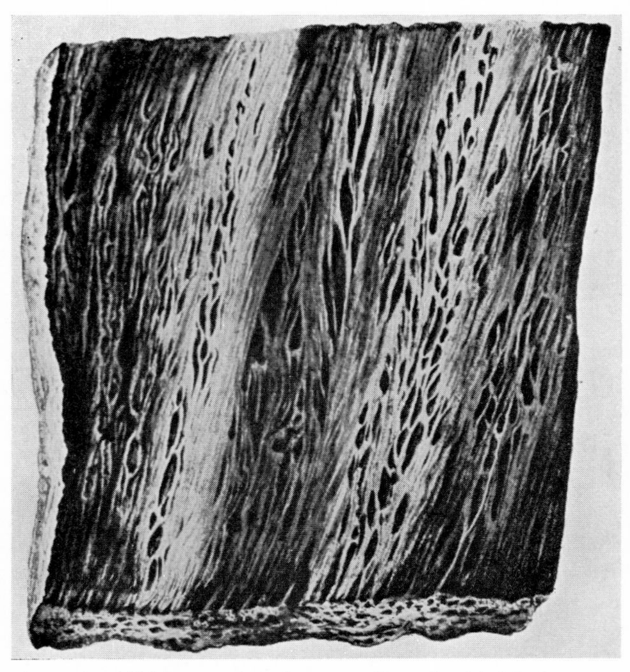

FIG. 96.—Thigh muscle of an ox affected with blackquarter. The cut surface is dry, and the muscle fibres, which present pale yellow and blackish streaks, are separated by gas bubbles.

signed as a dressed carcase to an abattoir with the history that a bruised leg or shoulder has been removed. The flesh of such a carcase may emit the typical rancid odour of butyric acid, though frequently the carcase shows no other change. Blackquarter may be confused with anthrax, but in anthrax crepitating swellings are absent, the blood is uncoagulated and the spleen is usually enlarged.

Judgment. If a live animal awaiting slaughter is found to be affected with blackquarter, slaughter and dressing of the carcase should be forbidden. Where disease is detected in the dressed carcase total condemnation is necessary, as the presence of fever, the marked rancid odour and the onset of early decomposition render it unfit for human food; no restrictions, however, need be placed on the removal of the hide to a tanyard. Carcases of calves from which a limb has been removed, but which possess a butyric-like odour, should be condemned.

BRAXY

Braxy, or " sickness", is an acute infective disease of sheep and occurs in Scotland, Wales, Ireland, and also in Denmark, Norway and Iceland, where it is termed " bradsot ", a term denoting rapid disease. The affection appears in the autumn and winter months, and chiefly affects ewe hoggs wintering on hill or upland grazings. Animals in good condition are probably more liable to contract braxy, which, before the introduction of preventative measures, caused a loss in Scotland alone of upwards of 150,000 sheep annually.

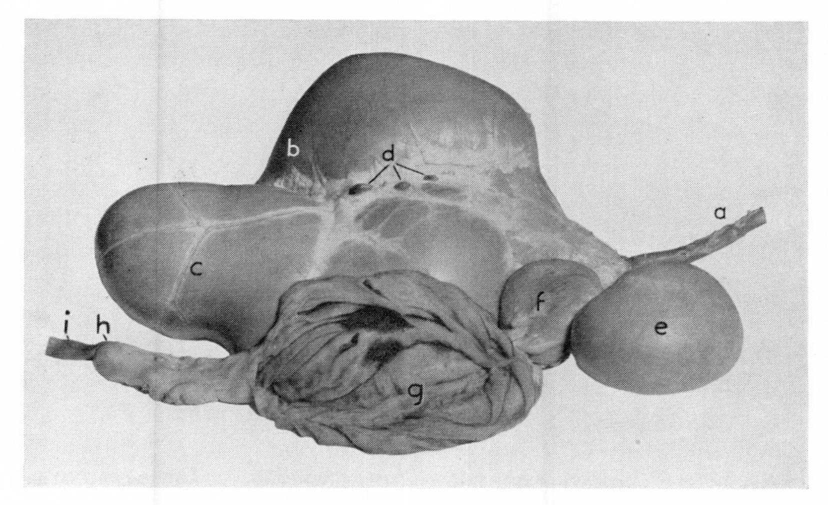

FIG. 97.—Stomach of sheep showing lesions of braxy on mucous membrane of opened abomasum (*g*) ; (*a*) oesophagus ; (*b*, *c*) left and right blind sacs of rumen ; (*d*) gastric (ruminal) lymph nodes ; (*e*) reticulum ; (*f*) omasum ; (*h*) pylorus ; (*i*) duodenum.

Pathogenesis. The disease results from the invasion of the body tissues by the micro-organism *Clostridium septique.* This bacterium is a normal inhabitant of the gut of all sheep in braxy areas, and only shows its pathogenic properties when, for any reason, there is a lowering of the vitality of the abomasal mucous membrane. The predisposing causes which assist the invasive powers of *Cl. septique* are obscure but are probably nutritional in nature.

Symptoms and Lesions. A characteristic of the disease is the shortness of the period between infection and death, and sheep engorging on frosted grass in the early morning are frequently found to be dead the next morning. A further characteristic is the rapid decomposition which occurs after death, carcases showing great abdominal distension within a few hours. On post-mortem examination there is an offensive odour when the abdomen is opened, and the peritoneal fluid, which is turbid and increased in amount, constitutes an almost pure culture of the micro-organism. Cloudy swelling of the kidneys, liver and heart may be observed, but the characteristic lesions are encountered in the abomasum, the mucous membrane of which shows patches of dark red discoloration, often situated where this stomach is in contact with the rumen.

Judgment. Braxy is unlikely to be encountered in meat inspection, for death occurs very rapidly after infection, though carcases of animals which have died but have been bled may occasionally be consigned to the slaughterhouse as casualties. The disease is not communicable to man, and advantage was formerly taken of this fact in Scotland, where animals dying of braxy were slaughtered and the flesh consumed, the disagreeable odour being removed by rubbing the carcase with salt, washing in water, and again salting and smoking. The disease, however, is toxaemic, and affected carcases decompose rapidly and should be condemned.

BLACK DISEASE

This braxy-like disease of sheep is caused by *Clostridium oedematiens* and occurs principally in Australia, Tasmania, and to some extent in New Zealand. Cases have also been reported from the United States, and the disease has also been reported in Scotland, in the northern parts of which it is regarded as a major problem. The affection is essentially an infectious necrotic hepatitis, and has been termed black disease on account of the black coloration of the inner surface of the skin when removed from an affected animal; this coloration is due to the marked and widespread engorgement of the minute blood vessels. Black disease occurs in areas in which liver fluke infestation is common, and shows a definite seasonal incidence which corresponds to the migration of immature flukes to the liver in the late autumn and early winter months. Active migration of these immature flukes through the liver gives rise to destruction of liver tissue, with the result that the spores of *Cl. oedematiens*, lying dormant in the liver, become activated, multiply rapidly and liberate a toxin which gives rise to necrotic areas in the liver tissue. These areas may be seen on the surface or in the substance of the liver and vary from ½ to 1 inch in diameter, on occasions 2 inches in diameter, and are yellowish in colour and surrounded by a dark areola.

Judgment. The production of the powerful toxin causes rapid death, and carcases of affected animals should be condemned.

INFECTIONS OF SHEEP DUE TO *CLOSTRIDIUM WELCHII*

Diseases due to *Clostridium welchii* in the lumen of the intestine cause widespread losses amongst sheep in Great Britain. The micro-organism only multiplies rapidly in the intestine when conditions are favourable, one of these conditions being a sudden change from an inferior to a rich diet. The most important affection of sheep caused by this bacterium is entero-toxaemia, and affected carcases are frequently brought to slaughter-houses as casualties ; other affections caused by the same micro-organism are pulpy kidney disease and lamb dysentery, but they are unlikely to be encountered in meat inspection.

Entero-toxaemia

This is known also as turnip sickness, and is a rapidly fatal toxaemia which is extremely common amongst store or fattening sheep during the autumn and late winter months. Farmers frequently confuse this disease with braxy, which it resembles in its onset and course, but entero-toxaemia is a distinct and separate malady.

Pathogenesis. Entero-toxaemia is caused by *Cl. welchii* which, under certain circumstances, multiplies rapidly in the abomasum and intestine, and produces a powerful toxin which is absorbed into the blood stream

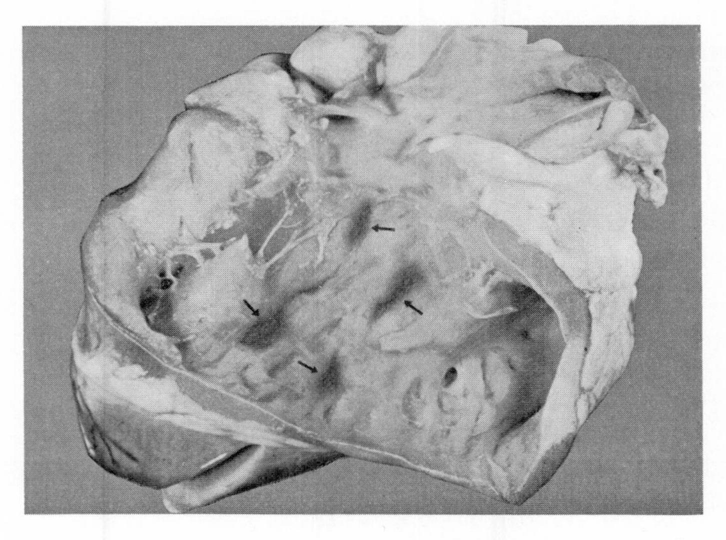

FIG. 98.—Heart of sheep showing subendocardial haemorrhages (indicated by arrows), a lesion frequently present in entero-toxaemia.

and quickly paralyses the vital centres in the brain. The affection is most frequent in hoggs in improving condition and often occurs soon after a change to better feeding, such as stubbles, green forage crops and trough feed, for the conditions most favourable for toxin production are when the intestine contains much highly nutritious food.

Symptoms and Lesions. Affected sheep are seldom seen alive. Typical cases show great pain, wild movements of head and limbs and gasping, while in other cases the sheep is found in a dull, sleepy condition and may show diarrhoea. After death the carcase becomes distended with gas, and characteristic post-mortem findings are congestion of heart and lungs, blood-stained pericardial fluid, diffuse or punctiform haemorrhage of heart and endocardium, and a haemorrhagic and pulpy state of the kidneys especially noticeable some hours after death. There are no constant abomasal or intestinal lesions. *Cl. welchii* toxin may be demonstrated in the gut.

Judgment. Carcases of animals which have been properly bled and promptly eviscerated are suitable for human food, though the kidneys should be condemned. Carcases showing imperfect bleeding should be condemned.

Pulpy Kidney Disease

This disease, also caused by *Cl. welchii*, occurs in lambs 6 to 16 weeks old. It causes sudden death and on post-mortem examination the kidneys are characteristically soft, pulpy and haemorrhagic.

Judgment. Similar to entero-toxaemia, but casualties from pulpy kidney disease are rarely brought to the slaughterhouse.

Lamb Dysentery

This is a highly fatal, infective disease which attacks lambs within the first or second week of life. It is caused by *Cl. welchii*, and produces death

SEASONAL INCIDENCE OF SHEEP DISEASES IN BRITAIN

DISEASES	JANUARY	FEBRUARY	MARCH	APRIL	MAY	JUNE	JULY	AUGUST	SEPTEMBER	OCTOBER	NOVEMBER	DECEMBER
Braxy . . .											■	■
Lamb Dysentery . .			■	■	■							
Pulpy Kidney . .				■	■							
Entero-toxaemia . .			■	■					■			
Pregnancy Toxaemia .		■	■	■								
Gangrenous Mastitis .			■	■								
Liver Fluke . .	■	■	■							■	■	■
Parasitic Gastro-enteritis	■	■	■				■	■	■	■	■	■

from septicaemia and toxaemia, with or without typical ulceration of the intestines. The disease is widely spread in Britain, lambs becoming infected within the first few days after birth and showing profuse diarrhoea and dysentery. On post-mortem examination there is enteritis and ulceration.

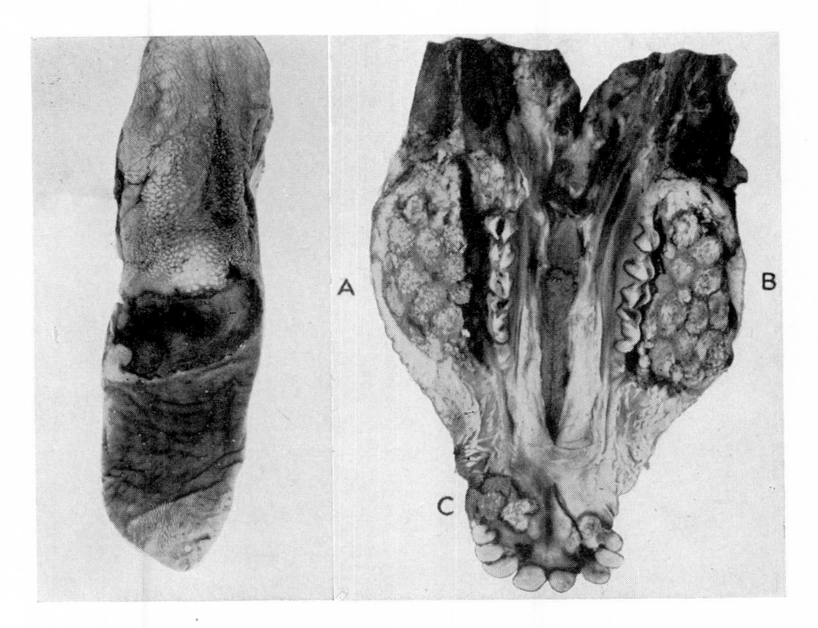

FIG. 99.—Calf diphtheria showing (left) extensive necrosis of tongue and (right) necrosis of the gums (A, B) and of the mandible (C).

Judgment. The disease occurs so early in the life of the lamb, and is of such an acute nature, that carcases are unlikely to be encountered in meat inspection. The carcase is immature and imperfectly bled, and is quite unfit for food.

BRUCELLOSIS

The term Brucellosis is now employed to include contagious abortion in cattle, together with abortion of an infectious nature in the goat and sow.

The organism *Brucella abortus* is responsible for contagious abortion in cattle, an affection which is world-wide in its distribution. In infected pregnant cows post-mortem examination reveals a viscid exudate, mixed with flakes of pus, between the uterine mucous membrane and the foetal membrane, and both foetal and maternal cotyledons are covered with a grey or yellow purulent material. Affection of the bovine testicle with *Br. abortus* is not uncommon and takes the form of necrotic and purulent foci of the testicular substance and globus major of the epididymis. The necrotic process may involve the whole testicle to form a pale yellowish caseous mass lying in the tunica vaginalis, the latter being filled with a sero-sanguineous exudate, and in chronic cases there is great thickening of the scrotal wall.

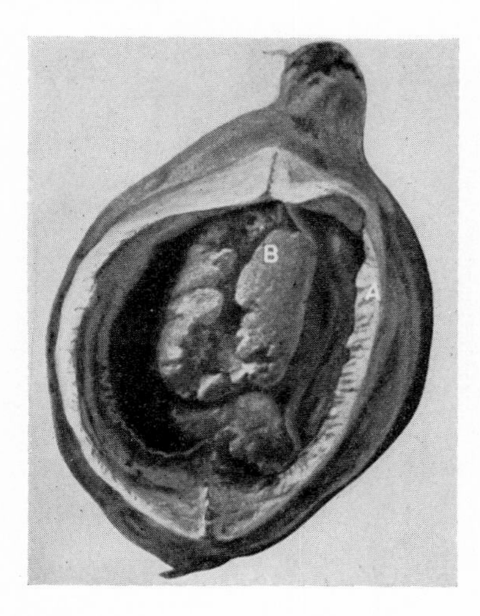

FIG. 100.—Scrotum of bull showing infection with *Brucella abortus*. At A can be seen great thickening of the scrotal wall, while the testicle, B, has undergone complete necrosis and has been converted into a cheesy mass.

In cattle in Africa, particularly in indigenous animals, chronic cystic formations occur due to *Br. abortus* infection. These lesions, known as hygromas, are essentially a bursitis, tenosynovitis or arthritis and are situated subcutaneously where the skin covers prominent bony structures. They are therefore found most commonly in the cervical region, knee, hock, stifle, or angle of the haunch, and possess a fibrous wall which contains a yellowish fluid and sometimes fibrinous masses varying in size from a rice grain to a hazel nut. In the abattoir a cyst situated between the two attachments of the ligamentum nuchae may be opened during the sawing down of the carcase, thus contaminating the neck region, and a procedure recommended in such cases is to excise the cyst, wash the carcase with a high pressure water spray and finally apply a spray of a 1 per cent. solution of lactic acid to the neck and forequarter.

Brucella melitensis was originally discovered as the cause of Malta fever in goats in that island, but these animals, though they act as carriers and excrete the organism in the milk, usually show no symptoms of the disease. In the last decade *Br. melitensis* in sheep has been recorded in Western Germany.

Brucella suis has produced outbreaks of abortion in sows in North America and all parts of Europe. The organism in swine may give rise to lesions in the vertebrae which bear a close resemblance to tuberculosis, and also to lesions in joints and bursae, but in some cases the only lesions present are chronic nodular formations in the spleen, up to $\frac{1}{6}$ inch in size and possessing greyish to yellowish-white contents, sometimes tinged with light green.

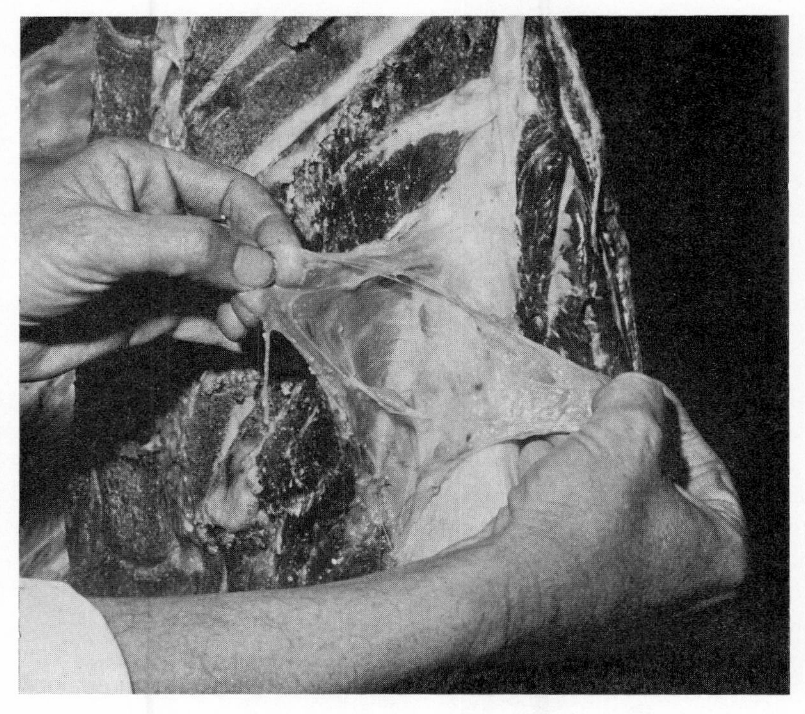

FIG. 101.—Hygroma, opened, situated on the withers of a bovine carcase. Brucella infection has involved the bursa situated between the two funicular portions of the ligamentum nuchae at their point of attachment to the superior spines of the dorsal vertebrae. Hygromas may contain viable *Brucella abortus* organisms and two pints or more of fluid.

Brucellosis in Man (Undulant Fever)

The types of brucella organisms found in human beings in a given area have roughly the same predominance as the animal population in that area (e.g. *Br. suis* in Iowa in the United States, and *Br. melitensis* in the Middle East).

Human infection with *Brucella abortus* is characterized by fever which shows marked irregularity of temperature and a tendency to recurrence. Infection occurs by drinking milk from infected cows or through handling of infected meat and animals. There are no records of man becoming infected through the consumption of meat of an infected animal. *Br. melitensis* is highly infective to man who may acquire the disease through the consumption of milk or milk products of infected goats, through airborne infection from faecal dust, or, as in Western Germany, in persons in contact with infected flocks of sheep. Human infection with *Br. suis* has been recorded in the United States in persons engaged on the meat inspection of pigs and in abattoir workers connected with scraping and dressing of pig carcases; no less than 50 per cent. of cases of human brucellosis in that country are attributed to a porcine infection. Both *Br. melitensis* and *Br. suis* are more pathogenic for man than is *Br. abortus*.

Judgment. The culturing of viable brucella organisms from the musculature of infected slaughtered cattle has been successful in only a small percentage of cases, and the number of organisms present is very small. Brucella organisms only remain viable for a short time in the muscles of a slaughtered infected animal, for the organisms are easily destroyed by the lactic acid which forms in muscle after slaughter. Refrigeration, however, will not destroy the organisms, and viable brucellae may be present in organs, muscle, bone and lymph nodes of infected carcases for periods in excess of one month. It has also been shown that the organisms can survive pickling and inadequate smoking. The fact that large numbers of organisms have been demonstrated in the organs and lymph nodes of infected animals has led to revision of the regulations of the German Federal Republic, which now prescribe that in a carcase known to be affected with brucellosis the lungs, liver, spleen, kidneys, intestine, udder and blood shall be regarded as unfit for human consumption, and, in addition, the lymph nodes of the carcase and organs shall be removed. Federal Regulations in the United States prescribe that carcases affected with localized lesions of brucellosis may be passed for food after the affected parts are removed and condemned.

CALF DIPHTHERIA

This affection occurs particularly in young calves, and is caused by *Fusiformis necrophorus* (*B. necrosis*), a bacterium which is widely distributed in nature and frequently present in the intestinal tract of healthy herbivorous animals. The same causal organism is also associated with such diseases as necrosis of the uterus and vagina in the cow, " black spot " on the cow's teat, bacterial necrosis of the liver in the ox and sheep (Fig. 65), necrotic ulceration of the tongue and rumen in adult cattle, and contagious foot rot in sheep (Fig. 62).

Pathogenesis and Lesions. The micro-organism is anaerobic and non-sporing, and is demonstrable in the lesions as filaments, 80 to 100 μ in length, which are particularly abundant at the junction of necrotic and healthy tissue. The disease is acquired by ingestion of infected food or drinking water, especially from infected buckets, and develops rapidly in the form of diphtheritic patches and ulceration on the tongue, mouth, pharynx or gums ; these lesions appear as grey necrotic areas which can only be scraped or peeled off with difficulty, bleed easily when removed, and are associated with a typical necrotic odour. Infection may extend to the intestines to cause similar lesions, but more commonly it extends to the lungs and causes rapid death from a septic bronchopneumonia. The necrotic areas involving the tongue (Fig. 99) may be distinguished from foot and mouth disease by the fact that they are yellow or brown in colour, are deep and well defined from the surrounding healthy tissue, while the epithelium bounding the lesions is not loose and ragged but is closely bound down to the underlying tissues.

Judgment. The disease in the early stages may be regarded as a local one, and it is sufficient to condemn the head and, if affected, the stomach, intestines or lungs. The affection, however, runs an acute course and is likely to lead to rapid wasting in the calf, an animal already deficient in adequate muscular development. Where there is emaciation, therefore, or where there are toxic changes in the form of cloudy swelling of the parenchymatous organs, with enlargement of the carcase lymph nodes, the carcase should be condemned.

CASEOUS LYMPHADENITIS

This is a chronic bacterial infection occurring in sheep and is caused by *Corynebacterium pseudotuberculosis* (*Bacillus Preisz-Nocard*), an organism about 1 μ long. The presence of a caseous material in affected lymph nodes has also earned for this disease the term pseudotuberculosis, and though the condition is rare in Europe, it is common in South America where it results in severe outbreaks and great emaciation ; it occurs also in Australia and New Zealand and is widely distributed in South Africa. The disease has not been shown to exist in Great Britain, but a condition resembling caseous lymphadenitis and caused by *Bacterium purifaciens* occurs in many parts of Scotland ; the disease appears yearly on some farms, being commonest in Scottish Blackface sheep and particularly in adult rams.

Method of Infection. Sheep become infected most frequently by cutaneous inoculation, especially through wounds of the skin at shearing time, or during tail-docking, castration and ear-tagging. The disease shows a greater incidence with age, for older animals have a greater opportunity of acquiring wound infection. In Australia the affection occurs mostly in Merinos, especially in ewes and old wethers whose loose skin frequently becomes nicked during shearing.

Lesions. In the majority of cases lesions are confined to the lymph nodes, chiefly those which are situated externally, the carcase nodes being affected in the following order of frequency: prescapular, precrural, superficial inguinal, ischiatic, and popliteal. The bronchial, mediastinal, iliac and lumbar nodes may also be affected but the mesenteric group are rarely found diseased.

Affected lymph nodes may be enlarged and contain a thick glutinous pus which is surrounded by a thick wall of connective tissue. The pus is of a greenish-yellow colour, later becoming inspissated and paler, while in older lesions it may become laminated like the layers of an onion, and eventually completely calcareous. Kidney lesions are not infrequent, and the lungs often contain small greenish-grey nodules in otherwise normal lung tissue, or large abscesses with pasty, odourless contents.

Method of Examination. In England and Wales the Meat Inspection Regulations 1963 prescribe that when the inspector has reason to suspect that caseous lymphadenitis or any other suppurative condition exists in the carcase of any sheep or lamb, he shall, in addition to carrying out the prescribed routine examination for such animals (*a*) examine by palpation as well as by observation such of the lymphatic glands as are readily accessible ; and (*b*) examine in detail the prescapular, superficial inguinal, supramammary and precrural lymphatic glands of a sheep, and in the case of a lamb, examine those glands in detail if he has found evidence of disease in the course of visual examination or palpation.

In Australia and New Zealand this procedure is followed, and experience has shown that lesions no larger than a match head in a superficial lymph node can be detected during palpation and that less than 1 per cent. of carcases so examined and passed may subsequently be found affected.

Judgment. The Regulations applicable to England and Wales prescribe that the inspector shall regard either of the following conditions as evidence of generalized caseous lymphadenitis :

(*a*) multiple, acute and actively progressive lesions of caseous lymphadenitis ;

(*b*) multiple lesions of caseous lymphadenitis which are inactive but widespread.

When the inspector is satisfied that a carcase or offal is affected with caseous lymphadenitis or any other suppurative condition and that the said condition is not generalized nor associated with emaciation, he shall regard the following parts of the carcase and offal as unfit for human consumption :

(*a*) any organ and its associated lymphatic gland, when the aforesaid condition exists on the surface or in the substance of that organ or gland ;

(*b*) in any case to which sub-paragraph (*a*) of this paragraph does not apply, the lesion and such of the surrounding parts as the inspector may think proper having regard to the age and degree of activity of the lesion. For the purpose of this sub-paragraph, an old lesion which is firmly encapsulated may be regarded as inactive. Britain, however, will not accept from abroad carcases of mutton or lamb where more than two lesions have been found during post-mortem examination.

CONTAGIOUS PLEUROPNEUMONIA

This affection is a disease peculiar to cattle, and takes the form of a chronic inflammation of the lungs and pleura. Contagious pleuropneumonia has not appeared in Great Britain since 1898, being stamped out chiefly by energetic slaughter and quarantine measures, and the disease in Europe is now only found in Russia, Spain and Poland, though indigenous in Africa, Australia and Asia.

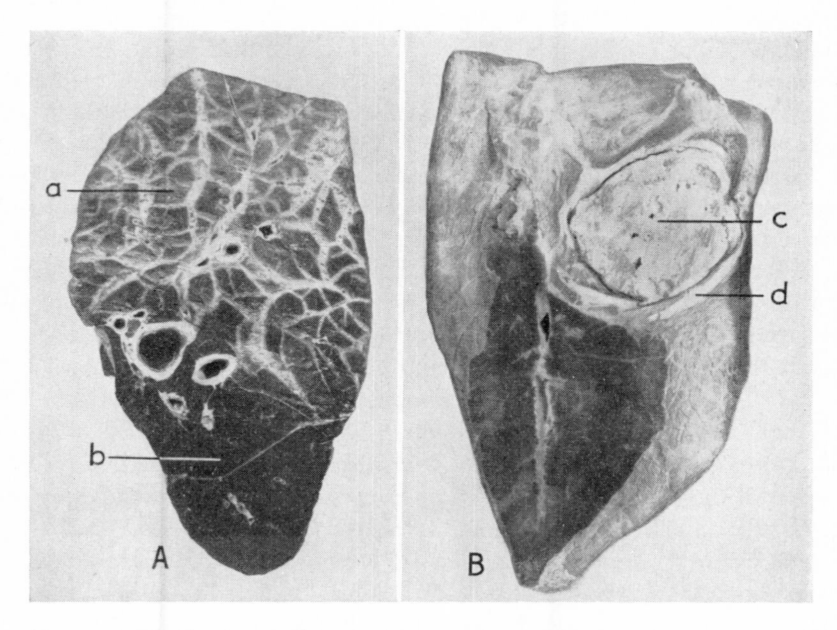

FIG. 102.—Bovine lungs affected with contagious pleuropneumonia. A. Acute stage showing (*a*) thickening of the interlobular septa, and (*b*) an area of unaffected lung tissue. B. Recovered case showing (*c*) sequestrum enclosed in a fibrous capsule (*d*) (P. L. Le Roux).

Pathogenesis. For many years the cause of the disease was attributed to a filter-passing virus, but it is now considered to be due to a motile micro-organism which, in certain stages, is so minute as to be filterable. It is generally agreed that the micro-organism gains entrance to the animal body by inhalation, and may be found in the lung tissue, pleural exudate, bronchial lymph nodes and the nasal discharge of affected animals.

Symptoms and Lesions. As the disease runs a chronic course the symptoms are not obvious, being chiefly manifested by a difficulty in breathing which, in the later stage of the affection, is accompanied by a bubbling sound resulting from the increased bronchial and nasal secretion. The mortality of the disease varies from 10 to 50 per cent., but animals which recover may act as carriers, especially where a chronic lung lesion communicates direct with a bronchus.

On post-mortem examination the characteristic lesions are found in the lung tissue and on the pleura, the left lung and especially its middle lobe being particularly affected. The lung shows various stages of hepatization, some of the lobules being light red, others reddish-yellow or greyish-yellow, and these changes are associated with great thickening of the interlobular lung tissue due to infiltration of the septa with a straw-coloured fluid. As the disease progresses, this fluid becomes replaced by connective tissue, so that the varying stages of the pneumonic process are separated by strong connective bands and the lung on section presents a marbled appearance. Pneumonic areas eventually undergo necrosis, the necrotic areas being firm, dry and 4 to 5 inches in diameter. These foci do not become gangrenous but are encapsulated in fibrous tissue to form a sequestrum, and, should this remain infective, recovered animals may thus act as carriers. The affected area of lung is invariably associated with a straw-coloured pleural exudate and an inflammation of the contiguous pleura ; this local area of pleurisy may extend to form chronic adhesions between the pleura and lung tissue, and it is a characteristic of these adhesions that they can be removed in layers.

Judgment. Contagious pleuropneumonia is not communicable to man, and the carcase of an animal which has recovered from the affection may be passed for food after condemnation of the diseased lungs and removal of the inflamed pleura. A condition of high fever may be present during the disease, however, and if the carcase is congested or if there is emaciation or serous infiltration of the tissues, it must be totally condemned.

FOOT AND MOUTH DISEASE

This is an acute, febrile disease caused by a filterable virus and affecting the cloven-footed animals, i.e. the ox, pig, sheep, goat and deer. It occurs occasionally in the rat and hedgehog and these animals may act as important carriers of the affection, but dogs, cats and fowls can only be artificially infected with difficulty and play no part in the natural spread of the disease. Infection of human beings occasionally occurs.

The disease is almost world-wide in distribution in spite of stringent measures to ensure its eradication ; even in Great Britain, where the disease is periodically stamped out, infection is reintroduced, and there can be little doubt that this reinfection is of foreign origin.

Foot and mouth disease is undoubtedly the most infectious of the so-called animal plagues and may occur from direct contact between affected and healthy animals, but airborne infection, except for short distances, is considered unlikely. Infection by indirect contact is of the greatest importance and may take place through contaminated straw, drinking water, stalls and footpaths, or by means of the clothes and boots of those attending affected animals. Regulations in Great Britain are therefore applied as counter-measures to these numerous avenues by which infection may be spread. The possibility of infection being introduced into a country and spread within that country by the agency of birds is considered likely, and the numerous outbreaks which have occurred in the autumn in cattle at grass in the south-eastern counties of England are almost certainly related to the autumn migration of birds from the Continent of Europe. Though movement of susceptible animals from one country to another is unlikely to carry infection, for rigid quarantine regulations on the part of the receiving country preclude this, imported hay or straw used as packing material, the wrappers of imported meat, or imported meat itself, are all methods by which the disease may be introduced. Indeed, the succession of outbreaks during the war of 1939-1945, occurring primarily in pigs, undoubtedly bore a relation to the great increase in the pig population in Britain and the feeding of these animals on swill which frequently contained the bones from imported meat.

Pathogenesis. The virus of foot and mouth disease is one of the smallest of the ultramicroscopic organisms, and is present in its greatest concentration in the infective fluid from the vesicles which characterize the disease. It is also found in the epithelium covering the vesicles, and in the circulating blood during the period of fever which precedes the appearance of the lesions. The infectivity of the virus declines as the disease progresses, and affected animals become non-infective some 4 to 5 days after the height of the disease; the bone marrow may, however, remain infective for 76 days after slaughter, though the virus is destroyed after 30 days if decomposition occurs. Under conditions of low temperature and dry atmosphere the virus may survive for some months outside the animal body, and the increase in the number of outbreaks in Great Britain in the winter months is undoubtedly related to the preservative action of low temperature on the virus. The virus of rinderpest is similarly preserved when held at low temperature (Fig. 110).

The virus is particularly susceptible to acidity, and in muscle is destroyed within 48 hours by the lactic acid which is produced in appreciable quantities a few hours after slaughter. If an infected carcase, however, be chilled or frozen immediately after slaughter, the virus retains its infectivity for some months in muscle and bone marrow, with certainty in bone marrow for 76 days and in frozen meat for at least 100 days. Quite apart from the persistence of infectivity of the bone marrow there is equal risk of other tissues, including the lymph nodes, kidneys and rumen, remaining infective for long periods. In articular joints the virus may survive at chilling temperature for 19 days, for the pH stability of a joint, together with its capsule, afford the virus protection against the natural inactivating properties of lactic acid and muscle enzymes. During the boning-out of meat the virus may be liberated from joints and contaminate other tissues ; on muscle fascia and fat stored at 33·8° F. it will survive 14 days, and on muscle fascia and fat stored frozen it will survive 21 days, but viable virus has not been found in infected synovial fluid spread on muscular tissue and stored at 33·8° F. for 11 days. Although quick-frozen meat and its wrappings are more dangerous than meat frozen by ordinary methods or chilled, the commercial refrigeration of imported meat must be regarded as playing an important part in maintaining the viability of the virus in infected carcases and organs.

The virus can be destroyed by most disinfectants, but it has been shown that an alkali is the most efficacious, whereas disinfectants which coagulate protein, as carbolic acid or bichloride of mercury, are less effective. It is recommended that a 4 per cent. solution of washing soda (sodium carbonate) dissolved in warm water, or a 2 per cent. solution of caustic soda be used, and formalin in 5 per cent. solution is of value in the disinfection of stacks of hay and straw.

Susceptibility. Cattle and pigs appear to be most susceptible to foot and mouth disease, sheep and goats probably less so. A strain of virus may at times appear to show a predilection for a particular species of domestic animal, but will eventually affect animals of other species; more commonly, animals of all the susceptible species will become affected if exposed to infection. Seven distinct types of the causal virus are now recognized, namely A, O, C, S.A.T. (South African Territories) 1, 2 and 3, and the Asian type, and the immunity created by each type is specific and gives little or no protection against an attack by viruses of the other types. The virus which is responsible for most of the outbreaks in Great Britain is type O, though type A is also encountered, and type C, an unusually lethal strain, has also been recovered. Speaking generally, foot and mouth disease in Britain is usually only fatal in the case of very young animals such as calves, lambs and piglets, and in these animals is septicaemic in nature and without vesicle formation.

Symptoms. These may be considered in some detail, as many outbreaks in Britain have been first detected in animals awaiting slaughter, and prompt recognition of affected animals is an important factor in control of the disease. The virus is capable of penetrating the intact mucous membrane, but infection of susceptible animals is facilitated by abrasions of the mucous membrane of the mouth and lips, and parts susceptible to mechanical irritation are therefore likely to show the presence of vesicles ; these include the feet, mucous membrane of the mouth and muzzle, the teats in cattle or the snout in pigs, and foot and mouth disease has been observed in pigs fed on crushed bones which is a foodstuff likely to have a severe abrasive action on the gums.

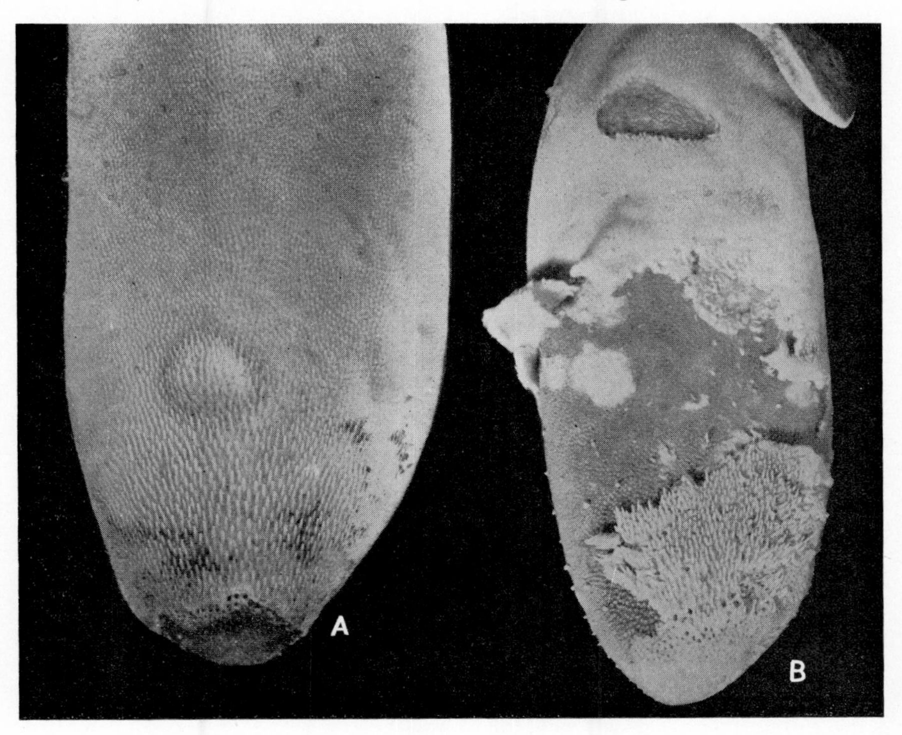

FIG. 103.—Foot and mouth disease of bovine tongues. (A) Tip of tongue shows ulceration and loss of epithelium, while above this can be seen an unruptured vesicle. (B) Freshly ruptured vesicle showing ragged edges of epithelium ; the fungiform papillae remain unaltered in the ulcerated area and can be seen at the lateral aspect of the tongue. (A, Crown copyright ; B, Dr. H. Magnusson.)

After infection an incubation period of 2 to 14 days is observed, and is manifested by a rise in body temperature ; at the end of this period the vesicles appear and the temperature falls.

The symptoms in cattle are chiefly associated with the position of the lesions. Primarily there is a period of general dullness, with lack of appetite and cessation of rumination ; though the animal feeds, it both chews and swallows slowly, and may occasionally open the mouth with a peculiar smacking sound. As the vesicles develop there is an increased flow of saliva from the corners of the lips, the secretion usually being thick, glairy and containing bubbles ; the single thread-like secretion frequently observed to be hanging from one corner of the lips in cattle is unlikely to be due to foot and mouth disease. Associated with the increased salivation is evidence of lameness, particularly when the animal is walking on hard ground, and an affected animal may suddenly lift up a foot and shake it as if in the attempt to dislodge a stone from between the claws.

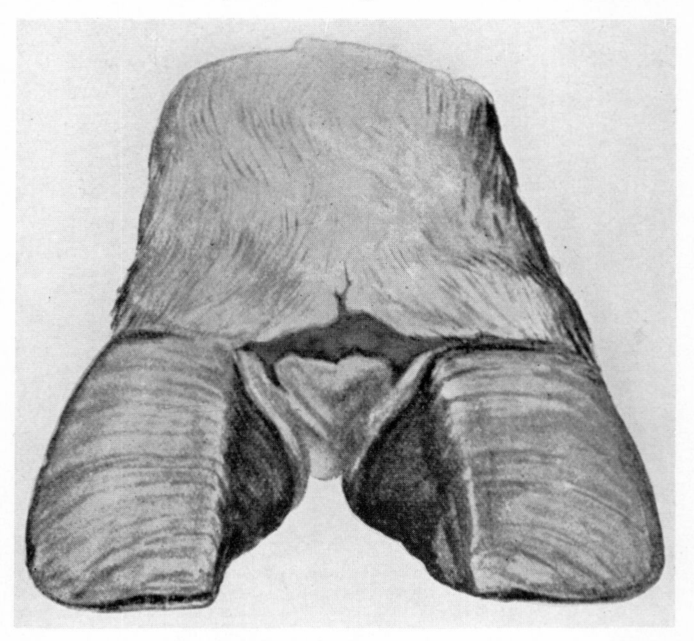

FIG. 104.—Foot and mouth disease of bovine foot. A freshly ruptured vesicle is seen in the interdigital space, with extension along the coronary band.

In sheep symptoms of lameness and the desire to avoid unnecessary movement may be observed, and in pigs suspicion should always be aroused where a number of animals show a marked disinclination to be moved. Salivation in the sheep and pig is not a symptom of the disease, but lameness in a number of these animals awaiting slaughter should always call for an expert examination.

Lesions. In the ox these are observable on the tongue, lips, dental pad and feet, and in the cow they may also be seen on the udder and teats. The vesicles in the mouth, which have a clean, white appearance, vary from half an inch up to 2 inches in size, and contain a yellow straw-like fluid ; these vesicles eventually rupture, leaving red, shallow painful erosions with ragged portions of epithelium attached to the edges of the ulcer. Lesions on the feet may develop simultaneously with the mouth lesions or they may appear some hours later, vesicles appearing between the clefts of the feet, on the heel near the supernumerary digits, or around the coronet ; where vesicles on the feet have not yet ruptured, pressure of the thumb will cause them to burst and discharge the yellow coloured infective fluid. When vesicles occur on the udder and teats of cows the udder is swollen and painful, while the skin around the vesicles is also painful and reddened.

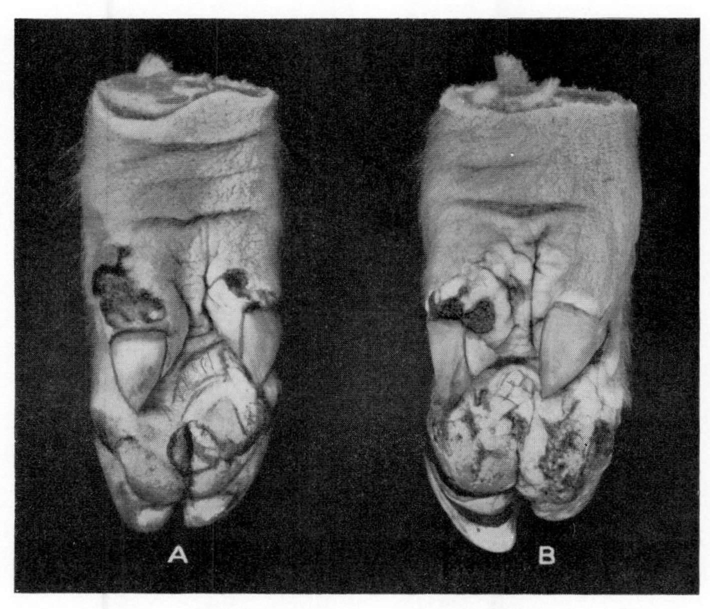

FIG. 105.—Foot and mouth disease of pig's feet. (A) Both claws have been cast, and there is ulceration in the region of the supernumerary digits. (B) The right claw and the horn of the left supernumerary digit has been cast, while the left claw is showing separation prior to casting. (Crown copyright.)

In foot and mouth disease of the sheep and goat the vesicles are much smaller than in the ox, are more transient, and though commonly observed on the feet they may be absent from the mouth. When the mouth is affected in sheep the lesion is found most commonly on the dental pad, the whole surface of which may become separated from the underlying tissues and can be removed with the finger.

In the pig the disease principally affects the feet, lesions being found around the coronet of both the main and supernumerary digits. Mouth lesions are not common in the pig, but vesicles may occasionally be seen on the snout or inside the nostrils, and in sows on the udder around the nipples. In both sheep and pigs it is common for the claws to be "cast" as a result of the disease, and in pigs, when the casting of the claw is gradual, the formation of new horny tissue takes several months and the tip of the old claw may be seen still encasing the new horny growth. This condition is known as "thimbling", and is strongly suggestive of a previous attack of foot and mouth disease.

Economics of Foot and Mouth Disease. Though the disease in Europe has from time to time assumed a particularly virulent form with up to 50 per cent. of deaths, the mortality rate is generally not high and, except in the case of infection due to the C type of virus, certainly not higher than 10 per cent. Complications after an attack of foot and mouth disease are frequent, however, and cattle show a marked loss in condition as a result of the fever, lameness, and difficulty in eating and swallowing.

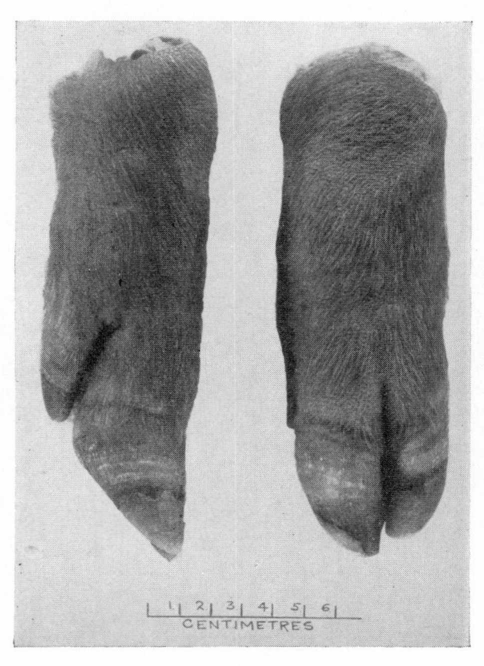

FIG. 106.—Pig's feet showing "thimbling" of the claws, the result of an attack of foot and mouth disease some 3 months previously.

Mastitis and loss of milk yield may also be observed in affected dairy cattle, and an infected animal after recovery may frequently only attain three-quarters of its previous milk yield, while sheep and pigs may lose their claws, with a resultant loss in bodily condition.

The disease in Great Britain and North America is sporadic, and the policy in these countries of immediate slaughter of affected and in-contact animals, with adequate cleansing and disinfection of the infected premises, is a justifiable economic procedure. Where the disease assumes an epidemic form the slaughter policy may be deemed impracticable and may be abandoned, but the financial loss due to the disease, as a result of its rapid spread, will inevitably be severe.

FOOT AND MOUTH DISEASE IN MAN. Though infection with the virus of foot and mouth disease is not common in man, it may be acquired by the consumption of milk from an infected animal, or even from butter or cheese prepared from such milk, and direct infection may occur in slaughtermen or laboratory workers. The affection in man usually takes a mild form, the symptoms being those of fever and dryness of the mouth, followed by the appearance of vesicles on the mouth, lips or tongue and also on the fingers at the base of the nail.

Judgment. In Great Britain the question of meat inspection of infected animals does not arise, for all affected and in-contact animals are destroyed by burning or burial under strict Government control. The fact that the disease has not been known to occur in man from the consumption of infected meat has, however, made it economically expedient in certain parts of Europe, where foot and mouth disease is endemic, to release infected carcases for food after destruction of the head and feet, udders, stomach, intestines and lungs.

In the malignant form of foot and mouth disease, where the death rate is high due to direct action of the virus on the heart muscle, experience on the Continent has shown that animals bled and eviscerated immediately after death can safely be passed for food, provided the bleeding of the carcase is satisfactory. The danger of the further spread of the disease by the agency of the bones and other tissues from these salvaged carcases is, however, considerable.

GLANDERS

This is a disease of the horse, ass and mule, occasionally of man, and has also been encountered in zoological gardens in carnivorous animals which have been fed on the meat of infected horses.

This disease, in the past, has caused serious mortality both in the equine population and in humans, but prior to the war of 1914-1918 was practically eradicated from Great Britain and Europe. During the 1914-1918 war, the intermingling of horses resulted in an increase in the number of outbreaks in these countries, but energetic slaughter and quarantine measures, aided by the diagnostic use of the mallein test, again succeeded in combating the disease, and Great Britain has been free of infection since 1928. The diminution of the horse population and the abolition of the communal horse watering trough are factors which have been concerned in lowering the risk of infection and the incidence of the disease. In most countries, including Britain, the disease is a notifiable one.

Pathogenesis. The disease is contagious, usually chronic in nature, and is caused by *Pfeifferella mallei* (*B. mallei*), a slender rod-shaped organism, 3 to 4μ long by 0·5μ broad. The bacterium is not particularly resistant to adverse conditions, being destroyed by a temperature of 130° F. for 10 minutes, whilst direct sunlight will destroy it in a few hours.

The micro-organisms do not multiply in the blood, but are carried by the arterial blood stream to certain predilection seats, these being the capillaries of the lungs or nasal mucous membrane, and other tissues in which the bacteria are likely to settle are the lymph nodes and the subcutaneous tissue of the skin.

Infection takes place from the excretions of infected animals, especially from nasal discharges or pulmonary expectoration. The common method is by ingestion of contaminated food and water, and though infection may also occur through abrasions in the skin, it rarely occurs by inhalation.

Symptoms. The term glanders and farcy is used to denote two manifestations of the same disease, glanders referring particularly to the affection of the nose and respiratory tract, while the term farcy is used in connection with the chronic cutaneous affection in which there is swelling of the lymphatic vessels and production of the so-called farcy buds.

Glanders may assume an acute or chronic form, but in the chronic form, the type more likely to be encountered in meat inspection, there are few characteristic symptoms. Small grey nodules which rapidly become ulcerative in character, may be seen inside the nostrils and give rise to a yellowish-brown, blood-tinged nasal catarrh. In farcy the cutaneous nodes vary from the size of a pea to a bean, tend to ulcerate, and occur particularly on the limbs, lateral aspect of the thorax, or lower part of the belly.

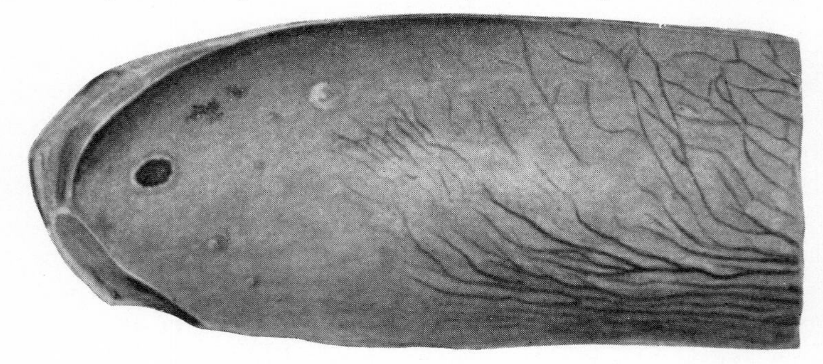

FIG. 107.—Nasal septum of horse, showing lesions of glanders. Nodules and an ulcer with a typical " punched-out " appearance can be seen, together with marked congestion of the nasal mucous membrane.

Lesions. In chronic glanders the commonest lesions occur in the lung and take the form of shot-like nodules up to the size of a pea, which are grey in colour and surrounded by a red area of congestion. These nodules vary in number from 20 to several hundred, their centres eventually degenerating into a yellowish material which stands out in marked contrast against the surrounding zone of hyperaemic lung tissue.

The lesions in the nose occur as ulcers which are in most cases confined to one nostril, have a characteristic " punched-out " appearance, and may heal with the formation of a scar. The submaxillary lymph node of the affected side is frequently enlarged and indurated, and may become firmly fixed to the jaw. Ulcers may also occur on the mucous membrane of the trachea, particularly on its ventral wall.

The cutaneous form of glanders, or farcy, is essentially a chronic lymphangitis, and may be seen in the form of nodules along the course of the subcutaneous lymphatics which resemble knotted cords. These nodules may suppurate, becoming ulcerative and discharging an infective purulent material.

GLANDERS IN MAN. This is usually acquired by cutaneous inoculation and occurs particularly in grooms, laboratory workers and veterinary surgeons. A glanders nodule develops at the seat of inoculation, with inflammation of the lymphatic vessels and lymph nodes, and from these the disease may extend to the nasal mucous membrane or lungs.

Judgment. On account of the infectivity of the disease to man, either by the handling of infected flesh or possibly by its consumption, affected carcases must be unhesitatingly condemned.

HAEMORRHAGIC SEPTICAEMIA OF CATTLE

This disease in cattle occurs in nearly all countries, though it is doubtful whether true haemorrhagic septicaemia exists in Great Britain. Haemorrhagic septicaemia is caused by *Pasteurella boviseptica*, which is a micro-organism belonging to a group of closely allied bacteria classified as the Pasteurella group. It is a short, almost oval rod, 1·2μ long by 0·3μ broad which, on staining with the aniline dyes, shows a deep coloration of the ends with a clear centre. The primary cases in an outbreak probably occur in animals which are carriers of the micro-organism, the resistance of the contact animals being so lowered under unfavourable conditions such as fatigue or changes in the weather that the infection rapidly assumes the character of an epidemic.

Symptoms. In addition to cattle the disease may infect deer, while it is transmissible to the horse, pig and goat and chiefly affects the young animals of these species. Haemorrhagic septicaemia may appear in the following forms: (1) The skin or subcutaneous form, showing fever, marked swelling of the head, neck, throat and dewlap; death in this form is rapid; (2) the pectoral form, in which there is high fever and persistent cough, death occurring within a week. Haemorrhagic enteritis, often manifested by the excretion of blood-stained faeces, is present in both forms of the disease.

Lesions. In the skin form the subcutaneous tissues of the head and throat are infiltrated with a clear, yellowish fluid, while the adjacent lymph nodes are greatly enlarged and may show the presence of petechial haemorrhages.

In the pectoral form of the disease, petechial haemorrhages are invariably present on the mucous and serous membranes and in all the organs; the lungs show a well-marked pneumonia with great thickening of the interlobular septa, and thus bear a resemblance to lungs affected with contagious pleuropneumonia. In both forms of haemorrhagic septicaemia the intestines, particularly the ileum, show a marked enteritis.

Differential Diagnosis. The presence of pharyngeal oedema and blood-stained faeces may confuse the disease with anthrax, particularly of the horse and pig. In anthrax of the horse and pig the micro-organisms may be demonstrated in the submaxillary lymph node, while in bovine anthrax the bacilli may be demonstrated in the blood, and enlargement of the spleen is a characteristic post-mortem lesion. Though the pectoral form of haemorrhagic septicaemia in cattle bears a resemblance to contagious pleuropneumonia, in haemorrhagic septicaemia the lung changes are acute and uniformly distributed, the bipolar organisms may be demonstrated in the blood, and there are multiple haemorrhages in all the organs and tissues. Many cases of so-called transit fever occur in Britain in recently imported animals and resemble the pectoral form of haemorrhagic septicaemia, but the predisposing cause of transit fever is prolonged and wearying transport, whereas the onset of haemorrhagic septicaemia is sudden and rapid and the affection is septicaemic in character.

Judgment. In true haemorrhagic septicaemia there is danger of spread of infection to other animals by the dressing of infected carcases, and for this reason the animal should be treated similarly to one affected with anthrax, and bleeding and dressing of the carcase should be forbidden. Carcases found affected should be condemned.

JOHNE'S DISEASE

This is a chronic infectious disease of cattle, characterized by persistent diarrhoea and wasting. The disease also occurs in sheep, running a much more acute course than in cattle, particularly in lambing or suckling ewes and in lambs; it also occurs in the goat but the affection is not transmissible to man.

The causal organism *Mycobacterium johnei* is an acid-fast bacterium resembling the tubercle bacillus so closely that the disease was at one time attributed to the avian form of the tubercle bacillus; it is now known to be a specific organism which is shorter than the tubercle bacillus, about 2μ long by $0{\cdot}5\mu$ broad, and found in typical clusters in affected tissues.

Johne's disease in cattle is most frequently observed in animals over $1\frac{1}{2}$ years old, being particularly common in second-calf cows, the effect of parturition being a possible factor in accelerating the progress of a disease that may be already latent in the intestine. The affection is less com-

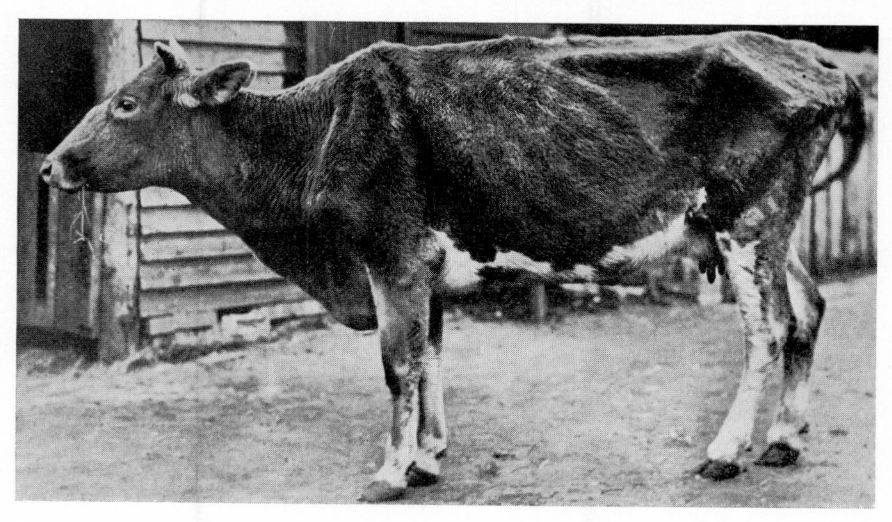

FIG. 108.—Cow affected with Johne's disease, showing typical wasting of buttock muscles and severe emaciation. Note the bright eye and that the animal has been feeding. (A. Norman.)

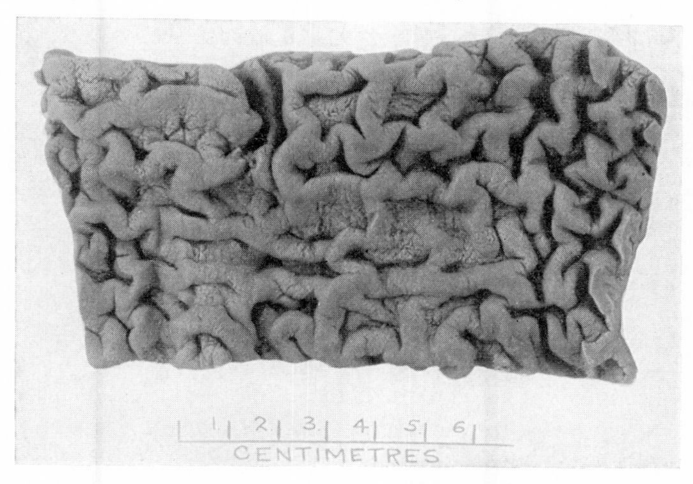

FIG. 109.—Small intestine of ox showing typical lesions of Johne's disease. The mucous membrane has an appearance resembling cerebral convolutions and is usually coated with a greyish-white or greenish mucus.

monly encountered in the heifer and bullock, but in Britain about 90 per cent. of cases of chronic persistent diarrhoea occurring in cows and cattle over 18 months old are due to Johne's disease. Infection is likely to be acquired in the first twelve months of life, but the disease develops so slowly that months may pass before an animal shows clinical symptoms. Infected pastures are regarded as unsafe for at least a year after affected animals have been removed from them.

Symptoms. Oedema of the intermaxillary space is the earliest symptom of Johne's disease, and early wasting of the buttock muscles is a diagnostic feature of the affection. Though an affected animal gradually loses condition, there is at first little interference with the appetite, and rumination does not cease; thus emaciation without exhaustion is a feature of this disease. Diarrhoea soon develops, this being periodic but persistent, foul smelling, dark in colour and homogeneous in structure with small bubbles appearing on the surface (Fig. 9). As the disease progresses there is pallor of the mucous membranes due to anaemia, and this is followed by emaciation. The emaciation and general tissue dehydration which occur are due to failure of the animal to absorb nutrient material and water from the intestines, but even in this stage of the disease the appetite may remain good and the temperature normal.

Lesions. These are not strikingly evident compared with the marked emaciation which typifies the disease in its later stages, and at times the intestinal mucous membrane, where the characteristic post-mortem changes occur, may show little change even in clinically severe cases. The earliest lesion is usually found near the ileocaecal valve, and though the ileum is chiefly involved, the caecum, colon and rectum may also be affected. In these portions of the intestines the mucous membrane may be four to five times its normal thickness, and raised in irregular longitudinal and transverse convolutions which cannot be obliterated by stretching the membrane. The surface of the convolutions, particularly where the large intestine is affected, may show areas of congestion, and the intestinal wall may be much thickened and show oedematous infiltration. The mesenteric lymph nodes are enlarged and oedematous, but the parenchymatous organs show little change, though pathological fatty infiltration of the liver may be seen in the last stage of emaciation due to the disease. It is a characteristic of animals affected with Johne's disease that loss of flesh precedes loss of body fat, and a further characteristic is that the carcase fat assumes a sickly yellowish-white coloration.

In sheep Johne's disease frequently coexists with severe intestinal parasitic infection and may be manifested by thickening of the ileum, often without corrugation of the intestinal mucosa. In sheep the intestine may be pigmented an intense yellow and though necrosis, caseation and calcification are never seen in cattle, they may be present in the mesenteric lymph nodes of affected sheep and calcified nodules may be found in the intestinal wall.

Judgment. Many bovine carcases encountered in meat inspection are " border-line " cases between poorness and emaciation, and present considerable difficulty in judgment. This is facilitated, however, if the decline in physical condition of the animal can be definitely attributed to infection with Johne's disease, for the disease is not communicable to man. In cattle over $1\frac{1}{2}$ years old, where examination of the carcase and organs reveals no obvious cause for the wasting it is advisable as a routine procedure to examine the mucous membrane of the ileum, when lesions of Johne's disease may frequently be demonstrated. Where such a carcase comes within the classification of " poor " it may be passed for food, but where there is evidence of serous infiltrations with a dampness apparent on the serous membranes of the thorax and abdomen, together with lack of setting, it is advisable to detain the carcase in a cool dry atmosphere for a period of 12 hours. In a number of cases considerable improvement in the appearance and dryness of the carcase will be evident after this period, and such carcases, having a value for manufacturing purposes, may safely be passed for food. Where there are definite indications of emaciation, or where, after the detention period, the carcase is still oedematous and shows lack of setting, it should be condemned.

MALIGNANT CATARRHAL FEVER

This is an acute, infective disease of cattle caused by an ultramicroscopic virus, and characterized by inflammation of the eyes, respiratory passages and brain membrane. The disease exists in northern Europe, Norway, Switzerland, Germany, Russia, America and several parts of Africa, and though sporadic in nature, may occur as a herd infection. It has not been recorded in Great Britain although a disease known as malignant catarrh occurs in Britain and presents identical symptoms.

Pathogenesis. Poor conditions of housing, contamination of the stalls, and impure water were formerly held responsible for the disease, but it is now known that the effects of these are limited to increasing the susceptibility of animals to attack by the virus. Young cattle are most susceptible, though the disease is not transmissible direct from animal to animal ; however, it is reported in Africa that apparently healthy sheep and wildebeeste may transmit the disease to cattle.

Symptoms and Lesions. The symptoms are those of an acute infective disease with elevation of temperature, lack of appetite, cessation of rumination and a diminution in the milk yield.

In the early stages ocular symptoms are observable ; the animal avoids light, there is marked lachrymation with eventual development of a whitish corneal opacity, and this, in animals that have recovered from the disease, may result in partial or complete blindness. The ocular symptoms are accompanied by a pronounced nasal discharge, at first mucoid but later becoming purulent and foetid and drying in crusts around the nostrils. The nasal mucous membrane is deeply congested and develops grey diphtheritic membranes which are sloughed off to leave ulcers. The buccal mucous membrane shows similar diphtheritic deposits, which are cast off to leave red erosions, while the mucous membrane of the respiratory tract, from nose to the smaller bronchi, reveals a catarrhal or diphtheritic inflammation. Involvement of the nervous system is shown by lassitude, or by excitability in the form of loud bellowing, grinding of the teeth and muscular tremors. The animal rapidly becomes emaciated, the mortality rate being between 20 and 90 per cent. and greatest when older animals are affected.

Differential Diagnosis. The lesions of the mouth and gums bear a strong resemblance to rinderpest, but gastric symptoms are marked in the latter affection, whereas in malignant catarrhal fever the presence of ocular lesions, with opacity of the cornea, together with the nasal affection and cerebral symptoms, render confusion unlikely. Malignant catarrhal fever may be distinguished from foot and mouth disease by the absence of typical vesicles and ulcers of the mouth and feet. In simple nasal catarrh diphtheritic lesions in the mouth and nasal passages are absent.

Judgment. Malignant catarrhal fever is not communicable to man, and in the early stages of the disease the carcase may be passed for food after condemnation of the head and lungs. As the disease progresses the animal becomes emaciated, and this, together with the high blood content, necessitates total condemnation of the carcase.

MALIGNANT OEDEMA

This disease occurs in the ox, sheep, pig and horse, and in northern climates is also responsible for severe outbreaks in herds of reindeer.

The causal micro-organism is *Clostridium septique* (*Bacillus oedematis maligni*), an anaerobic spore-forming bacterium with rounded ends and 3 to 5μ long by 0·8 to 1·0μ broad. *Clostridium septique* is also the cause of braxy in sheep, and though the bacterium is not found in the circulating blood of affected animals, it is widely distributed in the soil and is a constant inhabitant of cultivated land. Malignant oedema is therefore particularly associated with wound infection and is most likely to occur where there is laceration, with deep destruction of muscular tissue and effusion of blood, these forming a medium favourable for the growth of the micro-organism and the production of its toxin. Age appears to have no influence on the susceptibility of animals to malignant oedema, for cattle over 3 years of age are affected just as frequently as younger animals, and a particularly acute form of the disease occurs in the cow after parturition, infection being introduced into the uterus by unsterilized hands or instruments. Infection of sheep may occur after shearing, docking or castration, and the so-called " bighead ", which occurs in rams after fighting, is a form of this disease; death occurs more rapidly in sheep than in cattle.

In pigs the disease is usually acquired by wound infection, but may also occur by ingestion of the bacteria, which penetrate the mucous membrane of the stomach and produce oedema and gas formation in the stomach wall.

Symptoms and Lesions. Where the disease arises as a result of wound infection an oedematous area develops at the site of inoculation within 24 hours. This swelling is at first sensitive, but becomes softer and can then be incised in the living animal without pain. At a later stage the swelling may crepitate in a manner similar to the lesion in blackleg, and when incised there is effusion of a reddish-yellow fluid which contains gas bubbles and possesses a putrid odour.

In infection after parturition there is a thick, brownish-red discharge from the vagina, followed by a swelling on the vulval lips which is at first painful but later becomes cold, painless, blue in colour and crepitant. This form of malignant oedema is often incorrectly described as parturient blackleg.

In malignant oedema in pigs the stomach wall may show oedema and gas formation, and this may be associated with changes in the liver and kidneys, which become porous due to gas formation and constitute the so-called " foaming organs ".

Judgment. The disease runs an acute course, fever is present and the onset of decomposition is rapid. Carcases of affected animals should therefore be condemned.

RABIES

This is known also as hydrophobia and is an acute infective disease, nearly always fatal in animals and usually transmitted by a bite from an affected animal. Man is susceptible, and is usually infected by the bite of a rabid dog.

The disease is seen particularly among carnivores, including dogs, cats, wolves, foxes and jackals, for the chief method of offence and defence in these animals is by biting. At one time the disease appeared in Europe in the form of epizootics, but has been largely stamped out by strict precautionary and quarantine methods, though in southern and eastern countries, such as India, it is still of frequent occurrence, while in Russia the rabies problem is perhaps the most serious in the world. The last case of rabies in Great Britain occurred in 1922, the end of a serious outbreak which commenced in 1918 as a result of a dog being smuggled by aeroplane into Great Britain from the Continent of Europe.

Rabies is caused by an ultra-microscopic virus which is present in its most concentrated and purest form in the brain and spinal cord of affected animals, and is also found in the saliva and salivary glands, occasionally in the blood, but rarely in the milk. The presence of the virus, particularly in brain tissue, is associated with typical cell inclusions known as Negri bodies which are round, oval or triangular in shape and 1 to 27μ long by 1·5 to 5μ broad. On staining with eosin-methylene blue these bodies appear dark red in colour, while the brain cells and their nuclei stain blue. The presence of Negri bodies in the brain tissue may be regarded as conclusive evidence of the existence of rabies and, where the disease is suspected, the head of the animal is submitted to an approved laboratory where a microscopical examination can be made for the presence of these cell inclusions. Inoculation experiments on rabbits are also conducted for the presence of the virus.

Pathogenesis. The disease is commonest in the dog, 80 per cent. of the cases of rabies originating from these animals, and it can be transmitted to practically all mammals, including those utilized for human food. Infection of the food animals occurs in nearly every case from the bite of a rabid animal, and as the virus possesses an affinity for nerve tissue, especially that near to the brain and spinal cord, wounds situated on the lips, cheeks and nose are particularly dangerous.

After the virus is inoculated into the system through the bite of a rabid animal, it is conveyed by way of the nerves to the central nervous system, where it sets up the typical symptoms of the disease by damage to the nerve cells. The period of incubation is a long one, and in dogs the time elapsing between infection and the appearance of the first symptoms is usually between 2 and 6 weeks, but may extend to 6 months or over.

Sheep and cattle are most likely to be infected as a result of bites around the face, for the thick wool of sheep and the hide of cattle protect the other parts of the body from injury; it has been frequently observed in foreign countries that shorn sheep are more likely to be infected than sheep in heavy wool. It should be noted, however, that every animal bitten by a rabid dog does not contract rabies, and it is recorded in Austria that only 40 per cent. of horses, 50 per cent. of cattle and sheep, 36 per cent. of swine and 25 per cent. of goats which had been bitten became affected with the disease.

Symptoms. The symptoms of rabies in the dog, which is the animal chiefly affected, are not as important to the meat inspector as are the symptoms in the food animal, but the recognition of early symptoms in dogs is of value in preventing the spread of disease to cattle, sheep and pigs. Routine ante-mortem inspection of the food animals, particularly in countries where the disease is endemic, is of great value, for these animals may show typical symptoms of the affection though macroscopic post-mortem findings may be completely lacking.

In the carnivores the disease occurs in two stages, which are classified as furious rabies and dumb rabies. Furious rabies is preceded by a period of melancholy which lasts 1 or 2 days, this being followed by a period of rage or excitement in which the dog commences to wander or run, and may cover considerable distances without resting. The animal will attempt to eat indigestible articles as stones, rags or sticks, and should it encounter a flock of sheep or herd of pigs, may bite and injure many of the animals in a short time. Rabid dogs usually avoid human beings, however, and will attack them only when threatened. The furious period is succeeded by the so-called dumb rabies, in which the animal seeks a secluded spot and develops paralysis of the lower jaw; paralysis soon becomes generalized, and death takes place within 8 days of the onset of the symptoms.

Rabid cattle exhibit sexual excitement, bellowing and aggressive behaviour, and similar symptoms of excitement may be observed in sheep and goats. In affected pigs there is pronounced irritation and aimless wandering, which is followed by aggressiveness, paralysis and death.

Lesions. Post-mortem examination of rabid food animals which have died or been slaughtered reveals no diagnostic lesions. The stomach contains little food, and though the gastro-intestinal mucosa may show inflammatory change the characteristic changes in the brain substance are only evident on microscopical examination.

RABIES IN MAN. The disease in man is nearly always acquired from the bite of a rabid dog, though an extensive human outbreak in Trinidad in 1931 was found to have been transmitted by the bites of vampire bats. An incubation period of 14 to 90 days is succeeded by symptoms of both the dumb and furious type, and affected persons may exhibit itching in the region of the bite, with cramp, salivation and avoidance of fluids. In the outbreak of rabies which occurred in south-west England between 1918 and 1922 no less than 319 dogs became affected and 358 persons were bitten, but prompt vaccine treatment prevented the occurrence of any human deaths from the disease.

Judgment. This is facilitated where a food animal showing symptoms of rabies has a history of having been bitten by a rabid dog. Though rabies is a disease transmissible to man by inoculation rather than by ingestion, animals which show symptoms of the disease should be condemned. The Expert Committee on Rabies of the World Health Organization state that in the case of a meat-producing animal the flesh may be consumed during the following week after exposure to infection, or six months afterwards. The danger from such an animal is rather to those handling such meat than to those who consume it.

RINDERPEST

This disease, known also as cattle plague, causes enormous losses in the cattle population and may lead to the almost complete extinction of animals over large areas. It is an acute febrile, infectious disease, particularly of cattle, but occasionally causing ravages amongst sheep and goats; it is caused by an ultramicroscopic virus and is characterized by inflammatory necrotic changes of the mucous membranes.

The virus is present in the blood, tissue fluids and excretions of affected animals, but is not highly resistant to heat, drying and disinfectants and

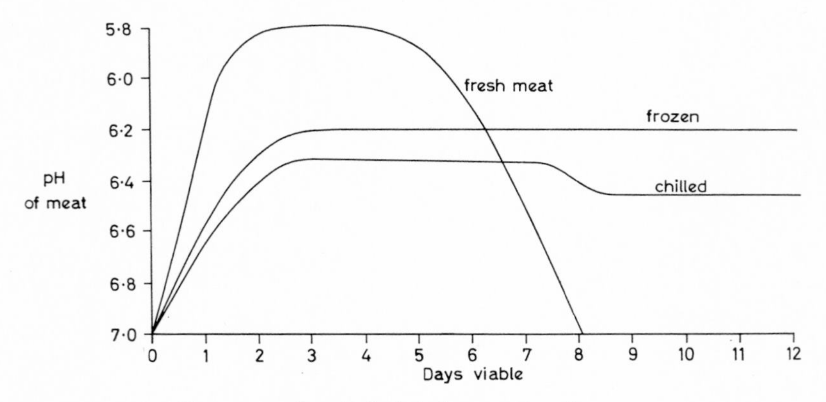

FIG. 110.—Survival of rinderpest virus in meat.

In an animal slaughtered while affected with rinderpest the formation of lactic acid and fall in pH of the muscle causes the virus in muscle to be fairly rapidly destroyed. But if the carcase is chilled or frozen immediately after slaughter the fall in pH is inhibited and the viability of the virus is preserved for prolonged periods. Immediate chilling or freezing of the carcase of an animal slaughtered while affected with foot and mouth disease has a similar preservative effect on the virus in muscular tissue.

rapidly loses potency at or about room temperature, being inactivated in dried secretions in 24 to 48 hours and in salted raw hides in 48 hours. At temperatures of 78° F. or over the virus will not persist in muscle or organs for longer than 10 days, but in chilled or frozen meat it will remain viable for at least one year. The greatest danger arises from the bone marrow, and also the lymph nodes in boned meat, because of the concentration of the virus in these tissues and its prolonged survival time when frozen.

Pathogenesis. The disease is spread by infected cattle and game animals which come in contact with susceptible cattle, but the susceptibility varies markedly and the affection assumes a milder form in permanently affected districts. The disease has an incubation period of 3 to 9 days, animals of all ages being equally susceptible, and though recovery from an attack confers a permanent immunity, the mortality rate from the disease may be up to 90 per cent. Infection usually takes place by way of the digestive tract, and in spite of the theoretical possibility that rinderpest might be introduced into a country through the agency of refrigerated meats or offals of animals slaughtered while affected with the disease, outbreaks in new countries have always been due to the introduction of living affected animals and in no case to infected meat or organs. Because of the fragility of the virus indirect contact in the form of human agency or fodder plays a less important part in the spread of rinderpest than in foot and mouth disease, and simple restrictions on the traffic of animals and their raw products can be relied upon completely to eradicate the disease.

Symptoms and Lesions. High fever, accompanied by a discharge from eyes, nose and mouth, results from the entry of the virus into the blood stream and leads to rapid emaciation. Further toxic effects are manifested by the destruction of the epithelium of the mucous membranes, leaving erosions, particularly in the mouth and digestive tract. The buccal mucous membrane becomes covered with soft, grey plaques, which give the membrane the appearance as if it were sprinkled with bran, these plaques coalescing into a soft, cheesy mass which is eventually desquamated to leave erosions with ragged edges. The necrotic process is also evident in the stomachs, the abomasum being congested and brick-red in colour, while small round sloughs are present on the folds of mucous membrane. The intestines are congested, and when the transverse furrows alone are inflamed the mucous membrane may present a typical "tiger-skin" appearance. Death from rinderpest usually occurs in 4 to 7 days.

Judgment. Though rinderpest is not communicable to man the febrile and toxaemic state of the carcases of affected animals justifies total condemnation.

SWINE FEVER

This is an infective disease of pigs, also known as hog cholera, and is caused by an ultra-microscopic virus. Swine fever is characterized by symptoms of a septicaemia in the form of multiple haemorrhages, while lesions in the form of lobar pneumonia and gastro-intestinal changes of a diphtheritic nature may also develop. The disease occurs nearly all over the world and, unless controlled by effective protective measures, assumes an epizootic form with severe loss, especially among younger pigs. In Britain there is no other disease of pigs which causes so many deaths at short intervals or such continued unthriftiness, whilst it is the only disease peculiar to pigs which affects animals of all ages.

Swine fever was recognized as a specific disease as far back as 1885, and was attributed to infection by *Salmonells suipestifer* (*B. cholerae suis*), for this particular micro-organism could be isolated in connection with the intestinal ulceration which is typical of the disease. Later research proved

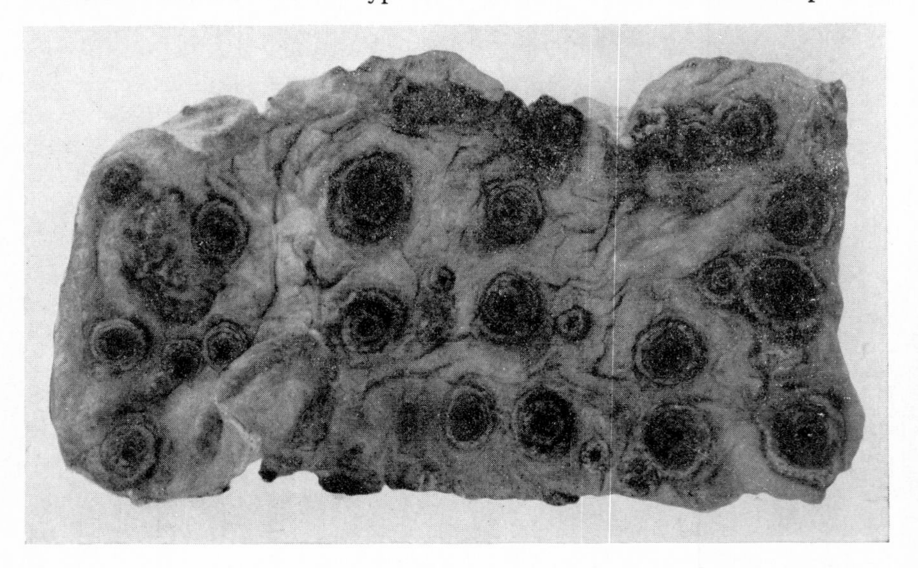

FIG. 111.—Mucous membrane of pig caecum showing a number of swine fever ulcers. In most cases of swine fever the ulcers are less numerous. (T. M. Doyle.)

that the disease was caused by an ultramicroscopic virus, but that *S. suipestifer* played a part in the development of the intestinal lesions. It was also shown that *Pasteurella suiseptica* was associated with the development of the typical lobar pneumonia, almost invariably present in a case of swine fever ; intestinal ulceration and lobar pneumonia, however, are both capable of being produced by the action of the virus alone and without the assistance of these secondary invaders.

During the febrile stage of the disease the virus is present in the circulating blood, in the organs and in all the excretions. The urine plays an important part in the spread of swine fever, but the faeces are of less importance as the virus is destroyed or weakened by the putrefactive processes of the intestine, and infective dung is innocuous within 1 to 2 days ; if infected pigs are removed from a piggery the premises will not remain infective for longer than 14 days. The swine fever virus is destroyed in the carcase within 1 to 2 days as a result of development of post-mortem muscular acidity, but in carcases of animals slaughtered in the incubative stage of the disease and immediately chilled, the bone marrow may remain infective for at least 73 days ; there is evidence that the virus can survive about 1500 days in frozen pork and at least 27 days in bacon which has been pickled, dried and smoked, for salting and pickling have a preservative action on the virus. The severe outbreaks of swine fever which occurred in Sweden in 1926 and 1927 were attributed to feeding on swill which contained scraps of North American bacon.

Susceptibility. Pigs of all breeds and all ages are susceptible, though in younger animals the infection is likely to run a more acute and severe course. Man and other animals are immune to swine fever.

The period of incubation is usually 5 to 9 days, but may extend to 28 days, infection taking place by way of the digestive tract through infected urine or other excretions. Market infection is one of the commonest methods of infection in young store pigs, and another method by which pigs may become infected is related to the prolonged infectivity of the virus in chilled, frozen or salted pork. The possibility of viable virus being carried to piggeries through swill obtained from restaurants and canteens, and containing infective pork or bacon scraps, must not be lost sight of, while " green " bone meal, i.e. unsterilized ground bones, is commonly fed to poultry and, as it may contain bones from infected pig carcases, is also a potential source of infection to healthy pigs. Castrators, too, may convey the disease from piggery to piggery, and as the virus may be present in the blood of apparently healthy contact pigs it is inadvisable that slaughtermen should also be pigkeepers.

Pathogenesis. After ingestion the virus penetrates the mucous membrane of the digestive tract, enters the blood stream and gives rise to symptoms and lesions of a septicaemia ; this is manifested by a rise in body temperature, congestion of the mucous membranes and haemorrhages in various parts of the body.

Symptoms. The disease may be peracute, acute, or chronic. In peracute cases, usually observable at the beginning of an outbreak, death takes place within some 3 days, and ulceration of the intestine and lobar pneumonia may be completely absent.

In acute cases there is evidence of fever with a rise in temperature to 105-108° F., and this is accompanied by great thirst and conjunctivitis, manifested by a muco-purulent secretion from the eyes. The faeces at first may be firm, but become fluid and of a yellowish colour ; symptoms of enteritis in pigs, especially when accompanied by pneumonia, should always arouse suspicion of swine fever. There is loss of control of the hind limbs, producing a staggering gait, and evidence of haemorrhages on the skin, particularly of the ears, shoulder, belly and root of the tail. These haemorrhages appear as a red rash, later becoming violet in colour, which is accentuated when the carcase has been scalded and scraped, and it is a characteristic in swine fever that surface markings on the skin, such as are made by a drover's stick or by the feet of other pigs, are almost black in colour and show up more prominently after scalding. Recognition of the skin haemorrhages is facilitated in dead unscalded pigs if a little boiling water be poured over the skin, and the hair then removed with a knife.

The chronic form of swine fever develops from the acute, and the only symptoms evident may be a short cough, periodic attacks of diarrhoea and the inability of the animal to thrive. Round, dark-coloured necrotic ulcers may be seen around the coronets and up to the knees and hocks, and should always be regarded as suspicious of swine fever ; necrotic skin lesions, however, may be present in swine fever without the co-existence of any intestinal lesions.

Lesions. In peracute cases the only lesions observed may be those of a septicaemia. These take the form of small haemorrhages of both serous and mucous membranes and kidneys, together with moderate swelling and congestion of the lymphatic nodes. In some peracute cases the intestinal mucous membrane may be intensely congested and of a port wine colour.

In less acute cases haemorrhages may be found on the skin, in the lung tissue, in the mucous membrane of the larynx, particularly the epiglottis, while they also occur in the trachea, digestive tract, pericardium, endocardium, bladder mucosa and kidneys. In the latter organ these haemorrhages give rise to the so-called " turkey egg kidney ". Petechial haemorrhages on the surface of the kidney are common in other febrile conditions of the pig, but it is stated by some authorities that, except in swine fever, these haemorrhages disappear when the kidney is immersed in warm water. In suspected swine fever the kidneys should always be sectioned, as in some cases petechial haemorrhages may be found in the substance as well as on the surface. The lymph nodes, particularly the bronchial and mesenteric, are swollen and oedematous and show a typical mottled red coloration, known as " marbling ", which primarily affects the periphery of the node but extends gradually to the centre ; this coloration is caused by the accumulation of red blood cells which have been transported by the lymph vessels from haemorrhagic areas to the associated lymph nodes. Haemorrhages or haemorrhagic infarcts may also be seen in the spleen, particularly at the edges of the organ, infarction being caused by proliferation of the endothelial cells of branches of the splenic artery.

The alimentary tract may show lesions as far forward as the pharynx, on which petechiae or yellow diphtheritic deposits may be seen. The

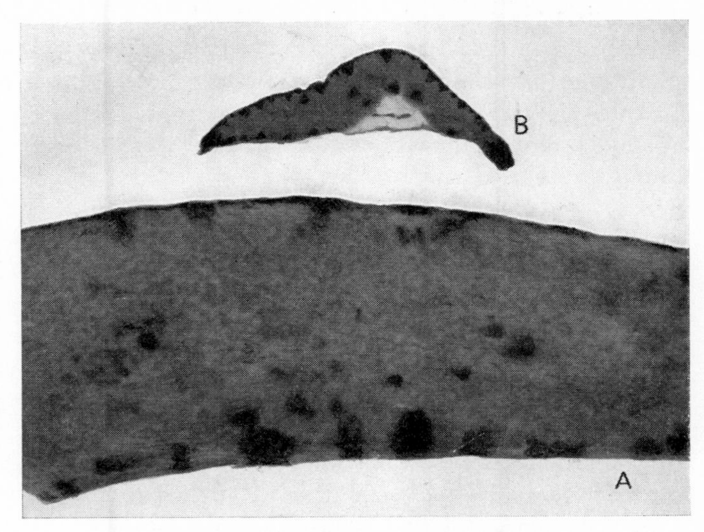

FIG. 112.—Haemorrhagic infarcts in pig spleen, from a case of acute swine fever. (A) surface of spleen; (B) spleen in cross-section.

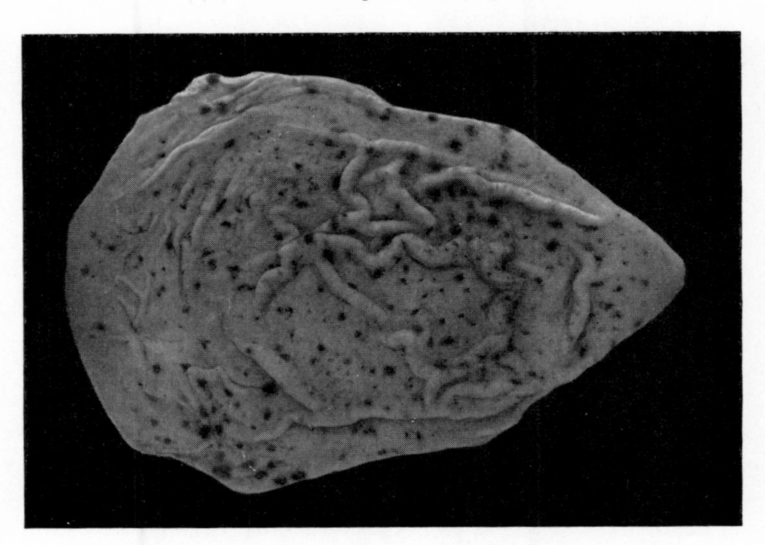

FIG. 113.—Mucous membrane of pig stomach, showing numerous haemorrhages in a case of acute swine fever. These usually occur in the cardiac portion of the stomach. (T. M. Doyle.)

stomach is deeply congested and may show haemorrhages or yellow fibrinous deposits, while the faecal contents of the caecum may be almost black in colour. The characteristic lesions may be seen in the neighbourhood of the ileo-caecal valve, the mucous membrane of which shows changes arising in connection with the small lymph follicles. These lesions, which originate over a haemorrhage in the submucosa, are evident as projecting button-like ulcerations and are dirty yellow, grey or black in colour ; they vary in size from a millet seed up to 1½ inches or larger and are firmly adherent to the underlying tissue, the more well-defined ulcers showing concentric ringing due to the progressive deposits of fibrin. In many cases the haemorrhagic base of the ulcer is visible on the peritoneal surface of the intestine and is a valuable diagnostic guide. The mucous membrane of the caecum, colon and rectum is deep red in colour and may show similar deposits. These so-called " button ulcers " are at times confused with the mucous plugs which are seen on the ileo-caecal valve, and at first sight appear to be caseous in nature. The latter, however, are a retained glandular secretion, and can be distinguished from the adherent necrotic lesions of swine fever by the ease with which they can be squeezed out from the mucous membrane.

The lungs may be adherent to the thoracic wall, and show numerous petechial haemorrhages with localized areas of pneumonia. In some cases the pneumonic process may involve a whole lobe, particularly an anterior lobe, the hepatized area appearing greyish-red and indurated ; in chronic cases of swine fever, however, the principal lesions are confined to the alimentary tract.

PROCEDURE WHEN A CASE OF SWINE FEVER IS DETECTED. In Great Britain swine fever is a notifiable disease, and any person having in his possession, or under his charge, an animal or carcase affected with, or suspected of being affected with swine fever must forthwith give notice of the fact to a constable of the police force of the area ; the same procedure must therefore be followed when the disease is encountered during routine inspection in the slaughterhouse. Though an inspector of a local authority possessing powers under the Diseases of Animals Acts may serve a notice on the occupier of the premises which house the suspected animal, declaring the premises an Infected Place, this should not be done in the case of a slaughterhouse except by an inspector of the Ministry of Agriculture, Fisheries and Food. The disposal of carcases of animals which have died of swine fever is, however, the responsibility of the local authority and should be done either by burning or by burial in quicklime, the procedure being clearly detailed in the Swine Fever Order of 1938.

African swine fever. This is a long-established disease of the wild pig and warthog in Africa ; on occasions it may infect the exotic domestic pig and in the latter animal the disease runs a rapid course and is almost invariably fatal. The causal virus is readily isolated from the tissues of pigs which have died from an acute infection, and also from the tissues of carrier pigs. The virus remains viable in infected carcases after 15 weeks chilling, and it has been recovered from hams for periods up to five months, and from the bone marrow of such hams for up to six months. In Africa the feeding of uncooked meat scraps has proved to be a means by which infection spreads from a primary outbreak.

Judgment. Though *Salmonella suipestifer* belongs to the group of organisms which include the bacteria responsible for food poisoning in man, there is little evidence that this bacterium is harmful to man, and the association of swine fever, where there is no evidence of septicaemia or pyaemia, with cases of food poisoning can therefore be discounted. In acute cases of a septicaemic character showing fever, evidence of petechial haemorrhages, lymph node enlargement and enteritis the carcase should be condemned, while the chronic cases of swine fever associated with extensive bowel ulceration and diarrhoea are often emaciated or too poor and undersized to be passed for food.

In a swine fever outbreak the apparently healthy pigs may be consigned by licence from the infected premises to a slaughterhouse for immediate slaughter, and though the lungs of many of these animals may show evidence of lobar pneumonia, the bleeding and setting of the carcase should be the criterion of judgment. It is the usual practice to " turn " the caeca of such animals and examine the mucous membrane for diphtheritic changes, but it is advisable to condemn the stomach and intestines whether lesions are present or not.

PIG PARATYPHOID

This disease, known also as necrotic enteritis, is often confused with swine fever and in Britain is perhaps the most important affection of pig breeding, pigs from weaning to 6 months of age being usually affected. It is caused by *Salmonella suipestifer*, which inhabits the intestines of many healthy pigs, the disease appearing when unsuitable conditions such as bad housing, vitamin or mineral deficiency, or heavy infestation with parasitic worms, lower the resistance of the animal to bacterial infection. After infection a pig will excrete large numbers of micro-organisms in the faeces and may affect other animals whose resistance is impaired; thus young affected pigs which are introduced direct into a herd without preliminary isolation may originate the disease. Pig paratyphoid is seasonal in incidence, being particularly common in the winter months, and usually assumes a chronic form, though less commonly it may run an acute course.

Symptoms and Lesions. The symptoms closely resemble swine fever, affected pigs beginning to lose condition between the fifth and ninth weeks of life, while they are listless, have a scurfy skin and excrete a yellowish diarrhoea.

On post-mortem examination the intestinal mucous membrane presents long streaks of irregular necrosis, at times patchy in distribution, which become converted into greenish-yellow ragged masses. Patchy haemorrhages and ulcers may occur in the intestine, but these ulcers are shallow, not raised or button-like as in swine fever, and are surrounded by a smooth raised border of normal mucous membrane. The skin lesions may take the form of fine pin-point haemorrhages which become apparent when the carcase is scalded and scraped, or there may be red discoloration in the

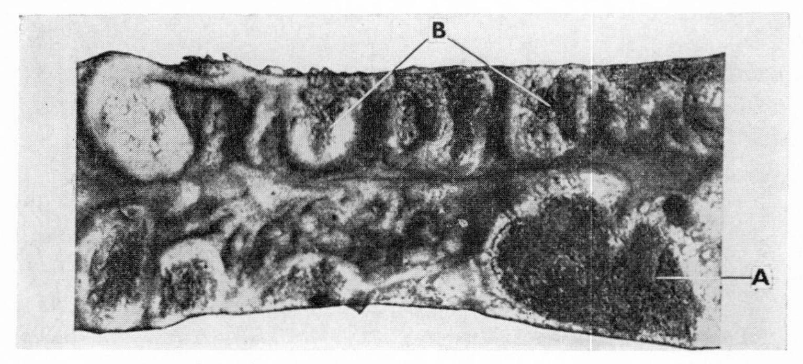

FIG. 114.—Intestine of pig affected with pig paratyphoid. A. Superficial ulcer with smooth raised border and soft necrotic deposits. B. Different stages of ulceration.

region of the ears, buttocks, legs and belly, and petechial haemorrhages may be present in the kidneys, though not usually so numerous as in swine fever. Skin ulceration does not occur in pig paratyphoid, and the mesenteric lymph nodes, though swollen, are less deeply congested than in swine fever and of a peculiar greyish-yellow colour.

Judgment. The disease is not a notifiable one, and is usually confined to store pigs in early life. Carcases which may reach the slaughterhouse are generally stunted, emaciated, and so lacking in muscular development that they should be condemned.

SWINE ERYSIPELAS

This is an infectious disease of pigs, septicaemic in nature, and occasionally infecting sheep, birds and man. The disease is widespread throughout Europe and is caused by *Erysipelothrix rhusiopathiae*, a slender rod-like organism, non-sporing and 1·0 to 1·5μ long. The organism is frequently present in the marrow of long bones of healthy pigs, and also in the pharynx and intestinal tract; when excreted with the faeces the bacterium is capable of multiplying under suitable conditions of moisture or warmth, and the faculty of the organism to live a saprophytic existence in the soil for at least a year accounts for the sporadic cases which occur on isolated farms, usually in the summer months from June to September. Predisposing causes such as bad housing, bad sanitation or fatigue may lower the

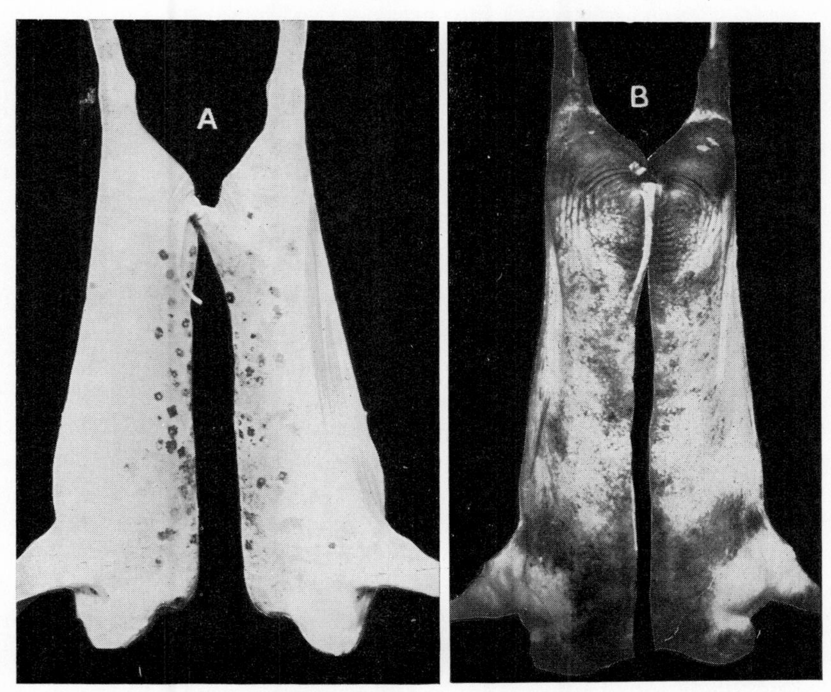

FIG. 115.—Pig carcases affected with swine erysipelas. (A) Mild or urticarial form, showing typical diamonds; (B) acute or septicaemic form. (A. C. F. Gisborne.)

resistance of the animal to an attack, and it is not uncommon for apparently healthy pigs consigned on a long train journey to arrive at their destination showing well-marked symptoms of acute swine erysipelas. The bacterium is easily destroyed by boiling water, and by the usual disinfectants within a few minutes, though it may remain alive in salted and pickled meat for 3 to 4 months, in buried carcases for 9 months and in frozen carcases for at least 10 months.

Pathogenesis. Infection is acquired through the ingestion of urine and faeces of affected animals, and recovered animals undoubtedly act as carriers. The disease has an incubation period of 3 to 5 days, and can spread from pig to pig. Frequently, however, only odd pigs in a herd are affected, and although the disease seldom attacks old sows and boars, or young pigs up to 3 months old, it has been observed that particularly well nourished pigs, whose powers of heat dissipation in warm sultry weather are relatively slight, are the most frequently affected.

Symptoms and Lesions. When the infective micro-organisms enter the blood in considerable numbers they give rise to a septicaemia, the bacterial toxins causing weakening of the capillary walls and the formation of petechial haemorrhages in the lungs and kidneys and on the serous covering of stomach and intestines; other septicaemic manifestations may be seen in the form of enlargement of the spleen and lymph nodes. In these acute cases, the majority of which are fatal in 2 to 7 days, the skin shows red patches over the ears, neck, abdomen, buttocks and under the thighs. The causal organisms can be found in the capillaries of the skin and all the organs, and are constantly present in the kidneys where a diagnostic microscopical feature is that they may be demonstrated in clumps and often within leucocytic cells. It is a characteristic of swine erysipelas that the skin discoloration and the petechial haemorrhages are more obvious in the dead unbled animal than in the pig which has been bled.

In those cases where the virulence of the organism is low or the powers of resistance of the animal are high the disease assumes a milder or urticarial form in which the bacteria tend to localize in the skin, producing red, slightly swollen areas which are rhomboid or diamond-shaped, whilst the blood vessels in these areas are dilated and congested and the skin is oedematous. These so-called diamonds appear on the sides, back and buttocks, being from ½ to 2 inches in diameter and apparent as flat, firm plaques when the skin is handled. The centres of these lesions tend to become paler, and in rare cases the inflamed skin areas may become necrotic, giving rise to scab formation and a bluish-red discoloration of the subcutaneous fat; the tips of the ears and tail may also become necrotic and be sloughed off. The skin erythema is essentially the same in both septicaemic and urticarial form, the condition differing only in degree and distribution, and though in the urticarial form of the disease the bacilli may be found in large numbers in the skin lesions, they are only occasionally found in the blood and organs and then in small numbers. In addition to the skin lesions there may be gastritis or enteritis, with a yellowish-green diphtheritic deposit in the caecum and colon, but ulceration or necrosis of the alimentary tract never occurs as in swine fever.

Chronic swine erysipelas arises as a result of an acute attack, and may be manifested by symptoms of cardiac disturbance. The animal is disinclined to move, resting on its belly rather than on its side, and although affected pigs may appear to recover they frequently die suddenly. In chronic cases the pericardium often contains a serofibrinous exudate, the epicardium being covered with a thick fibrinous deposit, and a verrucose or ulcerative endocarditis is frequently present, usually on the mitral valve. Wart-like vegetations, which usually contain the causal bacilli in large numbers, may be revealed on the valve after removal of adherent blood clots, and detachment of emboli from the affected valves may set up an acute attack of swine erysipelas with a recurrence of the typical symptoms of the acute disease and a diffuse or diamond-shaped discoloration and petechiation of the kidneys. A flare-up of a chronic case of swine erysipelas is probably one of the commonest causes of kidney petechiation, though such petechiae in otherwise normal pigs may be caused possibly by larvae of *Ascaris lumbricoides* (var. *suis*) which have entered the arterial blood stream from the lungs, or by larvae of *Toxacara canis* or *Toxacara cati*, common ascarids of the dog and cat respectively. Emboli from the cardiac vegetations may also give rise to infarcts, which are usually observed in the kidneys (Plate I), and in chronic cases of swine erysipelas a chronic villous arthritis may be seen in the joints of the fetlock, hock and stifle with replacement of the synovial membrane by red granulation tissue (Plate III). In hind limb affection the iliac nodes are much enlarged and reddish-brown in colour, while affection of the fore-limb may manifest itself by enlargement of the prepectoral node.

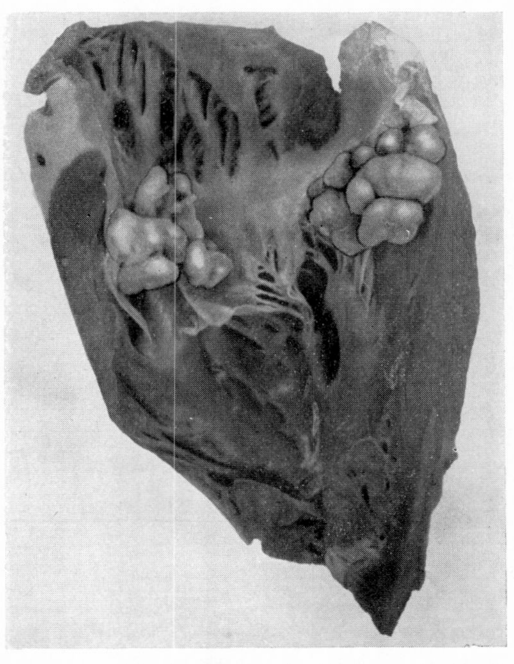

FIG. 116.—Pig heart, showing lesions of chronic swine erysipelas involving the tricuspid valve. Lesions of this affection are frequently more cauliflower-like in appearance. The histological report stated that the vegetations consisted of dense hyaline fibrin, were firmly adherent, and contained many slightly curved Gram positive bacilli (*E. rhusiopathiae*).

Though it is not usual to incise the heart in routine examination of pig carcases, the presence of endocardial vegetations may sometimes be suspected by dilatation and enlargement of the heart, for the production of a mitral stenosis leads to accumulation of blood in the left auricle, this being followed by stasis within the pulmonary veins and passive congestion of the lungs. Extension of stasis throughout the large veins of the body may finally result in passive congestion of the liver or in chronic enlargement of the spleen.

SWINE ERYSIPELAS IN MAN. Infection is conveyed to man by inoculation through abrasions of the skin and is seen as an acute erythema with itching and cellulitis, usually of the thumb or fingers. The disease is most common in abattoir workers and also in fish curers and manufacturers of ground fish meal, for the bacilli, probably originating from sewage, have been found on the skin of many salt-water fish. The English type of swine erysipelas organism tends to involve the joints and tendon sheaths of man, whereas the type of organism occurring in Poland often involves the heart valves and is frequently fatal.

Judgment. In swine erysipelas of the septicaemic form, in which there is great constitutional disturbance and death is likely to occur rapidly, the congestion and lack of setting of the carcase render it unfit for human food. In the milder urticarial form, or in chronic swine erysipelas, the carcase may be well nourished and well set, with little abnormality except for the skin or heart lesions, and a favourable judgment may frequently be given. Where urticarial skin lesions are present it is advisable to skin the carcase instead of scalding, and regard should then be paid as to whether the inflammatory changes associated with the reddened skin areas have extended to the subcutaneous fat. In such cases the discoloured fatty tissue may be trimmed off and the carcase safely passed for food.

SHEEP POX

The diseases classed as pox occur in all the food animals and in man, and are caused by an ultra-microscopic virus. The disease in man is known as variola or smallpox, while the poxes of veterinary importance are sheep pox and fowl pox, both being responsible for severe epidemics. In cattle and horses the disease is milder and the eruption is more localized, whilst swine pox in Britain is rare and is usually seen only in very young pigs kept under faulty conditions of feeding and housing. Sheep pox has not occurred in Britain since 1850, but has been known to exist in Europe since the 13th century and is still responsible for severe epidemics, particularly in the summer months.

Symptoms and Lesions. Infection is acquired by inhalation, the development of the eruption commencing after an incubation period of 6 to 8 days, and appearing on the skin where there is little wool, and on the mucous membranes. The skin around the eyes, cheeks, lips, inner aspect of thighs, posterior part of belly and under surface of tail are particularly likely to be affected, and these skin changes are accompanied by fever and a muco-purulent discharge from nose and eyes.

The eruption takes the form of a papule surrounded by a red ring or areola, which increases in size and rapidly becomes filled with a clear serous fluid to form a vesicle. As this vesicle increases further in size it becomes cupped or umbilicated, and eventually becomes purulent due to invasion by pyogenic organisms, the final stage being a degeneration of the pustule to form a crust which is cast off to leave a small red spot or cicatrix. The temperature of the animal falls when the vesicular stage is reached, and the wool over the pock becomes loose and is easily removed. In the affected areas of the animal body the skin and subcutaneous tissue may be oedematously infiltrated, particularly around the eyes, nose and mouth, and further complications may develop in the form of extensive haemorrhages on the skin or cutaneous necrosis, which in some cases is followed by gangrene. The mortality in certain outbreaks is about 5 per cent., but in extensive outbreaks associated with skin haemorrhages and secondary infection of the lungs it may be as high as 50 per cent.

Judgment. If sheep are slaughtered during the development of the pocks, the animal will bleed badly and the carcase should be condemned, but the carcase may be considered fit for human consumption if the pocks are healing and the body temperature has returned to normal. Where secondary complications exist, as in extensive septic or gangrenous infection, the carcase is unfit for food.

In Great Britain the disease is a scheduled one under the Sheep Pox Order of 1938, and the skin and wool, from the veterinary public health aspect, are of importance in the possible spread of the affection. Carcases intended for human food may therefore only be removed from an Infected Place if they are certified free from sheep pox and after the skin has been removed, while an affected carcase must be burned or buried in a manner similar to a carcase affected with foot and mouth disease.

TETANUS

This is an acute infective disease caused by *Clostridium tetani* (*B. tetani*) and characterized by spasmodic contraction of the voluntary muscles. *Cl. tetani* is a thick, straight rod, 4 to 8μ long by 0·3 to 0·6μ broad, and is strictly anaerobic, though it will grow and multiply in the soil at warm summer temperature. The disease occurs most commonly in tropical countries where it may even assume an epizootic character, but it is frequently encountered in northern climates and causes losses, principally amongst horses and sheep. It also occurs in cattle, more rarely in the pig, while man is infected by contamination of wounds with material containing the micro-organism or its spores. *Cl. tetani* is particularly abundant in the surface layers of soil, especially in manured fields and garden soil, and the bacterium can frequently be demonstrated in the intestines of healthy horses. *Cl. tetani* readily forms spores which are terminal, spherical in shape and about twice the thickness of the bacterium; the organism thus presents an appearance resembling a pin or a drumstick. These spores are destroyed by boiling water, though the digestive juices have little effect on them.

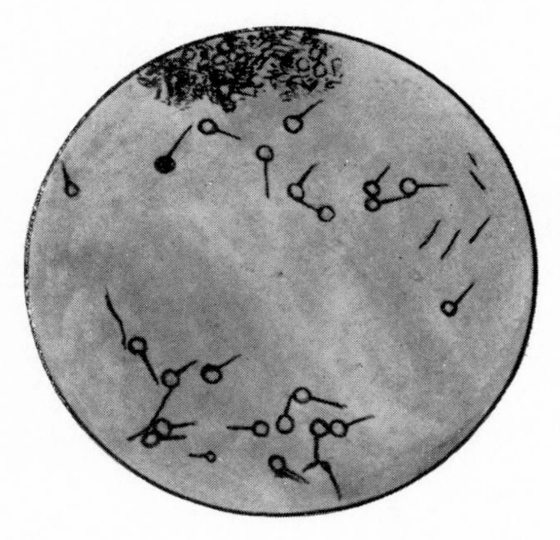

FIG. 117.—*Clostridium tetani* showing rods, many with terminal spore formation.

Cl. tetani produces a powerful toxin made up of two components, tetanospasmin, which causes the typical muscular spasms of the disease, and tetanolysin, which produces disintegration of the red blood corpuscles. The toxin is susceptible to heat and is destroyed by heating to 149° F.

Infection with tetanus is associated with injuries of the skin or mucous membranes, particularly in those wounds where there is haemorrhage and destruction of tissue. For this reason wounds of the feet in horses are a common cause of tetanus, especially where there has been deep penetration of the sole and where the animal has been engaged in spreading lime on fields. Fractures, castration, particularly by the rubber ring method in sheep, shearing wounds or difficult parturition are other common methods by which the micro-organism may gain entrance to the animal body and multiply under anaerobic conditions; infection may also occur in the new-born animal by way of the umbilicus. The period of incubation of the disease is from 4 to 14 days, but spores may remain latent in animal tissues for considerable periods and then, under suitable conditions such as cold, excessive heat or muscular exertion, become active and set up symptoms of the disease.

Symptoms and Lesions. Clostridium tetani seldom reaches the blood stream, but exerts its pathogenic effects by its toxin, which possesses an affinity for nervous tissue. The disease is characterized by the onset of muscular spasms, beginning in the region of the head and spreading backwards to other muscular groups. The muscles feel hard and board-like, while difficulty in opening the mouth, which is associated with spasms of the masseter muscles, is responsible for the common term "lockjaw". The above symptoms are accompanied by great excitability and increased respirations, and it is a characteristic of the disease that the temperature may remain normal until death, but then shows a rise of several degrees.

In cattle, retention of the foetal membranes and a resultant septic metritis is often associated with tetanus, the chief symptoms being cessation of rumination together with tympanitis and distension of the left flank. In sheep and goats the disease is manifested by a stiff, stilted gait, and in pigs by a pricking up of ears and tail (Fig. 9).

There are no characteristic post-mortem lesions of the disease, though pathological fatty change may be observed in the heart, liver and kidneys, and the muscles may be soft and of a grey or yellow colour due to hyaline degeneration. Animals which have died of tetanus show evidence of asphyxia, the blood being dark red and showing little tendency to clot, while petechial haemorrhages may be found on the serous membranes or heart, together with oedema and congestion of the lungs. It will be apparent that though tetanus may be recognized with ease in the live animal, its detection after slaughter presents considerable difficulty and it is therefore a disease in which ante-mortem inspection is of the greatest value.

Judgment. Tetanus is extremely unlikely to be acquired by man consuming the flesh of an animal affected with the disease, but the imperfect bleeding of the carcase, together with the poor durability and change in the colour of the musculature, necessitate total condemnation of the carcase and organs.

TUBERCULOSIS

BACTERIOLOGY.

Characters of bacilli and their staining reactions.

Types of bacilli and their pathogenicity for animals and man.

INCIDENCE.

Cattle, pigs, sheep and goats.

MODES OF INFECTION.

Cattle, pigs, sheep and goats.

PATHOGENESIS OF TUBERCULOSIS.

AFFECTION OF SPECIFIC PARTS.

Lungs—serous membranes—liver—spleen—kidneys—bones and joints—central nervous system—alimentary tract—female sex organs—male sex organs—udder—muscle—skin—other organs.

DIFFERENTIAL DIAGNOSIS.

Corynebacterium infection in pigs—Brucella suis infection in pigs—Parasitic infections.

JUDGMENT OF CARCASES AFFECTED WITH TUBERCULOSIS.

Localized and generalized tuberculosis.

Routine post-mortem procedure.

Procedure in England and Wales.

Code of judgment in England and Wales.

Code of judgment in Western Germany.

Bacteriology

Characters of Bacilli and their Staining Reactions

Mycobacterium tuberculosis is a slender, rod-shaped micro-organism, straight or slightly curved and 2·5μ long by 0·3μ broad. A characteristic arrangement of the bacilli in tissues and organs is one which resembles a bundle of faggots ; they may also be seen in pairs with the bacilli lying at an angle to each other, but they are rarely seen in chains. The bacilli are obtained in greatest abundance for microscopical examination by the technique of crushing a young growing tubercle, but in older caseous or even calcified lesions they are best demonstrated from scrapings of the inner aspect of the encapsulating fibrous wall. *M. tuberculosis* belongs to a group of bacteria which are characterized by the possession of a lipid material which is responsible for the resistance of the micro-organism to staining by ordinary laboratory methods. Staining is usually done by the use of hot carbol fuchsin, and it is a characteristic of micro-organisms of this group that, once stained, they resist decolorization even by strong acid ; they are therefore classified as the acid-fast group. *M. tuberculosis* is also alcohol-fast, and a common decolorizing agent used in staining the bacterium is 25 per cent. sulphuric acid in methylated or industrial spirit.

The acid-fast group of micro-organisms includes pathogenic and non-pathogenic bacteria ; the pathogenic group includes *M. leprae*, the cause of leprosy in man, and *M. johnei*, the cause of Johne's disease in cattle. Non-pathogenic members of the group are distributed widely in nature and are found in butter, dung or on vegetable plants, but they are of no importance in meat inspection.

As far as meat is concerned thorough cooking, boiling or roasting of small joints will destroy any tubercle bacilli present with certainty, and the usual pasteurizing temperature of 142° F. to 145° F. for 30 minutes provides an ample margin of safety in regard to milk. Methods of preservation of meat, particularly freezing and pickling, are of doubtful value in destroying tubercle bacilli, and *M. tuberculosis* has been shown to remain alive for over 2 years in carcases frozen at 15° F., and for 18 days in infected portions of pickled meat, while tuberculous organs in pickle for months may be still infective. Decomposition has no effect on the viability of the organism, and virulent tubercle bacilli have been found in decomposed bovine lung after 167 days, in putrid carcases after several years, and in carcases of tuberculous fowls buried 8 feet deep for a period of 27 months.

Types of Bacilli and their Pathogenicity for Animals and Man

Three types of tubercle bacilli concern man and animals, the human, bovine and avian. All three types are probably members of a common original strain, but have acquired different biological features by long years of adaptation in their particular host. A fourth type of tubercle bacillus occurs in fish, particularly in the halibut, and in other cold-blooded animals, but bacilli of this type are harmless for warm-blooded animals and man.

Man

Though the majority of cases of human tuberculosis are caused by the human type of bacillus, it is probable that all human beings are as susceptible to the bovine type as they are to the human, but the chances of infection by the bovine bacillus have been greatly reduced in most countries as a result of the eradication of the disease from the cattle population. It cannot be over-emphasized, however, that the bovine bacillus is probably just as virulent for man as the human bacillus and is a deadly and killing organism, while it must also be stressed that it is erroneous to believe that small doses of living bovine tubercle, taken accidentally with food, raise the specific resistance of individuals without producing disease.

In the past relatively few cases have been reported in which the avian bacillus has been shown to be the cause of tuberculosis in man, but in recent years an increasing number of human infections have been recorded due to the avian micro-organism. The findings of Nassal (in 1961 in the Freiburg area of Southern Germany) are tabulated below and show that amongst a farming community the percentage of human cases of tuberculosis due to the avian type of bacillus, and also to the bovine type, were higher than among a town population.

	Farming community	*Town population*
	Percentage incidence	
Human type .	69·5	84·1
Bovine type .	21·0	9·1
Avian type .	9·8	6·8

Cattle

The bovine form of the bacillus is the most pathogenic for cattle, and is the commonest cause of tuberculosis in these animals. Spontaneous disease in cattle due to the human micro-organism is rare but has been recorded several times, especially from sanatorium sewage or from tuberculous attendants ; natural infection with human type tubercle bacilli does not produce progressive disease in cattle but an infection which quickly heals, the lesions in cattle sensitized by the human bacillus being small and confined to the bronchial and mediastinal lymph nodes, while at times no lesions may be found. No case of generalized tuberculosis in cattle due to the human type bacillus has been recorded.

Infection of cattle by the avian bacillus has been frequently recorded, though its virulence for these animals is but slight. Lesions are usually localized and non-progressive, being generally found in the mesenteric lymph nodes and occasionally in the retropharyngeal nodes. They are seldom larger than a pea, and are usually encapsulated and calcified. When extension of avian infection occurs in cattle the serous surfaces of the body cavities are frequently involved, and lesions may be found in the udder, lung, liver and spleen.

PIGS

In Britain bacilli of the bovine type were formerly responsible for most of the cases of tuberculosis in pigs, but the position now is that over 90 per cent. of cases in pigs are due to the avian type micro-organism. In the United States, in which bovine tuberculosis has also been eradicated, the avian micro-organism is likewise responsible for practically all the cases of porcine tuberculosis. Infection of pigs by human type bacilli occasionally occurs, and though infections with the avian and human type micro-organisms are usually localized it is recorded in the United States that avian type bacilli in pigs can at times give rise to generalized disease.

SHEEP AND GOATS

Tuberculosis in these animals is usually caused by bacilli of the bovine type, though the goat can contract the disease from human type bacilli and this may assume a progressive, generalized and fatal form. In certain areas where avian tuberculosis is common in the United States the majority of cases of tuberculosis in sheep have proved to be due to bacilli of the avian type. Birds of all kinds are susceptible to the avian bacillus but are almost entirely resistant to the human and bovine strains; the exceptions to this are the cockatoo and parrot, which are susceptible to all three strains.

Incidence

CATTLE

The prevalence of bovine tuberculosis is attributable to one factor, the presence of "open" cases of bovine tuberculosis which disseminate widespread infection. Greater opportunities for infection exist in dairy herds than in cattle reared in breeding districts, and the prevalence at one time of the disease in milch cows may well have been related to intensive methods of production, including close housing, frequent pregnancies and excessive milk yields.

In Great Britain the proportion of tuberculous cattle has shown a gradual reduction since 1950 when the Tuberculosis Eradication Scheme was introduced, and at the end of 1960 all cattle were in officially tubercle-free herds, the total cost of eradication in Britain being estimated at £150 million.

In the United States, the effect of the eradication scheme on meat inspection has been to lower the number of carcases of beef condemned for tuberculosis from 40,746 in 1917 to 9,968 in 1936 and 244 in 1965. It is therefore estimated that some 40,000 carcases have been saved annually in recent years, the value of which represents a large dividend on the financial expenditure incurred on the eradication scheme. In 1964 in Western Germany the incidence of tuberculosis found in slaughtered cattle was 0·2 per cent.

Pigs

In Britain the incidence of swine tuberculosis was at one time closely related to the incidence of the disease in cattle, and tuberculous pigs were likely to be found where there was a high percentage of tuberculous cows and where dairy products, such as whey, were fed to pigs. The incidence was also related to the age of the animal, being lowest in pork pigs, higher in bacon pigs, and highest in boars and sows. The average incidence of tuberculosis in pigs, which was 1·64 per cent. in 1960, had fallen to 1·2 per cent. in 1965. In Northern Ireland the incidence was 0·69 per cent. in 1963.

In 1965 the average incidence of tuberculosis in pigs slaughtered in Danish abattoirs was only 0·18 per cent., though this includes a proportion of tuberculosis-like lesions caused by *Corynebacterium equi*. In 1964 in Western Germany the incidence of tuberculosis in slaughtered pigs was 0·3 per cent.

Sheep and Goats

The incidence of tuberculosis in these animals is very low and is related to the open-air life of the sheep and goat and the consequent rarity of exposure to infection. The statement that the goat is immune to tuberculosis is, however, incorrect, for the susceptibility of these animals increases if they are housed for more intensive milk production, and in Switzerland 0·25 per cent. of slaughtered goats were found affected in 1954. In 1964 in Western Germany the incidence of tuberculosis in slaughtered sheep was 0·01 per cent. and in slaughtered goats 0·2 per cent. In horses the incidence of tuberculosis in Switzerland was 0·04 per cent. in 1954, and in Western Germany 0·1 per cent. in 1964.

Modes of Infection

The methods by which tubercle bacilli gain entrance to the animal body may be classified as follows :

(1) Alimentary—infection by way of any part of the digestive tract such as the mouth, pharynx, tonsils or intestines.

(2) Respiratory—infection by way of the air passages.

(3) Genital—infection by way of the genital organs.

(4) Cutaneous—infection through the skin.

(5) Congenital—infection of the foetus while *in utero*.

By far the commonest methods of infection of the food animals are by way of the digestive or respiratory tract.

CATTLE

The question as to the relative frequency of infection by the digestive or respiratory route is controversial. The respiratory route is more likely to be the method of infection where cows are housed, especially in winter when the housing is almost continuous, or where one or two cows are actively disseminating infection. On the other hand, cattle at grass may occasionally become infected by ingestion, for the tubercle bacillus, under ordinary conditions on pasture, remains viable about 2 months in summer and 5 months in winter. Calves may become infected by the respiratory route if they are kept in close contact with cows suffering from open tuberculosis of the lungs, but the ingestion of tuberculous milk is also a likely source of infection. The retropharyngeal lymph nodes may become infected secondarily from lesions in the lungs.

Genital tuberculosis is transmitted and acquired during copulation, and is only likely to take place when the sexual organs of the male or female are tuberculous.

Infection by way of the skin is rare, though cases where tuberculous lesions in a carcase are confined to one prescapular lymph node or one precrural node may possibly be attributed to infection by this route. Similarly, tuberculous lesions in the superficial inguinal lymph nodes of bullocks may occur without evidence of any other lesions in the carcase, and infection of this nature is probably acquired by way of castration wounds. Infection of the parotid lymph node in cattle may occur as a result of dehorning.

Congenital infection in calves was at one time not uncommon in countries where there was a high incidence of bovine tuberculosis but very rarely occurred in animals of other species.

PIGS

The main channel of infection in pigs is undoubtedly the digestive tract and in some countries the feeding of cows' milk was a most important source of the disease. Infection of pigs with the bovine tubercle bacillus was, however, not necessarily acquired through cows' milk but occurred through the excreta of tuberculous cattle or from slaughterhouse offal, while in Britain and in the United States ingestion of food contaminated with excreta from tuberculous poultry accounts for most of the cases of tuberculosis of the submaxillary lymph nodes in pigs. Cutaneous infection can at times occur, and castrated hogs have shown tuberculosis of the spermatic cord through infected castration wounds.

SHEEP AND GOATS

Sheep chiefly become infected by way of the digestive tract, either by grazing on pastures after tuberculous cattle or poultry, or by consumption of cows' milk. Goats may become infected from a similar source.

Pathogenesis of Tuberculosis

Tubercle bacilli which enter the animal body produce a so-called primary lesion which generally occurs in the respiratory or digestive tract, and following this in the associated lymph nodes. This primary lesion is always present even though it may be small and unrecognized, and in cattle is found most frequently in the lung where it is often seen as a subpleural focus in the well aerated upper border of one of the main lung lobes (Fig. 70). The specific reaction of the body tissues to the multiplication of invading tubercle bacilli is manifested by a proliferation of the phagocytic cells at the point of arrest, resulting after a time in the formation of a nodule or "tubercle". Among the phagocytic cells there now appear multinucleated giant cells, and increase in the size of tuberculous foci is due to the increasing destruction of the normal tissue by the organisms and the fusion of adjacent lesions.

After about 3 weeks the tubercle is just visible to the naked eye as a grey translucent nodule, but with the onset of necrosis it undergoes a change in appearance and becomes opaque and grey or yellowish-white in colour. Necrosis is succeeded by caseation in which the necrotic tissue becomes cheesy, while if the tubercle does not disintegrate the proliferation of fibroblasts at the periphery of the lesion leads to the formation of a capsule of fibrous tissue which tends to delimit locally the spread of the disease process. At a later date caseous material may undergo calcification due to the deposition of lime salts, calcified lesions being paler than caseous ones and almost white in colour, and though virulent tubercle bacilli can be found in partially or completely calcified lymph nodes they are usually few in number and undergoing degeneration.

During the primary infection period the presence of the invading bacilli brings about a body resistance and this reaction tends to act as a dam by limiting the aggressive powers of the tubercle bacilli and localizing them to the site of infection ; thus the tuberculous process may be confined to the primary complex throughout the life of the animal. But if the host does not rapidly organize a defence against tuberculous infection the disease process may extend from the original focus to other parts or organs, the main pathways by which spread takes place being (*a*) by local contiguity, as in infection of the parietal pleura from a lesion in the lung, (*b*) by natural ducts, tubes or channels, as in the spread of infection from one part of the lung to another by coughing and aspiration, (*c*) by the lymphatic system, and (*d*) by the systemic circulation.

Entry of bacilli into the systemic circulation, the recognition of which is of paramount importance to the meat inspector, may occur in the following ways : (*a*) Tuberculous lesions may develop on the lining of a blood vessel or erode through the wall of a blood vessel, and thus it is possible for systemic infection to occur due to entry of bacilli into a capillary vessel from a single active lesion, or (*b*) bacilli which have been arrested in a lymph node may continue to multiply, break down the lymphatic barrier to enter the efferent lymph vessels of the node and be conveyed to the venous blood stream. This lympho-haematogenous route is the commonest one in the production of generalized tuberculosis.

If the body defences are adequate the disease will become quiescent, but should the body defences of the animal be lowered, either reinfection or superinfection may occur and this is associated with a profuse inflammatory exudate in the area where the invading bacilli have lodged. This exudate is disadvantageous in that it inundates the affected tissues with fluid and thus encourages widespread dissemination of bacilli by intracanalicular, lymphatic or haematogenous channels. The result of this breakdown of body resistance is that chronic tuberculous lesions, particularly in the lung, udder, uterus or kidney, develop into rapidly caseating lesions of the exudative type, and acute generalization therefore occurs and bacilli enter the blood stream in very large numbers. This may give rise to an acute miliary tuberculosis, with the presence of miliary tubercles in the lungs, kidneys, liver, spleen and other organs. More commonly, however, generalization gives rise to tuberculous lesions of what is known as the " breakdown " type and occurring as a caseous pneumonia (Fig. 121), caseous metritis (Figs. 119, 128), caseous mastitis, caseous pleurisy, caseous lymphadenitis (Fig. 118) or caseous nephritis. Lesions of the breakdown type (the *Niederbruchsformen* described by Nieberle) are characterized by the presence of dry caseous masses interspersed with small haemorrhages, and the caseation and exudation associated with such lesions facilitate erosion of the tuberculous processes into the neighbouring lymph vessels and thus produces lesions in the regional lymph nodes. The affected lymph nodes associated with breakdown lesions become hypertrophied and firmer in consistency, while the caseous material visible on section of the node may be interspersed with haemorrhages and may at times present a

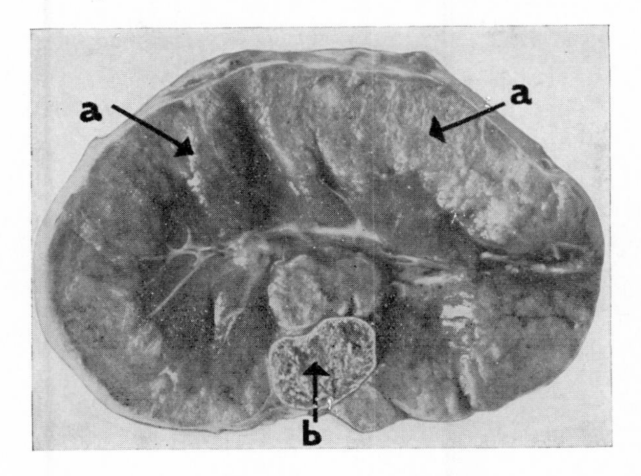

FIG. 118.—Bronchial lymph node of calf showing (*a*) acute exudative caseation at cortex of node, the so-called breakdown form of tuberculosis. At (*b*) is an encapsulated and calcified lesion from the primary infection. (Dr. Pallaske.)

marbled or radiating appearance due to thin isolated radiating lines of caseation alternating with areas of normal lymph node tissue. This is

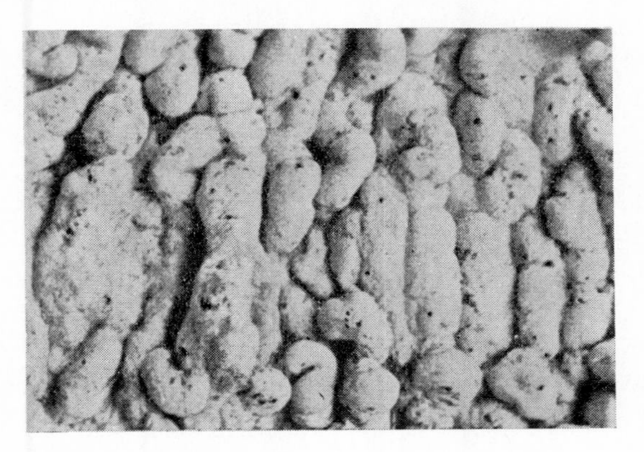

FIG. 119.—Tuberculous metritis in the cow. The lesions are of the exudative or "breakdown" type; the mucous membrane is thickened, thrown into folds and shows evidence of dry caseation interspersed with small haemorrhages.

known as stellate caseation and lesions of this type are active and rich in bacilli, calcification is incomplete or absent, and indicate that the defensive reactions of the body have been inadequate and that bacilli in considerable numbers have been entering the blood stream. It will therefore be apparent that in the judgment of tuberculous carcases it is important to recognize not only the disposition of the lesions but also their character, as this indicates the manner in which the body tissues have reacted to the invading organisms and whether or not a successful defence has been achieved.

Types of Tissue Reaction

The nature of the reaction of an animal to tuberculosis depends on two factors, the aggressive powers of the invading organisms and the defensive activities of the body. If the invading organisms are harmless or of moderate pathogenicity they are ingested by the body cells and destroyed, and the reaction in this case is therefore of a cellular or productive

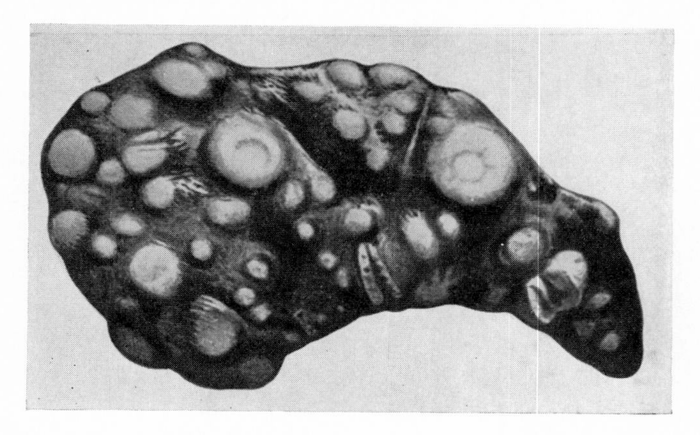

FIG. 120.—Horse spleen affected with tuberculosis. Owing to the high species resistance of this animal to the bovine tubercle bacillus the lesions are of a productive type, resembling metastatic tumours and showing no evidence of caseation or calcification. The centres may, however, undergo liquefaction with the formation of material resembling thick viscid pus.

type composed of giant cells and granulation tissue and of a local and circumscribed nature; where the organisms are markedly pathogenic, however, the tissue reaction is of an exudative type. Whether entry of tubercle bacilli into the animal body is succeeded by a reaction of the productive or of the exudative type depends not only on the type of bacilli (whether the bovine, avian or human type), but also on the species of the animal attacked and the degree of resistance induced by a previous invasion.

Species resistance is high in the horse and pig, and a reaction of a productive type is frequently manifested in tuberculosis in the horse, and also in tuberculosis of the pig when caused by the avian type of bacillus. Tuberculous lesions in the organs of these animals may therefore take the form of tumour-like nodules of various sizes especially in the spleen (Fig. 120) liver (Plate II) and lungs, the lesions having a fatty, glistening appearance when incised and showing no evidence of caseation or calcification. Similarly, the lymph nodes associated with affected organs may be enlarged, finely granular in appearance, and of uniform consistency and grey or greyish-red in colour, but caseation or calcification do not occur.

In cattle, species resistance plays no part in the pathogenesis of tuberculosis so that lesions may be either of the productive type or of the exudative type, depending on the degree of body resistance which has developed as a result of the original primary infection. If a high degree of resistance has been produced the effect of subsequent reinfection will be to cause lesions of a productive type, as seen in chronic tuberculosis of the pericardium (Fig. 124) or chronic tuberculosis of the udder (Fig. 130) or testicle, and a feature of such lesions is that the associated lymph nodes, though they may be enlarged and firmer than normal, show no evidence of caseation or calcification. On the other hand, should the resistance of the animal have been lowered due to various unspecific factors, the lesions of tuberculosis are of the exudative or breakdown type and show evidence of caseation and calcification, while similar macroscopic changes may be observed in the associated lymph nodes.

Though reinfection after recovery from a primary infection occurs in cattle, in pigs it is rare for reinfection to occur because of the relatively short life of this animal. Tuberculosis in pigs therefore runs the course of a primary infection, the primary lesion occurring in the digestive tract, frequently in the tonsillar tissue from whence it gives rise to lesions in the submaxillary lymph node. This primary focus may become quiescent and undergo retrogression and healing, but it may break down and lead to lympho-haematogenous generalization, sometimes of the miliary type, during the primary infection period. The character of the lesion of tuberculosis in pigs, however, differs markedly according to whether the bacilli are of the bovine or avian type.

As the bovine type of bacillus is highly pathogenic for pigs, its entry into the host leads to a tissue reaction of an exudative type in which there occurs typical tubercle formation (Fig. 125) with subsequent caseation and calcification. Lesions of the bovine type occurring in the lymph nodes are clearly defined and should the invading bacilli be particularly virulent the lesions, especially in the submaxillary and mesenteric nodes, may exhibit stellate caseation. The reason that tuberculosis of the bovine type in pigs frequently assumes a generalized form is that (*a*) the bovine type of bacillus gives rise to an exudative inflammation, the infiltrative nature of which leads to invasion of adjacent lymphatics and blood vessels by the tubercle bacilli, and (*b*) the disease runs its course during the primary infection period before the body has been able to mobilize its defence against the invading organism.

When tuberculosis of the avian type occurs in pigs, the low pathogenicity of this bacillus leads to a tissue reaction of the productive type. Affected lymph nodes, such as the submaxillary or mesenteric, are enlarged and firmer than normal but show no tubercle formation, though at a later stage the nodes may exhibit small discrete yellow foci or large areas of necrosis which occupy the centre of the node, are putty-like in consistency and readily enucleated from the lymph node tissue. The reason that tuberculosis of the avian type in pigs is less likely to become generalized than when infection is due to the bovine micro-organism is that the avian type of bacillus is of low pathogenicity to pigs and the tissue reaction is therefore of the productive type in which the peripheral cellular reaction and absence of exudation tend to limit further spread of the disease. Generally speaking, lesions of tuberculosis of the avian type in the organs or lymph nodes of pigs may be distinguished from lesions of the bovine type by the absence or paucity of typical tubercle formation, the tumour-like appearance of the lesions and the fact that they show little or no tendency to undergo caseation or calcification.

Affection of Specific Parts

LUNGS

In the adult bovine the primary or initial lung lesion may be situated in any part of the lung lobes, and consists of a limited area of bronchopneumonia, with involvement of the associated lymph node ; this primary focus may heal by fibrosis and calcification, but is much more likely to caseate and spread within the neighbouring bronchial and alveolar passages. The typical lesion so formed is seen superficially, or on the cut surface of the lung, as a cluster formation around a finer bronchiole, being clover-leaf in shape due to the filling of the related acini with caseous material ; the anatomical formation of such a lesion may be described as acino-nodular, being conspicuous by the way it delineates a lung lobule, and most lesions of progressive lung tuberculosis are similar, spread taking place by the bronchial passages and causing gradual destruction of the lung tissue by caseation and liquefaction. These areas of caseous bronchopneumonia are, however, likely to be delimited by the infiltration of a serous exudate into the surrounding interlobular septa, which become much thickened and tend to localize the bronchial spread ; at a later stage the infiltration is succeeded by the deposition of connective tissue which encases the broncho-pneumonic area and separates it from the surrounding healthy tissue. If a solid caseous area formed in the above manner becomes liquefied it may enter into a main bronchus with the formation of a cavity, and though cavitation is less common in the bovine lungs than in man, it sometimes occurs in the upper caudal parts of the main lung lobes, the cavity presenting a congested wall and containing a yellowish purulent material.

Foci of caseous pneumonia are also encountered, of varying size and of a slate-grey or yellowish colour, these pneumonic lesions being usually found in the lobes of the lungs and solidified into a compact grey mass which contains irregular cavities filled with foetid muco-purulent material.

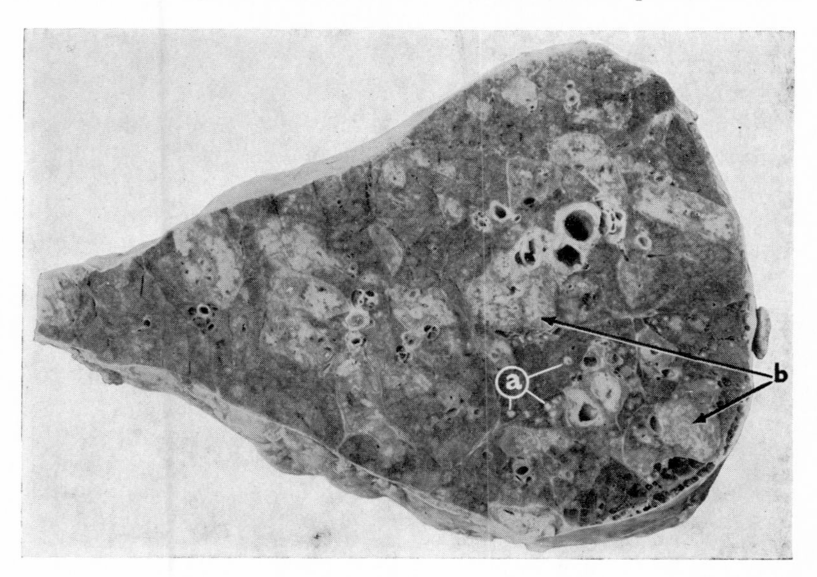

FIG. 121.—Section of ox lung affected with caseous tuberculous pneumonia. The small acino-nodular foci (*a*) are caused by aspiration of infective material from one part of the lung to another and these foci eventually coalesce to form large greyish-coloured areas of caseous pneumonia (*b*). Such lesions are of the typical exudative type and are likely to lead to haematogenous dissemination. (Prof. Cohrs.)

In some cases the anterior lobe of the lung is collapsed and violet-red in colour, the congested tissue having become occluded from the outside air due to obstruction of the principal bronchus.

The following macroscopic conditions must therefore be distinguished in the bovine lung :

(1) Isolated encapsulated and calcified foci with corresponding lesions in the associated lymph nodes and indicative of the primary infection. A compensatory lung emphysema often accompanies a widespread primary infection of the lungs.

(2) Scattered caseous foci of various sizes involving the acini of one or both lungs and caused by aspiration of infective material. These lesions spread intracanalicularly and, as they show no tendency to lymphatic or haematogenous spread, the regional lymph nodes are unaffected. If these nodes are found affected the lesions can be attributed to the result of an original primary infection and are of an encapsulated or calcified nature.

A more even distribution of caseous foci in one or both lungs is indicative of a breakdown of body resistance and the production of acute acino-nodular lesions ; this may result in a localized or haematogenous spread, depending on the severity of the disease, and in such cases of " breakdown " the regional lymph nodes are always affected.

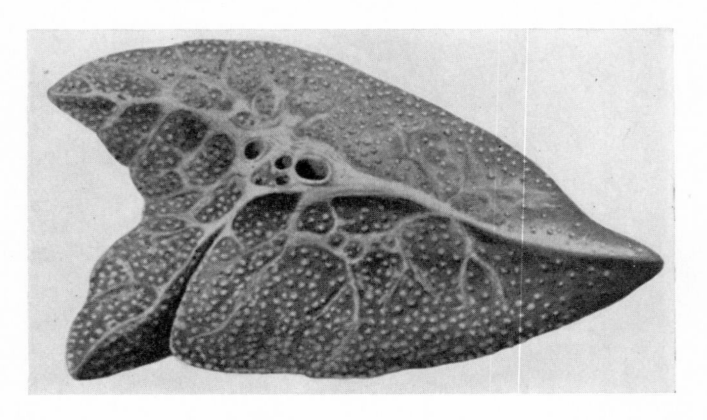

FIG. 122.—Miliary tuberculosis of lung of ox. The lesions are all of an equal age and size and uniformly distributed throughout the lung tissue.

(3) A condition of caseous pneumonia, manifested by large areas of caseous lung tissue interspersed with blood spots, resulting from coalescence of several caseous foci ; these are often sharply delimited from healthy lung tissue by a zone of inflammation and, in the later stages, by connective tissue. Lesions of this type are likely to give rise to massive entry of bacilli into the blood stream.

(4) Wide, evenly distributed dissemination of small, uniformly-sized crops of tubercles throughout both lungs, these being indicative of a massive haematogenous infection and constituting the so-called miliary tuberculosis. In this condition the lungs are usually enlarged and heavy due to emphysematous and oedematous changes.

The coughing up of tuberculous material may give rise to a tuberculous tracheitis or laryngitis, and tuberculous nodules or ulcers may be seen on the mucous membrane of the trachea, the ulcers being most frequently found in the retromucosal space adjoining the posterior tracheal ridge.

Plate II

1. Actinomycosis of udder of sow. The udder is indurated and contains numerous thick-walled fibrous nodules with purulent centres. The udder is the only common seat of actinomycosis in swine.

2. Mesenteric emphysema of small intestine of pig.

3. Pig liver showing tuberculous lesions of the productive type caused by the avian tubercle bacillus.

4. Tuberculosis-like lesions of submaxillary lymph node of pig caused by *Corynebacterium equi*. The necrotic foci are surrounded by a connective tissue capsule and easily removed from the lymph node tissue.

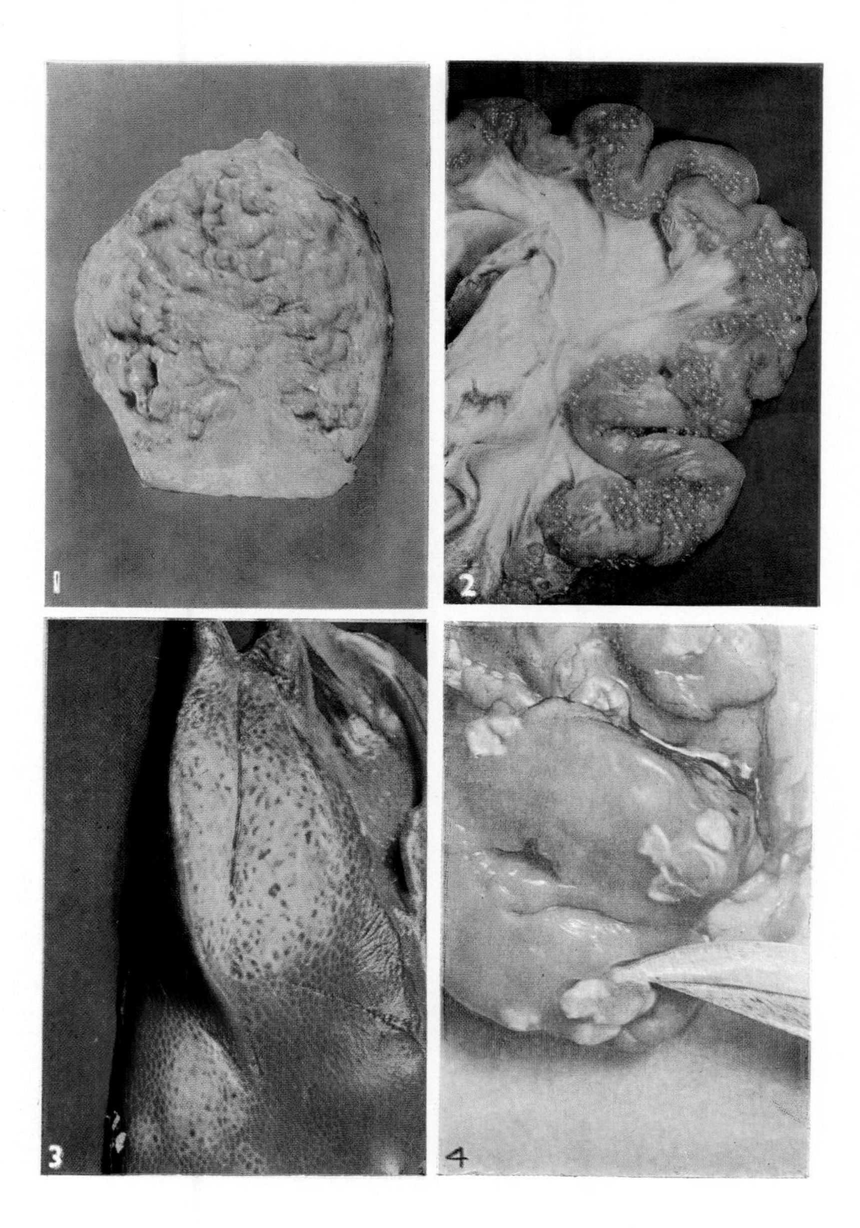

Tuberculosis of the lungs of pigs caused by infection with avian bacilli, and likewise tuberculosis in horses, is of a purely productive nature without caseation or calcification. The lung lesions have a fatty, glistening appearance and on section are not unlike metastatic tumours; when closely aggregated they simulate a lardaceous broncho-penumonia but the lymph nodes, though slightly enlarged, appear unaffected.

Pleura

Tuberculous pleurisy may arise early after a primary lung infection by direct lymphatic drainage from lung lesions to the visceral pleura, with

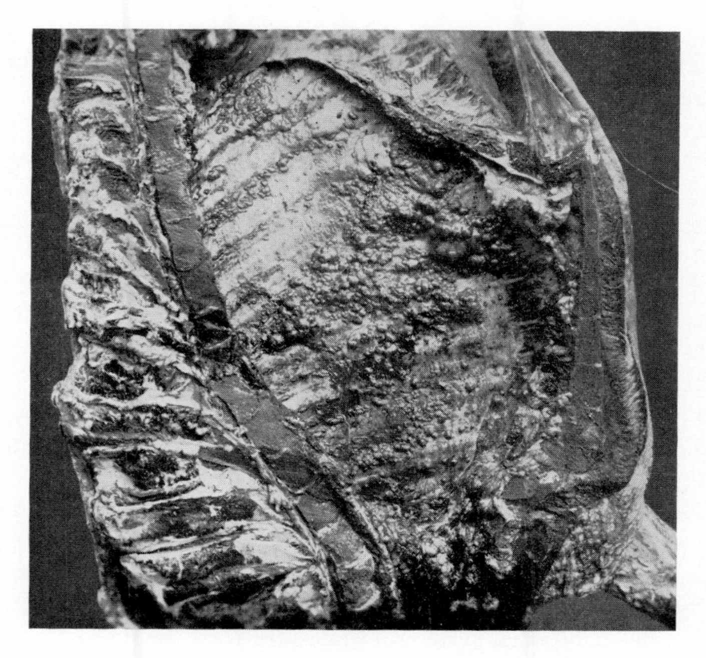

Fig. 123.—Bovine forequarter affected with chronic tuberculosis of the parietal pleura. (A. C. F. Gisborne.)

subsequent spread of the infection into the pleural cavity; it is significant that in bovine tuberculosis the visceral pleura is affected more frequently than the parietal pleura. Pleural infection may also occur by rupture of a lung lesion or a thoracic lymph node into the thoracic cavity, but it is considered unlikely that these methods play an important part in the production of tuberculous pleurisy in the bovine. Only rarely is the pleura likely to be infected from the peritoneum by way of the lymphatics of the diaphragm.

The early stages of tuberculous pleurisy are seen as soft, reddish, velvety granulations on visceral or parietal pleura or on both, but as the disease enters the stage of chronic generalization these lesions tend to coalesce, forming large caseous masses which vary considerably in size and constitute the typical " grapes ". On section these show caseous and calcified centres, and are associated with marked thickening of the pleural membrane which may be one-half inch in thickness ; tuberculous lesions of the bovine pleura rarely penetrate to the subpleural tissue, for growing lesions develop in the direction of the free space of the thoracic cavity. The acute form of tuberculous pleurisy is mainly encountered during late generalization, the serous membrane being thickened to one inch or more and composed of a dry caseous material interspersed with blood spots. Lesions of this type are likely to give rise to massive entry of bacilli into the blood stream.

In the pig tuberculous lesions of the serous membranes are not common and usually take the form of small, scattered, discrete nodules which may penetrate to the subpleural tissue. At times the lesions are so small that they resemble grains of sand when palpated with the tips of the fingers.

Peritoneum

Tuberculous peritonitis in the bovine is much less common than tuberculous pleurisy, and may occur at two distinct stages :

(1) It may arise in congenital infection or in calfhood by extension from a primary lesion in the liver, the peritoneal lesions in such cases being usually confined to those parts of the peritoneum and diaphragm which are in contact with the anterior surface of the liver.

(2) Tuberculous peritonitis is more likely to occur later in the disease process, and is then frequently widespread, affecting both visceral and parietal layers of peritoneum. Affection of the peritoneum may arise :

(*a*) By extensive breakdown of lung lesions, which results in ingestion of massive doses of bacilli into the digestive tract followed by infection of the mesenteric lymph nodes ;

(*b*) By direct extension of infection from a tuberculous abdominal organ such as the liver or uterus ; or

(*c*) By extension from pleura to peritoneum by way of the lymphatics of the diaphragm.

It will be apparent that lesions of both pleura and peritoneum may occur without entry of tubercle bacilli into the systemic circulation.

Pericardium

Tuberculous pericarditis almost always arises by direct extension of infection from a tuberculous pleurisy, and is characterized in the early stages by red, velvety patches near the base of the heart. As disease progresses these foci extend and become caseous, eventually encasing the heart in granulation tissue which contains numerous caseous areas. Tuberculous lesions of the endocardium or myocardium are rare, although foci may occur in the myocardium as an extension of a tuberculous pericarditis.

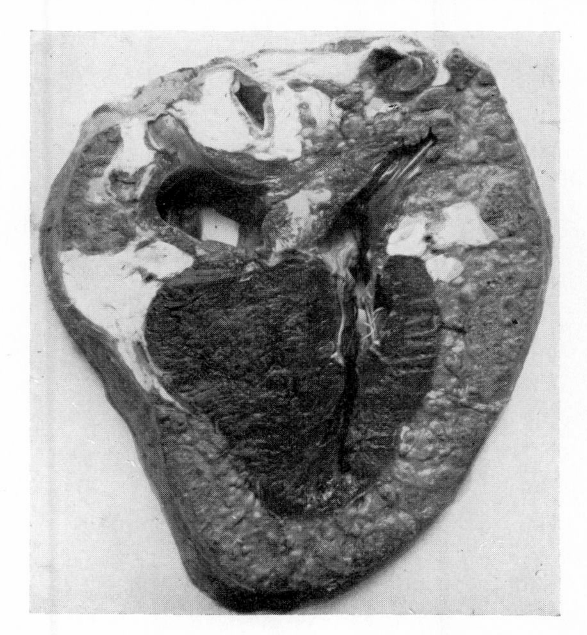

FIG. 124.—Tuberculous pericarditis of ox heart, the so-called armour-plated heart. There is present a chronic pericarditis of the productive type which has caused complete obliteration of the pericardial cavity and gross constriction of the heart. (G. O. Davies.)

LIVER

The liver may become infected in the following ways:

(*a*) In congenital tuberculosis, by direct infection *via* the umbilical vein;

(*b*) From primary intestinal tuberculosis, as the portal lymph nodes receive direct afferent lymphatics from the duodenum;

(*c*) By secondary infection of the intestines as a result of swallowing massive doses of bacilli, a condition usually associated with breakdown of lung lesions; this mode of infection of the liver entails the involvement of the mesenteric lymph nodes with subsequent entry of tubercle bacilli into the finer radicles of the portal vein; or

(*d*) By haematogenous spread.

Nearly all cases of tuberculosis of the liver occur as a secondary extension from tuberculosis of the peritoneum, intestine or mesenteric lymph nodes, and tuberculous lesions in the posterior mediastinal lymph nodes of cattle and calves may arise by lymphatic drainage from a tuberculous liver. Most commonly the liver lesions in cattle are seen as discrete, nodular, encapsulated foci which may be few or numerous in number, but in some

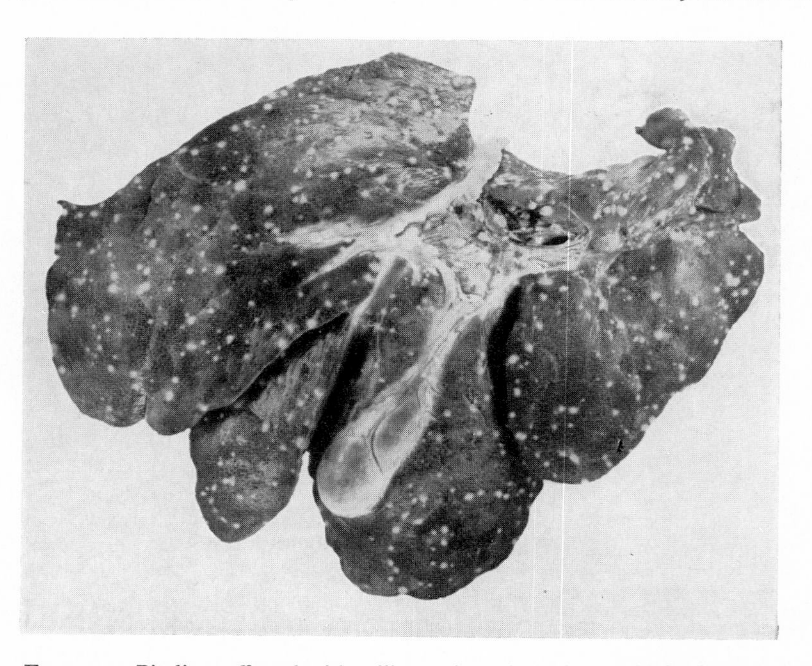

FIG. 125.—Pig liver affected with miliary tuberculosis due to the bovine type of bacillus. Haematogenous invasion of the organ *via* the arterial circulation may occur during the primary infection period with formation of very numerous uniformly-sized caseous foci throughout the organ, but in the pig there also occurs an isolated miliary tuberculosis of the liver when bacilli are transported to the organ by way of the portal vein.

cases they take the form of small encapsulated abscesses which are difficult to distinguish from abscesses caused by the ordinary pyogenic organisms.

In tuberculosis of the pig liver caused by the bovine bacillus the lesions are usually characterized by their small size, being generally little larger than a pinhead or barley grain, usually encapsulated and tending to undergo caseation and calcification. In avian type infection of the pig liver greyish-yellow tubercles may occur, but commonly the lesions are of the productive type (Plate II) resembling metastatic tumours or milk spots of parasitic origin, and the portal lymph nodes, though enlarged and firmer than normal, show no obvious degenerative change.

Spleen

In calves the splenic substance is more commonly infected than the surface and is usually regarded as indicative of a congenital infection, but tuberculous lesions in adult cattle are almost invariably confined to the spleen surface and result from an extension of a tuberculous peritonitis. Lesions of the splenic substance in adult cattle are uncommon, and a possible explanation to account for the rarity of such lesions is that tuberculous foci in the lung, which frequently give rise to generalization of bacilli throughout the body, may be so extensive that the animal dies before spleen lesions have time to develop. On the other hand, in congenital tuberculosis the lesions may become established in the foetal spleen whilst the lungs are functionally inactive, and pulmonary lesions are

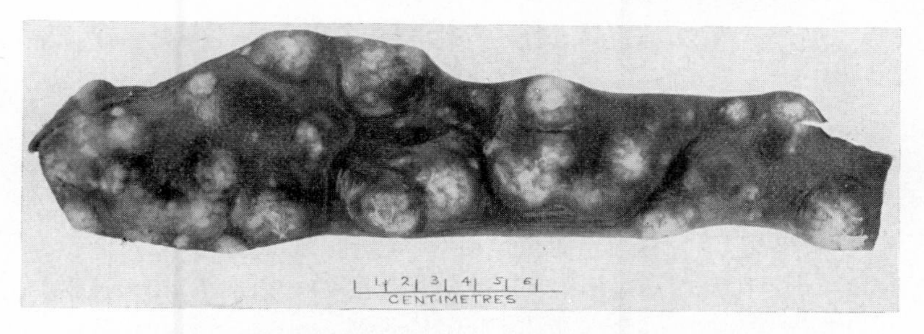

FIG. 126.—Pig spleen showing large, caseous tuberculous foci in the substance, indicative of haematogenous spread during the primary infection period.

therefore few in number or absent. Chronic lesions in the spleen substance of adult cattle are an indication that haematogenous infection occurred during the primary infection period but was not of a magnitude to prove fatal, and under the influence of the body resistance the splenic lesions became quiescent and underwent caseation, encapsulation and calcification. In the pig, lesions of the peritoneal covering of the spleen are rare, lesions of the substance being much more common and related to the tendency which swine tuberculosis of bovine origin exhibits towards generalization.

Kidneys

Infection of a kidney must only occur as a result of haematogenous spread and may take the form of small isolated nodules distributed irregularly through the kidney substance, but more commonly the tuberculous process is confined to one or more kidney lobes, the surface of which appears irregularly nodular and greyish-white in colour. On section of a kidney lobe the entire substance may show caseation, and should the disease process involve a renal papilla, other papillae become infected with the eventual production of a tuberculous pyelitis and descending ureteritis or cystitis, followed by excretion of tubercle bacilli in the urine. Tuberculosis of the kidney is invariably associated with lesions in the renal lymph node. A detailed examination of the kidneys of cattle and pigs is necessary whenever there is evidence of tuberculosis elsewhere but care should be taken not to confuse anaemic infarcts in the kidney of cows with lesions of tuberculosis.

Bones and Joints

In the ox tuberculosis is found most commonly in the ribs and vertebrae, but occasionally in the sternum and in the spongy tissue at the extremities of the long bones. Tuberculous cavitation of bone, or caries, is

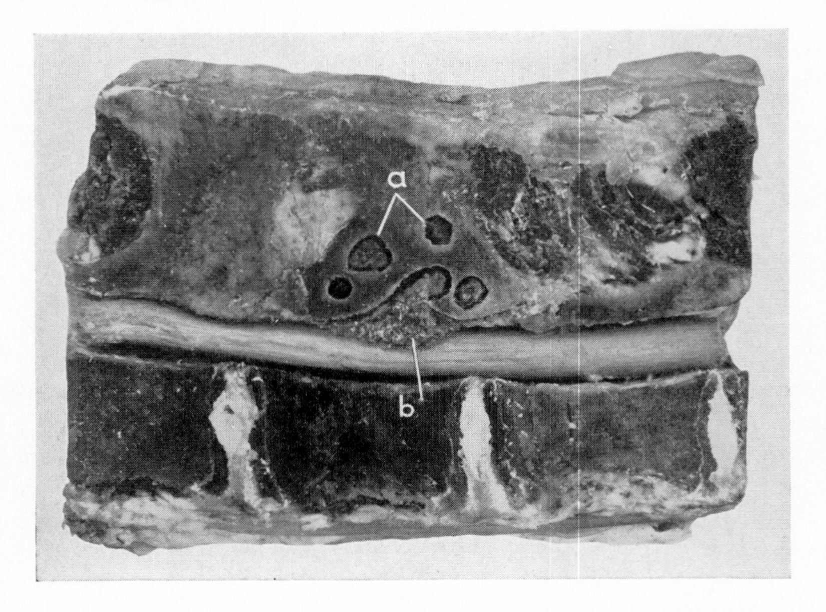

Fig. 127.—Tuberculous caries in ox involving arch of lumbar vertebra. Greyish-yellow foci (*a*) are enclosed in smooth-walled cavities from which the material can easily be enucleated. A caseous lesion (*b*) has eroded through the vertebra and extended downwards to cause constriction of the spinal cord.

characterized by a local destruction of bone with the formation of yellow granulation tissue, together with a thinning and rarefaction of the cortex and spongy tissue of the bone contiguous to the tuberculous lesion. Erosion by a tuberculous process through the epiphysis of a bone and into a joint cavity is responsible for the formation of a tuberculous joint, which is seen as a bulging of the joint capsule and enlargement of the joint, together with yellowish-brown proliferative growths into the joint cavity and destruction of the articular cartilage. In cattle the joints most likely to be affected are the knee, occasionally the hock and stifle.

In the pig tuberculosis of bone may be seen in the bodies and spinal processes of the lumbar vertebrae, and also the ischio-pubic symphysis; lesions in these locations are a suspicious indication that other bones of the skeleton, particularly the femur, may also be affected. Tuberculosis of the lumbar vertebrae may be a cause of prolonged recumbency in sows.

Central Nervous System

Tuberculosis of the central nervous system develops most commonly in the primary infection period and is therefore most often seen in calves and young cattle and indicative of haematogenous dissemination. Caseous foci may be found macroscopically in the cerebrum, cerebellum, mid-brain or pons, and rupture of such tuberculous foci may give rise to a diffuse tuberculous meningitis. Less commonly, a similar affection of the spinal cord and its meninges may occur and is caused by contiguity with tuberculous foci in the bodies or arches of the vertebrae.

Alimentary Tract

The bovine tongue is at times the seat of true tuberculous ulcerations, these being surrounded by hard indurated tissue, and the same condition may occur in the tonsils; such cases are associated with enlargement and caseation of the parotid or retropharyngeal lymph nodes.

Primary infection of the intestinal tract is rare, though secondary infection of the intestinal canal may occur in the adult bovine, and it is from this source that the majority of lesions in the mesenteric lymph nodes arise, while many lesions of the portal lymph nodes also occur in the same way. Secondary intestinal infection occurs usually from the swallowing of massive doses of bacilli arising from the breakdown of progressive lung lesions, and though in the majority of cases bacilli pass through the intestinal wall without causing permanent recognizable lesions, they may give rise to isolated nodules of the mucosa. These nodules, which occur particularly in the ileum but occasionally in the caecum, may coalesce to form ulcers of varying sizes which are round or oval in shape, have raised, irregular and slightly undermined edges and are covered with greyish muco-purulent material.

Female Sex Organs

Tuberculous lesions may involve the vagina in the form of nodules or ulcers, and tuberculosis of Gärtners glands occurs in conjunction with tuberculosis of the uterus ; the glands are hard and cord-like, and tuberculous material can be expressed from them by pressure with the fingers.

Tuberculous metritis may occur in the following ways :

(*a*) The uterus may become infected during haematogenous dissemination ;

(*b*) It may become infected from a tuberculous peritoneum, particularly where the posterior part of this membrane is affected, bacilli gaining entry to the uterus by way of the Fallopian tubes ;

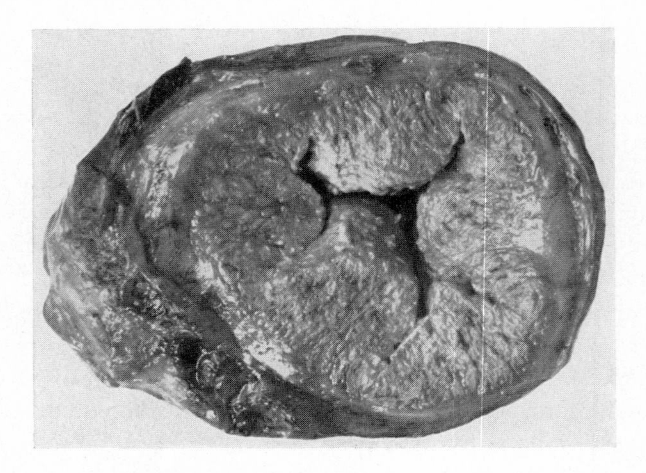

FIG. 128.—Acute caseous tuberculous metritis of cow. A transverse section of one uterine horn has been made ; the uterine wall has become thickened and rigid and the mucous membrane is affected with dry caseation and thrown into folds (see Fig. 119). Such lesions, being exudative in character, are likely to lead to haematogenous dissemination. (Dr. Pallaske.)

(*c*) Genital infection of the uterus may arise from service with a bull affected with tuberculosis of the penis, epididymis or testis ; cows in attested herds have occasionally become infected with primary lesions in the uterus due to introduction of infection during treatment for retained placenta or infertility.

Tuberculous metritis is usually bilateral and symmetrical, involving both uterine horns, and frequently originates at the greater curvature of the uterus in the region of the bifurcation of the cornua, a situation which corresponds to the areas of distribution of the uterine arteries. The affection takes the form of yellow spots, pinhead in size, on the mucous membrane, though in some cases the lesions are small, fleshy and translucent, but as disease progresses pea-sized nodules develop in the submucous tissue and give rise to prominences on the surface of the mucous membrane. At a later stage the mucous membrane is thickened and thrown into folds and the uterine cornua become thickened and rigid; thus the tuberculous process sooner or later involves all the coats of the uterus, and finally the peritoneum. Post-mortem examination of cows in an advanced degree of pregnancy and affected with tuberculous metritis almost invariably shows masses of tough, odourless, sticky pus in the uterochorionic cavity, this material being distributed particularly around the necks of the cotyledons.

Extensive lesions of haematogenous origin may sometimes be found in the ovary, which appears large, has an uneven surface and contains caseo-calcareous nodules or purulent masses. The Fallopian tubes are invariably affected in such cases, and are studded with granulations which are more or less confluent and greyish-white in colour.

Male Sex Organs

Tuberculosis of the male sex organs generally occurs as a result of haematogenous spread and involves the testis or epididymis, infection usually commencing in the latter structure and extending to the testis to

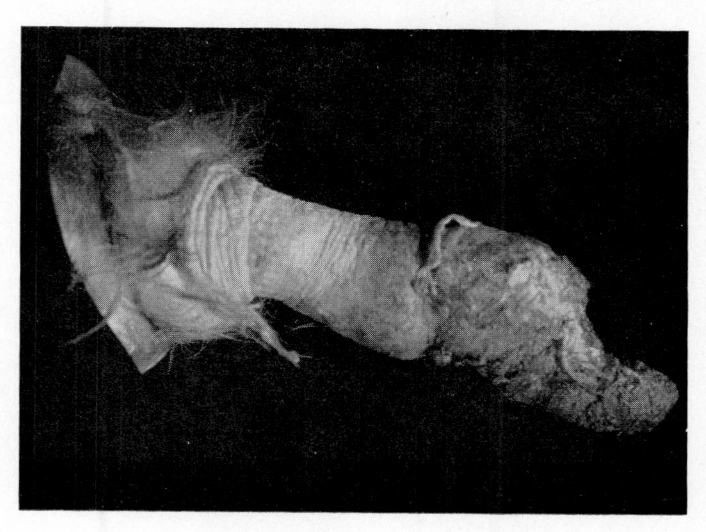

FIG. 129.—Tuberculous granulations on glans penis of bull, the result of a primary genital infection.

form miliary tubercles or larger nodules. In old bulls chronic tuberculous orchitis may be unrecognized, for being of a purely productive nature it shows a radiating, fatty and glistening appearance on section, while the regional lymph nodes are unaffected. Primary tuberculosis of the penis of the bull may be acquired during coitus and in such cases tuberculous lesions will be found in the superficial inguinal lymph nodes, while affection of the prepuce may be manifested by lesions in the precrural node.

Udder

The post-mortem recognition of tuberculosis of the udder is of importance, though at times it presents considerable difficulty. Tuberculous mastitis may occur in the following ways :

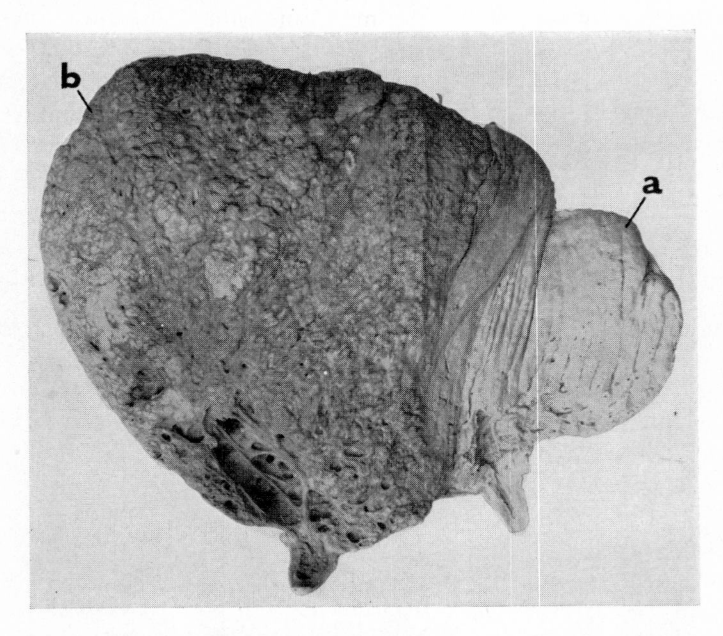

FIG. 130.—(*b*) Chronic tuberculosis of hindquarter of udder of cow, diffuse granulomatous form. This is the commonest form of udder tuberculosis and occurs in an animal which has developed a resistance to the disease as a result of a previous infection. Spread of infection throughout the udder takes place by way of the milk ducts and entry of bacilli into the lymph or blood stream does not occur. (*a*) Normal forequarter of udder. (Prof. Cohrs.)

(*a*) It may arise as a result of haematogenous spread, and 70 per cent. of cows proved to be excreting tuberculous milk are found on post-mortem examination to be suffering from generalized disease ;

(*b*) It may arise by lymphatic extension from an abdominal lesion, and in some cows primary lesions in the lungs with secondary lesions in the mesenteric lymph nodes and udder may be present with no other evidence of tuberculosis in the carcase ;

(*c*) Primary tuberculosis may occasionally occur through the teat, usually as a result of udder irrigation with an infected syringe, and lesions in such cases in tuberculin-tested herds are generally confined to induration of a quarter or quarters of the udder, with tuberculous lesions in the supramammary and internal iliac lymph nodes.

Tuberculosis of the udder may be recognized in its earliest stages by a sharply defined change in the udder colour, indicative of where the lesions are forming, from the normal yellowish-white to that of an orange-brown. Subsequent to this the affection may assume the following forms : (*a*) A chronic diffuse granulomatous form in which the cut surface, instead of the usual flaccid structure, shows great enlargement of the lobules which project firmly from the surrounding interlobular connective tissue, while the surface is dry and not milky ; (*b*) a chronic nodular form in which the cut surface shows the presence of nodules, frequently not very numerous and either caseous and calcified, yellow and caseous but not calcified, or of a tough and fibrous nature ; (*c*) an acute caseating form in which there is extensive destruction of lobular tissue with large areas of haemorrhagic necrosis, while softening may occur with the formation of liquefied caseous material, and calcification may be marked or absent ; (*d*) a diffuse tuberculous galactophoritis in which the change is confined to the milk duct ; in all types of tuberculous mastitis there is extensive tuberculosis of the duct system.

Tuberculous lesions of the supramammary lymph nodes are not present in the chronic form of mastitis, but are seen in the acute caseating form of the breakdown type which usually gives rise to massive blood infection. Tuberculosis of one quarter of the udder may be associated with a concomitant enlargement of the supramammary lymph node and iliac node of that side, and in infection of an anterior quarter the precrural lymph node may be infected.

Tuberculosis of the udders of the gilt or sow is sometimes seen and is probably the chief means of spread of the disease from pig to pig, i.e. from sow to her suckling litter.

Muscle

Muscular tissue very rarely becomes affected with tuberculous lesions, though caseous foci in the bovine tongue may occur through abrasions of the mucous membrane, and in the myocardium as an extension from a tuberculous pericarditis. Very occasionally foci of haematogenous origin have been observed, but lesions in muscular tissue arise most commonly by contiguity with tuberculous foci in serous membranes, joints or bone.

Skin

The so-called " skin tuberculosis " in cattle is an important condition in connection with tuberculosis eradication schemes, for a proportion of animals react to the several tuberculin tests due to the presence of these lesions. It is stated that the path of infection is probably by the skin and that cattle lose their sensitivity to tuberculin when the lesions are removed surgically. The number of cases of " skin tuberculosis " in the United States is said to have increased since the virtual eradication of tuberculosis from that country, and the affection is also said to be increasing in Great Britain, though probably not more than 50 per cent. of clinical cases of " skin tuberculosis " give rise to a reaction to mammalian tuberculin.

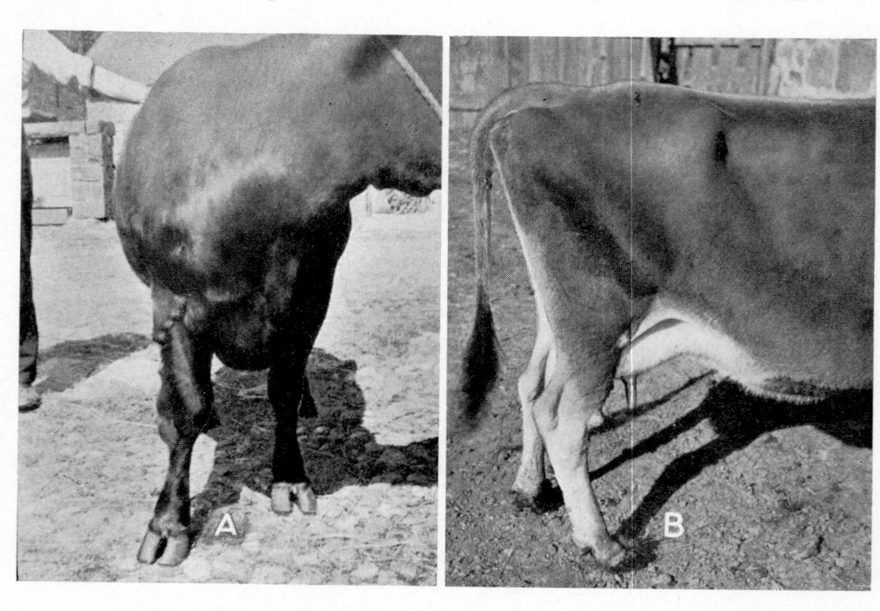

FIG. 131.—" Skin tuberculosis " : (A) on forearm of Shorthorn cow ; (B) on ante-lateral aspect of hind limb of a Jersey cow. (A : G. D. Coward ; B : Dr H. Magnusson.)

The lesions take the form of hard, painless nodules, varying in size up to that of a hen's egg ; they may be single or multiple, and in the latter case are seen in a chain formation usually following the line of a subcutaneous lymphatic vessel. The lesions are most commonly found on the limbs, particularly the fetlock, forearm, hock, and less frequently on the chest wall or shoulder, while they are subcutaneous or closely related to the skin and usually removed with it. In addition to the subcutaneous and intradermal positions in which lesions are usually found, they have been recorded in the prescapular, popliteal and submaxillary lymph nodes, muscles of the shoulder, and connective tissue surrounding the sheath of the metatarsus; such lesions are considered to have been extensions from typical skin lesions in the same animal. On section the nodules are found to consist of a fibrous wall, enclosing a centre which is most commonly caseo-calcareous, but in other cases the centre contains a thick, yellow glutinous pus and at times a dried material resembling powdered maize, or sometimes dry flake-like pellicles. Microscopically the structure of the lesions is indistinguishable from that of a tuberculous nodule, and though acid-fast bacilli can nearly always be seen histologically, no organism likely to be responsible for the lesions has so far been cultivated or been capable of transmission to other animals. Though ulceration of the nodules may occur, with the discharge of acid-fast bacilli in the purulent material, such animals do not come within the terms of the Tuberculosis Order in Britain, and the present weight of evidence is against the lesions being tuberculous. Though the recognition of skin lesions may play an important part in tuberculin testing of herds and in tuberculosis eradication schemes, in meat inspection the condition is only of local significance, requiring condemnation of the tissues adjacent to the seat of lesions.

Other Organs

Tuberculous lesions of the adrenal body, prostate gland, thyroid gland, eye or pancreas are usually indicative of a generalized systemic infection, though the latter organ may become infected by contiguity with tuberculous lesions of the liver.

Differential Diagnosis

A number of affections of the food animals give rise to lesions which may be confused with those of tuberculosis. Most of these affections are of bacterial or parasitic origin, but it may be accepted that in countries from which bovine tuberculosis has been eradicated only a very minute proportion of tuberculosis-like lesions in the internal organs of bovines are caused by the tubercle bacillus, while tubercles in the sheep lung are almost invariably the result of parasitic infection.

Bacterial Infections

Corynebacterium Infection in Pigs. Tuberculosis-like changes in the submaxillary lymph nodes of pigs have been recorded in Britain, Denmark, Norway and other countries, the lesions appearing as small, yellow, necrotic foci which are surrounded by a connective tissue capsule and easily enucleated from the lymph node tissue (Plate II). The affection is caused by the micro-organism *Corynebacterium equi*, which lives a saprophytic existence in the soil, young pigs acquiring the infection when they are running with the sow or when they are on free range and have access to earth. The condition may be confused with lesions produced in the submaxillary nodes of pigs by the avian type of tubercle bacillus but may be distinguished by examination of stained smears from the affected node. This is a routine procedure in Denmark where it has been shown that only a small proportion of the cases are due to tuberculous infection, the remainder to infection with *Corynebacterium equi*, and where the lesions are shown to be caused by the latter organism the head is released after removal of the affected node.

Brucella suis Infection in Pigs. Lesions which bear a close resemblance to tuberculosis but are caused by *Br. suis*, have been reported in the United States in the vertebrae of pigs. These foci appear as greyish-white or pearly-white abscesses and are usually found in the sacro-lumbar region, though occasionally in the carcase lymph nodes; they usually originate in the intervertebral spaces and thence extend to the bodies of the vertebrae. In some cases of *Br. suis* infection in pigs lesions are found in the spleen only.

Parasitic Infections

Certain parasitic infections of the food animals give rise to cheesy, sometimes calcareous, necrotic foci in various tissues, especially where the parasite dies and undergoes degeneration; this latter change is particularly likely to occur when parasites are found in organs other than those for which they have a predilection. The liver of the horse may show nodular or serpentine-like foci which are caseous or calcareous and caused by larvae of some types of strongyles. In other animals tuberculosis-like foci may be found in the liver due to invasion by ascaris larvae or, particularly in sheep, to wandering larvae of the lung strongyles. Irregularly distributed nodules and serpentine-like burrows, which are common in the substance and on the surface of sheep livers, are most likely to be caused by immature forms of *Fasciola hepatica* or of *C. tenuicollis*. The former parasite may also give rise to tuberculosis-like lesions in the liver of pigs, these foci taking the form of white spherical nodules, usually situated superficially and composed of a thick connective tissue capsule with brownish or yellowish semi-solid contents.

Hydatid cysts in the liver and lungs may degenerate to form a cheesy mass which is encapsulated in connective tissue; multilocular hydatid cysts, particularly, may bear a resmblance to tuberculosis but in the hydatid cyst the laminated cuticular membrane is still present even after the cyst has degenerated and can be readily picked up with a forceps. In most parasitic infections microscopical examination of the caseous mass will usually reveal some resistant characteristic portion of the causal parasite, and in degenerated tapeworm cysts it may be possible to demonstrate the presence of hooklets or of calcareous corpuscles from the neck portion of the tapeworm head.

The subpleural tissue of sheep lungs frequently shows grey, sharply delimited nodules caused by lung worms of the genus *Muellerius*, while a parasitic condition occurs in the lungs of pigs and appears as glistening, translucent nodules beneath the pleura, sometimes in the lung substance. These foci are common in young pigs and are often discrete, though sometimes aggregated or in long chains; no lesions are found in the lymph nodes of the lungs and the condition is attributed to larvae of the lung worm *Metastrongylus elongatus or M. pudendotectus* which have died in the smaller bronchioles with resultant nodule formation.

Judgment of Carcases Affected with Tuberculosis

There are two principles that must be observed in the problem of assessing the fitness or otherwise of tuberculous carcases for human food. The first and most important is to protect man against the possibility of infection due to ingestion of infected or contaminated meat or by any other means. The second principle, which has an economic basis, is to avoid any unnecessary waste of meat due to faulty or over-rigorous judgment.

Localized and Generalized Tuberculosis

Tuberculosis is to be regarded as localized if there is no evidence of recent passage of numerous bacilli into the blood stream, and an affected carcase is so classified if the lesions are localized and not numerous, where there is no evidence of recent distribution of tubercle bacilli through the blood or by other means to the muscles or to parts that may be eaten with the muscles, and if the animal is well nourished and in good condition. In such cases there is no proof or reason to suspect that the flesh is unwholesome and the disease may be regarded as localized and only those organs or parts affected need be condemned and destroyed. There is complete justification for the condemnation and destruction of organs affected with tuberculosis and also the affected parts of a carcase and the parts contiguous thereto, and an organ should be regarded as affected if lesions are found in the substance or on the capsule or in the associated lymph nodes. It is necessary to condemn an organ in which the lymph node is affected but no lesion visible in the substance of the organ itself, the justification for this action being that apparently normal organs of tuberculous animals may at times contain microscopic lesions or even isolated bacilli.

The presence of tuberculosis in the head of cattle or pigs affected with localized tuberculosis calls for a somewhat different approach in the matter

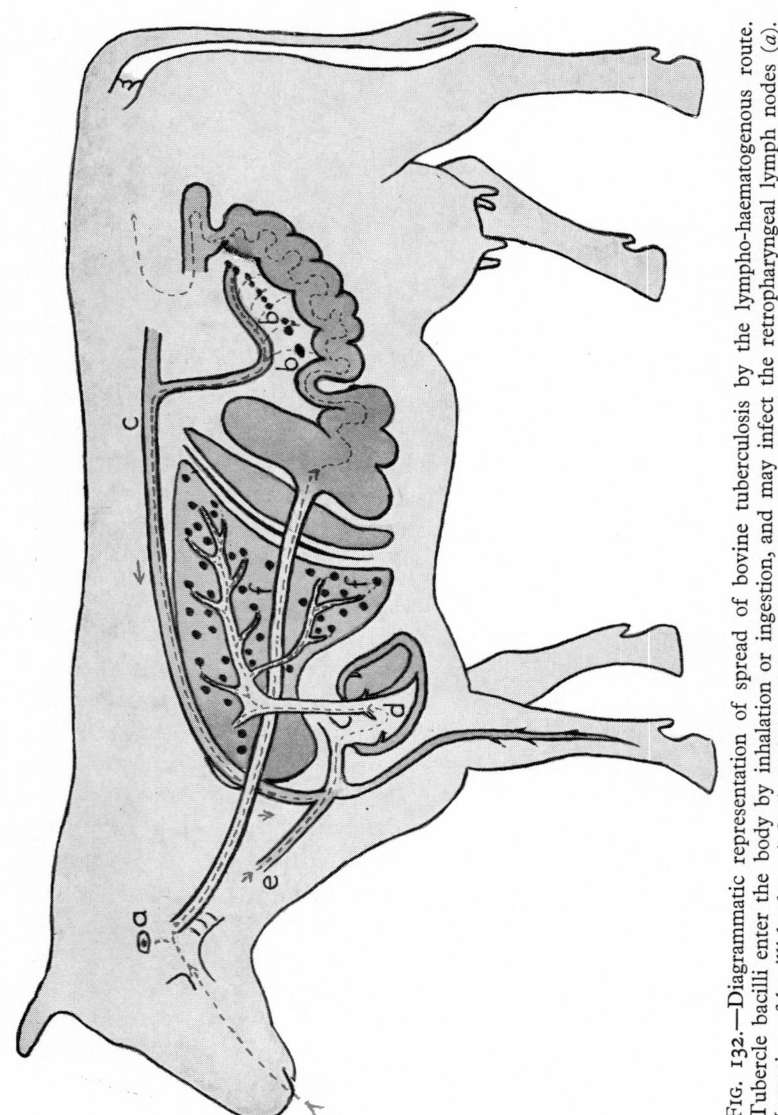

FIG. 132.—Diagrammatic representation of spread of bovine tuberculosis by the lympho-haematogenous route. Tubercle bacilli enter the body by inhalation or ingestion, and may infect the retropharyngeal lymph nodes (*a*). Ingestion of bacilli leads to infection of the mesenteric lymph nodes (*b*), with eventual passage of bacilli into the thoracic duct (*c*), and thence to the right ventricle (*d*). (Breakdown of tuberculous foci in the lymph nodes of the head may give rise to entry of bacilli into the tracheal lymph duct (*e*).) Entry of bacilli into the pulmonary artery causes haematogenous infection of the lungs which is manifested, if infection is massive, by numerous miliary tubercles scattered uniformly throughout both lungs (*f, f*). The development of generalized tuberculosis is, however, considered to occur more frequently from lesions in the lungs than from the alimentary tract (see Fig. 133).

of judgment, for visible evidence of disease is usually only found in the lymph nodes, i.e. the retropharyngeal in cattle and the submaxillary in pigs, and almost invariably these nodes have become infected from entry of bacilli via the tissues of the tonsils or pharynx. Where there is evidence that the lesion in the lymph node has become quiescent, indicated by the fact that it is small, inactive and calcareous and the lymph node itself is not enlarged, there is justification for releasing the head and/or tongue after removal of the affected node together with the contiguous tissue.

The presence of generalized tuberculosis may be assumed where there is evidence of recent passage of bacilli in considerable numbers into the systemic circulation. Significant of such invasion is the presence of numerous miliary tubercles in organs such as the kidneys, liver, spleen, sexual organs and bone. This constitutes a generalization of the acute type and is complete justification for condemnation of the carcase and all organs. Generalized tuberculosis may also be presumed to be present where there are acute infiltrative caseating lesions of the breakdown type, for these are an indication that there has been a recent collapse of the organic defences of the body and that bacilli will be present in the blood and muscular tissue.

Routine Post-Mortem Procedure

In order to assess whether tuberculous lesions are present in the carcase or organs of a slaughtered animal it is necessary to carry out a careful search for the disease, and once detected, to conduct a further examination in order to assess its disposition and extent in the carcase and the character of the lesions.

The initial duty in routine post-mortem inspection is to examine those parts or organs in which tuberculosis is most likely to occur, and inasmuch as the commonest portals of entry are by the respiratory or digestive tract it is essential in cattle and pigs to examine the head and its lymph nodes, the lungs and their associated nodes, the mesenteric chain of nodes, and the liver and its associated portal nodes. In some countries the first nodes incised in cattle are those of the lungs, this practice being based on the time-honoured contention that if no lesion of tuberculosis is found in the left bronchial node of cattle, the carcase may be regarded as tuberculosis-free and no examination for further lesions need be conducted. Though this rule may hold good in over 90 per cent. of cases, because by far the greatest number of primary lesions in cattle occur in the lung, it cannot be regarded as infallible, and for that reason every post-mortem examination in cattle and pigs should include not only inspection of the lungs but also the head, mesentery and liver, together with incision and examination of

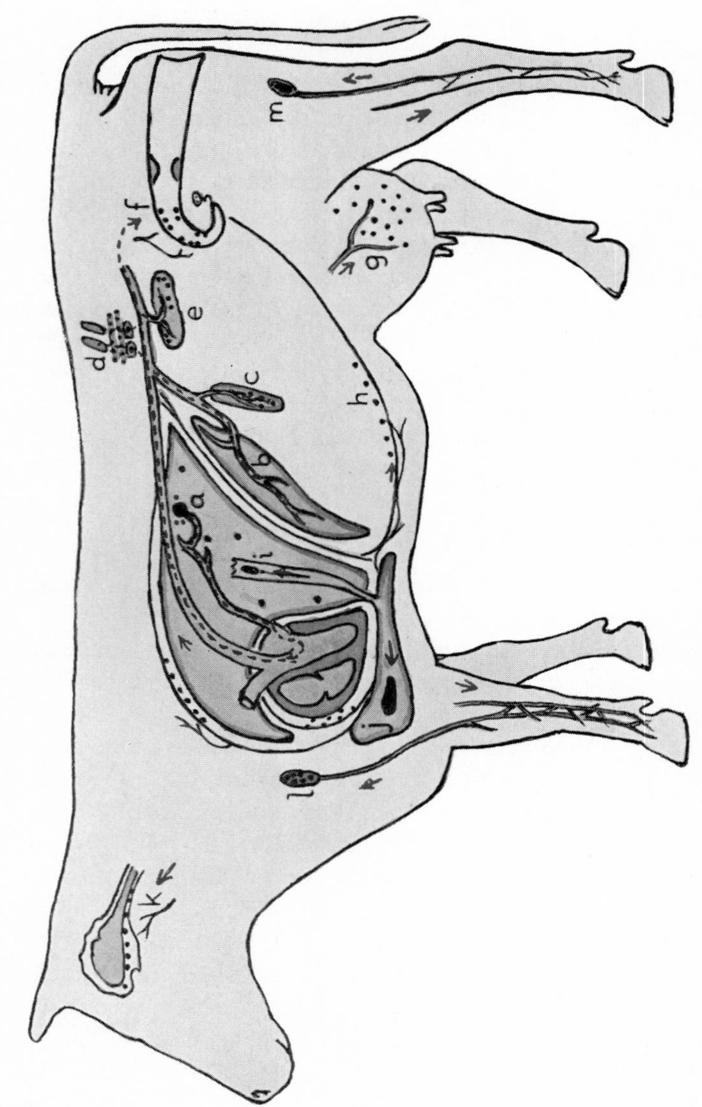

FIG. 133.—Diagram showing production of generalized tuberculosis from a lung lesion (*a*). If such a lesion erodes into a branch of the pulmonary vein, bacilli are carried to the left ventricle and enter the systemic circulation to involve the liver (*b*), spleen (*c*), bodies of vertebrae or other bones, particularly the tubular bones (*d*), kidneys (*e*), uterus (*f*), udder (*g*), ribs (*i*), and sternum (*j*). Entry of bacilli into the arteries of the limbs may eventually result in infection of the carcase lymph nodes, e.g. prescapular (*l*) and popliteal (*m*). Bacilli entering the anterior aorta may give rise to lesions in the brain or cranial bones, with eventual production of a tuberculous meningitis (*k*).
It is possible that the peritoneum (*h*) may also be affected by haematogenous spread.

the regional lymph nodes of these organs or parts. The present method of inspection in England and Wales is discribed below.

PROCEDURE IN ENGLAND AND WALES

This is laid down in the Meat Inspection Regulations 1963 and prescribes the method in which the head, thoracic and abdominal cavities and the organs and viscera therein shall be examined. In examining the udder of a cow or sow the inspector shall incise the udder and shall examine it by observation and palpation and shall examine in detail, i.e., by making multiple deep incisions, the supramammary lymph nodes. In the case of any female animal other than a cow or sow, the udder shall be examined by observation and palpation and, if necessary, the udder incised and the supramammary lymph nodes examined in detail. In bulls and boars the superficial inguinal lymph nodes shall be examined and, if considered necessary, the superficial inguinal lymph nodes of any other animal shall be examined. The justification for requiring inspection of these nodes in every routine examination is that in the cow a primary infection of the udder may occur due to the introduction of tubercle bacilli by a contaminated syringe, while in bulls a primary infection of the penis may occur as a result of service of a cow affected with tuberculous metritis.

When an inspector has reason to suspect that any part of a carcase or offal of any animal is infected with tuberculosis he shall, in addition to carrying out the detailed instructions laid down for the routine post-mortem examination of all animals, carry out the following :

(*a*) in the case of any carcase, require the carcase to be split, examine the vertebrae, ribs, sternum, spinal cord and, if he considers it necessary, the brain, and expose, and if a lesion of a kidney is visible or suspected, incise, the kidney ;

(*b*) in the case of the carcase of any bovine animal or horse, examine in detail the following lymphatic glands (being glands not already examined by him in accordance with the provisions of Part II of Schedule I of the Regulations), namely, the superficial inguinal, supramammary, prepectoral, presternal, suprasternal, xiphoid, subdorsal, intercostal, prescapular, iliac, sublumbar, ischiatic, precrural and popliteal, those glands which are least likely to show infection being examined first ;

(*c*) in the case of the carcase of any pig, examine in detail the following lymphatic glands (being glands not already examined by him in accordance with the provisions of Part II of Schedule I of the Regulations), namely, the superficial inguinal, supramammary, cervical, prepectoral, prescapular, subdorsal, sublumbar, iliac, precrural and, if he considers it necessary, the popliteal.

CODE OF JUDGMENT IN ENGLAND AND WALES

This is laid down in the Meat Inspection Regulations 1963 and prescribes that the inspector shall in determining whether tuberculosis is generalized take into account the source of the evidence of disease and the character of the lesions throughout the carcase and, in particular, shall regard evidence of any of the following conditions as evidence of generalized tuberculosis :

(*a*) miliary tuberculosis of both lungs with evidence of tuberculosis elsewhere ;

(*b*) multiple and actively progressive lesions of tuberculosis ;

(*c*) widespread tuberculous infection of the lymphatic glands of the carcase ;

(*d*) diffuse acute lesions of tuberculosis of both the pleura and peritoneum associated with an enlarged or tuberculous lymphatic gland of the carcase ;

(*e*) active or recent lesions present in the substance of any two of the following : spleen, kidney, udder, uterus, ovary, testicle, brain and spinal cord or their membranes, in addition to tuberculous lesions in the respiratory and digestive tracts;

(*f*) in the case of a calf, congenital tuberculosis.

Where the inspector is satisfied that a carcase or offal is affected with tuberculosis other than generalized tuberculosis or tuberculosis with emaciation he shall regard the following parts of the carcase and offal as unfit for human consumption :

(*a*) any part of the carcase infected with localized tuberculosis and any other part continuous thereto ;

(*b*) the head, including the tongue, when tuberculosis exists in any lymphatic gland associated with the head or tongue ; provided that, where in a particular gland or glands the lesion is small and inactive and the gland is not enlarged, the inspector may at his discretion regard the head or tongue, or both, as fit for human consumption after the removal of the affected gland or glands and the surrounding tissue ;

(*c*) any organ or viscera when tuberculosis exists in the substance, or on the surface thereof, or in any lymphatic gland associated therewith.

It is further prescribed that the inspector shall regard any part of the carcase and any offal or blood contaminated with tuberculous material as unfit for human consumption.

The conditions which an inspector is to regard as evidence of generalized tuberculosis are discussed below.

(a) Miliary tuberculosis of both lungs with evidence of tuberculosis elsewhere.

It is in the judgment of the lung lesions of bovine tuberculosis that the meat inspector is most inclined to err, and of all manifestations of the disease it is the recognition of those lung lesions which can properly be regarded as constituting miliary tuberculosis which presents the greatest difficulty. Acute miliary tuberculosis in cattle denotes a very heavy invasion of the blood stream with tubercle bacilli. Miliary tuberculosis is very unlikely to be confined to the lungs for although bacilli which are circulating systematically have invariably entered the venous system and are first arrested in the lungs, the lung is an imperfect filter and the condition is therefore characterized by the presence of a very large number of miliary tubercles, all of an equal age and size and uniformly distributed throughout both lungs together with miliary lesions in the visceral organs, particularly the kidneys and spleen. The search for evidence of miliary tuberculosis of the lungs should always be undertaken in natural light and tubercles are often readily detected by tensing the lung surface, when the tubercles will be apparent beneath the visceral pleura. This may be followed by incision of the lung tissue, but inasmuch as tuberculosis of the miliary type involves all the lung lobes, should the apical node be incised and reveal no miliary tubercles it may be assumed that the case is not one of miliary tuberculosis. Undue importance should not be attached, however, to the presence in the lung tissue of a number of tuberculous lesions which are shot-like, caseous or caseo-calcareous and up to a pea in size, for these lesions are indicative of a previous blood infection in which a relatively few bacilli have been concerned and which the animal has successfully resisted. Thus the diagnosis of miliary tuberculosis of both lungs should only be arrived at after very careful examination of the lung tissue and of the character of the lesion or lesions elsewhere.

(b) Multiple and actively progressive lesions of tuberculosis.

This section must be taken to include affection of tissues, organs and lymph nodes but the classification of the carcase as one affected with generalized tuberculosis is only justified when the infection is both multiple and actively progressive ; the presence of either of these conditions alone is not sufficient to warrant total condemnation. Multiple lesions should be taken to denote the presence of a lesion in several organs or parts but it should be noted that multiple lesions are the rule rather than the exception in a tuberculous carcase. Thus in a carcase it is common to find lesions involving the lungs, pleura, mesenteric nodes and liver, but on no account could this disposition of disease be classified as evidence of generalization unless the lesions were of an actively progressive nature. Indications that disease is both active and progressive may be assumed if:

(*a*) There is evidence of congestion of the surrounding tissue,

(*b*) the lymph nodes draining the area where the lesion is present are enlarged and oedematous,

(*c*) several small millet-sized lesions are distributed around an older caseous focus, and

(*d*) lesions are of the "breakdown" type, characterized by the presence of dry caseous masses interspersed with small haemorrhages and the lymph nodes associated with such areas are enlarged and show miliary tubercles or stellate caseation.

On the other hand, dry caseous lesions without haemorrhages, or lesions which are encapsulated or calcified, are indicative of a chronic healing condition.

(c) Widespread tuberculous infection of the lymphatic glands of the carcase.

The carcase lymph nodes are normally regarded as those which remain on or in the carcase after dressing, and include the renal and supramammary; they therefore comprise all the lymph nodes of the body with the exception of those of the head and those removed with the thoracic and abdominal organs during evisceration.

Judgment of carcases under this section calls for a sound knowledge of the areas and type of tissue drained by the carcase lymph nodes; the latter may be classified as follows, according to the nature of the tissue they drain:

(*a*) They may drain muscle exclusively, as in the case of the popliteal, axillary and prescapular.

(*b*) They may drain organs exclusively, as the renal lymph node.

(*c*) They may drain both organs and muscle, as in the iliac, ischiatic and lumbar nodes.

(*d*) They may drain lymph almost exclusively from the skin, as in the case of the precrural node.

The intermuscular or deep-seated nodes which drain muscle exclusively are the most important, for they are only likely to become infected if tubercle bacilli are present in the portion of muscle drained by the node.

The carcase lymph nodes draining organs exclusively, such as the renal node, are also important, for they indicate in this case that the kidneys contain or have contained tubercle bacilli, and infection of these organs is only likely to take place by the haematogenous route. In routine meat inspection, however, the renal node is not infrequently found infected, whereas examination of the kidneys shows these organs to be apparently

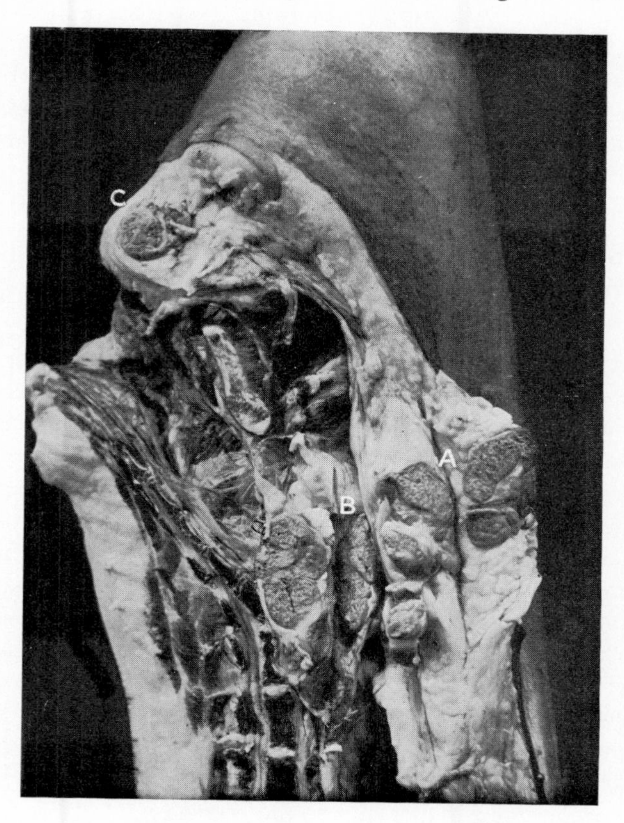

FIG. 134.—Tuberculosis in the carcase of a sow, showing multiple infection of the carcase lymph nodes. (A) supra-mammary; (B) iliac; (C) gluteal; this node is only present in 10 per cent. of cases. (A. C. F. Gisborne.)

normal. It must be remembered that the renal node is actually one of the lumbar chain, so that its affection may be the result of tuberculous spread within the peritoneal cavity and therefore of less serious import in the judgment of the carcase.

The significance of infection of carcase lymph nodes which drain both the muscle and organs is less easy to assess, for these nodes may become infected either from diseased organs or from the presence of bacilli in muscular tissue. Such lymph nodes, however, are most likely to derive infection from an organ, for tuberculosis of the internal organs is much commoner than tubercle bacilli in muscular tissue, and the detection of tuberculosis in a node of this group should always be followed by an examination of the organs it drains.

The group of nodes draining lymph from the skin are of little importance for the skin is least likely of all tissues to be affected with tuberculosis.

Widespread tuberculosis of the lymph nodes of the carcase is usually regarded as being present if there are lesions in two or more carcase lymph nodes in addition to two or more other lymph nodes not confined either to the thoracic cavity or to the abdominal cavity.

(d) Diffuse acute lesions of tuberculosis of both the pleura and peritoneum associated with an enlarged or tuberculous lymphatic gland of the carcase.

Acute tuberculous infection of the serous membranes takes the form of red, velvety granulations which may be spread over the greater part of the pleura and peritoneum. In a minority of cases such infection may be haematogenous in origin, and being also active it may be associated with the presence of tubercle bacilli in the muscular tissue. Though chronic lesions of the pleura or peritoneum are of less significance and are unlikely to extend to the subserous tissue, the removal of these membranes by stripping should, nevertheless, be regarded as unjustifiable unless the tuberculous areas are relatively small in extent and where there is no evidence of involvement of the associated lymph nodes of the carcase. Infection of the pleural membrane of carcases in which disease does not come within the category of generalization is better dealt with by the procedure known as ribbing in which the costal wall is removed and condemned, for in stripping there is likely to be extensive bacillary contamination of the underlying tissues during the operation.

(e) Active or recent lesions present in the substance of any two of the following: spleen, kidney, udder, uterus, ovary, testicle, brain and spinal cord or their membranes, in addition to tuberculous lesions in the respiratory and digestive tracts.

This paragraph contains a very necessary proviso, that the lesions which may be present in the spleen, kidney, etc., must be active or of recent origin. Provided the lesions are inactive or of a chronic nature, manifested by encapsulation or calcification, there is justification for the release of the carcase after condemnation of the affected organs or parts.

(f) In the case of a calf, congenital tuberculosis in calves.

Tuberculosis in calves is characterized by the predominance of infection of the lymph nodes and by the frequency of lesions in the abdominal cavity. Three forms of infection may be encountered on post-mortem examination: (*a*) Tuberculosis of the lungs and their lymph nodes, indicative of a respiratory infection; (*b*) tuberculosis of the mesenteric lymph nodes indicating an infection of alimentary origin; and (*c*) congenital tuberculosis acquired by the foetus *in utero*. It is the last form which is of the greatest importance in meat inspection.

The importance of the recognition of congenital tuberculosis in the calf is that it is a primary infection, and all forms of primary tuberculosis in the calf are frequently followed by haematogenous dissemination. Evidence of congenital tuberculosis in the veal carcase is therefore highly suggestive that the infection is of a generalized nature and is an indication for total condemnation.

Infection of the foetus with congenital tuberculosis appears to occur late in gestation, and only if the metritis is in an early stage, bacilli gaining entry to the umbilical vein from tuberculous lesions in the placenta, and giving rise to more or less numerous lesions according to the number of invading bacilli. It has been seen (p. 85) that by far the greater part of the blood in the umbilical vein passes through the capillary network of the foetal liver before being conveyed onwards to the heart, while only a small amount passes directly from the umbilical vein to the portal sinus (*sinus intermedius*), and thus by-passes the liver to reach the heart and lungs by way of the ductus venosus; it follows, therefore, that in congenital tuberculosis the liver or portal lymph nodes will become affected far more frequently than the lungs or other organs.

The spread of congenital tuberculosis throughout the foetus originates from the primary infection of the foetal liver and occurs by the blood stream, but bacilli may also be disseminated from liver to peritoneum by way of the lymphatics, the peritoneal lesions being smooth and creamy white, without evidence of degenerative changes, and confined to the posterior aspect of the diaphragm where it is in contact with the liver. In certain cases the thoracic cavity may also be invaded through the lymphatics of the diaphragm, giving rise to lesions in the posterior mediastinal lymph nodes, which are often greatly enlarged; the bronchial lymph nodes may be similarly affected, together with isolated nodules in the lungs, but lesions in the latter organ are usually superficial, while tuberculous pleurisy very rarely occurs.

As primary tuberculosis of the calf tends to become generalized there may be widespread infection of the carcase lymph nodes, and tuberculous lesions are frequently present in the kidneys and substance of the spleen. In the majority of cases where the bovine spleen becomes affected post-natally the tuberculous lesions are confined to the splenic capsule and very rarely involve the splenic substance, so that the presence of lesions in the spleen substance is strongly suggestive of congenital infection, a fact which should be borne in mind when tuberculous lesions are

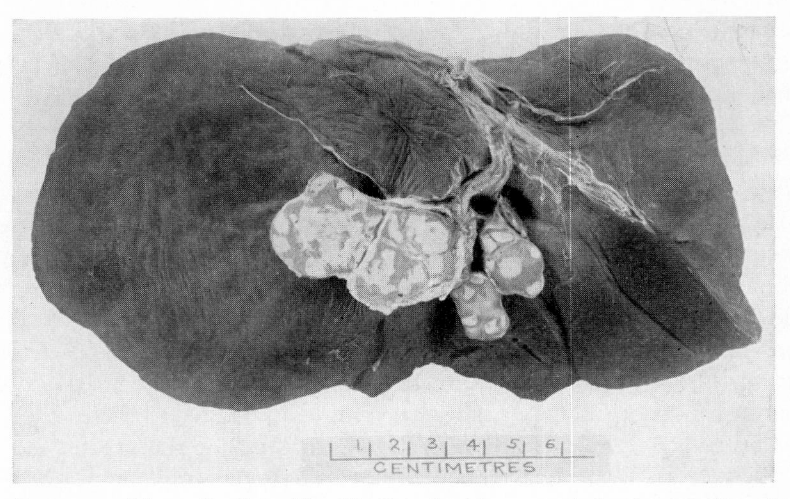

FIG. 135.—Liver of 2-day-old calf affected with congenital tuberculosis and showing enlargement and coalescing caseation of the incised portal lymph nodes. Caseous lesions were also found in the posterior mediastinal lymph node and two isolated nodules on the lung surface.

found within the splenic tissue of adult cattle. A feature of congenital infection in calves is that the parotid lymph node, which drains the cranial cavity, may not infrequently be found affected.

Tuberculous lesions in calves, or indeed in any of the food animals, are unlikely to be discernible macroscopically until infection is 3 weeks old, so that the presence of tuberculous foci in calves up to a fortnight old may be regarded as conclusive evidence of congenital infection. After that time the presence of lesions in the portal lymph nodes cannot be accepted as a definite indication of congenital infection, for in primary tuberculosis of alimentary origin these nodes may become infected post-natally by way of the lymphatics of the duodenum. In older calves up to 4 months old, a diagnosis of congenital infection can be made when the portal lymph nodes are relatively greatly enlarged, in some cases forming a mass half the size of the liver, and are caseous or caseo-calcareous, together with a widespread distribution of lesions in the lymph nodes and organs. In these older calves infection of any two of the following organs—liver, kidney, spleen—is regarded as evidence of congenital infection and it was contended by Nieberle that all calves, no matter what age, which show isolated lesions in the liver or portal lymph nodes are examples of true congenital infection.

In still older animals the pathological picture of congenital tuberculosis may be obscured by subsequent post-natal infection, and its recognition is thereby rendered more difficult. The calf born full-time from a slightly tuberculous uterus will, however, often commence to show symptoms of tuberculosis at 4 to 9 months, the first symptom being usually that of a meningitis.

CODE OF JUDGMENT IN THE FEDERAL GERMAN REPUBLIC IN RELATION TO CARCASES AFFECTED WITH TUBERCULOSIS

The judgment of the carcases and organs of animals affected with tuberculosis has been re-drafted and is considerably more severe than in the previous legislation of 1941. The latter Regulations, based on the researches of Nieberle and others, placed great emphasis on the qualitative aspect of the tuberculous lesion and on the importance of differentiating lesions which were acute from those which were of a chronic nature. These workers conceded that tubercle bacilli might enter the bloodstream and be spread systematically in any case where a lesion showed signs of activity, but believed that only a few bacilli were concerned in such occasional invasions and that the virulence of the organisms was attenuated by the increased resistance developed by the animal as a result of infection.

The provisions of the 1941 Regulations were severely criticized by some authorities who questioned the justification for releasing unconditionally those carcases in which the lesions present were apparently of a chronic nature. Further researches confirmed that this criticism was a valid one and that generalization from a chronic tuberculous lesion occurred more frequently than had hitherto been averred ; indeed, there was evidence that a single primary focus, even when encapsulated and calcified, could permit of entry into the blood-stream. From this followed the categorical statement that in every form of tuberculosis there is a possibility of tubercle bacilli being present in the muscular tissue, and as a result new regulations regarding tuberculous carcases were promulgated in 1961. These provide, as do regulations in all countries, that an organ is to be regarded as tuberculous if its associated lymph node is affected, and such organs must be condemned. If a carcase with tuberculous lesions is emaciated or cachectic the entire carcase and organs shall likewise be condemned, but in all other cases where a carcase is found affected with tuberculosis, the carcase shall be only regarded as conditionally fit for human consumption, irrespective of the nature, distribution or age of the lesions. It is then provided that the carcase shall be cut into small pieces, cooked thoroughly under official supervision, and sold on the Freibank to individual customers only for their own consumption. Such meat is sold at a reduced price, but sale to institutions such as schools, restaurants or hotels is forbidden.

Provided a Freibank system is in operation in a country this procedure cannot be questioned on either public health or economic grounds, and in those countries where bovine tuberculosis is, or is being, eradicated the proportion of animals to be dealt with is so small that consideration might be given, provided facilities for heat treatment and sale under official supervision were available, to reviewing their appropriate regulations regarding tuberculous carcases in the light of the finding of the German workers. Against this, it may be contended by a country that the incidence of the disease is so low that condemnations due to tuberculosis are no longer a major problem, that the procedure prescribed by the German regulations is unduly severe and ignores the aesthetic aspect, that beef and pork is usually cooked thoroughly before consumption and that the existing regulations of the particular country applicable to carcases affected with tuberculosis provide an adequate public health safeguard.

GENERALIZED SYSTEMIC INFECTIONS

Mode of Spread of Infections in the Animal Body

Bacteria may gain access to the animal body by a variety of routes, by inhalation, by ingestion, or by penetrating a surface directly through wounds or abrasions. The question as to whether further spread will take place depends (*a*) on the nature of the infective organisms, (*b*) on the degree of resistance the defensive mechanisms of the body are able to produce, and (*c*) on the type of tissue invaded. Bacteria are more or less specialized in their nutritional demands, and they are most likely to establish themselves in the animal body if they arrive at a site which best satisfies their biological requirements. Staphylococci, for example, may multiply rapidly in the skin to produce boils, but it is very unlikely that if swallowed they will establish themselves in the intestine ; the reverse is true of *Clostridium welchii*. Generally speaking, therefore, the actual site at which infection occurs depends largely on the nature of the infecting organism.

Every infection, of whatever nature, is initially a local one, and its importance in meat inspection is whether the infection has spread from its original site and whether it has become generalized. Any initial success on the part of the bacterium is manifested by extension of its activities around the original point of entry, i.e. the disease process spreads through contiguity of tissue; the question as to whether further spread will take place is influenced by the readiness with which the animal body is able to mobilize its cellular and humoral defences. Shortly before death, when the tissue reactions are on the point of exhaustion, it is common to find pathogenic bacteria, which had previously been kept localized, suddenly able to disseminate themselves rapidly and in great numbers to distant parts of the body, while after death the numerous bacterial species which are harmless residents in the various parts of the body soon spread from their original habitat. Any impairment of the nutritional state of the animal body is therefore reflected in the greater ease with which a disease process may become generalized.

Importance of the Type of Tissue Invaded

The site of the original infection is of prime importance as to whether the infection will spread throughout the body or will remain localized. Though some bacteria are extremely selective in their preference for the tissue attacked, others, such as the streptococci, are less limited in this way and may succeed in producing infection by way of almost any tissue to which they gain access. With such organisms much will depend on where this tissue is situated; if the initial infection is in the skin the opportunities for local extension and dissemination into the blood circulation are slight. The uterine mucous membrane, on the other hand, possesses a large vascular surface, especially after parturition, and septic infection of this organ is associated with conditions favourable for the initial multiplication of the organisms and ample opportunities for spread of the infection into the blood stream. Similarly, the udder substance presents a large vascular surface to infective organisms, and septic mastitis may thus frequently be associated with a massive entry of bacteria or their toxins into the systemic circulation. Again, in septic pneumonia the infective material may spread by contiguity if it pass up the bronchi and trachea and be then aspirated to another part of the lung; the infection may thus enter the lymph stream and systemic circulation to become generalized. Conversely, the bovine pericardium, though frequently infected as a result of traumatic influences, is for all practical purposes a closed sac which tends to encapsulate and localize the infective material contained within it, and for this reason traumatic pericarditis, even where the amount of infective material is large, is an affection not necessarily associated with spread of the causal organisms throughout the body.

TOXAEMIA

Some organisms have little tendency to spread from the original site at which they become established but produce poisonous substances or toxins in the course of their growth and multiplication, and these diffuse into the lymph and blood circulations to become distributed throughout the body. These toxins are classified as endotoxins or exotoxins, the distinction lying chiefly on laboratory evidence. For example, if a culture of *Cl. tetani* is allowed to grow for a period and the organisms themselves are then removed by filtration, the remaining fluid will be found to contain considerable quantities of the poison, which is biologically identifiable as possessing the characteristic properties of tetanus toxin; this is described as an exotoxin. A similar experiment with *B. anthracis* produces a negative result, and its endotoxin can only be liberated by methods involving the destruction of the bacterial cells. Endotoxins do not cause specific effects as do *Cl. tetani*, *Cl. welchii*, or *Cl. botulinum*, nor are their poisonous properties specific, while they are much less active and less poisonous than exotoxins. In some cases a local infective focus may contain a mixed bacterial flora, included in which are protein-splitting putrefactive bacteria, and absorption into the system of toxic products resulting from such protein breakdown may result in a marked and violent intoxication in the live animal and symptoms of severe illness; examples of this form of toxaemia, at one time designated sapraemia, are gangrene of the lung, gangrenous mastitis and certain cases of metritis or traumatic pericarditis. The significance of toxaemia in meat inspection is not so much the nature of the infecting organisms, but whether their metabolic products have produced generalized and systemic effects on the carcase. These may take the form of cloudy swelling or fatty change of the liver, kidneys and heart muscles, and other lesions that may be present in the bovine carcase are emphysema of the lungs, a marked distension of the gall bladder and enlargement of the carcase lymph nodes.

SEPTICAEMIA

Though the production of toxin is the main armament of some bacteria, the property of invasiveness is the most pronounced characteristic of others, and bacteria highly endowed with this penetrative power are the most likely to enter the blood stream and be carried to different parts of the body. The entry of bacteria into the systemic circulation is designated bacteraemia; it occurs commonly in exhausted animals or in cases of local trauma, but the number of organisms remains small and widespread injury to the body does not result. Bacteraemia may be a transient phenomenon if the organisms are rapidly taken up and removed by the phagocytic cells present in the blood and endothelial lining of the blood vessels; it causes little or no systemic disturbance and, from the point of view of meat inspection, is therefore of little significance. On the other hand, where organisms are escaping into the circulation faster than the phagocytic mechanism can remove them, the blood becomes heavily infected, the organisms more and more widely distributed and tissue damage is produced over wide areas. This condition is termed septicaemia, and has often been used to indicate a condition in which bacteria are not only present in the blood but are actively multiplying therein. It is doubtful whether this ever occurs, except shortly before death, and septicaemia may be better described as a more profuse and persistent bacteraemia.

Where a massive bacterial invasion of the blood stream is sufficient to overcome the defensive mechanisms of the body the bacteria exert toxic effects on the animal, though endotoxins have not the selective effects of exotoxins but are poisonous to tissue cells generally ; the changes manifested in the carcase by endotoxin action as a result of such an invasion constitute the classical lesions associated with septicaemia. In such cases primary morbid changes may be observed in the tissue which constituted the original point of attack; they may take the form of a metritis, arthritis or enteritis, or there may be septic changes of the skin or feet, or gangrene of the skin or udder. In addition to these primary septic conditions there may be observed certain symptoms and lesions which are common to all septicaemias whatever the nature of the infective organism or the site of the original infection. The animal shivers and shows a high fever which is often remittent in character ; there is an increase in white blood corpuscles but a diminution in the number of red blood cells due to the destructive influence of the invading bacteria, and this may result in anaemia. Petechial haemorrhages may be seen in the skin or serous membranes, while focal affections of various organs, e.g. patches of broncho-pneumonia or joint abscesses, may also occur. The liver or kidneys show cloudy swelling with a dull opaque appearance, and the spleen is generally soft and much enlarged.

The infective organisms in animal septicaemias are usually streptococci or staphylococci, but certain specific diseases, as anthrax or swine erysipelas, are septicaemic in nature and are of importance in meat inspection for they are diseases common to animals and man, and the latter may become infected by consuming the flesh of an affected animal or by accidental inoculation. Another important group of bacteria which cause diseases in the food animals are the salmonella organisms, for most types, in addition to giving rise to illness of a septicaemic nature in animals, may also set up severe gastro-enteritis in man which is sometimes fatal. It must also be realized that every systemic disturbance tends to lower the body resistance and cause disturbance in the equilibrium of the intestinal bacterial flora, with the result that salmonellae, though not the primary causative agents of the disease, multiply in the intestine and may enter the systemic circulation. Meat inspection records have abundantly shown that the flesh or organs of animals slaughtered while suffering from a generalized systemic infection, especially when due to disease of the intestinal or genital tract, are the most likely to give rise to severe gastro-intestinal disturbances in man. Animal infections of this nature include :

1. Septic Metritis. This is commonest in cows, being bacterial in origin, and usually occurs as a result of retained foetal membranes after calving, or through injury or rupture of the uterine mucous membrane during parturition ; less commonly it may arise as a result of decomposition of the foetus *in utero*.

Septic metritis is manifested in the live animal by high fever, greatly accelerated pulse, muscular weakness and severe depression, and in many cases the animal is recumbent and unable to rise. A marked symptom is swelling of the vulva, the lips of which are separated and the discharge therefrom, which is at first serous and of a yellow, red or chocolate colour, eventually becomes more abundant, pus-like and foul smelling. Tympanitis usually occurs if peritonitis is present, and when the temperature reaches 107-108° F. death often follows ; the course of such an infection rarely lasts more than 3 to 4 days.

On post-mortem examination the uterus is not contracted and is often two to three times larger than normal ; it contains a quantity of chocolate-coloured or greyish fluid which is composed of effused blood and the remains of the foetal membranes, and in some cases the quantity of fluid amounts to several gallons and emits a most repulsive odour.

The mucous membrane of the uterus, particularly the uterine horn which contained the foetus, is thickened, dirty brown or dark green in colour, and is softened and covered with diphtheritic exudates and blood clots ; these are chiefly found at the base of the maternal cotyledons, which appear grey, pulpy, and almost detached from the uterine mucous membrane. The walls of the uterus are thickened due to infiltration with inflammatory oedema, while the peritoneum, especially that portion covering the uterus, may be highly congested and covered with pseudo-membranous layers of fibrin. Toxic infection of the carcase is manifested by great enlargement of the iliac, lumbar, sacral and ischiatic lymph nodes, with generalized congestion of the carcase and degenerative changes in the parenchymatous organs.

Carcases affected with septic metritis must unhesitatingly be condemned, but care must be taken to differentiate this condition from chronic endometritis, which is common in cows and occurs frequently after contagious abortion or as an extension upwards of catarrh of the vaginal mucous membrane. Though chronic endometritis is characterized in the live animal by a mucopurulent or purulent discharge from the vulva, there

Plate III

1. Osteohaematochromatosis of the humerus of ox, a congenital affection of the skeletal system and attributed to porphyrin, an iron-containing pigment.

2. Chronic arthritis of stifle joint of pig and a frequent sequela to an attack of swine erysipelas. The patella has been reflected downwards showing that the synovial membrane of the joint has been replaced by red granulation tissue which bears a resemblance to turkish towelling. There is some erosion of cartilage on the articular surface of the femur.

3. Sternal segments of ox showing lesions of osteomalacia. The centres of the segments have undergone cavitation and are filled with a dark red jelly-like substance.

4. (*Left*) Tendo-vaginitis in the foreshank of ox. The flexor tendons and sheaths at the rear of the limb are suffused with a gelatinous exudate. (*Right*) Normal limb.

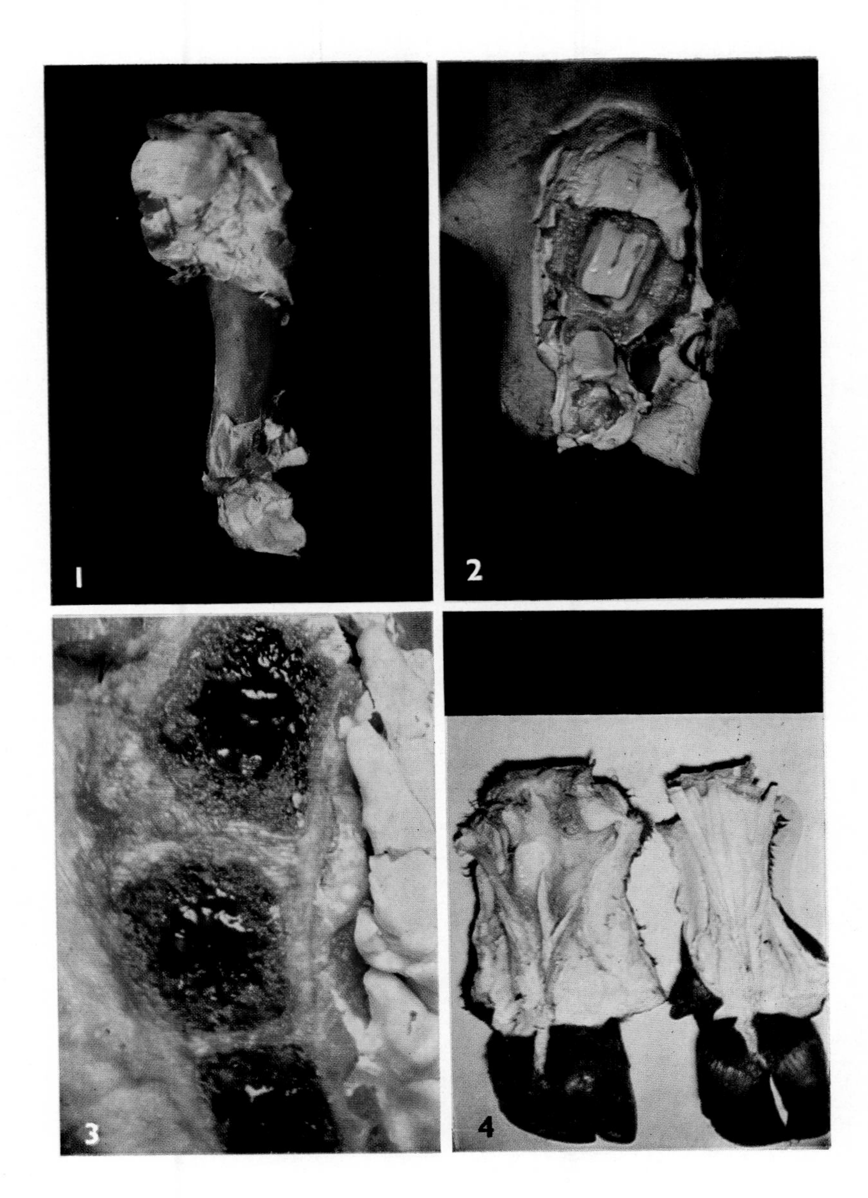
1
2
3
4

is a complete absence of the marked systemic disturbance associated with septic metritis; few old cows are free from chronic endometritis, and this affection may be regarded in meat inspection as a local one requiring condemnation of the uterus alone. Pyometra, characterized by the retention of a considerable quantity of pus in the uterus, is likewise frequently unaccompanied by systemic changes, and in the absence of these the carcase may receive a favourable judgment. The judgment as to whether meat is safe in septic metritis depends entirely, as in all septic infections, on whether or not the septic process has become generalized throughout the carcase, and this cannot be established with certainty except by bacteriological examination of the carcase and organs.

2. Septic Mastitis. This is a highly acute affection characterized by its rapid progress and severe systemic disturbance. It is essentially an involvement of the whole of the glandular tissue of the udder as well as the milk ducts, and is usually associated with infection by staphylococci. In septic mastitis a quarter of the udder, or sometimes the whole udder, is swollen, hot and painful, while the supramammary lymph nodes are swollen and oedematously infiltrated and the iliac and lumbar nodes usually enlarged. The secretion from the teats is red or yellow in colour, of a fluid consistency and with a putrid odour; purulent areas may develop in the udder tissue, and extension of the inflammatory process may be seen in the form of oedematous infiltration of the abdominal wall or inner aspect of the thigh. An attack of septic mastitis may be succeeded by gangrene of the udder which is characterized by a change in the colour of the organ to a violet-red and later to a greenish-black; the udder is cold to the touch, and on section the cut surface is both evil-smelling and very dark in colour.

Carcases affected with septic mastitis which show evidence of systemic invasion in the form of generalized carcase congestion, enlargement of the visceral and carcase lymph nodes, and degenerative changes in the parenchymatous organs should be condemned. Carcases showing gangrene of the udder must also be condemned, but the presence of thick-walled abscesses in the udder tissue, which are indicative of a previous attack of mastitis from which the animal has recovered, are only of local significance.

3. Septic Pericarditis. In the ox this is usually traumatic in origin, and though a number of cases of septic infection of the pericardial sac are encountered on routine inspection, the carcases frequently show no evidence of septicaemia. Such systemic changes as do occur in the form of oedema and emaciation are usually attributable to gross circulatory disturbance, or to absorption of toxins from the infective material. In the absence of toxic infection or of oedema or emaciation, a more favourable judgment may be extended to the carcase, for extensive pathological processes with formation of pus, as occur in this condition and in pyometra, are not so inclined to produce a generalized systemic infection as is generally supposed.

4. Septic Enteritis. In adult cattle the presence of a bloody diarrhoea together with high fever and marked constitutional disturbance is highly suspicious of a septicaemic condition. Enteritis in the live animal is manifested by diarrhoea, with foul-smelling faeces sometimes intermixed with blood or fibrin threads and containing masses of mucus. Emaciation rapidly supervenes and is usually followed by death in 5 to 7 days, but, more rarely, the disease may continue for some weeks with alternating

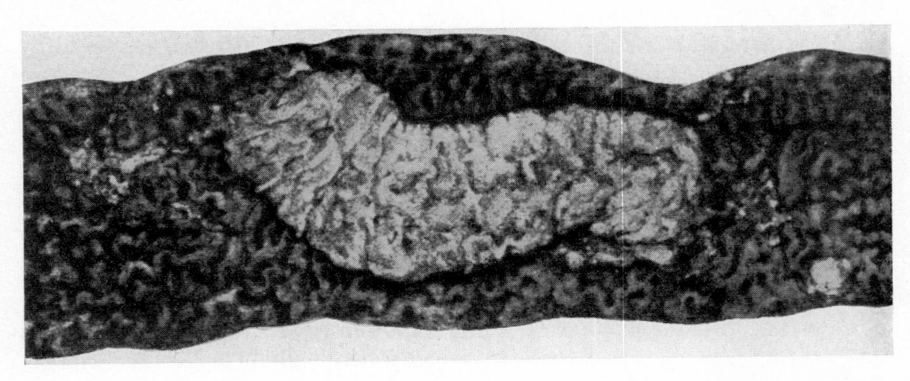

FIG. 136.—Small intestine of ox affected with septic enteritis. The mucous membrane shows intense congestion and is coated with a diphtheritic exudate.

constipation and diarrhoea, gradual emaciation, and occasional involvement of the joints and tendon sheaths (Plate III). Post-mortem examination reveals intense congestion of the mucous membrane of the small intestine, occasionally the abomasum, the mucous membrane being studded with petechial haemorrhages or coated with diphtheritic membranes. The mesenteric lymph nodes are greatly enlarged and infiltrated, and there may be enlargement of the spleen or effusion of blood beneath the visceral and parietal pleurae. In more prolonged cases necrotic foci may be seen in the liver and kidneys and constitute the so-called miliary organ necrosis. Such foci are regarded as pathognomic of an infection with *S. enteritidis* or *S. typhi-murium*, but they are frequently only discernible by microscopical examination. Carcases of animals affected with septic enteritis must be condemned.

5. Haemorrhagic Enteritis in Calves. This affection is known also as calf dysentery and is generally caused by *Salmonella dublin*; it is also known as calf paratyphoid and in South Africa *S. dublin* has been recovered from 95 per cent. of calf paratyphoid infections. On post-mortem examination the abomasum, especially near the pylorus, is red and oedematous, and its mucous membrane is loosened and may easily be stripped off with a knife. The mucous membrane of the small intestine is bright red and covered with tenacious mucus, while the intestinal contents are yellow or dirty grey, foul smelling, and mixed with flakes of mucus, gas bubbles and sometimes blood. An extensive acute swelling of the spleen may sometimes be seen and also miliary necrosis of the liver ; macroscopic lesions of this type in the liver are not likely to be observed in calves less than 14 days old but have been recorded in very young calves. The disease is associated with anaemia and emaciation and, being septicaemic in nature, the carcase must be condemned.

Haemorrhagic enteritis may be classified as a form of scour, of which the commonest form is white scour caused by *E. coli*. The colour of the faeces in white scour is due to the presence of purulent matter in the intestinal contents and the diminution in the secretion of bile. It is an affection which shows its greatest incidence in calves born from January to April, and as it is associated with great debility and emaciation the carcase should be condemned.

6. Septicaemia of the New-born Animal. Septic omphalophlebitis or navel ill, particularly in calves and pigs, is most frequently caused by the common pyogenic organisms, though at times by bacteria of the salmonella group. The infection is acquired shortly after birth and is usually of umbilical origin, the umbilicus being hard and swollen with infiltrated borders, while a sero-sanguineous or purulent fluid can be expressed from it. A large abscess may sometimes be found situated in the abdominal wall near the umbilicus, or abscesses may be seen in the substance of the liver. The umbilical vein is in places filled with blood clot which is partially or completely transformed into a dirty red, foul-smelling mass, and if the inflammation has extended to the peritoneum, adhesions may be found between the intestine, omentum and liver.

Simultaneously with infection of the umbilicus and umbilical vessels there may be observed a serous and occasionally a purulent inflammation of the joints. This arthritis occurs particularly in the knee, stifle, or hock joints, the synovial membrane being red and swollen and the synovial fluid thick, yellow or reddish, with the appearance of a hen's egg which has been mixed. The surrounding tissue of the joint is serously infiltrated, and icterus of the carcase may sometimes be observed. Such carcases are totally unfit for food.

7. Septic Wounds and Injuries, particularly of the joints or digits, predispose animals of all ages to septicaemia, and septic lesions of this nature call for a detailed post-mortem examination of the carcase and organs. In Western Germany no carcase found to be affected in any degree with one of the aforementioned conditions may be released for food until a bacteriological examination has been made of the carcase and organs.

Recognition of the Septicaemic Carcase

It is a characteristic of septicaemia in the food animals that though the ante-mortem symptoms are striking and excite suspicion immediately, the post-mortem changes are not nearly so obvious, particularly in cases of early slaughter when the carcase may show little but imperfect bleeding and a moderate degree of icterus. Of the lesions mentioned below, one or several may be absent, and judgment of septicaemia must be based on the sum total of the macroscopic changes presented by the carcase and organs.

The following symptoms and lesions are associated with cases of septicaemia in the food animals :

1. High fever is invariably present in the living animal, with a temperature up to 106° F. or 107° F. ; the carcase as a result is congested, bleeds badly, and rigor mortis is but slight or absent. Septicaemic carcases not infrequently show signs of icterus and therefore present a sickly, lemon-white appearance which is particularly apparent on the fat or serous membranes.

2. Petechial haemorrhages may be seen in the myocardium, liver or kidney cortex (Fig. 57), and in the serous membranes, particularly those covering the heart and lungs. More extensive effusions of blood may sometimes be seen in these serous membranes, and also in the omentum and mesentery.

3. The lymph nodes are enlarged, oedematous and may show isolated haemorrhages. In septicaemia caused by anthrax in the pig there may be a marked peritoneal effusion and haemorrhagic infiltrations in the neighbourhood of the mesenteric lymph nodes.

4. The liver, heart and kidneys show evidence of cloudy swelling, which, if the septicaemia has extended over several days, may be succeeded by pathological fatty change. In the early stages of septicaemia the liver is enlarged, its edges rounded and its capsule tense, but after 2 to 5 days the organ becomes smaller and the cut surface presents dark red portions alternating with those of a yellow colour, or it may be uniformly clay-coloured. The heart muscle is affected unevenly with cloudy swelling, parts being normal and other parts of a greyish-white colour, while the kidneys are pale, soft in consistency and enlarged, and the kidney capsule is easily stripped off. The spleen may be enlarged and of soft consistency with rounded borders, these splenic changes being particularly well manifested in the septicaemias of bovine anthrax and acute swine erysipelas, and in *S. enteritidis* infection in calves. In chronic salmonellosis in cattle a valuable diagnostic lesion is a thickening of the wall of the gall bladder.

5. Blood-stained serous exudates may be seen in the thoracic and abdominal cavities, and the rapid disintegration of the red blood corpuscles may frequently give rise to blood-staining of the intima of the large blood vessels.

6. The meat retains a permanent alkalinity and is soft, dark in colour, at times possessing a sweetish repugnant odour which is associated with the presence of acetone and may be accentuated by the use of the boiling test.

FIG. 137.—Petechial haemorrhages in ox kidney, from a case of septicaemia.

These changes may not be observed in animals which have undergone early slaughter.

Judgment. Septicaemic carcases are unfit for human food for two reasons : (*a*) the condition may be associated with entry of pathogenic organisms into the systemic circulation, and consumption of the meat of such animals is therefore dangerous ; (*b*) the congestion of the carcase as a result of pyrexia and imperfect bleeding, together with the alkalinity of the meat, so impair its keeping quality as to render it definitely unmarketable. In doubtful cases it is wise to detain the carcase for 24 hours, and to estimate the degree of congestion and setting at the end of that period. Accurate judgment of suspected carcases coming within the definition of " border line " can be made only if a bacteriological examination is carried out to determine whether or not salmonellae or other harmful bacteria are present, but an estimation of the hydrogen-ion concentration of the meat may also be of value, while evidence of imperfect bleeding may be deduced by subjecting portions of the meat to the haemoglobin-pseudoperoxidase test, the haemoglobin extraction test, or the Malachite green test. Where such tests are impracticable, the benefit of doubt in the judgment of a carcase showing lesions suggestive of septicaemia must in every case be given to the consumer, and the carcase should be condemned. The judgment of young calves suffering from any form of illness should always err on the side of safety.

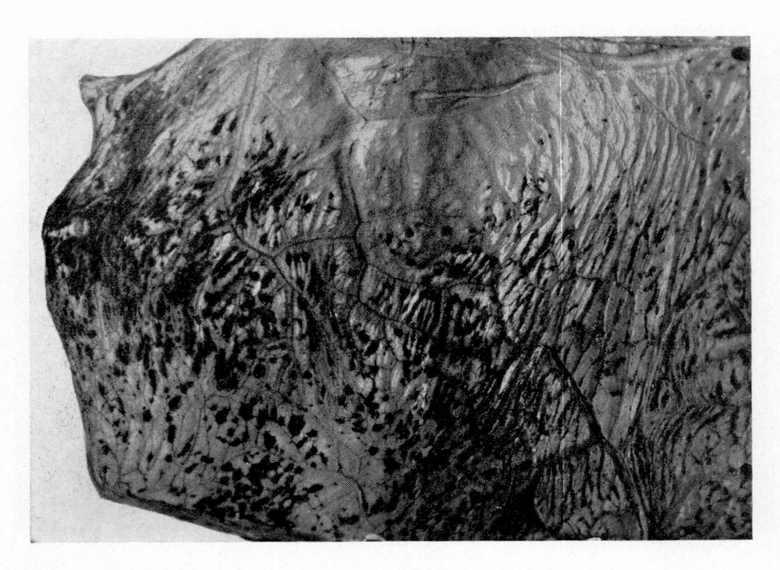

FIG. 138.—Extensive haemorrhagic effusions in omentum of calf, from a case of septicaemia.

The Regulations governing Federal meat inspection in the United States prescribe that all carcases of animals so infected that consumption of the products thereof may give rise to food poisoning shall be condemned. This includes all carcases showing signs of:

(1) Acute inflammation of the lungs, pleura, pericardium, peritoneum or meninges.

(2) Septicaemia or pyaemia, whether puerperal, traumatic or without any evident cause.

(3) Gangrenous or severe haemorrhagic enteritis or gastritis.

(4) Acute diffuse metritis or mammitis.

(5) Phlebitis of the umbilical veins.

(6) Septic or purulent traumatic pericarditis.

(7) Any acute inflammation, abscess or suppurating sore, if associated with acute nephritis, fatty and degenerated liver, swollen soft spleen, marked pulmonary hyperaemia, general swelling of lymph glands, diffuse

redness of the skin, cachexia, icteric discoloration of the carcase, or the like, either singly or in combination.

PYAEMIA

If pyogenic bacteria gain access to the blood stream from some suppurative focus they may result in the production of a thrombus, portions of which may be detached in the form of septic emboli. These may be carried by the blood stream until their further progress is arrested, resulting in the formation of metastatic abscesses in various parts of the body and the production of a condition known as pyaemia. Streptococci and staphylococci are the commonest of the pyogenic bacteria associated with pyaemia, but it may also be associated with organisms of the salmonella group.

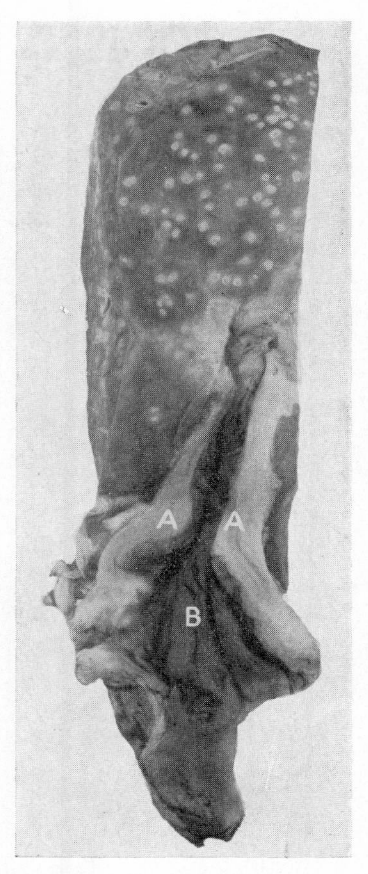

FIG. 139.—Portion of calf liver showing metastatic abscesses in a case of umbilical pyaemia. At (A, A) can be seen the thickened walls of the umbilical vein which contains (B), a semi-putrid blood clot from which septic emboli have become detached and have lodged in the liver parenchyma. From the anatomical relationship of the umbilical and portal veins to the hepatic circulation, liver abscesses of umbilical origin are usually located in the left lobe of the liver.

Pyaemia may be recognized in the live animal by the high fever, constitutional disturbance, and the presence of an area of local suppuration. In young animals this primary septic focus may be found in the umbilical vein; in older animals it may be found in the uterus or within the horn of the hoof, and should the infection be a particularly virulent one, it may cause the animal's death. In the pig, tail sores, septic infection of the feet, infected castration wounds and pig bites, the latter usually about the shoulder, are common causes of abscess formation and pyaemia, and pig carcases so affected should always be split and search made for secondary abscess formation. Post-mortem findings show an extension from the area of local suppuration to form haemorrhagic infarcts, which may be seen in the liver, kidneys or spleen and are the result of the arrest of septic emboli in the blood stream; the area of infarction rapidly becomes purulent, and similar metastatic abscesses may be seen in the joints. The presence of infarcts is often associated with an ulcerative endocarditis (Fig. 74), and the detection of wedge-shaped necrotic areas or metastatic abscesses in liver, kidneys or spleen calls for an examination of the heart cavities and valves.

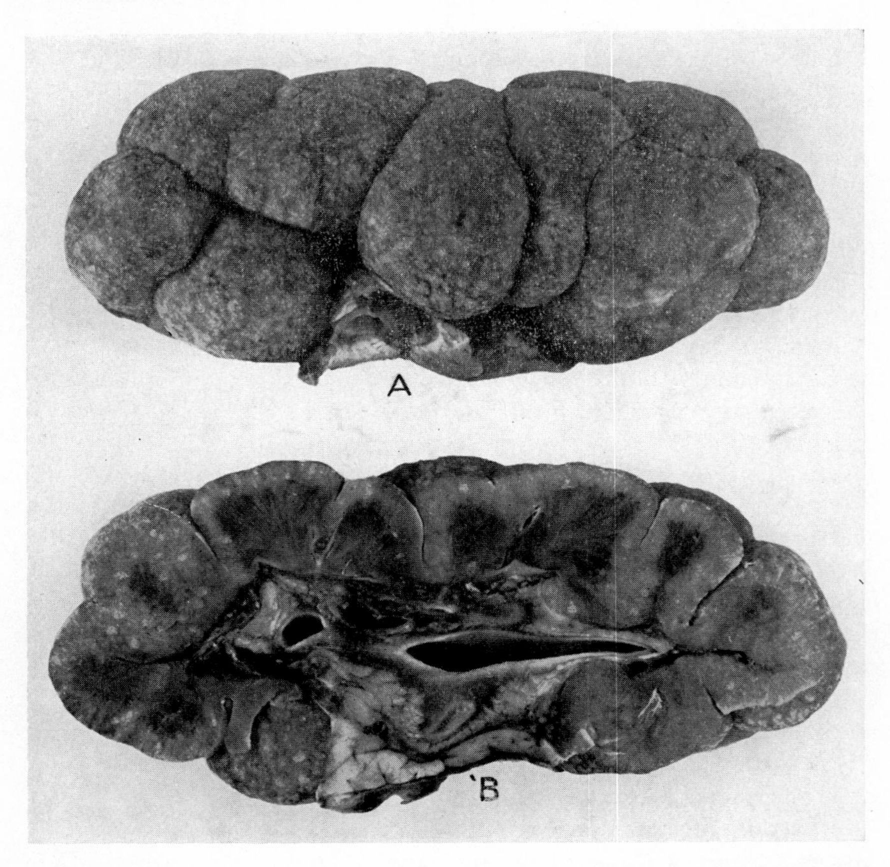

FIG. 140.—Kidney of one month old calf showing multiple abscess formation, the result of umbilical pyaemia. (A) surface of kidney; (B) section of organ, with numerous abscesses in the superficial and deep cortex.

An acute pyaemic infection exhibits the typical lesions associated with septicaemia, together with multiple abscesses. It may occur in the cow after parturition, usually arising by thrombosis of the uterine veins secondary to a septic metritis, and is manifested in the live animal by a hot, swollen and painful condition of the joints, particularly of the fetlock, hock and stifle. This state usually terminates fatally, post-mortem examination showing the formation of secondary abscesses in various parts of the body.

Pyaemia may also result in cattle if sharp foreign bodies of reticular origin penetrate the myocardium and introduce infection into a heart cavity. Infection of the new-born animal by way of the umbilicus may assume the septicaemic form (p. 315), or it may be seen as a pyaemia associated

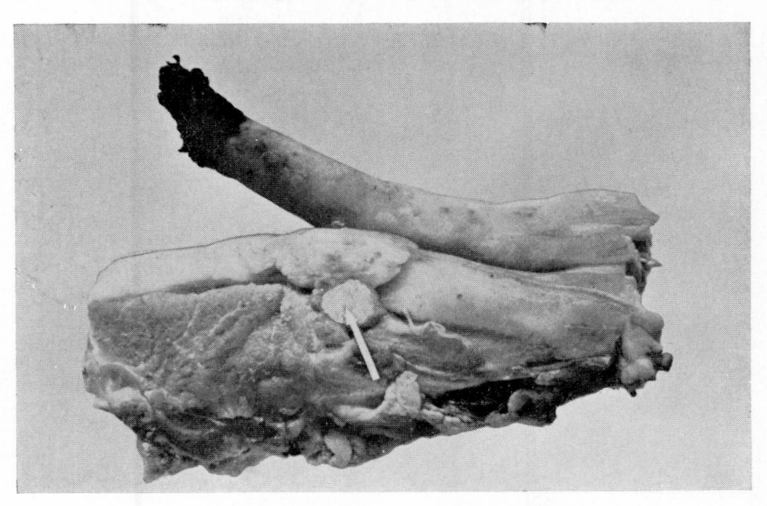

FIG. 141.—Necrosis of tip of pig tail. This may be caused by bites or may be a sequela to swine erysipelas and not infrequently leads to pyaemic abscesses in the lungs and elsewhere. It is a requirement in Denmark that when necrosis of the tail is encountered in slaughtered pigs the carcase shall be split and the ischiatic lymph node, if present, incised. The arrow indicates the site of a secondary abscess in the sacral region.

with multiple abscess formation. Pyaemia and ulcerative endocarditis are often associated with a haemorrhagic or purulent osteomyelitis, which is a suppurative condition of the bone marrow in which the marrow becomes yellow or chocolate-coloured and finally of a fluid and purulent nature.

Judgment. In acute cases of pyaemia, no matter what the cause, the carcase must be condemned. Care, however, must be taken to distinguish acute pyaemia from an old-standing chronic affection, for not uncommonly an animal recovers from pyaemia, the reparative process being manifested by encapsulation of the abscesses in white fibrous tissue. In chronic pyaemia, where the constitutional disturbance has subsided, and where the joints are not involved and the abscesses encapsulated in fibrous tissue, a bacteriological examination may warrant a more favourable judgment on the carcase.

CHAPTER VIII

PARASITIC DISEASES OF THE FOOD ANIMALS

Nematodes.

Ascaris—Roundworms of Stomach and Intestine in Sheep and Cattle—Stomach Worm Disease of Swine—Pimply Gut in Cattle and Sheep—Kidney Worm of Pigs—Thorny-headed Worm of Pigs—Lung Worms of Cattle, Sheep and Pigs—Onchocerciasis—Trichinosis.

Cestodes.

TAPEWORMS OF OX, SHEEP AND GOAT.
Moniezia expansa—*Moniezia benedeni*—*Thysanosoma actinoides*.
TAPEWORMS OF THE DOG.
Taenia pisiformis—*Taenia serialis*—*Taenia hydatigena*—*Taenia ovis*—*Taenia multiceps*—*Echinococcus granulosus* and hydatid disease.
TAPEWORMS OF MAN.
Taenia solium—*Taenia saginata*—*Diphyllobothrium latum*.

Trematodes.

Fasciola hepatica—*Dicrocoelium dendriticum*—Schistosomiasis in cattle and sheep.

Protozoa.

COCCIDIA.
SARCOSPORIDIA.
HAEMOSPORIDIA.
Redwater Fever.
Anaplasmosis

Arthropoda.

Ox Warble Flies—Horse Bot Fly—Sheep Nostril Fly—Sheep Maggot Fly—Contamination of Meat by Insect Larvae—*Linguatula rhinaria*.

A parasite may be defined as an organism which lives on another organism described as the host, derives nutriment from it, and confers no advantage in return. Though parasitic worms are responsible for a certain number of deaths in food animals, in many cases their deleterious effects are more insidious and lead to debility and digestive or respiratory disturbances, with retardation of growth and loss of condition, meat and wool. Parasitic worms, except possibly in the case of cattle, are the greatest single adverse factor influencing animal husbandry.

Parasites may affect the animal host in various ways :

(*a*) By sucking blood. The anaemia caused by extensive *Haemonchus contortus* infection in sheep is an example of this.

(*b*) By robbing the host of food. This effect is not of great significance, for though intestinal parasites are harboured by all young animals, they cause little harm unless the infestation is heavy.

(*c*) By mechanical injury to the host's tissue. An example of this is seen in liver cirrhosis caused by *Fasciola hepatica*, or in severe infestation of the liver with hydatid cysts. Mechanical injury to tissues may also permit the entry of pathogenic bacteria, and occurs in black disease of sheep, an affection caused by a combined invasion of the liver by *Clostridium oedematiens* and young liver flukes.

(*d*) By continued absorption of toxic products. The systemic changes associated with chronic fascioliasis of the sheep are attributed by some authorities to the continued action of toxic products from the flukes and invading bacteria, together with the blood-sucking capacity of the adult parasites.

The most important parasites in meat inspection are those which are transmissible to man by consumption of the flesh of affected animals, while other parasites, though not transmissible to man, may render the flesh or organs repugnant and therefore unmarketable. Extensive muscular sarcosporidiosis in the food animals is an example of a condition which is not considered dangerous to man but renders the flesh repulsive and therefore dictates its condemnation.

The parasites of importance in meat inspection may be classified as follows : (1) Nematodes or roundworms ; (2) Cestodes or tapeworms ; (3) Trematodes or flukes ; (4) Protozoa or single-celled organisms ; and (5) Arthropoda or joint-footed animals, including flies and linguatula.

THE NEMATODES

Ascaris

These are large, smooth, elongated worms with a short head and three smooth lips arranged around the mouth. These worms are not blood-suckers, but live on the semi-digested foods in the small intestines, and though they do not injure the intestinal wall, their life history is completed by the migration of the larvae through the lung tissue of the host ; it is during this migration that the most serious effects on the host are likely to occur. When present in large numbers the adult worms may cause intestinal obstruction, and perforation of the bowel at its mesenteric attachment occasionally occurs in the pig followed by a fatal peritonitis ; in this animal the adult worms may also invade the bile ducts (Fig. 78) and produce icterus. The parasite is also capable of producing toxic substances, and ascaris of the calf and sheep is said to produce volatile fatty acids which may impart a peculiar odour to the carcase and organs.

The species of ascaris encountered in meat inspection are : (*a*) *Ascaris lumbricoides* (var. *suis*) which inhabits the small intestine of the pig, being yellowish-white in colour and 6 to 15 inches long. Young pigs are most highly susceptible and are therefore most often affected, and though older pigs develop a strong resistance to this parasite a few adult worms may remain in the intestine of sows and are the main cause of the spread of infection. Though this parasite is anatomically and sereologically indistinguishable from *A. lumbricoides* of man, cross-infection from pig to man or man to pig does not occur ; (*b*) *Ascaris ovis*, which is probably identical

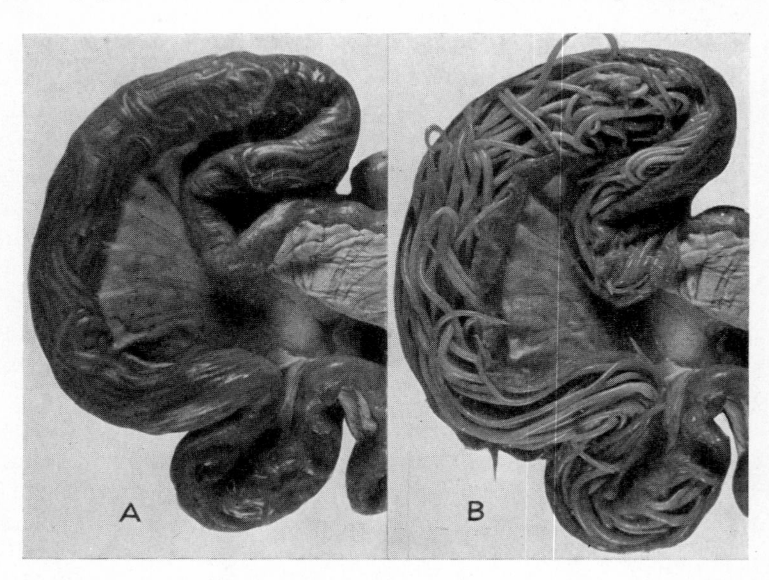

FIG. 142.—Extensive infestation of small intestine of pig with *Ascaris lumbricoides* (var. *suis*). (A) Unopened intestine ; (B) same intestine opened. The presence of the parasites in the intestine is frequently associated with a reddish slime and a distinctive odour on the wall of the intestine. (Dr. A. Jepsen.)

with *A. lumbricoides* (var. *suis*) and is found in the intestine of sheep but does not reach sexual maturity ; (*c*) *Neoascaris vitulorum*, which is translucent, reddish in colour, and inhabits the small intestine of the calf, but is rarely found in the adult ox. This parasite of young calves has a preference for tropical and sub-tropical areas and by producing unthriftiness is a serious economic problem in some countries ; (*d*) *Parascaris equorum*, which is found in the small intestine of the horse.

Life History. The sexes of *Ascaris lumbricoides* are separate, the female ascaris lying up to 1·4 million eggs daily. These eggs are excreted with the faeces but are not infective until they contain larvae, this stage being usually reached in 2 to 8 weeks, though under exceptionally favourable conditions it may occur in 10 days. Infection with this parasite is readily acquired if food is contaminated with faeces, and is therefore particularly likely to occur in the pig. Eggs in cultivated soil may remain viable for 4 or more years.

After ingestion of the egg by the host the outer envelope is digested by the intestinal juices, the larvae are freed and, penetrating the intestinal wall, are conveyed by the portal vein to the liver which they reach within 2 days of ingestion. Many larvae pass rapidly through the liver by forcing their way through the liver capillaries, but some are arrested and, by their irritation, give rise to areas of chronic focal interstitial hepatitis ;

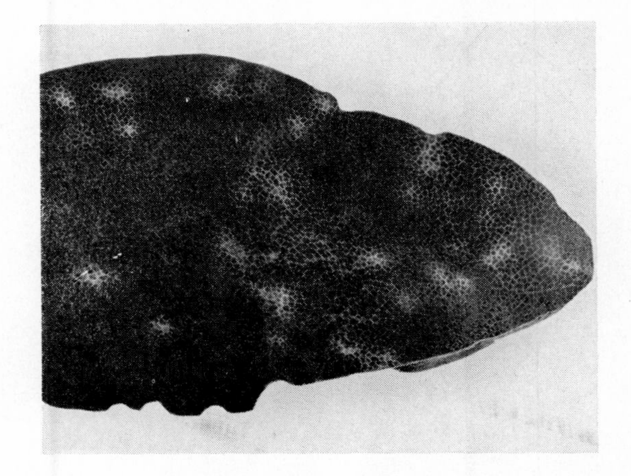

FIG. 143.—Lobe of pig liver, anterior surface, showing numerous milk spots caused by larvae of *Ascaris lumbricoides* (var. *suis*).

early lesions are haemorrhagic but later take the form of ill-defined, whitish foci in the substance and on the liver surface, and constitute the milk spots which are commonly seen in the liver of the pig.

Those larvae which pass through the liver enter the hepatic vein and posterior vena cava to reach the heart, and subsequently the lungs where they may be found as early as 3 days after ingestion. Some larvae may enter the arterial blood stream and lodge in kidneys and other organs where they give rise to haemorrhage and necrosis, but most of the larvae bore their way from the lung capillaries into the alveoli and are carried up the bronchi by the ciliated epithelium to the larynx, where they are swallowed ; they then proceed to develop into adult male and female worms within the small intestine, attaining sexual maturity in a few weeks. The total duration of this migration, from ingestion to finally reaching the small intestine, is about 14 days, and during this time the larvae grow from five to ten times their original length.

The passage of ascaris larvae through the lungs causes considerable systemic disturbance, which is an allergic reaction manifested by exudation with fever, cough, accelerated respirations and symptoms of pneumonia. The persistent cough and " pot-bellied " appearance of the sucking or newly-weaned pig is usually due to extensive ascaris infection, and when pigs of the same litter vary in size and condition ascaris infection during early life is the probable cause. The greatest harm is to pigs up to 4 to 5 months of age, and growth in animals which are moderately to heavily infested may be retarded to such an extent that they require 4 to 5 weeks longer to attain the desired weight than do pigs which are only lightly infested.

FIG. 144.—Two pigs from same litter and aged 5½ months ; the pig on the left is stunted due to severe ascaris infection. (R. Daubney.)

The incidence of virus pneumonia in pigs (Fig. 70) is ten times greater in animals in which ascaris larvae are migrating at the time of the virus infection than in pigs without ascaris larvae.

In the case of *Ascaris lumbricoides* of the pig and man the larvae follow the tracheal route described above and infection is acquired post-natally. On the other hand, the larvae of *Neoascaris vitulorum* follow the somatic route, passing through the intestinal wall of their host and thence distributed by the blood stream to the visceral organs and, via the placenta, to the foetal calf ; pre-natal infection appears to be the common method in the calf and post-natal infection would seem to be rare.

Judgment. There is little justification for condemnation of the intestines of animals which harbour ascaris. According to French authorities, the carcases of infested calves and sheep may be affected with a sickly or sour odour which does not disappear when the carcase is hung, and where such an odour is apparent after slaughter a period of 24 hours should be allowed to elapse and a boiling test then applied to a portion of the meat. In the absence of any abnormal odour, the carcase may be passed for food, but ascaris infection of the pig intestine does not appear to cause an abnormal odour of the flesh.

Roundworm Infestation of Stomach and Intestines in Sheep and Cattle

Extensive parasitic infection of the stomach and intestines is responsible for great economic loss amongst sheep and cattle, this being estimated in the United States at 110 million dollars yearly. Many of the cases of oedema and emaciation of sheep carcases encountered in meat inspection are probably due to this form of infestation, particularly when post-mortem examination rules out any evidence of fluke infestation of the liver or other obvious lesions of disease. Intestinal infection often coexists with infection by respiratory nematodes.

Roundworm Infestation in Sheep

The species of worms found in the abomasum are more pathogenic than those found in the small intestines, the most important being *Haemonchus contortus*, *Trichostrongylus axei* and *Ostertagia circumcincta*, of which the latter is the commonest species in Britain. *Haemonchus contortus* is the largest of the group, being 1 to 1¼ inches long, the thickness of an ordinary pin, and reddish in colour due to ingested blood.

Life History. A moderately infested sheep will excrete several million eggs daily, these developing into larvae under suitable conditions of warmth and reaching the infective stage in 1 to 3 weeks. Infective larvae, if situated in a moist, protected environment, may survive on pastures for upwards of 12 months, but larvae in exposed positions on grass have shorter lives and the great majority only survive 3 to 4 weeks. When the larvae are ingested they pass to the abomasum or small intestine of the sheep, where they become sexually mature in 2 to 4 weeks. Most adult animals carry a few worms and are therefore responsible for the continual reinfestation of pastures ; the effect of this is greatly increased under conditions of over-stocking, and the level of nutrition also has a marked effect on the resistance of lambs to roundworm infestation.

Pathogenesis. The adult worms bore into the gastric or intestinal mucous membrane and, in the case of *Haemonchus contortus*, suck blood from it; a moderate infestation of 3,000 worms depletes the animal of approximately one pint of blood per week. A further injurious factor in *H. contortus* infection is the continued bleeding from the points of puncture of the mucous membrane, and there are records in fat lambs and adult sheep of death occurring rapidly due to haemorrhage before the animals have had time to lose condition.

FIG. 145.—Suffolk sheep affected with emaciation due to parasitic gastro-enteritis. Note the oedematous swelling of the throat region. (G. H. Werts.)

Symptoms. The most consistent symptom is progressive loss of condition which may proceed to the stage of emaciation. Diarrhoea is usually seen in some or all of the animals of a flock, though it is not a constant symptom, and in some sheep severe infestation is accompanied by constipation. Anaemia and hydraemia usually develop and are manifested by paleness of the skin, conjunctiva and visible mucous membranes, while oedematous swellings may be seen in the dependent parts of the body, particularly under the lower jaw (Figs. 9, 176). Though the disease may run an acute course, the chronic form is much the commoner and is responsible for most of the poor thriving seen in lambs. Sheep, however, generally continue to feed until a very late stage of the disease.

ROUNDWORM INFESTATION IN CATTLE

As in sheep, the worms causing this condition are found in the abomasum and small intestine, those found in the abomasum being the more pathogenic. The most important are *Haemonchus contortus, Ostertagia ostertagi*, and *Trichostrongylus axei*. *Ostertagia ostertagi* produces small nodules in the mucous membrane of the abomasum, which are the size of a pinhead or slightly larger, and here the larvae spend the fourth stage of their development before returning to the lumen of the stomach. These parasites chiefly affect young animals, only exerting a pathological action when present in large numbers, and though calves are the most susceptible, young cattle of 15 months to 2 years of age are the most often affected. A predisposing factor is a low nutritional state occasioned by winter feeding on straw and turnips.

Post-mortem Findings in Cattle and Sheep. Sheep are the animals most likely to be consigned to a slaughterhouse as a result of parasitic gastro-enteritis, and the presence of emaciation, together with evidence that the animal has suffered from diarrhoea, is strongly suggestive of this condition. The abdominal fat is very scanty or has disappeared, the blood frequently appearing thin and watery, and the abdominal organs are generally paler in colour than normal. The mucous membrane of the abomasum may be inflamed, and a considerable quantity of blood is sometimes found in the stomach, while the mucous membrane, which may at times show small ulcers and punctiform haemorrhages, is covered with a thick layer of mucus. Scrapings from this layer compressed between two microscope slides will reveal the causal parasites, and the first 20 feet of the small intestine may at times show lesions of a subacute or chronic catarrh.

Judgment. All domesticated animals will be found to harbour worms of the digestive tract, and detection of these in the stomach and intestines does not justify condemnation of these organs, for the parasites are effectually removed in the preparation of the stomach for tripe and the intestines for sausage casings. The judgment of the carcases of animals affected with severe roundworm intestinal infestation depends on the degree of anaemia, oedema and emaciation.

Stomach Worm Disease of Swine

This affection is caused by *Hyostrongylus rubidus*, a small, filiform red worm, $\frac{1}{6}$ to $\frac{1}{3}$ inch long, and very common in pigs in Great Britain, Germany and North and South America. Stomach worm disease is manifested by a catarrhal or diphtheritic inflammation of the gastric mucous membrane, the pyloric portion showing mucoid, or sometimes dry, adherent deposits which are up to $1\frac{1}{2}$ inches in size and surrounded by a bright red zone of mucous membrane ; the reddish or brown-coloured worms may be seen in or beneath these areas.

The disease runs a chronic course, and severely affected young animals may show evidence of anaemia. Affected stomachs should be condemned.

Pimply Gut in Cattle and Sheep

This is also termed nodular intestinal worm disease, and is caused by parasites belonging to the genus *Oesophagostomum*. The condition is encountered in the ox, sheep and pig, and occurs in Europe, America, South Africa and Australia. *Oesophagostomum radiatum* causes pimply gut in the small intestine, caecum, and colon of cattle, being frequently encountered in Great Britain, whilst it is stated that nearly 50 per cent. of cattle casings in the United States are destroyed on account of this condition. *Oesophagostomum columbianum* is the cause of pimply gut in sheep, and though found in America and Australia, does not occur in Britain.

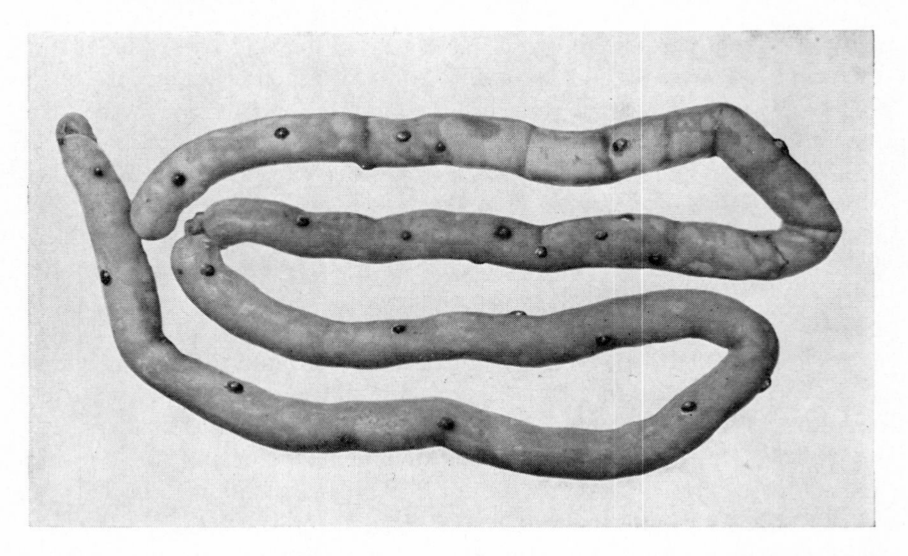

FIG. 146.—Small intestine of ox (everted) showing lesions of pimply gut caused by *Oesophagostomum radiatum*.

Oesophagostomum venulosum is common in the colon, more rarely in the small intestine of sheep and goats in Britain, but it does not give rise to intestinal lesions of a nodular form.

The intestinal lesions in pimply gut may be few in number or numerous, and a case has been recorded in the ox in which the small intestine was estimated to contain 4,000 nodules, while 1,000 were present in the caecum. The nodules vary in size from a pin-head to a pea, being greyish-white in colour and causing distinct elevations of the intestinal mucous membrane. A larva, $\frac{1}{10}$ to $\frac{1}{4}$ inch in length, may be found in the younger nodules, but the older nodules are filled with a cheesy or caseous matter which is greenish in colour.

Life History. Under favourable conditions of temperature and moisture the excreted eggs hatch within 24 hours, and the larvae, if ingested by the host, penetrate into the intestinal wall and eventually return to the lumen of the intestine where they attain sexual maturity. Those larvae which do not return give rise to the typical nodule formation.

Judgment. The intestines of the food animals are the main source of sausage casings, and bovine or sheep intestines affected with pimply gut are unfit for this purpose and should be condemned. In imported sausage casings the affection is usually removed during the scraping and cleaning process.

The Kidney Worm of Pigs

This parasite does not occur in Britain, being only found in countries with moist, warm climates such as Madagascar, Indo-China, Australia, the southern parts of the United States, and South America. The affection is now very common in Australia, where it constitutes a serious problem and it is stated that 62 to 84 per cent. of pigs in exporting districts are unfit for export due to this affection, and that 11 per cent. of slaughtered pigs are totally condemned as unfit for human consumption. In the southern parts of the United States the parasite is responsible for a loss of nearly 40 cents per head due to condemnations of livers, kidneys, kidney fat and loin trimmings in slaughtered pigs and in that country the loss due to condemnations of organs and parts is estimated at half a million dollars yearly. In Venezuela nearly 100 per cent. of pigs reared in the inland plains are affected with kidney worm disease, while in Costa Rica 80 per cent. of pig livers condemned are destroyed on account of this affection as also are a high proportion of the kidneys.

The adult parasite, *Stephanurus dentatus*, is a cylindrical worm $\frac{7}{8}$ to $1\frac{1}{2}$ inches in length, bluish or reddish in colour and possessing a mouth armed with bicuspid teeth. Pigs become infected through the skin or from the ingestion of living larvae, which are either swallowed with water or penetrate the mucous membrane of the mouth and are then distributed by the blood or lymph stream. The larvae are carried to the liver, where they remain for about 2 months and give rise to cirrhosis of the organ with the production of irregular areas of interstitial inflammation which resemble the milk spots caused by larvae of *Ascaris lumbricoides* (var. *suis*). At times the liver lesions may be as large as a haricot bean, each lesion containing one parasite, whilst the parasites may occasionally be found in the lungs or spleen, but sexual maturity is only attained by those worms which reach the perirenal fat, and worms in other situations cannot complete their life cycle. From the liver parenchyma the larvae migrate to the surface of the organ, bore through its capsule to enter the peritoneal cavity, and a large proportion of larvae reach the perirenal fat or the tissue around the ureters. In the latter location the larvae are found in small cysts which communicate with the ureter, and here the larvae attain sexual maturity, eggs being excreted by the host during urination.

On superficial examination of the ureters, or of the fat surrounding the kidneys, the adipose tissue appears thickened and distended, particularly on the left side, and palpation of this tissue reveals the presence of hard cord-like masses. Section of the fat shows the presence of numerous nodular cysts, which are about $\frac{1}{2}$ inch in diameter with viscid, greenish-contents and usually containing one female and one male parasite, but occasionally four or five. The ureters are thickened or may even be obliterated, and exposure of the mucous membrane shows numerous small tumours which possess a small orifice into which a probe can be inserted. In advanced cases the fat around the kidneys or ureters is honeycombed with numerous chambers which contain a creamy, greenish-coloured fluid and numerous parasites. Obliteration of the ureters may result in hydronephrosis, with conversion of the kidneys into fibrous sacs distended with urine, and in the walls of these sacs may be several purulent cysts containing adult worms.

Judgment. It is necessary to remove the affected tissues completely, and in bilateral hydronephrosis causing oedema or emaciation, or in severe cachexia due to extensive hepatic lesions, the carcase must be condemned. The effect of the parasite on the general health and condition of an animal may be so great that infected carcases can be detected by their appearance, which is less pleasing and leaner than that of normal pigs.

The Thorny-Headed Worm of Pigs

This parasite, *Macracanthorynchus hirudinaceus*, which is found in the small intestine of the pig, has been occasionally reported in man and occurs in Europe, North and South America and Australia, though there are no definite records of its presence in Britain. Superficially the parasite resembles ascaris, being a thick, cylindrical white worm, but it increases in width towards its anterior end, at which is situate a thorny proboscis possessing five or six circular rows of backwardly curving hooks. There is no intestinal canal, and food is absorbed direct through the body surface.

Life Cycle. The eggs of the adult worm are excreted and, if ingested by the larvae of various beetles, they hatch in the bodies of these larvae. The larval beetle then turns to a pupal stage and, later, into a mature beetle, the encysted worm larvae remaining unharmed within it. If the adult beetle is ingested by a pig the worm larvae are freed and become sexually mature in the pigs' intestine.

Lesions. The parasite attaches itself to the small intestine, boring its head deep in the mucous membrane by means of its proboscis, and giving rise to yellow foci of suppuration which are visible through the serous coat of the intestines and may be confused with lesions of tuberculosis. Perforation of the intestinal wall may even occur and give rise to peritonitis, while occasionally the parasite is found in the pelvis of the kidney.

Judgment. Infested intestines are unfit for use as sausage casings and should be condemned. Dropsy and emaciation of the carcase may also occur and necessitates total condemnation.

Lung Worms of Cattle, Sheep and Pigs

The roundworms affecting the respiratory tract of the food animals are numerous, some being responsible for serious epidemics of bronchitis and broncho-pneumonia. The affection in cattle is chiefly seen in young growing animals and is a disease of summer and autumn months.

The nematodes responsible for lung affections are all long, thin, smooth threadlike worms. The only lung worm of the bovine is *Dictyocaulus viviparus*, which is found in the calf and is responsible for the condition known as husk or hoose. The lung worms of sheep are : (*a*) *Dictyocaulus filaria*, which is a common parasite and responsible for severe outbreaks of hoose with extensive losses among lambs ; (*b*) *Protostrongylus rufescens*, which is the rarest of the three species of lung worms found in sheep in Britain ; and (*c*) *Muellerius capillaris*, which is probably the most commonly occurring lung worm of sheep, though its pathogenic action is slight ; the nodules and patches which are found in the lungs of large numbers of healthy sheep slaughtered for food are the result of *Muellerius* infection.

The lung worms of the pig are *Metastrongylus elongatus* (*M. apri*) and *Metastrongylus pudendotectus*, both of these parasites occurring in Britain, though the former is the commoner. The surface of affected pigs' lungs shows the presence of elevated, flat areas, which have a mother-of-pearl lustre and are commonest at the base of the lung. These areas are patches of chronic alveolar emphysema, prominent because of their pallor and large volume, and are caused by the fact that strong inspiratory effort permits air to enter the partly constricted bronchi but expiratory effort is too weak to expel the air and there is thus an increase in the intrapulmonary air-content. Foci of a nodular type may sometimes be seen in the lung substance or beneath the visceral pleura.

Pathogenesis. The adult lung worms inhabit the bronchioles and, together with their eggs and larvae, give rise to a catarrhal bronchitis.

Parasitic bronchitis of the sheep is usually due to the presence of *Dictyocaulus filaria*, and in nearly all cases a broncho-pneumonia is associated with it. On the other hand, the commonest lung lesions due to parasitic infection in the sheep are associated with the presence of *Muellerius capillaris*, which gives rise to infiltration of some lung lobules with an inflammatory exudate, this being manifested on the lung surface by pithy patches which correspond to the bifurcation of the finer bronchial

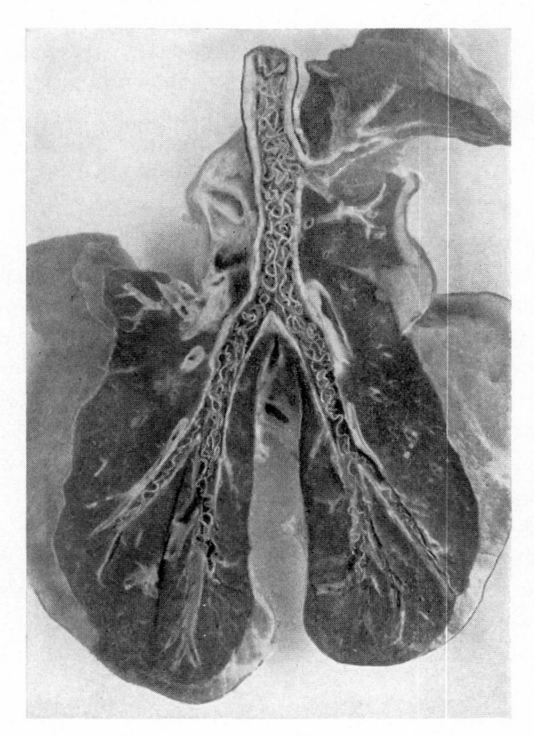

FIG. 147.—Lungs of a sheep affected with hoose. Numerous specimens of *Dictyocaulus filaria* are present in the trachea and bronchi. (Crown copyright.)

tubes ; these patches are greenish-grey due to the presence of eosinophils and contain eggs, larvae and adult worms. Numerous shot-like foci, which are the size of a millet seed to a pea and yellow or reddish-brown in colour, are also associated with these lobular infiltrations, though they occur at a later stage and are found chiefly on the surface of the lungs, especially at the lung margins. These foci, which are situated just beneath the pleura and are more or less confluent, eventually become caseous and finally calcareous, and contain the adult parasite which, having invaded the lung tissue from the bronchi, has died and become encapsulated. Part of the life history of *Muellerius capillaris* may take place in varieties of land snails and it is assumed that sheep become infected by ingesting the snails during grazing.

Post-mortem examination of animals affected with severe parasitic bronchitis will reveal general emaciation, the blood being thin and scanty with a serous effusion into the peritoneal and thoracic cavities. Section of the trachea and bronchial tubes shows a frothy exudate containing worms, and these may be so numerous as to obstruct the medium-sized and larger bronchi. The bronchial mucous membrane is oedematous and may show haemorrhagic streaks, together with areas of patchy pneumonia, while the edges of the lungs may present solid patches caused by infiltration of the inflammatory exudate into the alveoli.

Judgment. Few adult sheep, even when well nourished, are free from lung lesions due to *Muellerius capillaris*, and it has little deleterious effect on the animal's health. Sheep lungs, however, are an ingredient of white puddings, and extensively infested lungs should therefore be destroyed. Carcases which are oedematous or emaciated as a result of parasitic bronchitis should be condemned.

Onchocerciasis

This parasitic affection is caused by *Onchocerca gibsoni* and occurs in cattle in Australia, particularly in Queensland and New South Wales, while it has also been recorded in New Zealand and in the United States.

Onchocerciasis is essentially an infection involving connective tissue, and is manifested by typical nodules which are generally found in the region of the brisket or stifle. The condition was at one time of economic importance in Australia, for it necessitates removal of the brisket and plate before forequarters of beef, then known as Australian crops, are exported to Britain but losses due to onchocerciasis are now of little significance.

The male parasite is 1½ inches long and the female 36 inches long, but the length of the latter can only be estimated with difficulty as it is impossible to extricate the worm intact from the nodules ; it is a characteristic of the parasite that it shows a spiral thickening of the body, whereas nearly all nematodes show a faint transverse striation. The developmental cycle involves a biting midge, *Culicoides pungens*, the worm embryos being ingested by the fly and developing therein until they are almost adult ; they are then transmitted by the biting action of the fly to another bovine host.

Lesions. The worm nodules are found in the brisket, in the ligaments at the junction of ribs and costal cartilages, between the second and tenth ribs, and on the external aspect of the stifle joint. In the early stages affected ligaments appear thickened and dotted with haemorrhagic spots, which become caseous or calcareous and at times resemble lesions of tuberculosis. At a later stage the parasite becomes encased in yellow tumours which are the size of a pigeon's egg or larger, and consist of an outer wall of white fibrous tissue with a centre composed of a soft, spongy network in which one or two specimens of *O. gibsoni* are intimately entangled. These tumours may be flattened or of irregular shape, and are found in

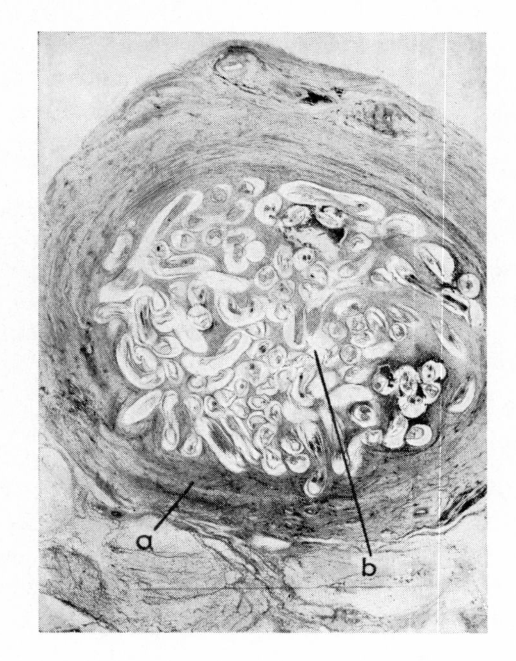

FIG. 148.—Section through an onchocerca nodule showing (*a*) fibrous capsule and (*b*) central spongy portion with sections of the parasite in many of the reticular spaces. × 3.

the subcutaneous connective tissue or in the connective tissue between muscles, but they never involve the muscular tissue itself. Lesions which are markedly fibrous generally contain numerous larvae, but nodules in which the connective tissue reaction is slight are usually sterile; the central spongy area, however, shows but little variation in diameter, even in nodules of different size.

In Australian meat inspection it is the practice to incise the superficial fascia on the lateral aspect of the stifle joint, a hook and thin-bladed knife being then inserted to remove as much as possible of the connective tissue and tendons on the outer aspect of the joint. The cavity is then palpated to ensure that all nodules have been removed and the incision closed by a metal pin, this being removed after the carcase has been chilled.

Judgment. The parasite probably only remains alive for a few hours after the slaughter of the host, nor can the infection be transmitted to man, but affected tissues are unmarketable and must be removed and condemned. In Australia, briskets and plates removed from forequarters

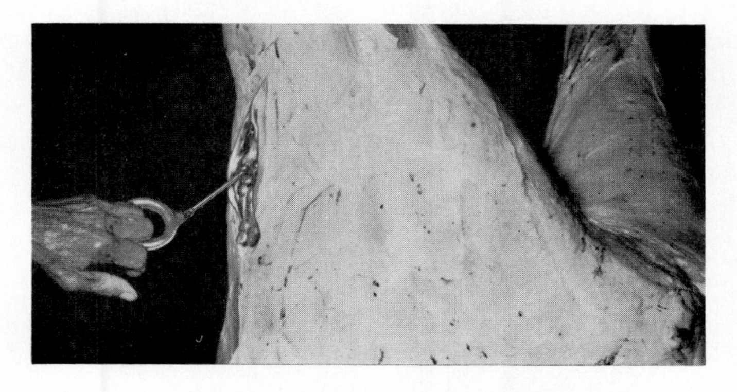

FIG. 149.—Examination for onchocerciasis in an Australian abattoir. An incision has been made into the lateral aspect of the stifle joint and a hook inserted, the tissues then being removed by means of a thin-bladed knife.

of beef prior to export of the latter to Britain are examined by incisions into the inter-muscular connective tissue and, if found free from nodules, are utilized locally for canning. Removal of the brisket and plate is not considered necessary where the beef is intended for the Eastern trade.

Trichinosis

This affection is caused by *Trichinella spiralis*, a small worm which in the adult form lives in the intestine of mammals, and in the larval form in the muscular tissue of the same host. The sexes of this parasite are distinct, the male being $\frac{1}{16}$ inch, the female about $\frac{1}{8}$ inch in length. It does not suck blood from the intestinal wall, for the mouth is round and unarmed, and though the preliminary symptoms in man may be that of an enteritis, the first symptoms usually observable are associated with the invasion of his muscular tissue by the embryo worms.

Trichinella spiralis is found in the intestine and muscular tissue of the pig, rat, mouse, dog, bear, wild boar, man, and other mammals. Though the parasite is essentially one of temperate climates it has been reported from almost every species of animal in the far north. In Africa it has not been recovered from domestic pigs south of the Sahara, but in East Africa it occurs in a number of wild carnivores including the leopard, jackal and hyaena. In Germany trichinosis in foxes is widespread and is regarded as more common than the affection in pigs, but in Britain it is probable that the rat is the mammal in which the highest incidence of trichinosis occurs. Cattle, sheep, and horses possess a certain degree of natural immunity to this parasitic infection, for if trichinosed meat is fed to these animals the adult worms develop in the intestines, but only rarely are larvae found in the muscles and then in small numbers. Similarly, birds harbour the intestinal form of trichinella after artificial infection, but larvae are only occasionally found in the muscles and are usually degenerated. Cattle, sheep, horses and birds therefore play no part in the spread of the disease, and the principal hosts for *Trichinella spiralis* are undoubtedly the pig, man and rat.

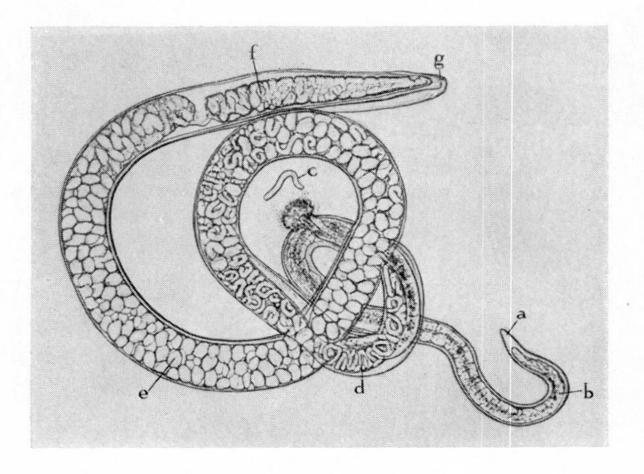

FIG. 150.—Adult female *Trichinella spiralis*. (*a*) Oral opening, (*b*) oesophagus, (*c*) new-born larva just expelled from vulva, (*d*) larvae in anterior portion of uterus, (*e*) fertilized and developing ova, (*f*) ovary, (*g*) rectum. × 100. (Dr. S. E. Gould.)

Life History. Adult trichinellae are only found in the small intestines, usually the ileum, of mammals which have recently eaten trichinosed flesh. When such flesh is eaten the larvae are liberated from their cysts by the action of the gastric juice, develop into sexually mature adults in the intestine, and copulate within a period of 2 days. The males die shortly after copulation, so that although the sexes are at first equal in number, within a fortnight of infection the parasites present are nearly all females The females have a duration of life of some 5 to 6 weeks, and penetrate the mucous membrane of the intestine *via* the crypts of Lieberkühn to reach the lymph spaces, where they give birth to 1,350 to 1,500 larvae. The larvae at this stage are $\frac{1}{250}$ inch in length and enter the mesenteric lymph stream to reach the systemic circulation by way of the thoracic duct.

The dissemination of larvae throughout the body is an arterial one, and where animals are artificially infected the embryos can be demonstrated in the blood of the heart, arteries, and capillaries, though they are unlikely to be encountered in the veins, for they become arrested in their passage through the muscle capillaries. The embryos show a predilection for striped muscular tissue, especially muscles poor in glycogen, and penetrate the walls of the capillaries, partly in a passive manner and partly by a boring action, to reach the surrounding connective tissue. They enter the sarcolemma which surrounds each muscle fibre, and may be observed penetrating this membrane 7 to 8 days after infected meat is ingested. At this stage the larvae are actively motile and have undergone no increase in size, but after entering the sarcolemma they become quiescent, commence to grow, and about 14 days after infection have increased from four to eight times their original size and then curl up within the muscle fibre in a typical spiral coil. It is from this characteristic coiled formation that the parasite derives its name, and in about 3 weeks the embryos are $\frac{1}{25}$ inch long and growth then ceases. In addition to dilating the sarcolemmal sheath of the muscle fibre, the embryo causes the muscle fibre to lose its typical cross-striation, the fibre degenerating to form a granular mass, while the muscle nuclei increase in number and in size.

Two months after infection the irritation set up by the presence of the embryo gives rise to a tissue reaction, and the embryo becomes enclosed in a muscle cyst which is lemon-shaped in form with its long axis parallel to the muscle fibres. The cyst is fully formed at 3 months, the capsule being about $\frac{1}{50}$ inch long by $\frac{1}{100}$ inch wide and composed of a structureless, hyaline material which is at first translucent. Cysts are not readily detected until 2 to 3 months have elapsed and they are not obvious until 6 to 8 months later. The poles of the cysts now become infiltrated with fat droplets, while at a later stage there is a deposition of lime salts, which involves both the cyst and the body of the parasite. Calcification in the pig may start five months after infection and be complete in nine months but the parasite may remain viable if the process of calcification does not involve the actual worm, and calcified trichinellae have been known to remain alive in man for 31 years, and in pigs for 12 years. Encapsulation is a necessity if the parasite is to survive within muscular tissue, and living larvae have regularly been recovered from cysts which have undergone calcification.

Location of Trichinella Cysts. By far the greatest number of cysts are found in striped muscle tissue, and though larvae have been found in the heart muscle, liver and stomach of artificially infected pigs, the numbers found in these organs are very small. Sites of predilection vary with the species of host. In pigs the skeletal muscles particularly liable to invasion are those concerned with respiration and are, in order of frequency, the

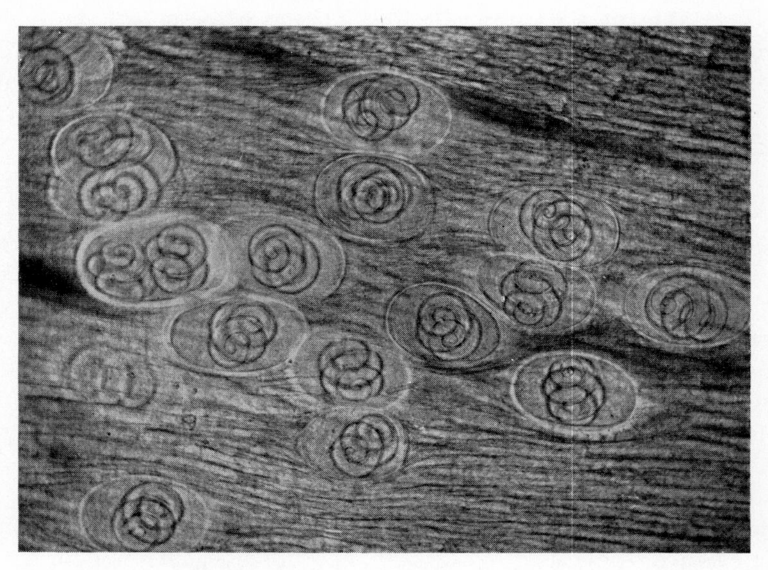

FIG. 151.—*Trichinella spiralis* cysts in skeletal muscle of rat. The cysts are about 3 months old, and calcification, which begins at the poles, has not yet commenced. One of the cysts to the middle-left of the illustration contains two parasites, though this is uncommon. × 45. (Crown copyright.)

pillars of the diaphragm (thick skirt), the costal portion of the diaphragm, the muscles of the tongue and larynx, and the abdominal and intercostal muscles. The frequency of infestation of these muscles is probably due to the fact that they are in constant activity and therefore receive an abundant supply of arterial blood, whilst the larvae are found in greatest numbers near the tendons and beneath the sarcolemmal muscular sheath, as it is here that the muscle offers its greatest resistance to their passage through the capillaries.

Methods of Infection. The pig is the only one of the common food animals which acquires a natural infection of muscular trichinosis from eating trichinosed flesh, and trichinosis in man is usually acquired by consumption of the flesh of this animal. Cattle, sheep and horses, being herbivorous animals and also somewhat resistant to the development of muscle trichinellae, play no part in the spread of the disease.

It is frequently stated that trichinosis in pigs is commonly acquired by the eating of infected rats. Though a pig may be readily infected should it eat a dead rat harbouring muscle trichinellae, this is not considered to be a common occurrence and the concept that the rat plays an important part in the epidemiology of the disease is largely discounted. A question of importance, however, is whether the pig can become infected by the eating of food contaminated with the excreta of trichinosed rats or mice. The faeces of these rodents can be infective, particularly in the first 24 hours after they have eaten trichinosed flesh, when cysts and larvae may pass undigested through the intestine.

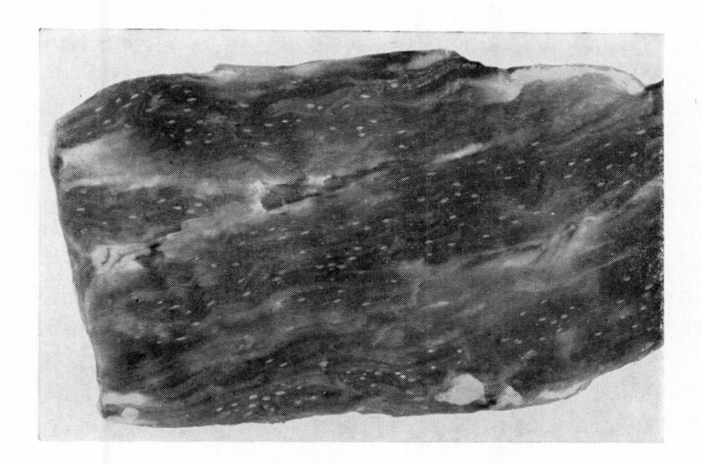

FIG. 152.—Trichinosis of muscle of pig. The trichinellae have become encapsulated and the cysts have undergone well marked calcification.

The more probable method by which pigs become infected with trichinosis has been elucidated by observations in America on the relationship between the incidence of the disease in pigs and the method by which they are fed. The investigation showed that (*a*) in pigs fed in woods and fields only 0·5 per cent. were infected; (*b*) pigs fed on grain but also receiving garbage and scraps from the farm kitchen showed an incidence of 1·0 to 1·5 per cent. of trichinosis; (*c*) pigs fed on uncooked swill showed an incidence of 4·5 to 5·0 per cent.; while (*d*) pigs fed on slaughterhouse offal showed the highest incidence, which varied between 10 and 20 per cent. According to United States authorities, not only is the incidence of trichinosis in swill-fed pigs more than six times greater than in pigs fed largely on grain, but the intensity of infection in swill-fed pigs is also much greater.

Trichinosis in the pig is therefore most likely acquired from the flesh of another pig, and it is considered that the usual method by which a pig becomes infected is through feeding on raw or unboiled garbage containing scraps of trichinosed pork or bacon which are either raw or insufficiently cooked. The rat probably acquires the infection from a similar source, and it has been shown in the United States that the heaviest infection in these rodents occurs around abattoirs, where rats have ready access to meat scraps and offals; infection may then be transmitted from rat to rat by cannibalism.

Though the outbreaks which have occurred in Britain in recent years are of public health significance, there is no evidence that any heavy infestation exists in the pig population. In Western Germany the incidence of the disease in pigs is decreasing and in 1965 only nine cases were recorded out of 18·4 million pigs slaughtered. In Denmark the parasite has not been recorded in Danish carcases since 1928.

PREVENTION OF TRICHINOSIS IN MAN AND ANIMALS. As the common method by which pig or man become infected with trichinosis is by consumption of infected pig flesh, measures directed towards lowering the incidence of the affection must either be based on ensuring (*A*) that pig flesh is trichinosis-free before it is released for sale; or (*B*) that all pig flesh and products containing pork are rendered safe before consumption.

(*A*) Naked-eye examination of carcases of pork cannot be regarded as a reliable method for the detection of trichinosis, because although cysts are just visible once they have undergone calcification, this change does not occur until after 8 months, often not until a year.

Routine laboratory examination of muscle from pig carcases was therefore instituted in some European countries with the aim of ensuring a trichinella-free product. The original method was by microscopical examination of portions of flesh the size of an oat grain, the material being obtained from the tendinous insertions of the pillars and costal portion of the diaphragm, the tongue and the pharyngo-laryngeal muscles; this muscular tissue was then compressed between two glass slides and examined under a magnification of 30 to 40. In Germany this method does not permit of examination of more than 45 pigs by one technician daily, and larger abattoirs now use a projection lantern or trichinoscope, specimens being obtained from the pillars of the diaphragm only and examined under a magnification of 70 to 80; using this technique the operator can examine 75 pigs per day. The prescribed technique under Federal German Regulations is to examine two specimens of muscular tissue from the pillars of the diaphragm, each specimen being the size of a hazel-nut and divided into seven portions each the size of an oat grain. The 14 specimens are then compressed between two glass slides, the degree of compression being such that ordinary newspaper print can be read through it. The examination of the 14 specimens shall occupy not less than 8 minutes and particular attention must be paid to the periphery of the preparation as larvae as yet unencapsulated may be found there as a result of the compression. In assessing whether or not trichinosis exists in a country believed to be free of the disease it is recommended that muscle specimens be obtained from older pigs, i.e. boars and sows. Routine examination of all slaughtered pigs has been compulsory in Germany since the last century, while in

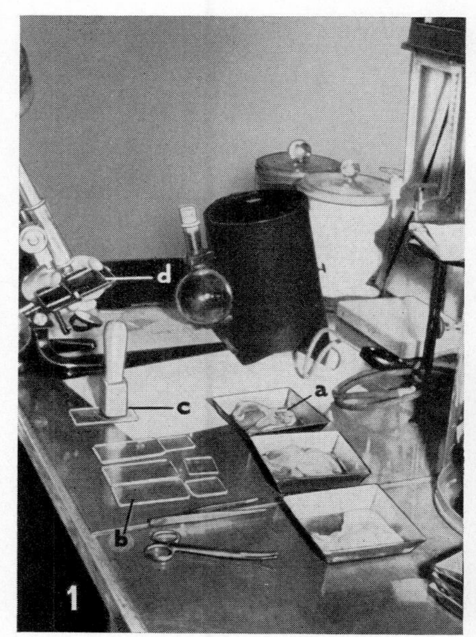

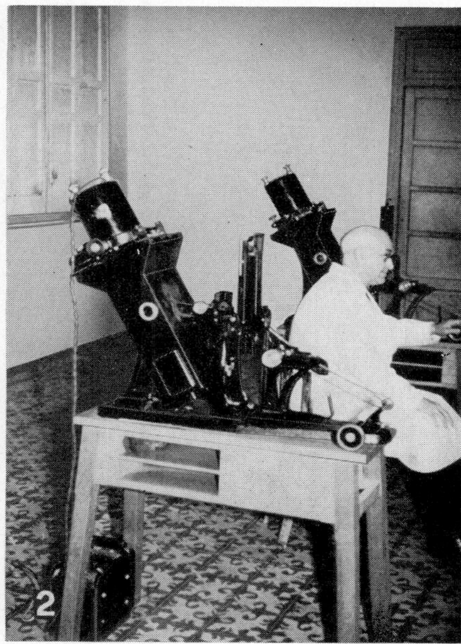

FIG. 153.—Trichina examination. 1. Examination of pig muscle in a small abattoir in Sweden. (*a*) Portions of diaphragm ; (*b*) slides between which specimens are placed, and (*c*) compressed ; (*d*) examination of specimen by microscope. 2. Examination by means of trichinoscope, Madrid abattoir.

Denmark it is compulsory in the case of sows and boars and in all carcases of pork weighing more than 220 lb. A useful laboratory method now employed in the United States and elsewhere for the detection of trichinella cysts in muscle consists in digesting the meat in artificial gastric juice, the parasites being then concentrated by chilling and centrifuging the solution.

The failure to find trichinella cysts by any of the above methods cannot be regarded as a definite guarantee that the meat is free from trichinosis, and in America it was estimated that in pigs whose diaphragms were microscopically examined by the Bureau of Animal Industry between 1898 and 1906, approximately one animal in seventy-five whose flesh was not found to contain trichinellae did actually contain the parasites, and these probably in sufficient quantity to cause clinical disease in human beings. Routine microscopical examination of pork was discontinued in the United

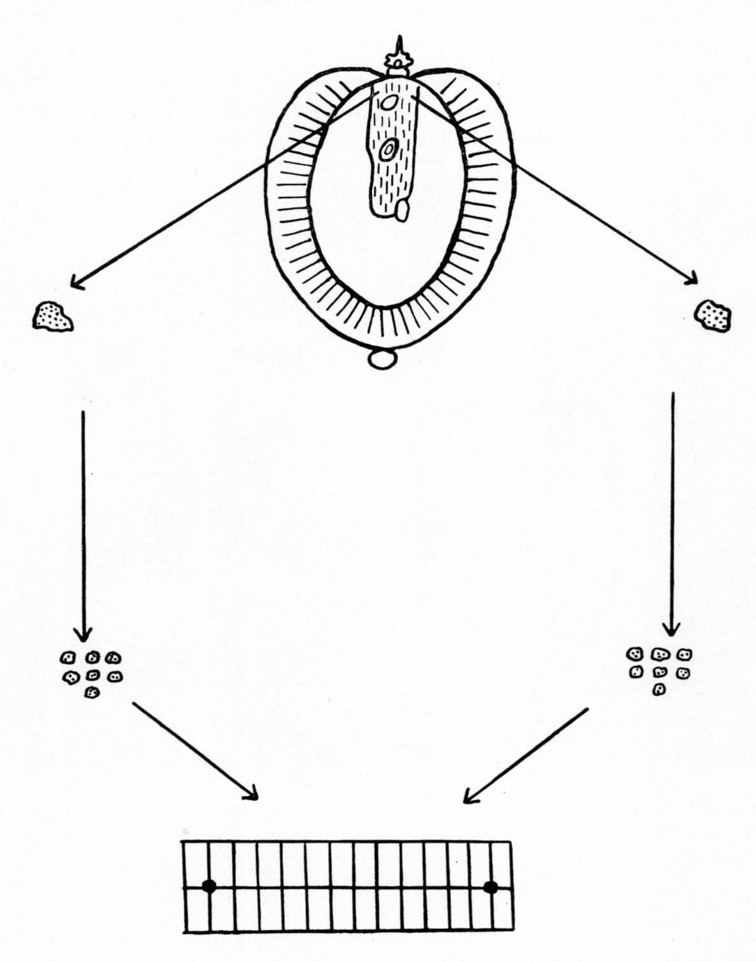

FIG. 154.—Technique for the obtaining of specimens of muscle from the crura of the diaphragm of pigs for trichina examination.

States after 1906, for it is deemed impracticable under high-speed American packing-house methods, while it is estimated that such an examination, costing 25 cents per pig, would require an annual expenditure of 5 million dollars over and above that already expended on Federal meat inspection. Though the technique for trichinella detection has been considerably improved within the last 40 years, there is at the present time no known practical adequate method for the inspection of pork, and the microscopical examination of portions of muscles from pig carcases, being a method which is inherently imperfect, may lend a false sense of security to persons addicted to eating raw pork and its products and thus defeat the very purpose for which the inspection was intended.

(*B*) Pig flesh which contains trichinella cysts or which, from the known incidence of the disease in any particular country, is likely to be infected, may be rendered safe for consumption either by refrigeration, by heating to a high temperature, or by salting. The holding of pork carcases at a temperature of 5° F. for 20 days will destroy all trichinella cysts effectively, though it is an unreliable method if the portions of pork or pork products are more than 6 inches thick; at a lower temperature of 0° F. pork and pork products are rendered safe in 24 hours. Thicker pieces of pork require a longer period of freezing before they are rendered safe, and it has been shown that if a barrel of meat at 32° F. be placed in a refrigerator maintained at 5° F., it requires some 7 days before the centre of the barrel is at the same temperature as that of the refrigerator.

Destruction of trichinella cysts in meat can be ensured by ordinary cooking or adequate frying, for the albumen of the parasite is coagulated if the temperature reaches 137° F. It is, however, essential that this temperature be attained at the centre of the meat, as it has been shown that cooking a 15 lb. ham in water maintained at 180° F. requires 2½ hours to raise the temperature at the centre of the ham from 78° F. to 137° F., and 3½ hours to raise the temperature from 46° F. to 137° F. Large hams which are not cooked for a sufficient time are therefore particularly dangerous, and an approximate guide as to the period necessary to destroy trichinella cysts by cooking is that large thick cuts of pork should be boiled for 30 minutes for every pound of their weight. The process should continue until the pork is no longer red, but white at both the centre and near the surface, for if pink in colour it has not been sufficiently cooked, and pork which has not been sufficiently cooked should not be eaten. The temperature necessary for the killing of the parasite may not always be obtained when sausages are fried, and it is safer to cut the sausages in half and to cook the halves thoroughly.

Salting, smoking and drying of meat may also be employed for the destruction of trichinella cysts. The lethal effect of curing is related to the desiccating properties of the salt, but it is a process which is only efficacious if the penetration of salt into the meat is complete, and live trichinellae have been found in meat pickled in brine for 2 months. A period of curing for 40 days at not less than 36° F., followed by smoking at 113° F. for 10 days, is necessary to destroy the cysts with certainty, while they can remain viable in decomposed meat for 2 to 3 months.

Other methods recommended for the control of the disease are the intradermal testing of pigs for trichinosis by a technique similar to that employed in the intradermal testing of cattle for tuberculosis, or by the irradiation of pork by high voltage X-rays. These methods, as yet, have assumed no practical significance, but there is evidence that exposure of carcases for a few minutes to gamma irradiation on their way to the chill room may be a practical means of controlling trichinosis, for the cost is estimated at not more than 0·25 cents per pound.

In the United States, where 80 per cent. of the pork produced is slaughtered at plants operating under Federal meat inspection, legislation requiring the cooking of garbage that is to be used as feed for pigs has been enacted in all 50 of the States. The boiling of swill containing meat scraps has also been compulsory in Britain since 1927 and in Canada since 1915, and this process not only renders the foodstuff more palatable and useful for pigs, but is also an important factor in controlling the incidence of human and porcine trichinosis and, in addition, fowl pest, swine fever and foot and mouth disease.

The measures which may be adopted to lower or limit the incidence of trichinosis in animals and man are:

(*a*) Swill or meat scraps should be thoroughly boiled before being fed to pigs.

(*b*) Meat foods which may contain trichinella cysts, and particularly pork or sausage, should be thoroughly cooked before being eaten by man, while in countries where the incidence of trichinosis in pigs is high the seriousness of the problem may justify treatment by refrigeration or other means of all pork and pork products usually eaten without cooking, before these are released for sale. Low temperature treatment, required in the United States for certain commercial products, demands a temperature not higher than 5° F. for 20 days. Alternatively, all parts of meat should be heated to a temperature of 137° F., and both these procedures may be practised by the housewife at home, in the former case by deep freezing for 20 days, and in the latter by cooking of pork until no trace of pink remains.

Differential Diagnosis. Calcified trichinella cysts are most likely to be confused with muscular sarcosporidia (*Sarcocystis miescheriana*), the latter being the commonest form of calcification occurring in the muscles of the pig. Sarcosporidial cysts, however, are more often visible to the naked eye, the capsule is composed of connective tissue fibres, calcification of the cyst takes place irregularly, finally extending to the poles, while the transverse striation of affected muscle fibres remains intact.

Calcareous concretions due to *Cysticercus cellulosae* in pork are invariably larger than trichinellae, lying between the muscle fibres and not within them, and microscopical examination will demonstrate the calcareous corpuscles and characteristic hooklets (Fig. 166).

Masses of tyrosin crystals sometimes seen in hams, either smoked or unsmoked, may resemble trichinellae, but there is no capsule formation, their crystalline nature can be demonstrated microscopically, and the crystals are readily soluble in acids or alkalies.

Trichinosis in Man

The evidence of *Trichinella spiralis* in the animal population of a country does not necessarily indicate that human infections occur at a similar level. There have been three outbreaks in Great Britain in man in recent years and an overall incidence of approximately 10 per cent. of infected cadavers reported in various cities such as Birmingham, Wolverhampton, Bristol and Cambridge. In the United States it is considered that the present human adult infection rate is 4 per cent. or less compared with the figure of 15 to 20 per cent. 25 years ago. In some South American States the human incidence reaches over 12 per cent. in the cities, in parts of Europe 11 per cent., and in Hawaii 7 per cent. In Africa, Australia and Asia, with the exception of Lebanon, Syria and certain districts in India, the incidence is negligible and the low incidence in the tropics, subtropics and in Moslem countries is due to the fact that pork and pork products are less frequently eaten.

The earliest symptoms in man may be those of diarrhoea and abdominal pain, and are associated with the adult worms penetrating the intestinal mucosa. The second stage, which occurs some 9 days after infected flesh has been eaten, corresponds to the migration of the larvae into the blood stream and is manifested by symptoms simulating influenza or typhoid fever, and, at a later date, by pains which resemble rheumatism. These symptoms are caused by the toxic products of those embryos which lodge in tissues or organs other than muscle and as a result are rapidly disintegrated by the action of leucocytes and connective tissue cells. The larvae may give rise to a myocarditis or a fatal encephalitis, about 5 per cent. of the human cases proving fatal, and it is beyond doubt that this parasite is the most dangerous nematode which infects man.

The seriousness of an attack of human trichinosis depends on the number of parasites consumed, their stage of development, and how the meat was prepared. The chances of a severe infection are greatest when a whole pig, as in home-cured bacon and ham, is consumed by a few persons over a fairly prolonged period, and clinical cases of trichinosis are almost always traceable to locally slaughtered pork which is eaten uncooked. The incidence of clinical trichinosis is generally higher during the winter when large quantities of these foods tend to be consumed, and in one outbreak in the United States it was found that a single animal eaten by 71 persons produced clinical symptoms in 56 of these persons with serious illness in 26 and two deaths. In the United States the significant reduction in prevalence, mortality and severity of trichinosis over the last 25 years is attributed to the legislative measures regarding heat treatment of garbage used in swine feeds, increased consumption of ready-to-eat pork products, and education of the public in the necessity for the proper cooking of pork.

FIG. 155.—*Trichinella spiralis* in human muscle showing calcification of cyst wall. Some of the adjacent muscle fibres are degenerating and have lost their typical cross-striation. × 240. (Dr. J. F. Brailsford.)

Judgment. Although the fat and internal organs, as distinct from the musculature, do not contain trichinellae, the entire carcase is dangerous and should be condemned. In the case of countries exporting pork to Britain, the latter country prescribes that a special examination of pork carcases for trichinosis shall be carried out, except when it can be established that there has been no case of trichinosis in the exporting country during the preceding three years.

THE CESTODES

A characteristic of the cestodes or tapeworms is that their parasitic tendencies have become so developed that they have lost all trace of an alimentary canal, and obtain their nourishment by absorption of the partly digested food of the host through their integument. Tapeworms vary very considerably in size, from $\frac{1}{4}$ inch in the case of *Echinococcus granulosus* to 30 feet in the case of *Diphyllobothrium latum.*

The adult tapeworm possesses a head or scolex, followed by a number of segments which vary from three to many hundreds. The scolex is modified to fasten the parasite to the wall of the intestine, generally the small intestine, and for this purpose it is usually provided with four circular suckers, but in certain tapeworms, as *Diphyllobothrium*, the scolex is provided with two elongated grooves known as bothria. Hooks or hooklets are present on the head of some species of tapeworms, which are then said to be armed, but most of the tapeworms found in the herbivorous animals are unarmed. In the armed tapeworms the hooklets are usually situated centrally to the suckers around a contractile organ known as the rostellum, and the shape, size and distribution of these hooklets form a useful guide in the differentiation of the various species of worm.

The head is followed by a neck which consists of young segments, these anterior segments being immature, the centre segments mature and both wider and larger, while the posterior segments are gravid and consist largely of fertile ripe eggs. Each segment contains both male and female generative organs, the male organs consisting of a number of testes, united by ducts, leading to the vas deferens, together with a seminal vesicle and a cirrus (penis). The female organs consist of vagina, uterus, oviduct and ovaries, the ducts of both male and female organs opening at a common genital pore which is usually situated at the lateral margin of the segment. After fertilization the ovum develops into a hexacanth embryo with six hooklets, acquires two enveloping layers and becomes an onchosphere. The ripe segments are excreted from the intestine either singly or in small groups, and although the actual segments can survive for only a few days, the ova contained within them are more resistant; under favourable conditions the ova of *Taenia saginata* can survive on pastures for 6 months, while the ova of *Echinococcus granulosus* may remain viable for over 1 year and can resist temperatures as low as 32° F. for 4 months.

Tapeworm ova require an intermediate host to complete their life cycle; when ingested by the host the hexacanth embryos are liberated, penetrate the gut wall by means of their hooklets, and are carried, usually by the blood or lymph stream, to reach a suitable part of the body for further development. Having reached a suitable position, described as a predilection site, they form a cyst or bladder worm which is the immature form of the tapeworm.

Tapeworm cysts in the food animals and man may be encountered in three forms :

(*a*) The cysticercus cyst which possesses an outer membrane enclosing a single scolex and a varying amount of fluid ; when ingested this cyst can give rise to only one tapeworm.

(*b*) The multiceps cyst (coenurus) which consists of a single cavity containing several scolices ; each of these scolices, when ingested, can give rise to an adult tapeworm.

(*c*) The echinococcus or hydatid cyst which contains brood capsules, inside of which scolices occur. The hydatid cyst may or may not contain daughter cysts which are identical in all respects to the mother cyst.

The presence of numerous tapeworms in the intestine may exert a deleterious effect on the host due to appropriation of nourishment, but such effects are rarely severe, and adult tapeworms in animals or man usually cause little more than inconvenience. Armed tapeworms, however, may give rise to inflammation of the mucous membrane of their host, the pathogenic effects being in direct relation to the number of tapeworms present. The importance of tapeworms in animals is that when the tapeworm ova are voided they may give rise to cysts in a suitable host, and such cysts may be injurious or fatal to man as in the case of hydatid disease, or injurious or fatal to animals as in *Multiceps multiceps* infection in sheep.

Tapeworms of the Ox, Sheep and Goat

The commonest tapeworm of ruminants in Britain, and the commonest tapeworm of sheep in Australia, is *Moniezia expansa*, though *Moniezia*

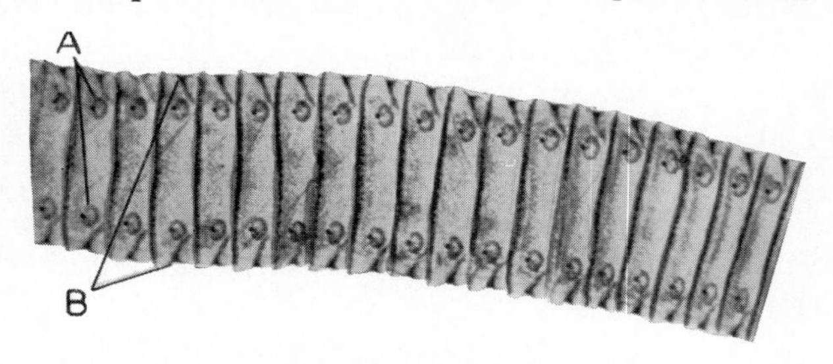

FIG. 156.—Mature segments of *Moniezia expansa*. Each segment contains (A) two sets of reproductive organs ; and (B) two genital pores. × 2.

benedeni is occasionally found. The former has a small head, with four prominent suckers, and may attain a length of 15 feet. In some districts in Canada 40 to 50 per cent. of sheep are found to be infested with *Moniezia expansa* and *Thysanosoma actinoides*, the latter being frequently found in the bile ducts and liver and the cause of considerable loss due to condemnation of affected livers. In certain parts of Africa *Stilesia hepatica* is very common in the bile ducts of sheep and goats and is likewise responsible for considerable losses due to liver condemnations.

The gravid segments of moniezia are passed out on to the pasture, and from them the ova escape. These are ingested by certain free-living mites of the genus *Galumna*, which are of common occurrence in herbage, and the intermediate stage of the tapeworm, known as a cysticercoid, develops within these mites ; the ox, sheep or goat becomes infested by the ingestion of mites carrying cysticercoids. The effects of moniezia on both cattle and sheep are generally considered slight and these parasites are therefore of but little importance in meat inspection, but occasional enzoötics do occur and give rise to anaemia, listlessness, loss of wool, diarrhoea and eventual emaciation.

Tapeworm of the Dog

These form a most important group from the point of view of meat inspection, and the dog also plays an all-important rôle in the occurrence of human hydatid disease. The tapeworms of the dog which are of importance in meat inspection are six in number.

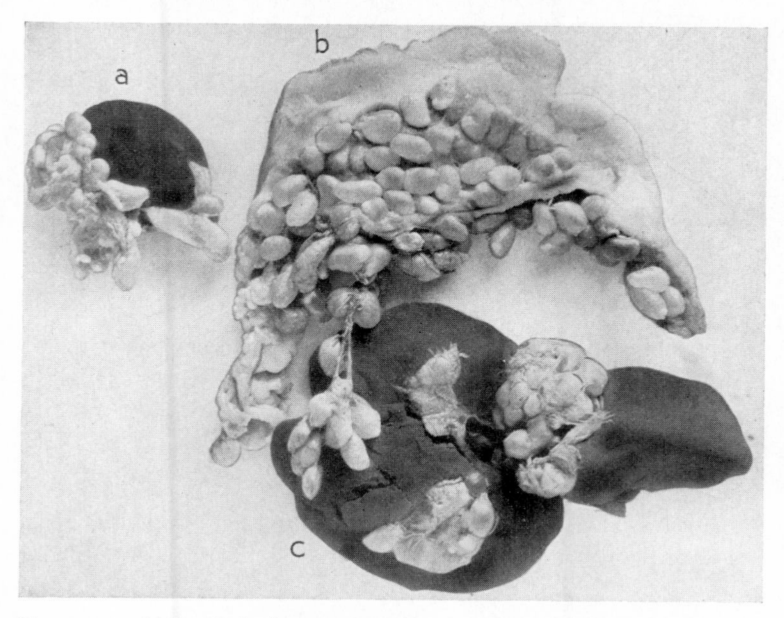

FIG. 157.—Abdominal viscera of rabbit showing subserous distribution of cysts of *Cysticercus pisiformis* in (*a*) kidney ; (*b*) omentum ; (*c*) liver.

1. Taenia pisiformis

Formerly known as *Taenia serrata*, this tapeworm is common in sporting dogs and is 2 to 7 feet in length, possessing a small head with four suckers and a crown of 34 to 48 hooklets. The segments are about 4,000 in number, the posterior border of the ripe segments being broader than the anterior and giving the worm a somewhat serrated appearance. This tapeworm is also found in the fox and other wild carnivores, and on rare occasions may occur in the cat.

Cystic Stage. This is known as *Cysticercus pisiformis*, the cyst being elliptical in shape, usually little larger than a pea and found in the hare, rabbit and, more rarely, the mouse. The cysts may be seen in the peritoneal cavity, occasionally free in this cavity but usually within the layers of omentum or mesentery, or beneath the serous capsule of the liver or kidneys. Only a few cysts are generally present, though in some cases

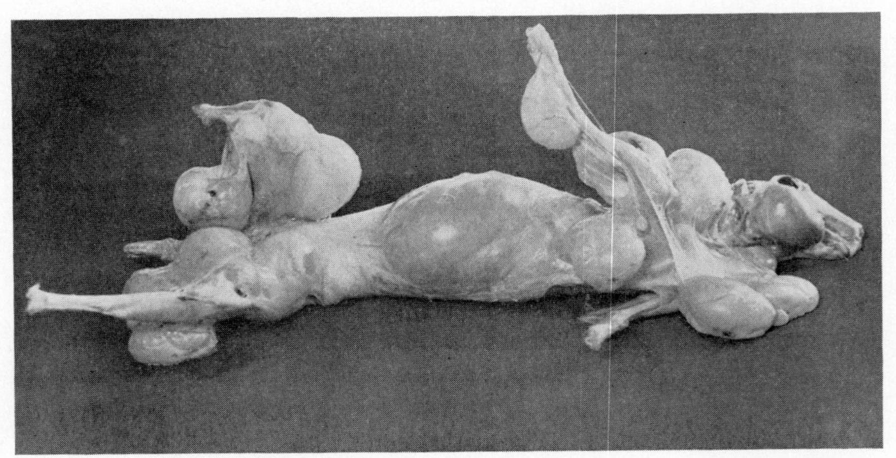

Fig. 158.—Rabbit extensively affected with *Multiceps serialis* cysts. See also Fig. 225. (Crown copyright.)

they are numerous, and when removed from the animal resemble a bunch of grapes. Affected hares and rabbits may be thinner than normal, but the cysts are not found in the musculature and only the affected tissues and organs need usually be condemned.

2. Taenia serialis

This worm is 8 to 30 inches long, is common in sporting dogs, and possesses a rather prominent rostellum with a double row of 26 to 32 hooks. It also occurs in the fox.

Cystic Stage. This is known as *Multiceps serialis* (*Coenurus serialis*), and occurs most commonly in the rabbit, the cysts after 45 days being as large as cherries and showing the first signs of scolex formation; the affection is also seen occasionally in the hare and squirrel. The usual seat for these cysts is the intermuscular and subcutaneous tissue of the back, loin, and hind limbs, but they may be found in other parts of the body, and not infrequently involve the external muscles of mastication where they give rise to a prominent swelling at the angle of the jaw.

The subcutaneous swellings caused by *Multiceps serialis* are obvious in the skinned or unskinned rabbit, and rabbit catchers and dealers at times puncture these cysts deliberately to mask the condition. In inspecting the animals with the skin on, the hand should be carefully drawn from head to tail, when the unpunctured cysts can be felt as fluctuating elevations, whilst punctured cysts will be evident by a depression in the muscle due to pressure atrophy. When the cysts are few in number the affected portion of the carcase may be removed and the remainder passed for food, but if the cysts are numerous the entire carcase should be condemned.

3. Taenia hydatigena

Known also as *Taenia marginata*, this tapeworm is 2½ to 17 feet in length and is the largest of the dog tapeworms. It is common in butcher's dogs and possesses four round suckers and a double row of 26 to 44 hooklets. The segments number about 400, the more posterior and sexually mature being oblong in shape.

Cystic Stage. This is termed *Cysticercus tenuicollis*, and is found in the ox, sheep, goat, pig and in wild ruminants. The cyst is one of the largest of the cysticerci, with a diameter of up to 3 inches, while the neck, as the name denotes, is very long and thin. After the ova are ingested the embryos pass through the intestinal wall, enter the portal vein and are borne to various structures, particularly the omentum, mesentery and liver. The cysts are situated subserously in these tissues and cause slight projection of the serous membrane, but although they increase the protusion of the membrane as they develop they always remain covered by it.

Development from ovum to bladder worm stage occurs in 5 to 6 weeks, and the cysts may therefore be encountered during the inspection of calves, sucking pigs or lambs. The soft consistency of the liver in these young animals offers but little resistance to the migrating parasite, which bores through the liver substance to reach the surface of the organ. Marked changes indicating the passage of the embryos may therefore be seen in the liver substance, particularly near the thin edge of the organ, and take the form of long serpentine tracts in the liver or on its surface, these tracts being at first dark red, but later of a brownish or green colour and giving rise finally to irregular areas of scar tissue. Those parasites which fail to reach the surface of the liver remain in the substance of this organ, but do not attain a greater size than a pea and rapidly degenerate. Severe infestation in the young pig may occasionally give rise to extensive peritonitis or death from acute haemorrhagic hepatitis.

Differential Diagnosis. *Cysticercus tenuicollis* in the ox may occasionally be mistaken for *Cysticercus bovis*, or in the pig for *Cysticercus cellulosae*. *Cysticercus tenuicollis*, however, is always subserous and never intramuscular, while the neck within the cyst is long and thin, the hooklets sickle-shaped, and the transverse processes of the smaller hooklets show a distinct cleavage at their extremity. In *C. cellulosae* the hooklets are scythe-shaped, and bifurcation of the transverse processes is absent. As all parasitic cysts tend eventually to caseate and calcify, *Cystercus tenuicollis*, particularly when present in the liver, may be confused with tuberculosis, but in the parasitic infection the portal lymph nodes are not involved while the degenerated material within the cyst can be readily removed and leaves evidence of a white, folded membrane which is the cyst wall.

Judgment. In most cases of *Cysticercus tenuicollis* infection the condition is a mild and local one and only requires removal of the cysts, but the omentum, if extensively affected, should be condemned. Cysts which develop on the anterior surface of the liver may become partly embedded in the liver tissue due to pressure of the diaphragm, and though careful examination will show that the position of the cysts is superficial and subserous, organs affected in this way should be condemned. Livers containing haemorrhagic or degenerated tracts due to migration of the parasite should be condemned, and the very rare cases in which oedema and emaciation occur require total condemnation of the carcase. In New Zealand the incidence of *C. tenuicollis* in sheep livers is high and responsible for severe losses due to condemnations, while in South Australia about one-third of sheep livers are condemned for this affection.

4. Taenia ovis

This tapeworm is 1½ to 4 feet long, with a very small head and 24 to 36 hooks on the rostellum ; it may reach egg-producing maturity in the dog's intestine 7 weeks after a cysticercus is ingested. The parasite is found in Europe, North America, Australia, Africa and New Zealand.

Cystic Stage. This is known as *Cysticercus ovis* and occurs in the sheep and goat, the cyst being ⅛ to ⅜ inch in size and ovoid in form ; development from ovum to cystic stage requires about 3 months. The cysts are essentially parasites of the intermuscular connective tissue and are most commonly found in the heart, mainly under the epicardium, and beneath the pleural covering of the diaphragm ; they also occur in the skeletal muscles, particularly the muscles of the flank, and in the tongue, muscles of the jaw and oesophagus. Cysts occurring in the heart muscles tend to degenerate early and may show well-marked degeneration in less than 3 months after infection. When degeneration occurs there may be present a quantity of greenish blood-stained purulent material which eventually undergoes calcification.

The affection in sheep is not very common and though the incidence in the Western States of North America is stated to be between 1 and 4 per cent., the incidence in 1965 in United States Federal abattoirs was only 0·1 per cent. of the 12·3 million sheep slaughtered. Examination in Britain during 1960 of some 59,400 sheep from various sources in the United Kingdom showed an incidence of infection of approximately 0·2 per cent.

Judgment. Detection of this parasite in routine inspection may be carried out by examination of the heart and diaphragm and incisions into the external and internal muscles of the jaw. The commonest locations are the heart and diaphragm, but when cysts are discovered in any position, especially in situations other than the aforementioned, as, for example, the muscles of the flank, it is recommended that several exploratory incisions be made into the carcase musculature. Affected organs must be condemned, while involvement of the skeletal muscles dictates total condemnation of the carcase. Regulations in the United States prescribe that if the total number of cysts in muscle and heart do not exceed five, the cysts may be removed and the carcase passed, but should more than five cysts be present the carcase must be condemned.

5. Taenia multiceps

This worm was formerly termed *Taenia coenurus*, and is 16 to 40 inches long, with a small head carrying four suckers and 22 to 32 hooklets. It occurs commonly in sheep dogs or in butcher's dogs, and is also found in the fox, jackal and coyote.

Cystic Stage. This is known as *Multiceps multiceps* (*Coenurus cerebralis*), and gives rise to a chronic affection of the brain tissue, almost exclusively confined to ruminants, and producing a disease known variously as gid, sturdy or turnsick. The cyst varies in size from a pea up to a hen's egg and is composed of a thin transparent wall, on the inner side of which are a number of small, white, irregularly grouped spots, up to 400 or 500 in number and each representing an invaginated larval tapeworm head. The affection is commonest in first-year sheep, but is less common in cattle, while horses and other grass eating animals show very little susceptibility to the disease ; it has also been recorded in man. Infection occurs as a result of ingestion of ripe segments of *Taenia multiceps*, usually through grass or water contaminated with infected dog faeces, the embryos being then largely disseminated in a passive manner by the blood stream.

Symptoms of sturdy may be manifested in sheep at two different stages of the affection. About 8 to 14 days after infection the embryos reach the brain tissue, and though in about 20 per cent. of cases this may give rise to symptoms of meningo-encephalitis, manifested by nervousness

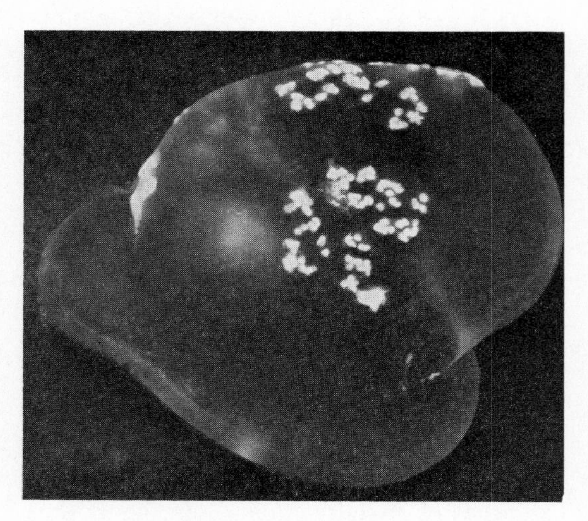

FIG. 159.—*Multiceps multiceps* cyst removed from sheep brain illustrated in Fig. 160. Numerous scolices are seen as white clusters on the inner wall of the cyst. × 2. (W. P. Blount.)

and excitability, the majority of sheep show no obvious symptoms. Post-mortem examination at this stage of the affection shows the brain to contain numerous narrow tunnels indicating the paths of the migrating embryos, and yellowish purulent streaks, together with vesicles little larger than a pinhead, are also apparent on the brain surface. After this primary acute stage of the disease there is a latent period of 4 to 6 months, this being succeeded by the chronic stage which is associated with the growth of the cyst and the production of pressure atrophy of the brain substance. Affected animals may squint, turn in circles or stagger, and persistently leave the flock, the direction in which the animal turns being often an indication of the situation of the cyst. Cysts situated in the cerebrum frequently cause the animal to move towards the affected side, and in animals exhibiting rotatory movements, described as "pivoters", the cyst is probably deep-seated, while forward movements with strongly-flexed head are usually associated with the presence of a cyst in one of the frontal lobes of the cerebrum; in advanced cases there may be actual deformity of the skull with softening of the frontal and parietal bones. The disease is progressive in character, and towards the end of the affection the animal remains lying on the ground, neither eats nor drinks and becomes greatly emaciated. An interesting observation has been made in Switzerland on the disease in the chamois, which, when affected, leaves the rocks on which it no longer feels secure.

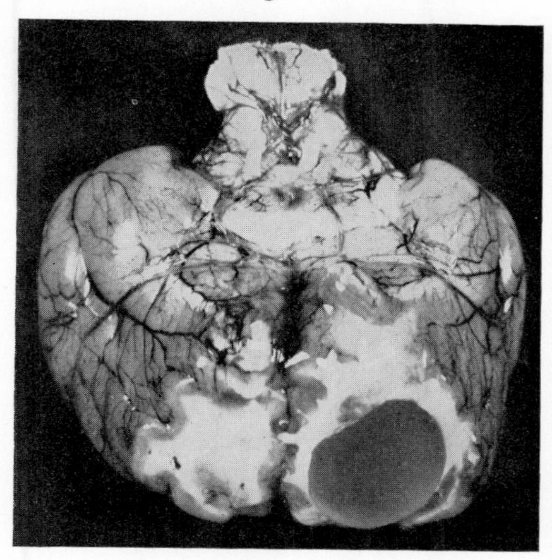

FIG. 160.—Brain of sheep affected with sturdy. The base of the brain is uppermost, and one large *Multiceps multiceps* cyst can be seen in the region of the olfactory bulb of the left cerebral hemisphere. Cysts in this position are usually manifested by symptoms of forward movements with strongly flexed head. (W. P. Blount.)

Post-mortem examination of a sheep which has shown typical symptoms of sturdy will usually reveal one large vesicle which is 2 inches or more in diameter, and only rarely are more than two cysts present. The commonest situation for these cysts is on the convexity of the cerebrum, but they are occasionally found in the cerebellum, or at the base of the bra in; they may even be found in the spinal cord, particularly in the lumbar region, and in this location are much elongated and associated with paralysis of the hind limbs. Though *Multiceps multiceps* has a predilection for brain tissue the embryos may invade other organs and parts, but unless the parasites find their way to the central nervous system they soon degenerate and either disappear or are seen as spherical encapsulated foci which are the size of a pea and consist of a greenish, pus-like material which later becomes calcareous.

Sheep which show symptoms resembling sturdy, but reveal no evidence of cysts when the brain is examined, may be suffering from " false gid ", a condition sometimes observed after dipping, and post-mortem examination in such cases shows an inflammation of the nasal passages with the presence of small abscesses in the cranial cavity, frequently beneath the cerebellum. Infection of the nasal passages or frontal sinus with the larvae of *Oestrus ovis* may also give rise to symptoms resembling sturdy. In South Africa sturdy must be distinguished from "pushing sickness" due to poisoning by such plants as *Matricaria nigellifolia* ("staggersweed").

Judgment. In the early stages of sturdy and before the onset of emaciation, it is only necessary to condemn the head. Carcases of animals which are emaciated due to this affection should be condemned.

6. Echinococcus granulosus

Known formerly as *Taenia echinococcus,* this is one of the smallest of the tapeworms, about $\frac{1}{4}$ inch in length and composed of a head and three segments, the head being armed with 30 to 36 hooklets arranged in two rows. The first and second segments are incompletely developed, while the last segment, which is gravid and contains up to 5,000 ripe eggs, is equal in length to the rest of the worm. The parasite is most commonly found in dogs, in rural rather than in urban districts, and is occasionally encountered in foxes and other carnivorous animals. In Australia the dingo is regarded as a suitable primary host for the tapeworm, as is the black-backed jackal in South Africa, but in the cat the tapeworm does not reach the stage of sexual maturity and this domestic animal therefore plays no part in the spread of the disease.

Echinococcus granulosus is not regarded as a common parasite in dogs in Great Britain or on the Continent of Europe, but in Beirut, in Lebanon, in 1948 32·4 per cent. of stray dogs were shown to harbour the parasite, which infests 20 per cent. of the dogs in New South Wales, 40-50 per cent. in South Australia and 29 per cent. in Punjab (India). The tapeworm is found in America, Africa, and also New Zealand where in the worst areas about 25 per cent. of dogs are affected, though the overall figure for the country is below 1 per cent. In Greenland 24 per cent. of dogs harbour the parasite, while in the coastal districts of Yugoslavia up to 50 per cent. of the dogs are affected. Examination in 1964 of 87 dogs on mid-Wales farms showed that 20 harboured the adult tapeworm. Several thousand adult worms may be found in the small intestine of an affected dog, and may give rise to an enteritis of an extensive and aggravated character. After ingestion of a hydatid cyst by a dog the scolex in the duodenum is stimulated by gastric juices, becomes aggressively mobile and attaches itself to the host's intestinal wall; in about seven weeks it develops into the adult tapeworm.

Cystic Stage. The immature stage of *E. granulosus* is known as the echinococcus, or hydatid cyst, and gives rise to hydatid disease. It is found in cattle, sheep, pigs, horses and occasionally in man; it is also found in many wild animals and has been recorded in the cat and dog. The distribution of hydatid disease throughout the world, whether in animals or man, shows considerable variation which bears a direct relation to the number of dogs and the frequency with which they harbour the adult parasite. Major centres of infection are North Africa, Central and East Africa, and South America. In Asia the major centres are considered to be Turkey, Lebanon, Irak and Iran.

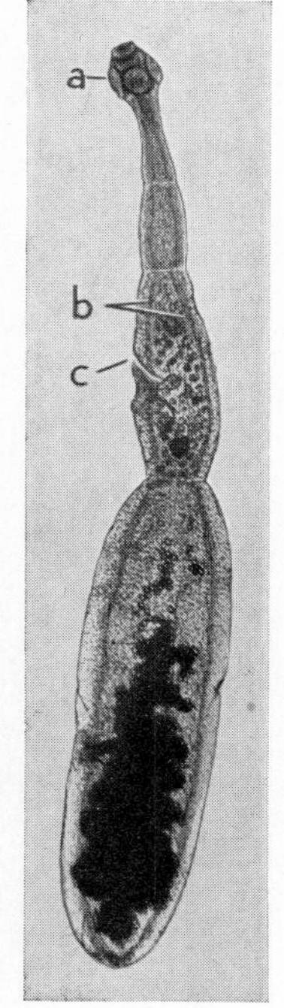

FIG. 161.—*Echinococcus granulosus*: (*a*) Head with four suckers and double crown of hooklets; (*b*) excretory canal of second segment; (*c*) genital pore. The black mass in the terminal segment is the uterus filled with ripe ova. × 11.

In cattle, the percentage of hydatidosis in France is 0·34, Switzerland 0·7, Spain 13 to 36, Italy 4 to 31, Greece 20, Yugoslavia 78 to 95, Kenya 28 to 41, South Africa 1·08, England and Wales 0·07 to 3·2 with an average of 1·13. In New Zealand a survey in 1958 showed that the incidence increased with age from 9 per cent. in cattle 1 to 2 years old to 74 per cent. in cattle 5 years or older. However, in more recent years the incidence has declined considerably and the disease is now uncommon except in older cattle.

In sheep, the percentage incidence in various countries is as follows: France 0·03, Italy 15 to 52, Morocco up to 43, Greece 54, Spain 2·8 to 40·6, Kenya 53, South Africa 0·92, Yugoslavia 35 to 72, Turkey 4, Australia 36, Argentina 11, Uruguay 58·1, with up to 100 per cent. in older sheep. In England and Wales the incidence in 1958 varied between 0·07 and 5·6 with an average of 1·41. In New Zealand the incidence is declining but is still as high as 58 per cent. in adult sheep. In lambs the infection rate is considered to be below 5 per cent.

In pigs, the percentage incidence of hydatidosis in France is 2·06, Zurich 0·36, Italy 1 to 8, Spain 1 to 2, South Africa 0·98, Argentina 20 and New Zealand 20. In England and Wales the incidence in pigs in 1958 ranged between 0·008 and 0·25 with an average of 0·05.

In horses in Holland the incidence of hydatidosis rose from 1·7 in 1945 to 3·2 in 1946. In Cape Town the incidence is 1·93 and in Switzerland (Lausanne) 1·8. An incidence of 55 per cent. was recorded in 1955 at one horse abattoir in Northern Ireland. In the Middle East 67·4 to 100 per cent. of camels are found affected. The losses due to condemnation of affected organs, particularly livers and lungs, is in some countries very considerable. In Montevideo the annual loss in livers condemned due to hydatidosis is £100,000, in New Zealand £400,000, and in New South Wales £107,000. In Yugoslavia animal hydatidosis is estimated to involve the country in a loss of some £7 million yearly.

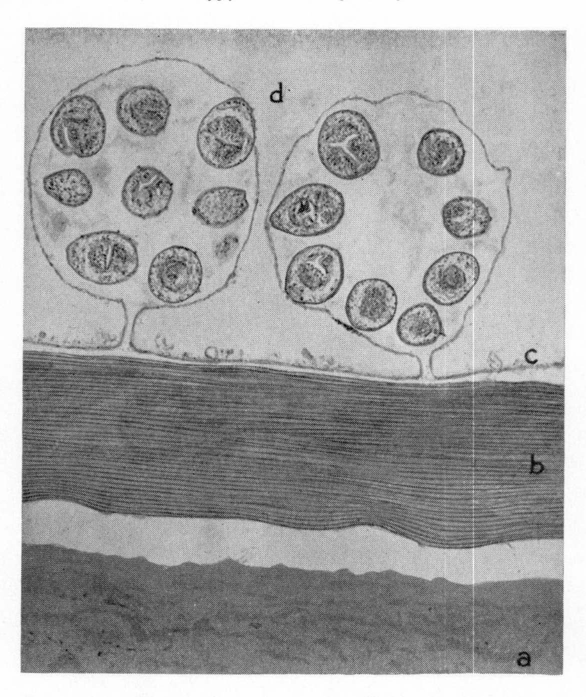

FIG. 162.—Photomicrograph of wall of a fertile hydatid cyst from sheep liver shown in Fig. 163. (*a*) Connective tissue capsule formed by reaction of host; (*b*) external cuticular membrane; (*c*) internal germinal layer attached to which are (*d*) two brood capsules each containing eight scolices. × 50.

Life History. After ingestion of ripe ova by cattle or other susceptible animals the embryos are released by dissolution of the egg shell, and invasion of the system takes place through the wall of the small intestine. Embryos enter the portal vein by the aid of their hooklets and reach the liver, where they become arrested in the liver capillaries, but the immature parasites have no selective affinity for any particular organ and the location of hydatid cysts in animals is controlled by the filtering action of the capillaries. Though the larger embryos become arrested in the liver, the smaller ones pass through the liver capillaries to reach the lungs, while those embryos which again succeed in passing through the lung capillaries enter the systemic circulation to reach the various organs of the body, including the kidneys, heart, spleen, bronchial lymph nodes in sheep, and more rarely the pancreas, bones and muscular tissue. It is also possible for embryos to enter the lymphatic circulation and be carried, via the thoracic duct and heat, to the lungs. In this way the lungs may be infected before or instead of the liver.

Structure of a Hydatid Cyst. This consists of:

(*a*) An external cuticular membrane, composed of a chitinous material which is concentrically laminated and whitish in colour.

(*b*) An internal germinal layer, much thinner than the cuticular membrane, and presenting a number of small papillae on its inner surface which represent the development of brood capsules.

(*c*) Brood capsules, which develop from the germinal layer and become hollow or bladder-like, being attached to the germinal layer by a short pedicle or stalk. Brood capsules may be just visible to the naked eye, and within each of them there develop a number of small scolices or tapeworm heads, usually five to twenty.

(*d*) Daughter cysts may also form within the parent cyst and develop either from shreds of the detached germinal layer, from brood capsules, or from scolices. Any factor which threatens the life of the parent cyst accelerates the formation of daughter cysts, and in the liver their formation is rapid if bile should gain entrance to the parent cyst.

The shape of the hydatid cyst is controlled by the organ in which it grows. When uninfluenced by pressure it is oval or spherical, but in the liver it may assume an irregular shape due to the presence of the bile ducts, and in bone it follows the structure of bony tissue and grows into the small crevices and channels. The size of hydatid cysts in animals ranges from that of a marble up to that of a child's head, but they are frequently the size of a goose's egg, and though they develop slowly it is probable that their longevity is limited only by that of their host; there is a record of a hydatid cyst in man which continued to grow for 43 years, but animals are usually slaughtered before sufficient time has elapsed for the full development of the slow-growing hydatid, and hydatid infection in animals is therefore less likely to produce marked systemic effects than in human beings. White nodules, as yet containing no fluid, may be seen in the liver 4 weeks after ripe eggs are ingested, while after another 4 weeks the cysts are $\frac{1}{10}$ inch in size and the centre cavity now contains a clear fluid. After 6 months some hydatid cysts may be $\frac{1}{2}$ inch in diameter and at this stage produce scolices and brood capsules and are infective to dogs.

Hydatid cysts may in time show degenerative changes in which the vesicular fluid disappears and the cavity contracts, becoming filled with caseous matter which may finally undergo calcification. Degeneration in a hydatid cyst is the result of bacterial infection conveyed from the intestine by the migrating embryos, and degenerative changes may be developing at the centre of a hydatid cyst at the same time as the cyst is forming daughter cysts in the periphery.

Those hydatid cysts which give rise to brood capsules or daughter cysts are described as fertile, but cysts in which these do not develop are known as sterile and are characterized by their smooth inner lining,

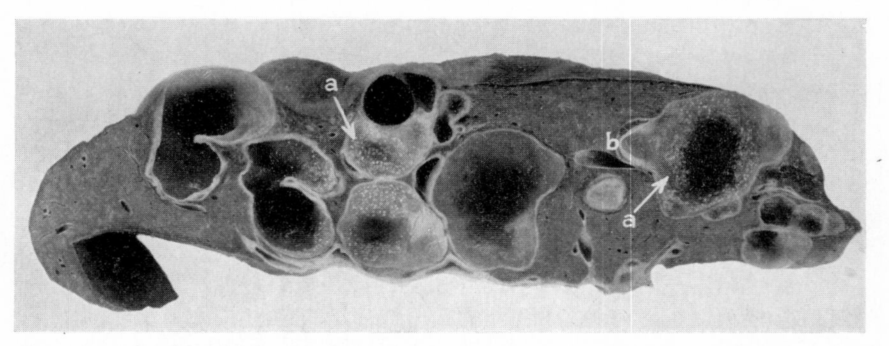

FIG. 163.—Section of sheep liver showing fertile hydatid cysts. The white spots on the germinal layer at (*a*, *a*) are brood capsules, and at (*b*) a growing cyst is assuming an irregular shape as it orientates around a bile duct.

usually with slight turbidity of the contained fluid. In Britain it has been shown that up to 90 per cent. of hydatid cysts in cattle are sterile, and in pigs 20 per cent., but in sheep only 8 per cent. of cysts are sterile and this animal is therefore the natural host for the hydatid cyst in Britain and is the chief source of infection. In Yugoslavia it has been shown that the fertility of hydatid cysts in sheep is seven times greater, and in goats five times greater, than in cattle, while in Italy it has been shown that brood capsules are present in a high proportion of cysts found in sheep and horses and in a low proportion of cysts found in cattle. In South Africa, on the other hand, it has been shown that 96·9 per cent. of uncalcified cysts in slaughtered cattle are fertile.

In New Zealand cysts in sheep are rarely infective to dogs until lambs are at least nine months old, but the majority of cysts remain fertile throughout the life of the sheep. In cattle in New Zealand the majority of cysts in older cattle are sterile.

Hydatid infection of the liver is always associated with a marked connective tissue reaction which encapsulates the cyst within a fibrous wall up to ½ inch in thickness. Affected livers are enlarged in proportion to the number and size of the cysts, and bovine livers of 200-250 lb. weight are recorded; in the pig the liver may weigh as much as 110 lb., and the affected organ, being usually markedly cirrhotic, may give rise to ascites.

Types of Hydatid Cysts. Hydatid cysts may take the form of a single cyst, which is frequently large and may be fertile or sterile; this simple cyst, known as *Echinococcus unilocularis*, is by far the commonest type of hydatid cyst found in the food animals. A second type of hydatid cyst is the multilocular form, known as *Echinococcus multilocularis*, in which the reaction of the host gains the supremacy, with the result that the original cyst is broken up into a number of small cysts separated by fibrous tissue; the cysts, which do not exceed the size of a pea, present a honeycombed appearance and are filled with a gelatinous material. This form of hydatid cyst occurs in man and has a relatively restricted geographical distribution in Europe and Northern Asia, chiefly in the Alps and Jura mountains, Soviet Russia and on islands in the Behring Sea. It is held that the adult tapeworm is a different species from *E. granulosus* and that its definitive hosts are not only dogs but also foxes and cats, with intermediate hosts in the form of field mice and other rodents. The status of a form known as *Echinococcus multilocularis veterinorum*, which resembles the human type of multilocular hydatid disease except that it is larger and occurs in cattle, is still *sub judice*.

Incidence of Affection of Various Organs. In sheep the lungs (Fig. 71) are affected with hydatids as frequently as the liver, the commonest form being the fertile simple cyst. In the ox the lung is affected more frequently than the liver, the commonest form of hydatid being the simple, small, sterile cyst, though larger cysts occasionally occur. In pigs the lung is affected less often than the liver, and the simple unilocular cyst is the commonest form encountered (Plate IV). In the horse the simple unilocular cyst is also the commonest form, the lungs being much more rarely affected than the liver.

HYDATID DISEASE IN MAN. The incidence of human hydatid disease in any country is closely related to the incidence of the disease in domestic animals, being highest where there is a large dog population and sheep are pastured in large numbers. The disease occurs frequently in Cyprus, Spain, India, South Africa, South America (particularly Uruguay), Australia and New Zealand. In the latter country about 70 cases are recorded annually, some 14 per cent. of these proving fatal, while 700 cases occur annually in Italy, 600 in Chile and 590 in Greece where the cost in hospital treatment and number of working days lost is estimated at £70,000 per year. In Britain some 1000 new cases were admitted to hospital between the years 1946 and 1957, the highest incidence occurring in South

Wales, and in parts of Southern Australia some 2 per cent. of human beings are infected.

Infection is acquired by man through the ingestion of ova from the dog tapeworm, and it is usually stated that contamination of watercress and lettuce, which are eaten without previous cooking, is a common method by which this can occur. It is questionable whether these foods play an important part in the transmission of the disease to man, nor can contamination of a water supply be regarded as a likely source of human infection, and a more probable method of infection is related to the uncleanly habits of the dog, which may transfer ova from its anus to its mouth by licking, and in turn transfer these ova to man by licking the person's hands or face. Contamination of the hairs on the dog's coat with ova from faeces is, however, considered to be the commonest source of human hydatid disease. The probability of this being the common mode of infection is confirmed by the fact that more than one case of hydatid disease frequently occurs in a family, and infestation often occurs during childhood, which is a period of general unhygienic behaviour. In their sacred book, the Koran, Mohammedans are enjoined to wash their hands seven times after touching a dog, and in France human hydatid disease is aptly termed *la maladie des mains sales*—the disease of soiled hands.

Another source of human infection, though probably less common than the foregoing, is from the fleece of sheep which have lain down in grass contaminated by sheep dog droppings. In Argentina and Uruguay 50 per cent. of the people handling cattle and sheep are infected, and the incidence in Argentina and Chile is said to be increasing. It has also been shown that domestic and wild rats and mice, and also cockroaches, avidly consume proglottides present on the surface of dog faeces and eliminate the proglottides in their faeces within 24 hours. The ova remain viable in this faecal matter for three months after they are expelled and the ingestion by man of food contaminated by the excreta of rats, mice or cockroaches may account for a number of the cases of human hydatid disease. The rarity of human hydatidosis in the United States is related to the fact that dogs are not used to tend sheep, all stray dogs are shot, and sheep are confined by dog and wolf-proof fencing. Cases of human hydatid infection in Britain show the average distribution of the cysts to be as follows : Liver 65 per cent., lungs 10 per cent., kidneys 7 per cent., other abdominal organs 8 per cent., cranial cavity 7 per cent. and bones 2 per cent.

Eradication of Hydatid Disease in Man and Animals. Regular inspection of all slaughtered animals and the destruction of organs containing hydatid cysts is the most certain method of interrupting the life cycle of the parasite and lowering the incidence of the disease in animals and man. In affected cattle and sheep the lungs contain hydatid cysts even more frequently than the liver, and as the lungs of these animals are usually sold as cat or dog meat, small undetected cysts, particularly in sheep lungs in which the majority of cysts are fertile, undoubtedly play a major part in the spread of the disease to dogs and thence to man. Under the United States Federal Regulation it is prescribed that dogs shall be excluded from slaughterhouses and meat works, while in Britain the Slaughterhouse (Hygiene) Regulations contain a similar provision but permit the entry of working dogs except to the parts of the slaughterhouse used for the dressing of carcases, the preparation or storage of meat, or where blood is kept for human consumption.

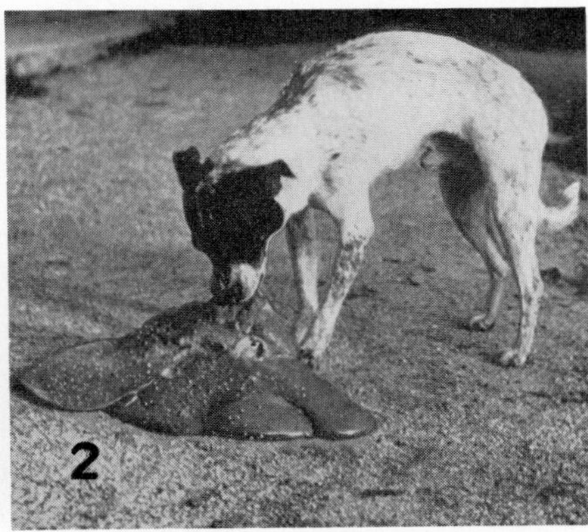

FIG. 164.—The rôle of the scavenging dog in the perpetuation of hydatid disease.
1. Dressing of ox carcase in a South American village.
2. Dog eating hydatid-infested liver from the ox shown in 1.

In New Zealand, hydatid disease in both man and animals is a major public health problem, for that country possesses vast numbers of sheep and the range and degree of moisture favour the survival of echinococcus ova, which may remain viable on pastures for over 12 months. Dead sheep or the offals of slaughtered sheep may thus be frequently eaten by dogs. Legislation was introduced in 1939 and it is an offence if a dog is allowed access to any raw diseased meat or to any raw offal, while dead animals must be buried within 24 hours. Local authorities register all dogs and supply a vermifuge, arecoline hydrobromide, at the time of registration. Similar measures have been adopted in Argentina, Yugoslavia and other countries in an attempt to reduce the incidence of the human disease, and in Bulgaria a campaign has lowered the number of infected dogs found from 46,000 in 1960 to 2,500 in 1963.

Judgment. Hydatid infection in the food animals is in nearly all cases confined to the lungs and liver, and infected organs must be condemned and destroyed, even when only a single superficial cyst is apparent, for hydatid cysts are as common in the parenchyma of an organ as on its surface. Emphasis must be laid on destruction, and it is not sufficient to bury these offals on a local refuse dump to which dogs may have access, for hydatid cysts in buried sheep lungs may remain viable for 9 days and in sheep liver for 7 days. In Uruguay, where the destruction of hydatid-infested organs is impracticable, it has been shown that cutting open the cysts and immersing the organ in a saturated salt solution will destroy the scolices and is a practical and effective procedure of rendering offals safe for feeding to dogs and a method which can advantageously replace confiscation or boiling. Cysts in organs left uncovered at normal temperatures cannot be considered inactive until a week has elapsed, though fly larvae are an important factor in the rapid destruction of cysts in unburied organs. If voluntary muscle is affected, or if the carcase has become emaciated or oedematous, total condemnation is necessary.

Tapeworms of Man

Three tapeworms occur in the intestines of man as a result of consuming affected flesh; these are *Taenia solium*, *Taenia saginata*, and *Diphyllobothrium latum*. The first two parasitic conditions of man's intestine are met with chiefly in countries where animals are kept under unhygienic conditions in the immediate vicinity of insanitary human habitations, and are therefore much commoner in subtropical and tropical Eastern countries than in Western lands. Though the incidence of human tapeworm affections in Western countries has been lowered by improved methods of disposal of human excreta and has now assumed almost negligible proportions, the practice of depositing human excreta in the open or spreading it upon fields as a fertilizer must be regarded as a likely method by which infection may be transmitted.

1. Taenia solium

This tapeworm inhabits the upper part of the small intestine of man, is sometimes referred to as the armed tapeworm and is particularly common in Central Europe and in India, China, U.S.S.R., Africa and Mexico. *Taenia solium* usually occurs singly in man's intestine and is referred to by the French as *le ver solitaire*, but in endemic areas several tapeworms, up to 25, may be found in one intestine.

The head of *Taenia solium* is globular and less than $\frac{1}{25}$ inch in diameter, while the rostellum is short and provided with a double crown of 26 to 28 hooks, and the neck is long and slender. The adult worm is 6 to 16 feet long and composed of 800 to 900 segments, the individual segments being distinguished from those of *Taenia saginata* by the fact that the gravid uterus has only 7 to 12 tree-like lateral branches on each side, whereas in *T. saginata* the lateral branches number 15 to 35. About 8 to 10 ripe segments are passed per day during defaecation, each segment containing about 30,000 eggs. Though this tapeworm is now very rare in Europe and the United States, it is of public health significance in meat inspection, for the cystic stage may also infect man and may occasionally prove fatal.

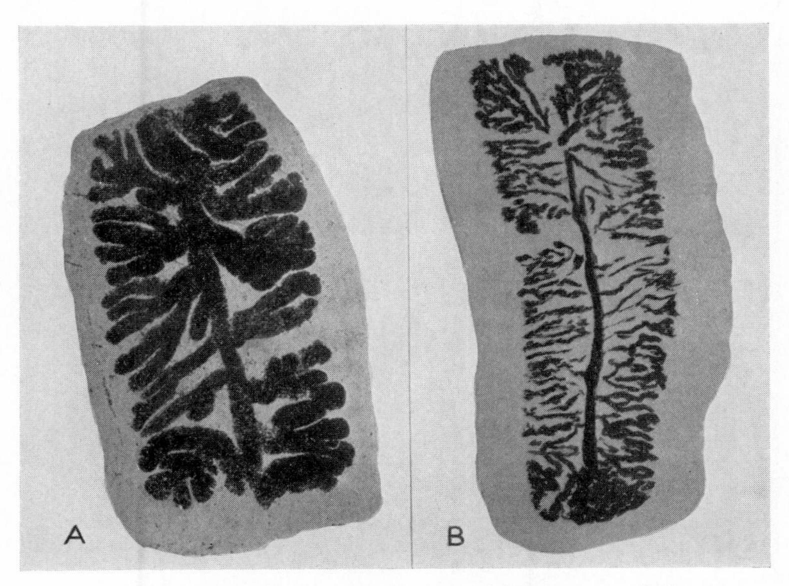

FIG. 165.—(A) Segment of *Taenia solium*; and (B) segment of *Taenia saginata*, showing gravid uteri and their lateral branches. × 6. (Dr. A. Jepsen.)

Cystic Stage. This is known as *Cysticercus cellulosae* and is found most commonly in the pig, though it can also occur in the cat, rat, monkey, while man and dog can also act as an intermediate host. It has also been recorded in cattle. In Mexico City 10 per cent. of the street dogs harbour cysts, while in Madras examination of 500 dog carcases showed seven to be affected. Infection in the pig is acquired whilst the animal is scavenging, the embryos passing into the systemic circulation, probably by way of the portal vein, liver and posterior vena cava. The cyst is of delicate structure and translucent, and the invaginated head or scolex, when developed, is seen through the cyst wall as a small white spot slightly larger than a pinhead in size. The scolex, like the adult worm, possesses four suckers and a double crown of 26 to 28 hooks.

The size of *Cysticercus cellulosae* varies with its stage of development; at 20 days the cyst is the size of a pinhead, at 60 days it is the size of a pea and the head is visible, while at 110 days all cysts are of approximately equal size and the scolex is developed and invaginated. The cysts are elliptical in form, and when fully developed are $\frac{5}{8}$ inch long by $\frac{3}{8}$ inch broad.

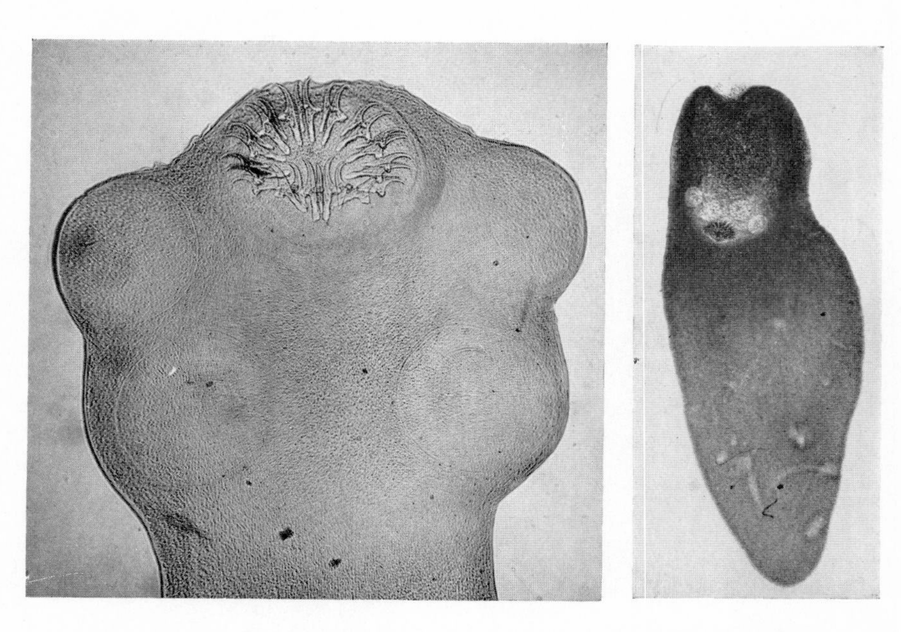

FIG. 166.—Photomicrograph of scolex of *Cysticercus cellulosae* showing four suckers and rostellum of hooklets. × 100.

FIG. 167.—*Cysticercus cellulosae* showing invagination of scolex within the cyst. × 9.

Location. The cyst has a predilection for skeletal muscle in preference to the visceral organs, the muscles most often invaded being those of the heart, diaphragm, tongue, neck, shoulder, intercostal and abdominal muscles. According to French authorities the incidence of cysts in infested pigs is as follows: heart 80 per cent., diaphragm and internal masseters 50 per cent. and tongue 40 per cent.; organs less often affected are the liver, lungs, kidneys, brain and eye. In some South American countries dealers detect the cyst in the live animal by an examination around the tongue, and dishonest pig vendors may prick these cysts to release the contents and mask the condition. Observers in many countries have also noted that the deep muscles of the thigh are often affected, and that freedom from infection of the tongue, neck, heart, etc., does not indicate the absence of cysts in the carcase musculature. The cysts in pig muscle, described as measly pork, may be scattered and few in number, or they may be present in enormous proportions, and one case of measly pork is recorded in which 3,000 cysts were present in 1 lb. of muscle.

The frequent occurrence of heavy infestations is explained by the fact that a person harbouring *Taenia solium* excretes 7 to 10 ripe segments daily. As each segment contains some 30,000 ova, a pig devouring a fresh human stool, which is a frequent occurrence in underdeveloped countries, may ingest no less than 300,000 tapeworm eggs. In addition, the freshly voided segments of *T. solium* are inactive and tend to remain in the faeces, so that pigs are more likely to acquire a massive infection than in the case of measles in cattle. In parts of Africa where the incidence of measly

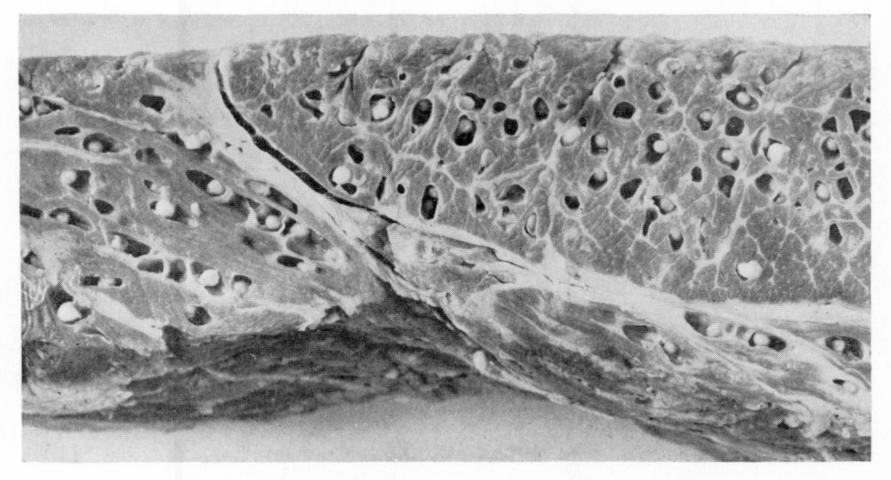

FIG. 168.—Measles of pork showing extensive invasion of muscle by *Cysticercus cellulosae*. Fibrous capsules have formed round the cysts and remain patent when the cyst is removed. The rounded white cysts contain the invaginated scolices. Natural size.

pork is unaccountably low it has been pointed out that there is competition between dogs and pigs for fresh human stools. Cysts of *Cysticercus cellulosae* can remain alive for some years, but where caseation or calcification occurs the parasite is no longer viable. If these dead cysticerci are numerous the muscles and heart may appear studded with white spots, and in severe infestation the muscles are soft and of a pale reddish-grey colour.

The incidence of pork measles in European countries is low, Denmark, Italy, Switzerland and Britain being free, while in others the incidence is usually lower than 0·5 per cent. In Western Germany in 1965 only 9 carcases were found affected out of 18 million pigs slaughtered, and in the United States in 1965 only one carcase out of 68 million slaughtered. The affection is common in the Balkans, Portugal, India and parts of Africa; in certain districts in West Africa up to 18 per cent. of pigs are affected, and though the average incidence in the main South African abattoirs was 4·6 per cent. in 1931, it had fallen to 1·48 per cent. in 1965. In Central and South American countries cysticercosis in pigs is a serious and ever-present problem, the incidence in native pigs in Venezuela being estimated at 15-20 per cent. and in Mexico 8-18 per cent. In one slaughtering plant in Mexico during 1951, 44 per cent. of pigs were found infected.

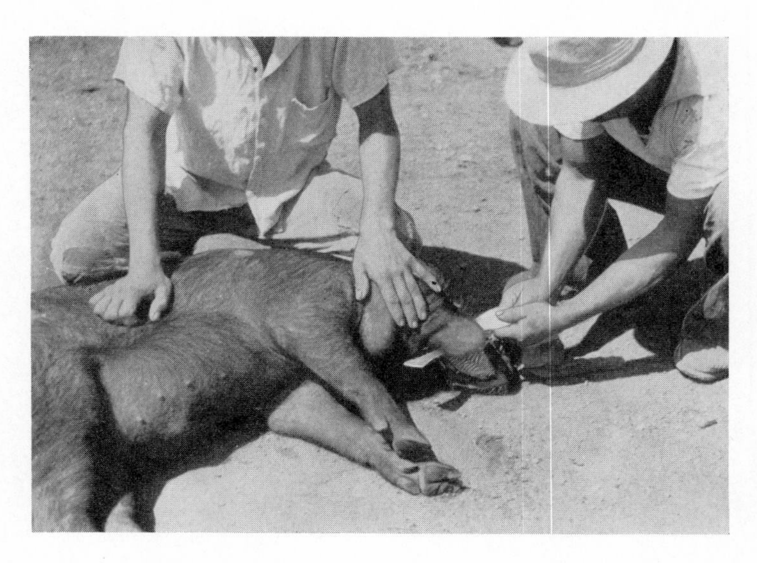

FIG. 169.—Examination of live pig for *Cysticercus cellulosae*. The prospective purchaser in a Central American market has inserted a metal bar between the jaws and is palpating the tongue for the presence of cysts.

Method of examination for C. cellulosae. The intercostal and cervical muscles and those of the diaphragm, abdomen and thigh may be satisfactorily inspected if the carcase of pork is split into two sides. The heart, tongue and larynx should also be examined. In Africa there is unassailable evidence that the muscles of the shoulders are frequently infected in pigs, and regulations in both South Africa and Rhodesia prescribe that the triceps brachii muscle shall be exposed by a deep incision about one inch above the elbow joint. Workers in South Africa have shown that if this shoulder cut were omitted from the routine incisions made in the examination of pig carcases, no less than 13 per cent. of carcases affected with measles would have been undetected and passed as free from cysticerci.

CYSTICERCOSIS IN MAN. Man not only harbours the adult *Taenia solium* in his intestines, but auto-infection with the tapeworm eggs can take place, with the result that the cysts develop in his muscular tissue and organs. This auto-infection may be caused by retrograde movements of the man's intestinal contents, thus conveying proglottides or eggs from the small intestine to the stomach, for the proglottides or eggs, though resistant to the alkaline juice of the intestine, are digested, and the embryos liberated if exposed to acid and alkaline juices successively. Auto-infection may also occur if ova are conveyed to the mouth by unclean fingers after defaecation, but the swallowing of ova through the agency of soil, water or vegetation appears to be the most likely method by which human cysticercosis occurs.

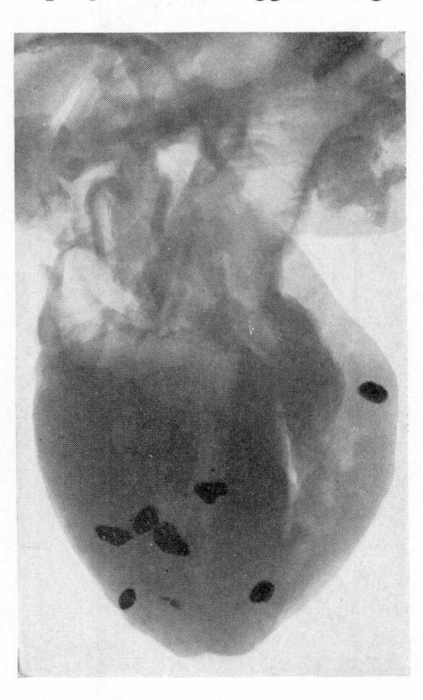

FIG. 170.—Radiograph of human heart showing several calcified *Cysticercus cellulosae* cysts in the myocardium. The patient had served 3 years in the army in India. (Dr. J. F. Brailsford.)

In man *Cysticercus cellulosae* infection is often limited to a single organ but may be found in muscle, particularly of the thigh or calf, or in the heart, liver, lungs, eye and brain. Routine inspection of pork carcases has done much to lower the incidence of *T. solium* in man and the consequent danger of auto-infection, but in 1950 Roblis, a brain surgeon in Mexico City, found that 25 per cent. of suspected brain tumours operated on were actually *Cysticercus cellulosae*, and 3-6 per cent. of all persons in the General Hospital were stated to harbour the parasite in various organs. Epileptiform symptoms due to the presence of the parasite in brain tissues are not likely to manifest themselves until degeneration of the cysts has occurred.

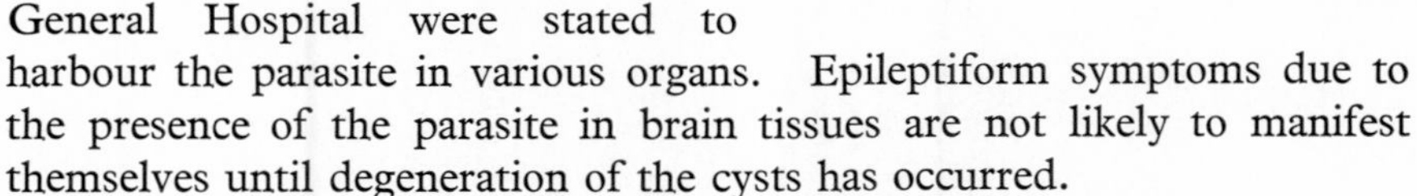

Judgment. *Cysticercus cellulosae* can be destroyed with certainty if the meat is heated to a temperature of 113° F. to 122° F., though the cysts have been found alive in the centre of a large joint of pork even after roasting. Pickling is reliable as a method of destruction if prolonged for 3 to 4 weeks in a brine composed of 25 parts by weight of salt in 100 parts by weight of water and the pieces of meat do not exceed 4 to 5 lb. in weight. The cysts can survive the death of their host for 6 weeks, and decomposition of meat is not a guarantee that the cysts contained therein are destroyed. Obviously infested pork flesh in repugnant even when the cysts have been rendered non-viable, and in Britain it is prescribed that affected carcases and organs should be condemned. United States regulations prescribe that affected carcases of pork may be passed for cooking, but if the infestation is excessive the carcase shall be condemned. In Western Germany a similar judgment is applied, and treatment of lightly infected meat by cooking or pickling, though not by freezing, is permissible by law and such meat is classified as conditionally fit and may only be sold on the Freibank. In some districts in Mexico the flesh of carcases of pork found moderately affected is cut into strips, the cysticerci removed by a stiff brush and the meat then fried.

2. Taenia saginata

This parasite, commonly known as the beef tapeworm, averages 10 to 25 feet in length and lives exclusively in the small intestine of man. The head or scolex, which bears four elliptical suckers, is not provided with a rostellum and no hooks are present. The segments number up to 2,000, and the uterus in each gravid segment possesses 15 to 35 delicate lateral branches and contains about 100,000 eggs. The gravid segments are up to 2 cm. in length, and in one month an infected person may excrete some 50 million eggs. The life cycle is similar to that of *T. solium* except that the larval stage, known as *Cysticercus bovis*, develops in the intermuscular connective tissue of the ox and rarely in other sites.

Cystic stage. *Cysticercus bovis*, or the beef measle, is a round or oval cyst and when fully developed consists of a scolex invaginated into a vesicle, or so-called tail bladder, which is filled with fluid. Surrounding this is an adventitious connective tissue capsule formed by the reaction of the tissues of the host. The cysticerci present the following macroscopic appearance, according to their stage of development:

(*a*) Very small cysts, about the size of a pinhead, with no scolex visible and surrounded by a delicate connective tissue capsule.

(*b*) Pinkish, oval cysts up to 1 cm. × 0·5 cm. in size, surrounded by a delicate translucent capsule through which the scolex can be seen as a white spot.

(*c*) At a later stage the capsule of the cyst becomes thickened, opaque and greyish-white in colour, and the typical cysticercus is enclosed within.

Cysticercus bovis is fully developed about 18 weeks after infection, but it is sufficiently developed for diagnosis to be made at about the sixth week. Degenerative changes may occur early and cysts in the first stages of degeneration have been recorded as early as 6 weeks after infection, though it may not occur until 7 months after infection has been acquired. Cysts in varying stages of degeneration from caseation to calcification are frequently seen, thus it is not uncommon to find:

(1) Oval cysts with a thick connective tissue capsule which is formed by the host's body, is difficult to separate from the surrounding tissue and contains a yellowish-green caseous material. A dead cysticercus, usually with scolex evaginated, may be found in association with this material.

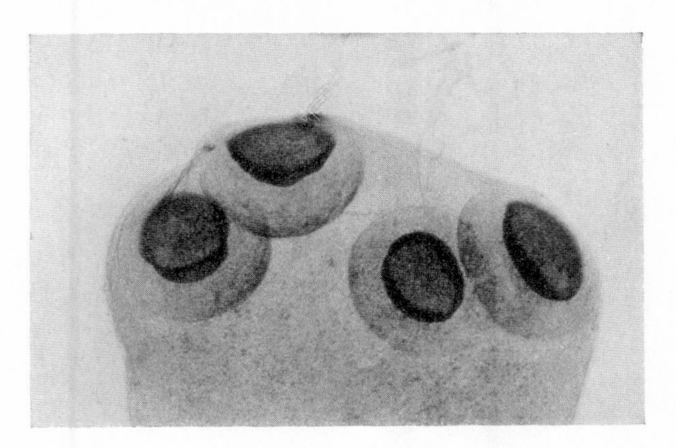

FIG. 171.—Photomicrograph of the head of *Taenia saginata* showing elliptical suckers and absence of rostellum and hooklets. × 80.

(2) Completely calcified cysts in which lime salts have been deposited and the cyst structure replaced by mortar-like concretions in the inter-muscular connective tissue.

Location. In *Cysticercus bovis* the cysts are not usually numerous throughout the bovine musculature, and they are most commonly found in muscles of mastication, particularly the masseter muscles, and in the heart, tongue, shoulder and diaphragm. The oesophagus is also a fairly frequent site and cysts have occasionally been found in fat, liver, lungs and lymph nodes. In cattle throughout Africa it has been shown that an important site for cysts are the muscles of the shoulder (*M. triceps brachii*), and that incision of these muscles is of particular value in the detection of slight infestations. Workers in South Africa showed that if this cut were omitted in routine post-mortem examination 47 per cent. of cattle slaughtered would have been passed as measles-free, while similar work done on cattle in Rhodesia showed that if the shoulder cut were omitted no less than 58·5 per cent. of measles-infected carcases would have been undetected.

It is somewhat difficult to reconcile the fact that, except for the African Continent, it is not considered necessary to incise the shoulder muscles in bovine carcases. The explanation for this may lie in the fact that a muscle in activity receives 10 to 20 times more blood than a muscle at rest, and a number of authorities now consider that there are no particular predilection sites for *Cysticercus bovis* and that the distribution of the cysts is controlled by the volume and intensity of the arterial blood ; in other words, that the distribution of the cysts is purely a mechanical one.

Workers in Kenya have shown that most cases of bovine cysticercosis are acquired in early calfhood, calves from birth to 28 days being highly susceptible to artificial infection. It is significant that the grazing habits of calves in Africa differ markedly from the manner in which calves are fed in Europe where they are housed from birth and during the first few weeks of their life have little or no opportunity for exercise. In the tropics and

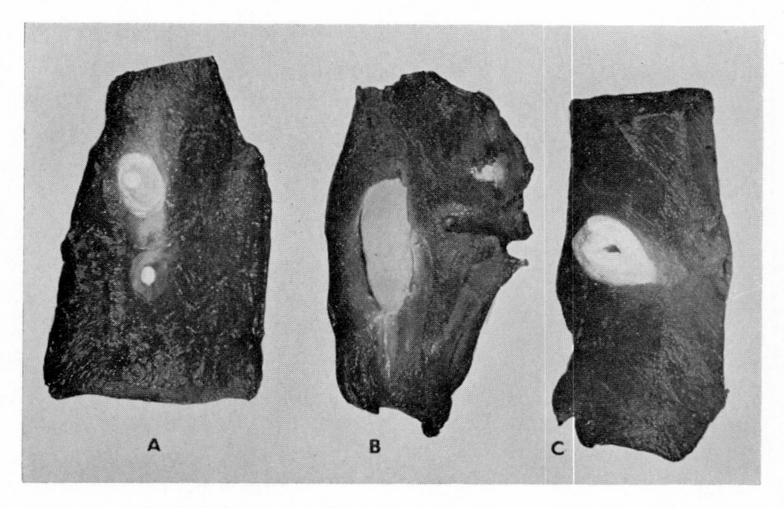

FIG. 172.—Cyst of *Cysticercus bovis* in various stages of development. (A) Two active and viable cysts in which the scolex of each cyst is clearly visible as a white spot through the translucent capsule ; (B) Cyst in which the capsule has become thickened, opaque and greyish-white in colour; (C) Cyst in further stage of degeneration with a thick connective tissue capsule and containing a yellowish-green caseous material. At a still later stage the cyst will undergo calcification.

sub-tropics, however, indigenous Afrikander or Zebu cattle graze for longer hours and travel greater distances than do animals in Europe. Under certain conditions, Afrikander cattle may cover a distance of 16 miles or more in their journey to watering points and back to grazing, so that the suckling calf, compared with its European counterpart, may be obliged to walk considerable distances at this early age and, as the leg muscles of such calves must receive large amounts of arterial blood, cysts are likely to be transported to the muscles of the limbs. Meat inspection records in Kenya show that the most important site for beef measles is the shoulder, followed by the tongue, heart and muscles of mastication. In Rhodesia it has been shown that the most frequently infected site is the shoulder, followed by the muscles of mastication, hindquarter, heart and tongue.

In countries where *Taenia saginata* is common and there are frequent and recurring opportunities for cattle to ingest the tapeworm ova, an active immunity is developed and the incidence of *Cysticercus bovis* follows a definite age pattern, being highest in young animals and then showing a progressive decrease in the older age groups. In 1965 in Prague the percentage incidence of *C. bovis* infection found in slaughtered cattle of various ages was : 1 year old 5·98, 2 years 4·28, 3 years 3·84, 4 years 3·17 and 5 years 1.28. In areas where the tapeworm is endemic, as in East Africa, it has been shown experimentally that after nine months of age animals which have acquired a natural infection can seldom be infected artificially. In non-endemic areas, however, as in Britain and the United States, even adult animals are susceptible to infection.

Incidence. *Taenia saginata* is a more common parasite than *Taenia solium*, having a worldwide distribution and found wherever beef is eaten. In Europe it is considered unlikely that the infection rate with *Taenia saginata* is higher than one per cent., but in Africa it is estimated that there are 12 million carriers of *Taenia saginata*, with a reported incidence as high as 30 per cent. in some African stockmen, while in the U.S.S.R. it is estimated there are 49 million carriers of the tapeworm. *Taenia saginata* tends to be particularly common amongst people who prefer their beef in an undercooked or even raw state.

Cysticercus bovis in cattle occurs in practically every country in the world. Prior to 1947 the parasite was rarely reported in Britain but the present incidence in cattle in Britain is of the order of 0·25 per cent., though this varies with the area. The proportion of cattle with cysticerci in Europe ranges from 0·3 to 14 per cent., and in the Federal German Republic the percentage incidence in 1957 was 0·62 but more meticulous inspection procedures were introduced in 1961 and as a result the percentage incidence in 1963 was 2·3. In Denmark the incidence in adult cattle was 0·66 per cent. in 1963. In South Africa the incidence in 1931 was 1·39 per cent. but by 1965 had risen to 3·03 per cent. with the highest average incidence of 6·94 per cent. in the Transvaal bushveld. Incidences as high as 50 per cent. are recorded in cattle in Tanzania and 80 per cent. in Ethiopia. In the United States the incidence in 1960 was 0·07 per cent. but by 1965 had fallen to 0·04 per cent.

There seems little doubt that ova from a relatively small number of carriers of the tapeworm are capable of becoming widely distributed and give rise to infection of large numbers of cattle. Indiscriminate defaecation by the human host may result in the distribution of ova or gravid segments on the land, or ova may be disseminated by sewage sludge or effluent, for although most worm eggs sediment within 1½ hours during the mechanical purification of domestic sludge, only a small proportion of tapeworm ova will sediment during this period. In heavily infested areas sewage treatment should include sand filtration, but most of the usual sewage treatment procedures, including rapid sand filtration, have not proved effective in eliminating tapeworm ova. When land is fertilized by sewage, cattle grazing on such land may therefore become infected, and dissemination of ova on to pastures by the flood water of polluted streams has also been recorded. It is known that ova may remain infective on pasture for at least 8 weeks, in liquid manure for 71 days, while Australian workers have found that the ova remain viable on dry sunny pastures for 14 weeks and there is evidence that they will live on pastures for 6 months if conditions are favourable to them. It seems possible that dissemination may also take place through the agency of insects or birds, particularly seagulls, feeding on contaminated material and as many as 150 ova of *Taenia saginata* have been recovered from the intestine of a naturally infected seagull; it is considered, however, that when cattle become infected on pastures soiled by birds only a small number of cysts will be found in the carcase. In some European countries a seasonal incidence of beef measles is recorded, the incidence being highest in the summer and autumn months when grass-fed cattle, whose opportunities for acquiring infection are greater than in stall-fed cattle, are being slaughtered. Infection with *C. bovis* can occur ante-natally in the calf, but ante-natal infection does not occur in the case of *C. cellulosae* in pigs due probably to the fact that the placental tissues of the gravid sow, consisting of six layers, provide an effective barrier between the blood circulations of mother and foetus.

Routine Measures. In the routine inspection of beef carcases there is a practical limit as to the degree of incisions which are permissible, for gross mutilation must necessarily lower the marketability of the carcase; as a result some of the light infestations may, on occasions, be undetected. In the majority of the infections in cattle in Europe only a small number of cysticerci are present, not infrequently a single cyst in the masseter muscles, while in cattle in Africa infestation is often confined to the muscles of the shoulder. Though routine meat inspection measures may not be an absolute safeguard in relation to the control of infection in man with *T. saginata*, there is no doubt that the cases of generalized infection in beef, and many of the light infections, will be detected by the techniques employed. A second line of defence, however, must be the housewife, for human infection with *T. saginata* can only be acquired if infected beef is eaten in a raw or undercooked state, and the thermal death point of the cysts, being 135° F. or over, is reached with certainty if beef is thoroughly cooked until it is changed to a uniform grey colour and the juice which

PLATE IV

1. Sarcocyst (*S. miescheriana*) in abdominal muscle of pig.
2. Hydatid cysts in liver of pig.
3. Lesions caused by *Linguatula* larvae in mesenteric lymph nodes of ox.
4. Chicken affected with caecal coccidiosis. The greatly distended caeca are seen on either side of the small intestine. In such cases oöcysts of *Eimeria tenella* (Fig. 180) can readily be demonstrated in the caecal contents which consist of cheesy masses of clotted blood and tissue debris.

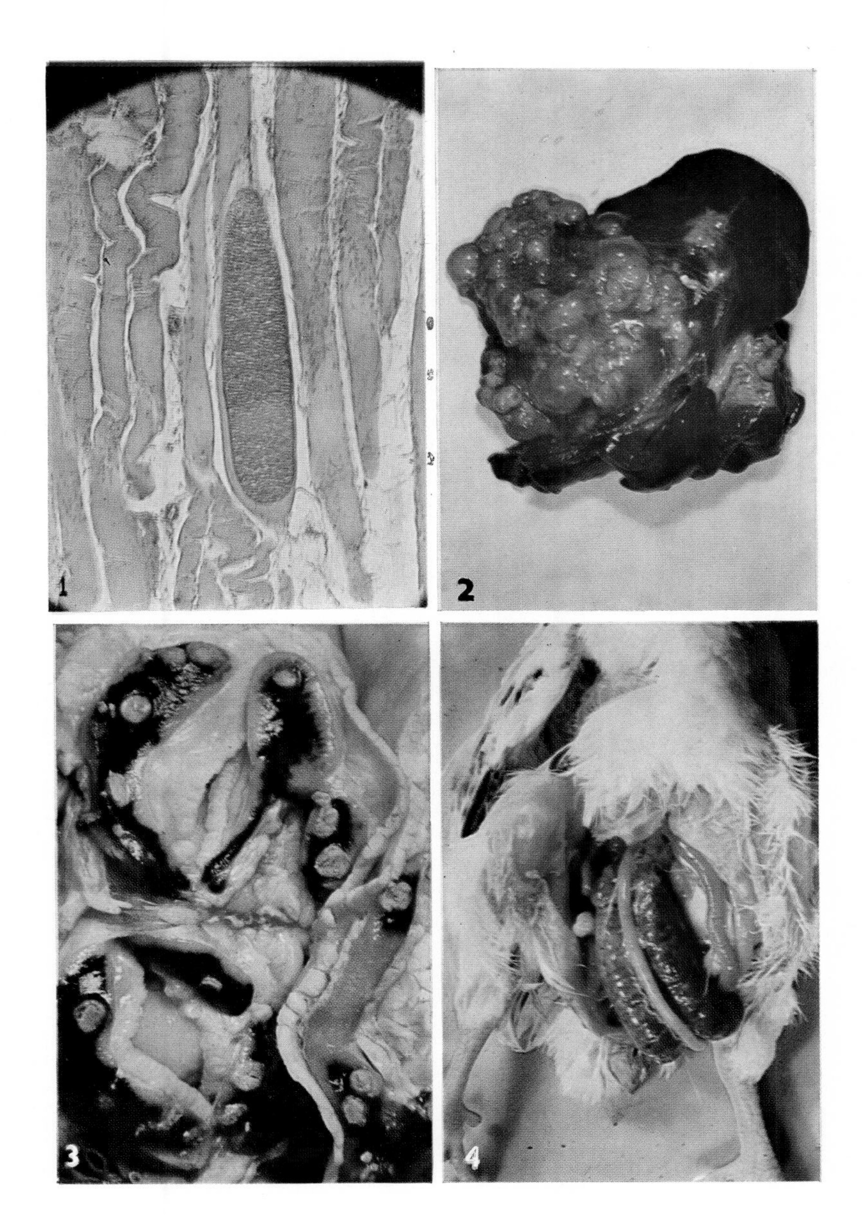

exudes when the meat is cut has lost its reddish tint; this indicates that a temperature throughout of 178° F. has been attained. In Denmark the incidence of tapeworm carriers has been shown to be higher in females, who become infected during the culinary preparation of raw beef, as the cysts tend to adhere to the fingers when infected meat is handled.

Method of Examination for Cysticercus bovis. In England and Wales the procedure for the routine examination of beef carcases requires several deep incisions into internal and external masseter muscles parallel to the plane of the lower jaw, and opening of the pericardium and examination of the heart muscles. In the case of an adult bovine animal the heart must be opened by an incision through the left venticle and, if considered necessary, further incisions shall be made into the heart muscle from the inside.

In Federal Germany the examination of calves under six weeks is confined to examination of the heart surface. All bovines over this age shall be examined as follows:

(*a*) A longitudinal incision through the pericardium and myocardium, opening both ventricles and incising the septum,
(*b*) two further incisions into the heart from auricles to apex,
(*c*) two longitudinal incisions through the lower surface of the tongue after its removal,
(*d*) at least two incisions parallel with the lower jaw through the inner and outer masseter muscles (i.e. eight incisions in all),
(*e*) examination of the muscular portion of the diaphragm after removal of its serous coverings, and
(*f*) examination of the oesophagus and of all visible muscular surfaces.

In the United States of America the prescribed method of examination of carcases for *C. bovis* is very similar to that prescribed in Federal Germany. In South Africa and Rhodesia the regulations are noteworthy in that a routine incision shall be made into the triceps brachii muscle of each side, the incision being made 2 or 3 inches above the point of the elbow and extending down to the humerus. In the event of cysticerci being found in the carcase in this or other prescribed routine incisions, seven further incisions, about one inch apart, shall be made into the muscles of the shoulder. The value of these additional cuts is in assessing the degree of infestations, and though these additional cuts, particularly the fourth, may outdo the initial cut in the number of cysts found, the primary cut remains the most important for the detection of slight infestations. It is beyond doubt that the shoulder cut should be insisted on in any of the African territories where *C. bovis* is prevalent; in Kenya a modification of the shoulder cut is prescribed, three routine incisions being made into the triceps brachii muscle and also an incision into the gracilis muscle parallel to the symphysis pubis.

Cysts in different parts of the body develop at different rates, while the onset of degenerative changes in the cyst appears to be influenced by the supply of arterial blood to the muscle in which the cyst is lodged. The greater the blood supply the more rapidly does the cyst degenerate and die; cysts in the cardiac muscle are therefore usually the earliest to undergo caseation and calcification. In endemic areas, such as East Africa, degenerative changes may be considerably delayed, and in an animal which becomes infected during the first 3 weeks of life cysts may remain viable for 30

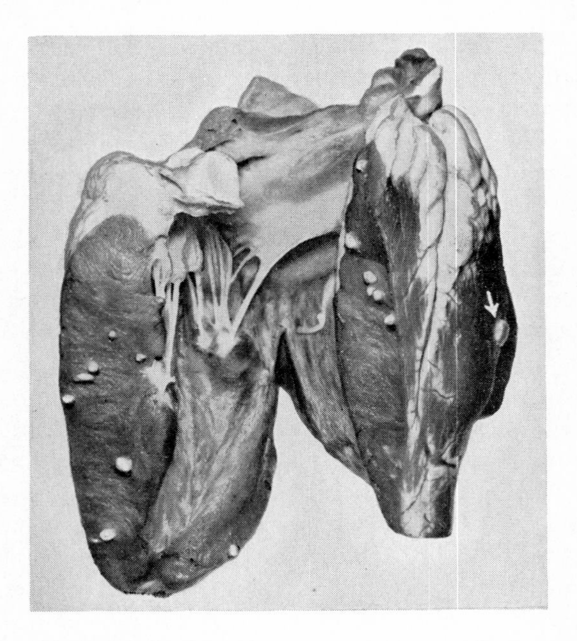

FIG. 173.—Degenerated cysts of *Cysticercus bovis* in wall of left ventricle of ox heart. One cyst, indicated by arrow, is visible beneath the epicardium. (E. F. McCleery.)

months, while some cysts in a proportion of cattle may survive for the entire life of the host. In Australia experiments have shown that 9 months is the maximum longevity for *C. bovis*. It is considered that only fresh viable cysts are infective to man, all later stages being non-infective, and if a test for viability is required this may be demonstrated in the laboratory by placing the cysts in normal saline solution to which ox bile (30 per cent.) or sodium taurocholate (5 per cent.) has been added. If the solution is incubated at 98·6° F. evagination of the scolex in viable cysts takes place within 1 or 2 hours.

Judgment. Meat inspection regulations in various countries concur in that total condemnation is necessary in *Cysticercus bovis* infestation when the flesh is oedematous or when the parasites, alive or dead, are generalized in the muscular tissues as well as in the so-called sites of predilection. In England and Wales it is prescribed that carcases shall be completely condemned if the disease is generalized in the meat substance; there are, however, no instructions as to the degree of infestation which shall constitute generalization. When infection is localized the parts of the carcase or the organs affected shall be condemned, and the remainder of the carcase and offal, with the exception of stomach and intestines, shall be placed in cold storage at a temperature not exceeding 20° F. for not less then 3 weeks, or at a temperature not exceeding 14° F, for not less than 2 weeks. Britain will not accept from abroad beef in which *Cysticercus bovis* has been found.

The Regulations of the Danish Meat Inspection code prescribe that carcases shall be regarded as having a generalized infection if more than ten cysts, whether alive or dead, are found. If less than ten cysts are found the carcase may be passed conditionally for treatment at an authorized meat factory or authorized cold store by refrigeration at 14° F. for not less than 10 days; the carcases of cattle over 2 years of age may be released without treatment if not more than ten completely degenerated cysts are found.

The regulations in Federal Germany state that generalization may be assumed if more than one parasite, alive or dead, is found in the majority of the surfaces revealed by the incisions made during examination. The stomach and intestines of such carcases may be passed for food if found free from cysticerci, while the blood, and also the bones if completely freed of soft tissue, may be released for human consumption. Where infection is classified as localized the carcase shall be pre-cooled at 32-35·6° F. for 24 hours then subjected to a temperature of not more than 14° F. for 144 hours, but in localized cases the liver, spleen, kidneys, stomach, intestine, brain, spinal cord, udder and fat need not be subjected to refrigeration provided they are free from cysticerci.

In the United States the Regulations state that generalization is considered to exist if incisions in various parts of the musculature expose on most of the cut surfaces two or more cysts within an area the size of the palm of the hand. If infection is localized the carcase and parts shall be held in cold storage at a temperature not higher than 15° F. continuously for not less than 10 days; this requirement applies also to lungs, fat, muscle of the oesophagus and heart, but other edible viscera may be passed unconditionally provided they are found to be free from infestation. A point on which there is not unanimity in all countries is the procedure to be applied when one single dead and degenerated cyst is discovered. It is now generally considered that inasmuch as live and dead cysts may coexist in the musculature of the same carcase there is justification in subjecting to freezing a carcase in which only a single degenerated cyst is found.

3. Diphyllobothrium latum

This tapeworm of man is 6 to 30 feet long and composed of 3,000 to 4,000 segments, while the head is $\frac{1}{10}$ inch long, oval or club-shaped in form, and possesses no hooklets. Two slit-like bothria are present, the uterus in each segment being situated centrally and rosette-shaped in appearance. The tapeworm is common round the lakes of Italy, Switzerland and Germany, and is also common in Central Europe, Poland, Finland, U.S.S.R., and in the Far East. A high incidence is found in Eskimos, and in Eastern Canada it is regarded as the commonest of the tapeworms of man. Fish-eating mammals act as reservoir hosts, including the dog, cat, wolf, seal and bear, but a large proportion of the eggs passed by hosts other than man are nonviable.

Cystic Stage. The eggs excreted by *Diphyllobothrium latum* possess a cap or operculum, from which emerges a ciliated embryo known as a coracidium, pollution of waters from which food fishes are obtained occurring by the discharge therein of raw sewage. This embryo swims in water and must quickly be ingested by a freshwater flea, of which *Cyclops strenuus* and *Diaptomus gracilis* are two suitable European species, before further development can take place. In the body cavity of the crustacean the embryo develops into a procercoid, and if the crustacean is eaten by a suitable fish, further development takes place and the embryo develops into a plerocercoid. The plerocercoid is about 1 inch long, greyish-white in colour, elongated and indistinctly annulated, and is found in the fatty mesenteric tissues, testes, ovary, or more rarely the muscles, of many species of freshwater fish including the trout, pike, perch, burbot, grayling, and freshwater eel ; the parasites may be recognized by their greyish-white colour and the transparent surrounding tissue. The larvae are killed in a few minutes at 122°F. but can survive the death of their host, and man becomes infected by consuming infected fish in an undercooked or raw state. Infection may thus occur by eating caviare or by eating raw burbot liver, as is done in East Prussia. This parasitic infection is of public health importance, for the adult tapeworm in the intestine of man competes with its host for vitamin B_{12} and may produce a severe anaemia ; affected fish should therefore be condemned.

PARASITIC CYSTS IN GAME ANIMALS. In Africa cysticerci have been found in the musculature of many species of game animals, including the warthog and members of the antelope family. In no case have the cysticerci proved to be *C. bovis* or *C. cellulosae* but have been identified as cysticerci of one of the closely related species of Taenia which occur in the large carnivores such as the cheetah, leopard, lion, hyaena and jackal. It cannot be assumed that the predilection seats of cysticerci in the musculature of game animals are necessarily similar to those in the domestic animals.

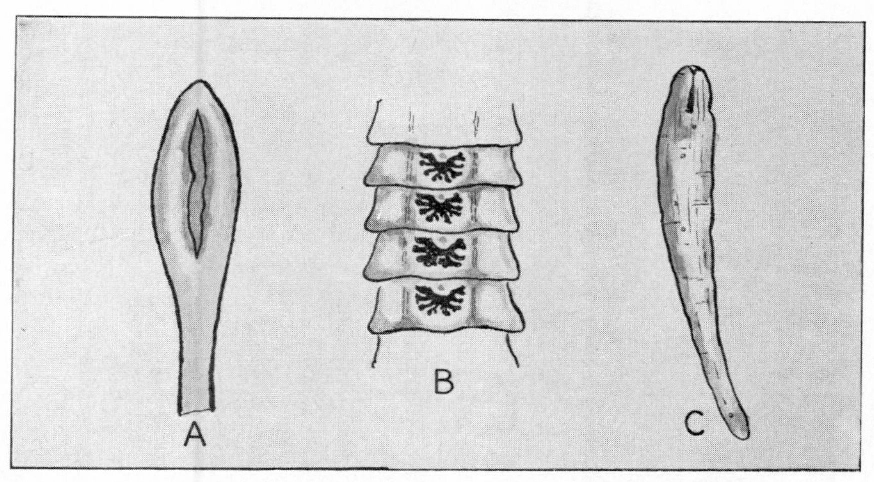

FIG. 174.—(A) Head of *Diphyllobothrium latum*. × 20. (B) Gravid segments showing rosette-shaped reproductive apparatus. × 3. (C) Plerocercoid. × 3.

THE TREMATODES

These are known commonly as the flukes, some of them being responsible for an acute and chronic inflammation of the liver and bile ducts, with resultant effects that are of considerable economic importance.

The principal and most widely distributed causal agent of severe liver infestation is undoubtedly *Fasciola hepatica*. *Dicrocoelium dendriticum* occurs but is of less pathological significance, while in North America and Europe the large American liver fluke, *Fascioloides magna*, is also found. *Fasciola gigantica* causes severe losses in cattle in Africa, and also occurs in the Philippines, Burma, India and the U.S.S.R.

FASCIOLA HEPATICA

This parasite is the common liver fluke, and is distributed almost universally throughout the world. It is pale brown in colour, flattened and oval in shape, being broadest anteriorly where it terminates in an oral sucker which surrounds the mouth ; a large ventral sucker is situated about $\frac{1}{10}$ inch behind the mouth. *Fasciola hepatica* is $\frac{3}{4}$ inch to $1\frac{1}{4}$ inches long and $\frac{1}{3}$ to $\frac{1}{2}$ inch wide, its eggs being brown, oval and provided with a lid or operculum. The cuticle of the adult parasite is studded with numerous backwardly-directed spines and these play an important part in the production of the typical liver lesions associated with the disease.

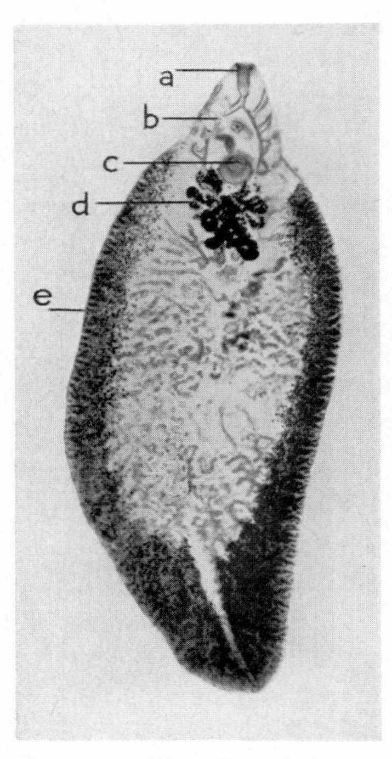

FIG. 175.—Adult *Fasciola hepatica* showing (*a*) oral sucker surrounding mouth; (*b*) branched intestine; (*c*) ventral sucker; (*d*) uterus containing ripe eggs; (*e*) yolk glands. × 3.

Incidence of Fascioliasis. In the years 1879-1880 liver fluke in England was responsible for a loss of over 3,000,000 sheep and, principally for this reason, investigations made into the life history of the parasite revealed an essential rôle played by its two hosts, the sheep and a variety of freshwater snail. Practical measures of control may therefore be based on the elimination of snails by the draining of pastures, together with the preventing of sheep from grazing on damp pastures which are liable to harbour the snail.

Though methods of combating liver fluke infection are now well known, the disease is undoubtedly one of the commonest parasitic conditions encountered in meat inspection. A survey made in Great Britain in 1942 elicited the following facts: in 73,372 cattle slaughtered (both home-bred and imported) no less than 17·6 per cent. of livers were found affected, and at least 1,500 tons of bovine livers are rendered unmarketable yearly in Britain, the loss in terms of retail price, i.e. 3s. per lb., being in the region of £500,000. This does not include the loss due to reduced meat and milk yield, and possibly calf production, of affected animals, but though these factors are ill-defined they are certainly large and, according to German authorities, the parasite is estimated to reduce beef production by 7 to 10 per cent. and the yield of milk by up to 16 per cent., while in sheep the loss of flesh is put at 25 per cent. In Northern Ireland, where the incidence of fluke disease in all cattle is estimated at 67 per cent. and in all sheep at 22 per cent., the loss of condition in cattle is stated to be about 5 per cent. and causes an economic loss of £2 per head. In Australia, with a sheep population of about 159 million, cases of chronic fluke infestation are rare due to the regular treatment of sheep in affected districts with carbon tetrachloride; there are, however, occasional heavy losses from acute fluke infestation. In the United States fascioliasis in sheep is not as prevalent as in Europe, due largely to the practice of grazing sheep on higher and drier pastures.

Animals Affected. *Fasciola hepatica* is most common in the sheep and ox, but occurs occasionally in horses, pigs, rabbits and hares, while a number of cases have been recorded in man. The affection is not uncommon in the liver of adult pigs, particularly sows and pigs which have access to pasture, but sheep possess the greatest susceptibility to fluke infestation and it is in these animals that the most severe symptoms and effects are observed.

FIG. 176.—Half-bred ewe showing oedema of throat (" bottle neck ") and dry, loose wool, the result of liver fluke infestation. Similar symptoms may be seen in severe roundworm infestation of the stomach and intestines. (W. Lyle Stewart.)

Life History of Fasciola hepatica. The adult liver fluke is hermaphrodite, and deposits ova in the bile ducts of its host, usually the sheep or ox. The number of eggs laid during the life of a single liver fluke may be over 1 million.

After passage of the eggs from the host by way of the bile and faeces, an embryo or miracidium develops whilst the egg is lying on the ground, and in 2 to 6 weeks in summer the embryo escapes from the egg shell by way of the operculum. This embryo is actively motile but dies within a few hours unless it encounters a suitable intermediate host, which, in the case of *Fasciola hepatica*, is a mud snail, *Limnaea truncatula*. The embryo enters the respiratory cavity of this snail, becoming transformed into an oblong sac known as a sporocyst, and in the next 2 to 4 weeks the sporocyst gives rise to six to eight rediae which are elongated structures each containing a sac-like intestine. In a further 4 to 6 weeks each of the rediae becomes actively motile, migrates to the liver of the snail, and eventually gives rise to fifteen to twenty cercariae. These have an oral and ventral sucker, a long tail and bifurcated intestine, and, escaping from the rediae, leave the snail and find their way to a grass stalk or aquatic plant. The period of development in the snail thus occupies 6 to 10 weeks.

The cercariae may either float on the surface of water or they may attach themselves to a blade of grass, becoming encysted by the excretion of an adhesive substance, and resembling grains of sand and of about the same size. The period of development from egg to encysted cercariae takes 2 to 4 months, and cercariae may remain alive in a pasture for up to 12 months, and even in dry hay for a few weeks. A pasture which is heavily waterlogged enables cercariae to encyst further up the blades of grass where they are more likely to be ingested by herbivorous animals, and in this way a wet summer or autumn is always of serious import to sheep grazing on fluke-infested land.

When grass or plants bearing cercariae are eaten by grazing animals, chiefly ruminants, the cysts are dissolved in the small intestine of the host, and the liberated parasites pass from the intestine to the liver and develop into adult flukes. The duration of life of an adult fluke in the liver may be up to 5 years.

Infection. Sheep are more likely to acquire infection than cattle, for they graze herbage more closely, and it has been observed that " parrot-mouthed " sheep, which cannot graze closely, are less likely to be affected. The occurrence of liver fluke disease in Britain is inseparably connected with the life history of the snail *Limnaea truncatula* which begins to be active in March or April and lays eggs which give rise to a generation of snails, these producing more eggs 3 to 4 months later; as several generations of snails are produced between March and October there is thus a great increase in the snail population. The emergence of cercariae from the liver of the snail begins early in July, and the first outbreaks of acute fascioliasis occur in sheep 6 to 8 weeks later. As *Fasciola hepatica* requires about 3 months to develop from the cercarial stage into the adult fluke, and as cercariae are scarce on pastures until July, the chronic form of the disease does not manifest itself until late in the autumn, while marked symptoms do not appear until early winter and become more serious as the winter progresses. The continued infectivity of pastures is maintained partly by the ability of the fluke eggs and infective snails to withstand adverse conditions, but chiefly by the repeated reinfestation of land by animals which, though clinically healthy, are fluke " carriers ".

Symptoms. Liver fluke infestation may assume an acute or chronic form, the first occurring within 3 weeks after infection and corresponding to the invasion of the liver by enormous numbers of young flukes. It has been shown experimentally that acute fascioliasis will occur in sheep if the number of cercariae invading the liver is 5,000 or more, and death may occur without

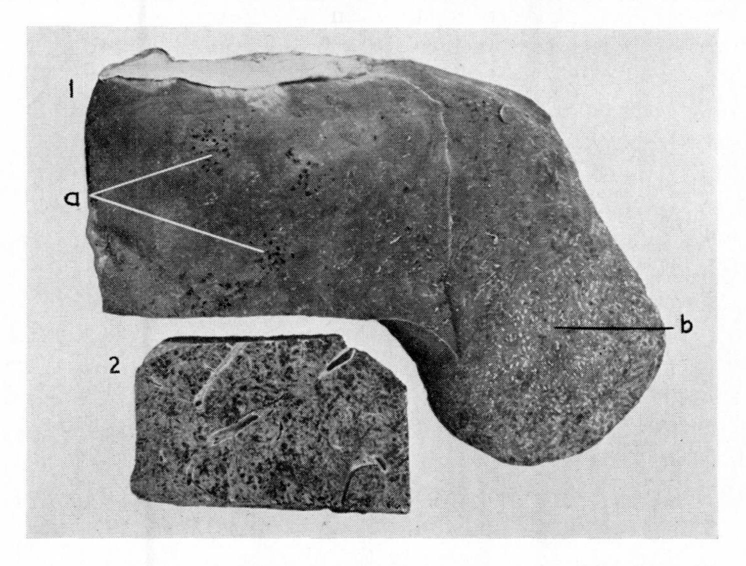

FIG. 177.—Liver of sheep showing effects of recent infection with immature flukes. 1. (anterior surface). The liver is swollen and congested and the serous capsule shows haemorrhagic spots (*a*), and is covered with fibrin (*b*). 2. (section). This shows numerous small holes which under pressure exude necrotic tissue and immature parasites.

any clinical symptoms being shown. More frequently, symptoms of fluke infestation are observed in the chronic stage of the disease which occurs some months later, and are manifested in sheep by a progressive anaemia with paleness of the conjunctiva, oedematous swellings of the eyelids, throat and brisket, and at times a pendulous condition of the abdomen. In spite of the anaemia sheep at this stage show a tendency to fatten, for the increased assimilation of fat-forming foods is facilitated as a result of stimulation by the flukes to the flow of bile. Following this period the animal becomes weaker, diarrhoea becomes evident, and the disease terminates in extreme emaciation and death. The systemic effects and the gross changes in the liver which are typical of this disease occur as a result of combined action of the blood sucking and tissue feeding capacity of the fluke, the irritant action of its suckers and cuticular spines, the continued absorption of metabolic products excreted by the flukes, and the effects of invading bacteria. Affected bovine animals, in contrast to fluke infestation in sheep, usually show little impairment in bodily health, and markedly cirrhotic livers may be seen in the best nourished animals. In general, liver fluke affection in cattle is less acute than in sheep, and whereas 50 adult flukes are capable of producing clinical symptoms in sheep, some 250 are necessary to produce the same effects in cattle. On the African continent, however, the infection in sheep with *Fasciola gigantica* is almost invariably of a peracute nature, for the ingestion of vast numbers of cercariae over a short period causes death from an acute haemorrhagic hepatitis. German authorities have shown that the incidence of " carriers " of salmonella organisms is four times greater in fluke-infested cattle than in cattle which are not affected.

Lesions. The liver is the organ chiefly affected by *Fasciola hepatica* and flukes reach the liver by boring through the intestinal wall into the abdominal cavity and entering the liver through its serous capsule. After a few days spent in the abdominal cavity the immature flukes make their way into the liver and wander about in the liver tissue for 5 to 6 weeks. The invasion of the liver by enormous numbers of young flukes gives rise to acute swelling and congestion of the organ and the production of an acute parenchymatous hepatitis, the serous capsule of the liver being at times sprinkled with haemorrhages and covered with fibrin. Section of the organ at this stage shows numerous sharply circumscribed small apertures which, under pressure, exude semi-fluid necrotic liver tissue and immature flukes. The parasites finally enter the smaller bile ducts and become sexually mature.

Liver lesions associated with the acute form of the disease are seen towards the end of the summer and are succeeded eventually by lesions of a chronic type in which the fibrinous deposit on the serous capsule of the liver becomes organized and gives rise to a chronic perihepatitis ; this is frequently manifested in both sheep and cattle by adhesion of the diaphragm to the anterior surface of the liver, or by adhesion of the liver and omentum. The presence of adult flukes in the bile ducts gives rise to mechanical irritation of these passages and results in a chronic, pericanalicular atrophying cirrhosis and the formation of connective tissue in the walls of the bile ducts and surrounding liver tissue.

In cattle the thickened and dilated bile ducts eventually become calcareous or " pipy " due to deposit of lime salts, and yellowish-brown bile containing adult flukes can be expressed when the ducts are incised. In the United States the common liver fluke affecting cattle is *Fascioloides magna*, which migrates through the liver tissue but does not invade the bile ducts. Livers affected with *F. magna* often show black melanin-like deposits, and sometimes a similar pigmentation is seen on the diaphragm or on the serous surface of the stomach where it is in contact with the liver. The black coloration is considered to be haematin, a broken-down blood pigment excreted by the parasite.

In chronic fascioliasis of sheep the liver becomes irregularly lobulated and distorted, but the bile ducts, though thickened, dilated and of a bluish colour, do not undergo calcareous infiltration, and "pipiness" is never seen in the livers of these animals. Less frequently the irritant effect of the immature parasites in the liver of the sheep is manifested by the presence of irregularly distributed foci which are initially haemorrhagic and appear as dark red tracts on the liver surface; they may be seen in the liver substance or beneath its capsule, frequently showing a serpentine-like formation and eventually becoming calcareous. The number of flukes present in an affected liver may be large, and over 1,000 have been counted in the liver of a sheep, and as many as 1,660 in an ox liver.

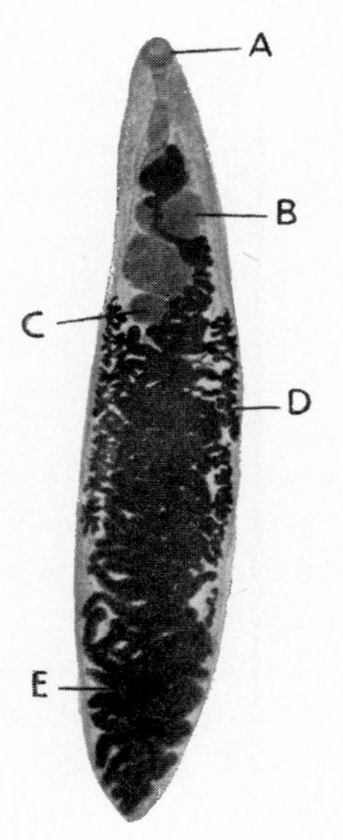

FIG. 178.—The small liver fluke, *Dicrocoelium dendriticum*: (A), anterior sucker; (B) testes; (C) ovary; (D) yolk glands; (E) uterus. × 10.

In the pig many immature flukes fail to reach the bile ducts and become encysted in the liver tissue where they form white, spherical nodules which are $\frac{1}{8}$ to $\frac{1}{3}$ inch in diameter, usually situated superficially, and composed of an outer fibrous capsule with brownish or yellowish semi-solid contents. The relative rarity of adult flukes in the bile ducts of pigs is probably due to the fact that a large proportion of immature parasites fail to complete their migration in this host.

Migratory Flukes. In cattle, immature flukes migrating through the liver parenchyma in their search for a bile duct may penetrate a radicle of the hepatic vein and be transported from the liver to the lungs by way of the posterior vena cava and heart. The flukes are found near the base of the lung, producing round cyst-like areas the size of a hazel nut to a tennis ball, and these, in the early stages, contain coagulated blood and immature parasites but later become calcified and exude a thick, dark brown slime when incised. In Britain about 2 per cent. of cattle with affected livers also have lesions in the lungs, but liver flukes are rarely found in the sheep lung due probably to the fact that the size of the parasite prevents it from entering the fine branches of the hepatic vein. Flukes may also be encountered in the mesenteric lymph nodes of both ox and sheep, being seen as green caseous nodules which are easily enucleated from the lymph node substance, and it is stated that green parasitic foci in the bovine mesenteric lymph nodes are more often attributable to migrating liver flukes than to linguatula larvae. More rarely flukes may be seen in the spleen, heart, serous membranes or subcutaneous tissue.

DICROCOELIUM DENDRITICUM

This parasite is slender and lance-shaped, and $\frac{1}{6}$ to $\frac{1}{3}$ inch long by $\frac{1}{10}$ inch wide; the intermediate hosts are species of land snails. The parasite is found in Northern Europe and in North and South America, but in Britain appears to be confined to islands of the west coast of Scotland. It is, in general, less pathogenic than *Fasciola hepatica*, due probably to the absence of cuticular spines, and the liver fibrosis is finer than in *F. hepatica* infection.

Judgment of Fascioliasis. Man is seldom infected by the common liver fluke and the number of cases recorded probably amounts to no more than 300. Infection in man is acquired by the swallowing of encysted cercariae and not by the consumption of animal livers containing the adult parasite, and man usually infects himself by eating watercress grown in water in which the snails are living and which is contaminated by the faeces of fluke-infested cattle or sheep, the latter being the principal reservoirs for human infection. Outbreaks of human fascioliasis have been recorded in Glamorgan and, on a more extensive scale, in France and Cuba, though usually not more than one or two flukes are present in the livers of infected persons.

Livers which are markedly cirrhotic, as shown by their toughness and unevenness of the surface, and livers which are markedly "pipy", must be condemned as unmarketable, though in bovine livers when the affection is confined to the bile ducts it is possible in many cases to remove these portions and pass the remainder for food. It may be noted that the parasites in the liver will not remain alive for more than a few hours after an infected animal has been slaughtered. The judgment of sheep carcases which are oedematous or emaciated as a result of fluke infestation depends on the extent of these pathological changes.

SCHISTOSOMIASIS IN CATTLE AND SHEEP

This affection is caused by the fluke *Schistosoma mattheei*, which is considered by some to be synonymous with *Schistosoma bovis* and differs from other species of the fluke family in that the sexes are separate, the male worm possessing a canoe-shaped groove in which the female worm is accommodated. The adult parasites are very frequently encountered in cattle and sheep in Africa and inhabit the finer branches of the mesenteric veins of their host, where it is not usual to encounter several hundred adult worms. The life history of the parasite is similar in many respects to *Fasciola hepatica* and symptoms are similar. Eggs laid by the adult female in the mesenteric veins may pass through the intestinal wall of the host to reach the lumen of the bowel and be excreted with the faeces. Some eggs, however, may be carried by the portal blood stream to the liver and give rise to a tissue reaction which initially causes the liver to become markedly enlarged and abnormally pale in colour. The eventual deposition of fibrous tissue in the organ produces a cirrhosis, but not infrequently eggs lodging in the liver tissue give rise to foreign body granulomas appearing as white pin-head sized foci. Livers severely affected with such lesions or with cirrhosis are unfit for food. Multiple areas of fat necrosis are not infrequently found in carcases of cattle and sheep affected with schistosomiasis, and in many cases the lungs and liver exhibit a grey, uniformly distributed pigmentation.

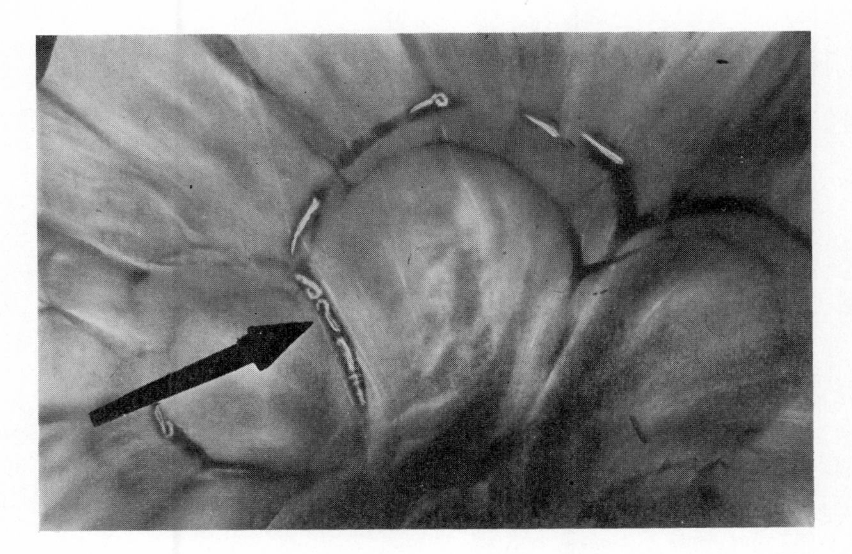

FIG. 179.—Adult male and female *Schistosoma mattheei* in the mesenteric veins of an ox. The parasites are about one inch in length and in the freshly slaughtered animal exhibit active movement.

THE PROTOZOA

These are the most primitive organisms of the animal kingdom and are mostly of microscopical size. They are single-celled, each individual being physiologically complete, and multiplication occurs by division or budding.

The protozoan parasites which are of importance in meat inspection are:

The Coccidia ;
The Sarcosporidia ; and
The Haemosporidia.

The Coccidia

These are cell-infesting parasites attacking the epithelium of certain of the food animals, the rabbit being the animal most frequently and most severely affected. Although coccidiosis is a common parasitic infection of rabbits and poultry, and also occurs in other animals, each coccidium is specific for its own host and cross-infection cannot occur. The chief coccidia capable of pathogenic action are as follows :

(*a*) EIMERIA ZÜRNII is the cause of red dysentery in cattle and occurs chiefly in southern England, Scotland, Ireland, Canada and North America. Cattle between 1 month and 2 years are most often affected, and though bovines of all ages may harbour coccidia, they usually show no clinical symptoms, and pathogenic action only occurs after mass infestation. This is likely to occur where hygienic conditions are unsatisfactory, but the disease is probably unrecognized in the chronic form and the unthriftiness is usually attributed to intestinal worms. Red dysentery is characterized by the presence of a haemorrhagic diarrhoea resulting from the injurious action of the coccidia on the epithelial cells of the mucous membrane of the large intestine, the detachment of these cells exposing the dilated capillaries and producing enteritis and subsequent systemic infection due to bacterial invasion. In acute bovine coccidiosis the mortality in affected animals may exceed 50 per cent.

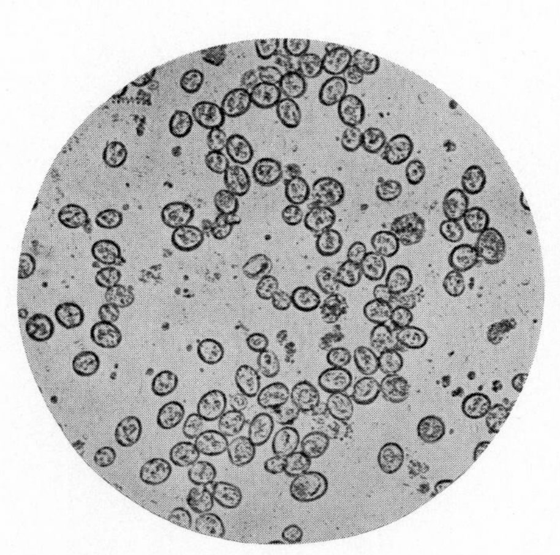

FIG. 180.—Sporulated oöcysts of *Eimeria tenella* from faeces of a fowl affected with caecal coccidiosis. Freshly excreted oöcysts are unsporulated and non-infective, but become infective when sporulation takes place, usually about 48 hours after excretion. × 100.

(*b*) EIMERIA FAUREI occurs in the intestine of sheep and goats, but is of little significance.

(*c*) EIMERIA STIEDAE is found in the liver of rabbits. It inhabits the epithelium of the bile ducts, the lesions being evident on the liver surface as irregularly-shaped whitish foci which, when opened, discharge a white creamy fluid containing numerous oöcysts. Microscopically the bile ducts show papillomatous ingrowths with the coccidia demonstrable in the epithelium. Liver lesions in rabbits are generally present along with intestinal coccidiosis caused by *Eimeria perforans*.

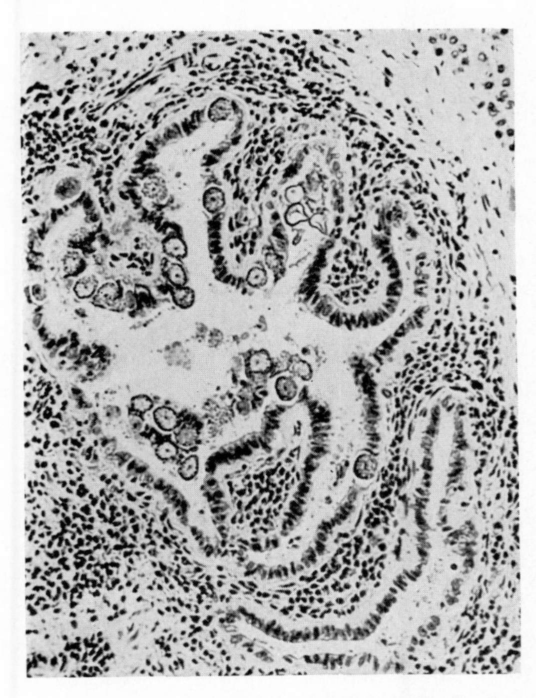

FIG. 181.—Photomicrograph of section of bile duct of liver of rabbit affected with coccidiosis. The duct shows several papillomatous ingrowths with numerous coccidia (*Eimeria stiedae*) in the cells of the epithelium. × 190.

Coccidiosis of the rabbit liver may be mistaken for tuberculosis, but lesions in coccidiosis are of irregular shape, are uniform in size and scattered evenly throughout the liver tissue. In tuberculosis, which is not common in the wild rabbit, the liver is studded with nodules which vary in size, occur in clusters or clumps and are often calcareous.

(*d*) EIMERIA PERFORANS occurs in the intestine of rabbits and gives rise to a severe intestinal catarrh. The anatomical changes are seen chiefly in the lower portion of the small intestine and caecum, the mucous membrane of which is red and swollen, and numerous coccidia can be found in the faeces and in scrapings from the intestinal mucous membrane. This intestinal form of coccidiosis is of much greater severity than the hepatic form, and the mortality in affected rabbits is in the region of 90 to 100 per cent.

(*e*) EIMERIA FUSCA, known also as *Coccidium fuscum*, is stated by German authorities to be the cause of the so-called " shotty eruption " which is seen on the skin of pigs (Fig. 63). This takes the form of round cystic papules around the tail and buttocks, varying in colour and size, and containing a brownish greasy material and curled-up bristles. The condition is said to arise in the sweat glands and is commonly encountered in Britain, but there is at present some doubt that it is caused by a coccidium.

The Sarcosporidia

These protozoa are parasitic in the striated muscle of vertebrates, and lie within the individual muscle fibres ; they are oval cigar-shaped tubes, known as Miescher's tubes, and are divided transversely into a number of chambers which are filled with small sickle-shaped nucleated bodies known as sporozoites or Rainey's corpuscles. These corpuscles eventually degenerate into a granular mass, and should calcification of the whole tube occur the lesions are just visible to the naked eye. A peculiarity of sarcosporidial infection is the ease with which various hosts can be cross-infected and experimental evidence, for example, has shown that sarcocyst infection may be transmitted to healthy pigs through the agency of dogs, cats, mice, rats, pigs and chickens, for if these animals are fed on infected pig flesh their faeces and urine are infective if ingested by pigs. The sarcosporidia of importance in meat inspection are as follows :

(*a*) SARCOCYSTIS MIESCHERIANA (Plate IV) occurs in the pig, the Miescher's tubes being about $\frac{1}{6}$ inch long by $\frac{1}{80}$ inch wide and found most frequently in the muscles of the abdomen and diaphragm, but also in the skeletal muscles. The larger sacs are visible to the naked eye as light-grey oblong dots in the darker muscular tissue, and may then be confused with calcified trichinella cysts. Calcified sarcocysts are the commonest form of calcification occurring in the muscles of the pig, the affection being quite common in swill-fed pigs in the United States and reaching an incidence of 75 per cent. in some localities, though it is stated that the incidence in pigs fed on grain is not higher than 5 per cent. Although this parasite was at one time found in 20 to 30 per cent. of pigs in Denmark, it is recorded that the affection is now much rarer.

(*b*) SARCOCYSTIS TENELLA. This parasite of the sheep and goat is larger than *Sarcocystis miescheriana*, being up to $\frac{3}{5}$ inch long by $\frac{1}{80}$ inch broad, and found chiefly in the oesophagus, but also in the tongue, pharynx, larynx, diaphragm and skeletal muscles. When found in the connective tissue of the oesophagus the sarcocysts are so large that they cannot escape attention and vary in size from a millet seed to a filbert; these large forms of the parasite, formerly considered to belong to a distinct species and in consequence termed *Balbiania gigantea*, have at first sight the appearance of a small abscess or a mass of fat, but microscopical examination of the milky contents of the cyst shows the presence of numerous sporozoites of varying size. Sarcosporidia are commoner in sheep than in any other food animal, being frequently encountered in the oesophagus of ewes, though they are seen less commonly in younger sheep.

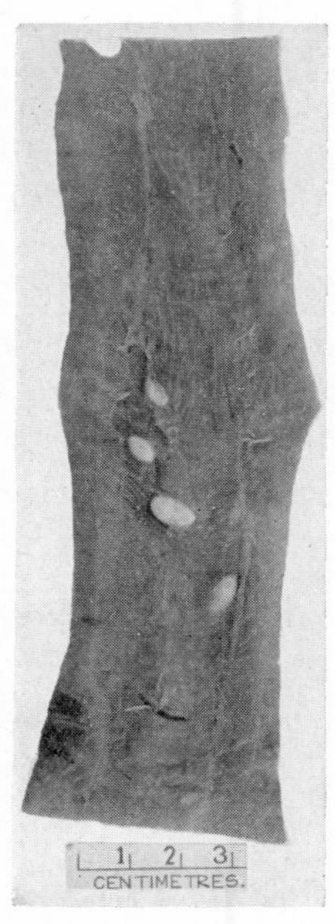

FIG. 182.—*Sarcocystis tenella* beneath serous covering of oesophagus of a ewe.

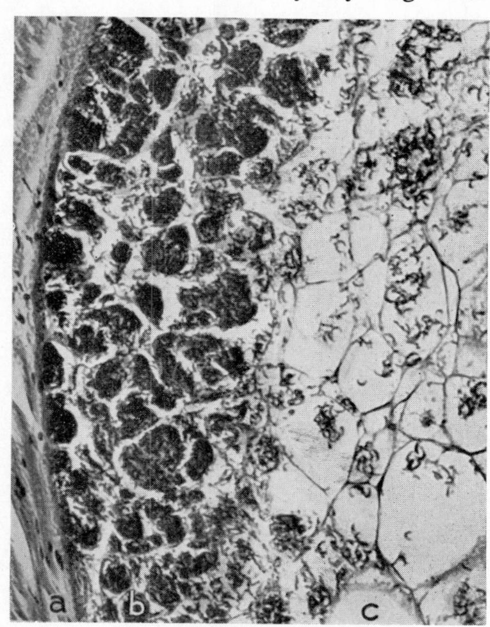

FIG. 183.—Photomicrograph of sarcosporidial cyst from oesophagus shown in Fig. 182. At (*a*) can be seen the cyst capsule; at (*b*) compartments densely filled with colonies of sporozoites, and at (*c*) compartments containing a few sickle-shaped sporozoites. × 190.

Sarcosporidia are also found in the musculature of cattle, chiefly in active muscles such as the tongue, heart, diaphragm and masseters; they are sometimes encountered in the latter muscles during routine post-mortem inspection, and slight infestations tend to disappear during overnight chilling. Authorities in the United States state that sometimes the muscle lesions may be concentrated in foci varying in size from a tiny group of three or four spots to a solid greenish area some inches in diameter; fat steers or heifers are most often affected, dairy cattle but rarely. Lesions designated as "sarcocysts" are not infrequently encountered in the inspection incision made in the shoulder during routine inspection of bovine carcases in Africa, these lesions being of a greenish colour, elongated along the course of the muscle fibres and sometimes widely distributed throughout the carcase musculature. Microscopical examination of these lesions has failed to reveal the presence of sarcosporidia, and though the cause of affection is obscure it is essentially an eosinophilic myositis which is probably of parasitic origin.

Judgment. A sarcocyst, *Sarcocystis lindemanni*, has been reported on a few occasions in the muscular tissue of man, and since the usual habitat of sarcocysts is the musculature of the animals commonly used for human food, infection in man might conceivably occur if infected flesh were consumed. Human infection might likewise occur if foodstuffs contaminated with the spores were consumed, but as the opportunities for such infections must be considerable it is thought that man is an unsuitable host for the parasite. Meat inspection regulations in most countries prescribe that when the affection is slight the carcase is passed for food after the removal and condemnation of all affected tissue, but if the infection is generalized the entire carcase and organs shall be condemned. In the case of lesions of eosinophilic myositis in the musculature of cattle a similar judgment should be applied.

The Haemosporidia

These organisms are parasitic in the blood stream, where they invade the red blood corpuscles, and are transmitted from the blood of one animal to another by a tick or fly ; large numbers of animals may thus become seriously or fatally attacked. The infection is known as piroplasmosis and is of wide distribution, though different species of the parasite are involved in different diseases ; bovine piroplasmosis is known as Texas fever in America, and as redwater fever in Britain, Africa and Europe.

REDWATER FEVER. This is a haemoglobinuria of cattle due to the presence in the blood corpuscles of a protozoan parasite *Babesia bovis*. The affection is common in southern and western England, in Wales and many parts of Scotland, but is most common in Ireland, and occurs in the spring in cattle aged 3 months and upwards, though it is usually a disease of adult cattle.

The parasites occur singly, sometimes in pairs in the red blood corpuscles, each parasite being pear-shaped and seldom exceeding $1{\cdot}5\mu$ in length. They may be found intracorpuscularly with their pointed ends in contact, the angle between the two organisms being obtuse, and for this reason the parasite was formerly termed *Piroplasma divergens*. Sometimes the organisms occur singly as rounded bodies 1 to 2μ in diameter, while less commonly they appear rod-shaped or lanceolate, and the parasites may be demonstrated microscopically if a blood smear be fixed with absolute alcohol and stained by Giemsa's or Leishman's method. Cattle acquire the infection from the bite of a tick, usually *Ixodes ricinus*, and infection occurs in localities where ticks capable of transmitting the disease are prevalent and where they have had the opportunity of ingesting babesia from infected cattle. Ticks abound chiefly in the grass and bushes of rough low-lying land and do not travel far on the ground, so that redwater is likely to be confined to certain districts or fields.

Ixodes ricinus differs in its life history from the American tick, *Boophilus annulatus*, which transmits Texas fever, by the fact that *Ixodus ricinus* is a

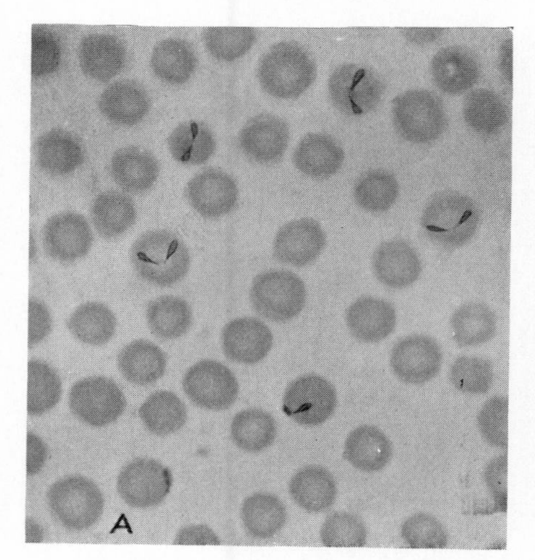

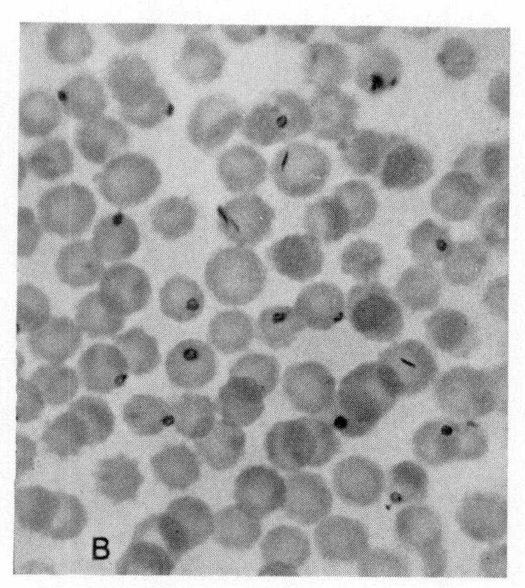

FIG. 184.—Blood smears from cattle affected with redwater fever showing (A) pear-shaped forms of *Babesia bovis*, and (B) spherical and rod-shaped forms.

three-host tick, leaving its host at each of its stages of development; it attaches itself to cattle during the larval, nymphal, and adult stage, and on each occasion it sucks the blood of the host and becomes engorged. The adult tick lays from 100 to 1,000 eggs during its life, the period from the egg to the dropping of the sexually mature tick to the ground being up to 3 years. *Boophilus annulatus*, on the other hand, is a one-host tick, and the various stages of its development take place on the one bovine host.

Symptoms. In acute cases there is an incubation period of 7 to 10 days, followed by fever. The urine is at first slightly darker than usual, later becoming red or even black in colour; this change is due to disintegration of the red blood cells resulting from the destructive action of the piroplasms, the liberated haemoglobin becoming dissolved in the blood plasma and excreted by the kidneys. During the height of an attack 5 to 40 per cent. of red blood corpuscles may be invaded with piroplasms, while the red blood corpuscles are reduced in number from 7 million per cubic millimetre to as few as 2 million and show marked abnormalities in their shape. Redwater may run an acute course with symptoms of anaemia and weakness, and death may occur in 3 to 4 days, or the disease may assume a chronic form in which haemoglobinuria is absent, but in either case recovered animals still harbour the parasite in their red blood cells and continue to act as " carriers ".

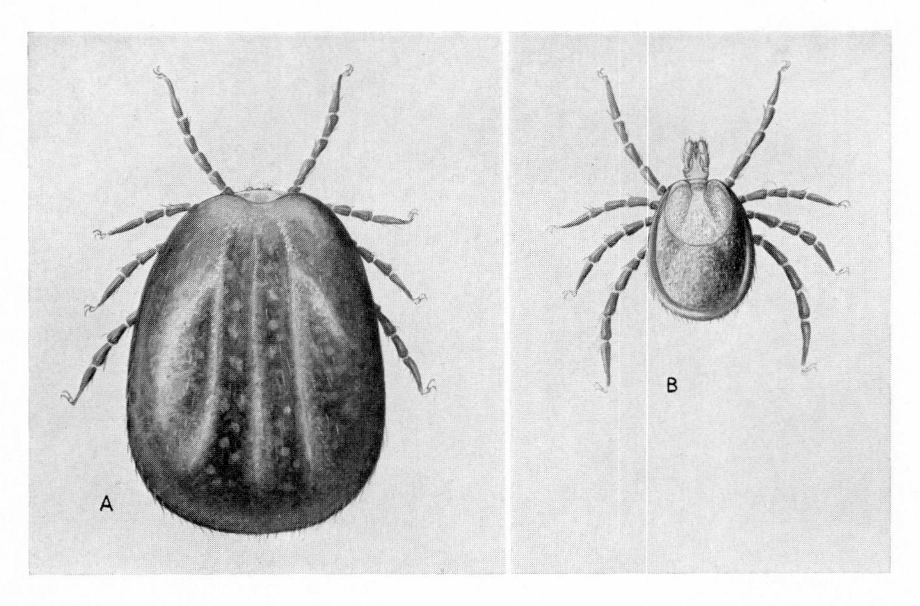

FIG. 185. *Ixodes ricinus*. (A) Engorged adult female. (B) Unengorged adult female. The male tick is somewhat smaller and does not swell in engorging. × 5. (Burroughs Wellcome.)

Lesions. In animals slaughtered within a few days of the onset of symptoms the carcase may set well and appear well bled, though there may be evidence of icterus. In later stages of acute cases the flesh may be pale and somewhat moist, and the blood, though thin, forms a firm clot. The liver is enlarged and icteric and in some cases has undergone cloudy swelling, while the kidneys may be only slightly discoloured but occasionally have a bluish-black coloration and possess a peculiar odour. A noticeable change occurs in the spleen which is markedly enlarged though the splenic pulp is firm.

Judgment. The parasite *Babesia bovis* is not communicable to man, and judgment of the carcase, if well nourished, must depend on the absence of icterus and degree of bleeding and setting. Where there is emaciation and the carcase fat is replaced by a yellow gelatinous material, the carcase should be condemned.

ANAPLASMOSIS

This is a disease of cattle, known usually as gall sickness, and occurs in Africa, Australia and the American continent. The affection is caused by a micro-organism *Anaplasma marginale* which parasitizes the red blood cells, but as these cells are broken down in the spleen there is no entry of haemoglobin into the blood stream and haemoglobinuria does not occur. Anaplasmosis is transmitted by ticks and runs an acute or chronic course, a long incubation period being followed by fever, icterus and progressive emaciation. Typical post-mortem lesions are impaction of the omasum, splenic enlargement, icterus, and distension of the gall bladder with thick clotted bile.

Judgment of carcases affected with anaplasmosis is similar to that of carcases affected with redwater but it is a wise precaution in both these diseases to confirm the diagnosis by microscopical examination of smears from blood and spleen. In the United States it is prescribed that carcases found on post-mortem to be affected with anaplasmosis shall be condemned, but carcases classed as recovered cases in which a slight yellow colour of tissues is evident on post-mortem shall be passed for food provided the yellow coloration disappears on chilling.

THE ARTHROPODA

The adult flies are of little importance in meat inspection, but in several of them the larval stage is responsible for damage of considerable economic importance, particularly in the case of the warble flies and sheep maggot fly.

Warble Flies

These are large, two-winged insects which torment animals during the summer grazing season, whilst their larvae, composed of twelve segments, have a temporary parasitic existence in the animal body. The ox warble fly is found all over Europe, Asia, Africa, Canada and the United States, though Australia, Argentina and New Zealand do not appear to suffer from its depredations. Norway, Sweden, Argentina and Czecho-slovakia are almost untroubled, and it is thought that the climatic conditions of these countries may have a bearing on the incidence of warble flies and their larvae, for they are countries which have remained virtually free of warble infestation without the aid of measures directed towards their eradication. The two common species are *Hypoderma bovis*, the large warble fly, and *Hypoderma lineatum*, the small warble fly, while a third species, *Hypoderma diana*, is found in Scotland. Though *Hypoderma diana* does not infect cattle as is generally believed, it has an economic importance, for the larvae, which inhabit the red deer and roe deer, have similar effects to those of *H. bovis* and *H. lineatum* and render deer hides useless for glove making and other purposes. On rare occasions larvae of *H. bovis* and *H. lineatum* are encountered in horses and in man, and Indian goats are sometimes severely infested with warbles.

Hypoderma bovis

This is the common European warble fly, which appears at the beginning of the summer and persists until the autumn (June to September). The duration of the life of the individual adult fly is only 2 to 7 days, but during that time the female attaches its eggs to the root of the hair in cattle, and close to the skin; *Hypoderma bovis* does not suck blood, and cannot feed on its host. As many as 370 eggs are laid by one fly during its life, the eggs being laid singly, usually on the outer aspect of the hind limb and, less commonly, on the belly. A week after the eggs are laid a larva hatches out, this being about $\frac{1}{25}$ inch long, and after entering the skin through a hair follicle by means of its cutting mouth hooks, commences to wander in the connective tissue of the animal, but never invades muscular tissue.

The path which the larvae of *Hypoderma bovis* subsequently pursues is still obscure, but larvae may be found in the thoracic or abdominal cavity within 2 months of entering the animal body. Unlike *Hypoderma lineatum*, they are never found in the oesophageal wall, but reach the back by way of the softer connective tissues, either through the crura of the diaphragm, the intercostal muscles at about the ninth rib, or by way of the spinal canal. Larvae may be found in the latter location between December and March, lying between the periosteum and dura mater, and at this stage are $\frac{1}{5}$ to $\frac{1}{2}$ inch in size. They migrate from the spinal canal towards the skin of the back by way of the intervertebral foramina, and are found on the back in two strips extending posteriorly from just behind the shoulders to the angle of the haunch, and extending laterally for 7 to 8 inches on either side of the vertebral column. Having reached the back the larvae produce a small hole in the skin, possibly by means of a dermatolytic toxin, and are thus able to obtain oxygen which is necessary for their further development; they become apparent on the skin of the back from mid-February till May, being visible for 28 to 35 days before they emerge from the back to pupate, while from the opening at the top of the walnut-sized swelling there is exudation of a sero-purulent fluid which mats the hair in the vicinity. The full-grown larvae, which are $\frac{3}{5}$ to 1 inch long and possess a tough outer skin, change in colour while still *in situ* from a yellowish-white to a brown or black. They are provided with transverse bands of spines by the aid of which they press themselves out of the skin aperture, drop to the ground and pupate ; the adult fly emerges from the pupa about 1 month later, the entire life cycle taking about one year to complete.

FIG. 186.—Single egg of *Hypoderma bovis* with two-lobed pedicle by which it is attached to an ox hair. × 32. (Crown copyright.)

HYPODERMA LINEATUM

This is a smaller fly, laying its eggs chiefly on the parts of the body which are in contact with the ground when the animal is lying, particularly the chest, belly, udder, elbow and fetlock ; the favourite location is the heel, and the parasite is therefore commonly known as the heel fly. The eggs are about $\frac{1}{25}$ inch long, and laid in rows of 6 to 14 on a single hair, from 400 to 800 being laid during the life of a single female. The life history of *H. lineatum* is similar to that of *H. bovis*, except that the larvae, after entering the body of the host, find their way to the oesophagus, where they are found in the submucous tissue between the mucous membrane and the muscular wall, and oriented along the long axis of the gullet. The pale, translucent larvae are easily demonstrated if the external connective tissue of the oesophagus is removed, and the oesophagus inflated after the manner of a pig's bladder and finally dried. The oesophageal larvae are $\frac{1}{5}$ to $\frac{1}{2}$ inch in length and are found in this location from December, when the peak incidence occurs, to mid-February, though odd larvae may be detected both earlier and later. Most of the larvae are found in the thoracic and abdominal portions of the oesophagus rather than in the cervical portion, and their presence in the oesophageal wall is sometimes manifested by an inflammatory exudate which extends to the mediastinum and gives rise to a yellow gelatinous condition of the mediastinal fat. The general pathogenic effects of *H. lineatum* are similar in every way to *H. bovis*.

FIG. 187.—Eggs of *Hypoderma lineatum* on ox hair. × 15. (Crown copyright.)

FIG. 188.—Hypoderma larvae embedded in fat on under-surface of ox skin. (Crown copyright.)

DELETERIOUS EFFECTS CAUSED BY THE WARBLE FLY AND LARVAE

(*a*) The condition known as " gadding " in which cattle hold the tail erect, rush about violently and kick with the hind legs towards the abdomen, is in part due to the ovipositing female fly, and though the presence of the adult fly causes little general disturbance in health, in dairy cows the quantity and quality of the milk is lowered by this over-excitement and exertion.

(*b*) The larvae, when present in the region of the back, have a deleterious effect on the animal's health, and in cows reduce the milk yield considerably; an average decline of 3·8 lb. (3 pints) in the daily yield of milk has been observed when more than thirty warbles were present in one animal. In the United States and in Germany the diminution in milk yield of affected animals is put at between 10 and 25 per cent., and Danish veterinarians also record a 25 per cent. decrease in the milk production of affected cows.

The effect on increase in weight of fattening cattle is also considerable, and it had been observed that over a period of 43 days affected animals showed an average gain in weight of 15 lb., whereas cattle which had been treated and cured showed a gain in weight of 46 lb. over the same period.

(*c*) Severe economic loss is caused by the damage to the hide, which is either received by the tanner with numerous small holes caused by the warbles or is deteriorated by the small, round, thin areas of scar tissue, the so-called "blind warbles" which are actually healed warble holes. The portion of hide affected (the butt) is particularly valuable for shoe leather.

FIG. 189.—Full-grown larvae of *Hypoderma bovis* removed from skin of back. Left—dorsal view; right—ventral view. (Crown copyright.)

The incidence of warbled hides varies throughout the year. In Britain the month of December shows the lowest average, 5 per cent. of slaughtered cattle being affected, rising in January to 20 per cent. and in April, May, June and July to 60 per cent.; thereafter the damage lessens each month but, taking the year round, more than one hide in every four in Britain is received with open warbles. Hides are graded according to the number

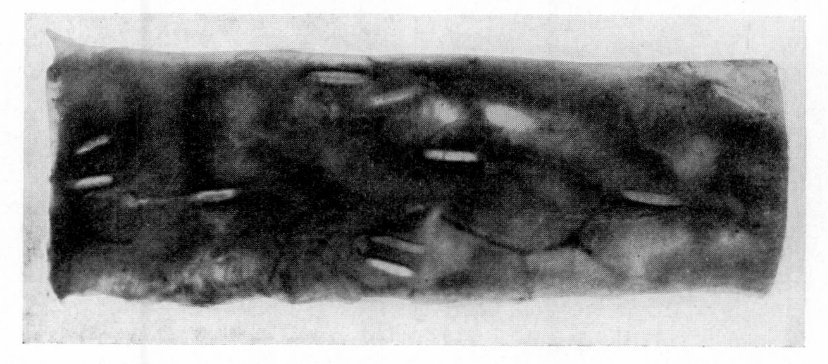

FIG. 190.—Larvae of *Hypoderma lineatum* in submucous tissue of bovine oesophagus. Some congested blood vessels can be seen and are the result of the inflammatory condition produced. $\times \frac{1}{2}$.

of warble holes present, an affected hide having a market value of 1d. to 2d. per lb. less than a "clear" hide, and as the average weight of an ox hide is 60 lb., warble damage may be responsible for a depreciation of 5s. to 10s. in the value of an individual hide. In the United States, hides possessing five or more warble holes are classified as grade 2 and are subject to a discount of one cent per lb., but a hide with numerous warble holes is not considered worth tanning and is sold for conversion into by-products. In 1960 it was estimated that about one-third of all cattle hides in the United States were damaged by warbles, while in Germany about 25 per cent. of hides show evidence of damage.

(*d*) Losses of minor significance are caused by the infestation of the oesophagus with immature hypoderma larvae, for the muscular coat of this organ, which constitutes weasand meat, is rendered unfit for use as a constituent of sausage. In America so-called grubby gullets are commonly encountered in packing houses in autumn and winter, and the serous coats of these cannot be used as a container for salami or bologna sausage. The larvae also cause damage to the subcutaneous and muscular tissue of the back, the deleterious effects chiefly involving the sirloin which is a highly prized portion of the carcase. The condition is described by slaughtermen as " licked " beef, and removal of the hide in affected animals reveals a mass of gelatinous material on either side of the vertebral column.

Figures indicating the total financial loss in a country due to warble fly infestation must only be accepted with great caution, for the losses due to decreased milk yield and damage to flesh are very difficult to estimate with accuracy. It is, however, possible to make a fairly reliable computation of the losses caused in hides by warble fly damage, though such figures are complicated by the fact that hides with open warbles cannot be used for upholstery, travelling cases, machinery belting and Service accoutrements, all of which require sound unwarbled leather, but can be used for boot soles by using the unaffected portions of hide. Again, there are probably as many hides with blind warbles as with open warbles, and these, too, though useless for upholstery, etc., may sometimes be used in footwear for heel pieces or inner soles (which are not subject to friction by contact with the ground).

Judgment. Prompt measures applied to the " licked " bovine carcase can bring about great improvement in the condition, and it should rarely be necessary to condemn portions of affected meat. As soon as possible after slaughter the gelatinous material on the back should be scraped off with a knife ; it is inadvisable to trim off this material, as the underlying muscle is thereby easily damaged. A piece of clean linen should then be applied over the warbled area and left on for 12 hours, and this has the effect of drying and considerably improving the appearance of the affected tissues. The use of mutton cloth or blotting paper is inadvisable for this purpose, as mutton cloth cannot be made to adhere to the carcase, while blotting paper cannot be removed intact from the gelatinous area.

Compulsory measure to combat damage due to warble fly infestation are now in existence in Belgium, Holland, Denmark, Germany, Russia, and in Great Britain under the Warble Fly (Dressing of Cattle) Order, 1948 and

Amendment Order 1960. As a result the average infestation in all parts of England and Wales fell from 31·5 per cent in 1960 to 18·9 in 1964.

The Horse Bot Fly

The bot flies belong to the same family, the Oestridae, as the warble flies, and the commonest example is *Gastrophilus intestinalis* (*Gastrophilus*

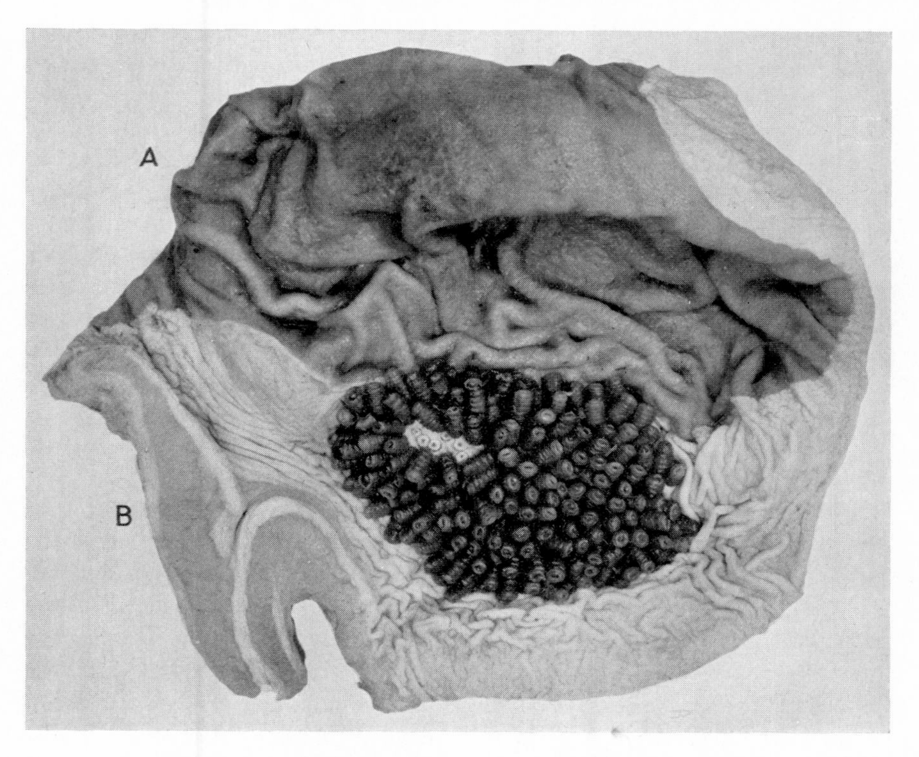

Fig. 191.—Mucous membrane of horse stomach affected with horse bots. (A) Pyloric end of stomach; (B) oesophageal (cardiac) end of stomach; the horse-shoe shape indentation at the bottom left of the illustration is the oesophageal opening. Several bots have been removed to show the circular pits where the larvae have been attached.

equi), the horse bot fly, the larva of which is known as the horse bot. *Gastrophilus nasalis*, though less common than *G. intestinalis*, also occurs in Britain and its larvae are found in a similar position.

The adult fly, which is on the wing from May to September, and is commonest about August, lays its eggs on the hairs of the anterior part of the horse's body, particularly the fore-legs, breast and shoulders. The eggs are yellow in colour and $\frac{1}{16}$ inch long, while the end which is unattached to the hair possesses an operculum. After being ingested the larvae bore through the buccal mucous membrane of the host and eventually reach the stomach, where they fix themselves to the oesophageal end by means of hooks with which the anterior end of the larva is provided. The fully developed larva is about $\frac{3}{4}$ inch in length, flesh-coloured or yellowish-brown, the segments of the body being provided with parallel bands of spines. A considerable number of bots may be found attached to the mucous membrane of the stomach, and up to 500 have been recorded, but the usual number is about 30; occasionally the larvae may be found in the pharynx. As the bots are usually situated at the oesophageal end of the stomach, which is less sensitive than the pyloric end and plays only a minor part in digestion, they cause little functional disturbance. The larvae remain in the stomach for about 10 months, then become detached and are ejected with the faeces, usually about June. Pupation takes place on the ground, the adult fly emerging from the pupa in 4 to 6 weeks. The incidence of the affection is at its highest when horses are kept constantly in the open and is seen particularly in animals which have had prolonged periods at grass.

Judgment. It is only necessary to remove the larvae from the stomach, as they produce no lesions either in the stomach, intestine, or in the carcase which warrant condemnation.

The Sheep Nostril Fly

Oestrus ovis is of world-wide distribution, with the exception of Australia, the larvae producing a chronic catarrhal inflammation of the nasal mucous membranes and adjoining cavities of the sheep.

The adult fly deposits living larvae upon the nostrils of sheep, these larvae being creamy-white in colour and $\frac{1}{16}$ inch long. They invade the nasal passages, even reaching the frontal sinus and horn cores, and feed upon the serous exudate and mucus which is produced as a result of their irritative action; when fully developed the larvae are $\frac{3}{4}$ inch in length, and up to 60 or 80 may be present in the nasal cavities, though the usual number is 3 to 6. Heavy infestation is associated with a muco-purulent nasal discharge and is manifested by frequent sneezing, tossing of the head, and even symptoms of brain irritation; the appetite is lost and is succeeded by weakness and emaciation, which may reach such a stage that the animal is unable to rise.

Judgment. Where sheep awaiting slaughter are suspected to be suffering from the affection, the head should be examined after slaughter by splitting the skull down the middle line. As the sheep head is utilized for food purposes in the form of broth and potted meat, the presence of larvae or of a muco-purulent inflammation of the nasal passages dictates condemnation of the head.

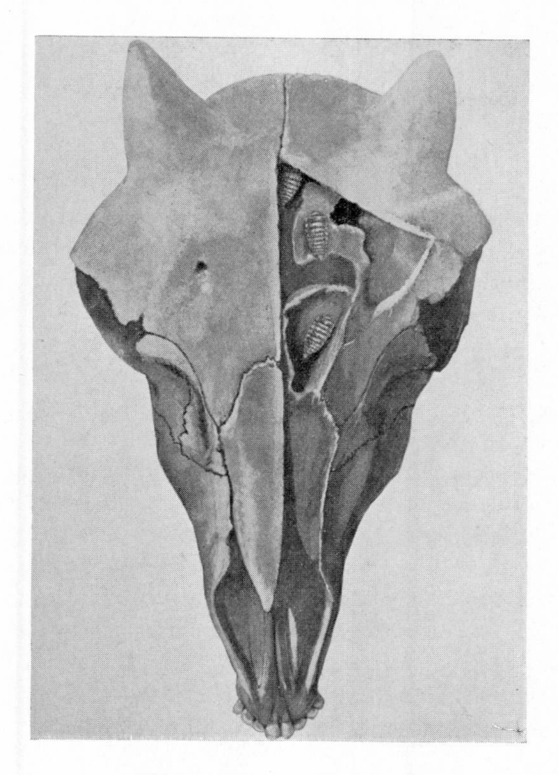

FIG. 192.—Head of sheep showing three mature *Oestrus ovis* larvae in frontal sinus. The most serious results occur when the sinuses of the head are involved, and symptoms of brain irritation may then occur. (R. B. Poole.)

THE SHEEP MAGGOT FLY

Lucilia sericata, the sheep maggot fly, is responsible for the deposition of larvae on sheep, producing maggoty or " fly blown " sheep. The affection is of considerable economic importance to the sheep farmer, for badly infested sheep do not thrive, and death occurs rapidly in a few days if animals are neglected or overlooked. Sheep maggot fly infestation is also known as " strike " and in Australia is responsible for such heavy losses that it is included among the notifiable animal diseases.

Affected animals are not commonly encountered in meat inspection, but where there is evidence of maggot infection, bearing in mind the tendency for the larvae to penetrate deeply into the connective tissue between muscles, an inspector should not hesitate to remove generous portions of muscular tissue from around the affected area. Sequelae in recovered animals sometimes take the form of chronic abscesses in the region of the chine, withers and back, but in the absence of toxic infection, for which the sheep kidneys are a valuable indication, the affected areas may be removed and the carcase released for food.

Contamination of Meat by Insect Larvae

The larvae occasionally found on raw or cooked meat belong to the sub-family Calliphorinae. The bluebottles or blowflies, of which *Calliphora vomitoria* and *Calliphora erythrocephala* are common examples, lay their eggs on meat, and these hatch within a period varying from a few hours up to 1 or 2 days, the shorter period occurring in hot weather. Under favourable conditions the larvae continue to grow and develop for 10 days before pupating, but growth ceases if the atmospheric temperature falls below 44° F. Larvae are found most commonly on the covered parts of the carcase such as the breast, under the diaphragm, or in pockets between muscles; they are therefore difficult to remove, and infestation in small veal carcases may be so severe as to necessitate total condemnation.

The grey meat fly, *Sarcophaga carnaria*, deposits living larvae on meat, and these are true flesh eaters and consume large quantities as they develop; a single larva can consume more than its own weight of meat in 4 hours.

The cheese or ham fly, *Piophila casei*, lays clusters of eggs in salted or smoked foodstuffs such as hams, or in dried beef or cheese; the eggs are deposited in damp crevices in the meat, or in pockets on the cut muscular surface of hams. The larvae developing from these ova are about $\frac{1}{3}$ inch long, being known as cheese or ham skippers, and feed on meat during their development. They leap considerable distances by seizing the edge of the anal extremity with their mouth hooks and releasing this when in a state of tension, but leaping only takes place at the end of the larval period, when the larva wishes to find a dry spot prior to pupation. Affected meat may be dealt with by trimming, which must be done generously as the larvae have a tendency to burrow deeply into the tissues; when the condition occurs in meat stores the meat should be immersed in boiling water or iced water before trimming, and in this way leaping of the larvae on to fresh meat foods may be avoided.

The larvae of the ham beetle, *Dermestes lardarius*, is $\frac{1}{4}$ to $\frac{3}{8}$ inch long with a wide, pale yellow band across the back, and is a troublesome pest in bacon, hams and cheese, while the flour mite, *Tyroglyphus farinae*, may be seen on meat if flour products and meat are stored together, and gives the meat the appearance of being covered with a grey powdery deposit.

Linguatula rhinaria

This parasite belongs to the Pentastomidia, which are closely related to the spiders, ticks and mites, but has become extremely altered owing to its parasitic mode of life. The chief significance of linguatulae in meat inspection is that the larval form occurs in the mesenteric lymph nodes of herbivorous animals, where it gives rise to lesions which may be mistaken for tuberculosis. The adult parasite is found chiefly in the nasal cavity of the dog, particularly in butchers' dogs, shepherds' dogs or hunting dogs; more rarely it is found in the nasal cavity of the horse, sheep, and occasionally man. The adult linguatula is elongated, with an enlarged and rounded anterior extremity at which is situated the mouth, furnished with four chitinous recurved hooks; the parasite then gradually tapers towards the posterior extremity and the integument is composed of about 90 segments. The sexes are separate, the male being white in colour and about ¾ inch long, while the female is darker, 3 to 4 inches long, and often shows a brown coloration of its centre due to the presence of numerous ova.

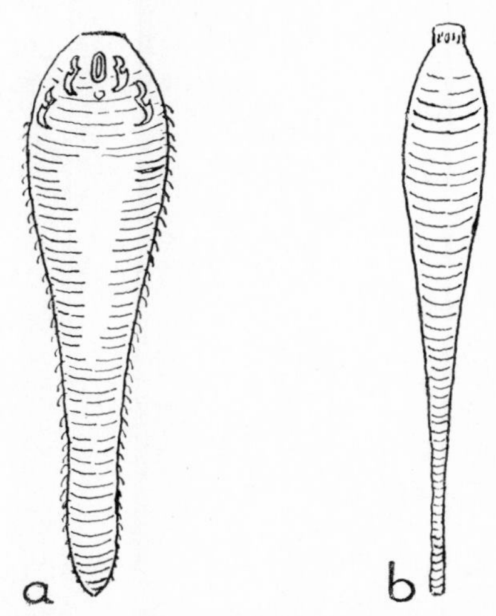

FIG. 193.—(*a*) Adult *Linguatula rhinaria.* Natural size. (*b*) Larval form (*Linguatula serrata.*) × 10.

Life History. The adult linguatula lives in the dog for about 2 years, the parasites being usually present in the folds of mucous membrane at the anterior part of the lower turbinated bone. Eggs first appear in the nasal secretions 6 months after infection, these being voided from the dog's nostrils by sneezing and nasal discharges; the number of ova so voided may be up to half a million. If the ova are ingested by an herbivorous animal the embryos are conveyed by the lymph and blood stream, and are usually found in the mesenteric lymph nodes of the host; they may also become lodged in the liver and lungs, and if they pass through the lungs and invade the arterial blood stream they may be found in the kidney, beneath the endocardium in cattle, in the spleen, or the mediastinal, prescapular, iliac, inguinal or lumbar lymph nodes.

The larval form of the parasite, known as *Linguatula serrata* (*Pentastomum denticulatum*) is ¼ to ⅓ inch long, and is chiefly found in the ox and sheep, but also occurs in the goat, pig, hare and rabbit. The larval forms in the mesenteric lymph nodes are seen as small nodules, particularly at the periphery of the nodes, and vary in size from a millet seed to a pea, being at first yellowish or green, but eventually become grey in colour.

The earlier yellow or green lesions are soft, and the parasite can be demonstrated in them microscopically, while the grey colour of the older lesion indicates the onset of pathological fatty change and calcification, but even after calcification has occurred the typical chitinous hooklets may sometimes be demonstrated by microscopical examination.

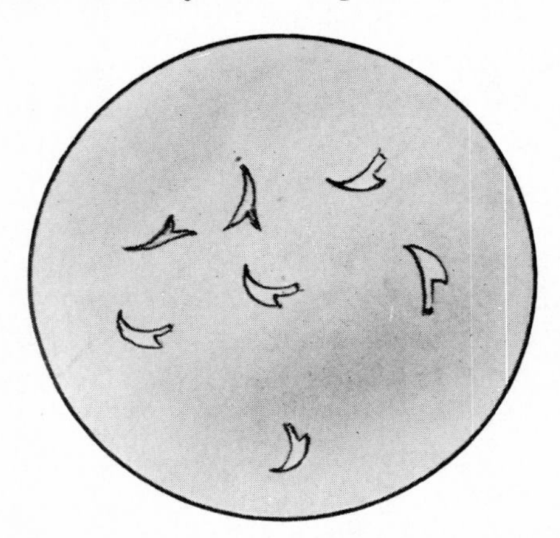

FIG. 194.—Hooklets of *Linguatula serrata* from a degenerated lesion in a mesenteric lymph node of the ox. × 15.

Differential Diagnosis. Though it is stated that parasitic nodules of the bovine mesenteric lymph nodes are more often due to undeveloped liver flukes than to linguatula larvae, examination of a microscopical preparation will demonstrate whether the nodule is due to fluke infection or linguatulae.

Yellow foci due to linguatulae may be distinguished from tuberculous nodules by the following : (*a*) Linguatula larvae are usually found at the periphery of the mesenteric lymph nodes, and can be easily shelled out with the point of a knife ; (*b*) the hooklets of the larvae can be demonstrated microscopically ; and (*c*) the nodules are yellowish, but more often green, and are soft in consistency ; they become grey when calcified, whereas tuberculous foci retain their yellow colour (Plate IV).

Judgment. Isolated foci in the liver, spleen or lymph nodes, etc., may be excised. When the mesenteric lymph nodes are found affected it is the usual practice to condemn and destroy the mesenteric fat. There is little justification for this, and a more reasonable procedure is to incise the mesenteric fat some 6 inches from its intestinal attachment, and the distal portion of this valuable edible fat, being free of lymph nodes, may then safely be passed for food.

CHAPTER IX

BACTERIOLOGY OF MEAT

1. Sources of Bacterial Contamination

In the live animal micro-organisms are present on the skin and hair and also in those cavities that communicate directly with the exterior by way of the natural body openings. Thus the alimentary tract, naso-pharyngeal cavities and external portion of the urino-genital tract harbour a characteristic bacterial flora which has become adapted to the particular environmental conditions. On the other hand those tissues and cavities which have no direct connection with the exterior are sterile, and provided the animal is healthy and in a physiologically normal condition no bacteria should be present in the blood stream, bone marrow, lymph nodes, or the thoracic or abdominal cavities, including the lungs, liver and spleen.

The importance of the rôle that bacteria play in relation to meat is that they are intimately concerned with spoilage and decomposition, and also with food poisoning. Bacterial contamination of meat may occur in several ways :

(*a*) The physiological condition of the animal immediately prior to slaughter has a profound effect on the carcase and subsequent development of deleterious bacteria, for early invasion of the blood vessels by micro-organisms from the intestines is likely to take place in animals weakened by long journeys or in animals which are ill prior to slaughter. In addition, the high pH of the flesh of animals slaughtered while exhausted or ill is favourable to bacterial growth and prejudicial to carcase durability.

(*b*) During the act of sticking of pigs it has been shown that bacteria enter the jugular vein or anterior vena cava and make their appearance in the blood, muscles, lungs and bone marrow. It is, however, questionable whether bacterial contamination of carcases by way of the sticking wound is of great importance.

(*c*) Under ordinary conditions the heaviest and potentially the most dangerous load of bacteria is in the animal's digestive tract. A fattening ox passes 90 to 100 lb. of dung daily and it is estimated that one ounce of fresh bovine faeces contains 1,500 million bacteria. One serious source of contamination from digestive material is the regurgitation which occurs when cattle are stunned and bled, and this causes severe contamination of the neck, throat and tongue. Recent work in Australia has shown that the level of contamination of beef carcases with intestinal organisms was often higher on the inner aspect of the neck than in other locations of the carcase, and a further significant observation was made that samples of ruminal fluid from cattle slaughtered at a number of abattoirs in Queensland showed that an average of 45 per cent. of samples contained salmonella organisms.

(*d*) Contamination of the surface of the dressed carcase from the outside of the hide is of considerable importance because the bacteria found on meat are identical with those found on the animal's hide. The hide bacteria, in turn, are dependent on the bacteriology of the soil of the pastures on which animals are fed. Stall-fed cattle in winter may carry considerable quantities of dung on their hides and it is estimated that $\frac{1}{10}$ of an ounce of soil can contaminate a whole side of beef to the extent of 200,000 organisms per square inch. It has also been shown that a clean knife on penetrating the hide may acquire 2 million organisms.

(*e*) Actual contagion with dirty hands, clothing, or equipment is another important factor in accounting for the number of bacteria found on meat. The use of wiping cloths, now expressly prohibited by most progressive countries, and of unhygienic knife sheaths can contribute materially to the surface contamination of carcases.

(*f*) Irrespective of whether cattle are dressed horizontally or on the line, the most important sources of contamination are from the digestive tract and the surface of the hide. In carcases dressed horizontally the highest bacterial contamination is found on the belly and legs, while in those dressed on the line the highest contamination is on the belly and shoulders. The contamination in on-the-line dressing occurs during removal of the abdominal organs and from the hands of the workers during manual propulsion of the carcase along the overhead rail. In line dressing the highest bacterial count of the air is obtained near the point where the hide of the animal is removed, but the higher the carcase is suspended the lower is the bacterial contamination of the carcase surface. Investigations made on behalf of the meat exporters in Australia and New Zealand are referred to on the following page, and show clearly how important are (a) the dirt brought on to the abattoir floor by the animal, and (b) the contamination that can occur on meat due to faulty handling, transport and storage.

Though line dressing of cattle in modern abattoirs does prevent the slaughtered animal from touching the slaughterhouse floor at any time, it is a fact that the frenzied tempo frequently associated with the procedure in factory abattoirs can be an effective means of pooling animal sources of salmonellae, of providing abundant opportunities for ante- and post-mortem transfer of these organisms, and of furnishing excellent media for maintaining their viability and promoting their proliferation. The more intense the productivity the greater is the salmonella hazard, and any error of hygiene in the chain of production may have consequence that are both serious and widespread.

(*g*) Bacterial infection of muscles may occur ante-mortem and be due to specific organisms which have been responsible for illness of the animal. Some, but not most, of these micro-organisms may belong to the group responsible for bacterial food poisoning in men. The technique by which carcases of animals suspected to have been suffering from a systemic affection are examined bacteriologically is dealt with on page 435. In addition, routine bacteriological procedures are of the greatest value in assessing the degree of surface bacterial contamination in abattoirs and meat processing works.

2. Sanitation in the Abattoir

An efficient meat hygiene programme does not begin in the abattoir but on the farm and must be maintained during transportation, in collecting centres and the abattoir—even as far as the consumer's home.

One of the main sources of carcase contamination in the meat plant is the live animal itself, this being particularly the case in winter months when animals are housed. A survey of 600 cattle hides in Northern Ireland in February 1965 showed that the average weight of manure, soil and other dirt adhering to them was 9 lb. with a range of 2-35 lb. Weights as high as 50 lb., even 80 lb., have been recorded. It is essential, therefore, that livestock be presented for slaughter in as clean a condition as possible, this being achieved by hygienic practices on the farm, in transport lorries and market pens, etc. In some countries it is the practice to pass cattle through water sprays in order to reduce this surface contamination. But while this may be suitable with soft dirt on hides it would only serve to make matters worse where dirt is firm and adherent. Again, spraying cannot be carried out with sheep, in which much of the soiling of the fleece is caused by internal parasitism.

FIG. 195.—Hygienic meat transport.
(By courtesy of Messrs. Smiths Litex Vehicles, Gateshead.)

Many countries have regulations which require frequent cleansing and disinfection of livestock vehicles. It is important that these are implemented not only from the animal hygiene point of view but also to eliminate the possibility of transfer of contagious diseases.

The work of Empey and Scott in Australia just prior to the Second World War dealt with the sources of contamination of meat in the abattoir and these can be summarized as follows :

(1) Dirt and skins of animals (approx. 33 per cent.)
(2) Pollution in the abattoir atmosphere (approx. 5 per cent.)
(3) The visceral content—in normal conditions (approx. 3 per cent.)

(4) Transport and storage (50 per cent. or more)
(5) Halving, quartering and packing of carcases (approx. 2 per cent.)
(6) Miscellaneous—utensils, personnel, etc. (approx. 3 per cent.)

It will be seen, therefore, that if the hide or fleece is heavily contaminated with faeces, the amount of transfer to the carcase by dressing operations is considerable, unless steps can be taken to reduce it by frequent washing of hands, clothing and equipment. After skinning as many as 10,000-100,000 bacteria per square centimetre can be found on the tissues, the contamination being greatest at the point of incision and lowest in the regions farthest from it.

Blades of knives can carry 80,000 to 40 million bacteria per blade; leggings of operatives removing hides after skinning 100 carcases in 6 hours have carried as many as 3×10^9 bacteria per gram of scrapings. The hands of meat operatives can carry as many as 2 million bacteria.

It will thus be evident that much of the contamination occurring in abattoirs is derived from the animals entering it. The accumulation of animals in lairages serves to further increase the possibility of carcase contamination unless strict attention is paid to cleanliness and the avoidance of overcrowding. It has also been shown that while the resting of animals prior to slaughter is an essential procedure in the production of a quality end-product, over-long retention only serves to increase the possibility of cross-contamination in which salmonella organisms are often incriminated.

It is important, therefore, to keep the initial contamination on the animals to a minimum and to supplement this with strict hygiene precautions at all stages in the abattoir itself.

Hygiene in the abattoir itself depends on many factors in addition to those outlined above, and include the area in which the plant is sited, its type of construction and layout, the size of throughput, type of equipment used, facilities for cleansing operations and last, but not least, the type of employees involved.

Before discussing the actual measures designed to reduce the amount of bacterial contamination in the meat plant it will be useful to define the meaning of certain terms. *Sterilization* refers to any process, chemical or physical, which destroys all living microorganisms. It is an absolute term, sterility meaning the absence of all forms of life. A *disinfectant* is an agent, usually a chemical one, which destroys bacteria (but not necessarily bacterial spores which are much more resistant to all forms of adverse agencies). An *antiseptic* has been defined as a substance which prevents or arrests the growth of organisms either by inhibiting their activity or destroying them; it is normally applied to agents used on living tissues. A *germicide* is a substance which will destroy vegetative bacterial cells but not necessarily bacterial spores and is thus akin to a disinfectant ; it is usually applied in relation to disease-producing bacteria. In recent years the term *sanitizer* has appeared in the literature in relation to food hygiene. It is a chemical agent which reduces to acceptable bacteriological standards the number of bacterial contaminants on surfaces in contact with food. Most sanitizers on sale are made up of combined detergent-sanitizing compounds.

A *detergent* is a cleansing substance which has the power to remove " soil " or dirt from surfaces. It may be natural or artificial and may be in the form of a powder, paste or liquid. The most effective general detergent is water, though the term is seldom applied to it. The artificial detergents may be simple inorganic chemical compounds such as washing soda (sodium carbonate), or more complex organic substances such as soap or mixtures of synthetic cleansing materials and lather-producing chemicals as in modern washing powders and liquids. Inorganic detergents include the carbonates, phosphates, sulphates and sulphonates of sodium and potassium, while the most important organic detergent is soap which is based on the combination of a fatty acid derived from various oils and fats and an alkali such as caustic soda or potash.

In order to be efficient a detergent or cleansing agent must possess the following properties :

(1) The power to remove " soil " from surfaces.
(2) The capacity to effect maximum suspension and deflocculation of " soil ".
(3) The ability to prevent scale formation in hard water systems.
(4) The means to ensure optimum rinsing.
(5) The potential to maintain relatively stable degrees of acidity or alkalinity.
(6) The ability to combine satisfactorily with sanitizing agents when both are used together.

Modern synthetic detergents, which have the property of producing abundant lather, consist chiefly of sulphonated fatty alcohols and adjuvant substances such as carbonates, silicates, phosphates, etc. Detergent action is measured by the ability of a substance to remove particles of dirt which are first of all loosened and then combine to form large globules. The detergent then encloses these in protective films and they become emulsified and are easily washed away.

The *sanitizing* agents commonly used in the food industry belong to four main groups :

(1) Halogen-based formulations.

(2) Quaternary ammonium compounds.
(3) Amphoteric compounds.
(4) Acids and alkalis.

The ability to sanitize is governed mainly by the concentration of the agent used, its temperature and time of application, the acidity or alkalinity of the solution and the presence of organic matter.

Of the halogens, chlorine and its compounds are the most important agents for sterilizing, disinfecting and sanitizing of food processing equipment and utensils, and for treatment of water supplies. Sodium hypochlorite as a 10 to 12 per cent. solution is perhaps the most important

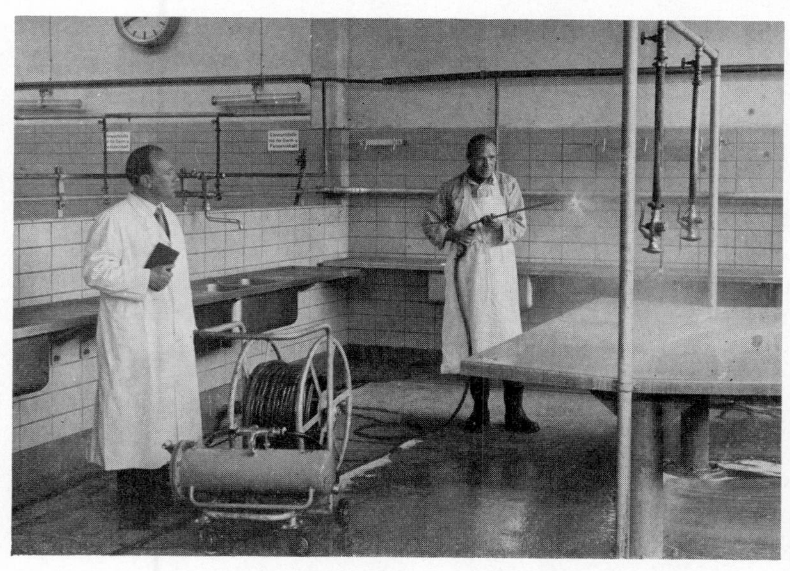

FIG. 196.—The use of an amphoteric compound in a meat preparation room. (*By courtesy of Messrs. Hough, Hoseason & Co. Ltd., Manchester.*)

source of chlorine in food plant sanitation. Organic matter inactivates chlorine and so it is important to have clean surfaces if it is to have a sterilizing effect. The efficacy of chlorine is reduced at pH value of 11 and over and so it is not used in the presence of over 2 per cent. caustic soda. Chlorine is somewhat corrosive to metals especially at high temperatures and for prolonged exposures. A solution of sodium hypochlorite containing 250 ppm of chlorine can be used effectively to disinfect clean equipment.

Quaternary ammonium compounds are most effective at pH levels near or just above neutral. They are inactivated by organic matter but not to the same extent as hypochlorite. They are able to form a fairly stable film which exercises a continuing bacteriostatic action. Although non-corrosive to metals, their efficiency is reduced with hard water and they are in general more expensive than the halogens.

Amphoteric compounds are either long chain substituted amino acids or betaines. They are surface active, compatible with all other detergents and sanitizers and remain unaffected by hard water.

It must be stated here that the use of a disinfectant or sanitizer must be preceded by thorough cleansing. Cleansing indeed must be a continuous process in the meat plant if optimum hygiene standards are to be achieved.

All buildings must be vermin-proof and kept free from flies. The surrounding area must be well maintained so that there is no risk to the plant from vermin or insects. Floor and walls should be of smooth impervious material, with corners covered. The use of porcelain tiles may be of advantage in certain places, but it is possible that modern epoxy paints which present a hard durable easily-cleansed surface may in time replace them. Tiles are apt to cause trouble if the grouting becomes defective and the tiles loosen. In so far as is possible no opportunity should be given for any dirt to collect—all areas should be capable of being easily and effectively cleansed. Maintenance should be of a high standard, whether this be related to equipment or to operations such as plastering, painting, etc. All paints used should be of a lead-free type.

Most countries in which meat hygiene is of a high calibre possess regulations which set standards for meat premises in relation to overall lay-out, type of construction, materials used, lighting, drainage, etc., as well as to the different types of departments to be included. These extend also to the types of equipment advocated, all these to be of a type which are durable, easily cleansed and non-toxic to meat products.

While the type of building and its equipment is important, so also are facilities for cleaning. An ample supply of good hygienic water is essential, this to be used through an adequacy of hose points. An ample supply of hot water is essential at a temperature of not less than 140° F., preferably boosted with steam to about 180° F. Steam by itself is not an efficient sterilizing agent, because when it comes into contact with a cold surface it is nothing more than a warm vapour. Water pressure must be high to enable accumulation of fat, blood, bone dust, etc., to be easily removed from floors and other surfaces. The usual method of applying hot water in meat plants is through high pressure jet cleaners. For greater efficiency the hot water is usually combined with a detergent, this being mixed in at a constant proportion irrespective of the water pressure.

Thorough cleansing using high pressure hot water is usually carried out at specified times when operations are suspended or at the end of the day's kill. Vertical hoses using hot water at lower pressures must be used to supplement these procedures and thus make the cleansing operation a continuous one.

The frequency of cleansing operations is stressed since no opportunity must be given for a build-up of bacteria to occur. Special attention must be given to trollies, hooks and gambrels, etc., which come into contact with the meat. These may be sterilized in in-place cabinets on the overhead

FIG. 197.—Using a steam-injected hose in an abattoir.
(By courtesy of Messrs. C. P. Equipment Ltd., Mitcham.)

rail or in the sterilization room where they are immersed in batches in tanks containing hot detergent solutions, hot rinses, derusting and oiling solutions. Hot water jet hoses may be used to clean certain types of equipment such as trucks, beef trees, etc., but these and smaller items such as meat containers, knives, scabbards, cleavers can be effectively sterilized in cabinets which utilize a hot water detergent solution.

The placing of the slaughter floor on an upper storey makes for a higher standard of hygiene as feet, hides, fleeces, etc., are discharged to the byproducts area below through a system of chutes. There is also less cross-traffic of trucks and personnel in this form of meat plant construction.

There is much to be said for having a sterilizing room or rooms managed by personnel specialized in the technology of sterilization. In this way a high standard of hygiene can be maintained since equipment and knives which have come into contact with contamination can be quickly changed

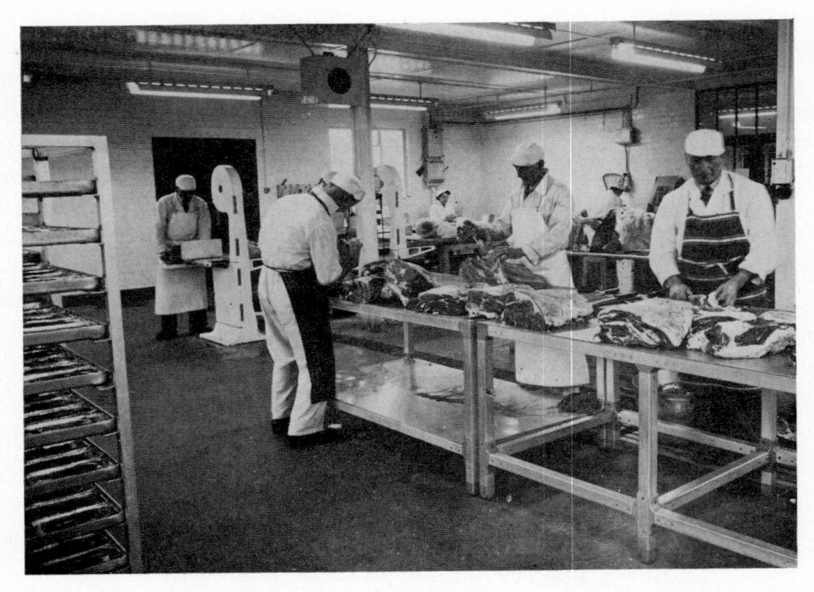

FIG. 198.—Clean personnel and facilities in a meat-cutting room.

FIG. 199.—A modern hygienic refrigerated meat cabinet in a retail shop. (*By courtesy of Messrs. J. & E. Hall, Dartford, Kent.*)

instead of leaving this to the operative engaged in the process of carcase dressing.

Important though the plant lay-out design and facilities are, they must be combined with a high standard of personal hygiene and responsibility towards cleanliness in the employees themselves. Most countries require food plant employees to have periodical medical examinations and to report the occurrence of certain diseases which might be responsible for the development of food-poisoning outbreaks. A sound training in the theory and practice of good hygiene is essential and operatives should have all the necessary facilities to achieve a high standard of personal cleanliness and a clean, workmanlike job.

The National Sanitation Foundation of the United States of America defines the term " sanitation " as follows :

" Sanitation is a way of life. It is the quality of living that is expressed in the clean home, the clean farm, the clean business and industry, the clean neighbourhood, the clean community. Being a way of life, it must come from within the people ; it is nourished by knowledge and grows as an obligation and an ideal in human relations."

3. The Assessment of Surface Bacterial Contamination in Abattoirs and and Meat Factories

Increasing attention has been directed in recent years to the use of rapid and simple methods of assessing the degree and nature of bacterial contamination that may exist on carcases, wall, floors, equipment and fittings, both in the slaughter hall and in those rooms where the meat or organs undergo further treatment before they are marketed for sale. The technique known as the media sausage method has proved simple, reliable and of inestimable value and is described below :

The media required is poured into an artificial sausage casing which has been sterilized by boiling, the casing being filled to capacity. A casing with a diameter of 3 inches is suitable for applying to large surfaces such as tables, walls and animal carcases ; but in some cases, as in the bacteriological examination of poultry carcases, a smaller diameter casing may be preferred. The sausage is then placed into a larger casing, the mouth of this being also tied firmly and the whole sterilized by steaming for 30 minutes on two successive days, thus ensuring that not only bacillary forms but also bacterial spores will be destroyed. The purpose of the outer plastic casing is to ensure sterility of the sausage during storage and transport, while the inner casing prevents bacterial contamination of the surface of the media.

Various media may be used, nutrient agar or blood for total counts, neutral red lactose agar for *E. coli*, brilliant green phenol red lactose agar for salmonellae, and malt agar for yeasts and moulds. In the assessment of the efficiency of the hygienic procedures in an abattoir it may be considered that the essential tests should be for (*a*) total bacterial count, (*b*) presence of salmonella organisms, and (*c*) the presence of faecal coli. The method cannot be used for assessing contamination due to anaerobic organisms.

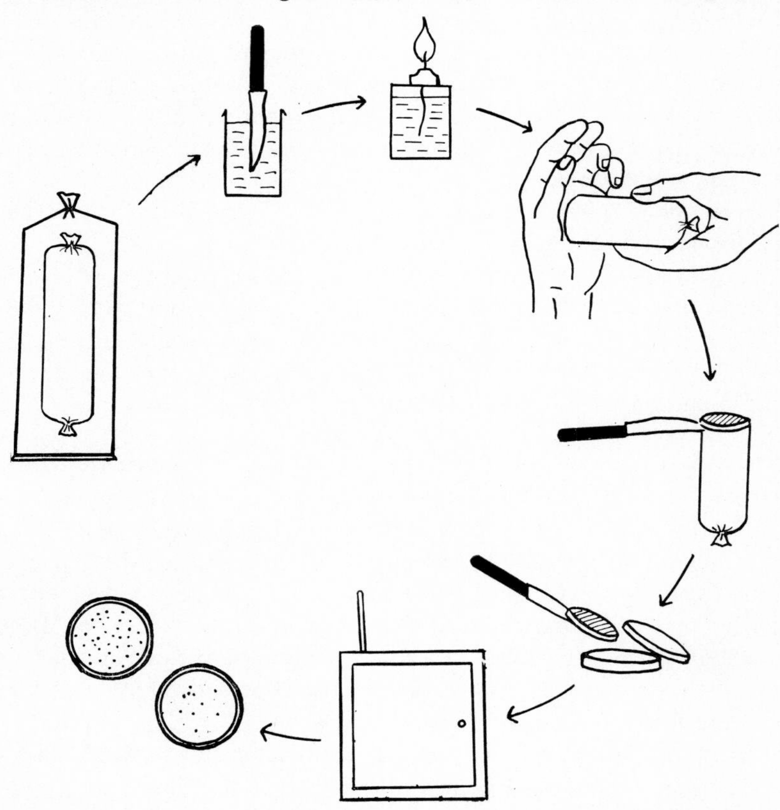

FIG. 200.—The media sausage method for the assessement of surface bacterial contamination.

The test is carried out by folding back the outer plastic container and the end of the inner sausage is cut across to present a smooth flat surface. The blade is flamed prior to the making of the cut, and between successive cuts is kept immersed in a solution of 70 per cent. alcohol; this avoids marginal infection of the edge of the media during slicing.

The cut surface of the sausage is then applied to the surface to be tested and maintained in contact for one second, then a slice of about $\frac{1}{16}$ inch in depth cut from the exposed end of the media, and this slice, contact surface uppermost, transferred immediately into a petri dish. The petri dish and media are then incubated for the prescribed time and at the appropriate temperature. The large surface of the media renders it easy to count the bacterial colonies, but the question will naturally arise as to the degree of bacterial contamination which should be regarded as permissible on carcases or on abattoir structures. Employment of the technique during various stages of operations, e.g. before the commencement of work, at the cessation of the day's work, and after subsequent cleansing procedures, should enable one to arrive at a criterion which can reasonably be maintained under everyday abattoir conditions. It should be borne in mind, however, that higher bacterial counts must be expected in the warmer months of the year. In Germany the degree of bacterial growth on media of 35·0 mm diameter is recorded in the form of a grade number as follows :

Growth	*Grade No.*
Negative	0
Slight growth (under 10 colonies)	1
Little growth (10-30 colonies)	2
Moderate growth (up to 80 colonies)	3
Heavy growth (over 80 colonies)	4
Complete coalescence of colonies	5

4. Methods of Limiting or Reducing Contamination

(*a*) The practice of allowing animals to rest in a lairage for not less than 12 hours after arrival has a threefold purpose :

1. The vascular engorgement of the subcutaneous and muscular tissues in reduced and better bleeding of the carcase is therefore ensured.

2. The period of rest tends to diminish the passage of bacteria from the intestines into the blood stream and ensures better durability of the meat.

3. The glycogen content of muscle, which becomes depleted by exhaustion, is wholly or partially restored and as a result there is adequate formation of lactic acid and the development of satisfactory post-mortem acidity.

(*b*) The accepted practice of allowing copious draughts of water to the animal awaiting slaughter is directed towards lowering the load of intestinal bacteria ; the vast majority of these consist of *E. coli*.

(*c*) Large number of micro-organisms of many kinds are carried into the abattoir by animals, and a considerable decrease in subsequent bacterial contamination of the surface of the dressed carcase may be ensured by subjecting the animals to an overhead spray and passing them through a water bath filled to the level of the animals' belly. It is important that the flooring of the lairage pens and of the race leading to the stunning box should be non-slip but at the same time readily cleansible. In Fig. 11 is illustrated a type of floor which satisfied both these criteria.

(*d*) The whole process of slaughter and dressing must aim at ensuring, as far as practicable, that the meat remains bacteria-free. In Germany the practice of leaving calves unskinned was at one time permissible on the grounds that this was necessary in order to preserve the natural colour of the flesh. It was shown, however, that the hanging and storage of unskinned calves could be a serious source of bacterial contamination, that meat colour was not affected provided the skinned carcase was properly refrigerated, and since 1961 the practice has been forbidden.

In modern works the bleeding of cattle is done while the carcase is suspended, the skin of the neck reflected and the oesophagus ligatured to prevent regurgitation of stomach contents. Cattle heads are usually removed while the animal is on the bleeding rail, but immediately skinning

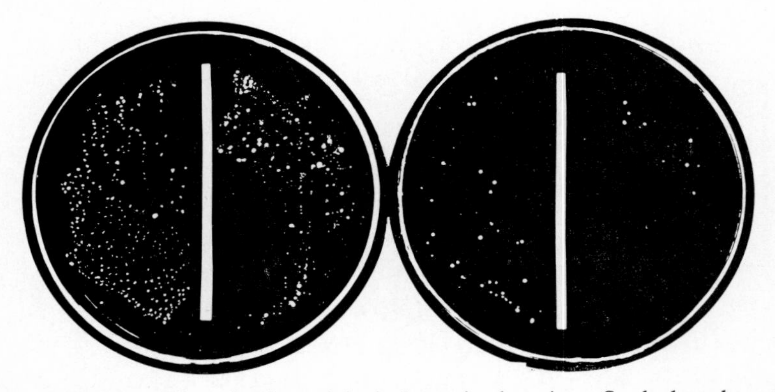

FIG. 201.—The value of routine bacteriological tests in abattoirs. Swabs have been taken from the inner surface of a knife sheath made of plastic (on left) and one made of stainless steel. The left side of each plate shows the bacterial growth prior to cleansing, the right the growth after cleansing. The plastic knife sheath shows a more severe bacterial contamination with only slight improvement after cleansing.

of the head is completed it is essential that the head, irrespective of the dressing procedure, be washed by high-pressure water spray. The abattoir floor, walls, meat hooks and inspection tables must inevitably become contaminated by the end of the day but the subsequent washing-down procedures are frequently unsatisfactory. Though washing-down followed by normal disinfection will reduce the bacterial load to some extent, only intensive cleaning under mechanical pressure will bring about a substantial reduction in the bacterial load. Tables and equipment of wood cannot be cleansed satisfactorily by any known method, nor can pitted floors or rusted iron hooks, and bacteriological tests of these have shown conclusively that they are undesirable under any circumstances. The following essentials are reiterated:

(i) Scalding and pressure cleaning of the slaughter floor, and frequent scalding of tools and equipment, are necessary if a low bacterial count is to be obtained.

(ii) Knife sheaths made of plastic are unsatisfactory and a one-piece sheath has been devised which is made of stainless steel and gives excellent results.

(iii) The washing of the dressed carcases by a fine spray at a pressure of 350 lb. per square inch will materially reduce the bacterial load of the carcase. The standard of purity of the water used for this purpose must be that of mains water, and the owner of one abattoir in Western Australia reported that after the filtration and chlorination of the water used for carcase washing was introduced the keeping quality of his beef, particularly the necks, was improved by 60 to 70 per cent.

(iv) The washing of edible offals such as liver, kidneys, hearts, thin skirt and tails is another important facet of satisfactory abattoir hygiene and it is essential that a continuous flow of clean water be used for this purpose. An excellent device for the washing of tongues is an inclined metal drum working on the same principle as a cement mixer though without the central agitator arms. The machine is provided with an inlet for water, the water then flowing out of the mouth of the apparatus, and the rotation of the machine, together with the flow of clean water, ensures a thorough washing of the tongue without the need for any manual operation.

(v) The provision of facilities for hand washing and knife sterilization is an essential requirement both on the abattoir floor and in meat processing rooms. In the larger plants in the United States of America there may be as many as 50 wash-hand basins located in readily accessible positions on the killing floor, whilst the regulations of the Federal German Republic now prescribe that wash-hand basins in processing rooms shall be so located that they are in the immediate vicinity of a worker. The necessity for observance of all the above practices has been amply confirmed, and preliminary washing of the live animals, rapid removal of hides and skins from the slaughter floor, thorough cleansing of premises, utensils and transport facilities, adequate supplies of clean water and supervision of cleanliness of personnel can reduce the abattoir contamination associated with slaughter by 80 per cent. or more.

(vi) In the slaughter and dressing of pigs the scalding water may at times contain salmonella organisms derived from the intestine of the animal, but the temperature of the water in the scalding tank is usually sufficiently high to reduce the vegetative population of micro-organisms. Further factors which reduce the bacterial surface load in pigs are the operation of scraping, and also singeing in the case of bacon pigs, and by these procedures the initial bacterial load on the skin is reduced by 99 per cent. A few aerobic and anaerobic spore-forming organisms, however, may remain embedded in the skin pores and can then cause deleterious changes during processing.

5. Significance of Bacteria in Meat

(A) FOOD POISONING

Food poisoning is as old as civilization itself, and from its earliest creation man acquired, by bitter experience, a considerable knowledge as to what food was good to eat and what should be left alone. Even for centuries B.C. it was recognized that the bodies of animals dying a natural death were not fit for food, for Moses commanded " Ye shall not eat anything that dieth of itself ". Unfortunately, after delivering this wise and far-seeing edict he prescribed further that " Thou mayest give unto the sojourner within thy gates that he may eat it, or thou mayest sell it unto a foreigner ".

Types of Food Poisoning

The term food poisoning, taken in its widest sense, includes :

(*a*) FOOD ALLERGY. Hypersensitiveness to certain foodstuffs is not uncommon, and the foodstuffs, generally protein in nature, include milk, eggs, cheese, fish, shellfish, pork and also mushrooms, tomatoes, etc. The tendency to become sensitive to certain foodstuffs may be transmitted from one generation to another, and a case is recorded where an allergy to hens' eggs persisted throughout four generations. It is stated that some 30 per cent. of all persons possess an allergy to certain foodstuffs.

(*b*) CHEMICAL CONTAMINATION is not common, and when it occurs is usually the result of accidental contamination or of some unforeseen chemical action between a foodstuff and its container. The metals encountered may be copper, lead, arsenic and antimony, but in England and Wales outbreaks caused by chemical contamination are usually due to the presence of zinc in acid fruits which have been stored or cooked in galvanized containers ; in Germany the storage of prepared foodstuffs in zinc containers is prohibited by law.

(*c*) INHERENTLY POISONOUS SUBSTANCES of normally edible plants and animals. These include certain fungi, berries, fish and shellfish.

(*d*) BACTERIAL CONTAMINATION. This is much the most important and frequent type of food poisoning, and may be due to living bacteria or the presence of bacterial toxins. In a literal sense diseases such as typhoid fever, dysentery, cholera (when conveyed by water), undulant fever and tuberculosis (when conveyed by milk), might be regarded as examples of food poisoning. It is customary, however, to restrict the term, with the exception of botulism, which is a disease " *sui generis* ", to mean an acute gastro-enteritis due to the ingestion with the food of certain micro-organisms, or of bacterial toxins resulting from the multiplication of those organisms in the food prior to its consumption.

Food poisoning, therefore, may take one of two forms, (*a*) an infection with living organisms, or (*b*) an intoxication by pre-formed bacterial poisons. The feature which chiefly distinguishes the two types clinically is related to the interval between eating the food and the development of symptoms. Where pre-formed toxins are present the conditions are somewhat analogous to poisoning by inorganic chemicals, and symptoms will develop very rapidly, usually within 4 hours or less. But if living organisms are ingested, some time will elapse before their multiplication in the body has proceeded sufficiently to provoke the usual reactions of diarrhoea and vomiting ; this period will naturally depend to some extent on the initial dose, but will seldom be less than 12 hours and may be much longer.

Bacteriology of Food Poisoning

The bacteria causing food poisoning may be classified as follows :

ORGANISMS CAUSING INFECTIONS

SALMONELLAE

The salmonellae constitute a large group of organisms of which more than 950 different types have been described. Salmonella bacteria are indistinguishable microscopically from coliform bacteria but they differ from them in their fermentative properties, and the individual types are identified chiefly by means of somewhat elaborate techniques of antigenic analysis. By no means all the types of organisms included in the genus salmonella are related to food poisoning. Some appear to be restricted to a single host species and are not found in other animals, amongst these being *S. abortus ovis*, causing abortion in ewes, and *S. gallinarum*, the cause of fowl typhoid. Conversely some salmonella types, e.g. *S. typhi*, which are associated with human disease are not known to affect animals. Many salmonellae, however, have a wide host range and these are the types which are commonly the cause of food poisoning.

Salmonella bacteria can exist for considerable periods in faeces and on pastures. *S. dublin* has been shown to survive in dried faeces for at least 3 years and on the walls of buildings for 10 months. Salmonella bacteria can remain alive in moist earth for one year, in dry earth for 16 months, and are not destroyed in carcases or offals maintained at chilling or freezing temperatures nor in the usual pickling solutions. They grow well on meat foods at ordinary temperatures, and Polish workers have shown by cultural methods that initially *Salmonella typhi-murium* increased in numbers in decomposed meat, reaching the highest level on the tenth day, but the numbers then decreased rapidly and none could be detected on the twentieth day. This observation may explain the difficulty of demonstrating *S. typhi-murium* in meat samples which have decomposed before they reach a laboratory, and it also provides an explanation of the fact that certain native tribes are known to consume the flesh of dead and decomposed animals without undergoing gastro-intestinal disturbance. Salmonellae are killed with certainty by the temperatures attained in commercial pasteurization and in the modern methods employed in the processing of canned foods.

Two types of salmonella are of special importance for they are pathogens of both animals and man, and together probably account for three-quarters of the outbreaks of food poisoning. These are:

1. SALMONELLA TYPHI-MURIUM (synonym *Bacterium aertrycke*). This organism is widely distributed, is a natural pathogen of rodents, especially mice, and has been found in cattle, sheep, pigs and various birds such as chickens, ducks, pigeons, parrots and canaries. In most countries it is the commonest salmonella isolated from cases of food poisoning in man and is a frequent pathogen of animals. The incidence of *S. typhi-murium* infection in calves has more than doubled in the last three years in Britain where for many years *S. dublin* has been the common salmonella of cattle.

2. SALMONELLA ENTERITIDIS (synonyms *Bacterium enteritidis*, *Gärtner's bacillus*). This organism is also widely distributed among domestic animals, is a natural pathogen of the rat, and has been found in cattle, pigs, goats and ducks, but its association with food poisoning outbreaks is very low compared with *S. typhimurium*. *Salmonella dublin* and *S. enteritidis* have given rise to outbreaks of food poisoning due to consumption of milk from infected cows.

Salmonella food poisoning is characterized by symptoms which do not appear until at least 12 hours have elapsed, and the illness is due to the growth of the organisms within the body, tends to be prolonged and is sometimes fatal. Infected persons may transmit the disease to others and for this reason food poisoning in Britain has since 1939 been included among the notifiable diseases.

DYSENTERY BACILLI

Organisms of this group are the cause of human dysentery, which is an ulcerative colitis characterized clinically by abdominal pain and diarrhoea, with blood and mucus in the faeces. Occasionally, however, they give rise to human illness of the food poisoning type, and one such outbreak, probably due to infected ice cream, occurred in Aberystwyth in 1942. They differ from the salmonellae in being non-motile and in their fermentation reactions which practically never proceed to the stage of gas formation, while final identification of the different strains depends, as with the salmonellae, on serological reactions. The group comprises a number of species of which *Shigella flexneri* and *Shigella sonnei* are common causes of dysentery in Britain ; the latter has been especially prevalent in recent years.

Organisms Causing Intoxications

In the past the investigation of food poisoning outbreaks has frequently failed to reveal the presence of any of the pathogenic bacteria of the salmonella or dysentery groups, and though other organisms might be present in abundance they were usually regarded as adventitious contaminants of little or no significance. It is now known, however, that certain organisms, not ordinarily regarded as of importance as pathogens, are, in fact, capable in certain circumstances of elaborating substances which are extremely irritant to the human gastro-intestinal tract. The most commonly implicated organism in this respect is *Staphylococcus pyogenes aureus*, but other organisms, besides the staphylococcus, appear to be able to give rise to this type of gastro-enteritis, and these include *Proteus*, streptococci, *Escherichia coli* and *Clostridium welchii*.

It appears that only certain strains of the organisms mentioned are capable of giving rise to toxins, and then only under limited conditions. It follows, therefore, that the mere presence of such organisms in suspected food, even in considerable numbers, is not, by itself, sufficient evidence that they are responsible for the toxic effect. The identification of toxigenic strains is at present a matter of considerable difficulty, and the only really critical test appears to be that afforded by human volunteers. Little has so far been learned as to the chemical nature of these toxins.

Staphylococci grow at ordinary room temperatures, and also in combinations of salt and sugar such as are present in cured meats and are inhibitory to many bacteria. They may produce a large amount of toxin if they are allowed to grow for 6 to 8 hours in a rich food medium and within the optimum temperature range of 68° to 105° F. Though the organisms themselves are readily destroyed at pasteurizing temperatures, the toxin appears to be heat-stable and is not inactivated by boiling or by being held at refrigeration temperature for long periods.

The incubation period of staphylococcal food poisoning varies from 2 to 3 hours, being followed by symptoms which persist for 8 to 24 hours but it is a form of food poisoning which is rarely if ever fatal, generally of very brief duration, and in which there are no sequelae. According to American authorities, food poisoning due to staphylococci is the commonest form encountered in that country and responsible for 90 per cent.

of the outbreaks. In recent years attention has been paid to the rôle of heat-resistant strains of *Clostridium welchii*, an anaerobic spore-forming organism, in causing food poisoning outbreaks of the gastro-intestinal type.

Sources and Modes of Infection

Infection of meat or other foods with bacteria capable of setting up food poisoning in man may arise in two ways:

(*a*) The Use of Diseased Animals for Food

Salmonella bacteria of the food poisoning type are not infrequently found in the intestinal tract of clinically healthy animals and it is probable that their presence is more common than has hitherto been supposed. In Britain from extensive surveys it is estimated that about 1 per cent. of cattle are latently affected with either *S. dublin* or *S. typhi-murium* and the carrier state in cattle was found to persist for at least one year. On the other hand calves that recover clinically from either *S. dublin* or *S. typhi-murium* infection almost invariably cease to excrete the organism. Clinically healthy animals which harbour salmonellae in the intestines will excrete the organisms intermittently in the faeces, but the organisms cannot normally increase in the intestines of healthy animals and are confined to the lumen of the digestive tract. Since evisceration after slaughter takes place without the intestines being opened, the flesh of clinically healthy animals which harbour salmonellae is unlikely to cause symptoms of food poisoning in man. Contamination may occur, however, in the dressing of the carcase, though the low pH of the flesh and the natural serous and connective tissues of the carcase constitute an adequate protection against growth and penetration of organisms.

Transmission of salmonella infection may take place from one animal to another when they are awaiting slaughter. This occurs through the agency of faeces, drinking troughs and the like, and infection is particularly likely to occur in pigs, probably in the lairage pens, during which time they are not fed. Infection can also occur in cattle awaiting slaughter and even in transport wagons. A severe outbreak of *S. typhi-murium* infection which occurred in Sweden in 1953 was attributed to the spread of infection in a slaughterhouse because of the abnormally long detention of cattle awaiting slaughter, insufficient cooling of the meat held in storage, and unusually high outdoor temperatures which favoured rapid growth of bacteria in the meat during its processing, storage, transport and holding in retail shops and homes. The avoidance of an excessively long period of detention in lairages and the prevention of overcrowding therein will considerably reduce the proportion of animals found infected at slaughter.

Should a clinically healthy animal harbouring salmonellae in the intestines be subjected to some untoward factor there is a disturbance in the equilibrium of the intestinal bacterial flora and the animal turns from an intermittent excretor to a constant excretor of salmonella bacteria. Organisms are now not only present in the intestines and mesenteric lymph nodes but also in the liver and gall bladder, and particularly the latter in which bacteria encounter optimum conditions for their growth. It is important to realize that the adult ox will excrete approximately one-half gallon of bile per day and that salmonella carriers are four times as common among fluke-infested cattle than among non-infested animals. Many observers have recorded the high incidence of salmonellae in the mesenteric lymph nodes of clinically healthy pigs, but healthy animals which are constant excretors of salmonellae are unlikely to be the cause of food poisoning, for the bacteria in the organs are few in number and the affected organs are in most cases cooked before being consumed.

It is known that any debilitating condition or disturbance of the intestinal functions will lower the resistance of the host and facilitate the passage of intestinal bacteria into the systemic circulation. Such debilitating factors include fever, extensive septic infections, prolonged starvation or fatigue, and there is evidence that a combination of the two latter factors will facilitate this passage more readily than will either factor alone. In such cases the defensive properties of the reticulo-endothelial system are impaired, so that if salmonellae are present in the intestine they may enter the systemic circulation by way of the lymph stream and radicles of the portal vein. In this way the organisms become established in the liver, gall bladder, kidneys, spleen, bone marrow, carcase lymph nodes and musculature, and consumption of the flesh or organs of such an animal, unless these are thoroughly cooked, may give rise to symptoms of food poisoning.

There are many animal diseases of a febrile or septic nature which have a marked debilitating effect and may convert a latent salmonella infection in the animal into an active and possibly fatal one. The conditions most likely to lead to systemic invasion of salmonellae from the intestines are, in the following order, affections of the intestinal tract, mastitis, metritis, slaughter after difficult parturition, diseases of the joints and of the tendon sheaths of hoof and claw, affections of umbilical origin, pleurisy, peritonitis, and systemic disease following suppurative conditions or gangrenous wounds. These affections are a very frequent cause of emergency slaughter, either on the farm or by consigning the ill animal to a slaughterhouse, and in Australia no animal slaughtered in emergency may be considered as fit for human food. It is probable that stress and strain play an important part in lowering the resistance of salmonella-infected calves, which may harbour *S. dublin* or *S. typhi-murium* without exhibiting clinical signs and then develop clinical symptoms as a result of these debilitating factors during transport from one part of the country to another. In Germany the carcases of all animals slaughtered in emergency must be examined bacteriologically before they are released for sale, and calves are regarded as the commonest and most dangerous source of salmonella food poisoning.

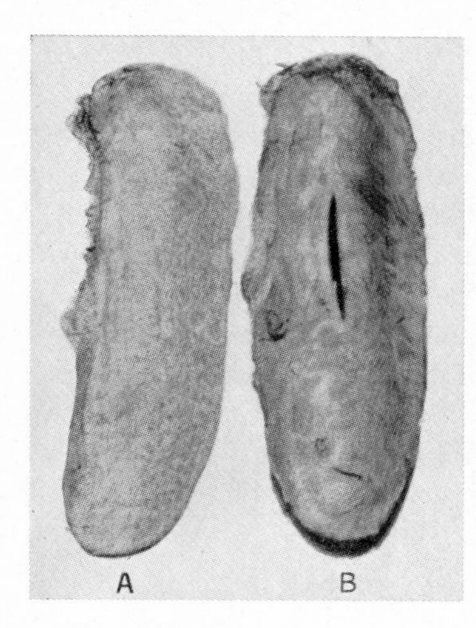

FIG. 202.—A. Spleen of cow, normal, showing sharp edges. B. Spleen from a cow slaughtered in emergency on account of septicaemia. Note the tense, swollen condition of the organ, indicated by the rounded borders and gaping of the incision made into the splenic substance. (Prof. Schönberg.)

Many cases of salmonella infection in animals prove fatal, but should recovery take place the animal may become a " carrier " and a residual salmonella infection may be present in the gall bladder, kidneys, spleen and carcase lymph nodes. Such an animal, by the regular excretion of salmonellae in the faeces, constitutes a serious source of infection to other livestock, but its flesh is unlikely to be dangerous as bacteria will have disappeared from the muscular tissue. A lymph node may, however, contain a few salmonellae and these may multiply and spread to the contiguous muscular tissue if carcases or joints are stored for long periods under unfavourable conditions.

Any entry of salmonellae into the systemic circulation, no matter to what degree, can obviously only occur if these organisms are originally present in the intestines. Where the entry of organisms is a massive one the classical post-mortem lesions of septicaemia will usually be manifested in the carcase and organs, except in those cases where the animal is slaughtered in the early stages of the affection and before the invading organisms have had time to produce readily recognizable lesions. Thus in order to decide whether a certain carcase or its organs is capable of giving rise to food poisoning if consumed a diagnosis of the pathological condition does not suffice, and a post-mortem examination of " border-line " cases should therefore be supplemented by a bacteriological examination to demonstrate the presence or absence of pathogenic organisms ; this procedure not only ensures the withdrawal of dangerous carcases from the market but also secures the release of many carcases which are shown to contain no organisms pathogenic to man. Generalized systemic affections, however, are in many cases associated with imperfect bleeding of the carcase and an alkalinity of the flesh, and these deleterious factors, even if salmonellae are shown to be absent, may so lower the durability of the carcase as to warrant its total condemnation. The extent to which diseased animals constitute a danger as a source of food poisoning therefore depends largely on the efficiency with which meat inspection is carried out and the success achieved in preventing the flesh of such animals from reaching the market. In France it is considered that the main salmonella danger is horse meat, for horses, more than other animals, are subject to primary and secondary salmonella infections or to a latent infection confined to the bowel. The very high incidence of salmonellae found in frozen horse meat, particularly the boneless type, imported into Europe from South American countries, would appear to confirm this; in Holland in 1966 the average incidence of infection found in frozen horse meat from three South American countries was 15 per cent. in the bone-in product, and 57 per cent. in the boneless.

(*b*) Contamination of Food from Extraneous Sources

There are almost innumerable ways in which this may occur. (i) It is difficult to estimate the importance of man himself as a source of infection, but there is sound basis for the axiom of the hygienist that food should be handled as little as possible. Chronic human carriers of the food poisoning salmonella types appear to be rare, though they do exist, and one human patient carried *S. typhi-murium* for 4 years, while convalescents have been found to carry *S. thompson* for up to 6 weeks. Again, the food poisoning outbreak in Wrexham in 1910, caused by consumption of pork pies, was traced to the head cook of the establishment who was a chronic salmonella carrier. In Britain and the United States the carrier rate in the general population of salmonella organisms has been estimated at about two per thousand. (ii) Carriers of the dysentery bacillus also occur, and outbreaks of food poisoning have been attributed to them. (iii) Staphylococci, on the other hand, are ubiquitous in nature, and human carriers of this organism are numerous and are undoubtedly the source of a number of outbreaks. Contamination of food may be traced to food-handlers with minor septic hand infections or severe nasal infection, with subsequent heavy growth of the organism on the food medium and production of sufficient enterotoxin to evoke symptoms of a gastro-intestinal nature in man. The nasal mucous membrane, particularly, is a likely source of staphylococci of human origin in food, and thus the hands easily become infected during the preparation of food. (iv) *Clostridium welchii* has been found in a variety of reservoirs, including faeces of human and animal origin, abattoirs, sewage and flies, and certain types of the organism produce spores which resist boiling for 4 or more hours. If the spores are present as contaminants on raw meat they may resist boiling or stewing, and should the meat be allowed to cool slowly overnight the spores will germinate into rapidly multiplying bacterial cells and produce large amounts of toxin.

An undoubted source of extraneous infection is the contamination of food with the excreta of rats and mice, for *S. enteritidis* and *S. typhi-murium* are responsible for much disease amongst these rodents. Examination in 1938 of 750 wild rats in Liverpool showed 7·3 per cent. to be harbouring salmonellae in the intestinal tract. These rodents may harbour the organisms for considerable periods as carriers, thus easily contaminating exposed and unprotected food, and in dried rat faeces the organism may remain viable for a year ; there is therefore ample justification for condemnation of foodstuffs contaminated by rats or mice, especially where the foodstuff is likely to be consumed without further cooking. It should be noted, too, that the so-called rat viruses consist of cultures of various strains of *S. enteritidis*, sometimes in the form of " grain bait ", sometimes as liquid suspensions for soaking bread or meal, and some outbreaks of food poisoning have been attributed to the careless handling and distribution of these preparations. The use of virus preparations for the destruction of rats and mice is therefore undesirable in all situations where foodstuffs are prepared, manufactured or stored. Dogs, and less frequently, cats, may suffer from salmonella infections and must be considered a possible source of human infection, and though the incidence of salmonellae in dogs is usually low in European countries, surveys in different areas in recent years have shown an incidence of from 1 per cent. to over 30 per cent., and more than 50 types have already been isolated from them, including the ubiquitous *S. typhi-murium*. Salmonellae will also survive in the house fly for the duration of the life of the fly, approximately 4 weeks, and such flies can infect food, water and other surfaces with which they come in contact. The faeces of infected rat fleas may contain large numbers of viable salmonella bacteria, and the organisms may also be found in the hind gut of cockroaches and infect the surface of foods.

To summarize, it will be seen that food poisoning may occur as a result of ante-mortem infection of an animal whose flesh is subsequently eaten, or it may occur by secondary contamination of the sound flesh or food. Of the organisms of the salmonella group, *S. enteritidis* is frequently associated with food poisoning of the first type while *S. typhi-murium* is more often associated with outbreaks due to contamination, and the majority of cases of food poisoning occur as a result of food, originally bacterially sound, becoming secondarily contaminated with organisms derived from outside the food. Outbreaks of infection with food poisoning organisms can, however, occur as a result of quite minor errors of technique in the manufacture of a variety of foodstuffs, and a point which has been repeatedly noted in investigation of food poisoning outbreaks is that foods subsequently shown to be contaminated with food poisoning organisms may show no changes in taste, smell and appearance, or changes of such slight degree that they may be easily overlooked.

Types of Food Implicated

Food poisoning rarely follows the consumption of fresh, well-cooked and untreated meat, the latter term denoting meat which has not been minced, rolled or stuffed, and in England and Wales by far the greatest proportion of the outbreaks associated with meat were related to processed or made-up meat foods. The frequency with which food poisoning is associated with such foodstuffs is related to the following facts :

(i) The salmonella group of organisms is pathogenic to bovines and pigs, and the flesh of these animals is a common ingredient of made-up foods. Sheep, on the other hand, are much less subject to salmonella infections and mutton is rarely used in foods of this type.

(ii) The preparation of made-up foods is often carried out as an adjunct to other businesses such as slaughterhouse work, and in this way specific infection is facilitated. Where food is prepared under unhygienic conditions there are innumerable opportunities for contamination by food handlers, rodents or flies.

(iii) The manufacture of made-up foods is associated with slight cooking, frequently followed by slow cooling, a procedure which promotes bacterial growth, while the high gelatine content of brawn and pork pies furnishes a suitable nutrient medium for the growth of organisms of the salmonella or staphylococcal type.

The information on the other foods associated with food poisoning may be summarized as follows : freshly cooked meat, freshly cooked fish, fresh vegetables, fresh fruit, and milk and milk products of all kinds are seldom dangerous. Canned foods, though generally very safe, are occasionally liable to contamination at the packing plant, while processed and made-up foods of any kind are always potentially dangerous and it is on these foods that public health workers should concentrate if they wish to reduce the present incidence of food poisoning.

Factors Controlling Food Poisoning Outbreaks

It will be clear that food poisoning cannot occur in the absence of specific infection of food. When such infection has taken place subsequent events will be determined by some further conditions. For example, if infection has been minimal, as it no doubt frequently is, some time will be required for the organisms to multiply in the food in order that they may be present in sufficient number either to cause infection of the person eating the food, or to produce sufficient toxin to cause poisoning effects.

The factors which chiefly determine the multiplication of pathogenic organisms are: (*a*) The presence of moisture. The bacteria concerned with food poisoning will grow on the damp surfaces of meat, and in the case of foods which are both damp and loosely packed, such as rissoles or sausage, they may show penetrative properties and spread throughout the foodstuff. (*b*) A suitable temperature range. This lies between 68° F. and 98° F., and in both Britain and Europe three-quarters of the outbreaks occur in hot weather, when optimum temperature conditions are present for bacterial growth. (*c*) The process of cooking. Cooking of meat is of importance, for the bacteria associated with food poisoning grow more luxuriantly on meat the protein of which has been broken down into its component parts by the cooking process; a substantial proportion of food poisoning outbreaks are due to reheated, "made over" or warmed up foods, particularly where meat has been placed in an oven for an hour or two and has not been cooked or eaten till the following day. (*d*) The time the food is kept before consumption. The larger the number of salmonella organisms ingested the shorter is the incubation period and the more acute the symptoms, and investigation of food poisoning outbreaks frequently elicits the fact that the food has been allowed to stand for some time before being eaten. Long storage and inadequate cooking must be regarded as the principal factors likely to increase the pathogenicity of a food when food poisoning bacteria are present, and staleness in foods is particularly to be avoided for it is associated with the multiplication of bacteria, some of which may be harmful to man. To prevent *Cl. welchii* food poisoning the cooking and storage of meat dishes are of paramount importance, and the period between cooking and eating should never be greater than one hour unless provision is made for storage at a temperature above 140° F. or in the cold.

Methods of Prevention of Food Poisoning Outbreaks

So far as meat is concerned the first essential is obviously an adequate system of inspection of the carcases of animals intended for food. In Germany during the 1914-1918 war the number of food poisoning outbreaks were comparatively few, for meat was rationed and the flesh of diseased animals that may have reached the consumer was eaten quickly. The subsequent lowering of the standard of meat inspection, forced upon that country by economic shortage, resulted in a rise from 142 outbreaks in 1915 to 1,459 in 1930.

Subsequent to the detection and detention of the carcase of a diseased animal, two alternative courses of action may be followed :

(*a*) To reject for food use all animals in which there is suspicion that pathogenic or non-pathogenic bacteria have given rise to a septicaemic or bacteraemic infection by gaining entry to the systemic circulation. This procedure is the one almost universally adopted throughout Britain and the United States and though wasteful it affords the maximum of safety.

(*b*) To distinguish between pathogenic and non-pathogenic infections by identifying the organisms by bacteriological means and to pass for consumption the flesh of those carcases which are otherwise marketable and which may safely be consumed. This is the method widely adopted in continental countries and its advantage is that much sound meat is saved which would otherwise be destroyed.

BACTERIOLOGICAL EXAMINATION OF CARCASES

BACTERIOLOGICAL FINDINGS IN SLAUGHTERHOUSE MATERIAL. In the healthy and physiologically normal animal those organs which have no direct contact with the exterior may be regarded as sterile, though the operation of slaughter and dressing may materially alter the bacteriological status of the animal and bring about the presence of bacteria in the blood, tissues and organs ; these organisms are usually a mixed flora of a non-specific type and are readily demonstrable by bacteriological means.

On the other hand, the bacteria present may be of a specific and pathogenic type and the presence of these in organs or tissues such as the spleen, muscular tissue or lymph nodes can only be attributed to the fact that a generalized septic or bacteraemic infection existed in the animal at the time of slaughter. Where such organisms are of intestinal origin their entry into the systemic circulation is explained by a breakdown in the natural resistance of the animal and emigration of the organisms from the intestinal tract ; haematogenous invasion may, however, occur from other naturally infected cavities of the body for the same reason.

As systemic invasion is most likely to occur in animals which are ill or exhausted, there are certain affections of animals where a bacteriological examination of the flesh and organs may be of material assistance to an inspector charged with assessing the fitness or otherwise of a carcase for human food. In some countries, as in Holland, such a bacteriological examination is optional and only undertaken when the inspector deems it necessary, but in other countries, as in Germany and Denmark, a bacteriological examination is obligatory when certain conditions are observed on post-mortem examination ; in Denmark this method of examination has been recognized as an official one since 1932, while in Federal Germany the provisions in regard to bacteriological examinations were re-drafted in 1961 and made considerably more severe.

INDICATIONS FOR BACTERIOLOGICAL EXAMINATION. There is no justification for conducting a bacteriological examination when a carcase and its organs exhibit marked pathological changes of a non-infectious nature or evidence of severe systemic disturbance. Such changes are themselves sufficient to justify condemnation of the carcase, and a bacteriological examination can never become a substitute for a careful organoleptic examination, its value being as a supplementary test to assist judgment of those carcases in which there is no more than a suspicion that a septicaemic or bacteraemic infection has occurred.

In Western Germany an obligatory bacteriological examination is required in the case of animals which

1. have been slaughtered in emergency ;
2. have been slaughtered on account of a disease associated with systemic disturbances ;
3. have been slaughtered on account of acute inflammation of intestine, udder, uterus, joints, tendons, claws and hooves, umbilicus, lungs, pleura and peritoneum, or because of systemic illness associated with suppurative or gangrenous wounds ;
4. have been slaughtered on account of fractures, external injuries (e.g. wounds, contusions), other lesions caused by external factors (e.g. foreign body in the oesophagus), or prolapse of internal organs (e.g. uterus, bladder, rectum) and in which resultant symptoms of illness (e.g. fever) have been detected ;
5. show pathological changes on post-mortem inspection that lead to doubt as to the suitability of the meat for human consumption, even though the animal was found healthy on ante-mortem inspection ;
6. have been shown by bacteriological tests to have been excreting food poisoning organisms prior to slaughter, or which emanate from a herd in which the presence of food poisoning organisms has been officially reported ;
7. have not been eviscerated within one hour of slaughter ; or
8. where the parts of the slaughtered animal necessary for post-mortem examination are absent or have been handled in such a way as to make satisfactory judgment impossible, and
9. where slaughter has taken place without the animal being subjected to the prescribed ante-mortem inspection.

MATERIAL SUBMITTED. The following samples shall be taken for submission to the laboratory for bacteriological examination :

1. Two complete muscles, with their fascia, one from a forequarter, and

one from a hindquarter, or cubes of muscle not less than 3 inches in diameter ;

2. the prescapular or axillary lymph node from the other forequarter of the carcase, and the internal iliac node from the other hindquarter, including the surrounding fat and connective tissue of the nodes ;

3. the spleen, which should not be incised except in cases where the organ is considerably enlarged, in which case a piece as large as the hand shall be taken from the diseased portion ;

4. a kidney ;

5. in the case of small animals, the whole liver with the gall bladder ; in other animals a portion of liver twice the size of a fist and including the portal vein, or the caudate lobe and including the portal vein, and also the portal lymph nodes and gall bladder ;

6. parts showing pathological change and which, in view of their position, are suspected to contain pathogenic bacteria, together with the associated lymph nodes (e.g. in the case of pneumonia, a portion of lung and associated lymph nodes) ;

7. a portion of small intestine together with a number of mesenteric lymph nodes in those cases where animals have suffered from enteritis and have been reported to be excretors of salmonella organisms, or animals known to emanate from a herd infected with such pathogens.

Laboratory experience has, however, shown that the liver frequently contains intestinal bacteria which have gained entry to the organ by way of the portal vein, and inasmuch as this invasion may occur after slaughter, the demonstration of organisms in this organ is of no significance unless these are of a specific pathogenic type. Similarly, the kidney should theoretically be of value for the purpose of bacteriological examination, but in practice it has been shown that bacterial invasion of the kidney substance readily occurs post-mortem by way of the kidney pelvis and renal tubules. The demonstration, therefore, of bacteria of a non-specific type in the kidney of slaughtered animals cannot be regarded as evidence that systemic invasion has occurred prior to the animal being slaughtered.

Attention should be drawn to the value of the marrow of long bones for bacteriological examination, for organisms which can be demonstrated by bacteriological means in muscle or lymph nodes can be even more readily demonstrated in the bone marrow. In addition, where joints of meat have been cooked it may be possible to isolate viable bacteria from the bone marrow, whereas in the meat itself the bacteria will have been destroyed by the cooking process. Examination of the bone marrow is of particular value in calves, and demonstrates, if positive, that infection had occurred ante-mortem and not subsequent to slaughter. In cattle and horses a first phalanx or metatarsal or metacarpal bone can be removed without interfering with the marketability of the carcase, and likewise a radius in pigs and radius or metacarpal bone in sheep can readily be obtained. Tissues and organs should be removed, allowed to cool, and if consigned to a laboratory should be wrapped individually in impermeable material surrounded by suitable absorbent substances.

TYPES OF BACTERIA FOUND. The bacteria found may belong to the non-specific group which comprises species that are non-pathogenic or only potentially pathogenic, and among these are streptococci of the viridans group, enterococci, *E. coli* in adult animals, clostridia, bacilli of the subtilis-mesentericus group and non-haemolytic staphylococci. These species of bacteria are present naturally in the intestinal flora and some, such as the non-haemolytic staphylococci, are part of the natural bacterial flora of the skin ; their invasion of the blood stream is of a secondary nature occasioned by some other pathological condition and does not indicate that the animal was affected with a generalized infectious disease.

The bacteria of the specific group include all species regarded as specific pathogens and amongst these are the haemolytic streptococci, pneumococci, haemolytic staphylococci, pasteurella, salmonella, *E. coli* in newborn animals, *Bacillus anthracis*, *Erysipelothrix rhusiophathiae*, Listerella and *Corynebacterium pyogenes*. The time taken for a bacteriological report is 24 to 48 hours and carcases may be detained in a cold storage chamber pending the results of the examination.

INTERPRETATION OF RESULTS. As the technical details in bacteriological examinations vary in different countries there are, as yet, no universally accepted criteria for the interpretation of bacteriological findings, though they follow certain general principles. When the samples submitted prove to be sterile the carcase and those organs which are unchanged may be released forthwith, provided the inspector is satisfied as to their fitness for food after a further visual examination.

When specific pathogenic bacteria are found in one or more samples, the carcase should be condemned, for this indicates that a generalized septicaemic or bacteraemic infection has occurred, even though the bacteria demonstrated may not themselves be transmissible to man.

Interpretation of cases when only non-specific, non-pathogenic bacteria are found is a matter of complexity but the spread of such bacteria throughout the tissues greatly favours spoilage and bacterial decomposition, particularly when due to clostridia which may develop anaerobically in the deeper muscular portions of the carcase ; it is now known that the presence of *Clostridium welchii* in meat, either fresh or used as a manufactured product, may give rise to food poisoning of the enterotoxic type. Condemnation of carcases shown to contain non-specific, non-pathogenic bacteria is therefore justifiable when the bacteriological results show that the infection is an extensive one, and a workmanlike code is followed in Danish regulations in which demonstration of non-specific bacteria from more than one sample submitted (the liver sample is excluded in this judgment) is considered evidence of extensive infection and classified as a high grade one and the carcase condemned. On the other hand, where growth of non-specific bacteria is reported from only one of the samples submitted the infection is classified as a low grade one and is considered insufficient to justify total condemnation.

The results furnished by a total of 50 laboratories in Denmark authorized to deal with bacteriological meat examinations showed that in 1965 of 17,778 suspected carcases examined 72·24 per cent. were found to be sterile, 10·62 per cent. had a low grade non-specific infection, 2·79 per cent. a high grade non-specific infection, while in 14·35 per cent. of cases the infection was shown to be due to specific pathogenic organisms. Thus approximately 83 per cent. of the carcases from which samples were obtained were either sterile or found to have a low grade infection, and only 17 per cent. of the carcases examined were found to be unfit for human food. Previous records have shown that a higher percentage of septic and bacteraemic infections were found among pigs than among cattle, but it should be pointed out that the pig carcases examined bacteriologically were predominantly young animals 6 to 7 months in age, whereas the bovine material comprised very few calves, as young calves of which there is any suspicion are normally condemned without bacteriological examination.

Further Methods of Prevention

Though bacteriological examinations are of the greatest value in the routine inspection of carcases, the way in which flesh is subsequently handled is of no less importance and bacterial contamination of sound food accounts for most of the outbreaks of food poisoning. Food should therefore be handled as little as possible, especially the made-up foods such as chopped meat, sausages, pies and brawn, and in this respect the provision of adequate washing facilities in food shops, canteens, etc., is of paramount importance.

The storage of food in a cool place, preferably by the use of refrigeration is advisable, for the temperature range for growth of the majority of pathogenic micro-organisms is 68° F. to 98° F., and adequate cooling will prevent the multiplication of such bacteria which otherwise may multiply and render the food dangerous. Non-sterile perishable foods should never be allowed to remain over 6 to 8 hours at temperatures within the above range, otherwise bacterial multiplication and development of toxins may take place to an extent sufficient to cause gastro-intestinal symptoms in man. In Germany it is illegal for minced meat to be prepared prior to the day of sale.

Finally, adequate cooking is a protection against food poisoning in so far as it is partly a sterilizing process, and salmonellae are easily killed at pasteurizing temperature. In England and Wales between 1949 and 1958 only an infinitesimal proportion of food poisoning was traced to fresh meat freshly cooked and eaten hot. While cooking may therefore be a protection, inadequate cooking may actually add to the danger, and *Salmonella dublin* has been shown to have remained viable in sausage gently fried for 15 minutes. Again, in the manufacture of meat pies it has been shown that if pre-existing infection of the meat exists, a slight departure from the normal boiling time or temperature may permit the survival of sufficient pathogenic organisms which may multiply later to the detriment of the consumer.

Botulism

Botulism derives its name from the Latin *botulus* = sausage, and differs markedly in its symptomatology and pathogenicity from the other bacterial forms of food poisoning.

The causal organism, *Clostridium botulinum*, was isolated by van Ermengem, in 1896, from a food poisoning outbreak which occurred in a Belgian village. At a festive gathering in this village certain members had consumed pieces of a raw ham, although the other ham and remaining joints of the same pig were consumed without harm. The incriminated ham was paler and softer than normal, had a rancid odour, and had been placed at the bottom of the pickling tub where the chances of contamination were obviously greater.

Clostridium botulinum is an obligate spore-forming anaerobe of the putrefactive type, and 4-6μ long by 0·9μ broad; it is a saprophyte and does not multiply in the human or animal body, so that infection from animal to animal, or from animal to man, cannot occur. The organism is classified into five types, A, B, C, D and E, the toxins of which can be differentiated from each other, and antitoxin prepared from one type of organism does not inactivate the toxins of the other types; only types A, B and E are associated with outbreaks of botulism in man, A being the commonest.

Pathogenesis. Botulism is set up by the action of a powerful exotoxin produced by the organism during its growth in food material. This exotoxin can resist the action of the gastric and intestinal juices but is destroyed in 30 minutes at a temperature of 176° F.

Method of Infection. The organism is a natural inhabitant of the surface layers of the soil and thus may easily be a contaminant of fruit, vegetables or other cultivated produce. It is also present occasionally in the intestines of the pig, ox and horse which feed on such produce, and Belgian authorities state that if pigs are slaughtered while digestion is proceeding, botulinus spores may gain entry to the blood stream and be present in muscular tissue. The frequency of its existence in the soil is shown by the fact that 64 specimens of soil collected from various parts of England showed 9 samples to contain *Cl. botulinum*, and where meat foods are infected, contamination by soil is therefore the most likely cause.

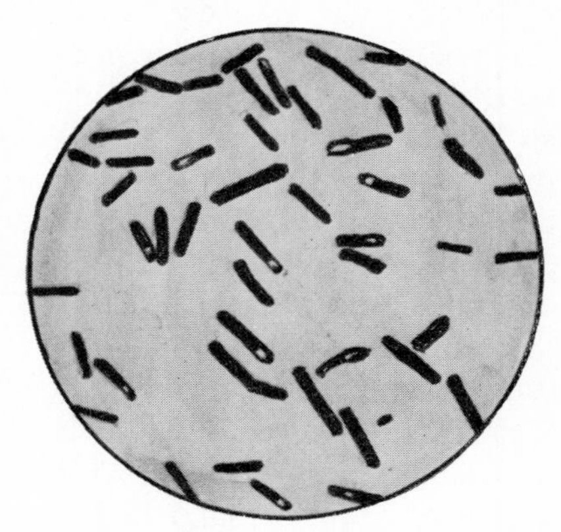

FIG. 203.—*Clostridium botulinum*, showing terminal or sub-terminal position of spores, which are thick-walled and wider than the bacillary body.

Types of Foodstuffs Implicated. Foods associated with anaerobic conditions and soil contamination, such as home-canned foodstuffs or hams and bacon stacked without air access, are particularly liable to be infected. In America most of the foodstuffs traced in connection with outbreaks of botulism have been found to be canned fruits and vegetables, while in Europe most cases have been due to sausages, hams, preserved meats, potted goose or duck or brawn. In Japan several outbreaks of botulism, type E, have occurred in recent years due to consumption of a home-produced food composed of rice, vegetables and fish, and the hygiene of sea-food is therefore a very important problem in that country. As the toxin of *Cl. botulinum* is destroyed in 30 minutes at a temperature of 176° F. there are few records of the disease having resulted from the consumption of food previously subjected to ordinary domestic cooking, and botulism does not occur as a result of consumption of fresh food, either cooked or uncooked. The incriminated food has in most cases been smoked, pickled or canned, allowed to stand and then eaten without adequate cooking.

On theoretical grounds botulism should be much more frequent than it actually is, for the organism, as already stated, is a common inhabitant of the soil and is sometimes found in the animal intestine, so that contamination of certain foodstuffs such as vegetables, fruit and sometimes meat must occur fairly frequently. Again, meat is a favourable medium for the growth of *Cl. botulinum*, and as the spores vary in their resistance to heat and may withstand boiling at a temperature of 212° F. for up to

22 hours, they are likely to survive any ordinary sterilization. One would therefore expect many samples of canned and bottled foods to be contaminated, for since anaerobic conditions obtain in these foodstuffs the organism, which grows well at 68° F., should proliferate readily and produce its toxin.

Botulism, however, is rare, its incidence being controlled by a number of factors : (1) The degree of contamination; the fewer the spores the more readily they are destroyed ; (2) the type of food, certain foods being more favourable to growth than others ; (3) not all strains of *Cl. botulinum* are capable of producing toxin ; (4) the thermal resistance of the organism ; this is lowered by decreasing the pH, i.e. increasing the acidity, or by increasing the concentration of sodium chloride. The fact that botulism is associated in practically all outbreaks with consumption of smoked, pickled or canned foods is not that these foods promote toxicity of the organism, but that they are foods which are most likely to be eaten " straight out of the can " and without a further heating which would be likely to destroy the toxin. Uncooked fresh foods are safe because they are eaten before the toxin has had time to develop, while if foods are cooked the toxin is destroyed.

In most, but not all, of the cases of botulism, the preserved foods have been noticeably spoiled, showing evidence of gas formation, break-down and rancidity. In canned goods contaminated with *Cl. botulinum* the can is often blown and the food soft and disintegrated, with an odour resembling butter or cheese, but although meat foods so contaminated often show evidence of spoilage, preserved foods such as beet, olives, spinach or string beans may contain potent *Cl. botulinum* toxin without the presence of obvious change in the appearance, taste or odour of the food. There is no record in Britain that canned food has ever been incriminated in botulism outbreaks, and only on two occasions have glass-packed foods been involved. In America the disease has been recorded more frequently, there being 140 outbreaks in Canada and United States between 1899 and 1925, the higher incidence being related to the common practice in these countries of home canning of fruit and vegetables. Here the temperature achieved during processing may easily be inadequate to destroy the spores of the organism, with resultant elaboration of the exotoxin under anaerobic conditions, and it is significant that in America the disease is commoner during the winter months, a period when home-preserved foods are most likely to be consumed.

Symptoms. The symptoms of botulism are produced by the action of a powerful exotoxin which possesses an affinity for nervous tissue. The period of incubation in man is usually under 24 hours, but may be longer, and is followed by a typical chain of symptoms which include thirst, nerve paralysis and great muscular weakness; in contradistinction to the symptoms in salmonella food poisoning, there is obstinate constipation and no vomiting. The fatality of botulism in man is much higher than in salmonella infection, and in America death occurs in from 60 to 70 per cent. of affected persons, the earlier the appearance of symptoms the higher being the mortality rate. In the Scottish outbreak which occurred at Loch Maree in 1922, the incriminated food was wild duck paste which had been used for the making of sandwiches, and this resulted in the death of all the eight hotel guests who had consumed the contaminated food. *Cl. botulinum*, Type A, was recovered from the remnants of the paste.

In horses and cattle the affection known as forage poisoning is caused by the ingestion of feeding stuff rendered toxic by infection with *Cl. botulinum*. In Western Australia botulism was recorded in sheep in 1928, and during succeeding years has been regarded as a source of greater economic loss than all other sheep diseases. There have been a number of reported cases of botulism on mink farms where the feeding of the animals on meat and fish scraps, often undergoing spoilage, may provide ideal conditions for the rapid formation of botulinum toxin, especially if the weather is warm; in Norway it is now illegal to use the meat of ill animals for mink food. Fowls may also become infected, usually through the consumption of decomposing preserved vegetables, the condition being known as limberneck, in which affected birds assume a very typical position, lying on their breasts with the head supported by the beak, and a further diagnostic symptom of the affection is that the feathers pull out easily.

Methods of Prevention. (1) The spores of *Cl. botulinum*, like most bacterial spores, are resistant to heat and can withstand boiling at 212° F. for 22 hours, but are destroyed with certainty at a temperature of 248° F. for 20 minutes; the greater the acidity of the food the more rapid is the destruction of the spores. These factors are taken into account in modern canning procedure, and the minimum standard of processing now universally recognized by reputable canners ensures the destruction of spores of *Cl. botulinum* in low acid and medium acid foods. The home canning of vegetables always constitutes a possible danger, and if cooking by steam under pressure cannot be ensured in home canning it is safer to substitute pickling or dehydration as methods of preservation.

(2) Pickled foods are rendered safe if the brine used contains not less than 10 per cent. of common salt; in weaker brines the micro-organism can continue to multiply.

(3) Preserved foods possessing rancid or other odours should be rejected. If a housewife tastes a faulty can of food which contains botulinus toxin and spits it from her mouth there is enough toxin remaining in her mouth to cause death.

(B) DECOMPOSITION

Decomposition of Meat

By this term is understood the breaking-up of organic matter, chiefly protein in character, by the action of bacteria which split the meat up into a number of chemical substances, many of which are gaseous and foul-smelling. In addition to protein, both fats and carbohydrates decompose by breaking up into simpler substances, and in the study of meat inspection regard must therefore be paid to the changes which take place in fat as well as in muscular tissue.

Protein molecules are broken up into simpler substances under the influence of acids, alkalis, superheated steam, digestive ferments or bacteria, the degree of decomposition varying greatly with the different agencies. Of these agencies the putrefactive bacteria carry the process further, breaking up the protein molecule into proteoses, then peptones, polypeptides, the amino-acids, and finally indol, skatol, phenol, together with various gases among which are sulphuretted hydrogen, carbon dioxide, methane and ammonia. It is the amino-acids, non-toxic in nature, which furnish bacteria with abundant and available nutritive material, and it is the presence of the products of their breakdown which is responsible for the typical appearance and odour associated with meat which has undergone decomposition. The recognized everyday signs of decomposition are marked changes of colour to a grey, yellow or green, a softening in the consistency of the tissue, a pronounced repulsive odour and an alkaline reaction due to the formation of ammonia.

After slaughter of a healthy animal decomposition eventually develops in the parts exposed to the air, the time that decomposition takes to develop being controlled particularly by the degree of heat and moisture, both of which are favourable for bacterial growth. The primary surface growth on meat is initiated by aerobic bacteria, among these being staphylococci, *E. coli* and *Proteus*, these aerobic organisms extracting oxygen from the meat surface and producing conditions suitable for the growth of anaerobic bacteria, an example of the latter being *Clostridium sporogenes.* Thus aerobic and anaerobic bacteria both play a part in decomposition, the aerobic bacteria on the surface creating the necessary conditions for the anaerobic putrefactive bacteria which, by their nature, can grow within the deeper tissues without the presence of oxygen. After surface putrefaction of meat has commenced the process spreads gradually by way of the nerve and connective tissue sheaths and along the surfaces of blood or lymph vessels. The rapidity of the extension of the putrefactive process throughout a carcase is greatly influenced by the condition of the animal before slaughter, and in exhausted animals or in those which have suffered from fever, especially if due to a septic cause, the meat is likely to show an alkaline reaction with the result that decomposition sets in very rapidly and quickly reaches the deeper parts.

A condition known in Britain as "heated beef", and in America as "sour side", is caused by inability of the freshly-killed carcase to dissipate heat rapidly and is brought about by hanging carcases too close to each other, thus preventing a proper current of air around the sides. The condition is also observed in rabbits, hares and game which are packed in hampers or baskets while still warm, and is known in the trade as "green struck".

In animals which have died and have not been eviscerated, both external and internal decomposition occur simultaneously, due partly to the high blood content of the meat and to the invasion of the abdominal veins by putrefactive bacteria from the intestines. The first bacterium to invade the carcase from the bowels after death is *E. coli*, which in warm weather may reach remote regions of the carcase with remarkable quickness, sometimes being found in the joints within 24 hours; these bacteria use up the oxygen in the carcase and pave the way for penetration of anaerobic bacteria, e.g. *Cl. welchii*, from the bowel. The presence of a greenish hue, first apparent on the kidney fat and peritoneal wall, with the diaphragm soft and flaccid and lying close to the ribs, is a strong indication that evisceration of the animal has been delayed and calls for a severe judgment on the carcase. Pigs which are the subjects of emergency slaughter during the summer months may show a greenness of the abdominal fat in 12 hours, particularly if the abdominal viscera have not been immediately removed. Lambs coming straight off grass and slaughtered in hot sultry weather have been known to exhibit evidence of incipient decomposition within one hour of being dressed.

In the case of shot deer which cannot be gutted immediately it is customary amongst sportsmen to incise the abdominal wall, as a current of air cools the abdominal viscera and delays emigration of putrefactive bacteria from the intestinal tract. Venison, which is particularly rich in connective tissue and therefore exceedingly tough after slaughter, requires conditioning by hanging before it is rendered palatable. It can hang for long periods without decomposition, and it is stated that the muscular tissue of deer possesses anti-bacterial substances which have an inhibitory action on a great number of putrefactive bacteria as well as on the bacteria responsible for food poisoning; in this way conditioning or ripening can take place in vension unassociated with decomposition. The smaller animals, as game or hares, lose heat rapidly after death, and at an atmospheric temperature of 61-65° F. small carcases such as rabbits cool to air temperature in about 12 hours, whereas larger carcases such as sheep require about 24 hours. As this rapid heat dissipation inhibits the growth of putrefactive bacteria it is practicable to consign feathered game and hares to market without removal of the abdominal viscera and packed in crates or baskets.

In sausage, decomposition in the early stages usually takes place simultaneously throughout the meat substance, but all the accepted changes associated with decomposition may not be present. Valuable indications of unsoundness in fresh sausage, as distinct from smoked, are (*a*) stickiness on the surface of the casing, (*b*) in the early stages, a sour rather than a foetid odour, (*c*) easy separation of the sausage meat from the casing, and (*d*) a grey colour on section of the sausage. The odour of early decomposition may be detected by the application of a boiling test, and is accentuated if a little limewater is added to the water before boiling.

Decomposition of Fat

The problem of fat rancidity crops up in the storage of practically every foodstuff. An unpleasant odour or flavour in a fat may be due to (*a*) absorption of foreign odours, as in the tainting of meat or butter stored in a chamber previously used for fruit, (*b*) atmospheric oxidation, (*c*) the action of micro-organisms, which may give rise to extensive hydrolysis of fat. A small content of free fatty acids has, however, little effect on flavour, and the probability is that the tainted flavour normally accompanying bacterial growth results from the absorption of nitrogenous products due to the breakdown of connective tissue.

Rancidity due to atmospheric oxidation does not require the presence of micro-organisms and is the most common type of deleterious fatty change; exposure to light is a factor which predisposes to oxidation of fatty tissues, and from this has arisen the practice of wrapping foods susceptible to atmospheric oxidation in green or red paper or in cellophane. Beef and mutton fats are relatively resistant, and cause little trouble except when such meats are frozen and stored at 14° F. for periods longer than 18 months, but bacon fat, particularly when exposed to light, is much more susceptible to oxidation. The type of feeding of the bacon pig also has an effect on the rapidity with which oxidation occurs in the finished product, for extensive swill feeding produces a soft fat containing a high proportion of unsaturated fatty acids, and these tend to be converted to aldehydes and ketones which impart to the bacon the acrid flavour associated with rancidity; the rapid onset of rancidity, together with a yellow coloration of the fat, has frequently been observed in carcases of pigs fed on cod liver oil or fish meal. A further deleterious factor in bacon manufacture is that during curing much of the natural resistance of the pig tissues to oxidation is broken down by the specific action of the pickling salts, and for this reason bacon fat is more liable to develop rancidity than pork fat. Even at 14° F. oxidation of bacon fat is appreciable within a few weeks, though if bacon is smoked subsequent to curing, the absorption of phenolic substances confers a certain amount of protection against oxidation during storage. The time factor in the curing of bacon and ham is therefore of particular importance, and bacon which undergoes a long period of manufacture, as Midland cured bacon which takes 3 to 5 weeks, is more liable to become rancid than Wiltshire bacon which is produced in 2 to 4 weeks. The still greater length of time taken to manufacture York hams, about 3 to 6 months, renders it essential that the fat of such hams be of excellent quality, because soft fat, which might be admissible in pork or Wiltshire bacon, will lead to noticeable rancidity before the slowly maturing York ham is ready for the market. Marked rancidity in pig fat is usually associated with a change in colour of the fat from white to yellow, and the rancid odour may be detected if a piece of fat is rubbed between the hands.

A further factor causing taint in fat is the activity of micro-organisms which produce hydrolysis, resulting in the liberation of free fatty acids. The development of this increased acidity is manifested by the production of a rancid odour and flavour, and the storage life of chilled meat is often limited by the appearance of taint in the fat. From experiments carried out on the fat of the kidney, brisket and back of the ox it would appear that such fat develops a taint when the amount of free fatty acids reaches 2·5 to 3·0 per cent., and the determination of the amount of free fatty acids present in fat is therefore a useful indication of change. The deep intramuscular fat of meat, as is seen in the marbling of prime beef, is not affected by hydrolysis or atmospheric oxidation and is therefore likely to remain sound for long periods, but the kidney and abdominal fat, being more exposed, is likely to develop rancidity early ; it is for this reason that these superficial fats are removed by the retail butcher before the carcase is hung up in the shop. Fats should be regarded with suspicion if they are found to contain over 2 per cent. of free fatty acids, though in routine practice the appearance, odour and flavour of the fat are the guides usually employed. Chewing of a small portion of fat may provide a valuable indication as to the presence of rancidity.

Bone Taint

The rapid dissipation of body heat from a freshly killed carcase is facilitated when the surrounding air is cool, dry and in rapid circulation. The rate of cooling is slow in heavy carcases owing to their greater thickness, and also in those which carry an excessive amount of fat, with the result that a high temperature may persist in the deep-seated musculature of these animals and give rise to deleterious change. This change, known as bone taint, is associated with the growth of putrefactive bacteria and occurs most commonly in the region of the hip joint of the ox and pig, but occasionally in the shoulder region of the ox.

Bone taint, or deep-seated spoilage of meat, is undoubtedly of bacterial origin and it appears that more than one organism or group of organisms may be involved, but the anaerobic spore-forming bacteria are the most important and, from the resemblance of these bacteria to those normally found in the faeces of animals, it seems probable that they emanate from the gut of the animals themselves. There is, however, still some doubt as to (*a*) how many of these bacteria were present in the living animal, (*b*) how many escaped from the intestines into the blood stream during the agony of death, and (*c*) how many were introduced into the blood stream during the act of bleeding. It appears likely that the organisms responsible for bone taint in cattle are actually ante-mortem invaders, being carried by the blood while it is still circulating and that their emigration from the intestines is facilitated by exhaustion of the animal prior to slaughter or by fright, shock, or even a sudden strain. (It has been suggested that the strain engendered by the steep ascent to the top floor of factory abattoirs may be an aetiological factor in bone taint by causing damage to the tissues at the upper extremity of the femur.) There is practical evidence that in some cases the putrefactive processes do commence in the blood vessels of the bone marrow, and the synovial fluid of the hip joint is also a favourable medium for bacterial growth for it has a pH between 7·0 and 8·0, which is the optimal range for many bacteria, whereas that of muscle in complete rigor is usually below 6·0. Recent evidence indicates that the lymph stream may also be of importance, for bacteria resembling those in taints have been isolated more frequently from lymph nodes than from bone marrow and muscle. These bacteria may therefore be present in the lymph nodes during life and, under suitable conditions, may spread to the surrounding muscular tissue. Bone taint is frequently encountered in hindquarters of beef imported into Britain, but is also seen in home-killed cattle, particularly in well-finished animals slaughtered in sultry weather during the months of July and August. The odour of bone taint is apparent in both the musculature around the femur and in the marrow of the bone and is very typical, being quite unlike the accepted odour of decomposing meat and resembling rather the sewage-like smell associated with gut-cleaning. The condition may be associated with a change in the muscle coloration to a grey, or at times a blackish-purple, but frequently the normal red coloration of the muscular tissue is entirely preserved.

In South American frigorificos the treatment of cattle before slaughter is directed towards the avoidance of bone taint by maintaining the subsequent bacterial contamination of the carcase at a low level, and also by aiding the rapid dissipation of heat from it after slaughter. Before these cattle are slaughtered they are given draughts of water and are run through a race, while immediately after slaughter the carcase is cooled rapidly to 35° F., and these precautions have done much to lower the incidence of bone taint in hindquarters of imported beef. Experimentally, the condition can be prevented by injection of one of the tetracyclines immediately before slaughter, and surface spoilage can be controlled by use of an antibiotic spray.

FIG. 204.—South American frigorifico practice, the cattle passing through a race and being sprayed with water prior to entering the lairage.

The smaller butcher in Great Britain aids dissipation of heat from the freshly killed carcase of beef by removing the kidney fat, together with the fat lining the pelvic cavity, and also by making an incision into the stifle joint, for the real danger spots in bone taint are the bone marrow and synovial fluid which are neutral in reaction, and once anaerobic bacteria gain access to these tissues only a rapid fall in temperature can arrest their growth. It is contended that to avoid bone taint the temperature at the centre of the round must not exceed 40° F. after 48 hours, and in carcases left to cool on the slaughter floor the internal temperature may be as high as 60° F. after 40 hours.

Bone taint is a local condition requiring condemnation of the affected tissues, but in many cases, when the hip joint or round of beef is affected, generous paring of the muscle around the femur is all that is necessary.

TAINT IN HAMS. This is also known as souring in hams, and is attributed by American authorities to contamination by *Clostridium sporogenes*, *Cl. putrefaciens* and *Cl. putrificum*, organisms which are proteolytic in action and break down proteins into amino-acids and ammonia; the taints in hams as well as in beef are fundamentally similar in origin, being in each case a deep form of decomposition which is unassociated with any surface change. Though the blood, marrow, muscle and bone of normal living pigs are free from ham souring bacteria, these micro-organisms may be present in such tissues soon after slaughter and develop rapidly along connective tissue bands between the muscle bundles. The sticking knife undoubtedly contributes bacteria to the blood stream, which can be demonstrated experimentally, for when pure cultures of uncommon bacteria are placed on the blade of the knife the bacteria can be isolated from the tibia and other long bones; the marrow of the femur, however, tends to harbour fewer bacteria than the tibia, and American authorities note that "tibia sours" are much the commoner. Too large a sticking wound also facilitates deep-seated contamination by ham-souring bacteria, for these organisms appear to resist the high bactericidal properties of pig's blood, and another factor which may be conducive to taint in hams is heavy eating, for French experience suggests that bacteria migrate from the intestine of pigs after feeding—*la bacteremie habituelle de digestion.*

A further factor which encourages bacterial growth within the pig carcase is that glycogen is less readily deposited in pig muscle compared with that of the ox, sheep and other domestic animals, while it is also lost more readily due to excitement and fatigue, with the result that pig muscle often fails to reach an adequate degree of post-mortem acidity, and the incidence of deleterious bacterial change is therefore high. Adequate and rapid refrigeration of freshly killed carcases of pork with prompt handling and careful sawing of the shank, together with bacteriological control of the pickling solution, have, however, done much to obviate this troublesome condition from commercially prepared bacon and ham, and have reduced all types of taint to a minimum. Though it is commonly contended that the slaughtering of gilts or sows during oestrum is likely to result in taint of the bacon or ham subsequently prepared, this it not borne out by bacon factory experience. In the case of the home-cured product, however, there is a possibility that the lowering of the glycogen content of the muscle due to the restlessness and excitement associated with oestrum may be a predisposing factor to the onset of adverse bacterial changes, for such carcases are not adequately cooled after slaughter and the cured product is usually hung for several months before it is consumed. The alleged dark flesh and lack of setting of carcases of cows affected with cystic ovaries may conceivably be due to the depletion of glycogen resulting from the excitement associated with nymphomania in which there are short and irregular intervals between heat periods and the periods themselves often prolonged.

Phosphorescence

This condition is caused by a number of organisms, one of these being *Pseudomonas phosphorescens*, which are widely distributed in nature, especially in sea water, and may infect a chilling room by the storage of fish therein. These organisms may, however, occur on meat without the previous presence of sea fish in the cold store, and are at times found in slaughterhouses, ice cellars, or where meat is regularly kept; being resistant to chilling room temperatures, their invasion of cold stores can be a matter of considerable inconvenience.

At the commencement of phosphorescence, which occurs in 7 to 8 hours when the condition is artificially produced, the surface of the meat, when seen in a dark room, shows luminous areas scattered over its surface and appears as if it were studded with stars. If decomposition develops in the meat the phosphorescence disappears.

Salted or stored meat may show various changes in colour due to bacterial action. Scattered areas, reddish in colour and not unlike beetroot juice, are caused by *Chromobacterium prodigiosum*, and a similar superficial change, but blue in colour, is seen as a result of surface contamination by *Pseudomonas cyanogenus*. *Pseudomonas cutirubra* appears to be the primary cause of " red mould " on charque, the dried salted beef of South America. Meat affected with phosphorescence or abnormal surface coloration is unsightly and repugnant, but if no putrefactive changes are present it may safely be dealt with by trimming.

The Danger of Decomposing Meat to Man

There is little doubt that the most serious illnesses which are caused in man by eating meat may be ascribed to infection or contamination of the meat by salmonella bacteria or *Cl. botulinum*, though such contaminated meat need not necessarily show gross signs of decomposition.

The presence of ptomaines, if they ever occur naturally in decomposing meat, will not produce illness, while the bacteria normally concerned with decomposition are not human pathogens nor are the cleavage products which arise from their enzymatic action poisonous to man. Though decomposition is an index of bacterial growth it is not an indication that the meat will necessarily be harmful; the question is simply one as to which bacteria are concerned in the bacterial contamination, for under special conditions certain of these can form poisonous products when growing in food. In the case of *Cl. botulinum* the illness produced is of a specific type, but in all other illnesses attributed to the eating of decomposed meat there are no specific symptoms and the affection is usually in the nature of an acute afebrile gastro-intestinal inflammation which is frequently of short duration but may prove fatal. The bacteria capable of elaborating poisonous products when growing in food include *Proteus*, certain strains of staphylococci, streptococci and coliform bacilli, but the nature and action of their toxins is not well known nor is it clear whether these toxins are elaborated in the bacterial cell and diffused into the surrounding meat or food, or whether they are products of decomposition of the protein of the meat itself. The presence of signs of decomposition in meat, being essentially an indication that bacterial growth has occurred, justifies the suspicion that harmful organisms may also have been present and multiplied and rendered the meat dangerous.

Another factor which dictates condemnation of decomposed meat is the aesthetic one. The appearance, odour and taste of decomposing meat is repugnant to most of the more civilized nations of the world, and in some individuals its consumption may be accompanied by marked psychological effects. A person purchasing meat expects a sound fresh product, and is entitled to demand that this requirement is observed. Decomposing food must therefore be regarded as unmarketable, with the proviso that those who by racial habit, inclination or birth prefer their food " high " are at liberty, if they so wish, to allow their food to decompose before consuming it. The position may be summarized by the statement that anyone selling a decomposed food is negligent in the legal sense of the word, and it may be regarded as an axiom that though in most cases eating of decomposed meat will do no harm, experience has shown that it can be responsible for human illness ; as it is impossible to state beforehand whether the bacteria present are harmful or not, decomposing meat should in all cases be condemned.

Judgment of Decomposition

The need has long been felt for a laboratory method by which the extent of spoilage in meat could be fairly accurately established. To be of practical value such a test must be short and simple and must provide results which would be unambiguous and thus could be interpreted with confidence. The laboratory tests which have been developed during the last 50 to 60 years include techniques of a chemical, bacteriological and physical nature.

The chemical methods suggested have included (1) tests based on the detection of free ammonia, and (2) the determination of the total amount of volatile bases produced during spoilage. In neither of these cases does the test give a clear indication of spoilage until the meat itself smells sufficiently to be condemned sensorily. (3) The determination of free amino-acid content as an indication of decomposition has been suggested but it is likewise unsuitable except as a guide to advanced putrefaction. (4) The production of indole, sulphur and other volatile products in decomposing meat has also been investigated, but although in fish there seems to be a relationship between spoilage and the amount of total volatile reducing substances and total volatile acids present respectively, such a relationship with regard to meat has not been established. (5) Tests for meat spoilage based on either the oxygen requirements of the meat or on its power of reduction have been in existence for some time but have not proved of practical value.

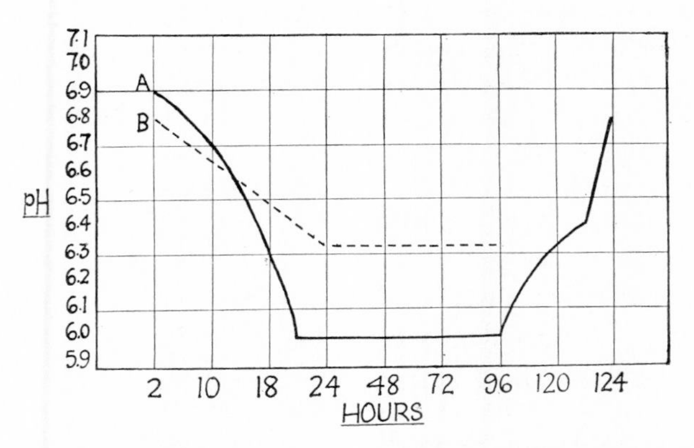

FIG. 205.—Variations in the pH of bovine muscle after slaughter; A. Carcase of healthy animal; B. Carcase of cow affected with septic mastitis. (After Schönberg.)

Bacteriological methods have been devised to relate bacterial plate counts to the quality of meat but these do not show any close agreement between the number of bacteria present and the degree of spoilage as assessed sensorily. It is, however, known that anaerobes cause putrefaction and the desirability of a test for anaerobes in meat comparable to the *E. coli* test in water analysis has been suggested. Of all the methods suggested to date which have claimed to assess satisfactorily the degree of freshness or extent of spoilage in meat, not one is sufficiently discriminating to replace sensory assessment and there is little doubt that the experienced inspector can arrive at a sound conclusion by estimating the texture, appearance, taste and odour of the food, with the use of a boiling test where necessary. It is, however, contended that in certain cases the estimation of the hydrogen-ion concentration of the muscle of suspected carcases may be of value.

Hydrogen-ion Concentration of Muscle. The hydrogen-ion concentration is an expression of the degree of acidity or alkalinity of a substance. The neutral point is 7·0, taking chemically pure water as a basis, and a pH below 7·0 indicates the degree of acidity, while a pH above 7·0 indicates the degree of alkalinity. Meat from freshly killed cattle has an average pH of 6·5 to 6·8 and sometimes up to 7·2. It is therefore slightly acid or slightly alkaline in reaction but the pH then falls rapidly, reaching its lowest level of 5·6 to 5·8 within 48 hours after slaughter. The pH then remains constant for some time, this period depending on whether the carcase has been properly cooled, and also on the degree of bacterial contamination and the storage conditions. Subsequently the pH begins to rise slowly due to autolysis and bacterial growth, and when a pH of 6·4 is reached there is suspicion of the presence of incipient decomposition, while when muscle reaches a pH of 6·8 or over, the objective signs of decomposition become apparent in the meat in the form of changes in odour, colour and texture; it is an unfavourable indication if the pH does not fall to 6·1 or below within 24 hours.

Estimation of the pH of meat is of value in the judgment of border-line cases, particularly of emergency-slaughtered animals, for it provides an indication as to whether or not the meat will possess adequate durability. In animals suffering from febrile diseases, or which are exhausted at the time of slaughter, the glycogen content of the muscles is low because the maintenance of this is dependent on a normal intake of food, normal metabolism and adequate rest. Thus excessive muscular activity or metabolic disturbances following on disease or physical strain will deplete the glycogen reserves and the pH of the flesh will remain at a high level.

Estimation of the pH of the flesh of suspected carcases, such as those found to be affected with a septic condition or animals which have been emergency-slaughtered, is carried out as a routine procedure in many continental abattoirs. This estimation may be made by means of an electrometric apparatus, which, though accurate, is expensive and therefore only used in large slaughtering centres, but in smaller or rural abattoirs the pH may be estimated with reasonable accuracy by simple forms of apparatus which rely on colour indicators for their interpretation. In Germany the indicator nitrazine yellow (1-10,000) is now widely used for it indicates the variations of pH between 6 and 7 and gives an immediate colorimetric result when a portion of meat is placed in a small porcelain dish and the indicator poured upon it. The sample of meat should be taken 24 hours after slaughter and should comprise a cube of gracilis muscle about $\frac{1}{3}$ inch square, this being removed from beneath the muscle surface and free from blood, fat or connective tissue. Meat with a pH of 6·0 produces a yellow coloration and is classified as of good durability; meat with a pH of 6·4 produces an olive-green coloration, is classified as of insufficient durability and is suspect, while meat with a pH of 6·8 shows a bluish-violet coloration, is considered of very low durability and is unfit for food.

In Denmark pH readings of over 6·5 are regarded as evidence that the flesh is of poor keeping quality and such meat may not be sold through ordinary market channels, but may be manufactured into sterilized canned products in special factories under the control of the Meat Inspection Service. The results supplied by one of the central laboratories of this Service showed that in routine determination of the pH of the flesh of 765 detained bovine carcases, a pH of 6·5 or over was encountered in 44 cases, while in 258 detained pig carcases the pH was 6·5 or over in 55 cases. Of this total of 99 cases in which an abnormally high pH was found, 21 cases coincided with bacteriological findings of a specific type or of a high-grade non-specific type, and in the remaining 78 cases the bacteriological findings were negative. An abnormally high pH was found to be associated most frequently with cases of peritonitis, enteritis, difficult parturition, arthritis and cases of uncertain diagnosis suspected of sepsis.

In animals slaughtered because of fractures of the lumbar vertebrae, pelvis or hind limbs it is common to find that owing to the inability of the animal to move the hind limbs the pH of the flesh of the hindquarters falls to the normal figure of about 5·8, whereas the struggling of the animal causes the pH of the forequarters to remain at a high level of 6·5 or more.

MOULDS

The formation of moulds on meat has been a grave problem to those exporting meat from South America, Australia and New Zealand to Britain, and has been the cause of very considerable losses. Though moulds are mostly harmless, for they do not produce toxins and do not cause food poisoning, they can assist in putrefactive processes, as in the encouragement of rancidity in bacon fat. In other cases they may impart a mouldy taste or odour to foodstuffs, mustiness in meat and foods being caused by organisms of the genus *Actinomyces* or *Pseudomonas*, and a small growth of *Actinomyces* in a storage room will cause rapid permeation of a musty odour throughout the room; this change is, however, usually confined to shell eggs, and moulds on meat are more likely to render the food unsightly than to render it unfit for human consumption.

FACTORS INFLUENCING MOULD GROWTH. The development of moulds depends on two factors, a suitable temperature and a certain degree of atmospheric moisture. Moulds first appear and grow most prolifically on the cut surfaces of the lean meat, and although the common moulds of imported meat are capable of growing on the meat surfaces at a temperature of several degrees below freezing-point, they also require atmospheric moisture, as without this they lose water by evaporation, wither and die. Again, although the spores of moulds may have a ubiquitous existence and often float about in the air attached to particles of dust, they cannot germinate without moisture.

Moulds on meat may therefore be prevented if the temperature and the atmospheric humidity are kept low, and, for this reason, proper ventilation in refrigerating and storage works is necessary so that circulating air may dry the surface of food and containers. The control of moulds in food products by the use of antiseptic substances has met with neither approval or success, as the concentration of antiseptics required to inhibit their growth increases rapidly as the humidity of the air increases.

The chief causes of mould on imported meat are : (*a*) exposure of the product to dust between leaving the ship's hold and the time of sale, (*b*) variations in temperature causing atmospheric condensation on the meat surface. Intermittent freezing, or fluctuations in the temperature of a refrigerating chamber, are common predisposing causes to mould growth, and most of the large consignments of meat found to be affected with mould in ships transporting foodstuffs to Great Britain have been subjected to variations in storage temperature as a result of the break-down of refrigerating machinery. Mould on imported meat is not usually associated with decomposition, for although mould will develop between 18° F. to 28° F., growth of putrefactive organisms only occurs at temperatures above freezing, and as the growth of putrefactive bacteria also has an inhibitory effect on the growth of moulds, the two conditions usually occur separately and within different temperature ranges.

Moulds are not uncommonly encountered in imported carcases of beef, mutton and lamb, but are much more likely to attack chilled than frozen meat. The important forms of mould are black spot, white spot, " whiskers " and the bluish-green moulds, among which is *Penicillium*.

1. Black Spot

This is the most troublesome affection of imported meat and is caused by *Cladosporium herbarum*. It is liable to attack quarters of chilled beef taken from ships and placed in cold store at a temperature above 18° F., for it is a mould some varieties of which will grow at 20° F., while all grow well in the neighbourhood of 32° F. In beef, black spot is commonly found on the neck, skirt and pleura, and in frozen mutton on the legs, inside the neck, or in the thoracic or abdominal cavities. These spots are about ¼ to ½ inch in diameter and occur on the surface of the meat, the dark colour being due to the threads of the fungus ramifying in the superficial layers of the meat, and from which layers the mould derives the moisture necessary for its growth. Black spot cannot be removed by gentle scraping with a knife, and microscopical examination shows that the threads of the fungus, dark green or olive in colour, are interlaced between the fat cells in the connective tissue on the surface of the carcase; they do not penetrate to a greater depth than $\frac{1}{8}$ inch, and the contiguous muscular and connective tissue is perfectly normal. Black spot may at times be accompanied by bacterial spoilage, which is a form of decomposition manifested by a softening, darkening and sliminess of the carcase surface and is associated with the growth of micro-organisms of the *Achromobacter* group (Fig. 216).

Black spot which is not too extensive and which is unaccompanied by decomposition may be dealt with by removal of the affected parts by trimming. This is invariably practicable in quarters of chilled beef, but in frozen mutton the mould formation may be so extensive on the inner aspect of the carcase, neck and pelvic cavity that total condemnation is required. Mould formation accompanied by bacterial spoilage requires more generous paring and, at times, condemnation of the whole quarter. It has been repeatedly borne out by practical experience that meat affected with mould, and subsequently refrozen after trimming or wiping, will develop mould more rapidly and in greater abundance than meat which, though mouldy, has not been so treated. Meat which has been trimmed or wiped to remove mould therefore requires a quick sale.

2. White Spot

This condition is caused by *Sporotrichum carnis* and is met with more frequently than any other defect of imported meat. It is seen as small, flat, woolly spots, frequently accompanying black spot on the same carcase and of similar size, but it is whitish in colour and entirely superficial in nature. The spores of *Sporotrichum carnis* can develop at 18° F., grow more plentifully at 28° F., and become profuse when the temperature is above 32° F.

The fungoid growth known as "whiskers" belongs to the closely allied genera *Thamnidium* (Fig. 216) and *Mucor*. The threads grow well at 32° F. and may project more than an inch beyond the surface of the meat, but they collapse on being brought into a relatively dry atmosphere. Though the growth of these moulds ceases at temperatures below 20° F., they retain their vitality, and proliferation then takes place if there is a break-down in the refrigerating machinery and a consequent rise in temperature above freezing-point; thus the presence of "whiskers" may be taken to denote that the meat has been exposed during storage to a temperature at or above 32° F.

Bluish-green moulds belonging to the genus *Penicillium* are seen frequently on cheese, unsound fruit, and also on meat. They are superficial in character and only grow with difficulty at 32° F., though conspicuous growths will occur at a slightly higher temperature.

The superficial nature of white spot, " whiskers " and the bluish-green moulds renders their removal easy, either by wiping with a cloth steeped in vinegar or salt water, or by trimming, and the latter procedure is often preferable, as mould on meat may be associated with a characteristic musty odour. In the treatment of imported forequarters of beef affected with mould, particular attention should be paid to the sawn surfaces of the vertebrae, especially the cervical and first four or five dorsal vertebrae, and all affected bones should be removed ; an affected pleura or peritoneum may be removed by stripping.

In spite of the non-pathogenic nature of moulds, it must be stressed that the meat may assume a mouldy odour and taste if the affection is extensive and of long standing. Moulds, too, may aid in the production of rancidity of fat, and in doubtful cases a portion of the meat should be subjected to a boiling test after the meat has been wiped or trimmed.

EMERGENCY SLAUGHTER

The importance of subjecting the carcases of animals which have undergone emergency slaughter to a careful and critical inspection was emphasized in 1876 by Bollinger, who pointed out that four-fifths of the cases of food poisoning in Germany were associated with the consumption of the flesh of animals which had undergone emergency slaughter. Striking confirmation of this was supplied by statistics prepared by Lydtin, which showed that the danger from meat of emergency-slaughtered animals, when compared with the meat of those slaughtered commercially, was 80 times greater in cattle, 12 times in calves, 100 times in sheep, 211 times in pigs, and 3 times greater in horses. As many animals suffering from illness of an acute febrile nature are slaughtered in an attempt to market the carcase, such cases add immeasurably to the responsibilities of the meat inspector if there are no facilities available for the bacteriological examination of the carcase and organs.

Generally speaking, animals are slaughtered in an emergency for two main reasons, accident or disease. Slaughter of a food animal on account of accident or injury is fully justified on economic and humane grounds, and most of the smaller food animals, i.e. sheep and pigs, are slaughtered for this reason. The commonest injuries encountered in the food animals are fractures of the limbs or pelvis, while extensive bruising may occur as the result of an accident or when an animal has become recumbent during transport by rail or road and has been trampled on by other stock.

Severe laceration and bruising, particularly of the head and throat region and hind limbs, is commonly seen in sheep worried by dogs, judgment in such cases depending on whether the animal has been promptly bled and eviscerated. Damage to the pelvis as a result of slipping is not uncommon in cows and usually manifested by a marked haemorrhagic effusion of the adductor muscles, while injury to the back may occur in heifers during the act of " bulling " or in sows during service by a boar. Other conditions where slaughter is advisable and where a favourable judgment may frequently be given to the carcase provided the result of a laboratory examination of specimens from the carcase is a favourable one, are animals overlain and nearly suffocated, an animal not quite drowned, and an animal struck but not quite killed by lightning.

Acute respiratory distress, with danger of asphyxia, may necessitate emergency slaughter and is seen in cattle as a result of tympanitis after consumption of fermentable fodder, or as the result of obstruction of the oesophagus with a portion of root; in the latter case the carcase frequently possesses a marked turnipy odour which is so strong as to necessitate total condemnation, and in addition rigor mortis passes off quickly and after 24 hours the carcase is often soft, flabby and has lost its bloom. Asphyxia in the cow may also result from the animal attempting to swallow the afterbirth, a portion of the membranes sticking in the oesophagus and pharynx and thus occluding the opening of the larynx. Acute respiratory distress in cattle may also occur from a sudden " flare-up " of tuberculous retropharyngeal lymph nodes.

Prolonged recumbency, particularly in the cow and sow, is a frequent cause of emergency slaughter and occurs most commonly after parturition. In cows recumbency may in some cases be attributed to injury to the lumbo-sacral plexus during the act of parturition, or to cases of milk fever which do not respond to calcium injections. It may also be the result of lactation tetany which may be seen in cows in springtime, usually about a fortnight after the animals are turned out to grass.

In sows recumbency may result from eclampsia, which generally occurs within 24 hours of farrowing, and at times it may result from pressure of tuberculous lesions on the lumbar region of the spinal cord. Recumbency may also occur in pigs due to heatstroke, and is often seen in pigs during transit to abattoirs in hot weather. Abscess formation, usually due to *Corynebacterium pyogenes*, is observed in a considerable proportion of emergency-slaughtered pigs and is probably caused by infection of wounds acquired during fighting or castration.

Affections which necessitate the emergency slaughter of sheep include pregnancy toxaemia, which occurs in ewes shortly before parturition, and entero-toxaemia which is seen in fattening sheep in the autumn and winter months. In lambs and older sheep paralysis of the hindquarters is frequently caused by pressure of an abscess on the spinal cord.

Slaughter because of acute illness may be encountered as a result of inflammation of the intestine, udder, uterus, joints, hoofs and umbilicus, or of affections associated with suppurating wounds, gangrenous lesions, penetrating wounds of the thorax or abdomen, prolapse of the uterus or transit fever. The chief causes of emergency slaughter in cattle are affections of the uterus and udder.

Many countries in Europe prescribe that no case of emergency slaughter may be passed for food until a bacteriological examination has been made of the carcase and organs, and in Denmark and Northern Ireland all cases of emergency slaughter must be accompanied by a veterinary certificate. In France it is illegal to slaughter an animal in emergency except at an abattoir, and a veterinary certificate must be issued to the effect that the animal was subjected to an ante-mortem examination before it was consigned for slaughter. In Western Germany it is prescribed that when an animal has not been subjected to an ante-mortem inspection, the carcase of such an animal must receive a bacteriological examination.

In England and Wales the Meat Inspection Regulations 1963 prescribe that where by reason of accidental injury, illness, exposure to infection or other emergency affecting any animal, that animal has been slaughtered for sale for human consumption in any place other than a slaughterhouse, no person shall remove or cause to be removed the carcase and viscera until it has been inspected in accordance with these regulations. There are, however, provisions that when an animal has been slaughtered in a place unsuitable for retaining a carcase, the carcase may be moved to some convenient place for inspection.

The Regulations referred to above provide an efficient safeguard against the dangers inherent in the flesh and organs of animals subjected to emergency slaughter, but in countries which have not included such provision in their public health enactments, ill, injured or dead animals may be conveyed to a slaughterhouse in the following ways :

The Animal May Arrive Alive but in a Moribund State

Cattle and sheep arriving at a slaughterhouse in a moribund condition usually stiffen immediately after slaughter, especially when they have suffered from digestive disorders and have been generously dosed with medicine. In very severe injuries or bruising the blood has a thicker and more viscous appearance, but in anaemia and redwater the blood is thin and watery. Judgment of carcases of animals which have arrived at an abattoir alive but in a moribund state depends upon (*a*) the bleeding and setting of the carcase, (*b*) the condition of the meat after quartering, and (*c*) the colour of the fat and serous membranes.

The Animal May Arrive Dead and Uneviscerated

Such animals may have been stuck and bled, or they may be unbled, but in all cases of dead cattle arriving at an abattoir, no matter what explanation is offered by the owner as to the cause of death, it is advisable to examine a blood smear from the ear or tail ; only when it is proved that the animal's death is not due to anthrax should the unloading of the animal from the motor wagon be permitted. Even then the evisceration of a bled animal should not be permitted unless death has occurred less than an hour or so previously ; coldness of the extremities and, in cattle, evidence of tympanitis in the left flank are indications that death has not been recent. Where cattle have been dead for more than half an hour and have not been bled, subsequent dressing should be forbidden, for the carcase will inevitably be condemned for imperfect bleeding.

In sheep which have been dead for some hours the wool is easily pulled out and tympanitis will be observed in the left flank. In such animals it is uneconomical to remove the pelt, for the carcase is unfit for food, nor does the value of the pelt justify the expense of dressing the carcase.

When the dead animal is eviscerated at the abattoir the uterus should be examined as to whether it is contracted or whether it is enlarged or flaccid ; in milk fever the organ is tightly contracted, but after recent parturition or in septic metritis it is flaccid, and in the latter affection may be two or three times larger than normal. The appearance of the fat and tissues should also be noticed when the animal is eviscerated. Discoloration of the fat and tissues in the pelvic cavity may be due to (*a*) difficult parturition, (*b*) septic metritis, or (*c*) fracture of the pelvis, a diagnostic feature of the latter condition in the bovine animal being that the affected leg or legs drop out at right angles. The intestines on removal may show a sloppy appearance in the wasted animal, and also in cases of enteritis or after large doses of purgative medicine.

After the carcase has been eviscerated and hung the degree of setting may be judged in the usual way by lifting the shoulder, but the well-nourished carcase may appear quite firm due to setting of the fat in the axilla, though the actual muscular tissue may be soft and spongy. Such carcases should always be quartered and a further examination made after 24 hours.

The Animal May Arrive in the Form of a Dressed Carcase

These carcases frequently present great difficulty in judgment, especially if they are unaccompanied by the internal organs. Examination of the head of cattle is important, for when they have been stunned prior to bleeding, either by mechanically operated instrument or by other means, there is evidence of haemorrhage in the space between the medulla oblongata and the occipital condyles. On the other hand, in cattle which have died or which have been bled to death without previous stunning such haemorrhage is absent. In dead eviscerated cattle, removal of the hide may have been delayed for some hours, and in such animals the carcase surface has a whiter appearance; failure to remove the hide at the time of slaughter may hinder cooling of the carcase, with resultant lack of setting which may be demonstrated by the ease with which the

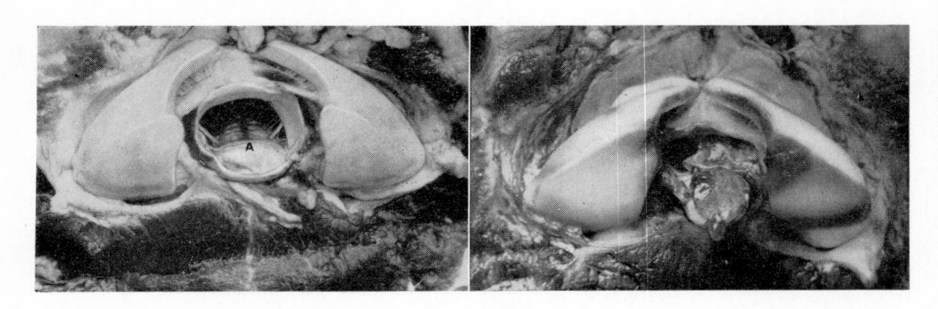

FIG. 206.—Haemorrhage around the medulla oblongata of an ox as an indication that the animal has been stunned prior to bleeding. The two illustrations are of the rear view of head and show the occipital condyles on either side of the medulla (A). The illustration on the left shows the absence of haemorrhage around the medulla of an animal which has died a natural death or has not been stunned prior to bleeding. The illustration on the right shows the haemorrhage produced by shock in an animal which has been stunned.

forelimbs can be raised. In dead, eviscerated cattle it is frequently observed that the two forelimbs have not contracted uniformly, flexion of the forelimbs together with a brownish-red coloration of the flesh being regarded as an indication that the animal was slaughtered *in extremis* after a long illness. It is most often observed where metritis and peritonitis have been succeeded by septicaemia.

Judgment of the carcase of an animal slaughtered on a farm is greatly facilitated if the internal organs accompany it, but in their absence recourse must be made to examination of the carcase lymph nodes for enlargement, haemorrhages or tuberculosis, and to the kidneys for the degree of bleeding. The degree of congestion and setting of the carcase should also be noted, and if a bovine carcase shows any degree of congestion a smear from a kidney or lymph node should be examined microscopically for anthrax. The vertebrae in cattle and pigs should be examined for tuberculous caries and the pleura and peritoneum for evidence of stripping, while an incision should be made into the musculature for the presence of any abnormal odour, and should this be detected a portion of meat should be subjected to a boiling test.

In emergency-slaughtered animals, only in cases where the animal has been but a short time dead, shows no evidence of disease, and in which the carcase sets and looks normal in every way, should one consider passing it for food. Where there is any evidence of post-mortem staining or of decomposition the carcase should unhesitatingly be condemned.

The Technique of Emergency Slaughter

Many animals which are slaughtered in an emergency on a farm and the carcase consigned to an abattoir, are condemned due to the owner's ignorance of the elementary principles of bleeding and evisceration. Where emergency slaughter becomes necessary, and the services of a skilled slaughterman are not available, the following procedure will increase the likelihood of the carcase being salvaged for human food.

Attempt may be made to salvage an animal even if it is not in prime fat condition, for although the dressed carcases of lean cows or store cattle are unattractive to the eye these carcases have a definite value as meat for manufacturing purposes. This applies also to store pigs and sheep, while animals which are badly lacerated or have fractured limbs may still be salvaged as the carcase can be jointed at the abattoir and the sound portions passed for food.

Bleeding. This is important, as on its efficiency depends the keeping quality of the carcase. Cattle, after stunning, should have the neck severed in a manner similar to the Jewish practice, this being done by cutting with a sharp knife across the upper portion of the throat and thus severing both carotid arteries and jugular veins. A wide cut should be made to ensure that these vessels are severed, and it should be continued deep down almost to the cervical vertebrae. Efficient bleeding may be obtained if the animal is then " possed ". This entails looping a length of rope around the upper foreleg and whilst pulling on this rope the operator places his foot in the animal's flank and presses vigorously in a forward direction. The process imitates a form of artificial respiration, and should be continued for 5 minutes at the rate of 15 posses per minute. Sheep and pigs should be bled by a transverse cut across the throat, and though these animals need not be possed, bleeding is greatly facilitated if they are hung head downwards to bleed.

After stunning or death in cattle, sheep and pigs, it is permissible, though inadvisable, for a maximum period of 20 minutes to elapse before these animals are bled. In cattle, should this maximum period elapse before bleeding, the process of possing must be more vigorous and prolonged.

Evisceration. A speedy removal of the abdominal and thoracic organs is essential if decomposition is to be avoided. In cattle an extensive incision should be made through the abdominal wall from sternum to pubis, and the abdominal viscera (stomach, liver, intestines, etc.) removed, care being taken to remove the rectum also. The diaphragm should then be incised to allow a current of air round the chest cavity.

In sheep and pigs the abdominal viscera should be removed, and the rectum and anus must be included, for decomposition develops rapidly in the hindquarters if these are allowed to remain. The diaphragm should also be cut through in these animals and the heart and lungs removed. In no case should more than 1 hour elapse before removal of the abdominal viscera. If bleeding and evisceration are carried out within their maximum prescribed periods cattle carcases may safely be left without further attention for 5 to 6 hours, or even overnight in cool weather, and sheep and pigs, if hung up, may be left for 24 hours. The hides of cattle may be left on and removed at the abattoir by skilled labour, while pigs which have been bled and eviscerated on a farm may be scalded, or if necessary, skinned, after arrival at the abattoir. Sheep skins may also be left on, though tardy removal of the skin of these animals, or failure to remove the intestines expeditiously after death, may impart a tallow-like taste to the mutton and, in addition, such carcases usually show early putrefactive changes.

CHAPTER X

TREATMENT AND DISPOSAL OF BY-PRODUCTS AND FATS

Though the animal by-product industry is a very old one and has made rapid strides in the last few years, there are few abattoirs in Britain which provide sufficient space and facilities for the treatment of by-products on the premises. Where an abattoir is already erected, a suitable by-products factory can be provided nearby but is more expensive to run due to cost of transporting raw material ; the smaller the abattoir the greater is the overhead cost of maintaining a by-products plant.

By-products may be defined as everything from the abattoir or butcher's shop that may not be sold directly as food. The need for efficient treatment of these products is based on, (*a*) the necessity for their rapid hygienic disposal, thus avoiding decomposition and the formation of obnoxious odours ; abattoir by-products, if not removed and treated in this way, become a serious source of contamination to fresh meat ; (*b*) efficient processing of abattoir by-products secures an economic return on material which would otherwise be wasted.

The need for efficient processing of by-products is agreed on both by the meat trade and by public health authorities, and where such a plant is erected and maintained by a local authority, any loss incurred, though unlikely, must be regarded as a charge against the local authority in carrying out its obligation in the ultimate hygienic disposal of unsound meat.

Buildings

Premises should be situated so that raw material can be conveyed to them with a minimum amount of handling, and they should be spacious, well lighted and ventilated, with impervious walls and floors ; the latter should be sloped to open channels leading through fat traps to the drains.

An abundant supply of steam and hot and cold water should be provided, and a point of importance is the position of the boilers supplying steam to the abattoir. These should be located near to the by-products plant so that all obnoxious vapours from the plant may be discharged into the boiler chimney. As most of the processes of by-products manufacture are classified as offensive trades, the fume control must be as complete as possible, though the melting of edible fat cannot in any way be classed as offensive and no form of control is needed. Similarly, tripe preparing cannot be classed as offensive, but the process of gut cleaning and the treatment of blood and inedible offals gives rise to offensive smells, and the two latter materials should be treated in enclosed steam-jacketed vessels, the fumes being suitably dealt with before being discharged into the open air. The secret of production of high-grade standardized animal by-products lies in prompt treatment of the raw material. Animal offals decompose rapidly, depreciating markedly as a result, and it should therefore be an axiom in abattoir control that no raw material should be left untreated after a day's slaughtering.

The following by-products require to undergo some form of processing before they may be utilized: fat, stomach and intestines, blood, bones, hoofs and horns, hair and bristles, hides, skins and condemned carcases.

Fats

BEEF FAT. It is desirable to include as much fat as possible in the edible category, and with the exception of the hide the most important abattoir by-product is the fat trimmed from the intestines and other internal organs of cattle. The value of this by-product is fully appreciated by the American meat works, where efforts are constantly being made to improve the methods of collecting the lower grade fats so as to transfer them to the first grade edible class. Edible ox fats are rendered down to yield premier jus, which is again separated into oleo oil and oleo stearin, but in war time all edible ox fat is converted into dripping. Fat which is unfit for use either as suet, dripping or premier jus, goes chiefly for soap manufacturing, though some of the very low grades are used for the dressing of leather; subsequent processing of these fats produces commercial glycerine, a valuable commodity used in many commercial processes, including medicinal preparations, nitroglycerine, gunpowder, cordite and dynamite. When every vestige of fatty material has been extracted the residual meat fibres, known as "cracklings" or "greaves", are ground and used for the feeding of poultry.

PIG FAT. Fat occurs in many regions of the pig carcase, the best quality fat being obtained from the peritoneal lining (leaf fat), the next best from the back fat, mesentery and omentum. The surplus fat of pigs is worked up into various qualities of lard, and a pig of 200 lb. live weight yields about 14 lb. of lard.

The process of rendering pig fat into lard is carried out by cutting up the fresh and clean raw fat into small pieces, as this hashing of fats promotes a rapid and uniform rendering. Rendering is carried out in steam-jacketed containers accompanied by stirring, for if heating of the fat is done over an open fire the value of the product is lowered due to overheating and discoloration. The liquid fat is run off, preferably continuously, into a jacketed tank where it is settled and cooled; rapidity of cooling is important, as crystals of stearin are formed when lard is allowed to cool slowly and the product lacks the smooth, white, uniform appearance that it presents when rapidly cooled.

MUTTON FAT. This is rendered in the same way as beef fat or lard, and though it is not converted into oleo oil or oleo stearin on account of its strong flavour, it may be used as dripping when blended with other fats. Mutton fat contains more stearin than ox or pig fat and, being a good deal harder, is used as a preservative layer on the top of glass jars of meat paste.

Stomach and Intestines

The stomach of the ox and sheep is made into tripe, the intestines into containers for sausage, while certain other commodities including rennet, pepsin, and surgical catgut, are obtained from the alimentary tract of the food animals.

RENNET. This is extracted from the abomasum of calves which have been fed exclusively on a milk diet, the stomach being washed, macerated in salt brine, and the rennet recovered in a dilute, impure form and finally concentrated to a powder by evaporation. Rennet is used by cheese manufacturers to coagulate milk, the soluble calcium caseinate in milk being split into insoluble calcium paracaseinate, or curds, and whey protein, or whey. Though it was the practice at one time to put a piece of dried rennet in milk for the purpose of initiating the process of cheese manufacture, this procedure has been replaced by the use of concentrated essences of standard strength prepared in recognized laboratories.

PEPSIN. The fundus, i.e. the portion of the lining of the pig stomach which lies between the cardiac and pyloric portions (and distinguished from these by its greater thickness and reddish-brown mottled appearance) is used for the making of pepsin. The mucous membrane, after careful removal and trimming off of connective tissues, is washed gently in cold water to remove dirt, chilled in ice water, then kept under refrigeration until ready for manufacture. The linings of 4 to 5 pig stomachs are required to produce 1 lb. of pepsin, the liquid extract being dried and made into tablets which are used medicinally in the treatment of human gastric disorders.

SURGICAL CATGUT. The material for surgical ligatures is obtained from inspected sheep, the process of manufacture being carried out under careful chemical and bacteriological control. The method is highly standardized, the intestines being kept at a temperature near to freezing so that fermentation and bacterial growth may be avoided. After being carefully cleansed the intestines are sterilized, sponged, dried and polished until absolutely smooth, then placed into sterilized containers which are finally sealed.

Blood

Though a considerable quantity of blood from slaughtered animals is utilized for the manufacture of black puddings and other types of blood sausage, many abattoirs are faced with the hygienic and economic disposal of the remainder. Occasional slaughter does not lend itself to the economic treatment of blood, as the quantities are small, and it is only in plants where the daily kill is large that full use can be made of blood by the installation of a plant by which the liquid can be dried.

The processing of blood can yield both inedible products and products suitable for animal feeding, but in either case a desirable abattoir feature is that animals should be bled at central points, an arrangement which secures a greater degree of hygiene and also facilitates blood collection. Fresh blood must be processed at the earliest possible moment, as otherwise it decomposes rapidly with an appreciable loss in its nitrogen content.

INEDIBLE BLOOD PRODUCTS. These may be prepared by two methods: (*a*) Blood is collected by gravitation into a steel tank from which it is blown by steam or compressed air to a storage tank and then to a further container where the blood is coagulated by live steam. After coagulation the blood is introduced into a blood press to dispose of the moisture liberated by coagulation and from there passes to a blood dryer and is then trucked to a grinding and sifting unit (Fig. 207). Five tons of raw blood yield one ton of the dried product which finds a ready sale in the artificial manure market.

(*b*) An alternative method of drying fresh blood is to subject it to a preliminary treatment in a drier and complete the process on a movable surface-evaporator table which has a canopy fixed over it and is 6 feet wide by 40 feet long. The table slowly passes from one end to the other, and the blood, being gently heated and subjected to a warm upward current of air, becomes dried without discoloration; this method gives a better product than by drying completely in the drier. An important factor in blood drying is that though blood may be rendered to a powder in various ways it is always necessary to coagulate the blood before it comes in contact with the heated surface of the drying apparatus, as otherwise it cannot be dried sufficiently for storage.

A more remunerative process than the above is the conversion of fresh blood into dried fibrin and a blood powder, or albumen, which is soluble in water. The proportions of the three constituents of blood are albumen 5 per cent., fibrin and corpuscles 13 per cent., water 82 per cent., and in the

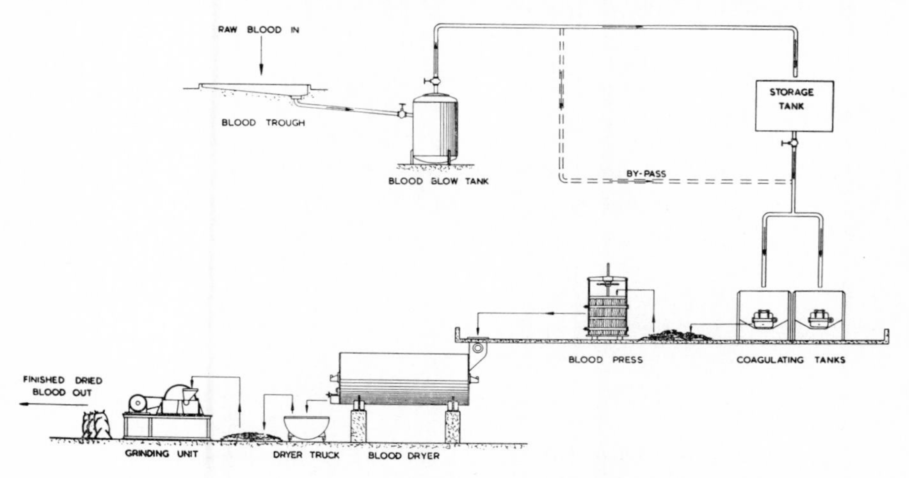

FIG. 207.—Layout of a blood drying plant. (Iwel Engineering Ltd.)

case of pigs the blood of 100 animals of average size yields 30 lb. of albumen and 78 lb. of fibrin and corpuscles. In order to extract the fibrin the blood must be caught and agitated immediately, while the fluid blood or plasma readily filters away from the fibrin and is dried in a heated vacuum chamber, thus yielding a product which keeps well and undergoes no change during prolonged storage. This blood albumen is 95 per cent. soluble in cold water and is used in aeroplane manufacture and work connected with plywood where gumming is necessary. Blood albumen also has a value as a clarifying agent for wines, in the preparation of certain sugars and photographic papers, and as a fixative for colours in cotton goods (gingham).

BLOOD MEAL. Edible blood meals, which must be prepared from quite fresh blood to avoid a high ammonia content and a consequent objectionable odour, are suitable as a feed for cattle and pigs, horses and poultry. The value of dried blood as an animal foodstuff is generally recognized, and a feeding mixture of two parts of blood and three parts of molasses is used in Denmark for cattle feeding.

Bones

Fresh bones are processed in bacon curing works, sausage factories and in modern abattoirs to yield a valuable edible fat, but bones prepared from dead or condemned animals are unfit for the production of edible products.

The processing of fresh bones, though not carried out on a large scale, takes place in a digester, the bones being filled into a bone cage which is then run over the open lid of the digester and lowered into it; the lid is replaced and the steam pressure inside raised to 25 lb. The fat which liquefies in the process is allowed to trickle off, 1 hour being sufficient to steam out all the fat which can be economically extracted, and this is then used for blending with lard or making into dripping.

If it is desired to obtain gelatine from bones this is done subsequent to the fat extraction and under carefully controlled pressure. A strong solution of gelatine runs off from the lower opening of the digester and is used in food factories in the making of brawn and pies; it is also used in ice-cream making, in the production of capsules for medicine, in photography, as a culture medium for bacteria and in the manufacture of smokeless gunpowder. Some of the gelatine used for these purposes comes from veal, for whereas 100 parts of beef yield only 6 parts of gelatine, 100 parts of veal yield 50 parts. However, most gelatine is now derived from pig skin.

After extraction of fat and gelatine the bones remaining in the digester are in a soft and chalky condition and are easily ground into bone meal, the main constituent of which is calcium phosphate. If the bone meal is adequately dried in a kiln, which is constructed of sheet iron trays and through which hot air is blown, it yields a product available for stock feeding, being known as feeding bone flour. If the bone meal is not dried rapidly it will contain about 18 per cent. of moisture and is known as steamed bone flour, which is used as a fertilizer. In Britain feeding bone flour is not now used by compounders as a source of minerals in animal food on account of the risk of it containing anthrax spores, while steamed bone flour has been to a great extent replaced by inorganic phosphates, which are free from micro-organisms. Calcined bone, obtained by the roasting of bones in the presence of air, is used in the manufacture of high class pottery and china, in the refining of silver and in copper smelting; bone charcoal is used in bleaching and sugar refining, and in case-hardening compounds in the manufacture of steel; special bone powders are utilized for the removal of fluorine from drinking water.

NEATSFOOT OIL. In this process the cattle feet are washed, scalded at 170° F. to facilitate scraping off of hair, boiled for 15 minutes to allow loosening and removal of the claws, and the feet then split. Prolonged cooking and settling yields a supernatant oil which is skimmed off and filtered, and being odourless, forms a valuable lubricant for delicate machinery; its chief application, however, is in the manufacture of leather.

Hoofs and Horns

Hoofs are removed from the feet by steeping in hot water, being then dried and sold to manufacturers of horn articles such as combs and buttons. White hoofs are particularly desirable for the above trades, whilst striped and black hoofs are dried in a steam drier and ground into hoof meal fertilizer; quantities of this material are exported from Denmark as a fertilizer for grape vines. Horns are sawn from the skull, graded and used for manufacture of combs, hairpins, other hair ornaments and buttons, or, if of low grade, as a fertilizer. Hoof and horn meal, as well as pig hair, have found wide usage in Great Britain for making foam type fire extinguishing fluids.

Hair and Bristles

Cattle hair goes with the hide to the tanners where it is separated from the skin by the use of lime or other chemicals, the crude hair being used by plasterers as a binding agent. For other purposes the hair requires purification, this being done by treatment with hydrochloric acid which removes the lime and impurities and sterilizes the hair. Cattle hair, when finally dried, has excellent insulating properties and is used as felt for placing beneath carpets.

In the pig the long bristles of back and tail are used for brush making, about 1½ to 2 lb. being obtained in the scraping of the pig carcase. Wild pigs yield the stiffest bristles and for this reason Russia was formerly the chief supplier of this material, though now much of it comes from Canada; shaving brushes, which at one time were manufactured from horsehair obtained from Siberia and China, are now largely made from pig bristles. The short hair of pigs is also purified by chemical means and is used for stuffing mattresses, or by furniture makers and upholsterers as a padding for chairs and cushions.

Hides and Skins

Though hides and skins do not come within the province of the meat inspector, except that they may act as carriers of certain infectious animal diseases, they constitute the most valuable material removed from the animal carcase. In American packing house practice it is estimated that the ox hide represents 12 per cent. of the value of the animal, the by-products 7 per cent. and the carcase 80 per cent. Generally speaking the ox hide weighs 10 per cent. of the carcase weight, or 7 per cent. of the animal's live weight, the outstanding hide for both quality and weight being from cattle of the Highland breed and frequently weighing up to 100 lb. Though great weight and thickness of the ox hide are related to the animal's resistance to untoward climatic conditions, these attributes are usually associated with the undesirable characteristics of coarse bone and slow maturing, and Highland cattle are not usually fat until 3 to 4 years of age. Herefords and Irish cattle also carry heavy hides, Shorthorns and other dairy breeds the lightest weights, but bull hides are not of great value owing to their irregular texture and strong growth marks in the region of the neck. Grass-fed cattle yield heavier hides than stall-fed animals of the same breed.

Ox hides arrive at the tannery, either fresh from the slaughterhouse, or salted and dried to prevent putrefaction. After soaking in water to cleanse and soften them they are placed in pits filled with milk of lime, where they remain 1 to 4 weeks, this process loosening the hair and opening up the fibre. The hair on the outside, and flesh and meat on the inside, is then scraped off and, after removal of lime by washing in weak acid, the hides are tanned. Tanning may be done by a vegetable process in which the barks of trees are used, or by a chemical process known as chrome tanning. The tannery process, from raw hide to finished leather, takes about 3 months. The hide from bullocks and heifers, when tanned, is used as sole leather or for belting. Sole leather is obtained from the butt, the area of the hide lying on either side of the backbone. Cow hides are often split and used for motor-car seats or for furniture upholstery, and hide-trimmings such as lips, etc., are used for the manufacture of gelatine.

The skin of a good bacon pig will average 4 feet by 3½ feet in size, pig skins making an excellent leather which is tough and particularly suitable for saddles, handbags, gloves and bookbinding. Pig carcases are rarely skinned in England, except where it is necessary to remove localized skin affections, and the tanning of pig skins is confined to Germany, and also to Scotland where skinning of bacon pigs is carried out prior to the preparation of Ayrshire roll bacon.

Sheep skins are made into leather for gloves, lamb skins being used for kid gloves, while sheep skins are utilized for chamois leather gloves by a process known as shammoying in which the skin is impregnated with fish oil to make it soft and pliable. The value of a sheep skin for tanning is in inverse proportion to the value of the wool for spinning and weaving purposes. Leather is also prepared from the skins of goats or kids and withstands considerably more wear than sheep skin and has a particularly attractive surface.

THE DISPOSAL OF CONDEMNED MEAT AND OFFALS

Though the hygienic necessity for forbidding the sale of food which is unfit for human consumption is fully recognized in all civilized countries, a study of animal disease enables the trained officer to distinguish between the following conditions :

(1) Meat or carcases that are sound and wholesome and which can be placed on the market without any restriction ;

(2) Meat or carcases that are affected with some condition which is too severe to permit of unconditional release but which can be sold to the public at a reduced price and subject to adequate public health safeguards ; and

(3) Carcases which are dangerous, or carcases which show such a deviation from the normal as to render them repugnant or innutritious to the consumer.

The meat inspection laws of the United States, Canada, Denmark, New Zealand, Italy, France, Switzerland and Germany recognize the economic and public health justification for this second classification, and the legislation prescribes, with varying modifications, the treatment which this meat must undergo before it is released for sale. Such meat, classified as " conditionally admissible ", is subjected to heat treatment by boiling, but in some cases it is rendered safe by adequate refrigeration, pickling or other means. This is the basis of the Freibank system which operates in Germany and Switzerland, and a similar procedure operates in Italy and is known as the Basso Macello.

Freibank System

This system became legalized in Germany in 1879 and entails the sale of (*a*) meat of inferior quality, and (*b*) meat which requires some treatment before sale, such meat being sold at a reduced price under strict Governmental or municipal supervision. The system has since been adopted by other countries in Europe and is the means of providing the poorer sections of the community with a safe, cheap and nutritious protein diet, though certain conditions must be rigidly observed, among these being that the sale of the meat is restricted to small quantities to any one person, while butchers, hotel and restaurant keepers are excluded from patronizing this source of supply. In some cases the premises where such meat is sold are within the precincts of the abattoir, in other cases they may be situated in a working class district, but it is obligatory that a notice be prominently displayed on the premises clearly indicating to the purchaser the treatment to which the flesh should be subjected before it is consumed.

In Switzerland meat and meat products classified as conditionally admissible may only be sold under official control. The prescriptions in the Swiss regulations under which meat is classified as conditionally admissible are :

FIG. 208.—A Freibank in Switzerland. Various products are exhibited for sale and the notice displayed on the wall reads : "Cooking Instructions !" "Cooking and roasting is not considered sufficient unless the innermost parts of the meat after treatment have attained a greyish colour in the case of beef or a greyish-white colour in the case of pork and the juice which exudes when the meat is cut has lost its reddish colour."

(1) Meat from an animal which has been injured and where several hours have elapsed between the accident and slaughter, always provided the animal had not been suffering from fever and the flesh is of normal appearance.

(2) Meat of animals affected with some organic disease accompanied by systemic disturbance but where there is no element of doubt as to the fitness of the flesh for human food and the flesh itself is not aesthetically repugnant.

(3) The meat of animals suffering from an organic disease such as affections of the intestines, uterus or umbilicus which readily lead to generalization, but where the symptoms, location of the disease and

condition of the lymph nodes furnish satisfactory evidence that no such generalization has occurred, proved, if necessary, by a bacteriological examination.

(4) The flesh of cattle affected with *Cysticercus bovis*, or the flesh of sheep or goats affected with *Cysticercus ovis*, provided there are only a small number of cysts in the predilection seats (masseters, tongue, heart and diaphragm).

(5) Pork slightly affected with *Cysticercus cellulosae*, provided the flesh has been sterilized by steam or has been salted for three weeks.

(6) The flesh of an animal which has been killed as a result of injury (e.g. lightning or accident) and eviscerated immediately, provided bleeding of the animal has been adequate and there has been no contamination of the flesh by contents of the stomach, intestines, urinary bladder, gall bladder or uterus.

(7) Flesh which, though not repugnant in appearance, is uniformly abnormal in colour, consistency, odour or taste (examples are the flesh of male goats, boars, rigs and cryptorchid pigs, healthy animals which are poorly bled, and animals affected with a pronounced degree of icterus).

(8) Meat which is abnormal in colour, odour or taste due to a specific feeding stuff or medicine, provided the feeding stuff or medicine is not harmful to man and the flesh is not repugnant.

(9) Flesh of healthy animals which have not been eviscerated immediately after slaughter and in accordance with Swiss Regulations ; also carcases which have been inflated by the mouth.

(10) Unaltered flesh of animals affected with tuberculosis :

(*a*) where there is chronic tuberculosis of an organ together with lesions of tuberculosis in isolated lymph nodes of the carcase;

(*b*) where there is chronic tuberculosis of the internal organs which is more widespread in character or with numbers of foci of a purulent or caseous nature ; also where there is tuberculosis of bone, provided the animal shows no evidence of emaciation.

(11) The flesh of calves, lambs, kids, pigs and foals aged from 8 days to 3 weeks, and also the flesh of other young animals in which there are no pathological changes but where the flesh is thin, flabby, discoloured and reddish in appearance.

(12) The flesh of animals cachectic as a result of illness, or of animals in markedly poor condition without any obvious illness.

(13) The flesh of pigs affected with swine erysipelas, pneumoenteritis or acute swine fever, provided there is no cachexia or evidence of severe systemic disturbance.

(14) The head, tongue and stomach, after scalding, of animals affected with foot and mouth disease, provided the extent of the lesions permit it.

(15) The flesh of animals with benign or slight anaemia.

In the Swiss abattoirs in 1960 of the 2,261,182 animals slaughtered, 99·1 per cent. of the carcases were released unconditionally after post-mortem examination, 0·26 per cent. were totally condemned, and 0·64 per cent. were released for conditional sale on the Freibank. In 1965, of the 2,689,906 animals slaughtered, 98·98 per cent. of the carcases were released unconditionally, 0·29 per cent. were totally condemned and 0·73 per cent. were released for conditional sale. The increase in the percentage of carcases totally condemned or released for conditional sale as compared with 1960 is due to the new meat inspection regulations which came into force in 1962 and impose a more severe judgment on certain diseases, including tuberculosis and cysticercosis.

Similar provisions exist in other European countries, and also in the United States where carcases or parts which on post-mortem inspection show lesions of disease too severe to be passed to be released unconditionally, but where total condemnation is unjustified, are marked " U.S. passed for cooking " and are only released after adequate heat treatment by this means. The affections in which this is permissible include certain cases of tuberculosis and caseous lymphadenitis, a moderate degree of icterus, certain cases of measles of beef and measles of pork, moderate infestation with parasites not transmissible to man (e.g. *Cysticercus ovis*), carcases of animals in an advanced degree of pregnancy, and carcases of animals which have within 10 days given birth to young but in which there is no evidence of septic infection.

Processing of Freibank Meat

The sterilization of meat which requires heat treatment before being released for human consumption is best carried out by boiling or steaming. The destruction of animal parasites such as cysticerci and trichinae may be effected with certainty if meat is subjected to a temperature of 170° F, and simple boiling of pieces of meat not more than 4 inches in diameter for 2½ hours will destroy parasites and will effectually inactivate most forms of non-sporing bacteria, including tubercle bacilli. Steam sterilization of meat, which entails heating by steam under moderate pressure (7 lb. per sq. inch) in an autoclave, is, however, more efficacious than simple boiling, and if portions of meat up to 6 inches in diameter are steamed for 2 hours it may be assumed that all portions of the musculature will attain the required temperature. It may be assumed that meat has been adequately cooked and has attained a temperature of approximately 176° F. if the deepest parts of the flesh are a uniform greyish colour and the juice which exudes when the meat is cut has lost its reddish tint.

In the case of meat affected with the more resistant spore-forming bacteria, as in anthrax, malignant oedema, or tetanus, no processing by heat or other means should be countenanced, and the meat from carcases affected with these conditions must be unhesitatingly condemned. Similarly, carcases affected with septic conditions or which are shown to contain organisms of the salmonella group must be regarded as definitely unfit for food. Diminishing use, however, is being made of the Freibank procedure in the United States, Canada, and a number of other European countries.

OTHER METHODS OF DISPOSAL OF CONDEMNED FOODSTUFFS

In some cases condemned meat is disposed of by treating it as trade refuse, and sending it to a refuse dump. No public health officer should countenance this procedure, and should not permit the practice, still existent in Great Britain, by which the carcases of diseased animals are allowed to be sent to foxhound kennels; nor is it sufficient to accept the assurance of those in charge of kennels that the meat will be boiled. Condemned meat must be rendered down by heat processing, or if this is impracticable it should be destroyed by burning.

Processing of Condemned Meat

The best and most economical method of disposal of condemned carcases and offals is by heat treatment in a jacketed vessel, as in this way complete sterilization is secured and the maximum return from the rendered down material is attained. Though a number of forms of apparatus exist for carrying out this process they all consist of two essential components, (*a*) a melter, which is actually a high-pressure steamer, and (*b*) an extractor, by which fat can be removed from the treated products.

In the Iwel-Laabs Dry Rendering process the melter is in the form of a horizontal steam-jacketed cylinder, fitted with a powerful central agitator shaft. The carcase meat and bones are loaded into the cylinder from above, the lid shut and clamped, and the material, coming in contact with the heated wall of the inner cylinder, is at the same time agitated by the moving agitator shaft. The water contained in the meat is converted to steam and, the fat being liquefied, the carcase literally " fries in its own fat ". The internal pressure is then released by means of a vacuum pump, and the process continued until the final products are dry

After drying, the machine is stopped and the discharge door opened gradually to allow the free fat to run off into the percolating tank and from there to the fat-receiving tank. The greaves from the charge are then discharged and allowed to drain in the percolating tank, the free fat held in them running through to the fat-receiving tank. This fat is then pumped by a fat-pump into a pair of settling tanks from which the fat is run off into drums or bulk storage containers. The greaves, after draining in the percolating tank, are loaded into centrifugal fat extractor baskets, wheeled to the centrifugal fat extractor and spun at a high rate, the excess free fat being thrown off and running to the fat-receiving tank. The heat from the steam used to drive the extractors keeps the fat flowing evenly, and the

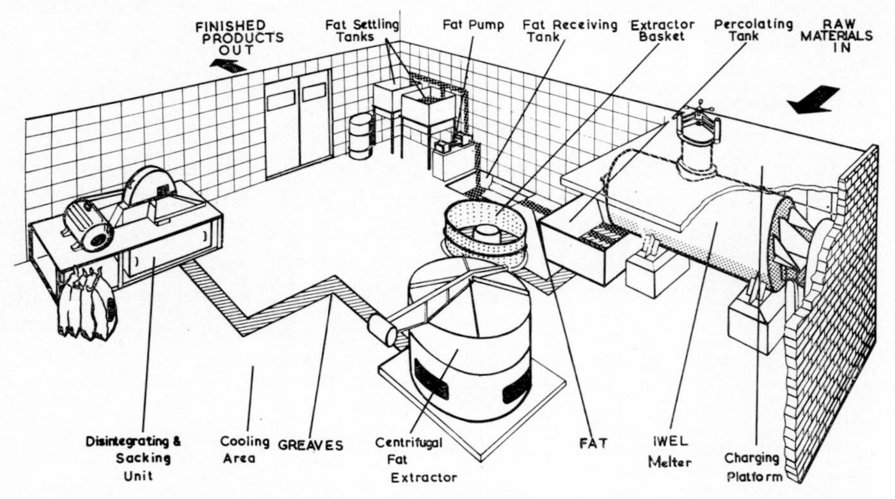

FIG. 209.—Layout of a by-products plant including a pressure melter and centrifugal fat extractor (Iwel Engineering Ltd.).

greaves, which when unloaded from the machine are hot, are emptied on to the floor to cool before being conveyed to the disintegrating unit for grading and sacking.

Other plants treat condemned carcases and other raw materials by chemical methods. One type, which can be used for all types of raw material, comprises a mixed method, namely steam sterilization following extraction with trichlorethylene.

Stale or decomposed bones are treated separately, being crushed and fed into steel extractors where they are treated by boiling benzine and the grease obtained, known as technical fat, recovered from the solution by steam distillation. The degreased bones are now conveyed to a revolving drum known as a polisher, which removes surface meat and fine splinters of bone. The bones are then passed into autoclaves of 4 tons capacity and treated alternately with high-pressure steam and hot water, this process removing the glue, which is then concentrated, chilled, cut into slabs and dried, to form the well-known sheet glue. A more satisfactory product, known as pearl glue, is prepared by dropping the liquid glue in white spirit (a high boiling paraffin) from a tower, the pellicles of glue thus formed being more easily dried and handled, and subsequently of greater durability than the sheet variety. The residue from the autoclaves is dried, and, if of low moisture content, is available as sterilized feeding bone flour, but if the moisture content is high and some decomposition takes place, the product is then sold as steamed bone flour for use as a fertilizer.

From the public health aspect it is essential that the collection and handling of the material should take place in a way that infection of other material, whether animals or human beings, is avoided, particularly as one of the end-products is meat and bone meal, which is used for animal feeding, and commercial products have frequently been shown to contain viable salmonella bacteria. By-products plants should therefore be strictly divided into two departments, the " unclean " department where infected materials are brought in, and the " clean " department where sterilized materials are treated or stored. In Denmark meat and bone meal, blood meal and similar products imported into that country must be re-sterilized before they may be offered for sale.

CHAPTER XI

THE PRESERVATION OF FOOD

The origin of methods for preserving foods in times of plenty for use in times of food scarcity is buried in antiquity. In Asia and the far north of Europe freezing and icing of fresh foods for preservation has been practised since time immemorial.

It is difficult to say which of the early methods of food preservation was the first to be devised, but it is probable that treatment of the food by drying, either in the sun or by a fire, was the first method to be discovered. Man, too, would probably soon observe that the foods of a low moisture content, as the nuts and cereal grains, could easily be kept wholesome by dry storage.

The primary purpose of food preservation is to prevent food spoilage. This spoilage may be slight with but minor changes in odour, flavour and texture, or it may be manifested by extreme changes, as in the decomposition of foods of animal origin, in the souring and curdling of milk, or in severe mouldiness of bread. Whether these changes are mild or extreme, the primary cause of food spoilage is the action of micro-organisms, either bacteria, moulds or yeasts, but as these are living organisms they can survive and develop only under favourable conditions of environment, and under unfavourable conditions they die or fail to develop. The conditions which are unfavourable to the growth of such micro-organisms are extreme heat or cold, deprivation of water and sometimes oxygen, excess of saltiness, or increased acidity of the medium in which the micro-organisms exist.

As the bacteria associated with decomposition only thrive in a certain degree of moisture and at not too low a temperature, the durability of carcases is increased by careful cooling in dry air directly after slaughter, the period just after slaughter being of prime importance as the heat and moisture of the freshly killed carcase provide optimum conditions for bacterial growth. The underlying principle of all food preserving methods, then, is the creation of conditions unfavourable to the growth or survival of spoilage organisms.

The recognized methods by which meat foods may be preserved are classified as follows :

(1) Preservation by drying.
(2) Preservation by salting and pickling.
(3) Preservation by cold.
(4) Preservation by heat.
(5) Preservation by chemicals.

Preservation by chemicals may be by artificial means, e.g. by the addition of sulphur dioxide to foodstuffs, but the addition of antiseptics and other chemicals, readily resorted to a few years ago, is now very greatly restricted by food regulations in most countries and does not come within the scope of a work on meat inspection. Chemical preservation by natural means, as in the smoking of meat and of fish is, however, of importance and is employed widely as an adjuvant to commercial salting and pickling.

1. PRESERVATION BY DRYING

Though this method would appear nowadays to play but a minor rôle in the preservation of meat foods, it should be realized that the whole vast process of refrigeration is largely based on preservation by drying, for in refrigeration the conversion of the water present in meat into crystals of ice deprives micro-organisms of a liquid medium in which they would thrive. Though the amount of water frozen out of the substrate is a very important factor in the limitation of bacterial growth at low temperatures, the reduction or inhibition of microbial metabolism by low temperatures cannot be ignored. Again, salting largely owes its preservative action in meat to the extraction of water from the meat substance by osmotic action.

Meat foods are not preserved on a commercial scale by drying and it is a method used chiefly by those who require a protein diet of great durability and lightness. In the jerked beef of South America the meat is cut into strips and dried rapidly in the air, while in the pemmican of North America, which may be made from venison, fish or beef, the meat is smoked before drying and is then pulverized and an equal amount of fat added. The biltong of South Africa is prepared mainly from beef, but also from the flesh of game animals and sometimes from zebra or ostrich. The strips of meat are first cured in salt, sometimes immersed in vinegar, and then dried, and in that country about 1½ million lb. are consumed yearly. There are two public health dangers associated with the consumption of biltong, the first being the possible contamination with salmonella organisms. Such contamination may be of primary origin, i.e., the organisms may be present throughout the muscular tissue of an animal killed while suffering from a salmonella septicaemia, and in such cases the organisms present in the flesh may resist the processes of salting, dipping in vinegar and subsequent drying and remain viable for 6 months or more. Salmonellae may also contaminate meat secondarily due to faulty methods of handling, preparation and storage but the danger here is of lesser magnitude since the ability of salmonellae to grow on and penetrate meat is not great in meat held at room temperature and a high degree of contamination is necessary to cause harm. When the secondary contamination occurs prior to curing there is greater potential danger than when contamination occurs subsequent to drying and it has been shown that meat which has been contaminated artificially with *S. typhi-murium* five hours before curing may still remain infective after 12 days, though when immersed in full or half-strength vinegar prior to the drying process the infectivity is reduced to 8 days.

Parasitic cysts, e.g. cysticerci, in meat are fairly rapidly destroyed when the ratio of salt to moisture in the meat is not less than 1 to 4, and at this concentration the cysticerci are viable after 16 hours, but 50 per cent. are destroyed after 90 hours, and all are rendered non-viable after 136 hours. The destruction of parasitic cysts in biltong may therefore be ensured by submitting the biltong to an adequate salt concentration followed by a holding period of not less than six days, but no evidence has yet been presented to show that the cysts found in the musculature of game animals in Africa are transmissible to man.

A number of frigorificos in Uruguay, and particularly in Brazil, devote much of their output to making charque, which is salted, sun-dried, fore-quarter beef from which the ribs are removed. This product is used extensively in the interior of Brazil because of the difficulties in transport of foodstuffs, and there are also considerable exports to the West Indies, particularly Cuba; though tough and stringy, it is not unpalatable if the excess of salt is removed by thorough soaking. In the Sierras of Peru charque is prepared for local consumption from the flesh of the llama and alpaca, and a similar product, known as chalone, is made from the flesh of sheep.

2. PRESERVATION BY SALTING AND PICKLING

Salt is the principal preserving material used in the curing of meats on a commercial scale, though it appears to have little directly harmful effect on bacteria, and the addition of large quantities of salt or sugar produces the same result as would be obtained by the extraction of water. This action is a physical one and is based on the fact that the osmotic pressure exerted by concentrated solutions of salt or sugar renders water unavailable to bacterial cells and thus inhibits their growth and multiplication. In a salt solution of a concentration above 25 per cent. practically all multiplication of bacteria ceases, for though water is at hand it is not available to bacteria ; thus bacterial growth is inhibited by pickling but the bacteria usually survive, and the dehydrating effect of salt is definitely greater than its germicidal action.

Ingredients Used in Curing

The preservation of meat by curing consists partly in drying the meat and partly in introducing a sufficiently high concentration of salt, saltpeter and sugar in solution into the meat substance. Of these constituents salt is the only essential ingredient in curing, and meat can be cured by salt alone.

(1) SALT. The difference between salting and pickling is that in the former process salt is applied to the surface of the meat in a dry form, whereas in pickling the meat is immersed in a salt solution ; the two processes differ markedly in the actual amount of salt which permeates the meat substance. The commoner salts have a high bacterial content which may prove troublesome, but the finest salts, prepared by a stoved vacuum process, are practically free from bacteria and are utilized for preservation of high class glass-packed foods.

Dry Salting. If dry salt is applied to meat it becomes dissolved in the meat fluid near the surface and then passes slowly inwards until the concentration of salt is approximately the same throughout the meat substance. Salt, when applied to the surface in this way, first of all draws out to the surface some of the meat fluids in which it dissolves, and a considerable amount of the moisture in meat is thus removed. This dehydrating effect is an important factor in preservation and it can be demonstrated microscopically that salted meat, compared with fresh meat, shows a diminution in the size of the intercellular spaces as a result of loss of water.

Pickling. When meat is immersed in a salt solution, i.e. brine, the salt passes from the brine into the meat fluids and eventually a certain amount of water from the brine also passes into the meat. Meat during pickling therefore shows a gradual increase in weight and, on microscopical examination, the spaces between the muscle cells are seen to be dilated due to absorption of water. The maximum increase in weight during pickling is obtained in about 3 weeks, though in the usual 4 days cure the gain in weight is not higher than 7 per cent., and about 2½ per cent. is lost during subsequent draining and stacking. Although the weight of meat is increased by pickling there is in this process a loss in extractives such as creatine and carnosine, and also in other nitrogenous compounds such as proteins, and in phosphorus and potassium salts; the loss is greater in pickled than in dry-salted meat, but meat preserved either by pickling or salting must be regarded as of slightly lower nutritive value than the corresponding fresh meat. As pickled meat contains more water than fresh meat or dry-salted meat, its keeping quality is lower than the dry-salted product, and it therefore requires early consumption, though its durability may be prolonged by smoking. Where durability is required, dry-salting of meat is preferable to pickling, but where a palatable article is demanded, not too salt to the taste and where the food is to be consumed in 4-6 weeks, then preservation by pickling undoubtedly produces a more attractive product.

(2) Saltpetre. This is available in two forms, as Bengal saltpetre or potassium nitrate, and as Chile saltpetre or sodium nitrate; saltpetre is also prepared commercially by fixation of nitrogen from the atmosphere. Though saltpetre exerts a slight preservative action on meat, its effect in excess is to make the meat very hard, and its chief purpose in meat curing, particularly of bacon and hams, is to impart an attractive colour to the cured meat and to bring about the change in flavour from pork to bacon.

Fresh meat owes its pink colour to the presence of myo-haemoglobin (oxymyoglobin), a colouring matter similar to that of the red blood corpuscles, and where fresh meat is cured by salt alone the myo-haemoglobin becomes converted into methaemoglobin and the meat assumes an unattractive grey colour; this change is particularly apparent when the meat is cooked. If, however, saltpetre is added to the curing solution the saltpetre is converted by bacterial action from a nitrate into a nitrite; chemical combination between the nitrite and the myo-haemoglobin forms nitric oxide haemoglobin, which is an unstable compound, but this is converted by cooking into a stable red pigment, nitric oxide haemochromogen, which gives the meat a permanent attractive pink colour.

It has been known for many years that an old nitrate pickle contained nitrite, the chemical change from nitrate to nitrite, both in the pickle and in the meat substance, being brought about by bacterial action. This change, progressing slowly at first, becomes quite rapid after the 33rd day, and for this reason old pickle liquors have long been considered as preferable for curing because of their more rapid colouring effect. Again, each time that meat is placed in the pickle, proteins and other substances diffuse out of the meat into the pickle, which therefore becomes more concentrated; older pickles therefore remove less protein and other substances from the meat than do new pickles.

The addition of potassium nitrate to pickling solutions has now been largely replaced by the use of sodium or potassium nitrite, and the superiority of nitrite as a colouring and preservative agent is recognized by the large bacon factories and packing houses. The advantages of nitrite are that its penetration is rapid, its preservative action is ten times as great as nitrate, its use is more economical and there is a marked improvement in the appearance of the meat. It is now generally agreed that the change in flavour from pork to bacon is due primarily to the action of nitrite on the flesh, whether produced from saltpetre or added as such, and that a satisfactory bacon can be made by using only salt and sodium nitrite; nor is bacterial action during pickling and maturing essential for the development of bacon flavour.

(3) SUGAR. Sugar is not an essential to curing but is widely used in methods of home-curing and in many bacon factories. It has the effect of keeping cured meat soft and may have been originally introduced to counteract the hardening effect of saltpetre. Its chief value, however, is to offset saltiness, and it also furnishes a medium for the growth of certain bacteria which may aid in the production of bacon flavour. On the other hand, the growth of putrefactive bacteria is inhibited in a medium containing sugar, since when sugar is fermented the production of acid is inimical to growth of putrefactive organisms.

Spices impart a desirable flavour to cured meats, and although many of the essential oils and other substances that occur in spices act as effective bacteriostatic agents, they cannot be depended on to have any preservative action in the concentrations employed in sausages and other foods. Indeed, spices may have a very high bacterial count and may contribute significantly to the total bacterial load of the unprocessed meat food.

COMPOSITION OF PICKLING SALTS AND BRINE

Whether the curing of meat is undertaken by dry-salting or by pickling, the chemical constituents, salt, saltpetre and sugar, are the same.

In dry-salting the ingredients are present in the proportion of 50 lb. of salt, 5 lb. of sugar, and 2 lb. of saltpetre. The latter ingredient may be replaced by $\frac{1}{2}$ oz. of potassium nitrite.

A pickling solution may be made by adding water to the same weight of the above ingredients to make up 20 gallons of solution. This is boiled and skimmed till clear, the solution then allowed to settle and the clear fluid decanted off. Sweet pickle, i.e. one containing sugar, which remains in a pickling tub or vat after the curing process is completed, contains many micro-organisms, together with nitrogenous and other foreign matter, and these may cause deterioration and souring of meat subsequently cured. It is therefore necessary for the pickle to be periodically strained, pasteurized and cooled, and finally filtered and standardized.

Types of Meat Foods Cured

While curing may be applied to all kinds of meat, it is best adapted to those meats containing a high fat content. Curing, therefore, yields excellent results when applied to pork or to fine-fibred beef intermixed with fat, and it is for this reason that brisket and flank of beef make an excellent pickled meat; on the other hand, lean beef, veal or mutton become dry and unpalatable as a result of the pickling process.

Methods of Application of the Cure

The dry-salting of joints of pork or beef yields a product which, when barrelled, is resistant to extremes of temperature and admirably suited for export. The surfaces of the joints of meat are rubbed with salt and the pieces packed in layers into barrels, each layer being covered with salt. A brine is formed by osmotic action, the water of the brine originating almost entirely from the meat.

Various methods have been devised to accelerate the penetration of the pickle, and in modern bacon factories the brine solution, which is a saturated solution of salt containing $1\frac{1}{2}$ to 4 per cent. of saltpetre and up to 500 parts per million of sodium nitrite, is introduced into the meat substance by means of a pump and a long perforated needle. Another method employed is by injecting the brine into the nutrient artery of the particular part and is known as arterial brining, a needle being inserted into the main artery of the ham, silverside of beef or ox tongue; by this method the brine injection of ham can be completed in 20 seconds, and the process is also applicable to ox briskets and bellies of pork. Considerable attention has recently been directed to the use of ascorbic acid in the pumping brine as a chemical reducing agent which is claimed to improve both colour form and stability. The use of ascorbic acid and its synthetically prepared twin, iso-ascorbic acid, is permitted in the United States in curing and pumping brines and cooked cured meats, and its use is also permitted as a thin covering applied by spray to the meat surface. Complex phosphates, of which sodium tripolyphosphate appears to be most effective, may also be included in the pumping brine with the purpose of increasing the water-binding capacity of the meat proteins and thus reduce shrinkage loss which is a particular problem in the canning of hams.

Effect of Temperature on Curing

Though high temperature accelerates the curing of meats it also favours bacterial growth. Conversely, a low temperature retards the curing process and at 30° F. it requires 160 days to cure a 14 lb. ham. Bacon factories maintain their pickling cellars between 38° F. and 45° F., for at this temperature the growth of micro-organisms is very slow, especially in the presence of salt.

Effect of Curing on Pathogenic Micro-organisms and Parasites

Pickling is of undoubted value in destroying parasitic infections of meat, but cysticerci in beef or pork are only destroyed with certainty by thorough pickling in a strong salt solution composed of 25 parts by weight of salt to 100 parts by weight of water. The joints of meat should not weigh over 5 lb. and the process should be continued 3 to 4 weeks, so that modern brine curing methods cannot be regarded as adequate. In trichinella-infected pork a period of curing for 40 days must be followed by smoking for 10 days at 113° F. with subsequent drying, and methods for rendering parasitic infections non-viable in meat should preferably be based on adequate cooking or refrigeration.

The effect of pickling on pathogenic bacteria is likewise unsatisfactory and cannot be relied on as a method of rendering suspect meat safe for human food. Cultures of anthrax bacilli are destroyed by salting in 24 hours, but when spore formation has taken place the organisms can resist this process for some months. Under natural conditions, as in the pickled meat of an animal dead of anthrax, the bacilli can survive 1½ months, and the pickling process has no deleterious effect on the spores. Tubercle bacilli retain their infectivity for 18 days when infected portions of meat are pickled, and tuberculous organs which have been in pickle for months are sometimes still infective.

Bacteria of the salmonella group are resistant to the measures usually employed for pickling and have remained viable for 80 days in a pickling solution of 10-13 per cent. strength. In Germany it is forbidden to use the flesh of emergency-slaughtered animals for pickling purposes. The causal organism of swine erysipelas, *Erysipelothrix rhusiopathiae*, may remain virulent in meat immersed in brine for 4 months, while the virus of swine fever will persist for at least 27 days in bacon processed commercially followed by drying and smoking.

Destruction of the virus of foot and mouth disease in meat may be ensured if pickling is carried out by injection at a sufficient pressure. In 1926, as a result of the tracing of foot and mouth disease outbreaks in Britain to imported Continental bacon, the British Ministry of Agriculture and Fisheries introduced legislation requiring that bacon and ham shall only be admitted into the country if pumped with brine under a pressure of 80 lb. to the square inch and subsequently pickled or dry-salted for not less than 4 days.

The Curing of Bacon and Ham

Bacon may be cured either by dry salting or pickling, the former method being usually employed in home curing, while the latter method is now generally carried out in bacon factories and packing houses. Pigs of 160 lb. dead weight are regarded as ideal for the British trade, white-skinned pigs being preferred to black-skinned breeds as the bacon rind has a whiter, more attractive appearance. A pig with light shoulders, long level back, deep and level flanks with broad hams is most likely to yield a carcase well endowed in the region of the most valuable bacon cuts, for in a side of bacon the collar and forehock together should weigh not more than 25 per cent. of the whole side.

For many years the fattening of pigs in Britain for bacon was unorganized, and there was difficulty in competing with the imported Danish bacon which was obtained from a commercial pig of uniform size and eminently suitable for British requirements. This pig, lean and about 150 lb. to 160 lb. dead weight, was produced as a mild-cured Wiltshire side, in which the complete side, including the ham but minus the head, was pickled, dried and sometimes smoked. Such mild-cured factory bacon contains as little as 2½ per cent. salt, whereas dry salted bacon contains as much as 15 per cent.

In modern bacon factory procedure pigs should preferably be taken to the factory the day before they are due for slaughter, though during the journey they suffer deterioration and damage from fighting, fasting and fatigue. Superficial damage from bruises and bites lowers the ultimate quality of the carcase and to obviate this the use of tranquillizers has been suggested. In Denmark use is made of a bit fitted into the animal's mouth. This prevents biting, being fitted when pigs reach the lairage pens, and the prevention of bruises and bite marks is of importance to the Danish export trade in Wiltshire sides, for bacon is not considered suitable for export if it shows more than one bruised area which is greater than 1·1 inches in diameter. Fasting causes tissue wastage and loss in weight of carcase, liver and kidneys, and only the weight loss in the liver and kidneys can be restored by feeding. The overnight rest helps to clear up any skin blemishes such as bite marks, scratches or bruises, so that after slaughter the skin, which forms the bacon rind, is free of unsightly markings. Pigs slaughtered on the day of arrival at the factory show every blemish on their skin after slaughter, and, in addition, the lack of proper resting prior to slaughter, together with the excitement and pyrexia which may occur in pigs not used to handling, are factors prejudicial to rigor mortis and also

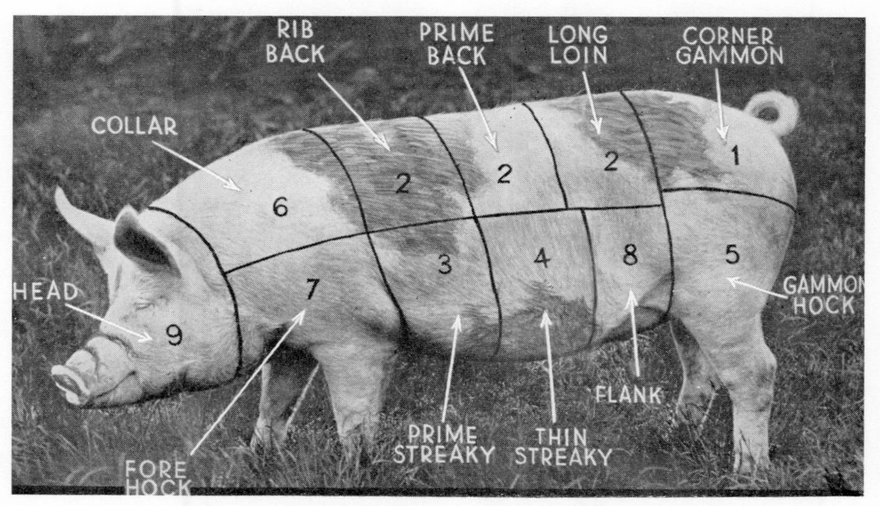

FIG. 210.—A good type of modern bacon pig with the retail cuts graded from 1 to 9 according to value. Note the light shoulder, good length, flat deep side and good ham.

affect the retention of the desirable red colour of the cut lean surfaces of the cured product.

Pigs slaughtered commercially are now usually stunned by the electrical method and, after stunning, a rear limb is shackled, the pig is elevated to an overhead rail where it is stuck and bled into a blood vat. After slaughter the carcase is lifted mechanically from the overhead rail into a scalding tank, the pigs in the tank being immersed at 140° F. for a period of 1 minute. The effect of scalding is to loosen the hair, but if kept longer than this period the carcase emerges " cooked " from the scalding tank, with the result that the bristles and scurf become set and scraping and cleaning is rendered impossible. After each day's kill the scalding tank is drained and replaced with fresh water, for the water in the scalding tank is a factor in the contamination of the surface of pig's flesh by spore-forming bacteria.

After scalding, the pigs are lifted mechanically into a dehairing machine and when the carcase has been scraped clean it passes out of the machine mechanically on to a table where scraping is completed by hand; the scraping table may be of any length, and has a movable top so that carcases are constantly on the move. The smaller types of dehairing machine are capable of dealing with a throughput of 80 to 120 pigs per hour, larger machines up to 300 per hour. Some of the packing plants in the United States now employ a technique which has replaced the scraping

FIG. 211.—Factory line procedure at a bacon factory in Denmark with a throughput of 800 animals per day. The slaughtered animals have been scalded, passed through the dehairing machine and singed, and are now being scraped and washed with a hose prior to evisceration. By these procedures the initial bacterial load on the skin is reduced by 99 per cent.

of pigs by hand or in the dehairing machine. After bleeding, the carcases are immersed in a hot adhesive compound composed of resin and oil which forms a seal-like coating over the whole carcase, heat turning the cutaneous moisture into steam which loosens the hair at the roots. After cooling, the carcase is stripped of the compound and a completely dehaired pig is the result. To prevent the compound entering the nostrils a rubber band is placed round the nose, and the compound can be reclaimed for further use by remelting and straining.

After dehairing, the carcase is hoisted on to a greased skid-rail and is transferred to a singeing plant, which consists of two vertical half-cylinders lined by fireproof bricks and has a throughput of 120 to 150 carcases per hour. The carcase is singed by a fired combination of oil and air at a temperature of 2,500° F. to 2,800° F., the effect of singeing being to colour the skin brown, to remove any hairs still remaining, and to exert a preservative action on the carcase. After leaving the furnace the carcases are sprayed with cold water and then scraped clean and white, this being done by hand in some factories but in large establishments by a back-scraping machine. In the case of the Midland "dry-cured bacon and hams" the singeing is done by flames of gas and compressed air on the blowlamp principle, the flame being run up and down the carcase to burn off any surplus hair which has not been removed by the dehairing machines and scrapers; this type of singeing does not discolour the skin. The dressing of the carcase and removal of the head and vertebral column are then carried out and the carcase finally split, the weight of by-products yielded in preparing a pig of 200 lb. live weight for bacon being about 50 lb. and including the blood, hair, fat and internal organs.

In most bacon factories all pig slaughtering is done early in the day so that carcases may be cooled in a natural draught until the late afternoon, the carcases being then moved by mechanical conveyors into chilling rooms at about 42° F. The day after slaughter each side of pork is placed on a bench, and the collar, or fleshy part of the neck lying between the head and shoulder, is removed and also the aitch or pelvic bone. The scapula is then removed, the shoulder joint being cut through with a cold chisel and the scapula extracted from the thoracic side, either by traction with a form of pliers attached to a belt around the slaughterman's waist or by other mechanical devices. The sternum is then removed and finally the feet or trotters, but the ribs may be left on the side, depending on the use to be made of the side; it may be rolled, or sold as "rib in" or "rib out" side of bacon.

The parts removed in preparing a dressed pig carcase of 150 lb. for curing weigh about 30 lb. and include the various bones, leaf fat, feet and tail. Thus the total weight of by-products, which include offal and bone, removed in preparing a bacon pig of 200 lb. live weight for curing is 80 lb. (50 lb.+30 lb.) or approximately 40 per cent. of the live weight of the pig. This may be expressed in another way by stating that the weight of the two sides of pork prepared for curing is about 60 per cent. of the animal's live weight.

Curing the Side of Pork

Whether bacon is to be cured by dry-salting or by pickling in a tank, the curing process is invariably accelerated by a preliminary injection of the pickle. This is done by means of a long hollow needle which is plunged into each side of pork in some 26 places, particularly in the very fleshy parts where normal penetration of brine is difficult; the pickle is injected into the tissues at a pressure of 85 lb., about 5 lb. of pickle remaining in each side of pork after injection. The space from which the scapula is removed, known as the pocket, is particularly liable to taint and is packed with salt, as also is the hip cavity. In dry-salt curing the meat is sprinkled with salt and saltpetre which is gently rubbed in by hand and the sides built up into stacks of six to eight, skin side downwards, the curing operation taking at least 10 days. In the preparation of mild cure Wiltshire bacon the sides are stacked in large tanks, 30 feet long and 10 feet broad, which are then flooded with brine. After immersion for 3 to 4 days the bacon is lifted out, drained by stacking skin upwards and allowed to mature for 7 days, the temperature of the cooling cellar being maintained at 42° F. This process of maturing is the most important stage of curing and is necessary for both bacon and ham, as during maturing the concentration of pickle tends to become uniform throughout the meat and the colour of the flesh changes from the dull pink of pork to the peculiar reddish tint of bacon. Most bacon is imported into Britain as pickled sides which are undried and unsmoked, drying and smoking being subsequently carried out by the wholesale provision merchant.

Curing of Hams

In the full Wiltshire side the ham remains on the side of pork and is cured with it, but the market in hams is a special one and both shoulders

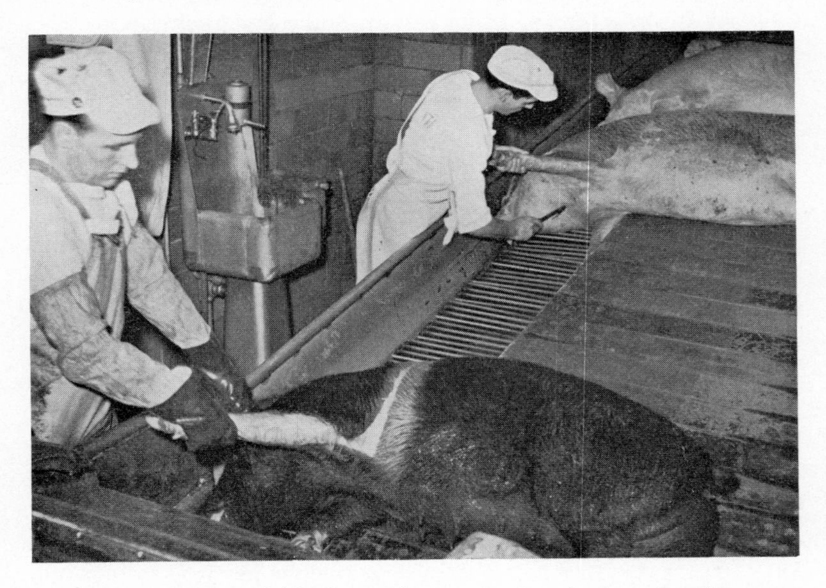

Fig. 212.—Sticking and bleeding of bacon pigs in a horizontal position on a movable conveyor, a technique developed to obviate internal ham bruising and blood splashing. (Hormel & Co.)

and hams may be cured separately. The curing process in hams is accelerated by the injection of brine which is directed in the region of the shanks and joints, an important measure directed towards the prevention of taint. In Scotland the curing of hams is conducted by holding them in pickle during the whole process, but the famous York ham, after a preliminary brine injection, is packed in dry salt and is allowed to mature in the factory for 3 months or over.

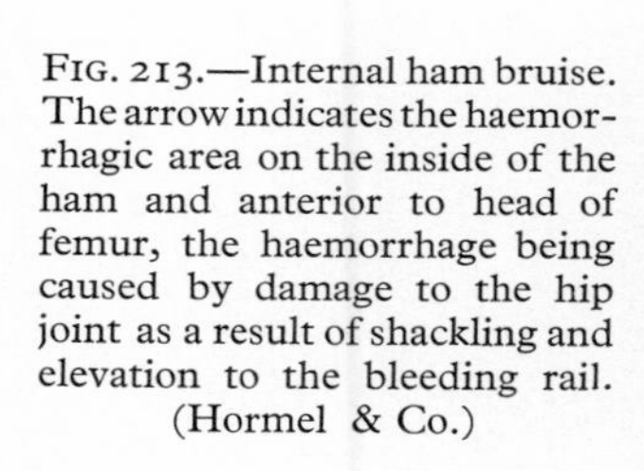

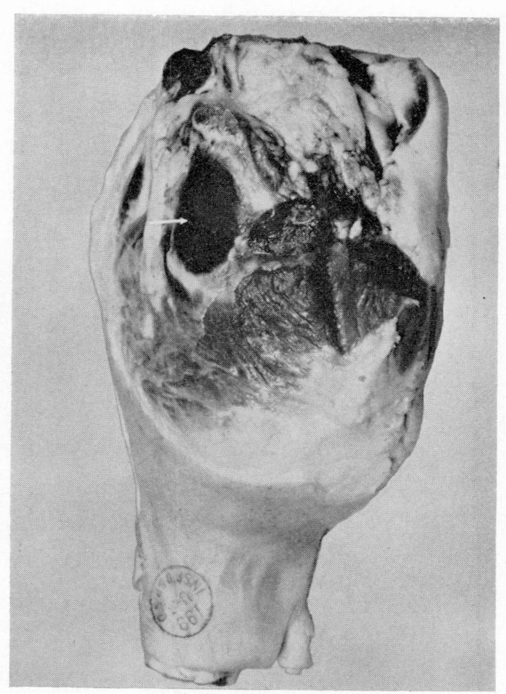

FIG. 213.—Internal ham bruise. The arrow indicates the haemorrhagic area on the inside of the ham and anterior to head of femur, the haemorrhage being caused by damage to the hip joint as a result of shackling and elevation to the bleeding rail. (Hormel & Co.)

A troublesome condition in hams, termed incorrectly ham bruise, is a haemorrhagic area seen at the inner aspect of the ham anterior to the head of the femur. It is caused by escape of blood-stained fluid from the hip joint as a result of tearing of the round ligament and rupture of the joint capsule, and is brought about largely by the process of shackling when the pig is hoisted to the vertical position for the purpose of bleeding. In the United States it is estimated that the loss due to this condition as a result of trimming of flesh is in the region of 0·5 dollars per ham, with an estimated national loss in packing plants in 1954 of 4 million dollars.

WATERY PORK

In pigs there may be wide variation in the amount of lactic acid formed in the muscles after slaughter and in the rapidity with which this occurs. In healthy rested pigs the amount of lactic acid produced shows a gradual increase after slaughter and brings about a fall in muscle pH from 7·0 to about 5·8 over a period of 12 hours. In certain pigs, however, particularly those which have been exposed to a high atmospheric temperature during transport or which are frightened or excited prior to slaughter, there is a considerable production of lactic acid and this brings about an unduly rapid fall in pH. In some cases the pH after slaughter may fall to 6·1 or below within 45 minutes and should this change be accompanied by a slow

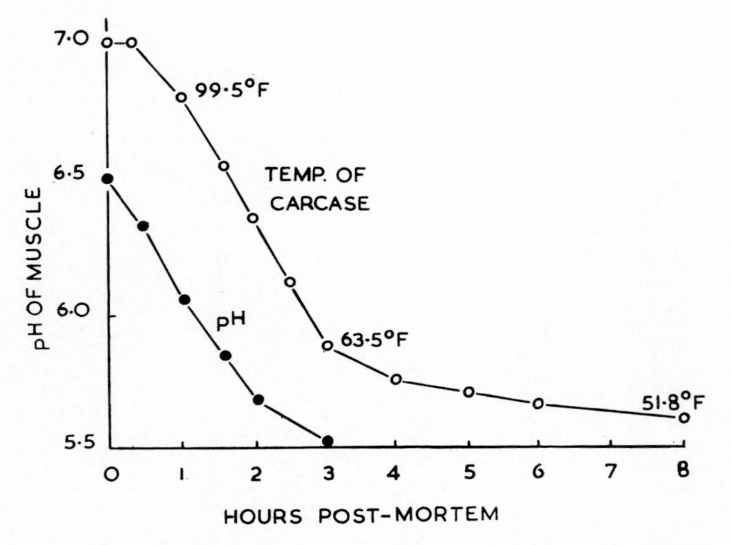

FIG. 214.—The occurrence of watery pork under abattoir conditions. The animal was excited prior to slaughter, resulting in a high production of lactic acid in muscle and a very rapid fall in the pH after slaughter. This rapid fall in pH occurred while the temperature of the carcase remained high, and these two factors caused the muscles to lose their water-holding capacity with the consequent production of watery pork.

reduction in carcase temperature the flesh of such animals is watery, has a pale unattractive colour and lack of flavour. This condition, known as watery pork, chiefly affects the leg, loin and fillet, and bacon and ham prepared from such pork shows similar unacceptable characteristics. In order to obviate the condition it is essential that the animal be properly rested and that the carcase, particularly in the summer months, be transferred to the chiller immediately to ensure rapid reduction in carcase temperature. It is perhaps unfortunate, however, that the modern bacon pig, carrying relatively more muscle and less fat than the older type of bacon pig, has relatively greater oxygen requirements, and certain breeds of pig, among these being the Danish Landrace and Pietrain in Europe and the Poland China in the United States, appear to be prone to rapid glycogen breakdown and the production of watery pork. A condition, which may be analogous to watery pork, is sometimes encountered in New Zealand in lambs slaughtered after an arduous journey, the carcase, particularly the shoulders, being unduly watery and to this condition the term travel oedema has been applied.

Smoking

The purpose of smoking bacon is to preserve, colour and flavour the meat. The bacon is dusted with pea-meal prior to smoking, which enhances the smoked appearance, the smoke being produced in rooms so constructed as to emit a cool smoke from smouldering oak or hardwood sawdust. Though bacon flavours are in part due to the pickling process, in smoked bacon they may also be due to the woods used in smoking, and hickory, maple and mahogany shavings are used in America, while juniper is said to be favoured in Germany, and birchwood in other parts of Europe. The smoking process occupies up to 3 days at a temperature of 85° F.

In smoke generated from wood the chief bacteriostatic and bacteriocidal substance is formaldehyde. Smoking of most meat products is accompanied by varying amounts of heat application in the smoke room, and the combination of heat and smoke usually causes a significant reduction in the surface bacterial population. In addition, a physical barrier is provided by superficial dehydration, coagulation of protein and the absorption of resinous substances.

Tyrosin Deposits on Brine-preserved Livers

These are occasionally seen on imported livers, either frozen or packed in brine, the deposits appearing as small white spots, usually smaller than a pin-head and scattered over the surface of the liver and on the inner lining of the large blood vessels. Their crystalline nature can be recognized microscopically, and treatment of a solution of these granules with nitric acid turns the solution, on heating, from a yellowish-green to a red colour. Tyrosin deposits are usually associated with prolonged storage and sourness of the organ, and if the latter condition is present the liver should be condemned.

3. PRESERVATION BY COLD

This process, the basis of the great industry of refrigeration, is certainly the simplest method for the preservation of food, and denotes the extraction of heat from a body, thus cooling it to a temperature below surrounding substances. By refrigeration meat can be preserved in a condition approaching its natural state for periods adequate for commercial requirements, its appearance and flavour are little altered, and no substance is added to the meat or any substance extracted.

The preservative action of refrigeration is based on the prevention of multiplication of harmful bacteria by the artificial lowering of the temperature. The failure of bacteria to grow at or below freezing temperature is chiefly based on the fact that the water which is necessary for bacterial growth becomes unavailable, for when beef muscle is frozen a portion of the tissue water separates as ice, amounting to 70 per cent. at 26° F., and to 94 per cent. at 14° F. A further factor is that the life processes of spoilage organisms are inhibited at low temperatures, though the actual lethal effect of low temperatures is but slight. Neither sharp nor slow freezing destroys the bacteria commonly found on beef carcases, and frozen meat which is thawed out, yielding an abundant supply of water in the process, forms an excellent medium for bacterial growth. In addition, the pH of muscle, which remains constant while the meat is frozen, falls rapidly after thawing, but then rises rapidly to create an environment which is also favourable to bacterial multiplication.

The surface growth of mould on meat is controlled not only by the temperature but by the relative humidity of the atmosphere. Some moulds are capable of growing on the surface of meat at several degrees below freezing point, but they require the presence of water in the surrounding atmosphere as otherwise they lose water by evaporation and wither away. For the prevention of mould the temperature must therefore be kept as low as possible and the relative humidity also low.

The refrigeration industry is presented with the following problem : (*a*) to preserve the meat at a temperature low enough to prevent the growth of spoilage bacteria and moulds, and (*b*) to avoid slow freezing if possible, as this will have the effect of altering the texture of the meat when thawed and lowering its keeping quality and marketability. The refrigeration process may be a natural one, as caused by climatic conditions (formation of ice), or it may be artificial, as is produced by mechanical means.

Mechanical Refrigeration

Refrigerating machines act in accordance with a physical law that the evaporation of liquid absorbs heat. Ammonia, which assumes the liquid form under high compression, is frequently used for this purpose, the release of pressure causing the liquid ammonia to vaporize and extract heat from the surrounding air ; the ammonia gas is then re-compressed by mechanical means and cooled to condense it to liquid ammonia to be utilized again.

The pipes in which the liquid ammonia is allowed to evaporate may be placed in the chamber which is to be cooled, either in a loft or on the sides or ceiling of the chamber, this being known as the direct expansion system, and outside heat is prevented from entering the chamber by lining it with insulating material. The method of refrigeration employed in the transport of meat by sea to Britain from America, Australia and New Zealand is known as the brine circulating system, the evaporator coils in which the liquid ammonia evaporates being immersed in a refrigerator tank filled with brine or with a solution of calcium chloride. The brine is cooled, circulates around the refrigerating chambers by means of pipes, and finally returns to the refrigerator tank to be recooled.

The temperature utilized in refrigerating chambers falls into two main categories according to whether the meat is chilled or frozen, but whichever method is employed it is important to keep the temperature constant, to maintain a good circulation of air which should be kept in fresh condition, and to adjust the humidity so that the air is neither too damp nor too dry.

Chilling is particularly useful when meat is to be preserved a relatively short time, for by this process the flavour, appearance and nutritive value of the meat are scarcely affected. In the chilled meat trade, by which most of the beef is imported into Great Britain, the temperature is maintained at about 30° F., the meat being preferably stored in the dark, for the effect of light is to accelerate the oxidation of fat, with the liberation of free fatty acids and the production of rancidity. The atmosphere is kept dry and this also hinders mould formation which is more likely to attack chilled meat than meat which has been frozen.

The chief types of meat foods preserved by freezing, as distinct from chilling, are mutton, lamb, pork and rabbits, but there are rather wide differences of opinion as to the proper temperature at which such meat should be frozen. The practice in Germany is to maintain a temperature of 21·2° F., in Australia 12·2° F., while in America much lower temperatures may be used in what are termed "sharp freezers"; frozen pork, for example, required for domestic use or export may be stored at 0° F., this low temperature preventing oxidation and resultant rancidity. During transport of frozen meat by ship a temperature of 16° F. to 18° F. is maintained in the holds, while the air is kept dry and in circulation.

Chilling and freezing are both reliable methods of mechanical refrigeration and render possible the importation of large quantities of beef, pork, mutton and lamb, rabbits, game and offals into Great Britain. The effect of chilling and of freezing on the meat substance is of importance for certain physical and chemical changes take place during these processes.

A. Physical Changes in Stored Meat

Meat, whether imported or home-killed, undergoes certain superficial changes as a result of storage, chief of which are shrinkage, sweating and loss of bloom.

Shrinkage. Shrinkage or loss of weight occurs as a result of evaporation of water from the meat surface, and carcases cut into quarters dissipate water vapour rapidly and continuously, the loss being even greater when the carcase is divided into retail joints. On the other hand, evaporation is inhibited by such membranes as the pleura and peritoneum, and in well nourished carcases the superficial fat and connective tissue aid appreciably in minimizing loss by evaporation, for the fat solidifies as the carcase cools and the connective tissue dries to a consistency resembling parchment. A freshly killed carcase dissipates body heat slowly, losing 1·5 to 2·0 per cent. of weight by evaporation during the first 24 hours of hanging, while further loss of weight during storage depends on the condition of humidity of the storage room, the drier the air the greater being the evaporation. The high velocity cold air system (Turbo-Chill) of reducing body heat of freshly killed animals entails supersaturation of the chilling room air with moisture to a level of 82 to 90 per cent. relative humidity, and this reduces the weight loss in beef carcases to about 1·3 per cent. Chilled beef from South America maintained at a temperature of 28° F. to 30·5° F. with carefully controlled humidity loses a bare one per cent. in weight over a 25 days journey. If shrinkage due to evaporation is to be avoided altogether, the consequent high humidity on the surface of the meat facilitates the formation of moulds, so that an accurate balance between temperature and humidity must be maintained; the dry, impervious film on the carcase surface is perhaps the best protection against the growth of spoilage organisms.

Sweating. This denotes the condensation of water vapour on meat which is brought out from a cold store into ordinary room temperature, and it has done more than any other factor to alienate the British butcher against the practice of refrigerating home-killed meat. This condensation, or sweating, occurs on meat due to the fact that the refrigerated carcase, being colder than the outside air, brings the temperature of the air below the dewpoint. In the winter months in Britain the dewpoint is generally below 40° F. and sweating is unlikely to occur, but in the summer months the dewpoint is always over 45° F., so that a chilled carcase which is brought out from a chilling room in summer will reduce the temperature of the surrounding air below 45° F. and moisture is deposited on the carcase. If the quarter or side is cut up immediately after removal from the chilling room the sweating will be extended to the individual joints.

Loss of Bloom. Bloom is defined as the colour and general appearance presented by the surface of a carcase when viewed through the semi-transparent layers of connective tissue, muscle and fat which form the carcase surface. If these tissues become moist the collagen fibres, which are a constituent of connective tissue, swell and become opaque and the meat surface assumes a dull, lifeless appearance. In addition to absorption of water, loss of surface bloom in beef carcases may be caused by dehydration or undue oxidation, but it may be prevented by avoiding temperature fluctuations that permit alternate drying and dampening of the carcase surface. It is also important to keep the relative humidity of cooling chambers high and ensure that there is circulation of air. Muscular tissue also tends to become brownish on exposure to air owing to the change of the myo-haemoglobin to the brown pigment methaemoglobin, but the actual amount of exposed muscle in a side of beef is so small that this change is of little or no consequence. Refrigeration has little effect on the carcase fat except in the case of frozen meat which has undergone a prolonged period of storage.

B. Chemical Changes in Stored Meat

The chemical changes which take place after slaughter are indicative of a slight degree of break-down in protein, due either to enzymes normally present in the flesh or to those produced by micro-organisms. The odour of the meat becomes progressively more marked but never disagreeable, and the flavour may be described as stale, rendering the meat unpalatable but not repulsive. The storage life of meat is more dependent on the chemical changes which take place in fat rather than in muscle, for fat rancidity, even in slight degree, is objectionable. The condition of the fat therefore determines the actual period for which a carcase may be stored, for whilst the lean muscle of a carcase may be still improving in flavour the changes in fat may be such as to render the meat repugnant and unmarketable. This change is most likely to occur in the kidney fat, and in hot weather the kidneys and fat of home-killed beef are removed soon after slaughter, usually by the retail butcher.

Physical and Chemical Changes in Meat in Relation to Conditioning

When meat is stored above its freezing-point at temperatures between 32° F. and 38° F. all the changes which usually occur at higher temperatures take place, but at a reduced rate. Atmospheric oxidation of fat, leading to rancidity, proceeds very slowly as meat is usually stored in the dark, and enzyme action in the fat which leads to the production of free fatty acids is also very slow. The action of bacteria is retarded but not arrested at these temperatures, while the proteolytic enzyme of the muscle fibres is definitely active and brings about a desirable change known as conditioning or ripening which is manifested by a marked increase in flavour, juiciness and tenderness of the meat. Conditioning is in no way brought about by bacterial action, and enzyme action is almost completely inhibited when the meat is stored at temperatures below freezing.

Tenderness of meat is influenced by the breed, age, condition of nutrition and amount of muscular exercise of the animal from which it

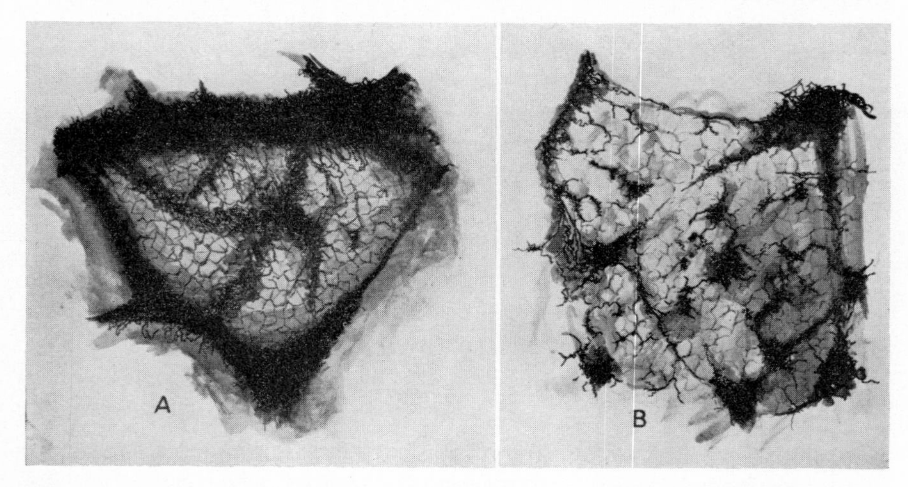

FIG. 215.—A. Cross-section of muscle of thin flank showing strong development of bands of connective tissue. B. Cross-section of muscle of the undercut, with sparse development of connective tissue. (Crown copyright.)

is obtained, and depends primarily on the amount of connective tissue present between the muscular fibres and, to a lesser extent, on the thickness of the muscle fibres themselves. The muscle of the thin flank, for example, is three times as rich in connective tissue as the muscle of the fillet or undercut.

Increase in tenderness of meat is produced by autolysis, or self-digestion, and is due to two causes : (*a*) The toughness of meat which occurs during rigor mortis is caused by the coagulation of muscle proteins, but this toughness disappears as rigor mortis passes off and the coagulated proteins are again rendered soluble. (*b*) Further tenderness is said to be produced by the softening and swelling of the collagen fibres, which are converted into softer and more digestible gelatine by the action of lactic acid, but another, and possibly predominant factor, is the effect of proteolysis by tissue proteinase, such as cathepsin, on the actual muscle fibres. The increase in tenderness due to the above factors will amount in raw beef, hung at ordinary room temperature for 8 days, to 30 per cent., and though increased tenderness will be produced in meat of both coarse and fine texture, the greater increase is in coarse cow flesh in which the increase in tenderness may amount to 50 per cent.

The procedure recommended for the commercial ripening of beef is as follows :

(*a*) The dressed carcase should be cooled for 1 to 2 days at 31° F. to 38° F.

(*b*) The sides or quarters should then be held for 10 to 12 days at 36° F. to 38° F.

(*c*) Before cutting up or removal for retail sale the quarters should be held at ordinary room temperature or, if that be too high, at 40° F. to 45° F. for 24 hours. In commercial practice conditioning of meat is limited to from 2 to 6 weeks, and when beef is cut into small joints the greatest increase in palatability is ensured by a storage period of about 9 days.

The tenderness, then, of meat, particularly of the coarser joints, may be greatly increased by conditioning, and the ripening which meat undergoes during the sea voyage is a factor favourable to the South American chilled meat trade. Conditioning of lean meat is of value in the preparation of canned meats for, if properly matured, the muscle fibres are softened, the meat is more easily sliced and the pink colour is more vivid. Again, the hanging of venison and game for long periods need not be regarded as evidence of a perverted taste but as an appreciation of the fact that improved flavours will develop, and that unless these foods are allowed to hang, the abundant connective tissue which is developed as a result of exercise will not be broken down into more tender substances and the food may therefore be so tough and stringy as to be almost inedible. Tenderness of meat can also be improved by hammering, which breaks down the muscle fibres ; by " quick " freezing before rigor mortis sets in (due probably to the mechanical effects of freezing) and by the application of the enzymes papain and bromelin obtained from the papaya and pineapple. Physical means of incorporating these enzymes into joints of meat are desirable but there is no indication that a subsequent holding period of from one to five hours prior to cooking has any effect for the enzyme does not start to become activated until a temperature of 170° F. has been reached.

Pre-Slaughter Tenderizing of Meat

A recent development in the tenderizing of beef comprises the introduction by gravity of a solution of papain into a jugular vein. Approximately 250 c.c. of the solution enters the vein in just under one minute, and it is then important that slaughter should take place in not less than 2 minutes and not more than 30 minutes if maximum tenderness is to be secured. A minor commercial disadvantage of the method is that the tongue, liver and kidneys of a treated animal become over-tender when cooked normally and require more controlled treatment.

Chilled Meat

It is the aim of the meat exporter, particularly the South American exporter of beef, to convey to Britain a product which has undergone as little change as possible in regard to appearance and palatability, but which shows at the same time an appreciable increase in tenderness; this aim is met by the exportation of meat in storage chambers which keep the meat cold but not frozen. By freezing, an inferior product is produced, and as meat freezes at a temperature of 29·5° F. the temperature in chilling is maintained slightly above this, usually at 30° F. Though bacterial growth is usually inhibited at chilling room temperature the meat continues to lose water by evaporation, and the air, becoming humid, creates a condition which is suitable for the growth of mould.

Durability of Chilled Meat

In commercial experience the storage life of chilled beef is only 35 days, so that if the period between slaughter and shipping of the meat from South America be put at 7 days and the period on board ship at 21 days, chilled beef can only have a safe life of some 7 more days. Beyond this time deterioration will make its appearance in the form of mould, bacterial slime and tainting of the fat, and chilled meat, on being landed in Britain, therefore requires a quick sale. Prior to the development of storage of chilled meat in CO_2 chambers the South American meat exporter had a great advantage over the exporter from Australia and New Zealand, for the many attempts made by the latter countries to introduce chilled meat into Britain had proved uneconomical owing to severe deterioration of the meat and condemnations as a result of mould. Consignments of South African chilled beef from Capetown to Southampton are, however, in transit only 17 days from the time of slaughter to exposure on British markets, an interval which is actually shorter than that of much of the South American chilled beef.

Bacterial Spoilage. Though mould formation is the commonest type of spoilage encountered in chilled meat, bacteria of the *Achromobacter* group may also set up a condition known as bacterial spoilage. The optimum temperature for the growth of these organisms is between 68° F. and 86° F., but they will continue to grow at a temperature of 32° F., the affection being manifested by small glistening brown droplets which eventually coalesce to form a brownish slime on the surface of the meat, with the production of a characteristic odour described as sour or " cold store taint " ; the slime is much more prone to occur on moist lean surfaces of cut joints than on uncut carcases and becomes visible when the number of organisms exceeds thirty million per square centimetre. Scrupulous hygiene in slaughtering methods has done much to lower the incidence of mould and bacterial spoilage in imported meat, and, by adopting standardized Argentine plant practices Australia has succeeded in conveying chilled beef to Britain purely by refrigeration and without the assistance of carbon dioxide storage.

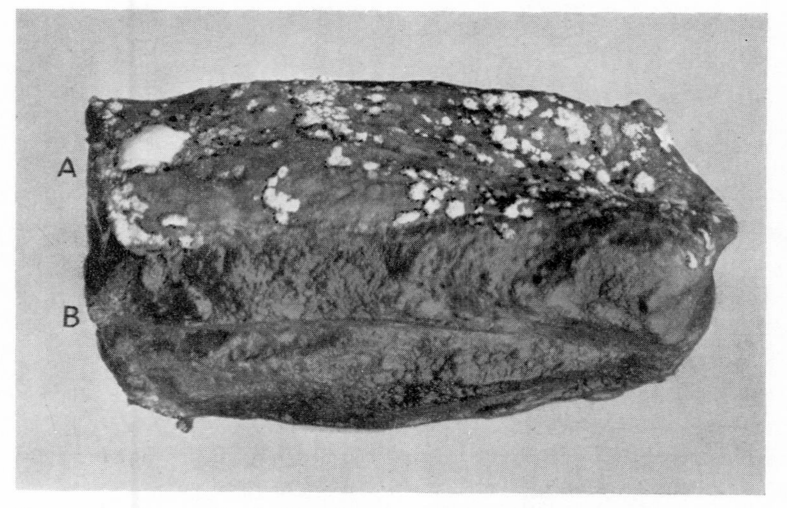

FIG. 216.—Joint of beef affected with mould and bacterial spoilage. The white areas on the fat (A) are colonies of the mould *Thamnidium*. The raised nodules and slimy areas on the lean (B) are colonies and patches of *Achromobacter*. (Crown copyright.)

OZONIZATION. A short period of treatment of meat with ozone in a higher concentration than could be used continuously, is effective in restricting the growth of mould and yeasts on the surface of meat, but its action on bacteria is only significant when the moisture content of the superficial tissues of the meat has been considerably reduced. The addition of ozone to the air in chilling rooms, especially where beef is being chilled prior to export to Britain, destroys surface organisms and obviates the stale odour often associated with chilling rooms, but it is not a suitable method where the storage time is to exceed a few days, for it produces discoloration of the lean meat and rancidity of the fat due to oxidation. Ozonization, however, is particularly valuable in the treatment of most forms of taint in frozen imported meat, including oil or fruit taint, though it is of no value in ammonia taint. Most taints can be dispersed entirely in 2 to 6 weeks by ozonization, depending on the degree of taint and the length of time which the meat had been exposed thereto. Though it is claimed by some that there is no damage to the appearance of the meat, there is little doubt that the slight and progressive oxidation, particularly on the fatty surfaces, becomes quite noticeable in about 3 weeks. The loss in sales value due to oxidation is, however, much less than the loss due to fruit or oil taint, and it is therefore sound practice to proceed with the treatment until all traces of taint have disappeared. In the detection of oil taint a small piece of fat chewed for a few seconds will in many cases give a better indication than the sense of smell.

Treatment of tainted chilled meat by ozonization is more difficult than in the case of frozen meat, for during treatment the meat undergoes a marked loss of bloom and, in order to avoid spoilage, the process must be carried out at a low temperature which causes the formation of ice crystals in the meat substance. Here again the loss in sales value of the meat is still less than the loss due to the taint itself. Ultra-violet lamps have been used to control microbial spoilage, especially in the ripening of meat at higher temperatures. The results are inconclusive, however, and the bactericidal effect is only superficial as there is little penetration into the muscle tissue, while surfaces shaded from the light remain unaffected.

Storage in Carbon Dioxide Gas. Great success in mould inhibition has been achieved by a process which depends on the ability of carbon dioxide gas, when present in high concentration, to prevent the growth of moulds. Facultative bacteria may or may not be inhibited by CO_2, while lactic acid bacteria and anaerobes are virtually unaffected. On the other hand, the highly aerobic bacteria and yeasts and moulds are selectively inhibited by CO_2, and the storage of meat in an appropriate concentration of this gas will therefore retard surface decomposition, though it will not inhibit deep-seated anaerobic spoilage. Mould growth can be arrested completely at 32° F. if a concentration of 40 per cent. of carbon dioxide be used, but in any concentration over 20 per cent. there is a rapid production of methaemoglobin on the exposed muscle and fat, while the bloom of the meat is lost. From experiments on the growth of moulds and bacteria, with analysis of the fat, it has been shown that in the presence of 10 per cent. of carbon dioxide the storage life of meat at 32° F. is double that of meat stored in ordinary air at a similar temperature, and in this way the storage life of chilled meat can be extended to 60 to 70 days.

Storage in a concentration of 10 per cent. carbon dioxide has made possible the transport of chilled beef to Britain from Australia and New Zealand and large consignments have arrived by this process and found to be in excellent condition, without deleterious effects on the bloom and free from mould, slime and taint. In the new, fast steamers some exporters are able to use carbon dioxide in as low a concentration as 5 per cent., but the need to provide gas-tight spaces in order to maintain the necessary concentration of CO_2 adds considerably to the cost of construction of the accommodation needed for the meat cargo. Though storage in low concentrations of carbon dioxide is applicable to most meats, including mutton and pork, it is unsatisfactory for the storage of bacon, as the problem here is not the prevention of microbial growth but the prevention of oxidation of fat.

Chilled carcases require an adequate supply of air around them whilst on board ship, and therefore must be hung on hooks. Frozen carcases, on the other hand, can be piled on the floor or on dunnage and require considerably less space. Dunnage is the term applied to loose wood laid on the bottom of ships' holds which serves to keep the cargo off the metal floor and out of bilge water. Frozen meat stacked without dunnage is likely to decompose, especially where there is heat infiltration from outside.

Frozen Meat

In Britain the price of imported frozen beef is considerably less than that of chilled beef, the discrepancy being attributed to the physical changes which meat undergoes during the freezing process, together with the inferior nature of the cattle slaughtered for the freezing industry. Experiments in Britain have shown, however, that where prime Aberdeen Angus bullocks were slaughtered and the carcases frozen there was practically no deleterious effect on the flavour, tenderness or palatability of the meat, and this fact strongly suggests that the unpopularity of frozen meat may largely be due to the poor original quality of the meat and its unattractive appearance. Further, badly stored frozen meat is notorious for its poor keeping quality after thawing.

Physical Changes in the Freezing of Meat

Two outstanding and unfavourable changes take place as a result of the freezing of meat:

(*a*) The physical state of the muscle plasm is considerably altered. The muscle plasm consists of proteins of the globulin and albumen class which, though normally soluble, become insoluble at a certain concentration. When meat is frozen below 28·4° F. the formation of ice crystals so raises the concentration of these proteins that they become insoluble, nor do they regain their solubility when the meat is thawed. A similar irreversible change may be observed if eggs are frozen and it is a well-known fact that when these are thawed the yolk becomes an objectionable pasty mass.

(*b*) The freezing point of meat lies between 30° F. and 28° F., ice crystals commencing to form in the meat at this temperature and continuing to form as the temperature is still further lowered; at 29·3° F., 35·5 per cent. of the muscle water is ice, at 23° F. the percentage of ice is 82, while at 14° F. the percentage of ice is 94. During freezing, the water present in the muscle fibres diffuses from the muscle plasm to form crystals of ice, the speed with which the freezing process is conducted having an important bearing on the size of the ice crystals and the future quality of the product. When meat is frozen slowly the largest crystals are formed between the temperatures of 31° F. and 25° F. and are largely located outside the muscle fibres; this temperature range is known as the zone of maximum ice formation, and where meat is subsequently stored within this range the ice crystals continue to grow in size during storage.

On the other hand, if meat is frozen rapidly to a temperature lower than 25° F. the ice crystals produced are small and lie mainly within the muscle fibres, while, if lowering of the temperature is sufficiently expedited, many of the crystals are ultra-microscopic in size, and all of them are smaller than the cells in which they are formed. Quick freezing of meat has made rapid strides and is applied to lambs, calves, pigs, poultry, fish and various wholesale cuts, the latter being distributed wrapped in cellophane or a latex rubber container base. The temperature of the food may be reduced by quick freezing to as low as — 50° F., rapid transference of heat being attained by contact with metal against which streams of brine at very low temperatures are directed; some methods use atomized sprays of cold brine and there is no distortion of the muscle cells and practically no "drip" on thawing. It is, however, unlikely that the quick freezing of whole quarters of beef will become a commercial proposition, for a temperature of — 464° F. would be required to quick-freeze a quarter of beef in 30 minutes.

"Weeping" or "Drip"

Weeping denotes the presence of a watery, blood-stained fluid which escapes from frozen meat when thawed and consists mainly of water, together with salts, extractives, protein and damaged blood corpuscles; the latter are responsible for the pink coloration of the fluid and are readily recognizable on microscopical examination. Weeping is an undesirable feature and is caused partly by the rupture of the muscle cells and tissues due to the presence of large crystals of ice, and partly by the permanent irreversible changes in the muscle plasm which prevent frozen muscle from reabsorbing water when the meat is thawed. The size of the ice crystals present in frozen meat bears a direct relationship to the damage done to the cells when the meat is thawed, and therefore to the amount of weeping or drip. If the meat is frozen slowly it will contain large ice crystals which will rupture mechanically the thin sheath of the muscle fibres, whereas if frozen rapidly the time taken in passing through the zone of maximum ice formation will be much less and the crystals, being small, will cause little or no damage. The amount of drip is greater in beef than in mutton, lamb or pork, but the better the original quality of a beef carcase the less on the average will be the drip from the meat after thawing. Quarters of frozen beef defrosted at 50° F. for 3 days and cut into large wholesale joints lose about 1-2 per cent. of their weight during the following day, while smaller joints of the retail trade lose 1·5-2·5 per cent.

The rate of thawing in both meat and fish is of less importance than the rate of freezing, for if large crystals of ice have already formed the damage done to the muscle is irremediable. It is claimed that drip is minimized if frozen meat be thawed very slowly, and one method employed for beef is to subject the meat to a temperature of 32° F. with 70 per cent. humidity, gradually increasing the temperature to 50° F. and the humidity to 90 per cent., the forequarter requiring 65 hours for complete thawing and the hindquarter 80 hours.

It is known that the faster the rate of breakdown of adenosine triphosphate in muscle the more rapid is the onset of rigor mortis and the greater the release of fluid from the muscles. If the rate of breakdown of ATP could be slowed, i.e. rigor mortis delayed, less free fluid would be available for drip formation on subsequent freezing and thawing. Again, meat which has a high pH prior to freezing has a low drip when thawed, and a useful diminution of drip from butchers' cuts can be brought about when the pH of the meat before freezing is 6·1 to 6·3. (See Fig. 50.)

Preparation of Frozen Meat for Export

All beef intended to be exported frozen should first be chilled, the time depending on the size and quality of the sides; 18 hours is not unusual, the important factor being to remove the animal heat. The beef is then quartered, placed in freezing rooms at a temperature of 0° F. or below, and finally enclosed in a bag of stockinette, and again in a bag of hessian; a temperature of 15° F. is maintained both during and after the voyage.

Carcases of mutton and lamb may be hung for a day or so at ordinary atmospheric temperature, being then frozen, enclosed in a stockinette bag before or after freezing and becoming hard frozen in 3 days. Modern

South American procedure is to chill carcases for a brief period immediately after slaughter and then place them in " sharp freezers ".

Practically all mutton, lamb and pork imported into Britain arrives in the frozen state, the meat substance of such carcases being much less damaged by freezing than in the case of beef, while the hard frozen condition of the carcases enables them to be piled on top of each other on board ship, thus achieving considerable economy in space.

Durability of Frozen Meat

Frozen meat stored too long becomes dry, rancid and less palatable, the most important change being the breaking down of the fat into glycerine and free fatty acids, with the production of rancidity. It is an axiom in the meat trade that the better the quality of meat the less trouble one encounters in its storage, and the condition of imported meat on arrival is also an important factor controlling its storage life.

It is generally accepted that frozen beef has the longest storage life and frozen pork the shortest. Under suitable conditions beef will store for a year, veal slightly less, mutton for 8 or 9 months, lamb 7 or 8 months, and pork about 6 months. Under exceptionally favourable conditions beef may be stored longer than a year without store-staleness developing, and recent experiments indicate that beef and poultry under suitable conditions can be kept solidly frozen, with their wholesomeness and nutritive value unimpaired, for 3 years or longer ; decomposition of both fat and lean, if it occurs, takes place either before freezing or after thawing. The main factors ensuring the best results in the storage of frozen meat are controlled humidity and temperature, an absolute necessity being that the latter remains constant.

With regard to the storage temperature of frozen beef, 10° F. or slightly above is considered suitable commercially, but scientifically a lower temperature of 0° F. to 5° F. would be preferred on all meats except pork. Pork for long storage is carried commercially in the United States at temperatures of 10° F. to – 10° F., the latter temperature being essential if pork is to be stored for a 6 months' period and rancidity and discoloration of the cut surfaces of the meat are to be avoided. Frozen offals and poultry which are suitably wrapped in greaseproof paper or waxed paper retain their bloom and show less storage effect than if packed without this wrapping, and can be stored satisfactorily for 12 months. Cured bacon will keep 3 to 4 months at 10° F. to 12° F., while sausages will keep 1½ months at 28° F. to 30° F.

Frozen meat after thawing is definitely less durable than the home-killed or chilled product, and in Germany it must be declared as such when sold. Similarly, in Britain all foreign meat must be labelled imported but the Regulation is not intended to warn the purchaser that the meat is of poor keeping quality but to prevent the butcher from substituting the frozen product for the more expensive home-killed or chilled meats.

Effect of Freezing on Pathogenic Micro-organisms and Parasites

Some bacteria are destroyed by freezing, but in others the effect of low temperature is merely to inhibit their growth and multiplication until conditions favourable to their growth appear. Freezing is therefore of no great value as a method of rendering a carcase affected with pathogenic bacteria safe for human consumption, nor are the bacteria commonly found on beef carcases destroyed by slow or sharp freezing. Anthrax bacilli can withstand a temperature of $-202°$ F., while organisms of the salmonella group can withstand exposure to $-302°$ F. for 3 days, and tubercle bacilli have been found to remain alive for over 2 years in carcases frozen at 15° F. The virus of foot and mouth disease can remain viable for 76 days if carcases of animals slaughtered during the incubative stage of the disease are chilled or frozen immediately afterwards. Under similar conditions the virus of swine fever may remain infective in the bone marrow for at least 73 days, and the virus has been shown to be viable in frozen pork for 1500 days. Freezing is, however, a valuable method for the treatment of meat affected with certain parasitic infections, and pork affected with *Cysticercus cellulosae* can be rendered safe if held for 4 days at 14° F. to 18° F., while carcases of beef affected with *Cysticercus bovis* can be rendered safe by holding for 3 weeks at a temperature not exceeding 20° F., or for 2 weeks at a temperature not higher than 14° F. Trichinella cysts in pork are destroyed by holding the carcase for 20 days at 5° F., or by quick freezing for 24 hours at 0° F.

Identification and Inspection of Imported Meat

Though the identification of imported meat in the form of carcases and quarters presents little difficulty, this difficulty is increased when the carcase has been jointed and is retailed as chops or steaks.

Fresh meat possesses a bloom or natural colour which is lacking in imported meat. The bulk of imported beef arrives in quarters, so there is a stale cut quartering surface, and the carcases are quartered leaving three ribs on the hindquarter. The stifle joint is not cut in imported beef, with the exception of chilled or frozen Australian beef in which the lateral aspect of the joint is incised and an examination made for the detection of onchocerca nodules. In this examination the underlying tissues are removed and the incision then skewered over the cavity which emits a drum-like note when tapped with the fingers. In home-killed beef in summer the stifle joint is often cut to encourage heat dissipation and avoid bone taint.

Chilled beef is hung in quarters during transport by sea, while frozen beef is stacked in the hold, and any prominences, such as the cod fat, lose all semblance of lobulation and the quarters present a torn, rough appearance.

Home-killed beef has a cold, dry, characteristic sheen on the surface, whereas chilled beef is cold and damp and is without this sheen ; frozen beef is cold, moist, possesses no sheen, and on thawing exhibits a considerable amount of " weeping " or " drip ". The muscular tissue is a bright red colour in home-killed beef, a bright red but occasionally a slaty blue in chilled, and pale red in frozen beef.

The amount of drip is least in home-killed beef, greater in chilled, and most abundant in frozen beef. The shrinkage of weight of these meats is therefore proportional to the amount of drip, though meat which has been " quick frozen " shows an almost complete absence of drip.

Home-killed meat turns a green colour when decomposing, but it is rare to observe this greenness in chilled or frozen meat, and the tendency for these is to decompose from the external surface, with the production of superficial blackish areas and slimy erosions.

A characteristic feature of imported frozen mutton and lamb is the ragged, dirty appearance and grey colour of the carcase surface, which is in marked distinction to the light sheen on the surface of home-killed mutton or lamb. This ragged skin, or bark, is usually trimmed from the smaller joints of frozen mutton before they are exposed for retail sale. Frozen pork has a darker skin than home-killed pork, and its muscle is paler and the fat is harder.

Affections of Imported Meat

A country engaged in the export of meat or meat products must maintain a high standard, particularly with regard to freedom of its products from bacterial, viral or parasitic diseases.

The conditions encountered from time to time in imported meat include abnormal odours, bone taint, brine staining, freezer burn, caseous lymphadenitis and moulds. With the exception of brine staining and freezer burn these affections have been dealt with on previous pages.

Brine Staining. Though brine or calcium chloride may be used in the brine circulating system for chilling or freezing of meat, calcium chloride is the liquid now more commonly used, and the term brine staining should be interpreted as including contamination of meat by either of these liquids. Meat stored in refrigerating chambers in which there are imperfect joints or leakages in the circulating system may become covered or partly covered with calcium chloride, which produces a characteristic dull or pale greenish colour on the carcase surface. The staining frequently penetrates the muscular tissue, which becomes darkened, and a feature of meat stained by calcium chloride is its extremely bitter taste. The staining of meat by sea water may be confused with that of brine stain, but in the former condition the taste is salty though not bitter, while the pale green colour is absent. Carcases or meat affected with brine stain may safely be released after trimming, though this may be impracticable in carcases of mutton where there is extensive staining of the pleura or peritoneum.

FIG. 217.—Carcases of imported mutton affected with severe brine stain. (Dr. M. T. Morgan.)

Freezer Burn. This is a condition which occurs on the outer surface of imported frozen offals, particularly livers and kidneys, and is attributed to loss of moisture from the outer tissues of the organs; it may sometimes be seen where a carcase is stored close to the opening of a cold air duct. Dehydration, or crystallization, takes place with great rapidity on the surface of offals, with the result that the surface of these becomes soft, spongy, and presents yellowish withered patches, while there is considerable wastage due to drip; this wastage may be as high as 3 to 7 per cent., and affected organs are usually so insipid and unpalatable when cooked that they require condemnation. Evaporation may be arrested and freezer burn avoided if the offals are enclosed in parchment paper before being packed in boxes, but the best method of prevention is to freeze the product on metal trays in coiled batteries installed in sharp freezers maintained at $-10°$ F. or lower. Freezer burn in frozen poultry can be avoided if the birds are packed in boxes lined with two layers of aluminium foil and grease-proof paper.

4. PRESERVATION BY HEAT

The underlying principle of all food preserving methods is either the creation of unfavourable environmental conditions under which spoilage organisms cannot grow, or the destruction of such organisms. Commercial canning is a method of food preservation in which carefully selected and prepared foods contained in a permanently sealed container are subjected to heat for a definite period of time and then cooled. In most canning processes the effect of heating on spoilage organisms is to destroy them, the permanent sealing of the container preventing reinfection of the food by further organisms.

Types of Container

As a food container the metal can possesses certain virtues possessed by no other type of container for heat processed foods. It has a high conductivity, which is of importance during processing, it cannot easily be broken and, being opaque, any possible deleterious effects of light on the foodstuff are avoided. The earlier types of metal container were made exclusively by hand, all seams being jointed by solder and the food packed into the can through a small hole in the end; the hole was then covered with a disc or cap which was soldered into place. The obvious disadvantages of these " hole and cap " containers were the difficulty of filling, and of efficient cleansing of the can before filling. Out of these disadvantages arose the modern " built-up " can, which has largely replaced the old form of can in which the cap was fixed by solder. The built-up can, also known as an open top or sanitary can, is useful for packs up to 10 lb. in weight, the principle being to roll or clinch the edges of the body and cover together under such strong pressure that an hermetic seal is formed, this being ensured by the presence of a sealing compound within the double seam (Fig. 219). The open top can is so universally used that few factories, except those engaged in milk and meat packing, now use any of the solder type.

Although the term tin can is applied to modern containers, this is somewhat of a misnomer as they are constructed of mild steel with a thin coating of pure tin, the actual amount of tin being only about 1·5 per cent. of the can's weight; it is important that the tin used should not contain more than one per cent. of lead. Coating of the steel plate is necessary to prevent corrosion, for steel is an unstable compound, and in some foodstuffs such as fish or fruit the tinplate is protected by a fish or fruit lacquer. Unsightly staining of the surface of certain foodstuffs, known as sulphiding, may also occur, and is avoided by use of a phenolic meat lacquer or a sulphur resistant lacquer. An alternative method of avoiding sulphiding is now being extensively employed for meat packs and consists of chemical treatment of the inside of the can to form an invisible protective film, the solution used being a strong alkali bath containing phosphates and chromates (Fig. 223).

The Selection and Treatment of Food to Be Canned

The food to be canned must be clean and of good quality, for the use of any material showing obvious signs of spoilage will result in deterioration

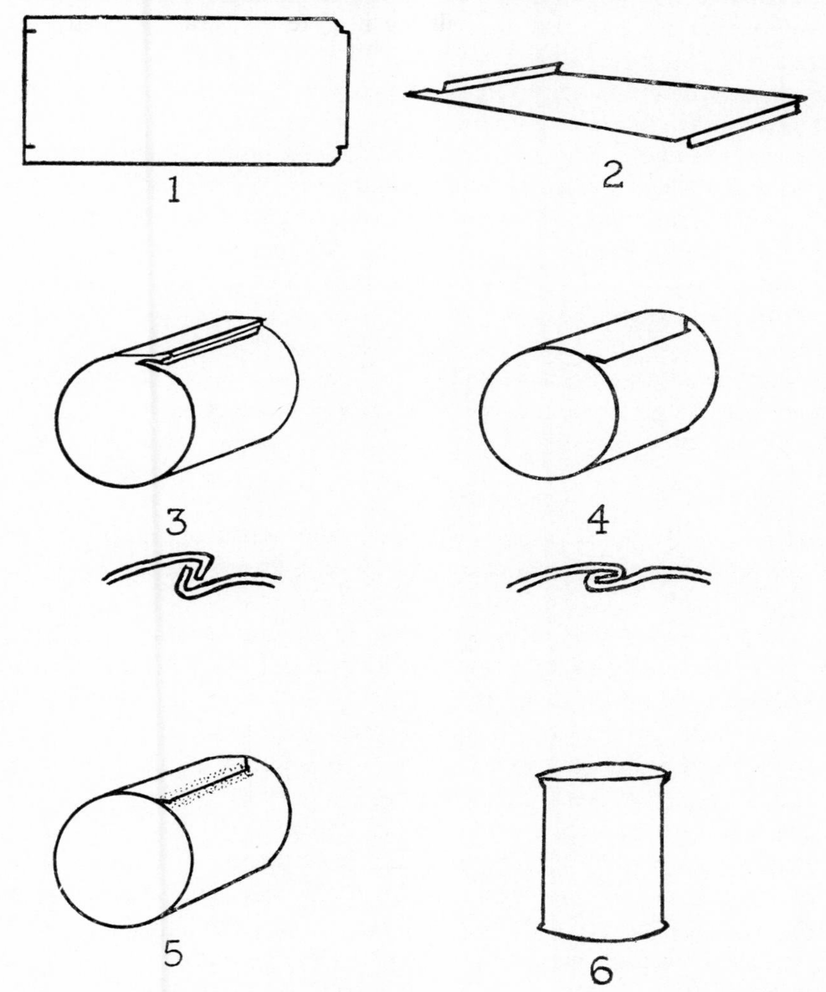

Fig. 218.—Stages in the manufacture of a "built-up" can. A machine known as a slitter cuts the tinplate into "body blanks". These are (1) notched; (2) hooked; (3) formed into a cylindrical body; (4) bumped, i.e. seam compressed; (5) soldered; (6) ends curved outwards to form a flange. (After Canned Foods Reference Manual.)

in quality of the product. Many foods, particularly fruit and vegetables, are scalded or blanched before treatment, the purpose of this being to cleanse the product, to produce shrinkage which permits adequate filling of the can, to remove gases from the food, and to prevent oxidative changes which might cause deterioration in the appearance and nutritive value of the food. In the case of meat foods a firm dry pack is required without any excess of free liquor in the can, and the moisture content of meat is therefore reduced by parboiling in steam-heated water ; by this process corned beef, i.e. pickled beef, will show a shrinkage of up to 40 per cent., ox tongues will shrink 32 per cent., and pork tongues 30 per cent. Highly fattened animals are not desirable for the manufacture of corned beef, as the meat is too fat and the finished product has an objectionable taste and appearance ; the meat is therefore obtained from cattle which are older and leaner than those furnishing the supply of chilled or frozen beef. The flesh of lean Criollo cattle is in greatest demand in South American canning factories, and these animals, which are derived from ancient Spanish stock, travel well and may be driven as much as 150 miles in 3 days.

After meats have been parboiled they are taken to the trimming table where inedible parts such as bones, cartilage and tendons, together with surplus fat, are removed.

Outline of Canning Operations

Cans may be filled either by hand or by automatic machinery, the next process being exhaustion or removal of air from the can before it is sealed.

1. *Exhausting*. Exhaustion is necessary because (*a*) cans sealed without previous exhausting may show such expansion of the contents during processing as to force the seams and produce a " leaker " ; (*b*) it produces a concavity of the ends of the tins so that any internal pressure may be readily detected and the can rejected ; (*c*) it lowers the amount of oxygen in the can and prevents discoloration of the surface of the food, and (*d*) in fruit packs it reduces chemical action between the food product and container, thus largely eliminating hydrogen swells. Although the production of a vacuum probably has very little effect on micro-organisms, the commercial packer, by long experience, recognizes the fact that tins containing a vacuum keep better than those from which the air has not been exhausted.

Exhaustion of a can may be carried out in two ways, by :

(*a*) Heat exhausting in which the contents are filled cold into the can, which is then passed through a steam-heated chamber before sealing. The ends of the can are loosely attached to permit of the escape of air, sealing being completed when the cans leave the exhauster, or

(*b*) Vacuumizing. In this process the cold material is filled into the can which is then closed in a vacuum-closing machine, the can being subjected to a high vacuum during the sealing operation.

2. *Processing.* With the exception of such foods as sweetened condensed milk or jam, all canned foods are processed, this being the technical term applied in the trade to the final heating given to the can and foodstuff after the can has been hermetically sealed. The term processing is an exact one, as it would be incorrect to describe the process as sterilization, and certain canned foods after processing may still contain living organisms. Although canned foods will keep with certainty if sterilized, it is the liability to alteration in the colour and texture of the food which compels the canner to limit the degree and duration of the heating to the minimum for his immediate object. Food to be canned is threatened on the one hand by spoilage due to bacteria, and on the other by danger of overheating; the canner therefore chooses a middle course, the minimum heat employed in processing being controlled by the nature of the food in the can and the types and number of bacteria likely to be present.

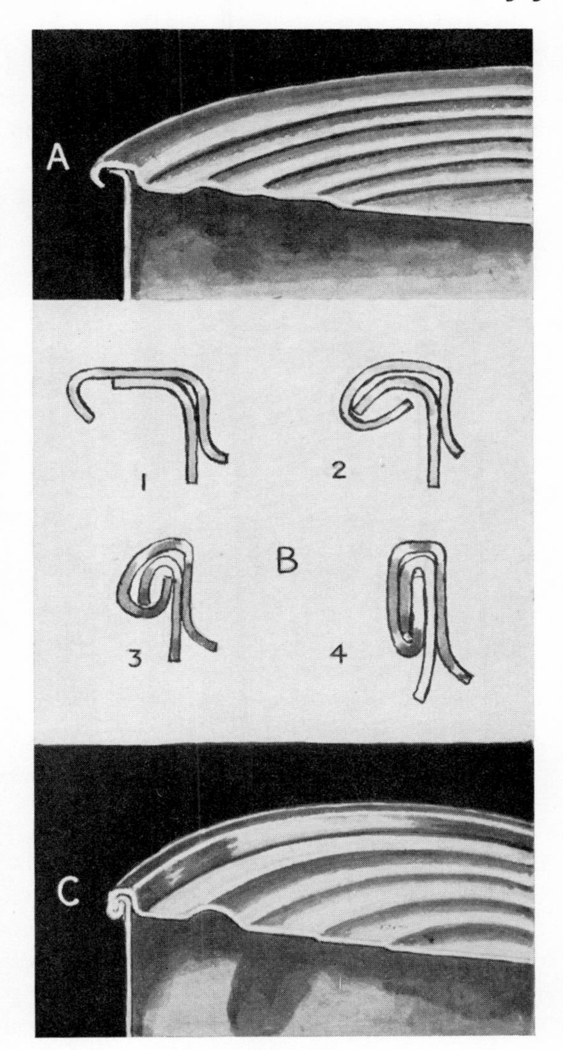

FIG. 219.—A. Relation of cover to can before sealing operation is commenced. The expansion rings on the cover lend elasticity to it and provide for expansion and contraction during and after processing. A fine film of plastic material, usually pure latex rubber, is placed on the upper edge of the outturned flange of the can.

B. Stages in sealing operation, in which edges of cover and can are rolled together to form a double seam, while the rubber compound forms a permanent hermetic seal.

C. Cross-section of closed "built-up" or sanitary can. (After Canned Foods Reference Manual.)

During processing, heat penetrates to the centre of the can by conduction and by convection currents. In solid meat packs the diffusion of heat is brought about by conduction and the process is therefore slow, but in more loosely packed foodstuffs the presence of channels permits

Fig. 220.—Battery of vertical processing retorts showing metal basket and time clocks to control processing period. (Metal Box Company.)

the passage of convection currents which facilitate the transfer of heat. Solids loosely packed in a liquid will therefore heat more rapidly than those which are tightly packed, and for this reason salmon which is solidly packed admits heat more slowly than where smaller pieces of fish are surrounded by liquid. Canned ham, being perhaps the largest and most solid pack of all the canned foods, requires particularly careful processing.

The acidity of the food contents also has an important bearing on the temperature required for processing. Acid foods, which include the common fruits, are easily processed, and it is only necessary to heat the sealed container long enough to permit the attainment of a definite temperature in the centre of the can. This temperature must be sufficient to kill yeasts, moulds and certain bacteria capable of growing in an acid medium, and is usually in the region of 200° F.

In non-acid foods, such as meat, the destruction of bacterial spores is slow, and these foods require temperatures of about 240° F. if adequate processing is to be obtained within a practical time limit. In commercial practice, metal baskets filled with cans are placed in closed retorts, which may be horizontal or vertical, and are then processed by steam pressure.

3. *Cooling.* Prompt cooling after processing is important, as it checks the action of heat on the food and prevents undue change in texture and colour. In addition, a marked internal pressure exists in the can when it is removed from the steam pressure retort, and rapid reduction of this internal pressure is ensured by prompt cooling of the cans ; this is done either by placing them under showers of cold water, by immersing them in a cold water tank, or in some cases by pressure cooling in the retort when the processing is completed. The standard of cooling water should be that acceptable for a public drinking water supply, i.e., it should be clean and wholesome, but the treatment required to attain this standard will depend on the type and source of water. Reliance cannot be placed on chlorination alone, for the addition of chlorine to water has little effect on any organisms if the water contains organic matter, and should the supply of cooling water be obtained from a river it will require sedimentation and filtration before final chlorinating. The amount of chlorine added to cooling water should be enough to produce, after 30 minutes contact time, a free residual chlorine content of 0·5 p.p.m. or more, and a chlorinated water supply should show no coliform bacteria in 100 ml. water, a standard readily obtained by effective treatment. In commercial practice cans are water-cooled to a temperature of 100° F., so that enough residual heat remains in the can to dry the exterior and prevent corrosion.

4. *Can Washing.* Cans which have just been cooled are dirty and greasy on the outside, and are therefore passed through a detergent bath to facilitate subsequent handling, lacquering and labelling. This bath is usually composed of soap or sulphonated fatty alcohols.

5. *Outside Lacquering.* Commercial lacquer or enamel is a coloured varnish containing vegetable resin or synthetic resin. Tins after removal from the detergent bath are washed, and lacquer may be applied to the outside of the tin to prevent external corrosion, particularly when the cans are destined for moist climates. Though external lacquering is not common in the canning of vegetables and fruits, it is almost universal in the salmon canning industry and is necessary not only because the English market insists on their shipments being finished in this way, but also because the loss through rust would otherwise be enormous.

Canning of Meats

Though corned beef is perhaps the best known of the canned meat products, considerable quantities of canned ham, ox, sheep and pig tongues and spiced hams are now manufactured, and form a nutritious and palatable product. The preparation of corned beef will illustrate the procedure normally adopted in the preparation of canned meats.

CORNED BEEF. Corned beef is prepared from beef pickled in salt, nitrite and sugar, is boiled for 1 hour and then trimmed of soft fats, tendons, bones and cartilage. The texture of the beef and the fat content depend on the taste of the country for which it is intended, some countries preferring a lean corned beef, others a grade with a higher fat content; that for the English market generally contains about 10 per cent. of fat. Pickling is essential, for without it the meat after processing would be very much shrunken and dark in colour, while the can would contain a quantity of liquid and dripping. After the meat is passed through a cutting machine

FIG. 221.—South American frigorifico practice. The carcases of beef have been boned out for the preparation of canned beef. The liquid in which the meat is parboiled prior to canning is concentrated to produce the commercial extract of beef. (Industrial Waste Eliminators Ltd.)

it is packed automatically into cans, the shrinkage from the original fresh boneless meat to its weight when finally packed being 40 to 45 per cent. The cans are then capped with the vent open, the vent being sealed whilst in a vacuum machine under a vacuum of 23 inches. In some cases exhaustion is carried out by leaving the vent open and placing the can in a process retort for 45 minutes at 220° F., the can being then removed and the vent closed as soon as it ceases blowing.

The subsequent method of processing varies in different plants. In some cases the corned beef cans are put into retorts and processed at a pressure of 9 lb. per square inch for 2½ hours or more, the time depending on the size of the can. A 1 lb. tin of corned beef requires processing for 2½ hours at 220° F., a 6 lb. tin requires 5 hours at 222° F., and a 14 lb. tin 6 hours at 227° F. In other cases processing is carried out in a hot water bath, the cans being immersed in boiling water for 3½ to 4 hours, the process in either case being followed by cooling, degreasing and lacquering.

CANNED HAMS. Hams are boned by hand and forced into a pressure mould to produce the required shape. The metal container for hams is double-seamed, though without a rubber gasket, sealing being done by

FIG. 222.—Canning of hams, Norway. The cans have just been removed from the retort where they have been exhausted by steam heating, and the vent holes are now being hand-soldered prior to processing of the cans.

hand-soldering followed by exhausting and soldering of the vent hole. The hams are finally cooked without pressure at 200° F. for several hours. Cooking at a higher temperature in a pressure retort is contra-indicated, for though it would lessen the length of the processing period, it would produce deleterious changes in the ham texture and heavy loss in weight due to exudation of fat and jelly. An increase of only 10 minutes in cooking time at these higher temperatures can result in an increased overall cooking loss of up to 5 per cent.

Foods Packed in Glass

A great variety of foods are packed in hermetically sealed glass containers, and though the treatment of these differs somewhat from foods packed in cans the principles of preservation are the same. The disadvantages of the glass container are that its greater weight, fragility, lessened output for the same amount of equipment and labour, together with the extra expense in packing, limit its use to the higher-grade products. Its advantages, on the other hand, are that it is less susceptible to attack by the product it contains, while the contents may be readily inspected by the purchaser. The metal caps of glass containers are usually of lacquered tin plate, a paper liner being placed inside the cap so that discoloration of the food, which may result from corrosion of the metal, may be prevented. The cap is firmly held against a rubber gasket on the rim of the glass container and thus forms an hermetic seal.

Glass-packed foods are processed for a longer period than canned foods but at a lower temperature, as there is risk of fracture of the glass, and both heating and cooling must therefore be carried out more slowly. The modern method is to process in steam-heated water on which air pressure is superimposed; at the conclusion of processing the steam is shut off and cooling carried out slowly by admitting cold water to the retort, but the air pressure is still maintained to prevent the cap from being blown off by the internal pressure which develops in the container.

Glass particles of appreciable size are but seldom found in food packed in glass, and particles, when present, are usually in powder form or of microscopical size. Foreign bodies such as glass, when present in the intestine, are orientated by the action of the muscular walls of the intestine so that they lie with their long axes parallel to the bowel wall, and not transversely by which they would be likely to do more damage. There is little if any evidence that glass in powdered or microscopical form is capable of exciting any injurious effect when swallowed in food, and the danger from glass particles in food has undoubtedly been greatly exaggerated. Elongated, coffin-lid shaped crystals of ammonium-magnesium phosphate and known as struvite are sometimes found in canned shellfish, usually after the can has undergone a long period of storage. These crystals, which are often mistaken for particles of glass but are distinguished by the fact that they dissolve readily in dilute acids, render the foodstuff unmarketable if they are present in considerable numbers.

Bacteria in Canned Foods

It was at one time thought that the keeping qualities of canned goods depended upon the complete exclusion of air. Later it was suggested that the heating destroyed all micro-organisms, while the sealing of the can prevented the entry of others, and that decomposition, when it occurred, was due to faulty sterilization or to entry of bacteria through a fault in the can. Neither of these views expresses the whole truth because living bacteria can often be found in sound and wholesome food, and bacteriological methods show that many canned meats or meat products contain living organisms, even after modern processing methods; the mere presence of living organisms is of little or no significance in assaying the soundness of canned goods.

The organisms responsible for spoilage in canned goods may be spore-forming and therefore resistant to commercial processing, or they may be non-sporing organisms which gain access to the can by leakages after processing. Aerobic spore-forming bacteria may be present in sound samples of canned goods, and living organisms of an aerobic spore-forming type have been demonstrated in a can of roast veal manufactured in 1824 and opened 114 years later, the contents being undecomposed even after that lapse of time. When present as spores these bacteria probably remain dormant under the anaerobic conditions of a properly sealed tin but, if supplied with air through faulty sealing, may develop and produce enzymes which decompose the foodstuff. Anaerobic bacteria may also be found in sound tins, though spoilage of canned foodstuffs, particularly meat, caused by anaerobic bacteria in pure culture is well known in the canning industry.

Non-sporing bacteria of proteolytic or fermenting types, as *Proteus* and *E. coli* may, if present, cause decomposition of canned foods, so that it will be apparent that no one type of organism is responsible for microbial spoilage. The problem of spoilage in canned goods is not the simple one of the presence or absence of bacteria of the decomposing type, but the problem as to why in some tins bacteria of this type decompose the contents, while in others they remain inactive. Though yeasts and moulds are of great importance as a cause of unsoundness in acid substances containing sugars, e.g. canned fruits, they are of little importance in the durability of canned meats and marine products. The presence of moulds in canned meat foods is evidence of the access of air after sealing and can make the food unsound; canned goods which, on opening, show evidence of surface mould should therefore be condemned.

Types of Spoilage

Canned goods are classified as spoiled when the food has undergone a deleterious change, or when the condition of the container renders such change possible. Spoilage may be due to a variety of causes, and spoiled cans may show obvious abnormalities such as distortion or blowing;

on the other hand, they may present a perfectly normal external appearance.

A can with its ends bulged by positive internal pressure due to gas generated by microbial or chemical activity is termed a " swell " or " blower ". A " flipper " is a can of normal appearance in which one end flips out when the can is struck against a solid object, but the end snaps back to the normal when very light pressure is applied. A " springer " is the term used to describe a can in which one end is bulged but can be forced back into normal position, whereupon the opposite end bulges. All blown cans pass successively through the " flipper " and " springer " stages, and these two conditions must be regarded as suspicious of early spoilage of the can contents. A change in the appearance of the gelatine surrounding meat packs is usually associated with the formation of gas, the gelatine being discoloured and more liquid in consistency; it should be remembered, however, that in hot weather the gelatine of meat packs is likely to be of a more fluid nature.

A " leaker " is a can containing a perforation from any cause, whereby atmospheric air may enter the can or its contents escape. An overfilled can is one in which the ends are convex due to overfilling, but filling by weight or accurate measurement has done much to obviate this condition and most tins classified as overfilled are actually in the early stage of blowing. Though an overfilled can cannot properly be regarded as a spoiled can, it must be differentiated from the can which is " blown ", and it emits a dull sound when struck, whereas a blown tin emits a resonant note. The term " slack caps " is used in the trade to denote a can which has a movement of one of the ends similar to a can in the early stage of blowing but it is now rarely if ever encountered, and the great majority of cans classed as slack caps are blown and should be treated as such.

Spoilage of canned goods may be of microbial or chemical origin or due to deleterious influences such as rust or damage.

MICROBIAL SPOILAGE. The factors determining microbial unsoundness in canned goods are:

(1) *The type of micro-organism.* Bacteria of the decomposing or fermenting type are the most important, while spore-forming bacteria are the most resistant. There are three main types of spore-forming organisms which can resist normal processing and may cause spoilage in canned foods: (*a*) gas-producing anaerobic and aerobic organisms with an optimum temperature growth of 98·6° F.; (*b*) gas-producing anaerobic organisms growing at an optimum temperature of 131° F.; both these types of organisms are associated with the form of spoilage recognized by blowing; (*c*) non-gas-producing aerobic or facultative anaerobic spore-forming organisms with an optimum temperature of about 131° F.; it is

this type of organism which produces the form of spoilage known in the trade as " flat-sours ".

(2) *The number of micro-organisms present.* Processing is not a substitute for cleanliness, and it is recognized by canners that a small number of bacteria are likely to be destroyed more easily by processing than are a large number. Bacteria subjected to heat or other harmful influences are destroyed in accordance with a definite law which prescribes that where two different suspensions of the same organism are subjected to heat under uniform conditions, the number of bacteria will be reduced by the same percentage over equal periods of time. This may be expressed in another way by stating that where two foodstuffs, one containing one thousand organisms and the other one million organisms, are subjected to heat, the former food will contain five hundred organisms and the latter half a million after treatment for the same period of time ; the heavier the contamination, therefore, the more difficult it is to produce a sound pack.

(3) *Efficiency of processing.* Insufficient processing must be regarded as a cause of unsoundness of canned goods, though not the all-important factor generally assumed.

(4) *Access of air to the can.* The bacteria found in canned meat or fish are nearly always secondary invaders gaining access to the food through a leaking tin.

Microbial spoilage may thus be due to under-processing or the result of leakage through the seam. Leakers may be detected by the disappearance of the vacuum from the sides and ends of the can, and bubbles appear if the can be held under water and squeezed. Another test for leakage is to heat the can until the temperature is 100° F. in the interior and allowing it to cool slowly, when, if a leak is present, there will be no concavity of the sides or ends ; the detection of leakers by striking the suspect tin with a mallet is now acknowledged to have little value in industrial practice. The commonest form of leaking is at the seams, and may sometimes be detected by the appearance of liquid or stain on the can surface. Mould formation on the surface of canned meats is also indicative of leakage through the seams, but cannot be detected until the can is opened.

The condition known as flat-souring in canned goods is manifested by the presence of a sour odour of the foodstuff, but without the can becoming blown, and canned foods susceptible to this deleterious change are those containing sugar or starches, and meat products such as sausages or pastes containing cereal. True flat-sours are caused by the growth of thermophilic organisms which attack carbohydrates with the production of acid but not gas, the exceptional heat-resistance of such organisms enabling them to survive the normal processing given to canned foods.

Sourness in canned foods may also arise due to leaking cans, or it may have developed in the foodstuff before processing; this latter form of spoilage is most liable to occur in cold-filled packs in warm weather, and its incidence is greatly increased by allowing the product to stand in open cans for even short periods prior to processing. In corned beef the presence of souring without gas production may be due to under-processing or leaking seams, but the development of pre-process souring is also a likely cause.

Flat-souring of canned goods due to thermophilic spore-forming organisms cannot be detected until the can is opened and its contents examined, but is unlikely to occur in temperate climates, as in Britain, unless storage conditions have been exceptionally hot; it is, however, of comparatively common occurrence in tropical and subtropical countries, or in cans imported into temperate climates from hot countries.

Chemical Spoilage. The condition in canned goods known as hydrogen swell may occur quite independently of fermentation or bacterial decomposition, and is associated with the formation of hydrogen gas in the can following on internal corrosion. Imperfections or scratches on the inner tin coating may expose small areas of iron, and, where the food contained is acid in nature, the acid may act upon the tin and iron which are in contact and thus produce an electric couple with the liberation of free hydrogen and blowing of the can. Electrolytic action is accelerated by the presence of atmospheric oxygen and by the red fruits due to their colouring matter, the anthocyanins; lacquering of the can also increases the rate at which hydrogen swells are formed, for cracks in the inner lining of lacquer serve to concentrate electrolytic action on areas of iron exposed by the cracks. Cans affected with hydrogen swell may show varying degrees of bulging, from flipping to blowing, and if the tin be punctured there is emission of hydrogen gas, which is odourless and burns on the application of a flame. The condition is chiefly associated with foods containing organic acids, particularly fruits, and the canned fruits in which this form of swell occurs are usually plums, cherries, raspberries, black currants and loganberries.

The range of acidity which is most favourable to the production of hydrogen swell lies between pH 3·5 and pH 4·5, and the less acid fruits therefore give more trouble than those of higher acidity, but with proper precautions there should be very little trouble from hydrogen swells in commercially packed English fruits until at least a year after canning. The condition is seldom encountered in canned vegetables and is practically unknown in canned meat foods, but it is sometimes seen in tinned sardines. Though the contents of a can in hydrogen swell may be quite harmless, the routine methods employed in the examination of canned goods render it impossible to distinguish between tins which are blown due to hydrogen swell and those which are blown as a result of deleterious changes due to bacteria or yeasts. All blown tins whether fruit, meat, vegetables or condensed milk must be regarded as unfit for food, and leakers, springers and flat-sours, together with tins whose contents show evidence of mould, should be likewise condemned.

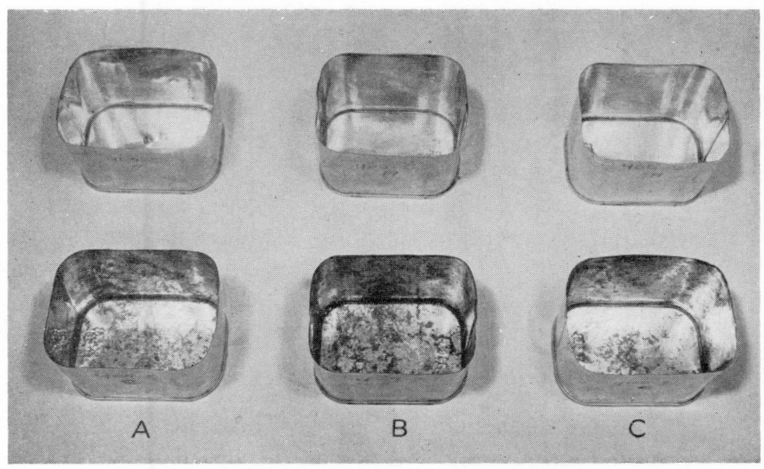

FIG. 223.—The advantage of a protective film on tin plate. The top row of cans was treated by a chemical immersion process, packed with corned beef, processed and opened after: A. five months; B. nine months; C. thirteen months. The inner surface of the cans shows complete freedom from sulphiding as compared with the lower control cans stored for similar periods. (Tin Research Institute.)

Sulphiding. Purple staining on the inner surface of cans in which sulphur-containing foods are packed is noticeable with all fish and meat products, especially liver, kidneys and tongue. It is due to the breaking down of sulphur-containing proteins by a high processing temperature, with the result that hydrogen sulphide is liberated and a thin layer of tin sulphide is formed on the inside of the can. This discoloration, which does not involve the foodstuff itself and varies from a light pink to a dark purple, may be accompanied by a blackening of both the inside of the can and surface of the foodstuff, these latter changes being due to attack of hydrogen sulphide on the steel base with the formation of iron sulphide; it is of more serious import than the deposition of tin sulphide, as it may lead to pitting of the steel and disfigurement of the surface of the meat pack. Discolorations of both types may be prevented by the use of a sulphur-resisting lacquer, the basis of which is copal gum dissolved in a suitable solvent to which are added substances capable of uniting with the volatile sulphur gases released while the food is being processed. Purple staining of the inside of the can is of no significance, while blackening of the surface of the foodstuff may be removed by trimming.

Rust or Damage. Cans showing external rust require careful consideration, and it is a condition particularly liable to occur beneath can labels when the adhesive contains hygroscopic substances. Cans in which the external surface is slightly rusted without noticeable pitting of the iron may be released for immediate sale and consumption, but if the rust be removed with a knife and inspection with a hand lens reveals the iron plate to be definitely pitted there is danger of early perforation and the cans should be condemned. Minute perforations of the tin plate, known as pin-holing, permit entrance of air and lead to spoilage of the can contents. Pin-holing may originate from the outside, but also from the inside of the can in parts where the tin plating has been imperfect or has been fractured during seaming, and in this case lacquer lining aggravates the trouble, as the cracks which occur in the lacquer aid in concentrating the chemical action on a small area. A can which is a leaker or pin-holed may occasionally seal itself by blocking of the holes with the contained foodstuffs, and may then proceed to blow; such self-sealing cans may blow at any period of their storage life, whereas an under-processed can will blow early in its life, generally within the first few months. Where unfilled cans are stored and allowed to rust internally before being filled the can edges may become rusted, with the result that during processing a chemical action may take place between the rust and meat juices and give rise to an unsightly grey precipitate of iron phosphate in the meat jelly.

Considerable significance should be attached to cans damaged by rough handling, the important factor in their judgment being the extent and location of the damage. Marked deformation of the seam of the can is attended by considerable risk of leakage, and cans showing seam damage should therefore be condemned. Slight indentations on the can body are permissible, but severe dents on the body may cause seam distortion with danger of leakage and such cans should be rejected; any can having a dent at one end should also be rejected for it is possible to reduce a springer to normal, at any rate temporarily, by hitting it upon the corner of a box. Nail holes in cans caused during the closing of packing cases may also be encountered, and such cans should be rejected even if the contained foodstuff appears perfectly normal. It is a wise axiom to reject any can which is in the least suspicious or which shows lack of concavity of the ends.

Durability of Canned Foods

All canned flesh foods improve by being allowed to mature, as, for example, sardines in which the bones and flesh become soft and the product more palatable; a popular brand of French sardine sold in the English market was said to have been matured in tins for five years before it was marketed. In most cases the turnover of stocks of canned foods is rapid, though if such foodstuffs are properly canned, packed and kept under favourable conditions, they should last for at least two years. The necessity for storage in a cool, dry environment cannot be overstressed, for heat during storage favours chemical action and development of springers or pin-hole leaks; the chemical rate of action in canned foods is doubled for each 18° F. rise in temperature, and whereas canned foods may be kept for 8 months at 45° F. they may not last 3 months at a temperature of 80° F. The increase in spoilage of canned foods in tropical climates is, however, mainly due to the action of thermophilic bacteria which show an optimum growth at 131° F., but these organisms do not normally develop at storage temperatures prevailing in Europe.

Vitamins in Canned Foods

From the nutritive point of view canned foods compare favourably with cooked fresh foods even as regards vitamin content. Vitamin A is insoluble in water and heat stable in the absence of oxygen, so that canning is less destructive to it than ordinary cooking. Vitamin B is very heat stable, but is water soluble; the only loss is therefore in the preliminary washing of foods to be canned. Vitamin C is readily affected by washing, heat and storage; cooking, whether domestic or in canning, therefore causes material loss of this vitamin, but many canned fruits and vegetables possess an adequate amount, and canning is not more prejudical to vitamin C than ordinary cooking. Vitamin D is heat stable, and undergoes no destruction in canning. Vitamin D_1 is water soluble, but has considerable resistance to heat in an ordinary acid medium; there is therefore some loss in canning but no more than in domestic cooking. The practical experience of the French Mission to Greenland in 1932-1933, when fifteen men lived for 13 months on canned foods, and almost entirely without fresh foods, is worthy of record, for no poisoning or nutritional defects resulted and the canned fruits and vegetables taken yielded sufficient vitamin C to prevent scurvy.

The Public Health Aspect of Canned Foods

Improvements in the canning industry during recent years, together with greater appreciation of its hygienic requirements, have done much to remove the prejudice in the minds of the lay public against canned foods, a prejudice largely based on the supposition that canned foods might cause food poisoning. Food poisoning is usually the result of improper handling of food during preparation or storage, and, with the exception of botulism, food poisoning outbreaks are in practically all instances caused by bacteria which are of low resistance to heat and would therefore be destroyed during processing. The salmonella group of organisms are destroyed with certainty by the temperatures attained in commercial processing.

The minimum standard of processing now universally recognized by reputable canners ensures the destruction of *Clostridium botulinum* spores in low acid and medium acid foods. A lower temperature is, however, permissible in the case of a few special packs such as cured meats, in which the curing salts have an inhibitory effect on the growth of the organism and the production of its toxin. In Britain there is no record that canned foods have ever been incriminated in outbreaks of botulism, and on only two occasions have glass-packed foods been involved. Public Health authorities in Britain have frowned on any development of the practice of home canning, but in America the widespread use of insufficiently processed home-canned foods has been the cause of many outbreaks, though no authenticated case of botulism involving commercially canned food has occurred in that country since 1925.

Staphylococci, and more rarely streptococci, are now recognized as a cause of food poisoning, and the majority of foods in which pathogenic staphylococci have been concerned were prepared or unheated foods, as cheese, salad, milk or ice-cream. These organisms are ubiquitous in nature, being found in air, water, milk and sewage, but their main source is the human or animal body where they are normally present on the skin, in the intestine, and in the respiratory tract. Staphylococci, however, are relatively susceptible to heat, and even the more resistant staphylococcal enterotoxin, which may withstand a temperature of 212° F. for 30 minutes, would be destroyed with certainty during commercial processing. Cans may occasionally become infected if these organisms gain entrance to a leaking can, and if this entrance is not accompanied by the multiplication of gas-forming bacteria the can will not " blow ", while its contents, though they appear normal, may contain vast amounts of the organism and its toxin. Most cases of food poisoning now associated with canned foods are the result of contamination of the foodstuff after the can is opened, but a number of cases of typhoid fever associated with canned foods have occurred in Britain in recent years. The outbreak in Aberdeen in 1964, in which there were over 400 confirmed cases, was attributed to the entry during the post-processing period of contaminated cooling water into a 6 lb. tin of corned beef of South American origin.

Viewing the question as a whole, it may be stated definitely that canned foods are considerably less likely to be a source of food poisoning than are ordinary fresh foods. The possibility of canned foods being rendered dangerous by secondary contamination with pathogenic bacteria also raises the question of the wisdom or otherwise of leaving food in a can after it has been opened. From the public health standpoint there is no reason why an open can, properly stored, should not be used as a food container, the only requirements being that it should be kept covered to prevent contamination and that the can and its contents should be kept cool.

5. PRESERVATION BY OTHER METHODS

ANTIBIOTICS

Antibiotics have many characteristics which place them in the category of approaching the ideal food preservative. In the required concentration they impart no flavours or odours to the food and do not discolour the product, while most of them are considered to be relatively harmless to humans. The range of effectiveness of antibiotics varies considerably, and with the appearance of the non-toxic broad-spectrum antibiotics such as chlortetracycline, oxytetracycline and chloramphenicol, their value in preservation has been amply demonstrated. It has been shown that infusion of beef carcases with the tetracycline antibiotics improves their keeping qualities and is efficacious in preventing and retarding internal spoilage in beef carcases. The technique may be modified to permit inoculation of the antibiotic into the living animal just prior to slaughter and thus spoilage organisms are inhibited before they have the opportunity of multiplying. Administration may be either intraperitoneal or into the tail of the animal, but the intraperitoneal technique is impracticable because of the time factor which cannot be easily afforded in commercial slaughter. It is, however, a procedure which could be adopted in countries lacking refrigeration and thus make it possible for the meat to be distributed to a much wider area than at present.

Extensive studies have also been made on the use of certain selected antibiotics for the preservation of foods such as poultry and fish. These antibiotics are added to water in a proportion of 5 to 40 parts per million, and poultry is dropped into the treated water; alternatively the antibiotic is added to ice in amounts of 2 to 5 parts per million, and fish is cooled and transported on the treated ice. Such treatment increases considerably the storage life of these foods, and in 1955 the United States gave authority for the use of certain antibiotics in the storage of fish, and more recently Canadian authorities have permitted the use of some in the preservation of fish and poultry.

An important limitation to the preservation effectiveness of antibiotics is that even the broad-spectrum antibiotics, though active against bacteria, are ineffective against other groups of micro-organisms such as yeasts and moulds. Objections to the use of antibiotics as food preservatives are also based on the fact that harmful effects may result from long-term inclusion of antibiotics in the diet, and the Federal Authorities of the United States sanction the use of chlortetracycline only when its complete destruction on cooking can be demonstrated. Another objection is that the widespread use of antibiotics in food will encourage the appearance of antibiotic-resistant strains among pathogenic bacteria present. There is also a danger that producers may be tempted to supplement good hygienic practices and refrigeration by antibiotic cover, and any attempt to use antibiotics in this way seems likely to increase the danger from salmonella-infected foods.

Radiation

Two sources of radiation exist, electrical generators (X-ray and cathode rays) and radioactive materials (gamma and beta rays) which, as by-products from nuclear reactors, may be quite cheaply available in the forseeable future. Such agents are capable of killing micro-organisms without significantly raising the temperature and hence make conceivable the preparation of sterile raw foods. During processing chemical changes occur, however, and these result in unpleasant odours and flavours, beef being particularly susceptible to such changes, pork and poultry less so. The increasing sensitivity to development of undesirable flavours is proportional to the increasing myoglobin content of the muscular tissue and is in some degree due to the action of proteolytic changes during post-irradiation storage. A considerable number of technological and chemical problems remain to be resolved before evaluation can be made of the practical value of radiation sterilization.

6. CHEMICAL RESIDUES IN MEAT

The inspection of meat in most countries of the world has been until recent years in the main a visual post-mortem procedure. But in its true form it should consist of an ante-mortem examination of the live animal before slaughter and a post-mortem inspection of the carcase and viscera as well as, in those cases requiring it, a laboratory examination—bacteriological, chemical or biochemical or a combination of these.

In the past the work of the food analyst was confined mainly to the detection of a few well-known entities—arsenic, lead, fluoride, rotenone, etc., but today because of the ever-increasing technological advances in agriculture a large number of substances can find their way into meat, and this state of affairs has thrown an extra burden on the shoulders of the meat hygienist.

Various chemicals are used at different stages in the production and processing of food. These include preservatives, stabilizers, emulsifiers, sweeteners, flavouring agents, tenderizers, colouring agents, spices, nutritional supplements, etc., and are permitted at certain levels by the law of the country concerned. In addition, however, farmers today are using several hundred compounds such as soil conditioners, tranquillizers, seed-treating compounds, chemical fertilizers, insecticides, herbicides, fungicides, soil fumigants, hormones, arsenicals, enzymes, antioxidants, heavy metals, and certain " growth promoters ". These substances may find their way into animals' tissues by direct routes such as injections or contact, or by indirect routes through addition to the animals' feed in which they may also be present in the original grain.

In order to control the levels of substances which may be deleterious to human health many countries have drawn up regulations stipulating tolerances for them, usually stated in parts per million, as well as withdrawal periods prior to slaughter. In the United States of America, for example, no new chemical additive that is toxic to human beings is permitted under the law to be used in foods. Of the substances that are considered as drugs or pesticides, only 17 are permitted to be present in meat, none are permitted in milk and only 2 are allowed in eggs.

It must be said that no chemical additive is safe under all conditions of use—there has to be a reasonable assessment made. And while as yet there have been no reports of any known detrimental effects on public health attributable to chemical residues in meat, nevertheless it is also true to say that no one can with certainty declare there are no ill-effects from long-term ingestion. Since most scientists regard nutrition as being the most important environmental factor in animal or human health it is obvious that any alterations in diet must be given the fullest attention. It is also possible that while the presence of any chemical at a particular level may not present a direct hazard it may, by acting as an " anti-vitamin ", make for a state of vitamin deficiency and thus cause an ill effect. Thus the nature of the substance, its level in the meat, its rate of excretion from the animal body, the nature of the metabolites formed (which may be more harmful than the parent compound) and the withdrawal period before slaughter are factors which have to be considered in determining its safety.

Cereals and vegetables grown on soils which contain high levels of selenium and fluorine often show fairly large amounts of these chemicals and have been known to cause harm in human beings and animals consuming them. The concentration of such substances in animals which have

TOLERANCES FOR PESTICIDES, DRUGS AND ANTIBIOTICS IN FOOD OF ANIMAL ORIGIN (UNITED STATES)

Residues Permitted (ppm) *

Chemical	*Red Meat*	*Poultry*	*Eggs*
Carbophenothion	0·1	—	—
Coumaphos	1·0	—	—
D.D.T.	7·0	—	—
Diazinon	0·75 Sheep only	—	—
Dioxathion	1·0	—	—
Diuron	Cattle, hogs, goats horses, sheep 1·0 meat, fat, meat by-products	—	—
Guthion	0·1	—	—
Lindane	4·0 hogs 7·0 others	—	—
Malathion	4·0	4·0	—
Methoxychlor	3·0	—	—
Toxaphene	7·0	—	—
Amprolium	1·0	1·0 liver, kidneys 0·5	—
Arsenic		0·5 meat 1·0 by-products	0·5 —
Chlortetracycline	Calves 1·0 muscles, fat 4·0 liver, kidneys Beef 0·1 kidneys, liver, muscles Swine 4·0 kidneys 2·0 liver 1·0 muscles 0·2 fat	4·0 kidneys 1·0 muscle, liver, fat, skin	—
Ethoxyquin	5·0	3·0 liver, fat 0·5 muscles	0·5
Oxytetracycline	—	3·0 kidneys 1·0 muscles, liver, fat, skin (total not to exceed 7·0)	—
Zoalene	—	Chickens 6·0 liver, kidneys 3·0 muscle 2·0 fat Turkeys 3·0 muscle, fat	—

* No chemical residues of any substance are permitted in milk.

eaten such grain and vegetables is, however, usually low and unlikely to present a hazard from the consumption of the meat.

Many of the chemical compounds used in livestock production are quickly excreted while others are not metabolized or excreted readily; it is the latter which present the greatest risk to public health. In some cases while they may not appear in the flesh they may be concentrated in certain organs, for example, the liver and kidney. Much depends on how they are used at the agricultural level. They may be applied correctly or wrongly and the wholesomeness of the meat product is influenced accordingly—for better or worse. While many are recognized to be simple and safe compounds others are of more complex structure and are known to be toxic to higher as well as lower forms of life. Some have not been used long enough for their safety or hazard to be assessed.

Some chemicals possess a high biological potency when used in animals, so much so that a few parts per million can produce physiological, pathological, pharmacological and/or toxicological change in the animal and its organs. For example, the implantation of the hormone hexoestrol in female cattle and sheep produces marked anatomical changes—enlarged pelvic area with distortion of the croup region and udder, etc. It is to the credit of those countries which banned the use of oestrogens in livestock production because of their possible carcinogenetic effect in human beings. Another possible effect of the use of antibiotics in animals immediately prior to slaughter is that signs of disease may be masked. With their present widespread use in those countries which either do not possess adequate legislation for their control or, possessing it, do not implement it, that serious diseases such as anthrax and salmonellosis may be suppressed is a real possibility. This indeed, is known to have occurred. It goes without saying, therefore, that ante-mortem examination of stock before slaughter becomes an even more essential procedure today, especially in the case of " casualty or emergency-slaughter " animals. The occurrence of resistant bacteria not only in animals but also in human beings as a result of the prophylactic use of antibiotics, is a further reason for recommending their use to be restricted to curative purposes.

Antibiotics, hormones, tranquillizers, arsenicals and heavy metals such as copper have been used as feed supplements and therapeutic agents to increase feed efficiency and carcase gain mainly in pigs and poultry. Chloramphenicol because of its toxicity and penicillin because of its tendency to cause allergy should not be tolerated in meat products.

In the assessment of the chemical residue problem the economic benefits in livestock production must be weighed against the stated real and potential hazards to public health. Only the least toxic compounds should be used, for example, the tetracyclines as antibiotics, these being also more

SHEEP

SC 6958

MEAT INSPECTION

OWNER	CLASS		Result of Inspection			Abscesses	Actinomycosis	Anaemia	Bruising, Localised	Bruising, Extensive	Cirrhosis	Colour, Abnormal	Congestion	Contamination	Cysts	Decomposition	Emaciation, Path.	Enteritis	Fascioliasis	Fatty Changes	Fever	Fibrosis
	Sheep	Lambs	P	S W	S P																	
Carried forward																						
TOTALS																						

susceptible to heat, disintegrating considerably at over 158° F. All these compounds should be used scientifically and be under proper legislative control, if indeed they have to be used at all.

It could be argued that since antibiotics and other substances currently employed in agriculture are designed to reduce a potentially pathogenic bacterial environment with which the animals have to contend, it would be much more sensible, more efficient and cheaper to deal with this outside rather than inside the animals. The real answer then would appear to lie with good animal husbandry in the form of sound breeding, feeding and a high standard of hygiene which will take care of the bacterial environment. As far as pesticides and herbicides are concerned there are those who contend that biological control would be more effective.

7. THE ROLE OF THE ABATTOIR IN INVESTIGATION AND CONTROL OF ANIMAL DISEASE

The primary function of meat inspection is to protect the public health but it has also an additional duty economically in that there must be no unnecessary condemnation of a valuable commodity. In recent years, however, more attention has been paid to another important aspect of

DEPARTMENT Date Inspector: 1249

																						OFFAL		PART SEIZED					REMARKS Livers		
Jaundice	Leukaemia	Lymphadenitis	Melanosis	Necrosis	Neoplasms	Odour, Abnormal	Oedema	Pigmentation	Pyaemia	Septicaemia	S. Arthritis	S. Mastitis	S. Metritis	S. Pericarditis	S. Peritonitis	S. Pleurisy	S. Pneumonia	Strongylosis	Tetanus	Toxaemia	Uraemia	Heads	Lungs	Hearts	Plucks	Stomachs	Intestines	Spleens	W	P	Kidneys

meat inspection—that of providing statistics which can be utilized for animal disease control purposes.

Many surveys have been carried out to determine the incidence of animal disease in different countries. Some of these have been related to random selections of farms while others have included meat inspection statistics. Not all disease incidences can be obtained from a study of the position on selected farms. Indeed the abattoir is the only place where certain conditions can be evaluated but as yet not enough use is being made of this valuable source of disease information, not only from a disease control point of view but also from the research standpoint. The United States Department of Agriculture's Consumer and Marketing Service publishes excellent " Summaries of Activities, Meat Inspection Division " which give details of the animals examined ante-mortem and post-mortem together with figures on reasons for rejection of the live animals and carcases and offal. All this provides much valuable information on the wide scale for which this very efficient meat inspection service is responsible. A picture is thus gained of the main reasons for condemnation of meat and offal and an opportunity afforded for investigation and possible control.

In Great Britain as yet no national meat inspection records are available. Only limited information is available from the annual records of city

CITY OF BELFAST MEAT PLANT

Form A.

Meat Inspection — Fatstock *Month ending*........................

	Cows	Heifers	Steers	Bulls	Calves	Sheep	Lambs	Goats	Pigs
Total Slaughter									
Tuberculosis						§§§§§§§	§§§§§§§	§§§§§§§	
C. Bovis						§§§§§§§	§§§§§§§	§§§§§§§	§§§§§§§
Fascioliasis									§§§§§§§
Cirr. Livers (Wt.)									§§§§§§§

CARCASE MEAT CONDEMNATIONS — HOME AND EXPORT

Class of Animal	Number of carcases		Weight Meat condemned	Reason for Condemnation	Weight Offal condemned (including Fluke)
	S.W.	S.P.			
Cows					
Heifers					
Steers					
Bulls					
Calves					
Sheep and Lambs					
Pigs					
Goats					
Totals					

General Remarks:

Signed.. Date.....................................

Do not include anything from Form B (Emergency Slaughter) on this form.

Offal Condemnations—CATTLE Date / /6 No 1601

SC 6454

Owner	Class*					Livers*		Lungs	Hearts	Reasons for Seizure					Weight (lb.)	Inspector
	C	H	S	B	Ca	W	P			Abscesses	Con-gestion	Fatty Changes	Fluke	Other Diseases		
TOTALS																

medical officers of health and from those abattoirs under the control of the Ministry of Agriculture. Most of these provide only an indication of how many tons of meat and offal were rejected as unfit for human consumption and the percentage of carcases totally or partially condemned for (*a*) tuberculosis and (*b*) diseases other than tuberculosis.

In Northern Ireland following an animal disease survey carried out on a random selection of 600 farms in 1954-55 and a close study of detailed records elaborated for 18 abattoirs, a national meat inspection recording system has been devised for the whole country. Forms have been made out for use by each abattoir from which a weekly return is made, all the resulting data being analysed at Ministry of Agriculture's headquarters in Belfast.

To be effective meat inspection records must commence with an adequate form which is easily completed by the meat inspector. The type of this varies in different countries and for differing circumstances depending on the type of abattoir, technique of inspection and slaughter etc. Line systems of slaughter demand a somewhat different system of recording from traditional booth systems. Examples of forms presently used in the City of Belfast Municipal Abattoir are given on pp. 534-537. It will be necessary to modify these once the city moves into its new meat plant which will be operated with modern line systems of slaughter.

From well-devised and standardized records used at individual abattoirs and regular returns to a central authority a clear picture of animal disease incidence as revealed at postmortem inspection can be obtained. Depending on the format of the individual records each abattoir can provide more detailed information on the disease picture in the livestock passing through it.

Examples of the type of information gained are seen in the following tables.

Fascioliasis or Liver Fluke

No significant reduction in the incidence of liver fluke infestation can be recorded for 1963, during which some 400 tons of cattle and sheep liver were condemned in Northern Ireland because of this menace; of this Belfast contributed about 94½ tons. The position of Belfast regarding incidence may be compared with other abattoirs (see below). Liver fluke, besides being the cause of much loss of edible liver, is also responsible for loss of condition, milk, wool and even progeny as well as death in its acute and subacute forms.

LIVER FLUKE IN CATTLE (NORTHERN IRELAND) 1963

Abattoir	*Total kill*	*Affected with fluke*	*Percentage*
Enniskillen	5,629	5,119	90·9
Lurgan	13,923	11,272	81·0
Strabane	2,149	1,716	79·9
Larne	3,830	3,036	79·3
Dungannon	8,981	6,997	77·9
Downpatrick	4,213	3,154	74·9
Ballymena Export	13,604	9,689	71·2
Coleraine	4,193	2,863	68·3
Dunloy	3,143	2,056	65·4
Belfast	63,091	38,420	60·9
Londonderry	8,327	4,911	59·0
Bangor	3,976	1,902	47·8
Ballymena	10,520	4,200	39·9
Newry	4,754	1,672	35·2
Newtownards	4,467	1,419	31·8
Lisburn 5/2	72	21	29·2
Banbridge	2,943	675	22·9
Lisburn 5/1	910	207	22·7
Totals	158,725	99,329	62·6

Bovine Cysticercosis

This disease is showing a gradual increase, not only at Belfast abattoir but also in Northern Ireland as a whole, a situation which can only be viewed with alarm. The percentage of cases detected at Belfast Abattoir during 1963 was 4·0 per cent., the average for the Province being 2·8 per cent compared with 2·5 per cent. in 1962. Besides being of great importance from a public health point of view in that, if infected meat is eaten raw or improperly cooked, it gives rise to taeniasis in human beings, the disease is also important economically, resulting in an average loss of £15-20 to the meat trade for each carcase which is subjected to refrigeration.

C. bovis was seen in generalized form in only two cases in Belfast in 1963.

BOVINE CYSTICERCOSIS (NORTHERN IRELAND) 1963

Abattoir	*Total kill*	*Cases of C. Bovis*	*Percentage*
Enniskillen	5,629	563	10·0
Newry	4,754	273	5·7
Belfast	63,091	2,505	4·0
Bangor	3,976	133	3·3
Ballymena Export	13,604	365	2·7
Downpatrick	4,213	109	2·6
Coleraine	4,193	88	2·1
Strabane	2,149	42	2·0
Larne	3,830	47	1·2
Dungannon	8,981	80	0·9
Londonderry	8,327	68	0·8
Banbridge	2,943	24	0·8
Lurgan	13,923	75	0·5
Newtownards	4,467	17	0·4
Dunloy	3,143	13	0·4
Ballymena	10,520	43	0·4
Lisburn 5/1/1	910	1	0·1
Lisburn 5/2	72	—	—
Totals	158,725	4,446	2·8

Tuberculosis

In pigs the extent of tuberculosis was 0·65 per cent. in pigs slaughtered in the municipal abattoir, the average for the Province (Local Authority abattoirs only) being 0·69 per cent. This condition in pigs was not encountered at 13 of the abattoirs making records, only 5 reporting the disease in 1963.

TUBERCULOSIS IN CATTLE (NORTHERN IRELAND) 1963

Abattoir	*Total kill*	*No. Affected*	*Percentage*
Ballymena Export	13,604	349	2·57
Newry	4,754	20	0·42
Downpatrick	4,213	12	0·28
Belfast	63,091	134	0·21
Dungannon	8,981	9	0·10
Larne	3,830	4	0·10
Bangor	3,976	4	0·10
Strabane	2,149	2	0·09
Enniskillen	5,629	4	0·07
Coleraine	4,193	3	0·07
Londonderry	8,327	5	0·06
Ballymena	10,520	5	0·05
Lurgan	13,923	6	0·04
Banbridge	2,943	1	0·03
Dunloy	3,143	1	0·03
Lisburn 5/1	910	Nil	—
Lisburn 5/2	72	Nil	—
Newtownards	4,467	Nil	—
Totals	158,725	559	0·35

It is, however, one matter to record this useful information, but quite another to make the fullest use of it. Certainly the pathological material available in abattoirs should be more fully utilized by veterinary research workers. But one important aspect of all this recording has not yet been exploited, namely the transmission back to the livestock producer of the disease data encountered in his animals at slaughter. This could be done direct for the more common diseases or via the owner's veterinary surgeon, especially where casualty animals sent to the abattoir with a veterinary surgeon's certificate are involved.

In Northern Ireland (where, for example, liver fluke is a major problem with an overall incidence of above 62 per cent. of cattle harbouring *Fasciola hepatica* and some 22 per cent of sheep), this could prove a major contribution to animal disease control by making tangible to the farmer those diseases which are not suspected by him to occur in his animals. Already a start has been made in a limited way in this direction.

It is an innovation, however, which requires good farm animal identification and can be more easily achieved where animals are consigned direct to abattoirs as is done for example through a meat marketing board. The current system of marketing certain livestock in the United Kingdom, viz.

REASONS FOR TOTAL CONDEMNATION OF CARCASES—CATTLE
(18 Local Authority Abattoirs in N. Ireland) 1955

Reason for Condemnation	*Number of Carcases*	*Per cent. of Total Seizures*	*Weight of Carcase Heat Condemned* (lb.)	*Per cent. of Total Condem-nations*
1. Specific infectious diseases				
(1)* Tuberculosis, generalized	336	79·0	142,476	80·8
Tuberculous emaciation	12	2·8	4,617	2·6
2. Degenerative and dropsical conditions				
(2) Emaciation, pathological	18	4·2	5,192	2·9
(3) Oedema, generalized	9	2·1	3,704	2·1
(8) Emaciation	4	0·9	1,332	0·8
Gangrene	1	0·2	390	0·2
3. Septic conditions				
(4) Septicaemia	7	1·6	2,785	1·6
Peritonitis, acute diffuse septic	3	0·7	1,585	0·9
Pericarditis, acute septic	3	0·7	1,265	0·7
Mastitis, acute septic	2	0·5	938	0·5
Metritis, acute septic	1	0·2	600	0·3
Pneumonia, acute septic	1	0·2	336	0·2
4. Inflammatory conditions				
(7) Peritonitis and pleurisy	5	1·2	2,060	1·2
Peritonitis	2	0·5	666	0·4
5. Injuries				
(6) Bruising, extensive and severe	6	1·4	1,858	1·1
6. Neoplasms	1	0·2	340	0·2
7. Miscellaneous				
(5) Fever	6	1·4	3,096	1·8
Leukaemia	3	0·7	1,422	0·8
Abnormal odour	1	0·2	448	0·3
Moribund and ill-bled	1	0·2	440	0·2
Bleeding, imperfect	1	0·2	302	0·2
Immaturity	1	0·2	56	0·03
Others	1	0·2	416	0·2
Totals	425		176,324	
Per cent. of total kill (56,604)	0·8			

* Figures in brackets refer to order of importance of individual conditions.

via auction marts, makes for difficulty. When a satisfactory and cheap form of farm animal identification is devised a real contribution to animal disease detection and control will be brought home to the farmer, and with subsequent investigational and advisory work a significant reduction in losses achieved.

CHAPTER XII

THE INSPECTION OF RABBITS AND HARES

Prior to the introduction of myxomatosis into Britain in 1953 large quantities of wild rabbits were killed annually in the British Isles and sent to towns and city markets. The demand in Britain for rabbits is now met almost entirely by imported supplies.

Imported Rabbits. Supplies of imported rabbits are obtained from Australia and Ireland, these arriving in flat wooden crates containing twenty-four unskinned or thirty skinned rabbits, the weight of the rabbits being approximately 60 lb. The supply of rabbits from New Zealand has ceased since that country has made it illegal to sell or export rabbit carcases or skins.

In Australia trapping begins in January and extends to the commencement of the breeding season in September. The rabbits are trapped during the night, removed from the traps immediately or early in the morning, killed by dislocation of the neck, paunched, and collected by a well organized system which facilitates delivery to chilling stores and then to central depots for grading and packing. Rabbits exported to Britain are unskinned and placed gut to gut, a procedure which combines efficient protection of the exposed flesh with a high rate of cooling. The temperature during freezing and storing before shipment is maintained at 10° F. or lower, while during the voyage from Australia to Britain, which occupies 5 to 8 weeks, the temperature of the holds is maintained at 14° F. As the demand for rabbits in Britain is mainly confined to the cold season the bulk of the Australian pack arrives in August or September, the period between the killing of the rabbits in Australia and their marketing in Britain being usually 4 to 5 months.

Australian rabbits are examined and graded under the supervision of Government Inspectors, this being carried out at the request of the packers and exporters. The various grades include classes which range from plump well-conditioned rabbits weighing 2½ lb. or over, down to animals of 1½ lb. weight.

Estimation of Age in Rabbits. In the young rabbit the ear is easily torn and bent, while the claws are smooth and sharp and break easily if bent sideways. If the jaws of the young rabbit are pressed together with the thumb and forefinger they break easily, and other signs of youth are the large knee joints, a short stumpy neck, soft brown fur and a sharp pointed nose. In the old rabbit the ears are dry and tough, the teeth long, the claws blunt and ragged, and the fur coarse and grey in colour.

Freshness in rabbits is manifested by a moist, bluish sheen of the flesh after skinning, and the carcase should have a sweet smell, be firm and cool to the touch, and the abdominal fat firm and white.

Causes of Condemnation

The bluebottle or blowfly, of which *Calliphora vomitoria* and *C. erythrocephala* are common examples, finds the flesh of the rabbit a favourable location for the deposition of ova, and maggots of appreciable size may develop from these in a few hours ; most condemnations of rabbits during warm weather are due to this cause. Decomposition is also a common cause of condemnation in warm weather ; the eyes appear dull, the fur is easily pulled from the skin, the interior of the rabbit is sticky and slimy, the liver a dirty brown colour, but the most useful guide is the presence of an offensive odour. Rabbits which have been imported frozen decompose more rapidly on thawing than do home-killed rabbits.

Mould formation is not uncommon in cold-stored rabbits and is due to errors in refrigeration on board ship. The condition appears as white spots, particularly on surfaces which have been originally frozen then defrosted and finally re-frozen, the mould developing rapidly and rendering the carcase quite unfit for food in a few days. Slight mouldiness may be removed by wiping, though severely affected carcases must be condemned. The English rabbit does not develop mould but undergoes decomposition before mould develops. Frozen rabbits may at times possess a musty odour which only becomes apparent after thawing, and such carcases must be condemned.

Yellow Coloration of Fat in Imported Rabbits. The fatty tissues of all the food animals eventually undergo certain deleterious changes when exposed to the atmosphere, chief of these changes being rancidity. The fat of rabbits may become rancid during storage at temperatures below freezing, but it may also undergo a change in colour, the exposed surfaces becoming light yellow to dark orange. The yellowing of the fat of rabbits in cold storage is a chemical reaction dependent on the temperature and duration of storage, and sufficient change in colour to affect the commercial value of rabbits will occur in 4 months at a temperature of 13° F., though no yellowing should take place for 6 or 7 months if the rabbits are stored at 7° F. The colour change is confined to the surface of the fat, and is usually associated with a sharp odour which resembles that of linseed oil and may also extend to the adjacent flesh ; the condition may be present without any accompanying mould or bacterial growth.

Yellowing of imported rabbits is unsightly and therefore renders the carcases unmarketable ; the British importers of Australian rabbits state that not less than 70 per cent. of crates contain affected animals, and that the annual losses amount to at least 5 per cent. of the total imports.

TUBERCULOSIS. This affection is rare in wild rabbits. The " spotted " liver commonly encountered in wild rabbits is in nearly every case due to coccidiosis.

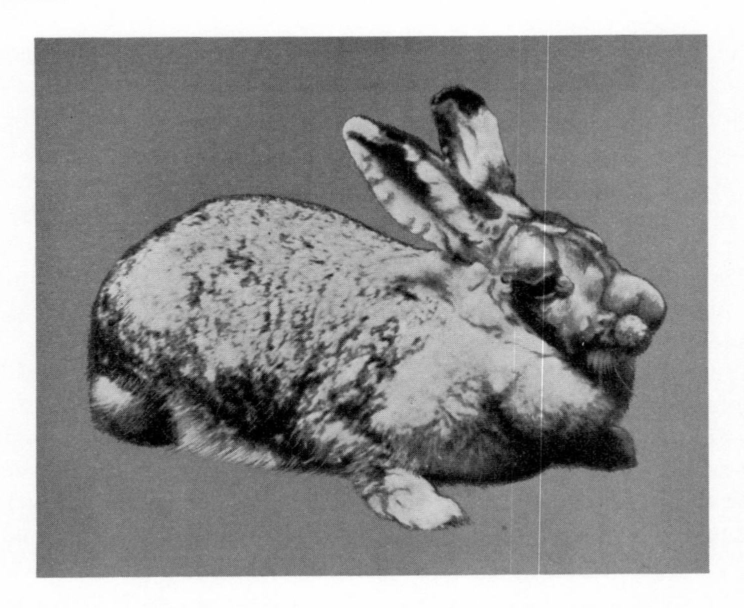

Fig. 224.—Rabbit affected with myxomatosis. There are extensive swellings involving the eyelids, nose and ears. (State Veterinary Journal.)

VENEREAL INFECTION OF THE RABBIT. Great prejudice still exists in the minds of many people against rabbit's flesh, largely due to the impression that rabbits suffer from syphilis. This is entirely erroneous for although a venereal infection known as rabbit syphilis does occur, and is caused by a spirochaete *Treponema cuniculi*, it is a local affection which produces moist scaly crusts on the vagina of the doe and prepuce of the buck and is not transmissible to man. In the well-nourished rabbit removal of the affected portions is all that is necessary before releasing the carcase for food.

MYXOMATOSIS. This disease has become widespread throughout Britain since being first introduced in October 1953 and is caused by a virus infection spreading rapidly under favourable conditions and causing a high mortality. The symptoms of the disease are characteristic, taking the form of a clear watery discharge from the eyes, the discharge then becoming thick and the eyelids encrusted with dry matter. Fleshy tumours develop in various parts of the body and cause swellings, noticeably at the base of the ears, on the nose, beneath the chin and also around the anus and genital organs. The period from infection to death is about 11 to 18 days.

Though no case of transmission of myxomatosis to man has been recorded, all carcases of rabbits and hares affected with this disease should be regarded as unfit for human consumption.

FIG. 225.—Rabbit affected with *Multiceps serialis* cysts which can be seen on the neck, shoulder and right buttock. The skinned carcase is shown in Fig. 158. (Crown copyright.)

COCCIDIOSIS. Coccidia may affect the intestines or liver of rabbits, *Eimeria perforans* affecting the intestine and *Eimeria stiedae* affecting the liver. In the well-nourished rabbit the liver alone need be condemned and the carcase passed for food.

MULTICEPS SERIALIS. The cystic stage of *Taenia serialis* of the dog is commonly encountered in the rabbit, cysts being found in the connective tissue of the lumbar muscles, muscles of the hind legs, and occasionally at the angle of the jaw. If only one or two cysts are present in the musculature and the rabbit is well-nourished the affected portions may be removed and the carcase passed for food.

CYSTICERCUS PISIFORMIS. The cystic stage of *Taenia pisiformis* of the dog (Fig. 157) is encountered in the peritoneal cavity of the rabbit, especially on the mesentery, the cysts being up to the size of a pea and filled with a clear fluid. Their presence rarely has any deleterious effect on the carcase.

Rabbits require condemnation if they are undrawn, i.e. still contain the gastro-intestinal and genito-urinary tracts. Emaciated rabbits must also be condemned, but a more generous judgment may be given in the case of localized abscesses due to abrasions, or in the case of bruises or gunshot wounds, and if these are localized it is sufficient to condemn the affected parts.

Hares

These possess an annual close season from 1st March to 31st July, both dates being inclusive. The young wild hare is termed a leveret and may be recognized by the narrow cleft in the lip, the presence of a small knob under the first joint of the fore-foot, and the fact that the claws can be easily cracked. A freshly killed hare is stiff and white, whereas a supple body and black flesh are indications of staleness.

Venison is the flesh of any kind of deer, and in both hares and venison the usual cause of condemnation is advanced decomposition.

CHAPTER XIII

THE INSPECTION OF POULTRY

THE EXAMINATION OF POULTRY.

DISEASES OF POULTRY.

Tuberculosis—Fowl Pox—Fowl Cholera—Fowl Pest—Diseases associated with Salmonella group of Bacteria—Coccidiosis—Blackhead—Gape Worm Infestation—External Parasites—Emaciation—Avian Leucosis—Tumours.

THE INSPECTION OF EGGS.

The term poultry applies to live or dressed domestic birds which have been bred and reared for edible purposes, and in its widest sense includes chickens, ducks, geese, guinea-fowls, pea-fowls, pigeons and turkeys. Of these the domestic fowl, particularly the old hen, is most likely to require the attention of the inspector.

Definitions

Milk-fed chickens, or petits poussins, are chickens 8 to 10 weeks old, about $1\frac{1}{2}$ lb. in weight, which have been fattened rapidly on a special diet of ground foodstuffs mixed with warm fat and milk. These chickens are a delicacy on the British market, which is largely supplied from France and Belgium.

A broiler is a young male or female chicken about $3\frac{1}{2}$ lb. in weight and 10 to 11 weeks of age. A cockerel is a male chicken too mature to be classed as spring chicken but not mature enough for the roaster class. A roaster is a young chicken weighing about 6 lb. and up to 8 months old. A capon is a male fowl from which the testicles have been removed surgically, and is characterized by the small head and the presence of undeveloped spurs, comb and wattles ; these birds are marketed at 7 to 8 months old and then weigh up to 10 lb. Caponizing, which encourages early fattening and the production of tender flesh, is usually carried out when the bird is 10 weeks old, though the use of an electric cauterizing needle, which is inserted into the testicle through an incision in the lumbar muscles, now enables the operation to be performed at 6 weeks and with less impairment to bodily condition. Boiling fowls consist of hens, having completed at least one laying season, i.e., approximately 18 months or more of age, and these should preferably be sent alive to the market, being in demand for poultry supplies on sea voyages and for slaughter for Jewish consumption.

Young hens may be recognized by the pliability of the posterior end of the breast bone which can readily be bent by the fingers, whereas in old birds it is hard and resistant ; pliability of the beak is often recommended as an indication of youth, but this is erroneous, for the beak of even young birds should be firm and hard, and softness and pliability are suggestive of rickets. The young bird has a smooth thin comb, smooth glistening feet and smooth legs, while in the old bird the feet are horny and the legs are rough.

Killing of Poultry

The wholesomeness of dead poultry and the colour, especially in the region of the crop, are adversely affected by the presence of food in the digestive tract before killing. The empty intestine is very resistant to the passage of bacteria from intestine to peritoneum, and starving of fowls for 24 hours before killing, together with an ample supply of water, ensures that the birds will have better keeping qualities and a more pleasant flavour.

Fowls may be killed by wringing the neck, by beheading, by sticking as in slaughter according to Jewish ritual, or by dislocation of the neck. The majority of fowls in Britain are slaughtered by the last method but are not bled, and when the head is dislocated the fowl is hung head downwards so that blood forms in a pocket between head and neck and unsightly external haemorrhage is thus avoided. Proper bleeding is not secured by this method and a better procedure is to suspend the bird by the feet, stun with a block of wood, attach a weighted blood cup into the upper mandible by means of a hook, and then sever the blood vessels of the neck. In large establishments poultry are stunned by electrical means, the stunner administering an electric shock at 90 volts for a period of half a second. When fowls are killed by cutting of the throat veins without pithing it is considered that a period of not less than $2\frac{1}{2}$ minutes should elapse between bleeding and scalding.

Bleeding of poultry vastly improves the appearance and whiteness of the flesh, and the flesh of unbled birds quickly loses its firmness, develops stale or other abnormal odours, and decomposition is more rapid ; the engorged small veins of the neck and the small haemorrhagic spots where the feathers have been removed from wings and thighs, together with a discoloured bluish-red or green coloured neck may all be associated with lack of proper bleeding. Bruising as a result of birds hitting sharp objects in their death struggles also reduces their quality.

During the process of cleaning poultry the peritoneum becomes heavily contaminated and the serous fluid forms an excellent medium for bacterial growth. Drawn birds will only keep for one day at 36° F. whereas undrawn birds will keep for 3-4 days, and some 56 per cent. of poultry dealt with in packing stations in Britain are dispatched without being eviscerated. When poultry are eviscerated hens are usually cooled before evisceration to minimize the spillage of liquid fat over operators and equipment. Fowls reared specifically for table purposes are eviscerated prior to cooling, and the market supply of pre-wrapped eviscerated birds is likely to increase until it constitutes the greater proportion of table birds.

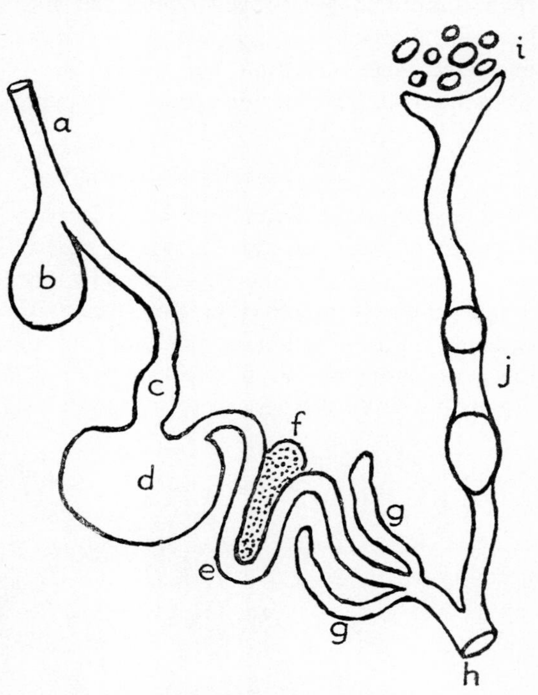

FIG. 226.—Digestive and reproductive systems of fowl: *a.* oesophagus; *b.* crop; *c.* proventriculus (glandular stomach); *d.* gizzard (muscular stomach); *e.* duodenum; *f.* pancreas; *g.* caeca; *h.* cloaca; *i.* ovary; *j.* oviduct containing two developing eggs.

FRESHNESS OF DEAD POULTRY

These have a light, bright, prominent eye and the feet should be moist and pliable. The flesh should give evenly when pressed with the finger, but as staleness develops the eyes become dark and sunken, the feet hard and stiff and the flesh loose and flabby. The flesh is darker in colour, often greenish in the region of the crop and vent, and an unpleasant odour becomes apparent. Greening of undrawn poultry is the result of biochemical activities of bacteria normally present in the intestines, particularly the caeca, and occurs in carcases where birds were inadequately starved before slaughter and inadequately cooled after plucking. As a result of bacterial metabolism hydrogen sulphide is produced and diffuses through the intestinal wall into the muscular tissue, where, in the presence of air, it combines with the pigments of blood and muscle to form a green pigment sulphaemoglobin. Greening around the vent is usually caused by intestinal contents which have been left in the rectum, but greening frequently develops as a patch on one side of the abdomen, usually the left side, for the tips of the caeca are nearest to the abdominal wall at this point.

COLD STORAGE OF POULTRY

Frozen poultry should be stored at an evenly maintained temperature not exceeding 15° F. Home-killed birds are not usually stored for longer than 3 months, but properly prepared and sound American poultry will keep for a period of 1 year without deterioration. Frozen poultry is only inspected with difficulty, but in the case of undrawn frozen birds it is recommended that an inspection be made by means of an abdominal "trier".

The Examination of Poultry

The routine examination of poultry which is exposed for sale is only carried out and, indeed, is only practicable in the wholesale markets of the larger cities, and is usually extended only to those birds which exhibit some obvious abnormality such as emaciation, tumours or oedema. The commonest affections of poultry encountered in routine inspection are emaciation, decomposition and oedema, and, of the internal organs, the liver most frequently shows abnormalities or lesions of disease.

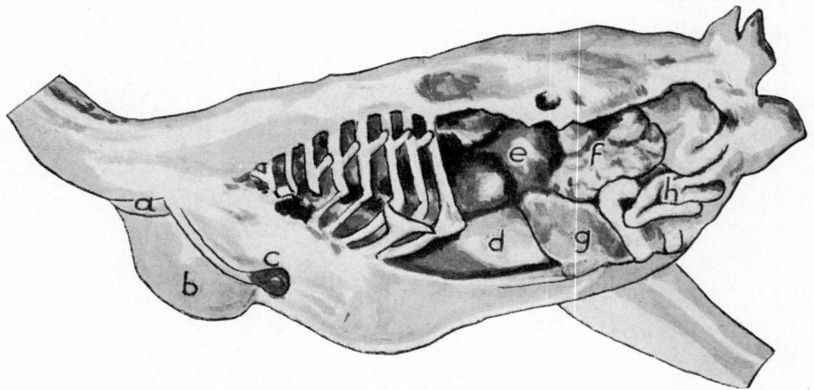

FIG. 227.—Dissection of left side of hen showing: *a*. oesophagus; *b*. crop; *c*. clavicle; *d*. liver; *e*. developing egg; *f*. oviduct; *g*. gizzard; *h*. duodenum. The anatomical relations of the abdominal viscera are of importance in the routine examination of undressed poultry.

Normally livers of fat poultry are soft and friable, and vary in colour from dark red to pale yellow or milkish-white depending on the character of the feed and the amount of fat the liver contains. The normal weight of the liver is about 2 oz., but an enlarged liver is present in many conditions, including tuberculosis and leucosis. In fatty change the liver is also enlarged and greasy, and it may be ruptured in early cases of tuberculosis, in pathological fatty change, or in fowl typhoid. In undrawn poultry this organ may be examined by the making of an abdominal incision large enough to permit of examination of the liver and other internal viscera, though too large an incision is to be avoided as it hastens putrefactive changes. In routine practice the incision is made on the left side, as a cut in the right flank may damage the gall bladder and contaminate the carcase with bile. In this examination the left leg is pulled back and an incision

FIG. 228.—Fowl affected with leucosis (" big liver disease "), showing great enlargement of liver. In this affection the spleen is also greatly enlarged and may be up to twenty times the normal size. (K. D. Downham.)

made parallel to the last rib and about 2 inches in length ; the incision is then enlarged by blunt dissection with the fingers until the liver can be satisfactorily examined. If the liver is free from disease and the bird otherwise normal the carcase may be passed for food ; if the liver is diseased the bird should be " drawn " and the other viscera examined, and if these are free from disease the carcase may be passed but the liver condemned,

Indication of disease in both liver and other viscera requires total condemnation.

Diseases of Poultry

TUBERCULOSIS

Avian tuberculosis was at one time a very common disease of poultry in Britain, but the sweeping changes in methods of poultry keeping, notably battery and deep litter systems together with disposal of laying stock at the end of the first or second laying year, have had a marked effect on the incidence of the disease, for pullets rarely become infected to such an extent that they disseminate widespread infection. Turkeys, guinea-fowls, pea-fowls, swans, and even pheasants under natural conditions if exposed to infection, are susceptible to the disease, whilst in captivity there are records of almost every type of bird becoming affected; out-breaks among ducks and geese, however, are relatively unusual. Avian tuberculosis in Britain is responsible for practically all of the cases of tuberculosis involving the submaxillary lymph nodes of the pig, and cases of tuberculous infection of bovines with the avian type of bacillus have also been recorded, the lesions being usually confined to the mesenteric or retro-pharyngeal lymph nodes, though generalization of the disease may occur.

Symptoms. Though avian tuberculosis is usually a slow insidious disease in which few symptoms are shown until the bird is over a year old, there is evidence that when poultry are reared on the deep litter method deaths do sometimes occur very rapidly in young birds. In some cases the bird becomes somnolent, unthrifty and emaciated, this latter change being particularly apparent in the pectoral muscles covering the sternum, and known to poultry keepers as " going light ". Loss of flesh, however, is by no means a constant symptom in tuberculous poultry, for very fat birds are sometimes found grossly infected, and rupture of the fatty and tuberculous liver or spleen is a cause of death of many birds. Anaemia also occurs, being manifested by pallor of the comb and wattles, and lameness may also be observed, this being unilateral and causing the bird to walk with a characteristic jerky gait. Intestinal tuberculosis also commonly occurs and is manifested in the live bird by a persistent diar-rhoea which contains large numbers of the infective micro-organism; infected faeces undoubtedly play the main part in the transference of the disease from bird to bird and from bird to cattle and pigs.

Lesions. It is a feature of tuberculosis in poultry that although the micro-organism can be recovered from tissues which exhibit no lesions, maeroscopic lesions are not likely to be evident in the organs until the later stages of the disease. On post-mortem examination the organ most frequently found diseased is the liver, which is affected in 90 per cent. of tuberculous fowls. Next in order of frequency is the spleen, affected in 74 per cent. of cases, the joints and bone marrow in 58 per cent., the intestines in 33 per cent. and the lungs in 17 per cent. of cases.

The rarity of pulmonary infection in fowls compared with the tuberculous process in cattle and pigs is noteworthy; nodules of the lungs and pleura of young chicks may be due to *Salmonella* infection (bacillary white diarrhoea) or to aspergillosis and are not likely to be confused with tuberculosis.

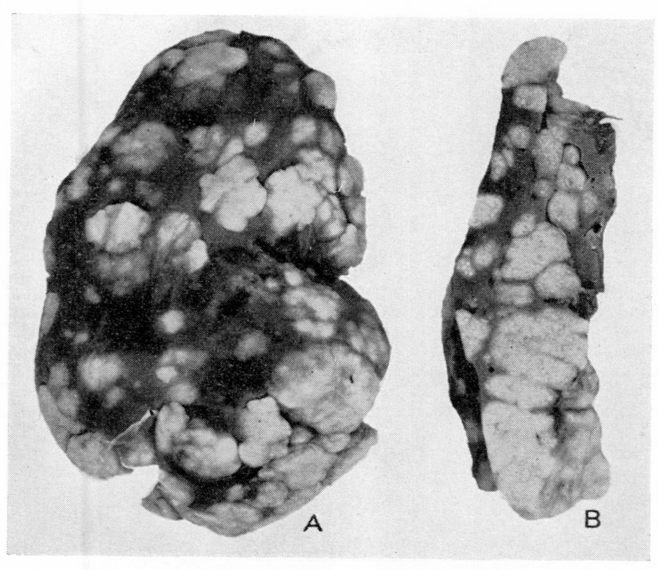

FIG. 229.—Tuberculous liver of fowl showing large, irregular caseous lesions which show a tendency to coalesce and can readily be enucleated from the liver tissue. A. Surface of liver; B. Cross-section.

LIVER. The liver lesions vary in size from a pinhead up to a walnut, and are yellow or yellowish-white in colour. The smaller nodules are not raised above the surface of the liver, but the larger ones may cause projecting nodes which are dense and difficult to cut, and on section show concentric ringing resembling agate or having the appearance of a polished surface of marble. Tuberculous lesions in the liver are sharply defined and can usually be readily enucleated, but they are not gritty on section, for calcification of avian lesions rarely occurs. In many cases the liver is markedly enlarged, though it may rupture with the production of a large abdominal blood clot and it is not uncommon to find the organ containing old blood clots indicative of a previous rupture of the parenchyma. Enlargement of the liver is also seen in leucosis, and in this affection the organ may at times show soft, grey areas of leukaemic infiltration, but these foci may be distinguished from tuberculosis by the fact that they are less sharply delimited from the healthy tissue.

SPLEEN. This organ, which in healthy birds is reddish-brown, rounded, and $\frac{3}{4}$ inch in diameter, is usually enlarged in avian tuberculosis, sometimes to the size of a hen's egg; the lesions are similar to those in the liver and are easily enucleated but usually protrude from the surface of the spleen.

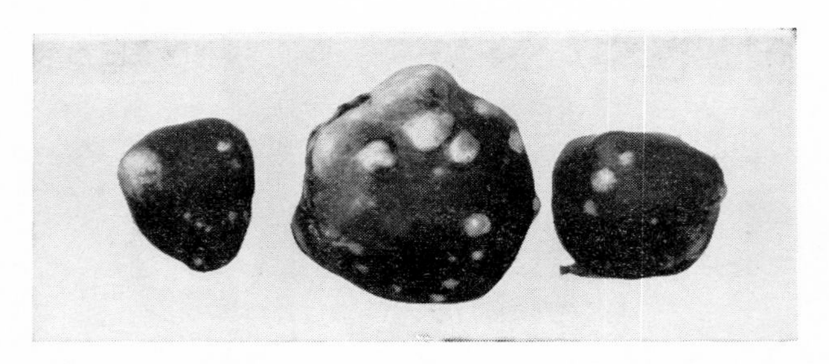

FIG. 230.—Fowl spleens showing lesions of tuberculosis. (W. H. Feldman.)

INTESTINES. The digestive tract is unquestionably the principal pathway by which infection enters the avian body, and the primary lesion may be looked for in the intestine. This primary lesion may not be

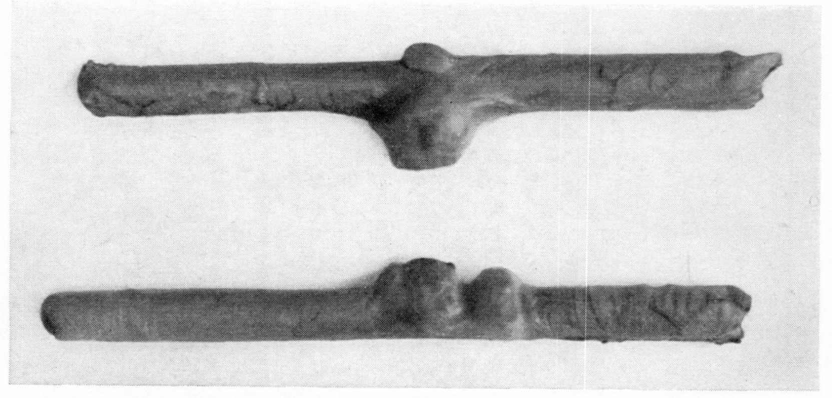

FIG. 231.—Intestine of fowl showing tuberculous lesions.

obvious, for tubercle bacilli may pass through the intestinal wall without causing macroscopic lesions, and as birds possess no lymph nodes (though they possess lymph plexuses), haematogenous dissemination readily occurs with spread to liver, spleen and bones. Though tuberculous lesions may arise in any part of the intestine, the commonest location is at the junction of the intestine and caeca. Nodules, varying in size from a millet seed to a golf ball or larger, are evident beneath the serous coat of the intestines, the larger lesions being brownish-yellow in colour and projecting outwards from the intestinal wall, but examination of these shows that the process commences as an ulcer, the margins of which have a rolled or rounded appearance, on the mucous membrane of the intestine; this ulcer becomes deep and pocket-like and filled with a caseous material from which numerous bacilli are discharged intermittently but persistently into the lumen of the gut. Large tuberculous nodules in the wall of the intestine may occlude the lumen of the gut, and fibrinous adhesions may be seen between several loops of intestine. Tuberculous lesions involving the intestinal wall may be confused with *E. coli* granulomata (Fig. 235),

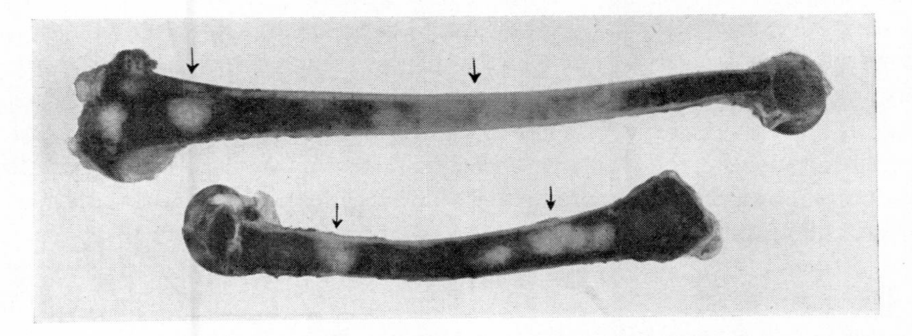

FIG. 232.—Tuberculosis of tibia (above) and femur of fowl. The bones have been split and the caseous lesions in the medullary cavity and spongy tissue of the epiphyses are indicated by arrows.

but the tuberculous lesions are easily enucleated from surrounding normal tissue and are invariably associated with tuberculous lesions in the liver and spleen. In *E. coli* granulomata infection the lesions are usually encapsulated and are found chiefly in the caeca and adjacent parts of the intestine, less commonly scattered throughout the intestines, and only very rarely in the liver and spleen. In leucosis nodules may also be found in the lower part of the intestine but they are of a soft consistency.

BONE MARROW AND JOINTS. It is possible that the bone marrow is the seat of tuberculous lesions as frequently as the liver, for histological examination of the bones shows tuberculous changes to be much commoner than can be detected macroscopically, and some authorities have demonstrated tuberculous lesions of bone in up to 95 per cent. of tuberculous fowls. The long tubular bones, particularly the femur and tibia, are the most frequently affected, and the majority of tuberculous fowls show bone lesions, even in relatively early cases of the disease. The lesions are frequently evident as light-coloured areas when the bone is examined externally, while on splitting the bone the medullary cavity is seen to contain caseous foci, white or yellow in colour, which are up to the size of a pea and contrast markedly with the soft brownish-red bone marrow. Lesions in the marrow of the ribs can often be seen if the tissues are held in front of a strong light.

JUDGMENT OF TUBERCULOSIS IN POULTRY. The absence of lymph nodes in poultry permits the passage of tubercle bacilli directly from the lymphatics into the systemic circulation, and early and widespread dissemination of bacilli may therefore occur even when lesions are few and apparently insignificant. On the other hand, the fact that tuberculosis caused by the avian type of bacillus has only been recorded in human beings on very rare occasions indicates the low pathogenicity of this type of bacillus for man. In the past the judgment of poultry affected with tuberculosis was governed by the extent of the affection and the nutritional condition of the carcase, but in view of the fact that there is the strongest argument for the complete eradication of tuberculosis from the pig population, the vast majority of such cases in Britain and many other countries being now due to the avian type bacillus, and in view also of the fact that the annual production of poultry for table purposes has increased so markedly in recent years and supplies are more than ample, there would appear to be justification for the condemnation of any poultry found affected with tuberculosis irrespective of the nutritional condition of the carcase or the extent or disposition of the tuberculous lesions. United States regulations prescribe that carcases of poultry affected with tuberculosis shall be condemned.

FOWL POX

This is caused by a filtrable virus, and occurs in one of three types, or in combination:

1. Skin Type. 2. Mouth Type. 3. Oculo-nasal Type.

The first form is characterized by wart-like nodules on the comb, wattles, eyelids and around the beak, and these lesions are found occasionally on the skin of the body, particularly the legs. Nodules, which at first are small and yellowish and later assume a cauliflower-like appearance, become darker in colour and are eventually shed, leaving a scab or scar.

Lesions in the mouth consist of a tough greyish-yellow diphtheritic membrane covering the floor of the mouth, and sometimes involving the tongue or extending backwards into the gullet. The oculo-nasal type of the disease closely simulates contagious catarrh and, in the absence of either of the two previously described types, cannot be distinguished clinically from this disease. There is considerable systemic disturbance in types 2 and 3, so that affected carcases may be sufficiently fevered to justify condemnation, but fowl pox is not communicable to man, and birds which are slightly affected, in good bodily condition and properly bled, may be passed for food purposes after removal of the affected parts.

FIG. 233.—Fowl pox, skin type, showing nodules on comb, wattles and edges of mouth. (J. E. Wilson.)

FOWL CHOLERA

This is a highly contagious, septicaemic disease of fowls, geese, ducks and turkeys caused by *Pasteurella multocida*.

It is relatively uncommon in home-bred poultry, although serious epidemics occur from time to time, and disastrous outbreaks have occurred in imported stock, particularly geese. There may be a reddening and congestion of the skin over the breast and abdomen of birds dying of the peracute disease, birds being usually in good condition and often in lay. Post-mortem examination reveals an extensive pneumonia with marked petechial haemorrhages in the epicardium, while the internal organs are intensely congested, and the liver, which is very friable, frequently exhibits minute areas of necrosis. In other cases there may be evidence of a severe haemorrhagic enteritis.

In less acute cases lesions are not so striking, and in these and in the more chronic cases loss of condition and abscess formation in the wattles is commonly noted. Carcases of affected birds, though not dangerous to man, are unfit for food and should be condemned.

Fowl Pest

The term fowl pest includes the diseases known as fowl plague and Newcastle disease, both being virus infections and responsible for rapid and heavy mortality. Extensive outbreaks of fowl pest, probably of foreign origin, occurred in Britain in 1947 and succeeding years, for poultry killed while affected with the disease or in the incubative stage may remain infective, the virus surviving in the skin of carcases stored at 34° to 36° F. for 96 days and in bone marrow for 134 days. In carcases stored at 4° F. the virus has been known to persist for 308 days. Fowl plague may affect domestic fowls, turkeys, geese, ducks, and guinea-fowls, the period of incubation varying from 2 to 7 days, and birds affected with the acute form are frequently found dead without exhibiting previous symptoms. Affected birds refuse food, are generally dejected and listless, and in some cases there is a discharge from the eyes and nostrils. Newcastle disease naturally affects the common fowl and may be transmitted to pigeons, ducks and geese ; the period of incubation is from 5 to 7 days, and though affected birds refuse food, they drink frequently and assume a sleepy posture with eyes half or fully closed. The wings and legs often become paralysed, but a characteristic symptom is a long gasping inhalation through the half-open mouth, and this is accompanied by gurgling and a frothy exudate from the point of the beak.

Lesions in affected birds take the form of collections of mucus in the nasal and buccal cavities, and the most persistent and typical lesion is the presence of petechial haemorrhages on the lining membrane of the proventriculus. The skin of the abdomen and thorax is often congested and discoloured, and carcases exhibiting such lesions indicative of high fever should be condemned. Fowl pest is, however, non-transmissible to man and in-contact birds may be salvaged for human food.

Diseases of Poultry Associated with the Salmonella Group of Bacteria

Poultry are playing an increasingly important rôle as a source of human salmonellosis and a number of diseases of fowls are caused by organisms of the salmonella group. In the United States poultry are regarded as the largest natural reservoir of salmonella organisms.

Within recent years salmonella infections in young chicks caused by organisms other than *S. pullorum* or *S. gallinarum*, have become more common, and *S. thompson*, a not uncommon cause of food poisoning in man, has been frequently implicated in these infections. Fowls may also acquire infection with *S. enteritidis* or *S. typhi-murium* (the salmonellae most commonly associated with food poisoning in Britain) by consumption of poultry food contaminated with the excreta of rats and mice, and infection with *S. enteritidis* may also occur in poultry by ingestion of certain rat poisons. Such salmonella infections may be responsible for a high mortality in chicks, while survivors may become symptomless carriers and thus constitute a danger to other poultry and to man.

Infection with *S. enteritidis* and *S. typhi-murium* is less common in the hen than in the duck, and in the latter bird frequently assumes an epidemic form. Eggs laid by infected ducks may contain virulent organisms of these types, for in some cases the ovaries are affected, but the chief method by which the duck egg becomes infected is contamination of the shell by faecal matter containing the micro-organisms during the passing of the egg through the cloaca. Bacterial penetration through the shell may also occur during storage or incubation, but even when this does not take place the contaminated shell is a possible source of human food poisoning if eggs are used in a raw state or when they are manufactured into dried egg powder. The greatest danger to man is, however, the stale infected egg which has been laid away from the nest and has been incubated on damp ground in the sun, for if consumed raw or lightly boiled it may contain large numbers of virulent organisms. Though hen eggs in shell form are but a minor cause of human food poisoning and may be largely disregarded as a vehicle for the transmission of disease, in Germany 50 million duck eggs were consumed annually and between 1932 and 1937 were responsible for a yearly average of 29 outbreaks of food poisoning. Legislation is now in force in Western Germany requiring duck eggs to be stamped with the words "Entenei—8 Minuten kochen" (duck eggs—cook for 8 minutes) before they may be offered for sale. In the German Democratic Republic the sale of duck eggs for human consumption has been forbidden since 1953.

Salmonella organisms in eggs are destroyed if the egg is hard boiled, and consumers should boil duck eggs 10 to 15 minutes before the shell is broken. Carcases of birds known or suspected to be infected with salmonella bacteria should not be passed for food, for if the flesh is incompletely cooked it may be the cause of food poisoning in human beings.

Coccidiosis

Coccidiosis is an important disease of poultry, and in the United States is responsible for a loss to stock owners of 5 million dollars yearly. It is recognized in two forms: Caecal coccidiosis caused by *Eimeria tenella*

(Plate IV, Fig. 180) and involving the caeca, and intestinal coccidiosis, caused by *Eimeria necatrix* and other species of *Eimeria*.

Caecal coccidiosis is of little importance in poultry inspection, as it is usually confined to chicks. Where the affection is found in older birds acute cases show distension of the caeca, the contents of which resemble clots of blood, and in chronic cases the caecal contents may be of a cheesy consistency. Intestinal or adult coccidiosis is primarily a disease of maturing birds, and frequently appears soon after pullets are confined to laying houses ; affected birds have an unthrifty appearance, with paleness of the comb, wattles, and a typical hunched-up appearance which is followed by emaciation. On post-mortem examination the mucous membrane of the small intestine is thickened and shows whitish-yellow or red spots or streaks, the intestinal contents varying from a clear yellowish exudate to a mass of clotted blood which often forms a solid fibrinous cylinder completely occluding the intestinal canal. The causal parasite may be demonstrated microscopically in scrapings from affected intestines.

Judgment of poultry carcases affected with coccidiosis depends on the degree of emaciation and anaemia.

Blackhead

This disease of turkeys, also known as entero-hepatitis, was termed blackhead as it was at one time supposed that the head appendages of an affected bird turned a dark purple or black colour. It is caused by a protozoan parasite, *Histomonas meleagridis*, large numbers of which are voided in the droppings of affected birds. Fowls are frequently carriers of this parasite, and outbreaks often occur in chickens between 6 and 16 weeks old. The parasite is frequently carried in the egg or larva of the poultry caecal worm, *Heterakis gallinae*, a nematode present to a greater or lesser degree in almost all fowls kept under intensive conditions in Great Britain. It is stated that blackhead in turkeys is endemic in parts of South Wales.

Lesions of blackhead are chiefly confined to the liver and caeca. The liver is much enlarged and shows numerous circular necrotic areas, which lie beneath the liver capsule, are up to one inch in diameter and yellowish-green in colour, the coloration being due to blood pigment while the concentric ringing usually seen in the lesions is due to extension of the necrotic processes. Both limbs of the caeca may be involved, but it is commoner to find only one affected ; the wall is thickened and may show yellow necrotic areas, while the caecal contents vary from sulphur-yellow fluid faeces to dry, crumbly, cheese-like material. In young turkeys and chicks the mortality is high and may reach 90 per cent., but in adult birds the symptoms are not so severe, and affected birds showing typical liver lesions may therefore be encountered in the market. In the well-nourished bird condemnation of the liver is all that is required.

FIG. 234.—Lesions of blackhead in liver of turkey. The entire surface of both lobes of the liver is covered with the typical necrotic areas. (Crown copyright.)

Gape Worm Infestation

This affection was formerly a serious one in young chicks in the first 8 weeks of life and reared on the ground. Birds are nowadays reared in very large numbers in brooders and do not reach the ground until 6 to 8 weeks of age, by which time they have reached a stage of " age immunity " to this parasitic infection. Adult fowls only harbour gape worms if fed on a very deficient diet, but adult turkeys, on the other hand, may be carriers throughout life. The casual parasite is a nematode, *Syngamus trachea*, the female worm being bright red in colour, 1 to $1\frac{1}{5}$ inches long, with the smaller male permanently attached *in copula*. Diagnosis can be established by the detection of these worms attached in pairs to the mucous membrane of the trachea or bronchi.

Syngamus trachea has been recorded in humans but is not communicable to man by the consumption of an affected carcase. Adult affected birds are usually so emaciated as to necessitate condemnation.

External Parasites

The only external parasite of poultry which is of importance in food inspection is *Laminosioptes cysticola*, an acarus peculiar to the fowl and living in the connective tissue between the skin and muscles of the body. The acarus exerts no deleterious effect on the health of the bird, but death of the parasite is accompanied by a tissue reaction which encases the acarus in smooth, white, calcareous granules up to $\frac{1}{16}$ inch in length and oval in shape. If infestation with these parasites is severe the carcase is rendered unmarketable and should be condemned.

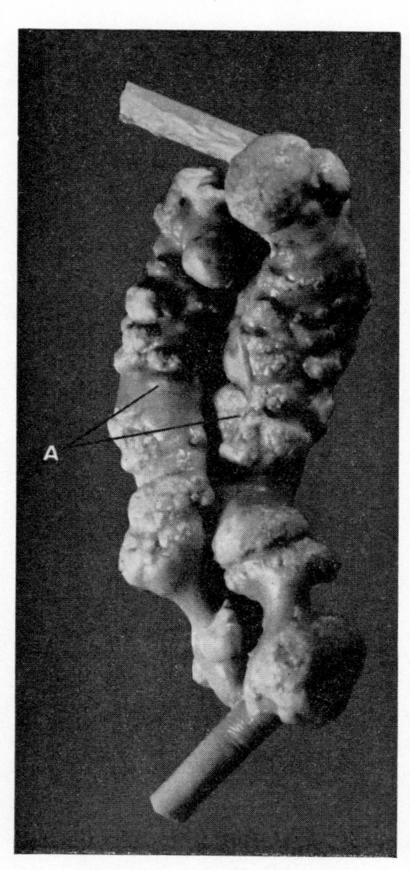

FIG. 235.—Caeca of fowl (A) showing *Escherichia coli* granulomata. The tips of the two caeca are seen at the upper part of the illustration in close contact with the ileum : their junction with the intestine at the commencement of the colon is seen at the lower part of the illustration. *E. coli* lesions may be confused with tuberculous lesions which involve the intestinal wall.

EMACIATION

This is a common cause of condemnation in poultry, especially in older fowls, and may be associated with the bacterial or parasitic affections already described, or may develop from irrational or insufficient feeding. It is difficult to draw distinction between poorness and pathological emaciation in the fowl, but the following code of judgment may conveniently be adhered to : A fowl in poor condition but showing no lesions of disease has a value for food purposes in restaurants or in the stock-pot and may be passed for food. A fowl in poor condition which shows definite evidence of any of the aforementioned diseases should be condemned. An emaciated fowl, even where no obvious lesions of disease are present, should be condemned.

AVIAN LEUCOSIS

This affection has been variously designated as fowl leukaemia, fowl paralysis, lymphomatosis and lymphocytosis and includes a group of neoplastic diseases resulting from proliferation of the essential blood-forming cells of the body and alterations to the bone marrow, liver and spleen. One form of the disease is known as big liver disease, the liver and other organs being enlarged and studded with firm greyish-white tumours, or the disease may take a diffuse form in which the liver and spleen, though greatly enlarged, are smooth, friable, show a strawberry-like mottling and vary in colour from cream to brown (Fig. 228). Other organs of the body, including the skin, may be affected. Another form of the disease is known as osteopetrosis and is characterized

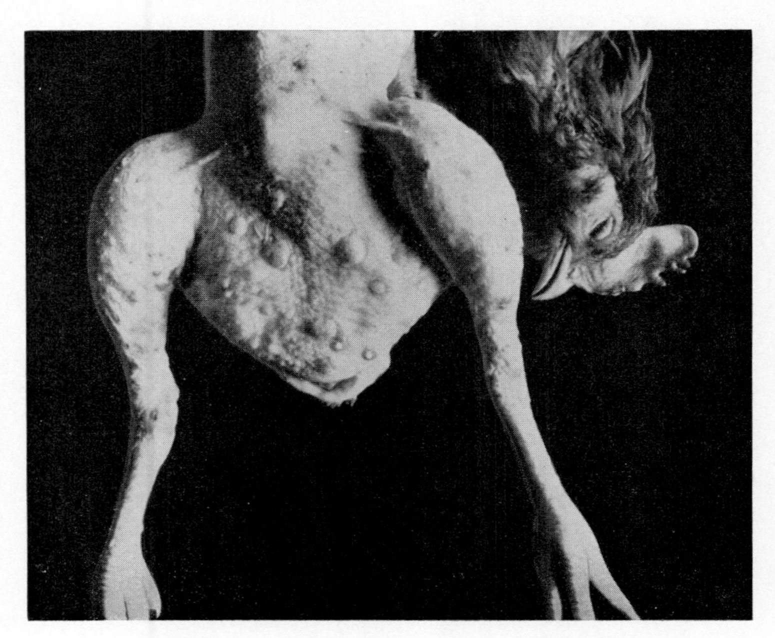

FIG. 236.—Lesions of leucosis on skin of abdomen of a fowl. The nodules consist of densely packed collections of lymphoid cells.

by the bilaterally symmetrical thickening of the long bones of the skeleton, this being especially obvious in the bones of the limbs, and it is a feature in the live bird that affected bones have a temperature some 6·5 °F. higher than unaffected bones and feel appreciably warmer.

Carcases of poultry affected with leucosis should be condemned.

TUMOURS

Tumours are commonly encountered in fowls and may be found in the liver, lungs, reproductive organs, muscular tissue and skin. Malignant neoplasms in the abdominal cavity, particularly when occurring in the reproductive tract, may give rise to ascites, and carcases showing pathological new growths should be condemned.

Other conditions which justify condemnation of poultry are marked abdominal dropsy, extensive fractures, severe bruising and discoloration, maggots or severe arthritis. Occasionally a fowl carcase may be seen with bluish-red patches on the abdomen which resemble bruises, and examination of the liver frequently shows that the organ is greatly enlarged and ruptured and the abdominal cavity filled with blood. The cause of this condition, as already stated, may be associated with tuberculosis of the liver, or with advanced fatty change or fowl typhoid, and affected carcases should be condemned.

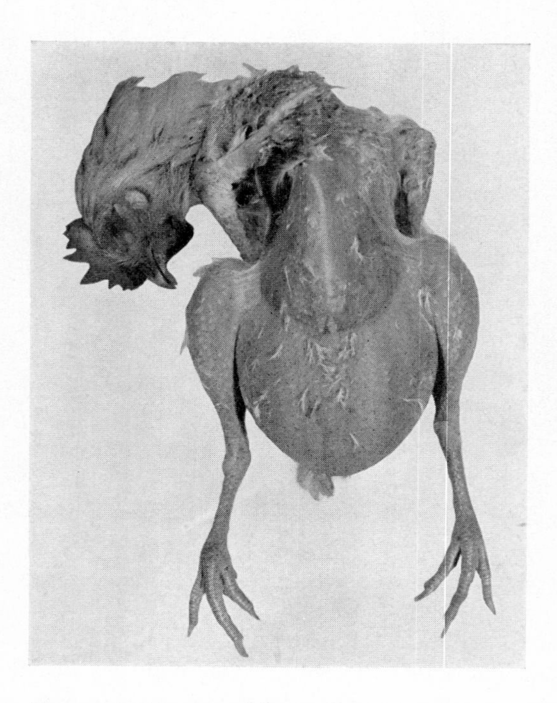

FIG. 237.—Carcase of fowl affected with ascites. The abdominal cavity shows great distension and contains 15 oz. of straw-coloured fluid. The affection is commonest in hens and usually arises secondarily from peritonitis or from chronic disease of the liver, kidneys or heart.

Peritonitis in fowls is usually associated with interference to the passage of the egg down the oviduct, but egg concrements, which are occasionally observed in the abdominal cavity of hens, are of no significance. Calcareous concretions, in addition to those affecting the skin and of parasitic origin, may be seen in the air sacs, pericardium, peritoneum, heart and kidneys, and if multiple dictate total condemnation.

The Inspection of Eggs

Eggs from the domesticated fowl form a convenient and concentrated article of diet, the average weight of a hen egg being 2 oz., of which 10 per cent. is composed of shell, 60 per cent. of white and 30 per cent. of yolk. The chemical composition of the hen egg is water 65·5 per cent., protein 11·9 per cent., fat 9·3 per cent. and ash and refuse 12·1 per cent.

As the ovum, or yolk, passes down the oviduct it receives the albumen, or white of egg, in about 3 hours, the shell membrane in a further 3 hours, and the shell covering after 15 to 20 hours. The shell of the hen egg is about $\frac{1}{60}$ of an inch thick and contains minute pores which, in the fertile egg, permit the passage of air through the shell to furnish oxygen to the developing chick embryo.

A newly laid egg possesses a surface bloom which is not present on imported eggs, and has a typical dull appearance due to a thin layer of protein material deposited on the shell just before the egg is laid. The presence of this gelatinous material tends to prevent entry of micro-organisms, but is removed mechanically by handling, particularly under damp conditions, and the egg thereupon becomes glossy. Though it is commonly asserted by egg dealers that a fertile egg has poorer keeping qualities than the sterile egg, and also that eggs from older fowls keep less well than from younger birds, both these contentions are incorrect. Battery-fed birds produce eggs with good coloured yolks provided the ration is suitable.

Large quantities of eggs are imported annually into Britain, the chief suppliers being Denmark, Holland and Ireland. These are fresh eggs which are not preserved in any way, and are imported in boxes of 120, known as long hundreds; if these eggs are kept dry and well ventilated and the boxes turned periodically, they will keep for several weeks. Eggs store best with the air chamber, situated at the broader end, uppermost, as when eggs are stored horizontally the yolk presses against the lower part of the shell and encourages decomposition at the point of contact.

PRESERVATION. The minute spores in the shell permit evaporation of water from the contents and also permit entry of micro-organisms which may cause decomposition. Methods of preservation of eggs are therefore based on the prevention of entry of micro-organisms or the inhibition of bacterial growth. Entry of micro-organisms may be prevented by coating the shell with wax, aluminium soap or petroleum jelly, and also by immersion of the egg in limewater (calcium bisulphite) or water-glass (sodium silicate). Eggs dipped in mineral oil will last 6 months and by water-glass eggs can be preserved for several years. The inhibition of bacterial growth may

1. Enlarged air space.

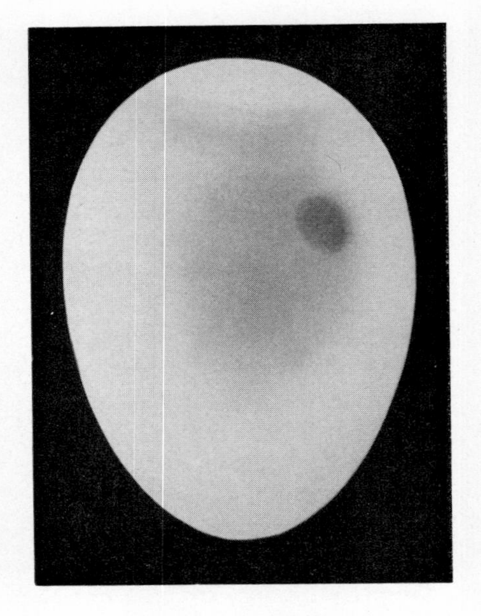

2. Large meat spot.

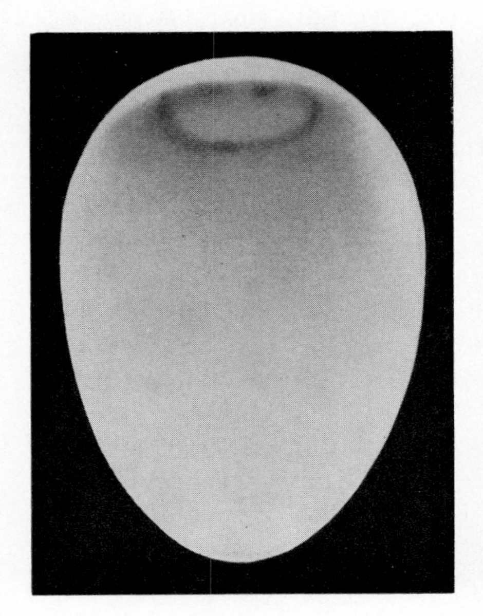

3. Mould.

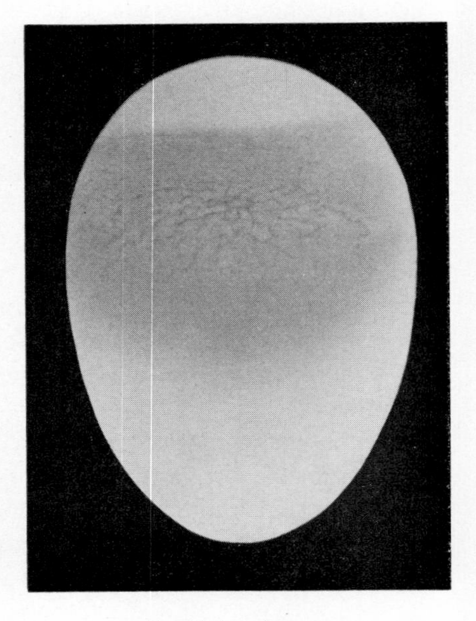

4. Fertile incubated egg.

FIG. 238.—Deleterious changes in hen eggs which may be detected by candling.

be secured by cold storage or by storage in a concentration of carbon dioxide gas or in ozone.

By far the greater amount of imported eggs, however, are preserved at chilling temperature, and cold-stored eggs imported into Britain from Australia, New Zealand and Argentina can be preserved for 9 months at a temperature of 32° F. At this temperature the egg contents are maintained in a plastic state, the temperature being low enough to inhibit bacterial growth but high enough to avoid cracking of the shell or coagulation of the egg protein.

The Examination of Eggs

The quality of eggs in shell is judged by their transparency to light, the examination being termed "candling" and consisting in holding the egg over a powerful light issuing from a box. When the fresh egg is candled the contents appear semi-translucent and without spots, the yolk being vaguely apparent as a sphere in the middle of the mass, while the air chamber can sometimes be seen and is $\frac{3}{5}$ inch in diameter and about $\frac{1}{8}$ inch in height. As the egg becomes older the yolk becomes more reddish or slightly marbled, and the air space becomes larger. This is due to evaporation and when thinning of the white occurs the yolk is brought in contact with the shell and decomposition can then occur. Rotten eggs appear opaque on candling, some having darker streaks or patches, and most of them have an enlarged air space. Other deleterious changes which may be detected by candling are the presence of cracks on the inside of the shell, or blood spots and meat spots. Blood spots are small haemorrhages always attached to the yolk and appearing as dark spots when the egg is candled. They are commonest in spring in first-year birds and as blood spots will eventually decompose and give rise to deleterious bacterial growth, eggs with blood spots should be condemned. Meat spots in eggs are considered to be portions of the shell pigment.

The density test for unsoundness in eggs is often recommended and consists in immersing the eggs in a salt solution of 2 oz. of salt to a pint of water. It is contended that an egg 24 hours old will just sink in the solution whereas an unsound egg or one over 3 days old will float easily, but the test is very unreliable.

Conditions Rendering Eggs Unsound

Mould. Stored eggs may develop mould growths on the surface of the shell, and these may penetrate through the shell pores and be seen on the inner aspect of the shell in the form of spots or patches which vary in colour. The mould *Penicillium* usually gives rise to yellow or blue spots, *Cladosporium* to dark green or black spots, and *Sporotrichum* to pink spots on the inside of the shell. Moulds may easily escape detection until the eggs are candled but they render the egg unmarketable and unfit for food.

Bacteria. The growth of *Proteus* or *Pseudomonas* in hen's eggs is associated with marked changes in odour and colour. The odour resembles that of faeces or of cabbage water, and the changes in colour are known variously as "black rot", "green rot" or "red rot"; "green rot" is the commonest of the deleterious changes in hen eggs in Britain or in eggs imported into Britain. These bacterial changes, which may be detected by candling, render the egg completely unfit for food.

The Danger of Tubercle Bacilli in Eggs from Tuberculous Fowls

There are numerous records of the finding of tubercle bacilli of the avian type in eggs laid by tuberculous fowls, and one observer records the isolation of this micro-organism in the eggs of 5·7 per cent. of tuberculous birds. It is doubtful if tubercle bacilli would be destroyed in the hen's egg by the ordinary methods of cooking, and it is probable that in infection of man by the avian bacillus the insufficiently cooked egg represents the greatest danger. Viable tubercle bacilli have been recovered from the yolks of eggs after eight minutes boiling.

Frozen Eggs

Small, dirty, cracked, leaking and other edible eggs of low market value are broken and frozen for use by bakers and confectioners. The frozen product may consist of a mixture of whites and yolks, or whites and yolks separately, and is packed into sterile 30 lb. tin containers which are filled to within 1 inch of the top and frozen to 0° F. The cans are sealed or soldered down and the frozen product, which is stored at 15 to 20° F., should retain its initial condition for over 1 year. From the nature of the raw product the bacterial content of frozen eggs is usually high.

Dried Eggs and Egg Products

Egg products such as whole dried egg, yolk, and albumen, both flake and powdered, are used largely in Britain and in recent years it has become increasingly evident that organisms of the salmonella group are frequently present in commercial egg products. During the Second World War imported spray-dried egg was examined and 9·9 per cent. of the samples from North and South America contained salmonellae, and evidence has continued to accumulate on the contamination of egg products with salmonellae and the dangers associated with the distribution of such foods, not so much in their being eaten uncooked as in the risk of bakery products becoming contaminated and the subsequent cross-contamination of unheated food materials such as imitation cream. Such dangers cannot be eliminated unless some method of treatment is applied to egg products to rid them of salmonellae, and as it is both possible and practicable to subject egg products to heat, such a measure would be expected to have effect on the general incidence of salmonella infections. It is also important from the point of view of livestock disease that when quantities of egg products are condemned as unfit for human food they should not be incorporated into feeding stuffs for poultry, and it is significant that the incidence in Britain of avian infections due to salmonella bacteria showed an increase of over 200 per cent. during the years 1941-1944, though the position has greatly improved during recent years, probably on account of the widespread adoption of fumigation of hatching eggs before or early in incubation. While the incorporation in poultry food of infected dried egg unfit for human consumption may be responsible for salmonellosis in poultry, particularly perhaps *S. thompson* infection, the isolation of *S. typhi-murium* from meat and bone meal suggests that these materials, as they are likely to be present in the poultry mashes produced by reputable firms, are of even greater importance. Similarly, such condemned foodstuffs should not be fed to pigs, as they may give rise to a salmonella infection in these animals, and suspicion should be aroused when pigs known to have consumed food containing dried egg powder show symptoms of pneumonia, skin discoloration, a discharge from eyes and nose, and excrete a yellowish-white diarrhoea.

INDEX

INDEX

(Principal references are shown in heavy type)

B

E

F

N

Q

R

S

T

U